The New Deal
and Its Legacy

Recent Titles in
Contributions in American History

THE NEW DEAL AND ITS LEGACY

Critique and Reappraisal

Edited by ROBERT EDEN

Contributions in American History, Number 132
JON L. WAKELYN, SERIES EDITOR

GREENWOOD PRESS
New York • Westport, Connecticut • London

#18780103

Library of Congress Cataloging-in-Publication Data

The New Deal and its legacy : critique and reappraisal / edited by
Robert Eden.
  p. cm.—(Contributions in American history, ISSN 0084–9219;
no. 132)
  Bibliography: p.
  Includes index.
  ISBN 0–313–26181–4 (lib. bdg. : alk. paper)
  1. New Deal, 1933–1939. 2. United States—Politics and
government—1933–1945. I. Eden, Robert. II. Series.
E806.N4145 1989
973.917—dc19   88–37377

British Library Cataloguing in Publication Data is available.

Library of Congress Catalog Card Number: 88–37377
ISBN: 0–313–26181–4
ISSN: 0084–9219

First published in 1989

Greenwood Press, Inc.
88 Post Road West, Westport, Connecticut 06881

Printed in the United States of America

Copyright Acknowledgments

The publisher and authors are grateful to the following for granting use of their material:

John A. Rohr, *To Run a Constitution: The Legitimacy of the Administrative State* (Lawrence:
University Press of Kansas, 1986). Courtesy of the University Press of Kansas.

Homer Cummings Papers (#9973), Manuscripts Division, Special Collections Department, University of Virginia Library. Courtesy of the University of Virginia Library.

Every reasonable effort has been made to trace the owners of copyright materials in this book, but
in some instances this has proven impossible. The publisher will be glad to receive information
leading to more complete acknowledgments in subsequent printings of the book and in the meantime
extends its apologies for any omissions.

To the memory of George Armstrong Kelly

"Quelle prise pouvaient-ils avoir sur de pareils hommes? l'Indien savait vivre sans besoins, souffrir sans se plaindre, et mourir en chantant. Comme tous les autres membres de la grande famille humaine, ces sauvages croyaient du reste à l'existence d'un monde meilleur, et adoraient sous différents noms le Dieu créateur de l'univers étaient en général simples et philosophiques."

In Memoriam

John Adams Wettergreen
1944–1989

Contents

Preface

Early in the spring of 1985, the Department of History and Political Science of Hillsdale College, in conjunction with the Center for Constructive Alternatives, published an invitation for paper proposals in several scholarly journals. The original invitation may serve as a measure by which to judge the current volume:

November 1986 will mark the fiftieth anniversary of Franklin Roosevelt's election to a second term as President of the United States. To many students of American politics, this election represents a critical moment in a critical phase of our history, the moment when the American people in effect ratified the leadership of an administration which advanced a new interpretation of traditional American ideals. Already in 1932, Roosevelt had called for "a reappraisal of values" or a "redefinition in terms of a changing and growing social order" of the rights proclaimed in the Declaration of Independence; in 1936, America seemed to answer this call.

To what degree Roosevelt's reappraisal of the American political tradition forms the basis of contemporary American politics is a difficult question; to address it adequately one must first ask whether the bewildering complex of policies we associate with the New Deal indeed rested on any coherent philosophy. In any case, the discontinuities between the New Deal and later versions of liberalism often seem at least as impressive as the continuities. Indeed, such discontinuities led many observers, beginning in the 1960s, to point to signs of decay in the public philosophy of the New Deal and of the political order associated with it, and to anticipate the emergence of a new alignment of parties and interests and of a new interpretation of the character and purpose of American democracy.

The question whether such a realignment is now in progress is an open one. Although the Republicans have improved their position considerably under Reagan's leadership, it is far from clear that they have laid the foundations for long-term dominance or that they have clearly defined their position with respect to the legacy of the New Deal. (Is Reagan a "New Deal conservative," as Samuel H. Beer has argued?) As for the Democrats, the disarray of their party is not a hypothesis of political scientists but a fact openly avowed by Democratic leaders. Thus neither party seems to have staked a clear claim to the enduring loyalties of a majority of Americans, and the evidence against "dealignment," or long-term decay of the party system itself, is far from conclusive. To restore the health of the party system would seem to require that parties appeal, not only to the immediate interests of the voters in general economic prosperity or in particular government benefits, but to the people's belief in a new expression of basic principles.

Such a renewal may require a thorough re-examination of welfare-state liberalism as it emerged in the New Deal period. In order to contribute to such a re-examination, the Department of History and Political Science of Hillsdale College, in conjunction with the Center for Constructive Alternatives, is sponsoring a series of conferences on The Legacy of the New Deal. The purpose of these conferences, to be held at Hillsdale College in 1986 and 1987, is to encourage a fresh examination of the intentions behind and consequences of New Deal politics and policies, to consider whether such an examination may shed light on the current condition of American institutions and public life, and to explore any implications relevant to choices faced by contemporary citizens, policy makers, and statesmen.

Approximately one hundred students of the New Deal responded to this invitation. Their proposals for papers were submitted to a jury of scholars. From the twenty-one papers eventually delivered at the Center for Constructive Alternatives seminars at Hillsdale College, eleven were selected for this volume.

To what degree do these essays together constitute that "thorough re-examination of welfare-state liberalism as it emerged in the New Deal period" that the conferences were intended to promote? The invitational statement obviously posed a challenge to the participants. It seemed appropriate to evaluate their responses to that challenge, as I have tried to do in chapter 1. Because the New Deal remains at the center of the debate over the American regime and way of life today, I have also attempted to indicate how the scholarly and philosophical controversies reflected in this volume illuminate and clarify that national debate.

Both as editor and as a participant in the conferences, I am indebted to Lissa Roche and Joseph P. McNamara of the Center for Constructive Alternatives. Understanding what the Puritan John Wise meant when he observed that "God made man to live bright and civil, with fine accomplishments," they have done their best to make the New Deal conferences a success. The Center provided many days of leisure in which the scholars represented here could share their knowledge, become acquainted, and engage in critical discussions. These informal meetings laid the foundation for the dialogue I have tried to reconstruct in chapter 1. On behalf of us all, I would like to thank the college and the Center for bringing us together and freeing us from mundane cares for a time.

Principal credit for the original conception and formation of the conferences is due Professor Ralph C. Hancock, now of Brigham Young University, and Dr. Thomas F. Payne, of the Vanderbilt School of Law.

Thanks are also due to Herman Belz (History, University of Maryland), Forrest McDonald (History, University of Alabama), George H. Nash (biographer of Herbert Hoover), and Jeremy Rabkin (Political Science, Cornell University).

Without the wisdom of these distinguished scholars, who served as consultants in planning and then as jurors, neither the conferences nor this volume would have been as instructive as they proved for all who took part. I am especially grateful to Marsha Boehmke for typing much of this manuscript.

I wrote the introductory chapter of this book during the summer of 1988, after my first year on the Hillsdale faculty. On coming to rural Michigan, I found here a remarkable climate of academic freedom. What I discovered, after almost three decades of study and teaching in prestigious North American universities, confirmed Eva Brann's observation: that the closing of the American mind, so eloquently described by Allan Bloom, was more evident and oppressive in the large universities, but that a different spirit has been preserved in some of our small independent colleges. In this regard, three individuals deserve special thanks, both for their friendship in supporting my work on this book, and for preserving such a radiant, morally demanding, and invigorating atmosphere at Hillsdale College: Professor John Willson, Dean John Reist, and President George Roche.

The New Deal
and Its Legacy

1

Robert Eden

Introduction: A Legacy of Questions

This book is a joint effort to reassess the New Deal project at the level of principle and in light of its consequences. It consists in the main of inquiries into the political thought of the New Deal architects of our present institutions—preeminently the thought of Franklin D. Roosevelt.

The chapters were written independently of one another from quite different perspectives. This chapter attempts to show how they may together inform and illuminate public controversy over the principles, political methods, and institutions that came out of the New Deal. As a companion to the volume as a whole, this chapter is designed to introduce the essayists and articulate the problems they pose for one another, on the hypothesis that this course should disclose some of the more challenging questions the New Deal poses for us all.[1]

Many studies of public policy written on the United States during the past forty years could have borne the title of this volume. The same could be said of much social criticism that appeared in these decades, and of several of the best essays in American political thought. For in the broadest sense, the legacy of the New Deal is the American regime as we have known it for nearly two generations. Yet despite intense critical reflection and incessant effort at reform, until recently the origins or foundings of our current political and constitutional arrangements in the New Deal were not subjected to sufficiently critical scrutiny; to most influential observers, they did not appear particularly problematic or question-worthy. The reason for renewed attention, however, is fairly clear: the public is almost as deeply divided by the programmatic legacy of the New Deal today as it was by the Depression in the thirties. It is to this fresh public interest and concern that these essays are addressed.

To appreciate the novelty of such concern, one should consider how dramatically prevailing assessments of the New Deal have changed over the past generation.

PUBLIC PERCEPTIONS OF THE NEW DEAL

Let us review, in this connection, some salient beliefs about the New Deal that were widely shared only a few years ago. Until roughly 1964 most Americans thought of the institutions that resulted from the New Deal primarily in terms of the safety net programs it put in place—chiefly Social Security—and its major regulatory initiatives as they bore on business, labor, and agriculture—the Securities Exchange Commission (SEC), the National Labor Relations Board (NLRB), and the Agricultural Adjustment Administration (AAA).[2] The permanent contribution of the New Deal seemed to be a rather modest regulatory framework intended to prevent the recurrence of depression nationally and to provide support to individuals when they could not work for reasons beyond their control. This was the welfare program that Americans knew and generally approved; when they spoke of the New Deal as the origin of the welfare state, this is the configuration to which it was linked.

To many observers, the New Deal by 1964 seemed comfortably conservative: what it had transmitted and preserved looked more significant than what it had originated; or rather, the innovations seemed to be instruments of continuity. Franklin Roosevelt had governed the country during a period of international economic turmoil and global war; at the end of his long term of stewardship, the Constitution and the party system were intact; the United States remained a constitutional democracy, secure in an almost unbroken political tradition, of government by deliberation and of free elections, that went back to the American Revolution. The Left was dissatisfied by New Deal conservatism and accused Roosevelt of preserving both capitalism and the spirit of bourgeois society. On the Right, even his most intransigent critics could find solace in the fact that FDR (by intention or neglect) had left most of the American heritage substantially intact.

Insofar as New Deal regulatory and redistributionist policies had modified the American economy, the effects appeared to be marginal and bearable, having little impact on entrepreneurial initiative, capital formation, or the commercial application of scientific discoveries and inventions. The productivity of the economy was not noticeably damaged by New Deal regulation; and in international trade the United States appeared to be more competitive than ever.

During this period the United States seemed to be restoring most Americans to the middle class or to what that status had been before the Depression. During the 1950s and 1960s that meant, in the first instance, having a home with the financial security to maintain it. The idea that the New Deal had seriously undermined property rights seemed to be refuted in the most practical way: a growing middle class with substantial and secure property appeared to be re-emerging; every rational and industrious American expected with good reason to own a home and car and then to set by substantial savings. While a closer look would have shown that the American middle class was composed of wage earners rather than property owners, during the 1950s and early 1960s the possibility of acquiring sufficient property to draw subsistence from it seemed increasingly within reach for many families. This prospect colored assessments of the New Deal program in retrospect; redistributionist policies did not then seem to endanger the property rights that mattered most to a majority of Americans.

In politics, as it then seemed to most influential observers, the New Deal had resulted in a broad consensus about public affairs, reflected abroad in a bipartisan foreign policy, and domestically in the willingness of the Republicans under Eisenhower to assume responsibility for administering the New Deal welfare state.

The political agreement seemed to express an even more impressive social consensus that many observers found oppressive. David Potter's *People of Plenty*, David Riesman's *The Lonely Crowd*, William H. White's *The Organization Man*, Louis Hartz's *The Liberal Tradition in America*, and Daniel Boorstin's histories all argued that the United States had emerged from the Depression years with a compelling, if not compulsive, unanimity regarding the commercial meaning and purpose of American life. Insofar as these authors saw a problem in the New Deal conception of self-government, the fault seemed to lie less in its "government" than in its "self"—a complacent notion of the conforming and consuming self. Though not all would have traced the origins of this doctrine to the New Deal, none questioned the success of the New Deal in transmitting it.

Even taking these critical voices into account, the regnant view in 1964 regarded the New Deal program as an attempt to restore the confidence of the American people in democracy and in their capacity to govern themselves under contemporary conditions. FDR seemed to have succeeded both in creating a new public consensus and in providing the ways and means that would enable self-government to survive both global depression and a world war. The portrait just given is not meant to deny the persistence of more critical views of the New Deal, some of which are reviewed in chapter 9. It is merely to recall that despite some forebodings of majority tyranny, and significant concerns in some quarters about the survival of individuality, a majority in the electorate and among the educated identified constitutional democracy with the New Deal welfare state and believed that the New Deal generally reflected a sound understanding of the nature, ways, and means of self-government.

What has become of this assessment of the New Deal?

By 1968 bipartisanship was already becoming a thing of the past. The consensus that had crystallized around FDR was shattered; the New Deal coalition had elected its last Democratic president. FDR's Herculean achievement in restoring the confidence and strength of liberalism suddenly appeared to be transient, if not wholly illusory and profoundly questionable. During the 1970s the crisis that had wracked European liberalism since the Victorian era was rapidly recapitulated, this time in a helter-skelter move by liberals toward the Left or (less commonly) the Right.

One remarkable feature of this unraveling of New Deal liberalism that had a profound effect on public assessments of the New Deal legacy was the discovery that programmatic reform could evidently be conducted through the courts and Congress without the kind of majority consensus on which New Deal institutions and programs had originally relied. While everything else in American society was collapsing during the 1960s and 1970s, the old New Deal programs seemed to take on a life of their own, as though freed from the trammels of majority consent, and many new ones sprang up, relying for political support only on organized minorities.

One measure of what has happened to the old New Deal program is that no one represents it. The major parties today define themselves by the stance they adopt toward the moderate New Deal program sketched above. The Democrats represent a programmatic critique of the moderate welfare state from the (putatively progressive) Left. Some important themes of that critique are discussed in chapter 12. The Republican program rests on a critique from the conservative Right, and merits attention here as an index of the shift in public assessments of the New Deal.

The platform of the Republican party articulated the challenge that Ronald Reagan meant to pose to New Deal liberalism during the presidential campaigns in 1980 and 1984.[3] As one commentary put it, the Republican platforms repudiated the intellectual consensus on which the New Deal and Great Society programs had been based, by rejecting its underlying idea: "the idea of government as an administrative body charged with reducing or eliminating economic risks, or of securing against the effects of bad choice or luck, is to a large extent the New Deal idea that was behind policies from Social Security to the convoluted farm price support programs of the 1970s."[4] Through the 1960s it had been widely believed that the New Deal was essentially moderate and limited, if not conservative. The Republican platform of the 1980s appealed to a newly persuasive public view, according to which the programmatic legacy of the New Deal was inherently expansive and potentially unlimited, primarily constrained by obstructions from without:

The New Deal primarily signified a new economic deal for the American people. It legitimized a role by government in the nation's economic affairs which government had never previously enjoyed. Even so, over a quarter of a century passed before the barriers to bona fide interventionism were effectively removed. With the influx of social science experts to Washington and the creation of the redistributive and regulatory Great Society programs in the 1960s, a bureaucracy blossomed in the national capital and the public sector began to grow at an astonishing rate. By 1980 over half the population of the United States were being sustained in whole or in part by programs of public support. The painful economic results of this trend, such as ever rising taxes, high interest rates, and above all increasing inflation, in turn generated a flood tide of dissatisfaction around the country which crested with Ronald Reagan's first election to the White House that year. This popular unhappiness with the results of redistributionist policies was, to be sure, no secret to most commentators at the time.[5]

In the Republican platform "this popular unhappiness" was addressed through a new definition of national needs and a commitment to contest redistributionist policies at every opportunity, on the conviction that special interests rather than the public good explained the staying power of New Deal programs.

Surprising as it might seem, that conviction was widely shared in both parties. Public interest organizations allied with the Democratic party, and analysts who urged "interventionist" reforms, such as Grant McConnell and Theodore J. Lowi, had argued for two decades that such programs were sustained by nothing other than the routine interest of the beneficiaries—by private rather than public needs.[6] To be sure, in conferences conducted at the Lyndon B. Johnson School of Public Affairs, one could still argue as though public disenchantment with the farm program, for example, were based on myth-mongering. But perhaps nowhere else could one say, with a straight face, "that these programs, controversial as some of them were, met a national need is seen in the fact that they have survived, fundamentally unchanged, for fifty years."[7] Shades in the mausoleum of the Great Society must have laughed to hear that. For most informed observers, and much of the public, the inertia of such programs rather proves that national needs are inadequately represented, and public spirit stymied or paralyzed, by current arrangements. As Don Paarlberg puts it in concluding chapter 2, "the question, therefore, is obvious: Have the New Deal farm programs become [so impregnably] institutionalized . . . that, despite their obvious failure, they cannot be basically changed?" That question is now commonly addressed to virtually every program of the New Deal, and indeed to its legacy as a whole.

THE WORLD OF REFORM IN CRITICAL SCHOLARSHIP

As the works of Grant McConnell and Theodore J. Lowi attest, critical scholarship accompanied and in some respects showed the way for major efforts to reform the regulatory framework into which the New Deal had subsided by the 1960s.[8] Their charge, however, was largely a transposition of the picture of the New Deal that I have just described as the dominant public perception in 1960. They shared the view that the New Deal was moderate, or hopelessly conservative, and that its program or public philosophy was defective precisely in generating the arrangements they delineated. "In politics," as Adolf Berle remarked, "you only get what you ask for: the problem is to ask the right thing."[9] McConnell and Lowi thought that the New Deal had asked the wrong thing, but had gotten substantially what it asked for.[10]

While public perceptions were changing, however, perspectives on the legacy of the New Deal were, in certain respects, shifting even more radically. One result, which I shall discuss in this section, was that scholars began to pay closer attention to precisely what the New Deal had asked for in politics, and to entertain the possibility that what we subsequently got (from the reinvigoration of interventionism in the 1960s and later) was substantially what the New Deal had been after. The inquiries in this volume broach some of the scholarly controversies that have arisen from this questioning of the New Deal roots of our current political and constitutional arrangements.[11]

The redirection of scholarly concern that is reflected in these essays can conveniently be introduced through a discussion of Peter J. Coleman's thesis.[12] In chapter 3 Coleman contends that the New Deal succeeded in establishing at the national level a political culture of interventionism that had already been in practice at the state and municipal levels for several decades in the United States, and at the national level in Europe and New Zealand. A review of his chapter will also help us to explore his controversial term *interventionism*.[13] He describes this international movement as follows:

The congruence of interventionism as a worldwide phenomenon can be explained by the emergence of processes and institutions common throughout the West. They include the rise of the social sciences, which gave activists a common methodology for analyzing society and its problems, a set of common assumptions concerning the capacity of human beings to engage in effective economic and social engineering, and a common will to reconstruct. Included as well was a massive increase in the volume and velocity of information available to lawmakers and those who would influence public policy, along with the rise of bureaucracies, private as well as public, with resources and skills dedicated to both disseminating information friendly to an expansion of the role of the state and a vested institutional stake in bringing that about. . . .

Though the interventionist thrust was in no sense coordinated, everywhere there sprang to life hosts of organizations dedicated to promoting this or that aspect of reconstruction. Mostly they owned their formation and drive to activists from outside the political establishment, though many of their leaders came from well-educated, middle-class and higher backgrounds—the sorts of people who saw it as their duty to be involved and who expected to be listened to. Such organizations often grew out of local activities—church groups, study circles, women's clubs, temperance societies, and the like. They discovered in their members common concerns and commitments to shared perception and goals, and then strengthened their efforts through like-minded people in regional, national, and sometimes international associational networks. Partly through overlapping memberships and other forms of cross-fertilization between institutions, the army of interventionism marched in the same broad direction, whether in searching for ways to improve the administration of industrial accident claims, provide better access to credit for farmers, increase the supply of higher quality, affordable housing for the urban poor, or protect female workers from exploitation.

For Coleman, the legacy of the New Deal was principally its inheritance; the accomplishment of the New Dealers was to place the "old wine" of interventionist practices into "new bottles" bearing a federal label.

With this serious argument Coleman has playfully reversed perspective on his fellow historians. In most accounts of the New Deal until very recently, the Depression or the crisis of American capitalism had been assigned the initiative. Urgent new realities precipitated the country into action, and the reformers were empowered precisely because they were ready to face these realities squarely, unhindered by the constraints of convention. The reformers and the electorate alike were compelled by emergencies to abandon more traditional approaches. On this view, material historical causes made the New Deal necessary. Because these historical developments threatened the destruction of constitutional democracy in the United States, the realistic modifications of the Constitution, of political parties, and of traditional democratic practices, which the reformers urged and the New Deal put in place, were said to be merely the necessary means to preserve democratic self-government under conditions of crisis. Elsewhere, liberal democracies perished for failing to adopt such measures; the New Deal innovations were necessary to avert a violent revolution such as the one that brought down the Weimar Republic or the short-lived Kerensky government in Russia.

Coleman's chapter helps us to understand that this plausible account is not entirely detached; it is essentially how the New Deal was seen from the perspective of what he calls "the world of interventionism." As his chapter indicates, the universities and professional schools were very much an integral part of the cosmopolitan "world of interventionism" from which the New Deal recruited so many of its staffs.[14] Until a few decades ago most scholars who studied the New Deal and taught courses on it would not have hesitated to locate themselves squarely within the community of discourse and professional activity that Coleman calls "the world of reform" or "the world of interventionism." Although they did not regard themselves as activists, but rather as scholars and teachers, they understood themselves to be participants in an unfolding culture or civilization in which the historical social sciences played a vital part, and in which the rise of the administrative state was the central political fact. Most American universities were proud to be centers of reform or at least centers of learning in which reform was promoted by a significant proportion of the faculty.

Having acquainted us with this "world" chiefly by offering biographies of its leading representatives, Coleman concludes by leaving us to judge "whether the wine was drinkable," that is, whether the transformation of national politics and administration brought about by the reformers was good or bad.

The other contributions may fairly be characterized as attempts to show how the study of the New Deal can illuminate this question. In chapter 4 Ellis W. Hawley reconsiders the interventionist critique of the New Deal failure to create an "administrative state." In chapter 5 John A. Rohr argues that the interventionist program would have undermined the legitimacy of "the public administration" by trying to displace the Framers' understanding of constitutional government; and he defends the Roosevelt administrations for resisting the reformers' project. In chapter 6 Sidney M. Milkis explores the impact of interventionist policies on the American party system. Charles R. Kesler argues, in chapter 7, that FDR only slightly modified the historicist public philosophy of

the reformers, above all Woodrow Wilson. John A. Wettergreen argues that
Roosevelt rejected the reformers' approach to regulation, in chapter 11.

It must be admitted, however, that the question has been significantly reshaped
by the other essayists. They have generally asked whether the national ascendancy
of interventionist policy is good or bad for constitutional democracy in the United
States, or for the American regime as an experiment in self-government. The
principal question that Coleman's essay poses may therefore be reformulated as
follows: *What does the emergence of "the world of reform" as Coleman describes it—this influential and resourceful new league of opinion leaders, human
service and policy professionals dedicated to the promotion and pursuit of the
activities of the administrative welfare state—portend for self-government in the
American political tradition?*

The prominence this question assigns to the reform movement indicates a
significant redirection of scholarly concern (as may be seen by comparing standard histories of the New Deal, or the crude sketch of prevailing approaches
given above).[15] It would be a misunderstanding, however, to presume that this
line of questioning downgrades the seriousness of the Depression or takes lightly
the political crisis that the New Deal addressed. As historians and students of
politics, all the contributors are well aware that such circumstances—necessities
or realities—provide one measure by which constitutions, political traditions,
and statesmen must be judged. It is a measure that applies to all; we make no
exception for the political culture of interventionism.

The perspective of interventionism appealed to some serious individuals because it promised to liberate their intellects from the authority of tradition. In
particular, it promised to liberate them from the vulgar world of political parties,
from the moral uncertainties of traditional statesmanship, from the mechanistic
rigidities of the founders' regime, and from the bourgeois world of Lockean
republicanism. During the New Deal era, it was claimed, the perspective of
enlightened administration enabled the reformers to face realities squarely, and
this claim was reflected in many subsequent accounts of the New Deal. These
"worlds," which seemed so confining, appear to us in a rather different light.
Many of the questions we seek to explore in this volume reflect the success of
the world of reform, attested in the fact that the coercive "realities" in public
and private life today are largely the institutional creations of the interventionists.
The authoritative commands that most citizens are called on to obey, issued by
courts, regulatory agencies, and Congress, are not less constraining than other
"realities."[16] The questions that we raise are intended to identify the assumptions
that prevented the New Dealers, and would prevent us, from confronting those
realities frankly and freely. Some of the chapters bring those assumptions to
light by adopting the perspective of American political parties (Milkis, Eden)
or of the anti-bureaucratic traditions in the American political tradition (Hawley,
Wettergreen). Others adopt the teaching of *The Federalist* (Rohr, Caton, Kesler)
or of John Marshall's jurisprudence (Shenfield). Others have attempted to recover
the perspective of traditional statesmanship by returning to the classical sources

on statesmanship that were available to the founders. A few remarks on the emergence of critical detachment toward the world of interventionism and on the reinvigoration of critical scholarship from each of these perspectives may help the reader to gauge the essayists.

The Study of American Parties

Elsewhere parties like the British Labour party and the German Social Democratic party (SDP) were much earlier made part of the world of interventionism. Until the New Deal neither of the major American parties had opened itself to the world of reform or offered itself as a vehicle by which interventionism could become a political force. A number of reform activists wanted a party to emerge on the model of the German SDP or British Labour; but in order to pursue that goal they had to overcome the established partisan habits and the vested interests of both the Democratic and Republican political parties. Middle-class Progressive reformers, of course, whether they were interventionists or not, had other objections to the parties as well. Had the New Deal simply extended interventionist politics from the state to the national level, as Coleman claims, it would have put itself on a collision course with the American parties, and would almost certainly have failed.

Many political scientists were delighted with the strategy that Roosevelt adopted to bring the world of reform into more fruitful collaboration with the parties. Although they were otherwise sympathetic to the world of intervention, as students of American political parties many were impressed with the New Deal precisely because Roosevelt took partisan politics more seriously than the Progressive reformers and those who sought to suppress the parties. V. O. Key in particular appreciated FDR's Southern strategy and agreed that a modification of the American party system from within was far more promising than a purification of the parties by regulatory reforms. During the 1950s and 1960s the legacy of New Deal liberalism seemed to be a restoration of the party system. The New Deal seemed to have strengthened a cleavage that cut across racial and regional divisions and promoted a new party competition on the New Deal issues.

The convergence between the path of the traditional political parties and the path of reform proved, however, to be transient. When reform liberalism once again turned against the world of the parties, in the 1960s and 1970s, it provoked a critical reappraisal of reform by political scientists who thought that weakening parties would weaken democratic political participation. To the extent that the legacy of the New Deal released the world of interventionism to do more damage to American political parties, students of party became outspokenly critical.[17]

Until 1968 elections at every level of government were conducted under roughly the same arrangements, constitutional and informal, that had prevailed before and during the New Deal. During the past two decades, however, the rules under which elections are held have been changed more dramatically, and more continuously, than at any time in American history.[18] In seeking to understand the accelerating attack on traditional parties, a number of distinguished political scientists began to reconsider the relation between the New Deal and Progressivism in the light of these changes, taking a closer look at the Progressive emphasis on administration at the expense of political parties, and on the regulation of parties as a way of weakening their impact or of strengthening independent voters and politicians at the expense of party discipline.[19] How revealing, and how challenging to received teachings on the New Deal, such a reexamination can be is clear from the essay by Sidney Milkis.

Lockean Republicanism

Coleman has, in effect, described the New Deal as a gradual, secular realignment that brought to power a new group of amateurs and professionals who were actively engaged in legislating and administering public policy and who shared an identifiable common outlook or concern.[20] One reason for its being described as a world was its self-conscious effort to define itself against its rivals, thereby differentiating and defending its unique concerns. By way of such cultural distinctions, the world of intervention insulated its members from the corrupting influence of other "worlds," and in the American case this meant from the traditions and teachings that had formed both the electorate at large and their representatives before the New Deal. Not only were the new professionals highly educated, but they also asserted a new definition of what it meant to be educated at all. Their insularity was particularly striking with regard to political education.

The term world is especially instructive because its origin in continental thought is easily traced, and familiar from the combination *Weltanschauung*, or worldview. The burden of the term is that culture and, especially, education shape our way of seeing in such a way as to form a world of what we see. Each such world is thus the product of a culture.

The movers and shakers of the world of reform shared a certain culture in common and worked collaboratively to bring a new world into existence. With the New Deal, according to Coleman, the culture of interventionism became the world of national administration and public policy.

As the term world intimates, there is a connection between idealistic reform or intervention, and a philosophy of history in which culture is a key term of distinction. The connection becomes more perspicuous when we reflect on the origins of culture as a central notion of social science. The origins lie in the doctrine of European idealism.[21] The foundations were laid by Rousseau, especially in *Emile*.[22] Rousseau there shows how education may effectively promote sound morality and insulate the properly cultivated individual from the corrupting effect of the arts and sciences.[23] The autonomy of culture from the domain of natural determinism is argued more systematically by Kant. He defends reason against Rousseau by demonstrating that ethical culture can be reconciled with and supported by philosophy and reason.[24] Idealism finally emerged as a comprehensive interpretation of all previous civilizations—indeed of all human culture—in the historical philosophy of Hegel.[25] In Germany the social sciences emerged from the Historical School through a polemical dialogue with Hegel; the centrality of culture in these social sciences is indicated by Max Weber's term for them in his methodological writings: *Kulturwissenschaften*, or cultural sciences.[26]

Although the interventionists were by no means all Hegelians, a diagram from Hegel may help to clarify their attitude toward the world of Lockean republicanism. Hegel had identified civil society as a preliminary moment or dimension of ethical life that would be subordinated to and subsumed within the state in a fully rational political society. In the cruder versions of this teaching that became common currency in the world of reform, the United States appeared as lacking an ethical life.[27] Civil society or "the system of needs" was equated with the liberal commercial republic delineated by Montesquieu. The kind of political society that the founders had attempted to secure and perfect by framing the U.S. Constitution, a political society in which a commercial way of life would predominate, was thus equated with and reduced to part of its political economy.[28] Hegel argued that the culmination or end of man's history was the state; in this perspective, a reform to displace the American regime with a modern administrative welfare state more like Bismarck's Germany could appear as progress toward the realization of human freedom.

The German Historical School indirectly provided the foundation for most of the institutional economics and public administration of the New Deal; German methods and doctrines had been vigorously adopted in leading American universities in the last quarter of the nineteenth century.[29] Although the Historical School repudiated the speculative side of idealism as well as Hegel's defense of reason, its leading exponents, above all Gustav Schmoller, labored mightily to refine the Hegelian *Rechtsstaat*, supplying the Bismarckean welfare state with publicists and civil servants.[30] Through the Historical School the *Rechtsstaat* was transmitted to the world of interventionism as its most advanced model of the administrative state; it guided reformers in conceiving their own role both in civil service and as contributors to enlightened administration through research and teaching.[31]

Thus Coleman's identification of interventionism with reform is apt because the world he describes was directed toward the realization of the interventionist state. The proponents of the new freedom of the new state were compelled by circumstances to work with American institutions; but they did not admire the principles of "the American political universe" (to use Walter Dean Burnham's phrase). In this respect they were pilgrims passing through the American regime, hoping to build their new City on the Hill. This project of edification led them to look on the city that happened to be on that hill—the liberal commercial republic and its representative institutions—as received historical material to be transformed or demolished. This new way of dealing with the founders' Republic was what "New Deal" meant to many of the best and the brightest during the thirties.

Because the Historical School was founded in a critique of rationalism and
an aversion to theory, the German philosophical tradition was not maintained
by the new cultural sciences with rigor, to say nothing of Hegel's depth and
subtlety. In this respect the *Rechtsstaat* had been disembrained. Max Weber's
methodological critiques attest that the thinking of the German Historical School
was fundamentally confused before it was exported to the United States.[32] But
for some reason American contempt for jerry-built goods did not affect the
prestige of German scholarly exports. The historical and institutional approach
in which Woodrow Wilson and other reformers were trained imbedded these
fundamental confusions in American scholarship. Because the Historical School
had turned away from philosophy toward history—or toward scholarly disciplines
based obscurely on the premises of theoretical historicism—the residual debts
to continental thought were carried over without critical scrutiny into the philosophical presuppositions of interventionism. In Woodrow Wilson's work on
The State the debts are writ large, but in less obtrusive ways historicism exercised
a shaping influence on scholarship and reform thought through the Progressive
and New Deal eras.[33]

The shift that the Historical School promoted, toward professional scholarship
and away from political philosophy, in certain respects postponed a reckoning
with the fundamental issues that the rise of interventionism posed. It may suffice
to raise one such fundamental issue. Many social scientists and historians inherited from the Historical School—if not from other sources—the belief or
assumption that political philosophy is impossible.[34] That prejudice generally
resulted in a certain contempt toward any political science that did not acknowledge the death of political philosophy. What did such an acknowledgment entail?
Taken seriously, it meant that the roots of the American regime, to the extent
that they were roots in political philosophy, were likewise moribund. The founders of that regime, who conducted a revolution and then saved or preserved it
by framing the Constitution of the United States, did not share this belief. Had
they shared it they could not, in conscience, have pledged their lives and sacred
honor in a Declaration of Independence that held certain propositions of political
philosophy up to the world as self-evident truths.[35] Today social scientists and
historians do not say such things, even in declarations of university policy, and
the reason is clear: no one stakes one's claim to be heard on a proposition one
knows to be impossible, absurd, or unverifiable. Intellectual honesty would
require of them, on the contrary, a public demand that the Declaration be di-
savowed as a condition of holding public office, on the premise that no intellectually competent individual could swear by these self-evident truths.

However this embarrassment is resolved, it is indisputable that New Deal
studies can no longer rest comfortably on the unnoticed authority or momentum
of the German Historical School, much less on deference to idealist philosophy
of history. One need not invoke disputes over public policy to explain how the
interventionist belief, that national salvation lies in the actualization of an administrative state, became the property of the intellectual rear. Harmony between

the university as a world of scholarship, and the world of reform once appeared to serve the quest for intellectual independence from the authority of tradition. But when the New Deal and the world of interventionism came into political authority in the United States, it began to speak with the voice of power and tradition, through the media as well as the universities. The quest for spiritual and intellectual independence that had drawn good minds to the world of interventionism before the New Deal thus led away from it. The essays to follow are by scholars who have learned to look with fresh sympathy into the world of American political parties and the world of the Founders; to reverse the angle of critical vision and scrutinize the world of reform from these once-despised perspectives.

That many of the essayists contribute to restoring the reasoned authority of the U.S. Constitution is one indication that the world of reform or of interventionism has ceased to command their intellectual assent; that the central ideas that gave that world coherence and direction have lost their hold over many fields of scholarship.

Statesmanship

The world of reform, as Coleman describes it, regarded politics as an extention of administration or as a means of institutional change. Accordingly, it was not only in tension with the world of party politics it was also set against the world of traditional statesmanship.

One avenue of approach to statesmanship had been through the classical historians, Tacitus, Sallust, Polybius, Plutarch, Thucydides, and Xenophon. The founders of the American Republic had lived with these works and looked to them for instruction and guidance. Charles Kesler, writing on the founders and the classics, has argued that classical political philosophy informed their understanding of virtue and the public good as well.[36] Whether one returns to the world of statesmanship as he does, through Aristotle and Plato, or (as Russell Kirk has done) through Edmund Burke, one encounters the objections alluded to above, especially from historians. Modern training in the field of history begins with the German Historical School, which appropriated these texts and claimed special authority to interpret them in the schools. The objection was that, because these authors spoke of themselves as historians, modern historical scholarship should be the proper arbiter of their content or teaching, whatever that content might happen to be.

The classical historians were not teachers of enlightened administration. From them, as Locke said, "one may learn great and useful instructions of prudence and be warned against the cheats and rogueries of the world." But in the world of reform those tasks were to be taken over by *Ideologiekritik*, cultural criticism, or debunking of myths, such as Thurman Arnold's debunking of "the folklore of capitalism." If they had to choose a companion with whom to study Tacitus, most of the contributors to this book would trust George Washington or Alexander

Hamilton (who read the classical historians for instruction in prudence and demonstrated prudence in their deeds) sooner than they would trust a modern historian
or philologist. They would make a sustained effort to prevent the presumptions
of modern historiography from interfering with what the classical historians try
to teach, in order to learn to "reason together" with the classics about prudence,
human excellence, and the world. In this vein John Wettergreen has written on
Thucydides, and Charles Kesler on Cicero.[37] Closer to modern times Hiram
Caton has written on the statecraft of Shaftesbury, on the founder of the liberal
commercial republic in Holland, De Witt, and on Sir Robert Walpole.[38] Morton
Frisch has written articles on Churchill's *Marlborough* and on Alexander Hamilton.[39] In the United States the principal attempt at a history that would establish
reform historiography as the portal to the world of statesmanship was Richard
Hofstadter's book *The American Political Tradition and the Men Who Made It*
(1955). Frisch has devoted much of his scholarly life to rescuing Franklin D.
Roosevelt's statesmanship from Hofstadter's condescensions and is the editor of
a volume intended to do the same for other American statesmen in reply to
Hofstadter.[40]

Thus a critical reassessment of the attempt to displace politics and statesmanship with administration underlies the effort that is made here, by several of the
essayists, to persuade New Deal scholars to accord greater prominence to FDR's
political thought. These scholars are familiar with the difficulties that FDR's
penchant for ambiguity and misdirection creates for anyone who would seek to
establish his intention. They do not find these difficulties to be categorically
different from the problems that arise in establishing the intention of most statesmen; that is why the classical historians remain instructive.

The reformers made allowance for politics, as they thought, by introducing
the notion of political leadership. Woodrow Wilson was primarily responsible
for transforming American liberalism by augmenting it with leadership, as
Charles Kesler and I have independently demonstrated.[41] Leadership may be
characterized as statesmanship reinterpreted from the perspective of the world
of reform. The perspective is part of a cultural education intended to preserve
the distinctive concerns of the interventionists—in Wilson's case, to prevent
them from being corrupted or influenced by the worldliness, pessimism, or self-
restraint of traditional statesmanship. To recover the perspective of the statesman
it may therefore be necessary to reconsider the notion of leadership and lay bare
its theoretical presuppositions, as I have attempted in another context.[42]

Thus the chapters after Coleman's are attempts to take the measure of the
New Deal and its consequences from a critical distance, adopting neither the
perspective nor the assumptions of the political culture delineated by Coleman.

Our survey has served so far to introduce the essayists. But it may also help
to make explicit a number of questions that this volume raises for New Deal
scholarship, especially as regards FDR. Many of the New Dealers clearly belong
within the world of reform that Coleman has limned. But does Roosevelt himself?
In this regard Coleman's thesis obviously contradicts one's commonsense impres-

sion that Roosevelt was far more immersed in the world of party politics, and more attentive to the rationality of Lockean republicanism, than the members of his own brain trust. And although his rank as a statesman is disputed in these pages, Churchill's high estimate of Roosevelt should give one pause.[43] During the New Deal an insular world of interventionism did not simply expand, in a big bang, to become the new American political universe. Roosevelt brought together the different "worlds" sketched above. On many occasions that produced conflict and brought disagreements to a head; at other times Roosevelt succeeded in obscuring the boundaries that divided his allies; sometimes he just preferred to govern by a policy of divide and rule. Each of these worlds became stronger. The party system, which had been in decline, was at least temporarily reinvigorated by this policy; the world of reform, as Coleman argues, went from power to power. Roosevelt's determination to fight and win World War II revived the world of traditional statesmanship as an imposed emergency could not have done. At one time the best political science departments in American colleges and universities mirrored Roosevelt's policy by attempting to bring together the study of political parties, the study of diplomacy and statesmanship, and the interventionist political curriculum. Perhaps one should not expect accomplishments of this character to reverberate forever if they are not repeated and reaffirmed.

Although the administrative state is not the official subject of every essay in the book, all the contributors take enlightened administration as their theme in one way or another in order to consider what the administrative project of the New Deal has meant for the American experiment in self-government. Accordingly, we devote considerable attention to the Brownlow Commission Report and executive reorganization. The chapters by Ellis Hawley, John Rohr, and Sidney Milkis present three appraisals of the origins of an American administrative state during the New Deal. They broach one of the central concerns of the book in trying to define what the New Deal or FDR meant by enlightened administration, and to what extent he meant by it what the Progressive reformers meant.

NEW DEAL POLITICS AND PROGRESSIVE PUBLIC ADMINISTRATION; ROOSEVELT'S COMMISSION ON EXECUTIVE REORGANIZATION

The most thoughtful of Roosevelt's speeches introduced the New Deal to a Progressive audience by announcing that "the day of enlightened administration has come."[44] What, then, did FDR understand enlightened administration to be? Or, to refocus the question, what kind of administrative state did FDR attempt to institute? The first to explore this question is Ellis W. Hawley, professor and chairman in history at the University of Iowa.

In chapter 3 Hawley analyzes the many anti-bureaucratic formulae that the New Dealers juggled, to show that the state-building program of Progressive political scientists did not become a major part of Roosevelt's program until the late New Deal, and then in such an altered form that most New Deal scholars overlooked it until recently.

Hawley's argument is addressed to current spokesmen for the world of reform, such as Theodore J. Lowi. According to Lowi, an aggressive administrative state capable of acting in the public interest against big labor, big business, and big agriculture could not be raised on the New Deal foundation. A fundamental break with the New Deal's public philosophy and modus operandi was therefore required. Lowi's influential critique, which urged the radicalization or completion of the New Deal effort to establish an administrative state, was simultaneously a prospectus for the new regulatory and redistributionist undertaking of the 1960s and 1970s.[45]

Lowi was not the first analyst to express interventionist misgivings about the New Deal, but he was the first to make disenchantment with Rooseveltian politics fully respectable for liberals. After Lowi's critique no self-respecting liberal could defend the moderate New Deal consensus (sketched at the beginning of this chapter) unless he was willing to become a neo-conservative. For Lowi held that the original New Deal was badly compromised and unwilling to back liberal justice with a sword.[46]

Hawley does not deny that Roosevelt compromised, but he questions whether the proponents of the administrative state grasped the significance of his compromises. They think that Roosevelt's policy impeded the development of a true administrative state in the United States. Hawley contends that this is a misapprehension of what the New Deal accomplished. He freely acknowledges that the New Deal was far more open to anti-bureaucractic "formulas" than were the Progressive founders of the modern doctrine of public administration. But FDR did not take enlightened administration to mean what the Progressives meant by public administration. Hawley discerns a deliberate and circumspect effort on the part of the New Dealers to respond to the anti-statist and anti-bureaucratic strains in American political thought, an effort that more recent interventionists have failed to understand.

The strategy that the New Deal devised combined populist appeals to the anti-bureaucratic and anti-business strains in the American political tradition, with initiatives in state-building—a strategy for advancing the administrative state within a Jeffersonian democracy that proved to be unbeatable. Roosevelt merged these opposed elements in an effective regime. The New Deal succeeded, according to Hawley, in founding a permanent administrative state precisely because FDR abandoned the doctrinaire European model, fighting with, rather than against, deep-seated American hostility to bureaucratic government.

One might derive from this chapter a prescription for continued state-building. In order to be radical, one must conserve New Deal modes and orders; for what is apparently most conservative in the New Deal, its evident compromise with Jeffersonian traditions, turns out, on closer inspection, to be precisely what was most subversive of those traditions. Rooseveltian indirection should and must be imitated.

Hawley's meditation on the New Deal as an effective strategy for proponents of the administrative state culminates in his remarks on Roosevelt's campaign for executive reorganization. That campaign, as Barry Karl, Richard Polenberg, and Sidney Milkis have demonstrated, places FDR's understanding of enlightened administration and his intention to create an administrative state in a new light.[47] The presidency that executive reorganization brought into being—even after Roosevelt's initial design was turned back by Congress—provided the foundation for the perpetuation and expansion of the New Deal program. It was intended by Roosevelt to do so. This discovery alone, when taken seriously, is sufficient to make FDR's political thought a serious problem for interpretation, for it indicates that Roosevelt had a comprehensive, architectonic understanding of the problems he faced and of the constitutional resources with which they might be solved.[48]

Before we turn to John A. Rohr's interpretation of this problem, let us underline the questions with which Hawley's account leaves us.

Hawley's argument stops short of the radical interpretation one might draw from it. To what extent was FDR's stance toward these American anti-bureaucratic traditions manipulative and designed to undermine them? Or, alternatively, to what extent did he accept anti-bureaucratic solutions because he thought they were superior and would bear the weight of experience? Hawley does not say whether the anti-statist formulations that the New Deal adopted are to be recommended for their intrinsic worth, because they add something to the administrative state that it lacks.[49] Reading his account, one cannot tell whether he thinks that the unmodified administrative state needs these democratic additions to be choiceworthy. Are American anti-statist formulations merely of instrumental utility to mollify and paralyze opponents? Does Hawley find in the populist and often conservative strains in the anti-statist tradition something of permanent worth for a republican and democratic people?

Hawley's chapter is the first of three reappraisals of the Brownlow Commission Report in this volume. The strategy Roosevelt pursued between 1937 and 1938 by means of the Brownlow Commission deserves this attention in a consideration of the New Deal legacy because executive reorganization was one of the most important instruments in Roosevelt's design to shape and determine his own legacy.

In chapter 5 the case for the New Deal version of the administrative state is argued in terms of constitutional legitimacy by John A. Rohr. Rohr exhorts us to approve the New Deal as a deliberate and circumspect effort at constitutional reform, that is, as an effort to introduce the administrative welfare state into the constitutional order and to secure its constitutional legitimacy.[50]

Rohr contends that New Deal practice, exemplified in the Brownlow Commission Report, was superior to the science of public administration that it took over from Progressive political scientists. The modern, value-free, realistic science of administration promoted by the Progressives was inferior, Rohr argues, because it failed to secure modern bureaucracy squarely on the foundation of the Constitution. Progressive public administration is crippled by problems of legitimacy that can only be solved by repudiating Progressive theory, or the Progressive animus against the constitutionalist political science of the framers. This solution was first approximated in practice by the New Dealers, although Rohr admits that New Deal theory was less than explicit in abandoning the Progressive science of public administration. Rohr argues that the public administration should be rescued from the Progressive theorists and placed squarely on constitutional foundations as our closest approximation to the high-toned government for which *The Federalist* contended.

On the central issue of constitutional interpretation, the Progressives were curiously in agreement with the Vanburenite strict constructionists whose party politics and congressional government they opposed. Both agreed that the original Constitution was fundamentally an alternative to enlightened administration, and that to introduce effective administrative institutions it would be necessary to break through the constraints of the Constitution. The Jeffersonians were determined to keep the Constitution that way, and the Progressives were determined to circumvent it. But they agreed that the original intention had been to make it work in that way. Rohr argues that this premise is unfounded. He is unwilling to accept a view of the Constitution that requires us to ignore pressing public necessities or to choose between constitutional legitimacy and great public needs. Viewing the Constitution as a thoughtful framework capable of meeting such necessities, he would rather look in the Constitution for its method of anticipating and providing for them. The alternative that he faults in Progressive theory is one that identifies great necessities and then compels us to adopt a manipulative and instrumental view of constitutional legitimacy to do the necessary thing. As he makes explicit, once we adopt this premise, "the creation of an administrative state" has to mean the destruction or suppression of the form of government established by the Constitution.

Rohr denies that such a Damoclean choice is posed. He argues that the Constitution we have inherited from the Founding—the Constitution of *The Federalist*—is a form of the administrative state, or rather, in Hamiltonian terms, an "administrative republic."[51] If Rohr is right about this, the New Dealers were right to abandon the Progressive animus against the Constitution because the animus was entirely misplaced. Yet it is not clear from his account that the New Dealers understood this. The discrepancies to which he draws attention, between *The Federalist* and the Brownlow Report, suggest that the commissioners were as impatient with constitutional government in the Hamiltonian form as they were with the Jeffersonian version. However this may be, the thrust of his argument is to carry us through and beyond the New Dealers to an adequate understanding of our constitutional order. He attempts to raise important questions that have been submerged by our use of the term administrative state or welfare state.

What did the founders mean by administration? What is the connection between administration and politics on the founders' view?[52] As Rohr indicates, many of the features we associate with the administrative state are in fact provided for by the original Constitution; they seem especially to be clear from the original Constitution "in speech," by which Rohr means "in theory"—the Constitution of *The Federalist*. In order to understand those administrative features (including the strong executive for which *The Federalist* provides), Rohr urges us to begin with the political science on which they rest and that made them intelligible to the framers. According to *The Federalist*, the strong executive is most of all dependent on the articulation of separated powers of government. This is because the legislative branches both in the nation and in the states will enjoy great political advantages and will tend to accumulate popular power. Separation of powers is not, as the Progressives argued, the source of congressional government; it is, on the contrary, the basis for the strong executive within a republican government.

The questions raised by John Rohr are engaged from a different perspective in chapter 6 by Sidney Milkis. Rohr and Milkis disagree with Hawley, but for diametrically opposed reasons.

Rohr notices that the Progressive theory of administration is capable of producing a constitutional order that makes no compromise with the Anti-Federalist and Jeffersonian tradition, perhaps a rational-legal bureaucracy that suppresses republican citizenship.[53] He denies that the New Deal order was based on that theory of administration. He goes so far as to argue that Anti-Federalist arguments for the promotion of civic virtue could be accommodated by teaching the civil servants who staff the public administration to look on their work as an exercise of republican virtue and as a task of representing the people. In the perfected New Deal order, on Rohr's reading, the Jeffersonian side of the American political tradition would be preserved, transmuted, in a representative bureaucracy. The Hamiltonian side of *The Federalist* would replace Progressive theory. In this way the founders' Constitution as understood by both Federalists and Anti-Federalists would be recovered as the constitutional armature of the modern welfare state with which we are familiar.

Sidney Milkis challenges Rohr's project on at least two grounds. First, it fails to encompass Roosevelt's thinking on the informal or working constitution, "the effectual truth" of power relations in the American two-party system. To understand the Brownlow Commission initiative as a change in the formal constitution, Milkis contends, one has to consider the purpose of executive reorganization as an effective answer to the power of parties over the President, over Congress, and hence over the long-term programs of the New Deal. Executive reorganization was intended to break the hold of the parties in "the councils of power."

This leads to Milkis's second ground for challenging Rohr: political parties in the American mold had been the chief mode of popular participation in political affairs. To break the hold of the parties by means of a permanent and fundamental reordering of governmental relations was the purpose of executive reorganization;

this meant loosening the hold of the parties on the habits and political manners of citizens. The weakening of parties that followed in the wake of the New Deal was therefore not accidental. On Milkis's analysis, the most serious casualty was the kind of participation that Jefferson had thought crucial to the American experiment in self-government, participation that actually molded republican character. This casualty is not measurable by the founds a party controls or by its capacity to control access to the electoral process. A party can be an effective organization without significantly shaping the character of its members, without attaching them more firmly to a republican constitution, and without eliciting their deeper loyalties. It may simply be a purpose-oriented institution, like a business.[54] But the American parties, which traced their origin to Jefferson, were never simply that. Nor, as Tocqueville remarked, were they purposive in the manner of a military machine. Even when they dragged the moral tone of American society down and became primarily a stage for advancing the personal ambitions of their members, Tocqueville still found them to be the primary schools of democracy, in which Americans learned the art of association or citizenship.[55] In Milkis's view, the New Deal initiated a long-range project for undermining parties of this latter character.[56]

Milkis's concern with parties may seem irrelevant to Rohr's theme, until we ask why *The Federalist* did not rely heavily on constitutional "legitimacy." Rohr argues cogently that the public administrators will never be regarded as lawful rulers until they accept the law to which the people are attached, the Constitution. His unspoken premise is that the people will continue to be attached to this law. Perhaps so. Milkis, if I understand him correctly, agrees with Tocqueville that it is through the life of association that the people come to be attached to the Constitution. The Jeffersonian parties were modes of affirming such attachment to the law, and not only for the instrumental purpose of turning it against partisan enemies.[57] Once such parties have been undermined, popular attachment can no longer be presumed.

On Milkis's reading, the New Deal was sufficiently indebted to Progressive theory to share its animus against both the Jeffersonian parties and the Founders' Constitution. FDR was more effective, however, in directing this animus. Instead of learning from experience what Rohr thinks the New Dealers learned—practical moderation and a skepticism about theoretic politics (lessons that would have brought them closer to the Constitution)—Milkis finds that they learned realism and Machiavellian prudence. FDR discovered the effectual truth about how to get around the fundamental law and to befuddle the principles at issue. Milkis thus answers in the negative the question we raised for Hawley: FDR adopted anti-bureaucratic formulations primarily for manipulative purposes. The radical advice one might draw from Hawley's analysis thus proves, on Milkis's account, to have been nearly Roosevelt's intention. After executive reorganization what FDR did by improvisation could henceforth be done deliberately and regularly; the logic of presidential responsibilities in the new office would lead even Republican Presidents, like Nixon and Reagan, to weaken the political parties and republican citizenship still further.

By focusing in detail on the evidence of Roosevelt's intention, Milkis enables the reader to judge for himself whether the executive reorganization plan was vital to the New Deal and to its institutional legacy. His is also the first essay to confront the Hillsdale invitational statement squarely by arguing that the New Deal altered the conditions for partisan realignment by deliberate structural innovations in the U.S. constitutional order.[58] He thus prompts us to reflect on the significance of the New Deal as the first realigning endeavor in American political history that made the executive central to its long-range program.

The New Deal was the first realignment to focus national attention on the potential of the presidency to extend the political capability of a democratic people by enacting a major legislative and administrative program over time.[59] The thrust of the first two realigning movements had been explicitly in the opposite direction. In 1800 the Republicans, under Jefferson and Madison, had campaigned to dismantle the Hamiltonian program and to prevent the development of an executive establishment at the national level. The purpose of presidential party leadership in the Jeffersonian mold was to capture the executive office in order to contain and minimize its constitutional potentials, especially its potential to strengthen the role of the executive in constitutional government.[60]

Van Buren reasserted this deconstructive policy when he restored the party conflict to center stage after 1828. Whatever one may say about the slavery issue and the rise of the Republican party during the 1850s, the restoration of a strong executive as the point d'appui for a new national program was unanticipated, and indeed Lincoln's adroit use of executive power surprised most of his Republican colleagues. Some of the strongest threats to the presidency came in fact from the Republicans in Lincoln's cabinet. Most of what Lincoln accomplished in consolidating the executive power was unforeseen and eventuated in the course of a war no one wanted. In 1896 the realignment that brought urban immigrants into the Republican fold was led on a pronouncedly modest and inactive platform by William McKinley. It opened a period of remarkable executive activism, but only by the accident of Theodore Roosevelt's ascent from the vice-presidency. Thus before the New Deal none of the programs to which the electorate had subscribed during a realignment had dramatized or called for a substantial exercise of the executive power that had been formally provided by the original constitutional plan.

This capacity was enucleated in the original Constitution but never wholeheartedly endorsed until Franklin Roosevelt, with fine panache, made the presidency central to the New Deal program. But the New Deal was not only first; it was conscious of being first. Roosevelt understood that initiating a new direction meant to counteract the traditional pattern of realignment and the habits that had sustained it. The New Deal was therefore also the first realigning effort to come to terms with the weight of this history of realignment in American politics. To say that previous realignments had been attempts to dismantle the executive power or to prevent it from developing along the lines of the original Federalist constitution, and that the New Deal was the first great effort to reverse this emphasis, is to say that established partisan habits were a serious threat to the New Deal; they rendered doubtful the transmission of the New Deal; they threatened the dismantling of its institutions; they were a major obstacle, at least in potential, to the continuity of the New Deal or its permanence. A realignment along the old lines could have canceled the "New Deal legacy" before it was firmly established. Had Roosevelt not considered this danger and prepared for it he would have been highly imprudent indeed. FDR was more aware than other New Dealers of what Jefferson had accomplished, and hence more thoughtful in finding a remedy.[61]

The dialogue betwen Rohr and Milkis may cause us to reflect with FDR on what Jefferson accomplished, and to ask whether the remedy that the New Deal framed, through executive reorganization, was as antithetical to republican citizenship as Milkis contends. It will be recalled that Rohr was reluctant to read the Constitution in such a way that great necessities would force us to break its mold. The Jeffersonian interpretation was, in certain respects, intended to compel us to do just that—to so construe the Constitution that it would permanently reinforce republican virtue. Van Buren wedded the American parties to the Jeffersonian interpretation of the Constitution. Both attempted to set the constitutional instrument against any long-range policy that might endanger republican virtue. This meant that the task of political science and the legislator's art was biased by all the habits of party life toward an Anti-Federalist policy. The spirit of *The Federalist*, by contrast, was to confront the recurrent necessity for such long-range policies and encourage a republican people to submit to the challenge that necessity posed to its virtue. As one distinguished commentator explains *The Federalist*'s political science,

The task of "reflection" . . . is to take account of things in nature and by chance that cannot be chosen and to match them with things that can be chosen. A republic might prefer to live by itself, under a homogeneous majority, and with virtues to keep it moderate. But a regard to the necessities of international relations and of human nature will reveal that these desirable things are beyond the power of human choice. Reflection, then, in the form of political science, will teach a republic not to choose what is, abstractly, most choiceworthy, but to be content with, or indeed make the best of, a large territory, a diverse people, and a spirit of interest and ambition.[62]

On this reading the executive is central to the constitutional order as a means of preserving the possibility of self-government, of reflection and choice, within a world that only grudgingly or sparingly permits self-government, a world dominated by accident and force.

It is especially in the executive that republican choice is given a new capability. For the executive not only provides decisions in emergencies as one ingredient of "energy" but also, as another ingredient, the duration of administration that makes possible "extensive and arduous enterprises'' (*The Federalist* 72). Such enterprises are familiar to us today as the long-term programs of legislation and administration—the New Deal, the Reagan Revolution—which always have their origin in the executive branch. Precisely the branch that most recognizes the limits to human choice arising from emergencies best extends human choice in the capability to set a general direction for policy now and in the future. An able executive will improve upon the occasions of his decisions. He will make his quick reactions consistent with his general program, so that his quickness is not merely willful but somehow connects to his lasting intent.[63]

THE NEW DEAL REALIGNMENT AND AMERICAN CONSTITUTIONALISM

If Roosevelt's attempt at executive reorganization thus raises the problem of how republican choice can be sustained within a world of accident and force, students of the New Deal face this problem in even more dramatic form when they attempt to judge his political and moral rhetoric. To clarify the issues raised by New Deal rhetoric, it will helpful to compare some remarks by Russell Kirk on the New Deal.[64]

Almost every essay in this volume might be said (in Kirk's phrase) to provide "instruction to seekers after prudence, pointing the way toward right conduct through knowledge of the blunders and successes of the past."[65] Kirk objected to a particular strain in New Deal rhetoric that seems to amplify the role of accident and force. By arguing from the compulsion of circumstances, Roosevelt and the New Dealers at times justified their reforms not because they were rationally defensible and choiceworthy measures but because movement and action were necessary to avoid revolution or civil war. Kirk joined the debate over these asserted necessities by reopening the question, Did the New Deal avert a violent revolution in the United States?

In answering this question, Kirk found it in certain respects unnecessary to be close to the center of power to judge democratic statesmen:

Neither will it do to rely altogether upon the memoirs of leading men of the period, few of whom were perfectly ingenuous; nor upon "court histories" of that period. For in a democracy, the beliefs, interests, moods, and passions of the mass of the people are more powerful causes of historical events than are the polemics of eminent politicians and publicists.[66]

FDR's prudence is generally held to be superior precisely in gauging these powerful causes, "the beliefs, interests, moods, and passions of the mass of the people." Kirk challenged this received assessment by giving an account of popular moods and passions, as he observed them himself during the Thirties. According to Kirk, the American people were more deliberate, more attached to constitutional forms, more law-abiding, more skeptical of appeals beyond their political experience, more dubious about the scope of theory in practical affairs than New Deal alarms let on. Kirk intimates that the American people understood themselves better than the New Dealers, and chose sensibly, despite the hysterical rhetoric about violent revolution, for the moderate optimism of the New Deal program. His implied argument is that FDR did not sway the masses away from violent revolution but, rather, was swayed by them to adopt the course he took. According to Kirk, Americans were not thrown far out of the course of their established political and moral habits by the depression. They sensibly repudiated Herbert Hoover, welcoming the new administration because its program was one of hope and confidence. The electorate was never stampeded out of their sound civil habits by the hardships of the depression.

To judge this assessment, one has to establish what this New Deal rhetoric meant in the context of American traditions. On this important question, the essayists are in disagreement. As I read them, John A. Wettergreen and Hiram Caton would be inclined to say that the metaphor serves a fairly clear purpose: to alert the electorate to the need for constitutional initiatives—the need to affirm and do again, on a lesser scale, what the American people did in adopting the Constitution in 1789. On this view, the rhetorical prospect of violent revolution was no different from the rhetorical prospect of dissolution under the Articles of Confederation that Publius repeatedly sketched in *The Federalist*. The New Deal rhetoric was a way to bring forward an unwelcome choice that a republican people would normally prefer to postpone—a way of precipitating another choice against the Anti-Federalist tradition, or against our tendency to defer any issue that might compel us to acknowledge that a free people is bound by necessities.[67] Perhaps during the thirties the political maturity of the American people was shown in taking this rhetoric as it was intended.

In chapter 7 Charles Kesler brings to life one of Roosevelt's most important programmatic statements by comparing it systematically with Woodrow Wilson's public philosophy. Focusing on one of the few texts that reveals FDR's political thought and intention, the Commonwealth Club Address of 1932, Kesler asks to what extent that speech can be understood as a Wilsonian manifesto. "Almost entirely" is his controversial answer.

As Kesler reminds us, Roosevelt built on a Progressive, Wilsonian tradition that took seriously the problem of cultural milieu and received political tradition. The Wilsonian notion of "public philosophy" was at once a way of characterizing the received cultural milieu as a product of culture and of setting it up for attack.[68] Public philosophy is a dressy term for public opinion, and publics are fickle, especially in a democracy. Wilson discovered how to turn a perceived weakness of democracies (the weak-mindedness of democrats or their manipulability by demagogues) into a respectable opening for strongminded opinion leaders.

The intention of Kesler's analysis is to direct our attention to the problem of natural right in Wilson's repudiation of the Declaration of Independence, which he argues FDR seconded and in certain respects renovated. The crux in interpreting the Commonwealth Club Address, Kesler contends, is to decide what FDR meant when he described the essential task of statesmanship as the "redefinition of rights." Kessler finds that this new task required a fundamental departure from the American political tradition and was therefore Roosevelt's most enduring and revolutionary contribution to the American regime. In this speech on progressive government, Roosevelt radically reinterpreted the Declaration by replacing its principles of natural right with an historical process: history becomes the source of guidance for political action and sanctions an enterprise of continuous redefinition of rights. Thus the impermanence of all rights, or the complete politicization of rights, appears to Kesler to be the essential legacy of the New Deal. In this key manner, Roosevelt was not attuned to the American consensus on basic principles, but at war with it, laying the foundation for more innovative redefinitions of rights by LBJ, John Rawls, and more recent opinion leaders.

Kesler brings to light these philosophical underpinnings of Wilsonian liberalism in part because conservative Burkeans will be loathe to challenge them. As he has argued, disciples of Burke on the right have more in common with their counterparts on the left than they recognize.[69] For Woodrow Wilson, as Kesler remarks, was consistently a devotee of Burke, and the essential task FDR derived from Wilson was a Burkean task. If the true conservatism is Progressivism, as Wilson claimed, then it should follow that the most effective radicalism will be Burkean as well, and for Kesler this describes the ineffectual predicament of many conservative critics of the New Deal. Kesler would agree that the rhetoric about immanent revolution was merely "Democratic boiler-plate," but he shows that the more important part of Roosevelt's rhetoric was his success in silencing the Declaration of Independence, or rather, redefining the rights it enunciated. Kesler would say that American conservatives have followed in FDR's wake by silencing the Declaration themselves. The conservative Burkean statesmen, Kesler thinks, joins in the demolition while claiming to minimize it, making it appear that rights have gradually redefined themselves—whereas FDR took credit and sought popular gratitude for the generosity of his innovation. For Kesler, this again describes the ineffectual predicament of conservative critics of the New Deal.

In chapter 8 Arthur Shenfield turns us to the Supreme Court, furthering our inquiry into the Progressive legacy with a critique of Oliver Wendell Holmes's jurisprudence and its reception in New Deal cases.

Shenfield would defend the Constitution on its original principles; though an Englishman himself, he does not assert (as Jeanne Kirkpatrick and Russell Kirk have asserted) that the rights proclaimed in the Declaration of Independence and vindicated in the American Revolution were merely the Rights of Englishmen. Shenfield finds a continuity between the jurisprudence of John Marshall and the exercise of judicial review by the pre-New Deal Court, on the argument that the Court's development of the doctrine of substantive due process was not fundamentally out of line with the founders' political economy; more precisely, he identifies the political economy of Adam Smith with the political science of the framers.[70]

At first glance, however, Marshall's jurisprudence seems to reflect a more restrained and moderate understanding of judicial review. In regard to economic doctrine, one may recognize a similarity between Marshall's decisions protecting national commerce and decisions against populist majorities within the states during the 1890s.[71] But substantive due process jurisprudence represented a type of judicial review—of constitutional interpretation—much closer to the judicial review of the New Deal Court.[72] The difference between substantive due process and substantive equal protection, on Shenfield's reading, would seem to be that the former was defensible by the founders' political economy.[73] Even granting that this were so, it cannot be denied that judicial activism since the New Deal has built on the foundation laid in the 1890s.[74]

It is worth noting that during this period "the Supreme Court did not look upon *The Federalist* as the authoritative commentary on the original intention of the framers and ratifiers of the Constitution, nor did the justices turn to it for guidance on controverted questions of constitutional interpretation."[75] Perhaps one reason that they did not may be, as Edward J. Erler has argued, that during these five decades, the Court was engaged more or less continuously in a violation of the letter and the spirit of *The Federalist*'s teaching on separation of powers.[76]

In chapter 9, Hiram Caton asks to what extent the New Deal needs to be understood in conjunction with the conservative opposition in order to locate it in the American political tradition.

Caton's survey of conservative opposition to the New Deal is an argument that the growing political strength of American conservatism has not been matched with proportionate intellectual accomplishments. This is not because conservatives were weak-minded but because the framework of thought they adopted required them to jettison the rationality of American enlightenment, including the political science that informed the Constitution. They have been in the compromised position of a conservatism that repudiates the greatest institutions and political traditions of the nation for whom they claim to speak. Having abandoned their vocation to conserve what is best, they should not be surprised when the electorate refuses to entrust them with the responsibility of governing.

Caton traces the conservative repudiation of the Federalist legacy to two sources: one, the dependence on European conservatism for intellectual sustenance, as in Russell Kirk's famous preference for Edmund Burke; and the other, on the libertarian side, the mistaken belief that Adam Smith was a sufficient guide or shield for a modern commercial economy.

Shenfield and Caton disagree as to the place of Adam Smith's political economy in *The Federalist* and in the Constitution as originally ratified. Shenfield argues that laissez-faire economics, properly understood, was fundamental to the original constitutional tradition.

According to Caton, the New Deal refurbished and empowered the original Constitution and governmental program by freeing it from the encumbrances of Smithian political economy and the rest of the baggage of Jeffersonian agrarianism.

Caton argues that the rigid identification of the original constitutional scheme with what came to be known as laissez-faire economic doctrine was a profound modification of the original principles of the founders' political science. It was an attempt to combat the Federalists and Alexander Hamilton by excluding the Hamiltonian critique of Adam Smith from Republican orthodoxy, and eventually from Republican constitutional historiography. Shenfield accepts this Jeffersonian revanche as correct when he claims that the founders had read Adam Smith, implying that they agreed with Smith on fundamentals. But, as Caton notes, Smith's political economy was a critique of the Court Whig approach to political and economic modernization. The Court Whigs under the leadership of Walpole had launched England on the course of capitalist development; Federalist political economy under the leadership of Hamilton was a continuation of Court Whig policy. As Caton shows in detail in his comprehensive history of *The Politics of Progress*, Smith failed to understand the Baconian dimension of modern capitalism, or its connection to mastery of nature; in particular, Smith prepared the way for Malthusian pessimism because he neglected the role that was to be played by natural energy sources, newly tapped by modern science, in capitalist production. To Smith, as to the Physiocrats, agriculture seemed to be the primary foundation of a modern economy, and his teaching therefore became the authoritative doctrine of Jeffersonian critics of the modern commercial republic. Like Forrest McDonald, Caton contends that Smith dominated Jeffersonian reaction against Federalist political economy, and that the New Deal return to Hamiltonian views on the regulatory powers of the general government were, on this score (as the New Dealers argued), a genuinely conservative reading of the Constitution: it restored the Court Whig and Federalist understanding of the liberal commercial republic.[77] Insofar as Shenfield binds the Constitution to Smithian economics, Caton would contend that he is in the awkward posture of defending a system of policy that was, in fundamental respects, at war with the politics of progress and of the liberal commercial republic, and that put the Constitution at war with it as well.

What concerns John Wettergreen is not so much the problem of violent revolution raised by Russell Kirk and New Deal rhetoric, but the revolutionary implications of what the Depression did (despite the New Deal) to the American middle class by destroying its economic independence and reducing everyone to the status of a wage earner or salaried employee. Taking a page from Aristotle's *Politics*, he reminds us in chapter 11 of what experience and common sense taught the founders, that even with the best constitutional arrangements, the fate of a commercial republic would depend on the virtue of its middle class and on the participation of its middle class in public affairs. In the final analysis, constitutional government is self-government. The great threat to self-government that the Depression posed was the destruction of the economic foundations of an independent middle class by destroying their savings and forcing the sale of their properties.

One of the questions Hawley does not raise concerns the moral content of the objections to bureaucratic administration or the state that gave anti-statist formulations their cutting edge and polemical bite. His essay is open to the interpretation that such moral considerations are merely an obstacle that astute state-builders should humor without giving them weight. John Wettergreen is less equivocal on this score. His essay spells out why the bureaucratic formulations that Progressives had earlier advanced were abandoned by the New Dealers. His contention that such measures had proved their political bankruptcy and inef-fectiveness puts Hawley's discussion in a new light; from this perspective, the synthesis of anti-statist and statist measures that the New Dealers sought was more rational and enlightened than either of its components taken alone.

What Wettergreen has in view throughout his essay is the character of the regime that a regulatory arrangement supports. He is also concerned with what labor and capital were willing to do to the U.S. Constitution, a nonviolent revolution that was averted by Roosevelt. Wettergreen contends that regulatory policy is at the heart of regime politics in America, and that the changes labor and capital respectively proposed during the New Deal would have transformed the United States into a socialist regime by making labor and capital wards or adjuncts of the government. Roosevelt's regulatory policy in framing the SEC and NLRB succeeded in preventing the real threat of revolution in the 1930s, which would come not from discontented mobs led by demagogues, but by organized interests trying to secure themselves through an illicit and unconsti-tutional alliance to government.

No one seriously challenges John Wettergreen's claim that the New Deal failed to prevent the Depression from destroying the economic independence of the American middle class or from converting it into a stratum of wage earners without substantial savings or property. In that respect all Americans seem to be more subject to accident and force—less free to reflect and choose a career or course of conduct—because they have no visible means of support. To use Max Weber's formulation, no one is economically dispensable, and this affects not only one's availability for citizenship or politics but one's ability to step back and meditate on the general direction of one's own life.[78]

In chapter 4, Ellis Hawley raised the possibility that administrative state-builders or interventionists might be more effective if they imitated the New Deal. My opening description of earlier public perceptions of the New Deal was designed to recall what one might well have learned from FDR's respect for anti-bureaucratic tradition and from his practice was the art of consensus politics. What the reformers learned instead is the subject of chapter 12, which points to considerations of democratic honor that contemporary social scientists have ig-nored in discussing realignment. This dimension of the New Deal drama is explored in order to demonstrate that the New Dealers themselves—beginning with Roosevelt and Felix Frankfurter—attached great weight to the political question of who deserves to be honored. Since 1968, I contend, presidential contests have been regarded primarily in this light within the Democratic party; the Democrats took this concern to an extreme by leaving the presidency to the Republicans, making the campaign chiefly a vehicle for establishing the respect-ability of new types of candidates.

The reform effort of recent decades abandoned the quest for consensus as Roosevelt understood it, as an agreement between citizens, about ruling and being ruled in turn, defining who is eligible to be entrusted with public offices. The recent Democratic assumption has been that no honorable agreement between the majority and minorities can be reached on this matter. Chapter 12 seeks to show how democratic honor and consensus politics are connected by showing how Roosevelt connected them. It also attempts to explain the ambiguity of Roosevelt's consensus politics by considering how his example was imitated by the interventionists who remade American institutions after 1964. Their recent reforms have made it difficult for Americans as a majority to share any idea of honor in common and in public; they have simultaneously made consensus politics newly problematic.[79]

CONCLUSION

Taken together, the essays that follow Coleman's indicate how the world of interventionism that Coleman describes was received by the New Deal, forming and being formed by it. They ask whether, or to what extent, the New Deal realignment succeeded in converting the disciples of that world into defenders of free government and American constitutional traditions; and they debate the quality of Franklin Roosevelt's attempt to fashion a new world of liberalism. The invitational statement from Hillsdale asked what light a reassessment of Roosevelt and the New Deal might shed on the practical political tasks Americans face today. What can we learn from this volume about realignment and the tasks of statesmanship bequeathed by the New Deal?[80]

In considering Milkis's essay, we found in it an effort to come to grips with what was distinctive about the New Deal realignment that might help to explain the apparent discontinuity in the cyclical pattern of realignments in American political history. Milkis centered his inquiries on the connection between executive reorganization and the decline of parties, exploring FDR's strategy for transforming the capability of the presidency in the light of his intention to insulate the New Deal program from the influence of the traditional American party system. Realignment as a recurrent historical pattern had been the result of repeated efforts, by Jefferson, Madison, Van Buren, and others, to secure sound republican habits of self-government through a distinctive kind of political party. Milkis argues that such parties and the habits they nurtured were the target of New Deal efforts to transform both the formal or parchment constitution and the informal or working constitution. It is his thesis that Roosevelt substantially succeeded, until a conservative presidential party emerged under Ronald Reagan, to challenge the New Deal program systematically. His essay prompted us to reflect on the significance of the New Deal as a circumspect attempt to forestall a traditional partisan realignment, which would have probably undermined any long-term program initiated from the executive branch. We conclude that if a new realignment is to be attempted, the precondition of its success would be the emergence of a Hamiltonian opposition to the New Deal within one of the major parties. This is so because the traditional Jeffersonian parties under which previous realignments had taken place—the last being the New Deal realignment headed by the party of Jefferson and Jackson—could not compete with the formidable combination of politics and administration that Milkis describes. A new form of constitutionalist party, one not opposed in principle to a strong constitutional executive, would have to be built.

Charles Kesler suggested the direction for a principled repudiation of the New Deal program that would be open to such an opposition party: namely, to refound the strong constitutional executive squarely on the principles of the Declaration of Independence, repudiating the Wilsonian public philosophy that FDR brought forward into the New Deal and, indeed, challenging the historicist notion of public philosophy itself because that notion demotes the Declaration to the marginal status of mere received opinion.[81]

Our practical objections to the interventionist approach to the study of politics and realignment may be summed up with a hypothetical example. Certain tasks of statesmanship requiring initiative and concerted political effort—including intervention by government into the course of history—are difficult to conceive and probably impossible to execute if one adopts the perspective of the world of reform. The most substantial example in the United States was the consolidation of a political majority opposed to the extension of slavery, which led to electoral victory in 1860 and provided the political basis for a war against secession. For the reasons we have touched on earlier, the interventionists studied by Coleman would not have intervened by founding a political party dedicated to the principles of the Declaration of Independence; they could not have imitated the traditional American political parties along these lines because, as we have noticed, they were profoundly cut off from the world of American parties and wanted to be liberated from it. For similar reasons they would not have intervened—certainly not to the point of risking a civil war—in order to defend the majority principle of Lockean republicanism. Nor could they have prepared themselves for any intervention that required them to perfect their capacities as statesmen; for as we have seen, they regarded the world of statesmanship as alien both to the proper political education and to their principal tasks. They would not have intervened to preserve the Union, or, more generally, the liberal commercial republic for which the Constitution had been framed, because they were transfixed by an alternative regime, of Hegelian lineage, the administrative state. For all these reasons the world of interventionism could not have done what Abraham Lincoln did—end slavery while preserving the founders' republic.

It is therefore incorrect to suppose, as the New Dealers evidently did, that a strong executive program in line with the Hamiltonian understanding of the constitutional order could only be based on Wilsonian principles, which Kesler shows were historicist principles. A republican constitutional order based on the principles of natural right articulated in the Declaration of Independence—on principles of justice—could be reinvigorated by a program for the reassertion of

Lockean republicanism, without reverting to the weak executive of Jeffersonian politics. That had already been demonstrated by Abraham Lincoln. But it is a formidable objection to interventionist politics that such a reassertion is as unthinkable from an interventionist perspective as it was from the standpoint of John Randolph of Roanoke or John C. Calhoun.

The subsequent chapters suggest the elements of such a realigning program that would come to terms with the New Deal legacy in practice by intervening on behalf of justice.

In reflecting on the potential dialogue between Arthur Shenfield and Hiram Caton as revealed in their essays, we noted that in the United States Adam Smith's political economy had buttressed the Jeffersonian opposition to the strong constitutional executive and that a rethinking of Smith as an analyst of capitalism or of the modern Baconian collaboration between science and commerce would be a precondition or concomitant of a realignment designed to put the capability of the constitutional executive to work on the problems generated by the New Deal legacy.

In John Wettergreen's chapter, one major task of the executive, the formation of regulatory frameworks that are consistent with the Constitution and with the character of the American regime, came into focus. To the extent that regulatory institutions are the skeleton of the New Deal legacy, and that such appropriate limits cannot be set to regulation on the basis of received New Deal principles, the task of realigning statesmanship in the executive branch must be to assert limits to regulation. The dialogue between Frisch and Wettergreen over the effect of the New Deal on the spirit of the American middle class brings us to one last dimension of realignment. If republican self-government is to continue after the Jeffersonian political economy based on agrarian foundations has disappeared, clearly one critical question is whether the political virtues of an independent citizenry can be cultivated in the American middle class. The Country Whig program that Jefferson consolidated in America was predicated on the belief that a republican standard for distributing offices and honors could only be undermined by a strong constitutional executive. Jefferson attempted to make the American presidency a symbol of executive self-abnegation: the president would not use his quasi-monarchic prerogatives to foster a stratum of courtiers and officeholders such as Robert Walpole had used to strengthen the British executive. The monarch as a source of benefices and titles was the great bugbear of Jeffersonian republicanism. The essential point was that political virtue required both economic and psychological independence, and that citizens who were beholden to a strong executive for income and honors would be crippled by such dependency. That is why Wettergreen and Milkis would be skeptical of John Rohr's suggestion that we look to civil servants for the republican virtue that was of concern to the Anti-Federalists. Regulatory policy is critical not only to protect the citizen from the economic power of corporations, labor, and big agriculture but also to protect the citizen who participates in such organizations from the politically crippling effects of dependence on government. This is the permanent truth in Jefferson's quest for some class or group that would nurture republican virtue. If we cannot look to "yeomen," or to an agrarian middle class, to protect and nurture such virtue, we must ask more seriously than the New Dealers how the political moderation of a middle class in the Aristotelian sense can be promoted in a liberal commercial republic.

The favorable public assessment I have sketched at the beginning of this chapter was a reflection of the standard of honor to which most Americans think they should be held; it is a standard of middle class moral and political virtue. They thought that the New Deal had been an attempt to assert and defend that standard, and they have been looking for a party, a president, and a Congress to be their standard-bearer ever since. If we may be permitted to ignore our differences and sum up the practical lesson in a sentence: The political and constitutional legacy of the New Deal currently seems to be to leave the majority that is trying to live by that standard with a potentially capable executive, but without adequate means of common deliberation and public judgment.

NOTES

1. The papers represent a selection of submissions in response to an invitation; one purpose of this chapter is to assess how the essays, taken together, measure up to the challenge posed in the invitational statement, which is given in the Preface to this volume.

2. Grant McConnell's critique of the New Deal regime was, therefore, divided into three parts: agriculture, labor, and business. McConnell, *Private Power and American Democracy* (New York: Vintage Books, 1966).

3. The Republican platform of 1988 is a reassertion of the platforms of 1980 and 1984, with only a few marginal modifications; compare the *New York Times*, August 11, 1988, A1, A14.

4. Douglas A. Jeffrey and Dennis Teti, "A Political Party in Search of Itself: Republican Realignment and the Dallas Platform of 1984," in *The 1984 Election and the Future of American Politics*, ed. Dennis J. Mahoney and Peter W. Schramm (Durham, N.C.: Carolina Academic Press, 1987), 56.

5. Ibid.

6. McConnell, *Private Power*; Theodore J. Lowi, *The End of Liberalism: The Second Republic of the United States* (New York: W.W. Norton, 1979).

7. Wayne D. Rasmussen and Gladys L. Baker, "The New Deal Farm Programs: The Myth and the Reality," in *The Roosevelt New Deal: A Program Assessment Fifty Years After*, ed. Wilbur J. Cohen (Austin, Tex.: Lydon B. Johnson School of Public Affairs, 1986), 216.

8. McConnell, *Private Power*, 54, 69, 336–68; Lowi, *The End of Liberalism*, 273–74. Lowi's contribution to a new regulatory politics is dissected in Harvey C. Mansfield, Jr., *The Spirit of Liberalism* (Cambridge, Mass.: Harvard University Press, 1979), 28–51. See also Brand's thoughtful reassessment of Lowi's critique of New Deal corporatism in Donald R. Brand, *Corporatism and the Rule of Law: The National Recovery Administration* (Ithaca, N.Y.: Cornell University Press, 1988), 1–30.

9. Beatrice Biship Berle and Travis Beal Jacobs, eds., *Navigating the Rapids 1918–1970: From the Papers of Adolf A. Berle* (New York: Harcourt Brace Jovanovich, 1973).

10. McConnell, *Private Power*, 54, 336ff.; Lowi, *The End of Liberalism*, 53, 71, 84.

11. The most widely recognized instance of such closer attention to what the New Deal had asked for is the work on what FDR sought from executive reorganization. See the works in the bibliography of this volume by Barry Karl, Richard Polenberg, and Sidney Milkis. We begin with executive reorganization in chapters 5 and 6, discussed in the next section of this chapter. See also Ellis W. Hawley, "The Corporate Ideal as Liberal Philosophy in the New Deal," in *The Roosevelt New Deal*, 851–83.

12. In his book developing this thesis, Coleman equates interventionism with reform, as his title suggests: see Peter J. Coleman, *Progressivism and the World of Reform: New Zealand and the Origins of the American Welfare State* (Lawrence: University Press of Kansas, 1987). I have followed his lead in using them interchangeably.

13. The disputes to be reviewed concerning Coleman's essay are controversies over his definition of interventionism, inter alia. Disputes over the constitutionality of intervention are coeval with the Constitution. The assertion that the governing activities defined by the founders' conception of limited government were not interventionist, or that they were circumscribed by a market economy governed by natural laws that the statesman could not alter was a product of Adam Smith's teaching as adapted by the Jeffersonian opponents of Hamilton. This circumscribed view of the scope of legislation and statesmanship was further reinforced in conservative circles by the reception of Edmund Burke's teaching. In these pages we reopen the debate over these fundamental issues. In my judgment, an adequate critique and reappraisal of the New Deal conception of interventionism would have to explore thoroughly the issues discussed in this chapter concerning the nature of enlightened administration, the idea of the administrative state, the character of administration under the founders' Constitution, the role of the executive in extending a republican people's capacity for considered choice, and the nature of realigning statesmanship. Here we broach these issues rather than attempt a definition of the controversial term interventionism.

14. Cf. Paul B. Cook, *Academicians in Government from Roosevelt to Roosevelt* (New York: Garland, 1982); John A. Rohr, *To Run a Constitution: The Legitimacy of the Administrative State* (Lawrence: The University Press of Kansas, 1986), 55–110.

15. Arthur Schlesinger, Jr., *The Coming to Power: Critical Elections in American History* (New York: Chelsea House, 1971), 456–68; Albert U. Romasco, *The Politics of Recovery: Roosevelt's New Deal* (New York: Oxford University Press, 1983); Kenneth W. Davis, *FDR: The New Deal Years, 1933–1937* (New York: Random House, 1986), 1–15.

16. Much imagination has gone into the task of obscuring the coercive side of interventionism or, as Morton Frisch says, into crafting a "soft despotism" such as Tocqueville envisioned. Those who prize their intellectual and spiritual independence of political authority should be the first to see through these devices.

17. Charles O. Jones, "Can Our Parties Survive Our Politics," in *The Role of the Legislature in Western Democracies*, ed. Norman J. Ornstein (Washington, D.C.: American Enterprise Institute, 1981); James W. Ceaser, "Political Change and Party Reform," in *Political Parties in the Eighties*, ed. Robert A. Goldwin (Washington, D.C.: American Enterprise Institute, 1980), 97–115.

18. Abigail M. Thernstrom, *Whose Votes Count? Affirmative Action and Minority Voting Rights* (Cambridge, Mass.: Harvard University Press, 1987); Ward E. Y. Elliott, *The Rise of Guardian Democracy: The Supreme Court's Role in Voting Rights Disputes*,

1845–1969 (Cambridge, Mass.: Harvard University Press, 1974); James Piereson, "Party Government," *Political Science Reviewer* 12 (1982): 2–53.

19. James W. Ceaser, *Presidential Selection: Theory and Development* (Princeton, N.J.: Princeton University Press, 1979); Ceaser, *Reforming the Reforms* (Cambridge, Mass.: Balinger, 1982). See also Richard M. Pious, ed., *The Power to Govern: Assessing Reform in the United States* (New York: Academy of Political Science, 1981); Elliott, *Rise of Guardian Democracy*.

20. V. O. Key introduced the term secular realignment to describe shifts in electoral habits resulting from gradual changes in the socioeconomic interests of voting groups: as an immigrant group moved into the middle class, the change in its interests would be reflected in new party affiliations or voting habits. See V. O. Key, Jr., "Secular Realignment and the Party System," *Journal of Politics* 21 (1959): 198–210. I adapt it here to describe the formation of a political class whose professional interests are closely connected with the expansion of the welfare state.

21. A condensed and relatively accessible account may be found in Allan Bloom, *The Closing of the American Mind: How Higher Education Has Failed Democracy and Impoverished the Souls of Today's Students* (New York: Simon & Schuster, 1987), 141–93, 298–305. A more comprehensive scholarly account is given in George Armstrong Kelly, *Idealism, Politics and History: Sources of Hegelian Thought* (Cambridge, Eng.: Cambridge University Press, 1969).

22. Jean-Jacques Rousseau, *Emile: or On Education*, trans. Allan Bloom (New York: Basic Books, 1979), 11–22.

23. Ibid., 171–75; Jean-Jacques Rousseau, *The First and Second Discourses*, ed. Victor Gourevitch (New York: Harper & Row, 1986), 28–115.

24. Susan Meld Shell, *The Rights of Reason: A Study of Kant's Philosophy and Politics* (Toronto: University of Toronto Press, 1980).

25. Kelly, *Idealism, Politics, and History*.

26. Robert Eden, "Weber and Nietzsche: Liberating the Social Sciences from Historicism," in *Max Weber and His Contemporaries*, ed. Wolfgang J. Mommsen, Juergen Osterhammel and R. S. Whimster (London: Allen & Unwin, 1987). See also Wilhelm Hennis, "A Science of Man: Max Weber and the Political Economy of the German Historical School," in *Max Weber*, 25–58; Manfred Schön, "Gustav Schmoller and Max Weber," in *Max Weber*, 59–70. In France the declension from Montesquieu and Rousseau to the founding of social science took a somewhat different path. Stephen P. Turner, *The Search for a Methodology of Social Science: Durkheim, Weber, and the Nineteenth-Century Problem of Cause, Probability, and Action*. Boston Studies in the Philosophy of Science, vol. 92 (Dordrecht: D. Reidel, 1986).

27. The reformer's view of Hegel was, in many respects, a crude and vulgarized picture that cannot be taken as gospel. By contrast, Michael Oakeshott understands Hegel's political philosophy as the most coherent and thoughtful articulation of civil association, and contends that Hobbes and the founders of modern liberalism were defenders of the same morality of individualism that Hegel subsequently defended in his *Philosophy of Right*. See Oakeshott, *On Human Conduct* (Oxford: Clarendon Press, 1975), 257–63. For an account deeply indebted to Hegel that rejects the crude picture of American civil, ethical, and religious experience, see George Armstrong Kelly, *Politics and Religious Consciousness in America* (New Brunswick, N.J.: Transaction Books, 1984).

28. Michael Oakeshott's remark that the American founders were endowed with "civil knowledge to the point of genius" is an indication that Hegelian thought could lead to

a different assessment of the American regime; but see Oakeshott, *Rationalism in Politics and Other Essays* (New York: Oxford University Press, 1981), 26–28.

29. Cook, *Academicians in Government.*

30. The world of interventionism in its German form was one target of Max Weber's effort to restructure the social sciences and to defend politics against enlightened administration or rational bureaucracy. See Robert Eden, "Doing Without Liberalism: Weber's Regime Politics," *Political Theory* 10 (August 1982): 397–407.

31. Kent A. Kirwan, "The Crisis of Identity in the Study of Public Administration: Woodrow Wilson," *Polity* (Spring 1977): 321–43; Kirwan, "Historicism and Statesmanship in the Reform Argument of Woodrow Wilson," *Interpretation* 9 (September 1981): 339–51.

32. Max Weber, *Roscher and Knies: The Logical Problems of Historical Economics*, trans. and ed. Guy Oakes (New York: Free Press, 1975).

33. Kirwan, "Historicism and Statesmanship." See also Charles R. Kesler, "Woodrow Wilson and the Statesmanship of Progress," in *Natural Right and Political Right: Essays in Honor of Harry V. Jaffa*, ed. Thomas B. Silver and Peter W. Schramm (Durham, N.C.: Carolina Academic Press, 1984), 103–27; Dennis J. Mahoney, "A Newer Science of Politics: *The Federalist* and American Political Science in the Progressive Era," in *Saving the Revolution: The Federalist Papers and the American Founding*, ed. Charles R. Kesler (Glencoe, Ill.: The Free Press, 1987), 250–64.

34. Leo Strauss, *Natural Right and History* (Chicago: University of Chicago Press, 1953), 9–36.

35. Michael P. Zuckert, "Self-Evident Truth and the Declaration of Independence," *Review of Politics* 49 (Summer 1987): 319–39.

36. Charles R. Kesler, "The Founders and the Classics," in *The American Founding: Essays on the Formation of the Constitution*, ed. J. Jackson Barlow, Leonard W. Levy, and Ken Masugi (Westport, Conn.: Greenwood Press, 1988), 57–90.

37. John A. Wettergreen, "On the End of Thucydides's Narrative," *Interpretation* 9 (August 1980): 93–110; Charles R. Kesler, *Cicero and the Natural Law* (book in mss, Claremont-McKenna College).

38. Hiram Caton, *The Politics of Progress: The Origins and Development of the Commercial Republic, 1600–1835* (Gainesville: University Presses of Florida, 1988).

39. Morton J. Frisch, "The Treaty of Utrecht in Churchill's *Marlborough*," *Polity* (February 1978).

40. Morton J. Frisch, *Franklin D. Roosevelt: The Contribution of the New Deal to American Political Thought and Practice* (Boston: Twayne, 1975); Frisch, "Roosevelt the Conservator: A Rejoinder to Hofstadter," *Journal of Politics* 25 (1963): 361–72; Morton J. Frisch and Richard A. Stevens, *American Political Thought: The Philosophical Dimension of American Statesmanship* (New York: Charles Scribner's Sons, 1971).

41. Robert Eden, *Political Leadership and Nihilism: A Study of Weber and Nietzsche* (Gainesville: University Presses of Florida, 1984), 1–35; Kesler, "Woodrow Wilson," 103–27.

42. Eden, *Political Leadership and Nihilism*, 211–35; see also Ceaser, *Presidential Selection.*

43. "It may well be that President Roosevelt felt that an adequate history of his administration could be written only by a statesman." Edgar Eugene Robinson, *The Roosevelt Leadership, 1933–1945* (Philadelphia: J.B. Lippincott, 1955), 9.

44. Franklin Delano Roosevelt, *Public Papers and Addresses*, ed. Samuel Rosenman, 13 vols. (New York: Random House, 1938–50), 1932 vol., 752.

45. Lowi, *End of Liberalism*, 84, 273–74.

46. Ibid.

47. Cf. Barry D. Karl, *Executive Reorganization and Reform in the New Deal* (Cambridge, Mass.: Harvard University Press, 1963); Richard Polenberg, *Reorganizing Roosevelt's Government: The Controversy Over Executive Reorganization, 1936–1939* (Cambridge, Mass.: Harvard University Press, 1966); Sidney M. Milkis, "Franklin D. Roosevelt and the Transcendence of Partisan Politics," *Political Science Quarterly* 100 (Fall 1985): 479–504; Milkis, "The New Deal, Administrative Reform, and the Trancendence of Partisan Politics," *Administration and Society* 18 (February 1987): 433–72.

48. As Charles Kesler remarks in chapter 7, the prevalent view among New Deal historians is that FDR was an improviser who lacked any such comprehensive understanding or theory.

49. Hawley's analysis is thus compatible with Romasco's portrait of Roosevelt as a political tactician who responded directly to the domestic balance of power, giving the most powerful faction at the moment his entire attention. Cf. Romasco, *Politics of Recovery*.

50. Rohr's position is developed more comprehensively in his book *To Run a Constitution*; I have drawn on it for points left undeveloped in his chapter.

51. Harvey Flaumenhaft, "Hamilton's Administrative Republic and the American Presidency," in *The Presidency in the Constitutional Order*, ed. Joseph M. Bessette and Jeffrey Tulis (Baton Rouge: Louisiana State University Press, 1981), 65–112.

52. Cf. John. A. Wettergreen, "Constitutional Problems of American Bureaucracy in *I.N.S. v. Chadha*" (Paper presented at the Annual Meeting of the American Political Science Association, New Orleans, La., September 1985.)

53. Cf. further Rohr, *To Run a Constitution*, 161.

54. See John A. Wettergreen, "The American Voter and His Surveyors," *Political Science Reviewer* 7 (Fall 1977): 181–227.

55. Alexis de Tocqueville, *Democracy in America*, trans. George Lawrence (New York: Doubleday, 1966), vol. 1, pt. 2, chs. 2, 4; vol. 2, pt. 2, chs. 2–7.

56. The gravity of this concern is underscored if we agree to Milkis's implied premise that such parties are the only form of association that can provide an effective channel for democratic participation.

57. Tocqueville, *Democracy in America*; see also Robert Eden, "Tocqueville on Political Realignment and Constitutional Forms," *Review of Politics* 48, no. 3 (Summer 1986): 348–72; Eden, "Partisanship and the Constitutional Revolution: The Founders' View Is Newly Problematic," in *Constitutionalism in Perspective: The Constitution in Twentieth Century Politics*, ed. Sarah Baumgartner Thurow (Lanham, Md.: University Press of America, 1988), 51–65.

58. See the preface, above, for this invitational statement.

59. Neither Woodrow Wilson nor Theodore Roosevelt had presided over a realignment. Their success in strengthening the presidency was thus transient by FDR's standards. The letter to Roy Stannard Baker that Milkis discusses is important evidence on this subject.

60. Even when Jefferson departed from his program dramatically, as in purchasing Louisiana, he did so with an eye to containing the executive. See Major L. Wilson, *Space, Time and Freedom: The Quest for National Unity and the Irrepressible Conflict, 1815–1861* (Westport, Conn.: Greenwood Press, 1974).

61. See Charles R. Kesler, "The Reagan Revolution and the Legacy of the New Deal: Obstacles to Party Realignment," *1984 Election*, 245–64.

62. Harvey C. Mansfield, "Republicanizing the Executive," in *Saving the Revolution*, 172.

63. Ibid., 173.

64. See Russell Kirk, "I Must See the Things; I Must See the Men; One Historian's Recollections of the 1930s and 1940s," *Imprimis*, Hillsdale College, vol. 16, no. 10 (October 1987).

65. Ibid., 1.

66. Ibid.

67. See the passage at n. 62 above.

68. See Kesler, "Woodrow Wilson," 103–27; Eden, *Political Leadership and Nihilism*, 1–15, 29–35.

69. Kesler, "Woodrow Wilson," 103–27.

70. See the Supreme Court's opinion in *Allgeyer v. Louisiana* (1897), which Christopher Wolfe calls "the first clear cut decision based on" substantive due process:

The liberty mentioned in that [the Fourteenth] amendment means, not only the right of the citizen to be free from the mere physical restraint of his person, as by incarceration, but the term is deemed to embrace the right . . . to enter into all contracts which may be proper, necessary, and essential to his carrying out to a successful conclusion [of various purposes]. . . .

Such a statute as this in question is not due process of law, because it prohibits an act which under the Federal Constitution the defendants had a right to perform. . . .

In the privilege of pursuing an ordinary calling or trade and of acquiring, holding, and selling property must be embraced the right to make all proper contracts in relation thereto.

Quoted in Wolfe, *The Rise of Modern Judicial Review: From Constitutional Interpretation to Judge-Made Law* (New York: Basic Books, 1986), 150.

71. Wolfe, *Rise of Modern Judicial Review*, 144–48.

72. Ibid., 39–72, 144–63.

73. The difficulty of sorting out the political economic doctrines of the framers is well brought out in Forrest McDonald, *Novus Ordo Seclorum: The Intellectual Origins of the Constitution* (Lawrence: University Press of Kansas, 1985), 97–142.

74. Wolfe, *Rise of Modern Judicial Review*, 323–26.

75. Mahoney, "A Newer Science of Politics," 250.

76. Edward J. Erler, "The Fourteenth Amendment and the Protection of Minority Rights," *Brigham Young University Law Review* 3 (1987): 977–1001.

77. Hiram Caton's interpretation is secured by Hamilton's repudiation of Adam Smith in his *Report on Manufactures*, which precipitated Republican opposition, and by his observation that Smith provided the doctrinal foundation of planter opposition to Hamiltonian commercial policies: Smith was at base a physiocrat who believed that agriculture, rather than industry and commerce, was the essential foundation of a productive economy. Caton, *Politics of Progress*, 348–56.

78. Hans H. Gerth and C. W. Mills, *From Max Weber: Essays in Sociology* (New York: Oxford University Press, 1958), 85.

79. I have drawn out the implications of this analysis for consensus politics more fully in "Dealing Democratic Honor Out: Reform and the Decline of Consensus Politics" in

Remaking American Politics, ed. Richard A. Harris and Sidney M. Milkis (Boulder, Colo.: Westview Press, 1988), 52–85.

   80. See the preface to this book.

   81. See Eden, *Political Leadership and Nihilism*, 1–35.

Don Paarlberg

Tarnished Gold: Fifty Years of New Deal Farm Programs

The essence of the New Deal farm programs was the effort to raise the incomes of farmers by reducing supplies and thereby increasing prices. Markets had failed, it was charged, and the remedy was for government to establish prices and control acreage. There were other New Deal initiatives, but the price-fixing and supply-control efforts of the Agricultural Adjustment Administration were central.

I feel qualified to discuss the past half-century or more of the New Deal farm programs; they parallel my adult life. Part of the time I was a farmer operating under their rules. Much of the time I was in the university, teaching and doing economic research on these programs. For sixteen of these years I was in Washington, helping to administer them. Since 1976 I have been in retirement, observing them with as much detachment as one can acquire after long involvement.

A VERY REAL CRISIS

The Great Depression laid the basis for the New Deal farm programs. Only the older people can recall it. A few figures will help to calibrate the disaster. From 1929 to 1932 the index of prices received by U.S. farmers fell 56 percent. I was farming then in northwestern Indiana with my father and brother, and keeping farm records in collaboration with Purdue University. The return to labor and management on our farm in 1932, a year of good crops, was a negative $1,203.

Farmers, needing help, undertook a number of desperate acts. In a dramatic protest against foreclosures, they threatened to hang a federal judge. They overturned milk trucks, picketed packing plants, and boycotted farm sales. The mood was ominous. There was anger, frustration, and insistence on action. The Great

Depression was worldwide. In Italy and Germany representative governments were replaced by dictatorships. The American political and economic systems were threatened.

What was the cause of the agricultural disaster? Among farm economists there were two leading schools of thought. One, led by George F. Warren of Cornell University, assessed the problem as general, resulting from the collapse of money and credit. The remedy, said this group, lay in a changed monetary policy. With this diagnosis and prescription I agree.

The other school, led by John D. Black of Harvard University, diagnosed the farm problem as arising within agriculture itself, the result of surplus production. The remedy, according to this group, consisted of reducing supplies so as to increase prices.

Belief that the problem was a phenomenon of money and credit had much to support it. The stock of money in the United States fell by one-third. Similar declines in the stock of money occurred in other countries. Prices fell for virtually all commodities, farm and nonfarm, whether they were abundant or in short supply. They fell in every country for which statistical information is available. But neither farmers nor farm politicians understood the complexities of money, credit, or central banking.

The contention that the problem was overproduction was, to farm people, quite persuasive. They knew that excessive production meant low prices and reasoned that with prices low, production must be excessive. But this superficial diagnosis rested on a poor foundation. Total agricultural production during the five first and worst years of the Great Depression was actually 2 percent below the production of the five preceding years.

Something had to be done. It was felt that with the low prices of internationally traded farm products, American agriculture could not compete in world markets. The proposal was that we should establish a domestic price structure basically higher than in the rest of the world and cut production approximately to what could be sold domestically, selling abroad such driblets as would be taken at our higher prices. Intervention in the market system on this scale could not be accomplished by individual farmer decisions; it had to be done by government. Consensus formed around this idea. The Agricultural Adjustment Act, based on this principle, was passed by the Congress on May 12, 1933.

Those who bore responsibility for our money and credit system were happy with the surplus diagnosis for low farm prices; it reflected acceptance of a micro diagnosis for what was in fact a macro problem. It helped to place the onus for the farm disaster on the impersonal forces of overproduction rather than on their own inept monetary management.

It would have better had our monetary and credit system been so managed that the Great Depression would have been averted. Granting the fact of the Great Depression and its disastrous effect on agriculture, it would have been better to put a government check in each farmer's mailbox and avoid tampering with the market. Accepting the existence of the depression and the fact of government price-fixing and production control, it would have been better to terminate the programs with the outbreak of World War II, when the depression disappeared. We missed all of these better options and continued the programs for more than fifty years.

NEW DEAL FARM POLICY

Passage of the New Deal farm program was a major change in the farm policy agenda. For seventy years after passage of the Morrill Act, which set up the land grant colleges, the farm policy agenda had been agricultural development; the components of that policy were research, classroom teaching, on-farm education, and improvement of agricultural resources. Professor Earl Heady of Iowa State University has called this "the best, the most logical, and the most successful program of agricultural development anywhere in the world."

This historic agenda, based on increased production, individual farmer decision, and competitive markets, was not compatible with the ideas underlying the New Deal farm program. Quickly the historic farm policy agenda was nudged aside.

The key words for the new farm policy agenda were relief, recovery, and reform. Relief was to come from a number of sources, including the Federal Emergency Relief Administration. Recovery was to be accomplished by the transfer of decision-making from the market to the government, specifically price support and production control. Reform was to come from modifications of the competitive system that would reduce the likelihood of another debacle. Reform consisted not only of price supports, but also of new institutions of farm credit, new tenure arrangements, federal crop insurance, and special help for the disadvantaged sectors of agriculture.

I recall well the revival of hope on the farm front that accompanied passage of these New Deal programs. Farmers were given a role in working out their own chosen solutions to their problems. They were put on committees by the thousands. They elected officers, attended meetings, and spoke their minds. Government checks began to flow. The hemorrhage of farm foreclosures began to abate. On every hand was evidence that the government cared. The Great Depression dragged on, but the mood changed for the better on American farms. The New Deal farm programs were, in the early years, accompanied by better morale and some improvement in economic conditions on American farms.

But now the early years are far behind. What has been the long-term experience with these programs? What of the New Deal farm policy agenda of relief, recovery, and reform?

Relief came with the Federal Emergency Relief Administration, the flow of government checks, and innovative lending on the part of the new credit agencies. On that score the New Deal must be given high marks. Recovery was only partial until the outbreak of World War II, seven years after the passage of the

New Deal legislation. Agricultural recovery from the Great Depression must be credited more to the stimulus of war than to management of supply and price. What of reform? It was, for the greater part, aborted. The agricultural elite, generally the large landowners, managed to retain most of the program benefits themselves rather than share them with tenants or employees. The Resettlement Administration and its successor, the Farm Security Administration, both intended to lift the status of agriculture's disadvantaged, were closed out. Today's incarnation of these two agencies, the Farmers' Home Administration, has been co-opted by the agricultural establishment. The New Deal farm programs, intended to lift average farm income, actually widened the income gap between top and bottom. Relief was achieved, recovery occurred for other reasons, and reform miscarried.

UNINTENDED RESULTS

With the passage of time, a new and unadvertised agenda emerged. The programs became preferential, profligate, and perennial.

They were preferential to start with; they began by designating six "basic crops"—cotton, corn, wheat, rice, peanuts, and tobacco. Dairy products soon joined the group. Left out of the program were more than 100 other crops and all the livestock products. More was left out than was included. The omitted crops not only were left out, but also had to bear the burden of the increased output that occurred on acres diverted out of the basic crops. Producers of cattle, hogs, and poultry had to accept the higher feed cost that resulted from reduced corn acreage. The programs were preferential in a flagrant fashion. The top 1 percent of the farmers got 21 percent of the benefits. In yet another way the programs were discriminatory. They raised the retail price of food. The average food consumer had less net income than the big farmers who got most of the program benefits. So the program transferred income from those who were poorer to those who were wealthier. Despite the New Deal rhetoric about helping the Forgotten Man, the farm program was and is regressive. Not only are the average incomes of the chief program beneficiaries above those of the average food consumer, but also the average equity of farm families is higher than the average of the nation's families—almost four times greater, as recently reported by Mary Ahearn of the Economic Research Service of the U.S. Department of Agriculture.

The programs became not only preferential, but also profligate. Estimated calendar year 1986 governmental outlays to the farm sector, including about $12 billion of direct payments and approximately an equal sum in commodity loans, were approximately $25 billion. This was almost as large as net farm income. The programs have also become perennial. They have continued for more than fifty years. They continued after relief had been supplied, recovery achieved, and reform forgotten.

There are other indictments of these programs. By pricing ourselves out of foreign markets and reducing crop production, we have conceded market growth to rival exporters: the Canadians, the Argentinians, and the European Economic

Community. We have held the umbrella for the cotton growers of Brazil, the wheat growers of Australia, the corn growers of Western Europe, and the tobacco growers of Africa.

The independent spirit of American farmers has been undermined by these programs. The programs have grown to such size that producers of wheat, corn, cotton, and rice are now reliant on government for the bulk of their net incomes. The programs are "voluntary," but the penalties for nonparticipation are now so great that a farmer who wants to be self-reliant is nevertheless virtually forced to sign up. This subversion of formerly independent farmers is one of the worst attributes of the programs.

Another adverse aspect of the programs is the lax manner in which they are run and the consequent erosion of respect for law. The programs are administered at the local level by farmer committee members who are reluctant to impose penalties on their neighbors. So farmers, with no restraint, rent their poorer acres to the government and pour the fertilizer on their better acres. The government pays for a 20 percent reduction in acreage and gets less than a 10 percent reduction in output. There is a $50,000 limitation on payments, so big farmers divide the overgrown superfarm —on paper—among wife, children, and tenants, collecting $50,000 on each bogus farm, again without restraint. Farmers talk frankly with equal parts of cynicism, humor, and guilt about farming the government.

It was claimed for these programs that they would bolster farm income, keep farmers from going broke, and thus keep the people on the land and preserve the family farm. What are the facts? When the program began we had 6 million farms. Now we have about 2 million.

With the advance of farm technology, and the consequent increase in farm size, agriculture is becoming industrialized, a trend that no farm program can be expected to avert. In Grandfather's day it was common for the farm operator and his family to supply all the factors of production—land, labor, capital, and management. This was in fact the underlying concept of the family farm. But with the industrialization of agriculture, farms have grown to such size and capital needs have become so great that the ordinary farm family cannot supply all these factors. Land, labor, capital, and management are now being split up and supplied by different entities, much as is the case in factory production. The only way the family farm can be preserved is to redefine it. A modern definition is this: A family farm is one on which the operator and his family supply the majority of the labor and management. This leaves unspecified the suppliers of land and capital. With this modern definition, most of the dwindling number of farms are still family farms.

Some of the antics of the commodity programs are so ludicrous as to be almost unbelievable. The dairy programs are perhaps most fantastic. We supported the prices of dairy products with the intention of increasing the incomes of dairy farmers. But, as would be known by every student who has taken a beginning course in economics, the result was to stimulate production, reduce consumption, and pile up surplus. The surplus of butter, cheese, and dried milk was then donated to welfare people. This proved to be an inadequate outlet, so these products were donated overseas. The surplus was still growing so we bought and slaughtered whole herds of dairy cattle. Thereupon the beef cattle producers, who are self-reliant and have neither price support nor production control, complained of this subsidized competition with their product and the government responded by purchasing beef for donation to the school lunch program. This did not adequately alleviate the complaints of the beef producers so the government exported beef from the slaughtered dairy cattle, a strange action, since we have a deficit for beef and import substantial amounts. Our forced exports of dairy beef disturbed other beef exporters, making an additional problem for the multinational trade negotiations in Geneva. All of these strange actions were undertaken because we would not take the simple effective step of lowering the official price.

Meanwhile those dairymen who stayed in business anticipate a reduced supply of milk and a better market. They are increasing their herds and laying the basis for a larger supply of milk. Like the sorcerer's apprentice, they have heard the signal for delivering more water (milk) and have heard no credible signal for stopping.

The commodity programs create surplus. They make a burden of what should be a blessing—our capability to produce food.

It is not as if we lacked precedents for commodity programs and so had to learn the principles of price competition by pioneering experience. In the 1920s the Stevenson Plan reduced the supply and raised the price of rubber in the Malay States, and so stimulated rubber production in a rival country, Java. Some years later the Brazilians restricted the supply and raised the price of coffee, putting a competitor, Africa, in the coffee business.

The United States is not alone in these antics. The Europeans, with their Common Agricultural Policy, are on a course similar to ours. Canada, Australia, and Argentina tailgate on us. For fifty years we have almost unilaterally adjusted production, supported the price, carried the stocks, and paid the bill. Other exporters moved in to take the markets from which we withdrew.

There were agricultural economists who warned about these programs from the beginning, among them G. F. Warren and F. A. Pearson of Cornell University and T. W. Schultz of the University of Chicago. As the years have gone by, other agricultural economists have opposed them: D. Gale Johnson, G. E. Schuh, Varden Fuller, Bruce Gardner, and now recently Willard Cochrane, who has courageously reversed his earlier position. Political scientist Charles M. Hardin has given these programs scholarly and unfavorable examination. Every secretary of agriculture since World War II has spoken out strongly against them: Benson, Freeman, Bergland, Hardin, Butz, Knebel, Block, and Lyng. Every president, Democrat and Republican, beginning with Eisenhower, has tried to scale them back. But these voices have been overwhelmed by the tide of political advocacy, aided by the funds of political action committees.

OUR MODERN DILEMMA

Why have the programs continued so long, despite their obvious failure? There are some politically powerful farmers who, in the short run, gain by them. The public thinks well of farmers and is under the illusion that with these programs, we protect the family farm. We are riding a tiger and fear to dismount lest we get clawed. There appears to be more political advantage in continuing the programs than in taking the tough steps necessary to correct them.

These can no longer be correctly called New Deal programs; they have been adopted by most of the Republican farm politicians. As an observer, I can no longer find credible differences in the Congress between the farm politicians of the two major parties.

These programs, at their beginning, were innovative, addressed to the severe problems of an unfortunate minority, and were intent on coping with a truly disastrous situation—all attributes of what has come to be considered the liberal movement. They had the support of well-meaning politicians who sought to rectify a terrible problem. But during the past half century the programs have been co-opted by the agricultural elite and are now programs of the privileged. Farm lobbyists, knowing that farmers have the goodwill of the public, have estimated the value of that sentiment at so many billion dollars and are selling it off at so much a year. They need to kow that they can't sell off an asset and still continue to possess it.

Currently there is authentic economic distress in agriculture. In my judgment, a major cause is ill-advised macroeconomic behavior. During the seventies expansionary credit and monetary policy caused inflation. Farm operators judged that this pattern would continue, and borrowed heavily, hoping to repay with cheaper dollars. The expected inflation did not occur. We were racing down the highway, exceeding the speed limit. Then the monetary authorities put on the brakes, throwing farmers—and others—against the windshield. To this macro problem is added a micro problem—excess agricultural production, resulting in part from the stimulus of artificially high price supports here and abroad. As was the case fifty years earlier, farm politicians and farm lobbyists are trying to correct agricultural distress with commodity programs, which in some measure caused them, were unable to prevent them, and cannot cure them. Less than one-third of the government payments currently go to farmers who are experiencing financial stress. Efforts to target the programs to those in real difficulty have been ignored. Currently the greatest difficulties are with the protected products—corn, wheat, cotton, rice, dairy. The unprotected products that have been selling in competitive markets—hogs, cattle, poultry, and most fruits and vegetables—are doing fairly well. One would think that this obvious fact would cool the ardor for the big commodity programs, but this has not been so.

The liberal myth is that competitive markets are selfish and are contrary to the public interest. Government programs, think the liberals, take economic activity out of the competitive environment and transfer it to the public sector, where every person has a vote, assuring that the public interest will be uppermost. The chief lesson to be learned from this review is that for the farm programs, this myth is not true.

These programs have been built into land values, mortgaged indebtedness, living levels, community services, political careers, government jobs, and farmer expectations. Have we passed the point of no return? Is our reliance on these programs now so great that escaping from them would entail pains greater than we would be willing to bear?

There have been attempts to scale back our dependence on these programs, to buy our way out, to lay down a plan for a gradual withdrawal. Up to now these have failed.

The Food Security Act of 1985 as conceived by the Reagan administration is a plan for withdrawal. Boldly and wisely, it lowers the level of prices for the supported crops. It attempts to scale back our excess agricultural capacity with a conservation reserve to convert 50 million acres of unneeded cropland to trees and grass.

But contrary to the administration's wish, the Act holds target prices at a high level, making it by far the most expensive farm program in history. The Act is considered by the farm lobby as a model for free-spending farm programs indefinitely into the future. The farm lobby doesn't want to be escalated out of these programs any more than a typical drug addict wants to undergo detoxification.

The proper course, in the opinion of this observer, is to proceed as follows:

1. Adopt fiscal and monetary behavior that avoids the roller coaster rides of the past.
2. Stay the course set by the Food Security Act of 1985 insofar as it lowered loan levels.
3. Reduce direct payments to farmers.
4. Use the savings thus achieved to
   a. cut the deficit and
   b. assist deeply indebted farmers by stretching out and renegotiating their loans, using the Farm Credit System in that undertaking.

Perhaps at some point the public will become concerned about the cost of these programs, will come to see that they are preferential and profligate, and will rebel at their perennial nature. But cost is not the constraint it once was, since we no longer cover the costs with taxes, but increasingly finance them with deficits.

If the programs are to be cut back and reformed, the effort will have to be applied from outside the farm sector; the farm lobby will never discipline itself. One hopes that if reform occurs, the programs would be so changed as to reduce the instability, a legitimate objective. The purpose should be to cut down the amplitude of price fluctuations around the equilibrium level, rather than to attempt to raise the level itself.

But maybe this is too much to hope. Some thirty years ago President Eisenhower learned that there was a tea-tasting unit in the Department of Commerce, placed there in the early days of the Republic to assure that the tea merchants of China and India did not sell us low-quality tea or stretch out the product with some adulterant. The President, intent on economy, thought that this was an agency that could be abolished, and so intended. But the grocery chains rose in protest; their quality control and pricing schedules had become institutionalized around this governmental unit. Rather than use his political capital on this small issue, the President capitulated.

The question, therefore, is obvious: Have the New Deal farm programs become equally institutionalized so that, despite their obvious failure, they cannot be basically changed?

3   *Peter J. Coleman*

The World of Interventionism, 1880–1940

The most fundamental characteristic of the New Deal was the massive federal intervention in so many aspects of American economic and social life. The depth and breadth of involvement was absolutely staggering. The government deprived Americans of their cherished right to hold gold, declared a bank holiday, re-organized the banking system, insured bank deposits, and regulated the securities industry. Manufacturers had to conform to codes of good behavior, farmers had to restrict output. Broadcasters were licensed; airlines could operate only along routes allocated by a federal agency. The government also embarked on a massive regional plan in the Tennessee Valley, put young men to work on conservation projects, created jobs by spending millions on public works, and even found ways to employ writers and artists. These and a host of other federal activities seemed to set off the New Deal as a major turning point in American history. Here, apparently, was a revolution as profound in its impact as independence itself.

Plausible though these assessments may seem, the truth is very different. The New Deal is better seen not as a beginning but as a culmination, as an American version of a worldwide phenomenon. The modern interventionist state had been evolving in the Old World no less than in the New since at least the 1880s. At the height of the Industrial-Capitalist Age, all countries in the West—Great Britain, Germany, Argentina, Canada, and New Zealand, as well as France, Denmark, and the United States—began using the power of the state to achieve broadly similar goals. Because each country had distinct cultural, institutional, and political traditions, along with distinct histories and perceptions of its own problems and needs, the thrust of interventionism was nowhere the same either in timing, technique, or content. What made the New Deal seem to be a revolutionary turning point was the pace and comprehensiveness of change and the vast increase in the reach of federal authority. But the United States was merely doing in its own way what other countries and indeed individual American states had been doing for more than a generation.

But there is a much deeper historical problem to solve than merely placing the New Deal in this particular time and space. The more fundamental question concerns causation and origins. Did interventionism here and elsewhere represent a return to the ancient concept of "commonweal" as the arbiter in human relations, whether between citizen and community or between citizen and state authority?

The answer is an ambivalent yes and no. To the extent that the New Deal had a welfare component, one can argue that it prefigured the coming of modern welfarism and thus harkened back to the colonial concept of community as embodied, for example, in the idea of Massachusetts as a "commonwealth." And to the extent that some New Dealers envisaged a reconstructed America based on a purposeful, comprehensive, and integrated redefinition of what constituted the "good" society, one might argue that the interventionism of the thirties had its roots in a hallowed tradition dating back to Tudor times and beyond.

THE ROLE OF THE PAST

Although Americans have long been accustomed to using historical precedent as a way of legitimating policy, a sense of history and of historical truth has never been a national trait. Except in myth-making, the collective American memory is extraordinarily shallow and runs backward in time over only a limited distance. So it seems unlikey that the New Dealers brought past and present together in a seamless web of historical continuities. Indeed, a dominant characteristic of the New Deal was the absence of a coherent, integrated philosophy and program. Pragmatism, compromise, ad hoc invention, moderation, and political opportunism seem more aptly descriptive.

Pragmatic though it may have been, the New Deal nevertheless built on the experience and practice of the Populist-Progressive years, roughly 1880 to 1930. Those decades more powerfully shaped the America we inhabit than any period since the formation of the Republic. They, rather than the decade of the thirties, were the watershed years separating the past from the present. It was then that we began redefining "the promise of American life" by embracing an ideology of rising expectations and by demanding of our institutions policies designed to achieve those goals. To be sure, we may have had to wait until the affluence and bright optimism of the fifties to realize these objectives, but the aspiration had been rooted in the national consciousness for two generations.

Over time, what had begun in the eighties of the last century has come to include today's greatly expanded safety net programs (aid to dependent children, Medicaid and Medicare, Head Start, retirement benefits, hot meals for schoolchildren, unemployment insurance, job training, and so forth). It includes a managed economy as well (the tax code, fiscal policy, export credits, import quotas, and similar efforts to promote or protect business activity, along with programs to protect the environment, bring safety to the workplace, and under-write the risks of farming). In the Populist–Progressive–New Deal years, inter-ventionism stopped far short of such policies, but America nevertheless moved unmistakably toward the present.

For example, we began redefining rights: Americans began demanding min-imum standards of living, whether income, housing, or public sanitation. Babies had a right to life, to grow up, marry, raise children of their own, and to live on into a secure old age. If that could not be achieved by private effort, then government would have to guarantee it by legislative fiat. Similarly, regulation became a way of American life—in mines, factories, packing houses; hours of work, rates of pay, the employment of young people and women as well; banking, insurance, utilities, railroads; even in competition itself, through the anti-trust laws, the Bureau of Corporations, and the Federal Trade Commission.

A WORLDWIDE TREND

There was nothing uniquely American about this interventionist trend. It was ubiquitous throughout the West and reflected a growing disenchantment with Adam Smith's "simple and obvious system of liberties," most especially in the Anglo-American world, though even there the rejection of classic liberalism was, in many respects, more apparent than real. Several points need to be made about the power and endurance of the ideas associated with what became the Manchester School of Economics. First, though we like to think that notions of freedom, liberty, and individualism have existed since time immemorial, the fact is that they are recent inventions and ones very much at odds with most human ex-perience. What we have come to think of as "inalienable rights," especially in America, are as much a true fruit of the Age of Expansion as the discovery of the Americas or Asia. So, too, with the "idea of progress" and the belief in the efficacy of the free market. All these concepts are the very epitome of modernity and had time to put down only superficial roots before coming under attack. As a consequence, the interventionist assault on the Smithian system was as swift as it was easy. It may not have seemed so at the time—witness the long struggle to secure union recognition and collective bargaining in the United States—but one must be struck by the fact that sooner rather than later reformers secured their every objective, winning over legislators and judges alike.

Second, the interventionist task was made all the easier by the persistence after independence and at all levels of American political life of what might be called the "positive Hamiltonian state." Generation after generation of Amer-icans looked to their governments for an astonishing array of measures aimed broadly but not exclusively at encouraging economic development.

The Congress, as is well known, dispensed its favors far and wide and with a lavishness bordering on indecency: tariffs for manufacturers, patents for inventors, protection for coastal shipowners, advantages for shipbuilders, subsidies for railroads, land for homesteaders, pensions for veterans, civil courts for litigants at much less than the real costs of the services provided, endowments for universities, harbor and river improvements for shippers, Indian removals for farmers and ranchers, and on and on. The list is almost endless.

State legislatures were no less committed to the growth ethic, spending lavishly to support the development of the transportation network; granting toll roads, canals, and railroads the power of eminent domain; investing in or subsidizing manufacturers; giving prizes and bounties to support agricultural improvements; promoting exports through systems of grading and inspection; supporting the development of mill sites and reservoirs; and granting business enterprises corporate privileges, including the power of perpetual succession and limited liability. Local authorities engaged in parallel policies, often in concert with state legislatures, particularly in the field of transportation, but they also regulated public markets, promoted gas and water utilities, sponsored harbor and wharf improvements, and in a host of other ways assumed large responsibilities for community growth and welfare.

Nor should it be forgotten that governments imposed corporate franchise taxes for the support of higher education and charitable organizations; made some provision for the care of the poor, old, widowed, orphaned, and infirm; protected natural resources through conservation legislation; and acted to restrain the employment of children. Even before the Civil War, American governments had begun to regulate banks, insurance corporations, and railroads. This regulation can be seen as an extention of the traditional policy of regulating utilities, such as grist millers, and the owners of toll roads, bridges, and canals.

In short, laissez-faire best described the ideology, not the practice, of most nineteenth-century Americans. Growth and progress were much too important to be left to chance.

Third, for very different reasons, classical liberalism gained only a slight following on the European continent and proved an even more tenuous guide to public policy. Feudalism, mercantilism, and community persisted there much longer than elsewhere. Neither industrialization nor urbanization had the atomizing effect it had in Great Britain or the United States. Moreover, Rousseau's concept of a social compact withstood the challenge of Adam Smith's system of free markets. And so modernity came to Europe only slowly. Portugal and Spain remained almost medieval until relatively recently; Germany and Italy did not begin to modernize until after unification; Eastern Europe, including Russia, remained in the grip of the landed aristocracy well into our own century; and France, which threw off feudalism only as late as 1789, nevertheless replaced it with statism, cultivating and relying on what might be called the Napoleonic tradition of centralized interventionism. In any event, in France and elsewhere in Europe classical liberalism was a British idea and for that reason suspect as an alien import.

But if the ideologies of classical liberalism, laissez-faire, and free markets were something of straw men throughout the Western world, there was no gainsaying that by the closing decades of the nineteenth century, capitalism was everywhere under attack as a flawed system of organizing economic, political, and social relationships. The attack came from all sides and from all classes—from the rich no less than the poor, owners no less than workers, landlords no less than tenants, the Right no less than the Left—though no two groups saw the problem in quite the same way.

The "lower orders," of course, had the most powerful reasons for dissatisfaction, though, ironically, they were probably better off in 1880 than they had been in 1780. But the rhetoric of capitalism had taught them to expect more out of life than the system seemed capable of producing year in and year out. Their fundamental objection was that the cyclical economy put them at risk by denying them continuity of employment and income. Ordinary folk still accepted the proposition that the poor would always be with us, but they could see all around them that a new kind of poverty was on the rise. Its causes were no longer rooted in individual character defects—laziness or alcoholism or infirmity or old age—but in what we would now call structural defects in the economic system. Some kind of corrective action was imperative.

The demand for state intervention was not confined to working people and their sympathizers. Businessmen everywhere were deeply troubled by problems that emerged within the capitalist system itself. These concerns included excess capacity, with the resulting fierce struggle for markets at home and abroad, the impetus to cartelization and other forms of collusion, sharp business practices, inequities in the availability of credit, the squeeze on smaller firms, and the rising costs of entry to the marketplace. In the abstract, capitalists both large and small much preferred a system in which market forces, whether free or rigged, alone determined success or failure. But in practice, and on particular questions, they, too, were drawn to government as arbiter, regulator, and promoter. For reasons of self-interest, capitalists themselves retreated selectively from their strident rhetoric of laissez-faire by choosing interventionism when they thought it would do them some good and rejecting it when they thought the costs would outweigh the benefits. The trend was worldwide.

This was particularly evident in the agricultural sector, where for many farmers, especially in New World countries, the returns did not seem commensurate with the risk and effort, especially as compared with rewards in commerce, finance, and manufacturing. In common with factory workers and other employees, small farmers sought income and security, most notably during the developmental years. They believed, when they were starting up as petty capitalists, that once established, they could survive on their own through hard work and ingenuity. Even estate holders in the Old World came to look to the state for support and protection, in their case as a reaction to the flood of farm commodities entering the market from abroad. But there were collateral farm issues as well, varying from place to place and broadly concerned with the "quality of rural life." In Old World countries it manifested itself in efforts to halt the drift to the cities and emigration overseas through the revitalization of the village community. The New World parallels were broadly similar and involved transportation improvements to give better access to markets, along with government investment in the community infrastructure to overcome rural isolation and cultural deprivation.

Whether in the Old World, or the New, the crucial causative force promoting interventionist agricultural policies appears to have been a failure of expectations. The market system was not living up to its supposed promise. Exacerbating this disenchantment was the new presumption that the world owed farmers, above all others, a favored place in the sun. Government intervention appeared to many farmers, large no less than small, the method best calculated to achieve that goal.

CAPITALISM, SOCIALISM, AND OTHER INFLUENCES

In short, the origins of modern interventionism can be traced to a profound crisis in late-nineteenth-century capitalism. Failures of performance sapped confidence in the system and exposed it to political interference. That businessmen themselves frequently led the charge underscores the argument that a broad consensus existed for modifying the economic and social order.

In many places growing fear of the Left intensified the interventionist trend. Generally speaking, social democrats, not radicals, dominated political life. They sought to reform capitalism, not overturn it. But criticism from the Left produced a siege mentality in both business and politics and led to strategies of co-option as the best way to defend capitalism. The most dramatic example was Bismarck's Germany, where the counterattack on socialism brought massive restraints on employers and foreshadowed the welfare programs that were to become commonplace elsewhere over the next century. It is not without point that the politics of co-option also animated much of the New Deal. Franklin D. Roosevelt's critics from the Right may have seen him as an enemy to his own class, but it is widely believed that his policies saved American capitalism from its own worst self.

However, there is a profound paradox in this line of analysis. For all the failures of capitalism, it was the system's success that made the interventionist state possible. The prodigious productivity of the market economy provided the essential resource base for a significant resurgence in government activity and a fundamental shift in its purpose.

Mercantilist interventionism in earlier times had been concerned overwhelmingly with building national wealth and power. Whether manifested in acts of trade, sumptuary laws, wage and price regulations, the relief of the poor, or controlling the pace of agricultural change, rulers preoccupied themselves with political goals. Regulators saw social and political stability as means to larger ends: peace at home; power abroad.

Several things had changed by the late nineteenth century. Two deserve particular mention. First, some interventionists began taking note of social and economic distress and devising ways to relieve it out of humanitarian rather than political considerations by laying the base for latter-day welfarism. Second, policymakers had (or thought they had) the administrative apparatus to make intervention work, which had not been true in the Age of Mercantilism. And they had the financial resources produced by capitalism's success to back the effort. Governments now dared to think that they could have a consequential impact on everyday affairs. They could raise sufficient revenues to finance their programs, and productivity and profit margins made it possible to expect business to absorb whatever burdens—regulatory costs, for example—that came with intervention. The worldwide debate concerned itself only a little with whether or not to expand the sphere of the state. The real issues were by how much, when, and to what purpose.

If the affluence capitalism provided made the interventionist state financially possible, human arrogance made it thinkable. As an abstract matter, human beings had since the eighteenth century believed in their capacity to exert substantial control over their world, but it was not until the closing decades of the nineteenth century that this confident belief in the power of reason began to shape public policy in ways leading to modern interventionism. The achievements of science and technology obviously had a powerful influence on the process. It was not difficult to suppose that if men could devise ways to vulcanize rubber, perform surgery under anesthesia, mass-produce steel, or transmit messages by undersea cable, they could deal just as effectively with social and economic questions.

To do that, they had to develop knowledge about human behavior and relationships, the analytical methods to investigate the causes and consequences of social and economic problems, and the scientific principles on which to ground public policy. What is so significant about the emergence of the social sciences is that from the outset, they were heavily biased toward problem-solving. There was no point in studying society unless the resultant knowledge could be applied. That is why these new disciplines attracted men and women who were interventionist by inclination or training. Moreover, the social sciences supplied journalists, clergymen, legislators, and other reformers with essential information, ideas, and arguments. If scientific knowledge and theory could reduce infant mortality or increase industrial productivity, surely there was no reason to doubt the human capacity to reduce poverty or increase employment.

Finally, a fundamental change in the nature of political life was an additional causative factor. It manifested itself earliest in New World countries but was everywhere evident in the decline in deference to traditional authorities in the rising claims on government by spokesmen for small farmers, workers, petty businessmen, women, and other powerless groups. The democratization of politics moved public affairs in this direction, but there was more to it than that. To return to an earlier point, the rejection of the primacy of the market as the arbiter in the outcomes of life came into play. Poverty or unemployment or slum housing or rack renting or sweated labor or land monopoly or inequalities of wealth were no longer automatically accepted as the inevitable human condition. The immutable natural order came under attack as distinct, organized interest groups began formulating their agendas of expectations and demands. Increasingly, the art of politics became populist in the sense that elections hinged on putting together coalitions of disparate constituencies. Retaining power depended on catering to their demands. Politicians had to act in new ways. They had to articulate the interests of their constituents; they had to demonstrate responsiveness. Not that all politicians were swept up in this tide. There was still a place for the resisters. They could block, delay, or, as a last resort, modify any particular demand, but over the long term, interventionism everywhere meant the new politics of activism.

To summarize: the worldwide impetus to reform had its causes in dissatisfactions with capitalism, in the accumulation of resources sufficient to finance interventionism, in the presumption that human problems had rational causes and were, therefore, solvable by rational solutions, and in the decline in political deference and passivity.

What common elements can be identified in the programs that interventionists adopted to move their countries toward the modern welfare state? A useful first approach can be found in the traditional categories of land, labor, and capital, though not all reform components fit perfectly within this framework.

The universal land issue, as already indicated, was income and security. In some places, particularly in New World countries, there was in addition the problem of monopoly, which manifested itself in attacks on alien, absentee, or corporate ownership, or simply in complaints about the concentration of holdings in the hands of a few. The most common objective in these cases was the creation of opportunities for the landless, but there was also talk of land nationalization based on the ideas of Alfred Russel Wallace and income equalization through taxation—the theories of John Stuart Mill and Henry George.

In general, the significance of these collateral issues lies not so much in the legislation they inspired as in the way they shaped attitudes toward state intervention and strengthened demands for programs responsive to rural needs. There were exceptions, of course. The Mexican and Russian revolutions, to cite two examples, spoke powerfully to breaking up the great estates and redistributing the land to the peasants, either by individual title or by collectivization. But the compulsory repurchase of large holdings in New Zealand, for example, was more important as a symbol of political concern than as a solution to landlessness. So, too, was the 999-year lease of public land, which was a sop to nationalizers and survived only until tenants could muster the political strength to force the government to offer them the right to buy freehold title. Similarly, the progressive land tax placed an inconsequential burden on large estate holders and did little to redistribute New Zealand property. The story was much the same in the United States, where the attack on railroad landholdings and tax avoidance or on alien and absentee owners had greater rhetorical than practical impact. And even in California, where there was talk of breaking up the great Mexican land grants, the state's acquisition of properties for subdivision into working farms never evolved beyond a few demonstration projects.

A much more important manifestation of the interventionist impulse was the attack on the problem of income and security through the subsidization of agriculture. The primary technique used in both the Old World and the New was the harnessing of science and education to the task of increasing the productivity of land and labor, the systematic improvement of processing techniques, and the investment of public funds in the search for and promotion of market opportunities. In the newer countries, especially, governments also subsidized agriculture by supporting the development of transportation networks, as in the land grants to the transcontinental railroads in the United States or in the subsidization of freight rates in Australia so that drought-stricken livestock could be fed. That is, farmers, processors, and merchants all looked to the state for a variety of services. Departments of agriculture organized and coordinated state efforts; universities engaged in research and set up demonstration projects to educate farmers in the new techniques; governments imposed health standards on the dairy and meat industries both to protect the public and to expand sales, especially in international markets; and diplomats assumed new duties—the promotion of agricultural exports. Everywhere the objectives and techniques were similar as governments assumed greatly enlarged responsibilities for rural welfare, including the welfare of the processors and distributors serving the needs of primary producers.

To this trend must be added state efforts to increase the supply of rural credit. Methods varied from country to country. Nevertheless, a common theme can be identified. The universal starting point was the perception that capitalism produced either a maldistribution or an insufficiency of credit. Generally speaking, creditworthy merchants and manufacturers had all the capital they needed, and on attractive terms. Farmers, by contrast, especially the little man, did not, and when they could borrow, they paid dearly for the privilege. Because bankers and private lenders showed little willingness to correct the imbalance, it behooved government to take corrective action, meaning that the rural sector had a legitimate claim to special treatment. The demand manifested itself as early as the 1850s in Louis Napoleon's France, where Saint-Simon's commutarianism influenced the creation of state banks. In the Low Countries and Scandinavia rural cooperatives became the credit vehicle; in New Zealand the government borrowed on the London money market to supply farmers with loans at substantially lower than commercial rates; and in the United States the federal government collateralized farm commodities—cotton, wheat, and corn—so that producers could get working capital to make next year's crop and perhaps even invest in improvements. In the meantime, it was hoped, they would not have to dispose of their harvest at distress prices. Comparable concerns shaped public policy throughout the world of agriculture.

Similarities in the world of work are no less evident. As in farming, the common denominators were income and security. Everywhere involved in one way or another was a rejection of market forces as the sole determinant of the job contract and the interposition of the state between employer and employee. And as in farming, crucial presumptions underlay public policy. The first was the conclusion that capitalism had failed to produce work for all those who offered their services and second, that capitalism had also failed, partly through the same oversupply of labor, to distribute national income in a defensible way. It was not just that too many workers lived out their lives on the margins of existence. In the United States there was a challenge based on the Lockean-Jeffersonian ethical tradition that productive work should be justly rewarded. And the Left everywhere rejected the market as the mechanism for determining wage levels.

Corrective action throughout the world of reform followed broadly similar lines and usually involved some mix of humanitarian, practical, and ideological considerations. The abolition of child labor was a common goal. Given the gradual reformulation of the meaning of childhood in the nineteenth century, there were sound humanitarian and social reasons for keeping children out of the labor force. However, it is realistic and not necessarily cynical to say as well that the reform also reflected a practical response to the scarcity of adult employment. If the competition of children could be eliminated, there would be more jobs for their older brothers and sisters as well as for their parents. Moreover, child labor would no longer depress adult wage rates.

Similarly, efforts to abolish night work for younger workers and women and to limit the length of their work week had humanitarian as well as practical resonances. In addition to health and reproductive considerations, these restrictions affected adult male workers as well by abolishing the night shift in manufacturing plants, such as cotton mills, which relied heavily on the labor of women and young people. The common characteristic of these laws was the categorization of the labor force by age and gender.

Other laws depended on the categorization of the workplace itself and were concerned with another aspect of security—safety and health. Hazardous occupations—mining and transportation, for example—were typically the first categories to be regulated. From that beginning the trend was usually toward comprehensive industrial codes specifying minimum standards for such matters as sanitation, ventilation, lighting, and safety. The most advanced legislation established maximum hours for all workers rather than just selected categories, and in some countries the retail trade became subject to comparable regulation.

The enactment of mandatory systems of workmen's compensation supplemented and strengthened these codes. The basic principle was that the employer became absolutely liable for all work-related injuries. Benefits were payable according to a fixed scale. This concept became as common in countries with a Roman law tradition as in those with an Anglo-Saxon legal heritage. Other considerations aside, these requirements gave employers a vested interest in job safety. The safer the operation, the lower the costs of doing business.

The late nineteenth century also saw considerable efforts to deal with the income side of the labor question by mandating minimum wage standards. The solution was both conservative and radical. Conservative insofar as it neither altered the reward system nor redistributed national income. But it was also radical in that government intervened to guarantee workers a minimum level of welfare. As in the question of hours, the most common approach used the categorization principle to single out particular industries for regulation and women for special protection. They were the industries in which exploitation was most rampant and in which women had the least leverage. There were moral imperatives as well. Many reformers linked prostitution to poverty. It was also assumed that setting a wage floor beneath female workers would have a ripple effect on all employees. However, once established for one category of industry or worker, the logic of reform was to extend the minimum wage principle to all occupations and all workers, as happened during the New Deal, for example.

The third common, though by no means universal, line of intervention involved attempts to resolve disputes between labor and management. Three principal models can be identified: voluntary mediation, as in Massachusetts; compulsory investigation, as in Canada; and compulsory arbitration as the technique of last resort, as in Australasia. Whatever the method adopted, intervention rested primarily on the presumption that lockouts and strikes were no longer the exclusive concern of workers and owners. All disputes, though some much more obviously than others, affected the public interest. The state, therefore, had an obligation to promote harmony. There were other motivations as well, ranging from fear of capital's excessive power to fear of labor's potential for revolution. In most countries these systems of modifying industrial relations were probably of limited practical consequence. Much more important was the assumption by the state of new power and responsibility and the blurring of distinctions between the public and the private.

Some governments also began tackling joblessness itself, typically in one of three ways. In the Anglo-American world the traditional idea of poor relief survived into the Age of Industrial Capitalism, though in much attenuated form. In theory communities remained responsible for the welfare of their residents, but in practice needs overwhelmed resources, especially in the industrializing cities, where rapid economic change fragmented the old values, and in the moving American West, where traditional institutions failed to take root. In Great Britain the Benthamite workhouse was deliberately designed to discourage supplicants. When the system became so scandalous that it could be tolerated no longer, the Lloyd George Liberals created the dole, a public handout financed from the general fund as a way of supporting those out of work. In nineteenth-century America, by contrast, local authorities increasingly walked away from the welfare problem, abandoning the delivery of services to churches and other charitable agencies and only supplementing such relief with public soup kitchens, shelters, and make-work jobs when conditions reached the crisis point.

A second model emerged in Germany in the 1880s with the enactment of a system of unemployment insurance. Income benefits then became a matter of right, but the right had to be bought by weekly contributions to the fund out of wage deductions.

Perhaps the most useful way to examine the common elements in reform programs affecting business is to start from the premise that the common goal was the preservation and reformation of capitalism rather than its overthrow and replacement by some other system, most notably a collectivist one. But this conservative objective rested on the perception that capitalism was working less than perfectly, that the system gave few signs of correcting itself, and that the state would have to mandate change if catastrophe were to be averted. This premise does not preclude active participation by capital in the reform process; nor does it preclude selective public ownership.

A major reform thrust, therefore, was the rationalization of business—an attempt to bring order out of chaos. It took a number of forms. Much of the labor legislation can be characterized this way. By prescribing higher standards in wages and working conditions, the state favored the larger and more efficient firms, which were already in compliance or which could easily do so. Similarly, laws protecting consumers from spoiled meat, adulterated foods, or dangerous pharmaceuticals put many small firms at risk. And laws regulating retail trading hours eliminated the competitive advantage of small, family-operated businesses over department and other large stores. To these measures can be added the enactment of codes proscribing sharp business practices, which if they did not necessarily favor the strong over the weak, at least sought fairness, order, and stability in the marketplace. Even the various approaches to the emergence of the very large firm fall into the same pattern. The problem was to find ways to obtain the benefits of bigness, efficiency, and rationality while at the same time leaving the doorway of opportunity open to smaller firms and newcomers.

Another way of making this point is to say that the state began asserting its primacy over private capital. In effect, government subjected business to performance standards. That assertion found different expressions in different countries, but the underlying objectives were similar. In the railroad industry, for example, and in utilities (gas, water, electricity, and grain elevators) the technique was public ownership and operation in some countries but regulation in others. The common denominator was the idea that these services were so essential to the public welfare that society had to insist that they operate accordingly. In insurance, mortgage lending, and housing some countries turned to state competition to force underwriters, lenders, and landlords to reduce their charges and in that way to perform satisfactorily. Elsewhere the same goal was sought through public regulation. Similarly, building codes set performance standards for property owners, and zoning laws subjected them to uses embodying standards of community welfare over private rights. Even the conservation movement, whether manifested in the preservation of recreational land or in the management of natural resources, reflected the same trend: the subordination of private claims to the larger public interest.

In addition, most countries revolutionized their tax systems. For the first time they forced capital to contribute significant amounts to the public treasury. In the past, revenues had come from four major sources: levies on wealth, most notably land, but also such items as carriages, chimneys, windows, or silver plate; custom duties on imports, such as wheat, manufactures, and luxury goods; excise taxes on selected consumer products, such as alcohol, salt, and tobacco; and user fees, such as stamp duties on various kinds of transactions. These crude fiscal arrangements, regressive though they may have been and bearing more heavily on the poor than on the rich, probably worked well enough in preindustrial societies, were suited to the administrative skills and resources of the time, and produced enough money in peacetime to meet ordinary public needs.

However, by the closing decades of the nineteenth century, traditional forms of taxation were becoming grossly inadequate, considering the additional responsibilities being thrust on governments. Worse still, with the rise of corporations, property was often in untaxable forms, such as inventories, machinery, receivables, and intangibles, most notably goodwill, franchises, and securities. And with princely incomes being earned from commercial, financial, and industrial enterprises, states came under pressure everywhere to raise their funds from new sources and in demonstrably more equitable ways by shifting the burden to those best able to pay.

The result was the imposition of a broad range of new taxes—inheritance taxes, and levies on personal and corporate incomes, on business franchises, and on all forms of personal property, whether owned by individuals or by firms. As compared with modern rates of taxation, these innovations pressed taxpayers very modestly, but in some countries the demand for greater fairness led to the establishment of the principle of graduated taxation—the more one owned or earned, the higher the rate. Some countries went still further by giving serious consideration to taxing the "unearned increment," or what we would today call capital gains from land transactions.

But whatever the particular strategies used, new fiscal regimes were becoming commonplace. They were to have the profoundest of consequences. They subjected capital itself to the obligations of modern citizenship, and capitalists to larger contributions to the public purse. More important, over the longer term the enlarged tax base financed an incremental growth in state interventionism. Modern governments, as we well know, have an infinite capacity to discover and then devour every potential revenue source.

Finally, notice the universal development of programs dealing with the problems of dependency. Throughout the world of reform, state intervention hinged on the perception that neither capitalism nor charity could deal adequately with the needs of the aged, the orphaned, the widowed, the disabled, the sick, or the unemployed. A few innovators aside, businessmen generally rejected responsibility for such problems, and charitable organizations, even if they possessed the will to respond, lacked the organization and resources to be effective. In the new economic order, needs were far too massive for traditional solutions. Perhaps more important was the revolution in the perception of dependency. In the emerging politics of the late nineteenth century, citizens in need began asserting claims on society as a matter of right rather than of charity. Responses to these demands varied from country to country. Most commonly, the state invoked the insurance principle, thereby rationalizing the creation of welfare payments on rights earned through contributions to the program, but in other systems, legislatures looked to the general pool of revenue for funding. Rights lay in citizenship, not in premium payments, though benefits were often conditioned on financial need and moral rectitude. Either way, the Western world began moving toward modern welfarism.

VOLUNTARISM AND STATISM

The stress on state interventionism as the common response to the crisis of capitalism does not mean that reform took place exclusively on that stage. On the contrary, enormous private efforts were simultaneously at work as people everywhere sought to order their lives and define their relationships within an ever more complex world through membership in voluntary organizations. Several points need to be made about this trend. First, voluntary though they may have been, most were occupational, such as associations of chartered accountants or brotherhoods of teamsters; fraternal, such as benevolent organizations based on religion or ethnicity; or issue oriented, such as chambers of commerce, beautification societies, study circles devoted to particular reforms, or temperance alliances. In the emerging interest-oriented politics of the late nineteenth century, those nodes of associational power constituted a vital new force for change, especially in the ways that political parties organized themselves and formulated their platforms.

Second, most voluntary organizations came to set standards of behavior or performance for their members. This was especially true of the occupational organizations—such as societies of civil engineers, iron molders, or master plumbers—where a desire to associate with people engaged in common lines of work probably brought members together in the first place. But what began in the bonds of recreational fraternalism led in due course to the assumption that the interests of the group were synonymous with the interests of the community.

Third, it was then a relatively short step from that perception of the members' collective needs to the promotion of those self-serving interests through legislative rather than private means. A classic example would be the regulation of the American grain trade. Chicago merchants, wanting to expand the volume of their business, organized a board of trade to police its members' activities, but when some of them refused to comply and scared off potential customers with their shady practices, the board lobbied the Illinois legislature to regulate the industry. With variations, that example could be duplicated many times over. Today, for instance, building codes everywhere protect the jobs of skilled construction workers, though their original purpose was quite different—public health and safety. The same codes also stipulate that construction permits will be issued only when the plans are drawn by registered architects, thereby protecting those highly paid professions from the competition of mere draftsmen and other even less qualified interlopers. Similarly, in many places barbers and beauticians enjoy the protection of state licensing laws, seemingly enacted to protect the public's health, but of more importance today as guaranteeing a supply of paying students for the operators of vocational schools and restricting entrance to those semiskilled occupations. Admission examinations for most professions—accounting, dentistry, engineering, law, medicine, and surveying—serve identical functions in those lucrative fields. In theory, licensing was supposed to guarantee that clients would receive the highest quality of professional service; in fact, licensing has served to restrain competition and guarantee work to those admitted to practice.

In other words, in time, voluntary organizations became vehicles helping to move Western societies along the road to modern statism. That many of them were resurrected versions of ancient medieval guilds simply underscores the fragility and tenuousness of classical liberalism.

THE ROLE OF PROGRESS AND THE "NEW LIBERALISM"

The processes by which the United States began its march toward the interventionist state had more in common with similar trends abroad than it had differences. Indeed, the parallels are striking. They also say something important about both the origins of the New Deal and the institutional and consensual base from which it built.

What we have labeled Populism and Progressivism in the United States and thought of as distinctively American movements in both causes and manifestations were in fact no more than our particular expressions of the universal transformation of liberalism from one set of values as a guide to public policy to something utterly different. Why and how that happened is complex, but the simplified, shorthand explanation is as follows.

At the birth of the American Republic and for some considerable time afterward, liberalism here, as elsewhere, was a revolutionary and dynamic force for change. In the past, government had been a repressive and tyrannical instrument dedicated to its own preservation, often dynastic, most commonly maintained by defending the influence, privileges, status, and wealth of the entrenched vested interests who formed the bulwark of its support. Think of the feudal regime in France. By the eighteenth century authoritarianism came under attack as reformers began to argue that the best way to alter the human condition was by reducing government to its barest essentials and by enlarging to the greatest extent possible the domain of individual choice and freedom. Every aspect of life—association, religion, speech, behavior, commerce—had to be made absolutely free of government restraint. Those were the principles we enshrined in the Bill of Rights and incorporated in Anglo-American common law in the nineteenth century.

This unleashing of individual ambition and energy had prodigious results. There was a "great leap forward" in national income and wealth; standards of living bounded upward as well. Great cities sprang up where there had once been only swamps. Busy canals linked the interior with the seaboard, vessels plied the Great Lakes, and steamboats brought a thriving commerce to the Mississippi Valley. Railroads and telegraphs snaked westward to the Pacific and southward from Canada to the Gulf of Mexico. Factories and mills poured out a cornucopia of finished goods to supply an ever more numerous people. And a fertile land flooded the world with an abundance of fiber and food on a scale unparalleled in human existence. Americans had every cause to celebrate their triumphs at the stunning centennial exposition at Philadelphia in 1876. Each passing decade had brought fresh confirmation of liberalism's success. Confirmation came as well from the arrival of millions of Europeans sweeping in from the Atlantic to share the New World's bounteous opportunities.

But these successes came at a fearful cost. Everywhere the gulf between the very rich and the very poor grew steadily wider. Hardest hit were the newcomers to America or citizenship—Old World immigrants, many of whom suffered outrageously from various forms of discrimination and exploitation, and former slaves, all of whom suffered deprivations, most notably in the denial of human freedom and dignity, including the opportunity to share equally in the nation's abundance. Taxation pressed hardest on those least able to pay. Smokestack industries fouled the air and poisoned the water. All too many children, if they survived infancy, grew up hollow of cheek, rickety of limb, and malnourished in mind no less than in body. In the South crop liens and sharecropping held small farmers in the bondage of permanent poverty; in the West producers groaned under the combined weight of high interest, freight, and processing rates, and rigged prices for such essential supplies as barbed wire, fertilizer, implements, and machinery; and everywhere in rural America land and commodity prices plunged ever downward as deflation and free markets extracted their cruel toll. Meanwhile in the nation's factories and mines and on its railroads thousands died horrible deaths or suffered fearful injuries, most of which went uncompensated on liberalism's curious legal theory that employees freely accepted the risks inherent in the workplace as part of the job contract. And in the cities slums proliferated, exposing native- and foreign-born alike to liberalism's urban exploiters, the quick-money developer and the uncaring landlord. Cesspools, rats, overcrowding, disease, poverty, and death became a way of American life. These and a host of other social and economic problems plainly demonstrated that the new system did not work. Either it was fatally flawed or it had gone berserk.

Classical liberalism then made a 180-degree turn. The New Liberalism replaced the older concepts of freedom—laissez-faire in business, individualism and self-reliance in personal behavior, and the liberty to pursue one's own self-interest—with their opposites—management, order, control, community, public welfare, and statism. Our ancestors of a hundred years ago did not pluck this New Liberalism out of thin air as a set of abstract principles to redirect public and private energy. On the contrary, Americans observed the condition of their lives, judged it to be in various ways unsatisfactory, and resolved to reform it. The most thoughtful, educated, and articulate of them formulated critiques, putting into words their longings for a new economic, political, and social order. They drew, of course, on a long-established American tradition of reform—abolitionism, temperance, education, and women's rights, for example—but they drew as well on ideas from abroad, so that the New Liberalism of the United States—our Populism and Progressivism—meshed almost imperceptibly into the worldwide thrust toward the interventionist state. In reformulating the meaning and content of freedom, and in assigning to government a much larger role, Americans also contributed powerfully to foreign thinking and behavior; witness the influence of Henry George, Edward Bellamy, or the Industrial Workers of the World beyond these shores.

Indeed, interventionism was an international phenomenon precisely because it drew so powerfully on one of the most striking features of late–nineteenth-century life, the emergence of an international information network. This First Information Revolution was comparable in its own way to the revolution wrought in our own times by the computer. Travel became cheaper, faster, safer, and more comfortable; human interaction became commonplace where it had once been unusual. Messages could be transmitted by telegraph and cable over long distances and almost instantaneously, thereby providing peoples of the Western world with timely intelligence. The introduction of inexpensive, speedier postal services, facilitated in part by the establishment of the International Postal Union, also greatly enlarged the flow of data and ideas, the more so because the writing and receiving of letters survived as a widely shared human pleasure. The development of high-speed presses and cheap printing papers added to the explosion of information, especially through the mass circulation of newspapers, magazines, and books. Public libraries expanded their activities as well, some of them financed through the generosity of Andrew Carnegie, and adult education programs spread like wildfire through such organizations as Chautauqua, the Workers' Education Association, the Cooper Union, and the Lyceum movement. The cumulative impact of this revolution was breathtaking as the volume and velocity of information increased exponentially. In one way or another this first Information Revolution touched every human life, but nowhere was its impact felt more deeply than by those involved in creating the interventionist state. Over a generation and more they shared a common search for a reformulation of the idea of the ''just society,'' the strategies by which a consensus for change could be brought about, and the policies required for its establishment. Speaking in the broadest terms, they rejected the negative concept of freedom espoused by classical liberals, calling it the freedom to starve, to fail, to be out of work, to risk one's life in factory or mine, or to live in dangerous housing. They replaced it with a positive concept, seeking to create minimum standards of human well-being as an essential prerequisite to the true exercise and enjoyment of liberty. That was best accomplished, they believed, by greatly expanding the role of government.

Reformers disagreed only on the kind of state most likely to achieve these goals. The most radical of them on the Left envisaged a collectivist society ranging in structure from Edward Bellamy's nationalist clubs to Karl Marx's communism. At the opposite end of the spectrum were the radical conservatives, most notably in Germany and in Eastern and Central Europe, where interventionism manifested itself in statism by the incorporation of occupational constituencies, such as bankers, industrialists, merchants, and workers, into ordered relationships with centralized authority embodying a supranational purpose and will.

But the majority of reformers occupied more centrist ground, seeking some mix of public and private activity capable of reining in the worst excesses of capitalism. These social democrats included such types as Henry Demarest Lloyd in the United States, with his vision of a cooperative commonwealth to be achieved by lifting behavior to higher ethical standards; David Lloyd George in Great Britain, with his program of tax reform and national insurance as a way of providing what we would today call a safety net; or Richard John Seddon in New Zealand, whose mix of humanism and pragmatism helped that remote South Pacific colony to become what outsiders called ''the world's most advanced democracy.''

The international information network provided an essential data base for these various programs of intervention, which helps to explain the similarity of theory and practice across national boundaries. The spectacular growth of the social and medical sciences was crucial to this process. They provided the methodology for the examination of human problems; theories of the causes of disease, explanations of political behavior, analyses of institutional relationships, understandings of economic behavior, and interpretations of the working of society itself; and, of profound significance, they also formulated proposals for change. Universities everywhere trained graduate students in the new disciplines and sent them out into the real world to observe, investigate, report, and, in many instances, involve themselves in the reform effort. Research institutes poured forth a flood of papers on every manner of question—from the causes, incidence, and costs of industrial accidents to the relationships between poverty, disease, juvenile delinquency, and adult criminality. Labor economists studied the causes of lockouts and strikes and proposed methods of achieving industrial harmony; social workers investigated wages and the cost of living and sought ways to alleviate distress; sociologists assessed the costs of rural isolation and deprivation as a first step toward proposals for the enrichment of farm life; and tax specialists examined the distribution of income and wealth with a view to devising more equitable and efficient revenue systems. And everywhere these experts organized themselves in professional societies, the better to gather and disseminate their data, theories, and recommendations for the reformation of the world of capitalism.

Typically, the knowledge base so laboriously accumulated in the academy percolated outward into the arena of practical politics. Beyond the traditional modes of disseminating information—public and private correspondence, word of mouth, newspapers, magazines, journals, public meetings, study clubs, and pulpits, for example—there was a striking proliferation of reports issued by all manner of agencies and organizations concerned with reform of one kind or another—bulletins of departments of agriculture, health, and public welfare; bureaus of labor statistics and municipal and legislative research; industrial and mine safety boards; trade unions; consumer organizations; trade associations; and suffrage groups, to name but a few. Universities and colleges created undergraduate courses and text materials to study public issues, and intercollegiate and inter–high school debating conferences served as additional forums for the wider dissemination of reform ideas. Similarly, commercial publishers responded to the public's craving for guidance on public issues by commissioning the preparation of home study libraries, and booking agencies did a lively business in arranging public lectures. Conferences of activists and experts gathered locally, regionally, nationally, and internationally to share experiences, ideas, and information and to consider policy choices. Those who could not themselves attend were often able to follow the proceedings in newspaper accounts and conference reports. Additionally, governments everywhere appointed commissions of inquiry on all manner of questions to investigate, report, and recommend. In short, the worldwide army of reconstruction-through-state-interventionism marched on information.

The striking feature of this process was the systematic and organized way in which this information was gathered and disseminated. In large measure that was because of the rising importance of the bureaucracy, one of the most innovative developments of the late nineteenth century. We see the bureaucracy quite differently—as a stultifying, frustrating institution. We too easily forget how efficiently the new agencies harnessed human energy and creativity in the task of managing and disseminating information. No small part of that success came from the power of money. By today's standards agency budgets were miniscule, but dedicated and mostly talented officials had more resources at their command than ever before and considerable latitude to spend it where it would do the most good. The time had not yet arrived when internal institutional needs absorbed much of the budget, leaving slender pickings for the delivery of services, and most agencies had yet to be taken over by lawyers and other administrative types who could happily spend their lives picking bureaucratic nits.

The power of information emanated from the bureaucracy, most of all. No small part of that influence came from the fact that these agencies attracted experts dedicated to applying their knowledge and skills to the task of economic and social reform. Interventionist by either inclination or training, they eschewed merely administrative functions and were not prepared to sit passively on the sidelines. Even librarians became activists in their own way, as can be seen from the large number of bibliographies on reform issues they compiled. In the beginning, at any rate, many bureaucrats tried to do much more than merely implement policies made elsewhere. Rather, they either made policy themselves, as was so often the case with state industrial commissions, which usually operated under broad legislative mandates, or they lobbied politicians to enact policies based on their expert knowledge.

The creation of the California workmen's compensation system is a classic example. The governor appointed a board to implement the statute, but the members, led by A. J. Pillsbury, judged the measure to be unsound and proceeded on their own initiative and without mandate to replace it with one of their own design, which they then rammed through the legislature in Sacramento. Or consider the celebrated Ballinger-Pinchot controversy during the Theodore Roosevelt administration. Factionalism, personal animus, and party politics aside, the dispute really boiled down to a quarrel over which group was more dedicated to the new interventionism—to the conservation of natural resources, to land-use planning, and against the "interests." It is not without point that the apparent victor in this impassioned struggle, at least until the Ickes report in 1940, was Gifford Pinchot, whose Forest Service publicity juggernaut crushed the opposition. This was persuasive testimony indeed to the power of the new bureaucracy to exploit the opportunities created by the Information Revolution and, not incidentally, to educate voters to a wider acceptance of the principle that the nation's heritage had to be managed by the state for the public benefit and protected from the ruthless exploitation of private predators.

The Pinchot example also demonstrates how quickly some of these new agencies became politicized, at least in the sense that they had to divert some of their energies to securing legislative appropriations. That was a crucial spur to their activist drive, for they had to cultivate the support of key politicians and constituencies by concentrating as much of their resources as possible on programs that would produce tangible results. For many agencies, departments of agriculture, for example, demonstration projects and field trials were highly visible ways of justifying their budgets because farmers could readily make the connection between scientific research and agricultural efficiency and productivity. Similarly, bureaus of labor could demonstrate the link between better safety practices and reductions in the incidence of industrial accidents. But for many agencies, including agriculture and labor, gathering and disseminating information were the cheapest and most effective ways of building support, the more so because they could incorporate in their publications data reported by investigators elsewhere. For example, the findings of inquiry commissions in one country fed into the information network encircling the globe. Thus field work conducted in New Zealand on the compulsory arbitration of labor disputes reached American audiences via reports originally issued in the United Kingdom, New South Wales, and Victoria.

But the Information Revolution and the state interventionism it spawned had its impact through individuals as well as institutions. Of the hundreds of examples that could be cited, six lives illustrate the range of activity and the interconnections on which the New Deal built.

First, the case of Henry Demarest Lloyd, who can be thought of as the journalist as reformer. Although he died half a century before the New Deal began, his interventionist message helped to shape the thinking of the generation that survived him. Lloyd began his career as a financial writer for the *Chicago Tribune*, but his liberal views soon put him at odds with his father-in-law, the paper's editor. Lloyd then left the *Tribune* to pursue his own vision—an America striving for and reaching its high destiny as a humane, just, and caring society. He set out to expose the nation's warts and to hold up foreign models as examples of the greatness the Republic could achieve. Throughout, he perfected the case study method of firsthand reporting to give his writing vivid authenticity and to make his reform message more appealing to the reading middle class. Thus he exposed the problems of concentrated wealth and power by investigating John D. Rockefeller's Standard Oil Company, and he laid bare the exploitation of Pennsylvania's miners in his moving descriptions of industrial warfare in the anthracite region. He also visited the British Isles to report on land reform programs, Switzerland to examine democracy in action, and Australia and New Zealand to shame and inspire his fellow citizens into reinvigorating their efforts to reconstruct the United States.

Along the way, Lloyd developed a warm admiration for William Pember Reeves, New Zealand's first minister of labor, 1891 to 1896, the politician responsible for the enactment of the most comprehensive set of laws touching the lives of working people that the world had yet seen. Poet, journalist, Fabian, and historian as well, Reeves went on to careers in diplomacy, education, and banking. He served as the colony's agent-general in Great Britain, as director of the London School of Economics (an influential forum of the New Liberalism), and on the London board of the National Bank of New Zealand. He wrote many articles on antipodean reform as well as a well-received two-volume study on *State Experiments in Australia and New Zealand* (1902), lectured on reform topics in both the United Kingdom and the United States, and corresponded with a wide circle of reformers, including Henry Demarest Lloyd in Chicago, who, after a visit to Australasia in 1899, sought to "New Zealandize" America through articles, books, lectures, and his considerable powers of moral suasion. Thus Reeves spread the interventionist message far beyond his native shores, becoming in time a minor elder statesman of the movement.

Economist John Bates Clark followed a very different career trajectory, but one no less influential in its own way in bringing the power of the state to bear on social and economic problems. Trained at Heidelberg and Zurich as well as at Brown and Amherst, he became a major figure in the development of economics as a discipline and profession, particularly by drawing on his continental experience to link the "dismal science" to ethical considerations. The author of many articles, monographs, papers, and widely used texts, he helped to organize the American Economic Association in 1885 and served two terms as its president in the next decade. More radical in his early career than in later life—witness the Christian socialist sympathies reflected in his first articles and books dealing with the philosophy and distribution of wealth—he nevertheless remained dedicated to the causes he espoused, such as state intervention to control bigness in business and promote fairness in competition, and to international peace through arbitration rather than force. As a teacher at Carleton, Smith, and Amherst colleges from 1875 to 1895 and thereafter at Columbia Unviersity, he sensitized his students to the ethical problems of capitalism and set them to thinking about ways to reform the system. His 1914 book, *Social Justice Without Socialism*, was representative of the social science writing of the time and the molding of American thinking along the interventionist lines that was to culminate in New Deal activism.

Clark had some influence on Thorstein Veblen at Carleton and much on Vida Scudder at Smith. In 1884 Scudder went on to postgraduate studies at Oxford, where she, like so many Americans, fell under the spell of John Ruskin. She returned to America fired with radicalism from what she had heard and seen. Appointed to the Wellesley faculty in 1887, she won distinction as a scholar in both literary and religious studies, combining her research with a brilliant though controversial career as a teacher. Students flocked to her lectures, becoming deeply involved in the connections she established between literature and social thought. Over a classroom career lasting for almost forty years, she brought successive generations of young women from high-status families to an awareness of the powerlessness of ordinary people and gave many of them the determination to apply their training and dedicate their lives to the cause of social and economic justice.

Scudder taught as well by example, for she had an active career beyond the classroom, drawing many of her students and colleagues alike into the world of urban reform and the life of Christian socialism. She helped to organize what became the College Settlements Association, which drew its inspiration from the example of Oxford students living and working in London's slums, and she devoted much time and energy first to social work on Rivington Street in New York City and then to Dennison House on Boston's South Side. A deeply committed member of the Rev. William D.P. Bliss's Christian socialist circle, which campaigned tirelessly for reform, Scudder also served as a delegate to the Boston Central Labor Union and helped to organize the Women's Trade Union League, the Episcopal Church Socialist League, and the League for Industrial Democracy. Scudder's life thus embodied many of the diverse strands of thought and action on which New Deal interventionism built. They included, first, an intellectual component: a radical critique of the injustices perpetuated by capitalism and a vision of a more caring, equitable economic and social order, which she transmitted to her students and the larger public through her lectures and writings. Second, there was her leadership in the settlement house movement, which deepened her understanding of the complex causes of urban poverty and gave an outlet to her ameliorative impulse. And third, she learned, along with so many others in the movement, such as Jane Addams, Florence Kelley, and Julia Lathrop in Chicago's Hull House, that only so much could be accomplished by treating poverty's symptoms. Hence her involvement in the trade union movement, which she saw as a vehicle for mobilizing support for fundamental improvements in the lives of the working poor.

Similarly, I. M. Rubinow's career illustrates from yet a fourth perspective how the New Deal had its roots in the previous reform generation and how long it could take to bridge the gulf between idea and fulfillment. Born in Russian Poland in 1875, Rubinow came to the United States in 1893, where he earned an accelerated baccalaureate at Columbia University in 1895 before going on to New York University, where he took a medical degree three years later. Radicalized by his experience in caring for New York's poor, he gave up doctoring to campaign for a comprehensive program of social insurance. To that end he became an expert actuary and statistician. At one time or another until 1919 Rubinow held positions in the federal and New York City governments, worked for a private insurance company, served as a consultant to state workmen's compensation boards, chaired the rate-making committee of the casualty underwriters' trade association, helped to draft the standard health insurance statute sponsored by the American Association for Labor Legislation, and served as the secretary of the American Medical Association's social insurance committee. Along the way he found time to take a doctorate at Columbia University, published authoritative studies on health and social insurance programs, and founded the Casualty Actuarial and Statistical Society of America. His most lasting achievement was the publication in 1911 of a massive two-volume study of European social insurance programs, which he directed for the U.S. Bureau of Labor. It helped to lay the basis for American workmen's compensation laws and, eventually, the Social Security system.

The extraordinary range and depth of this career, which has been only partially described here, underscores the importance of the flow of information from abroad into the American reform milieu. Rubinow's New York experience taught him that voluntary organizations—settlement houses and charitable agencies—provided no enduring or satisfactory solutions to the newly emerging problems of dependency in the cauldron of urban slums around him—not for age, accident, illness, orphanage, unemployment, or widowhood. Only compulsory programs of social insurance, he came to believe, could insulate suffering humanity from life's misfortunes and do so with certainty, dignity, and self-reliance.

That the remedies Rubinow so vehemently and so passionately advocated came so slowly to the United States says a good deal about the fiscal, philosophical, and constitutional restraints of the decades before the Great Depression. It also speaks to the flaws in his temperament and his lack of political skills.

Experts may propose agendas; they do not always control timetables. And their contributions may be easily forgotten. By the time Social Security came in America in 1936, Rubinow had been edged aside as a liability rather than an asset in winning over political support and public opinion.

The sisters Edith and Grace Abbott paved the way for the New Deal in yet other ways. Each left the prairies of Nebraska to take advanced degrees at the University of Chicago; as residents of Hull House each came under the influence of Jane Addams, Sophonisba Breckinridge, and Julia Lathrop; and each helped to shape public attitudes favorable to an enlargement of state activity by contributing to an informed awareness of the causes of social distress in America.

The elder of the two, Edith (1876–1957), made her principal contributions as a scholar and educator. Deeply influenced by Beatrice and Sydney Webb at the London School of Economics and by her life in an East End settlement, in 1908 she returned to Chicago by way of Wellesley College to become associated with the School of Civics and Philanthropy, which in 1920 merged into the University of Chicago as the School of Social Service. Dean from 1924 to 1942, she worked hard to make social work education as fully respectable as other professional training by insisting on a curriculum built around the social science disciplines, particularly economics, political science, and sociology and by stressing the need for rational solutions to social problems, such as could be designed only when based on sound field research.

Edith practiced what she preached. She published over a long career more than a hundred articles and books, founded and edited the influential *Social Service Review*, and organized the distinguished Social Service Series of research monographs to disseminate the findings of graduate students and others. Her own studies on jails, delinquency, and truancy aside, her most influential work and the one that established her scholarly reputation was *Women in Industry* (1910), which provided convincing proof for her thesis that females on both sides of the Atlantic had long worked outside the home, that they had always been exploited as a powerless group in the labor force, and that their welfare could best be protected by legislative intervention.

Grace Abbott (1878–1939) made her mark as a social worker, administrator, and political activist. She, too, joined the Hull House circle, where she supported the Chicago garment workers' strike in 1910 and 1911 and later campaigned for Theodore Roosevelt and for the right of Illinois women to vote, but in the years from 1908 to 1917 she was best known for her work on behalf of the Immigrants' Protective League, which she headed. She also taught a course on immigrant issues at the School of Civics and Philanthropy, persuaded the Illinois legislature to regulate employment agencies, studied immigrant backgrounds in Eastern Europe, and in 1915 published *The Immigrant in Massachusetts*, a study commissioned by the legislature. Two years later she left for Washington, D.C., and the Children's Bureau, where she was mainly responsible for implementing the new child labor law. That effort came to an abrupt end in 1918 when the U.S. Supreme Court declared the measure unconstitutional. Grace soon returned to Chicago and Hull House to become director of the Illinois Immigrants' Commission and then succeeded Julia Lathrop in Washington as the second head of the Childrens' Bureau. She also served from 1923 to 1924 as president of the National Conference of Social Work, an influential agency for social welfare reform. An effective administrator, Grace worked with the states to set up cooperative programs of infant and maternal care under the Shepphard-Towner Act. Although Congress withdrew funding in 1929, she succeeded in preventing the transfer of child care responsibilities to the Public Health Service, which she regarded as lacking in commitment to infant and maternal welfare, and she remained in Washington long enough to help draft portions of the Social Security Act before taking up a professorship at the University of Chicago's School of Social Service.

Thus Grace, like her sister Edith, built on the endowment of political and social concern bequeathed by their Nebraska parents and given focus and direction by her Hull House life. From involvement with immigrant workers in Chicago's neighborhoods, she took up their cause in Springfield, realizing that only the state could give them the protection they needed. Service in Washington followed when the federal government assumed some responsibility for the welfare of mothers and babies.

What one sees in these six careers and so many like them is a generation of activists coming to maturity in the Populist-Progressive decades and then projecting their ideas and programs to the national level, sometimes before and sometimes during the New Deal era. Each launched a reform career around a set of perceptions about the problems of capitalism, defined the issues, and designed strategies for change, such as regulation of the workplace, the control of big business and the preservation of competition, the establishment of social insurance programs to secure minimum levels of human well-being, the protection of immigrants from exploitation, and the use of scientific methods to improve the delivery of public welfare services. Common to these careers, as well, was the effective use of specialized knowledge and training in the dissemination of information by which to educate voters and their representatives to an acceptance of an enlarged role for government.

THE INEVITABILITY OF INTERVENTIONISM

The argument laid out here can be summarized in a series of interlocking propositions. First, for reasons both philosophical and practical, arising mostly from dissatisfactions with capitalism, all societies in the Western world began moving inexorably in the late nineteenth century toward state interventionism. With important country-to-country differences in timing, causation, and content, legislatures began expanding the reach of government by imposing various kinds of restraints on business; by recognizing and giving official status to various categories of private organizations, which then looked to government to shape the environment in which they functioned; and by assuming larger responsibilities for the well-being of diverse constituencies, whether farmers, immigrants, miners, mothers, or tenants.

Second, the congruence of interventionism as a worldwide phenomenon can be explained by the emergence of processes and institutions common throughout the West. They included the rise of the social sciences, which gave activists a common methodology for analyzing society and its problems, a set of common assumptions concerning the capacity of human beings to engage in effective economic and social engineering, and a common will to reconstruct. Included as well was a massive increase in the volume and velocity of information available to lawmakers and those who would influence public policy, along with the rise of bureaucracies, private as well as public, with resources and skills dedicated to both disseminating information friendly to an expansion of the role of the state and a vested institutional stake in bringing that about.

Third, though the interventionist thrust was in no sense coordinated, everywhere there sprang to life hosts of organizations dedicated to promoting this or that aspect of reconstruction. Mostly they owned their formation and drive to activists from outside the political establishment, though many of their leaders came from well-educated, middle-class and higher backgrounds—the sorts of people who saw it as their duty to be involved and who expected to be listened to. Such organizations often grew out of local activities—church groups, study circles, women's clubs, temperance societies, and the like. They discovered in their members common concerns and commitments to shared perceptions and goals and then strengthened their efforts through like-minded people in regional, national, and sometimes international associational networks. Partly through overlapping memberships and other forms of cross-fertilization between institutions, the army of interventionism marched in the same broad direction, whether in searching for ways to improve the administration of industrial accident claims, provide better access to credit for farmers, increase the supply of higher-quality, affordable housing for the urban poor, or protect female workers from exploitation.

Fourth, in the decades after 1880, the United States, along with other countries in the West moved down this road toward today's interventionist/welfare state. From the perspective of 1932, the nation may not have traveled very far as compared with some foreign countries, but at all levels of government, from city hall to Congress, many enlargements of the sphere of government had been proposed, some programs had been put into effect, and, most important of all, a generation of Americans had been exposed to the theory and practice of the New Liberalism. The problems of the twenties, which culminated in the Great Crash and the Great Depression, simply gave added focus and urgency to policy trends long under way. Although not voiced in the political campaigns of the fall of 1932, it seemed certain that the new President and Congress, whomever they were to be, would respond to the worldwide crisis with some sort of New Deal. By inaugural day the forces of history were in flood tide. There was only one question for the incoming administration to answer: not whether interventionism would increase, but what forms it would take.

Much of what we have come to think of as a Democratic New Deal might just as well have been Republican, and much of what we have believed to have been a sharp departure from American political norms was no more than an extension and nationalization of programs long established or proposed at the state and local levels of government. For example, the Wagner Act and the creation of the National Labor Relations Board in 1936, perhaps the most fundamental alteration in industrial policy since the formation of the Republic, drew on mediation concepts and policies dating back to the late nineteenth century in Massachusetts, New York, and other states. Similarly, the abolition of child labor, the concept of minimum wages, the provision of various forms of social security, and support for farmers were American goals with long histories. Indeed, many states had implemented such programs a decade or more earlier and the Congress itself had tried but failed as early as 1916 to do away with the employment of children.

To be sure, there were some apparent new departures after 1932, such as the creation of the Securities and Exchange Commission or the Tennessee Valley Authority, but even these policies were not as new as some supposed. After all, state regulation of banks, insurance companies, and railroads began before the Civil War. Grain merchants, among others, began to be regulated during Reconstruction, and the Populist-Progressive era brought many demands for programs with an extraordinarily "modern" ring. Nor was there anything very new in the thirties about the call for regional development, as one sees in the long history in the West of irrigation projects and the management of forest and other natural resources. For example, William E. Smythe of San Diego spoke out for such programs at the turn of the century, anticipating the Civilian Conservation Corps with his proposals to put the army of unemployed to useful work on developmental schemes. Others, such as Harris Weinstock and his half brother, David Lubin, anticipated New Deal agricultural policies by urging cheap loans for farmers, government programs to market farm commodities, breaking up large estates into working farms for the landless, and more humane living and working conditions for migrant farmworkers.

The point, of course, is that the New Deal was not so very new. In many ways it merely poured old wine into new bottles. It is for others to say if the wine was drinkable.

4   *Ellis W. Hawley*

The New Deal State and the Anti-Bureaucratic Tradition

As we reconsider the New Deal from the perspective of more than fifty years, we need to look anew at the New Deal state as it took shape in the years between 1933 and 1939. Indeed, the time seems particularly ripe for this. For not only have we come to realize that we know too little about it. We are also learning again about the value of state-centered studies; or, as the current movement in history and the social sciences puts it, about the necessity of "bringing the state back in."[1]

For a time, studies of the state—that is, of governmental structure, apparatus, and workings—had fallen into disrepute. The state, it was said, was only a tool, or a register of the forces in society. For the Marxists, it was a tool of the ruling class; for pluralists, a register of the contending interests in society; for others, a register of the impact of social movements. The explanation for what the state did lay elsewhere, and therefore it did not really deserve much study. Recently, however, this view of the matter has been changing. The structure of the state does demonstrably make a difference; government officials are not simply tools or registers. They can, and do, act independently to alter governmental outputs. Hence it behooves us to understand a nation's polity as well as its society if we are to understand its historical behavior; and in what follows, I seek to make some contribution toward a better understanding of the changes in our polity that took place during the New Deal period.

In American popular thought the state that came out of the New Deal has usually been seen as a result of bureaucratization reaching the national level and establishing itself there as a central feature of modern American life. The assumption underlying this view—an assumption that seems to underlie these seminars on the New Deal legacy—is that the growth of government in the 1930s moved us toward the kind of bureaucratization characteristic of the "welfare state'' elsewhere, and that the consequences lie at the heart of current political cleavages. Yet we have also had a considerable body of scholarship in recent years that directly challenges this assumption and stresses the failure of the New Deal to construct a true administrative state of the type that emerged elsewhere. The emphasis in this scholarship is on the divergence between the path that America has followed since the New Deal, and the path taken by state-builders in other industrialized democracies.[2] We have had a line of thought, in other words, that would favor undoing the New Deal, not because it led us into the errors being committed abroad, but because it erected obstructions in the path of needed institutional development.

Can these two approaches be reconciled? Can the New Deal state be represented both as a product of bureaucratic formation at the national level and as a result of anti-bureaucratic traditions seeking to prevent and find substitutes for bureaucratic development? I believe that it can; and my thesis in what follows is that seeing it in this way can add important dimensions to our understanding of the New Deal. More exactly, I shall look first at the heritages of state-building and opposition to bureaucracy that existed at the beginning of the New Deal; second, at the continuing interplay between the search for an administrative state and the quest for ways to do without one, during this period; and third, at the results as they became parts of the government. Understanding these matters will help us to reach a better understanding not only of the history of state-building in the 1930s, but also of the legacy from the period.

ROOTS OF THE ADMINISTRATIVE STATE

We may begin by noting that the United States in 1933 did not yet have an administrative state, at least not in the European sense. We did, however, have a considerable history of efforts to build and legitimate one. As a nation, we never had the monarchical or military bureaucracies that elsewhere became the foundation for administrative states. Our revolution had been directed against them, and in the nineteenth century we developed our own peculiar form of the modern state. It lodged power not in a bureaucratic elite, but in patronage-based political parties, local governmental units, and a strong judicial system. Modern bureaucracy here had emerged primarily in the private sector, largely in connection with the rise of big business, rather than in the public. And those who had seen bureaucratic expansion as the answer to our national problems had not been able to put much of what they advocated into practice before 1933. True, they had established bridgeheads in the public sector, notably in new forms of municipal government, in the creation of various regulatory commissions, in some public support for data production, and in measures aimed at bringing business methods into governmental work. But the administrative apparatus created was not a large one, and it remained highly fragmented, narrowly constrained, and linked to or dependent on the forms of governmental power that had been established earlier. The nation lacked the kind of autonomous administrative establishment to be found elsewhere, and it retained much that was hostile to the acquisition of one.[3]

This is not to say, however, that the United States of 1933 had escaped the influences that contributed elsewhere to the rise of administrative states. To a degree, it had shared in the revulsion against laissez-faire policies, against partisan politics, and against legalistic constitutionalism, revulsions that had helped bureaucratic elites to acquire power in other nations. And the result was the emergence here—particularly in portions of the business community, the new technocratic professions, and segments of the intellectual community engaged in discourse with their counterparts abroad—of reform policies that deplored America's lack of an administrative establishment and looked to developing one as the path to greater efficiency, harmony, and rationality. Such prescriptions had been part of the agitation for reform during the so-called "Progressive era" preceding World War I. They had continued to find advocates in the postwar period, some of whom invoked the war experience to support their arguments. And they were available in 1933 as prescriptions the New Deal might adopt.[4]

Developments from 1930 to 1933, moreover, had created wider openings for such policies. The persistence and deepening of the Depression lent credence to those who blamed market failure. They also created greater impatience with government as it existed; and they had discredited President Hoover's notion that correctives could be coaxed from the nation's private sector. By 1932 there was much discussion of the need for national economic planning and a national welfare system; and in a number of the schemes for meeting this perceived need, a central role was assigned to a new administrative state. In theory, in other words, the new duties could and should be performed by a special group of officials, who were to rise above the bickering of special interests, construct new institutions to serve the public or national interest, and thus become the enlightened controllers and guardians that were needed in a modern industrial society. America's liberal creed and institutional structure, it was argued, had once served it well. But the time had now come to join other democratic nations in developing a "new liberalism," one that recognized the realities of industrial urban life and capitalist development and that made a national administrative establishment a prime tool in securing further national progress.[5]

The New Dealers had at hand, then, a heritage of efforts to implement bureaucratic government, a set of proposals that were the product of this history, and a political crisis that provided a greater opportunity to set them in motion. They also had at hand the personnel with which to fashion new institutions. As some authors have pointed out, the New Deal could draw on skilled professionals and technicians who were unemployed.[6] And among the New Dealers were a number of people already inclined toward administrative statism. They were to be found in the Brains Trust that provided Roosevelt with ideas during the 1932

campaign; among the reformers now converging on Washington; and among the
"experts" being summoned there, especially experts with credentials in such
disciplines as public administration and institutional economics.

Yet, while these resources were at hand, the New Deal did not turn out to be
a straightforward push to create a new administrative state. Also at hand were
opposed public policy traditions, a heritage combining the promise of social
rescue and renewed progress with appeals to anti-bureaucratic values—formulations, in other words, that were supposed to save us not only from the anti-
social workings of the market, but also from bureaucratic tyranny. As I see it,
four such formulations stand out; and each of these proved to have important
implications for what followed.

One such formulation, clearly evident in 1933, was the notion of a "business
commonwealth," meeting the needs for planning and welfare through business-
led corporative (as opposed to government-run bureaucratic) institutions. This
is sometimes seen as an importation from the fascist, social Catholic, and neo-
capitalist movements in Europe; and it did, of course, bear certain resemblances
to them. But it also had firm roots in the American past. It was the latest in a
line of similar formulations reaching back to the crisis of the 1890s—formulations
that would make temporary use of government to coax needed social machinery
from the new organizations that had formed in the private sector. And like its
antecedents, it could and did appeal not only to private sector elites of various
sorts, but also to the anti-bureaucratic symbols deeply embedded in American
political discourse. The institutions envisioned, so the argument ran, would make
possible new forms of "self-government," "community action," "responsible
individualism," and "modern democracy." And these would then allow us to
have continuing order and progress, while retaining our safeguards against bureaucracy.[7]

A second formulation, also clearly apparent in 1933, although in different
circles, was what we might call the "populist commonwealth." This, in theory,
could make planning and welfare unnecessary by returning power to the "people" and their "communities" and conclaves. Envisioned here was a reformist
state that would use its power to establish a "people's" money, a "people's"
tax system, a "people's" antimonopoly law, and other "people's" instruments—
all working to destroy the corporate power that had allegedly put the people in
chains and robbed them of their capacity to prosper. But at least as the rhetoric
had it, none of this would mean power for a new administrative class. On the
contrary, as in a line of similar formulations reaching back beyond the 1890s to
the early days of the republic, it would save us from the anti-democratic designs
of pretentious "experts" who had helped to forge the chains in the first place.[8]

A third formulation, even more in evidence than the two already noted, called
for a temporary or emergency form of the administrative state. The underlying
assumption in this case was that unusual circumstances had created a "crisis,"
which required a temporary departure from our normal methods of governance
and decision-making. In part, the analogies drawn here were to the temporary

structures of management that had arisen to keep order and provide relief in the wake of natural disasters. But in larger part, they were to the administrative apparatus that had been established and used during World War I, in the national emergency of 1917 and 1918. Most of the wartime machinery had been set up outside the regular agencies of government; it had amounted in effect to borrowing private sector administrative resources for public purposes; and it had then been abolished once the emergency had passed. Its construction and usage had been such (or so the argument ran) that it had not brought the evils and dangers inherent in bureaucratic government. And the argument was now that we could be rescued by a similar apparatus, which again would be so constructed and used as to be anti-bureaucratic in its larger effects. As in the case of the other formulations, this was, in theory, a way to have one's cake and eat it too.[9]

Finally, entering the picture as a fourth formulation was a conception of expanded government in which public administrators would be used to implement the designs of deserving interest groups but would not be given the kind of power that would enable them to become a bureaucratic establishment running an administrative state. They would, in other words, remain tied to and take their identities from the groups that they served, would be constrained by a continuing division of powers, and would be coordinated by political brokers as opposed to master administrators. Envisioned was a kind of "interest group commonwealth" or what some writers later called the "broker state." We would be rescued from the intolerable features of the market economy through a politically brokered administrative expansion, which would allow groups in need of protection or enhanced economic power to acquire them. But the expansion would be such that power would remain in the hands of politicians and interest-group leaders. We would be saved from bureaucratic statism.[10]

What the New Deal really had at hand, then, was not only a set of prescriptions for giving America an administrative state, but also formulations for using government in ways that were supposed to allow us to continue without such a state. It could seize on the latter without ranging itself against the anti-bureaucratic tradition. And in practice, much of the New Deal state grew out of efforts to apply these formulas. I would argue that this was true of all three phases into which historians usually divide the New Deal (1933–1935, 1935–1937, and 1937–1939). I want to turn next to the details of this practice. By examining it, we can begin to understand how the New Deal state arose within a political culture that retained strong strains of anti-statism and why some now regard it as having erected obstacles to modern state-building, rather than advancing that process.

EARLY NEW DEAL POLICIES

During the first phase of the New Deal, what historians usually call the First New Deal, running from the Hundred Days of 1933 to early 1935, these notions

that salvation and renewed progress could come without resorting to administrative statism were clearly evident. There were, as we look back on the period,
opportunities for building a genuine administrative establishment or at least for
laying the groundwork on which one might subsequently have been erected. The
Economy Act of 1933 gave the President extensive powers to reorganize the
executive branch. The new agency for public works and resource planning had
some potential for becoming the national planning board envisioned in schemes
for administrative direction. And the support for bureaucratic regulation that led
to measures like the Securities Exchange Act had at least some potential for
producing a much larger and more coherent regulatory complex. If Roosevelt,
in particular, had conceived of the New Deal as administrative state–building,
or if he had been very receptive to those who did, more of this potential might
have been realized. But neither was the case, and the extraordinary presidential
power that might have been used for such ends was not. The grant of power
under the Economy Act was turned to what one scholar has called "picayune
purposes."[11] And for the Roosevelt of this period, the formulations that would
allow us to continue without an administrative state proved far more attractive
than the prescriptions for giving us one.

More specifically, the administrative complex that emerged during this initial
period was largely shaped and justified by a mixture of the "emergency management" and "business commonwealth" ideas. One component in the mix was
Roosevelt's invocation of the war analogy to call for an emergency government
capable of waging a "war on the depression," a government that, as authorized
and established, did resemble the one that Roosevelt had been part of (as assistant
secretary of the navy) in 1917 and 1918. Once again we had an array of new
agencies, theoretically established for emergency purposes; and as in the earlier
case, these were set up outside the regular agencies of government, were reliant
on a temporary "nationalization" of private sector administrative resources rather
than on a regular civil service, and were supposed to pass out of existence after
this war had been won.[12]

The other component in the mix was Roosevelt's embracing of the idea that
corporative institutions could combine self-government with a capacity for national management and that such institutions could become established through
a temporary use of governmental power to promote the process. The early New
Deal agencies, in other words, were to function not only as emergency managers,
but also as institutional "midwives," leaving us with new societal formations
capable of channeling market forces into constructive paths and keeping them
out of destructive ones. And Roosevelt, whose earlier work with business associations had involved attempts at such promotion, was now to serve as general
supervisor of these institutional midwives.[13]

The heart of the early New Deal state, to be still more specific, was the
administrative apparatus to carry into effect the National Industrial Recovery
Act, the Agricultural Adjustment Act, and the Federal Emergency Relief Act.
These were the key measures intended to alter social outputs; and in the machinery

for their implementation, we have the clearest examples of this mixture of the emergency and midwife states, both supposed to save us from the kind of bureaucracy that we had always been reluctant to establish. The National Recovery Administration (NRA) was in large measure modeled on the War Industries Board of 1918, but was also thought of as a midwife helping an organizational society give birth to new planning, regulatory, and welfare institutions. The Agricultural Adjustment Administration (AAA) was thought of in much the same way, although in its case the administrative resources temporarily "nationalized" were primarily those of the farm organizations and agricultural colleges, not those of the food processors, as had been the case during World War I. And the Federal Emergency Relief Administration was conceived of not as the nucleus of a new social service state, but as a provider of temporary aid to community-centered welfare institutions and as an agency that might in the process help new institutions of this sort to be born. In all three cases one finds an overlay of anti-statist rhetoric attuned to the anti-bureaucratic symbols and traditions long embedded in our political culture.[14]

If these structures were the heart of the early New Deal state, however, they were not the whole of it. Also helping to shape and justify some portions of it was the neo-populist thinking to be found in a variety of protest groups and congressional initiatives. Some of this was embraced by New Deal policymakers, mostly, it seems, with the idea of containing or co-opting its supporters. And what resulted were tools that, in theory, could be used to alter social outcomes by loosening the grip of the "money power" on "the people" or by protecting virtuous competitors from the continuing machinations of "corporate power." To be more specific, we got legislation empowering the president and the treasury to implement populist monetary remedies, legislation under which the district courts might act as agents of social rescue from the "money lenders," legislation divorcing investment from commercial banking, and a combination of legislation and executive action that added neo-populist enclaves and sounding boards to the structures being created by the NRA and AAA. The early New Deal state was hardly the "people's state" envisioned in neo-populist thinking. But it contained a number of concessions to such thinking, and these concessions brought into it another variation on the nation's anti-bureaucratic tradition.[15]

From the beginning, moreover, Roosevelt's experience as a politician made him receptive to the fourth formulation allegedly capable of improving on market performance while retaining safeguards against bureaucratic statism—to the idea, in other words, of a politically brokered administrative expansion driven by interest group desires, kept safe by constraints against its coalescence into a bureaucratic establishment, and harnessed to national purposes by political leadership and finesse. Even as he embraced the emergency and midwife concepts, and made concessions to neo-populism, Roosevelt found room in his program for an administrative expansion geared to interest group initiatives. One thinks particularly of such new administrative units as the Railroad Retirement Board, the Federal Coordinator of Transportation, and the Federal Grazing Service. And as interest group and interagency conflict rose within the major structures created in 1933, generating in the process a variety of similar initiatives, the President's role as manager and aggregator of these began to overshadow his roles as emergency chieftain, supervisor of midwives, and "people's" tribune. The broker state, justified by conceptions of interest group liberalism and administration by conflict, was in the making.[16]

Much of the early New Deal's administrative apparatus, then, was erected in the name of anti-bureaucracy; and when the expectations aroused were not fulfilled, two competing lines of explanation arose and by 1934 had become parts of an ongoing internal debate. One stressed the apparatus's lack of administrative capacity, both as initially established and as supplemented by such powerless coordinating bodies as the National Emergency Council. The needed capacity, it claimed, could come only through the lodging of more planning, adjustive, and directive power in the hands of qualified bureaucratic elites. The other line of explanation seized on the anti-bureaucratic components in the formulations and insisted that these were in practice being eroded. According to it, the problem lay with power-hungry bureaucratic aggrandizers who were seeking to turn economic self-government into government control, people's tools into bureaucratic ones, emergency administration into a bureaucratic establishment, and properly constrained administrative expansion into a power base for bureaucratic elitism. Such were the arguments now coming from the NRA code authorities and AAA committees, from neo-populist protest groups, and from defenders of interest group autonomy and vested institutional power. And given the resonance of these in our political culture, they helped to sustain institutional obstacles to the prescriptions for greater "administrative capacity."[17]

Hence, as early as 1934, the administrative creations of the New Deal were being denounced not only for their interference with free-market forces and established ways, but also for the obstacles they had erected in the path of modern state-building and good national management. It was a situation that would continue and in time have its counterpart in scholarly discourse.

AN ADMINISTRATIVE STATE IN THE MAKING

During the New Deal's second phase, what historians usually call the Second New Deal of 1935 and 1936, the effort to accommodate the nation's anti-bureaucratic tradition would persist. But in this period the convergence of several developments did bring forth something closer to the administrative states operating elsewhere. One such development was adverse court decisions rejecting the legal basis of the emergency and midwife concepts and putting much of the First New Deal's administrative system out of business. Of particular importance here was the decision overturning the NRA, *Schechter v. U.S.*, 295 U.S. 495 (1935). Another development was the changing political configuration, marked especially by a loss of business power and prestige, the emergence of anti–New

Dealism in the business community, and political gains for labor and other proponents of greater economic and social democracy. By 1935 this altered configuration had not only changed the makeup of Congress and the pattern of presidential policy advice, but also made reliance on private sector administrative resources increasingly difficult. And third, new links were being forged between would-be administrative state–builders and those making gains in the political arena. Key groups of industrial relations specialists, social work and social science professionals, legal technicians, and resource-usage experts were now having considerable success in selling bureaucratic prescriptions—with appropriate roles, of course, for their specialties—to the labor movement and to reform-minded politicians and legislators.[18]

Essentially, it was the convergence of these three developments that gave us what most historians would regard as the heart of the New Deal state as it was operating by the end of 1936. From it came the Wagner Labor Relations Act and the new bureaucracy for regulating industrial relations and collective bargaining. From it came the Social Security Act and the new bureaucracy to administer programs of social insurance; and from it also came new powers for the bureaucracies associated with the Securities and Exchange Commission and the Federal Reserve Board, a new jobs program that brought federal officials as well as federal funds into local communities, and an altered farm program that assumed the need for a permanent bureaucracy as opposed to an emergency structure or a midwifing operation. Policy, as expressed in laws and administrative decisions, was, for a while, being made by people who believed that federal bureaucracies had—or could acquire—the competence to perform these new social duties and function as effective national tools. Those who had seen the United States as lagging behind in this regard now believed that it was catching up. And New Deal lawyers seemed convinced that the shaky legal basis for these new national tools could be solidified through skillful litigation leading to the acceptance of new constitutional doctrines.[19]

During this period an American administrative state did appear to be in the making, and by 1937 the equation of this with progress was being asserted and celebrated in books like James M. Landis's *The Administrative Process* and Thurman Arnold's *The Folklore of Capitalism*.[20] Yet, as we look back on the period, it is also apparent that the emergence of these new bureaucracies was neither the whole of New Deal state-making, nor a development that was giving us anything approaching the full-fledged administrative state. For one thing, remnants of the earlier formulas for letting us do without such a state persisted and continued to shape some laws and administrative instruments. And for another, the new bureaucracy was still highly fragmented and particularized and still subject to the constraints of other forms of institutional power. It had, as later critics would put it, a "hollow core,"[21] a void where there should be a national planning agency and machinery for harmonizing agency goals with national ones; and it had to operate in an environment in which much of America's

nineteenth-century state had survived and a good deal of power was still lodged
with judges, party politicians, legislative committees, and local governmental
units.

The persistence of the earlier formulations can be readily noted in measures
that were important, if not central, parts of the Second New Deal's measures.
The continuing effort to contain and co-opt neo-populist initiatives left its mark
in the Revenue Acts of 1935 and 1936, in another farm bankruptcy law, in
protective measures for ''independent'' merchants, and in portions of the new
Banking Act and Public Utility Holding Company Act. All of these were supposed to create new people's tools for use against the money power and economic
imperialism. The emergency concept continued to be evident in a reemployment
apparatus that was supposed to disappear when the economic pump had been
primed and relief was no longer needed—not become a continuing tool for macro
economic and manpower planning. And a mixture of the midwife and empowered
interest group solutions continued to be evident in measures that were supposed
to improve the performance of ''sick'' industries by salvaging elements of the
NRA apparatus and continuing to entrust private sector administrative resources
with public duties. Action of this sort was taken for such industries as petroleum,
forestry, trucking, bituminous coal, and some foodstuffs.[22]

The other point about the New Deal state in this period—that the new bureaucracies did not add up to anything approaching a full-fledged administrative
state—was not only a point stressed in continuing calls for administrative reform,
but one evident in a variety of failed bureaucratic visions that ran afoul of
persisting critiques and constraints. The bureaucracies of the Second New Deal
were forced to function largely as a collection of political interest groups, not
as a unified structure engaged in national management and recognized as an
indispensable ''fourth branch'' of government. And those who would equip the
government with a centrally placed mechanism for national planning, hopefully
by strengthening and broadening the pioneering work of such agencies as the
National Resources Committee and the Tennessee Valley Authority (TVA),
found themselves repeatedly frustrated. New openings had appeared in 1935,
openings through which bits and pieces of a ''national bureaucracy'' could be
and were slipped. But these bits and pieces still had to accept narrowly constrained roles and accommodate themselves to a political framework and culture
that, in many respects, were hostile to their presence.[23]

Even in this second phase, then, the rise of the New Deal state was not
accompanied by a repudiation of America's long-standing and deeply rooted
antipathy toward governmental power exercised by a bureaucratic elite. The state
assumed a number of new social duties and added bureaucratic machinery to
assist in performing them. But the earlier formulas for securing a good society
without entrusting power to bureaucrats persisted. And the new ''national bureaucracy'' had to accommodate itself to a milieu supportive of anti-bureaucratic
values and to operate without the mechanisms it needed to begin functioning as
a system of national management.

A HOLLOW CORE

The third phase of the New Deal, from 1937 to 1939, has usually been seen as a time when the reformist expectations aroused by the electoral outcomes in 1936 were frustrated by revivals of conservative strength, and when the consequent stalemate pushed Roosevelt into such strategies to maintain the system as compensatory spending and lending, anti-trust action, and consolidation of previous gains. In most histories of the period the battle over administrative reform is mentioned but relegated to a decidedly peripheral place. There are scholars, however, who believe that it does not belong there. Historians like Barry Karl, in particular, would assign it a much more central place, and on the basis of their work, it does seem possible that the events of this period can be given a quite different reading.[24] It can be seen as a time when serious efforts were made to fill the "hollow core" in the state's bureaucratic apparatus, when we might have developed—but did not—the managerial component characteristic of modern states elsewhere, and when our failure in this regard meant that subsequent American state-building would stay within the patterns discernible in the earlier New Deal period.

One thing distinguishing this period from its predecessors was Roosevelt's close relation for a time to people who would bring "top-level management" to what the New Deal had wrought and would create an "up-to-date, efficient, and effective instrument for carrying out the will of the nation." In 1936 Roosevelt had responded to proposals for the study of management problems by creating the President's Committee for Administrative Management, chaired by public administration expert Louis Brownlow. After the election he had embraced most of the committee's recommendations and made them the basis of a government reorganization bill sent to Congress in January of 1937. The goal, according to the bill's drafters and proponents, was to "develop" the presidency "on the side of management and administrative supervision as well as on the political side." And to do that the bill proposed to create a number of new managerial tools and mechanisms, not just for a particular President, but for the office as an institution. Among these were to be a new managerial staff and stronger mechanisms of fiscal control; a national planning agency having both adviser and directive powers; and a greatly strengthened organizational capacity able to mold politicized semiautonomous administrative units into a harmonious structure of national management.[25]

This effort to fill the hollow core with professional managers and planners has usually been seen as an isolated initiative unconnected to other measures being pushed at the time. But again, some historians have begun to question this view by pointing out that three other attempted reforms during this period amounted to attacks on power structures that were seen as obstacles to the attainment of national management. One was the court reform sent to Congress some three weeks after the government reorganization bill. This, in essence, would restaff the courts with jurists who saw no constitutional barriers in the way of an expanding domain of administrative law and managerial power. The second was party reform, an initiative that finally led to the attempted "purge" of 1938. It was intended essentially to break the obstructive power of the Southern political organizations and the people they sent to Congress. And the third was the scheme to establish regional planning institutions, commonly referred to as the TVA's Seven Sisters. This was a scheme that, in its early versions, would have created a network of regional and local planning authorities responsive to central direction by a national planning board and posing a direct challenge to the whole structure of state and local influence on resource distribution.[26] Had all these initiatives been successful, this period might have become a truly revolutionary one in establishing and legitimating the kind of institutions that our anti-bureaucratic traditions had long taught us to fear and shun.

These potentially revolutionary initiatives, however, were not successful. As one might expect, they aroused the ire of the power-holders under attack, proved vulnerable to new invocations of traditional anti-bureaucratic rhetoric and wisdom, and produced only minor changes in the polity that they were intended to transform. The expectation that Roosevelt's extraordinary success at the polls could be translated into an instrument of transformation, supported by the people and the experts alike, proved to be a faulty one; and with the coming of new economic setbacks in late 1937, Roosevelt found his capacity to win legislative victories further diminished. Under these circumstances, moreover, he had soon fallen back on the earlier formulas. During the first half of 1938 he lent sporadic encouragement to a new crop of corporative schemes for national management through private sector resources. Some of his advisers thought that he wanted to revive the NRA. During the same period he called for a new set of emergency tools and for more people's tools to cope with the machinations of corporate power. And, viewed in retrospect, his legislative successes in 1938 were essentially of the type that allowed other bits and pieces of a national bureaucracy to slip through and accommodate themselves to a political framework and culture that remained hostile to bureaucratic ideals. What was new, by the end of the period, was the rise of the notion that coordination could be achieved through the management of spending, taxing, and anti-trust decisions. But the thrust of this thinking and what it produced was toward helping to keep the hollow core hollow. It was not, and would not be, filled.[27]

In this third period, then, the anti-bureaucratic tradition continued to play an important role in shaping the New Deal state. As of 1939, to be sure, a limited Reorganization Act had passed; a new executive office of the president had been established; and—of greatest importance—a new majority on the Supreme Court was stretching the Constitution so as to make room legally for the New Deal's bits and pieces of a national bureaucracy. But none of this had superseded earlier formulas for doing without a bureaucratic state. Nor should it obscure the fact that efforts to realize the managerial vision embraced by Roosevelt in early 1937 had come off second best in the clash with traditional power-holders who invoked traditional anti-bureaucratic rhetoric and wisdom. America's bureaucratic creations on the national level, most of them products of New Deal action, could not be integrated into a larger structure responsive to state managers. And this meant, as Barry Karl notes, that they would continue to be "managed" by a political system responsive to the pressures and powers of party organizations, interest groups, and the local elites who ran the nation's cities and states.[28]

THE ANTI-BUREAUCRATIC TRADITION VS. THE GROWTH OF GOVERNMENT

When we look more closely at just how the New Deal arose and survived, three conclusions are worth noting.

One is the degree to which reality does not correspond to the received picture— that an American version of the administrative or managerial state came into its own in the 1930s and has remained a central feature of the American polity ever since. There were elements in the New Deal trying to change the polity in this way, and at times Roosevelt was receptive to and supportive of them. This was especially true in the year 1937. But the anti-bureaucratic tradition and what it had produced in the past not only constrained such initiatives, but also became internalized in the New Deal constructions that were supposed to provide viable alternatives to bureaucratic statism. The state that emerged had a "hollow core" where the state managers were supposed to be; and along with its bits and pieces of a national bureaucracy, it had accumulated a variety of accretions that resulted from efforts to apply the corporative, neo-populist, empowered interest group, and emergency formulas.

Second, a closer look at the New Deal state provides us with a better under-standing of how the use of governmental power can grow within a political framework and culture that retained much of its hostility to state managers and bureaucratic ideals. It can grow, as the workings of the New Deal demonstrated, by being lodged in or linked to emergency managers, private sector administrative resources, people's tools, deserving interest groups, or survivals of our nine-teenth-century state, all of which claim to have an anti-bureaucratic function and have shown some capacity to make this claim credible. It can grow particularly at a time when much of the population is disillusioned with market-oriented economic policy and legalistic constitutionalism, as was the case from 1933 to 1939. We may need to rethink our views about the growth of government since the New Deal and our strategies for influencing the growth process by considering the circumstances of the New Deal period.

Finally, a better understanding of the New Deal state as it took shape between 1933 and 1939 can help us in our efforts to understand the polity we have today. There have, of course, been changes. We have had other bursts of governmental expansion, notably in the early 1950s when we added the national security state; in the mid–1960s when we added the minority rights and Great Society programs; and in the early 1970s when we added the new regulatory complex concerned with environmental protection. But the main contours of the American state that emerged during the 1930s and 1940s are still with us. We have not moved on to a managerial state in the sense of filling the hollow core with managerial institutions run by state managers and planners. The reforms along this line that have come out of a series of study commissions have been minimal. Nor have we departed from the strategies that allowed the New Deal to expand the usage of governmental power while accommodating anti-bureaucratic traditions. Not surprisingly, New Deal state-building has been and continues to be attacked both from a libertarian perspective and from a managerial one.

NOTES

1. See especially Theda Skocpol, "Bringing the State Back In," *Items* 36 (June 1982); Peter Evans et al., eds., *Bringing the State Back In* (New York: Cambridge University Press, 1985); Charles Bright and Susan Harding, eds., *State-Making and Social Movements* (Ann Arbor: University of Michigan Press, 1984); Roger Benjamin and Stephen Elkins, eds., *The Democratic State* (Lawrence: University Press of Kansas, 1985); Edwin Amenta and Theda Skocpol, "States and Social Policies," *Annual Review of Sociology* 12 (1986): 131–57.

2. See, for example, Barry D. Karl, *The Uneasy State* (Chicago: University of Chicago Press, 1983); Otis L. Graham, Jr., *Toward a Planned Society* (New York: Oxford University Press, 1976); Robert B. Reich, *The Next American Frontier* (New York: Times Books, 1983); Theda Skocpol and John Ikenberry, "The Political Formation of the American Welfare State in Historical and Comparative Perspective," *Comparative Social Research* 6 (1983): 87–148; Norman Furniss and Timothy Tilton, *The Case for the Welfare State* (Bloomington: Indiana University Press, 1977).

3. See Stephen Skowronek, *Building a New American State* (Cambridge: Cambridge University Press, 1982); Charles C. Bright, "The State in the United States during the Nineteenth Century," in *State-Making*, ed. Bright and Harding, 121–58; Karl, *Uneasy State*.

4. Edward Berkowitz and Kim McQuaid, "Businessman and Bureaucrat: The Evolution of the American Welfare System, 1900–1940," *Journal of Economic History* 38 (March 1978): 120–41; Anna Orloff and Theda Skocpol, "Why Not Equal Protection?" *American Sociological Review* 49 (December 1984): 726–50; John W. Chambers, *The Tyranny of Change* (New York: St. Martin's Press, 1980), 1–42; Charles Hirschfield, "National Progressivism and World War I," *Mid-America* 65 (1963): 139–56; Daniel T. Rodgers, "In Search of Progressivism," *Reviews in American History* 10 (December 1982): 113–32.

5. Graham, *Toward a Planned Society*, 4–27; Lewis L. Lorwin and A. Ford Hinrichs, *National Economic and Social Planning* (Washington, D.C.: Government Printing Office, 1935); Arthur M. Schlesinger, Jr., *The Crisis of the Old Order* (Boston: Houghton Mifflin, 1957), 130–39, 184–203.

6. See Elizabeth Sanders, "Business, Bureaucracy, and the Bourgeoisie: The New Deal Legacy," in *The Political Economy of Public Policy*, ed. Alan Stone and Edward Harpham (Beverly Hills, Calif.: Sage, 1982), 115–40.

7. Charles F. Roos, *NRA Economic Planning* (Bloomington, Ind.: Principia, 1937), 1–23; J. G. Frederick, *Readings in Economic Planning* (New York: Business Bourse, 1932); Kim McQuaid, "Corporate Liberalism in the American Business Community,"

Business History Review 12 (August 1978): 342–68; David A. Horowitz, "Visions of Harmonious Abundance" (Ph.D. diss., University of Minnesota, 1971); James Weinstein, *The Corporate Ideal in the Liberal State* (Boston: Beacon Press, 1968). See also my discussion in "The Corporate Ideal as Liberal Philosophy in the New Deal," in *The Roosevelt New Deal*, ed. Wilbur J. Cohen (Austin, Tex.: Lyndon B. Johnson School of Public Affairs, 1986), 85–103.

8. Alan Brinkley, *Voices of Protest* (New York: Alfred A. Knopf, 1982), 143–68; James Turner, "Understanding the Populists," *Journal of American History* 67 (September 1980): 354–73.

9. William E. Leuchtenburg, "The New Deal and the Analogue of War," in *Change and Continuity in Twentieth-Century America*, ed. John Braeman et al. (Columbus: Ohio State University Press, 1964), 80–143; Gerald Nash, "Experiments in Industrial Mobilization, WIB and NRA," *Mid-America* 45 (July 1963): 157–74; Graham, *Toward a Planned Society,* 9–17, 23.

10. Graham, *Toward a Planned Society,* 65–67; Grant McConnell, *Private Power and American Democracy* (New York: Alfred A. Knopf, 1966), 4–7, 158–65; Theodore Lowi, "The Public Philosophy: Interest-Group Liberalism," *American Political Science Review* 41 (March 1967): 5–24.

11. Peri E. Arnold, *Making the Managerial Presidency* (Princeton, N.J.: Princeton University Press, 1986), 82–83.

12. Leuchtenburg, "New Deal and Analogue of War," 107–32; James Holt, "The New Deal and the American Anti-Statist Tradition," in *The New Deal*, ed. John Braeman et al. (Columbus: Ohio State University Press, 1975), 1:31.

13. Holt, "New Deal," 33–35; Hawley, "Corporate Ideal," 89–90; Schlesinger, *Crisis of Old Order,* 374–75.

14. For detailed accounts of each, see Leverett S. Lyon et al. *The National Recovery Administration* (Washington, D.C.: Brookings Institution, 1935); Edwin G. Nourse et al., *Three Years of the Agricultural Adjustment Administration* (Washington, D.C.: Brookings Institution, 1937); Theodore Whiting, *Final Report of the Federal Emergency Relief Administration* (Washington, D.C.: Government Printing Office, 1942).

15. Albert U. Romasco, *The Politics of Recovery* (New York: Oxford University Press, 1983), 46–50, 114–56; Brinkley, *Voices of Protest,* 111, 247–48, 254; William E. Leuchtenburg, *Franklin D. Roosevelt and the New Deal* (New York: Harper & Row, 1963), 50–52, 60, 67–68, 74–76.

16. See McConnell, *Private Power,* 202–11; Wesley Calef, *Private Grazing and Public Lands* (Chicago: University of Chicago Press, 1960); Earl Latham, *The Politics of Railroad Coordination, 1933–1936* (Cambridge, Mass.: Harvard University Press, 1959); William Graebner, *A History of Retirement* (New Haven, Conn.: Yale University Press, 1980), 156–80; Francis Perna, "The National Recovery Administration: The Interest Group Approach to Economic Planning" (Ph.D. diss., Cornell University, 1981).

17. Arnold, *Making Managerial Presidency,* 89–92; Romasco, *Politics of Recovery,* 206–13; McConnell, *Private Power,* 235–39; Ellis W. Hawley, *The New Deal and the Problem of Monopoly* (Princeton, N.J.: Princeton University Press, 1966), 101–26; Brinkley, *Voices of Protest,* 154–56; Peter Irons, *The New Deal Lawyers* (Princeton, N.J.: Princeton University Press, 1982), 156–81, 215–34; Kim McQuaid, "The Frustration of Corporate Revival during the Early New Deal," *Historian* 41 (August 1979): 682–700.

18. Irons, *New Deal Lawyers,* 215–34; Theda Skocpol, "Political Response to Capitalist Crisis," *Politics and Society* 10 (1980): 167–201; Arthur M. Schlesinger, Jr., *The*

Politics of Upheaval (Boston: Houghton Mifflin, 1960), 270–74, 319–20; Howell J. Harris, "The Snares of Liberalism? Politicians, Bureaucrats, and the Shaping of Federal Labor Policy in the United States," in *Shop Floor Bargaining and the State,* ed. S. Tolliday and J. Zeitlin (New York: Cambridge University Press, 1985), 143–66.

19. Skocpol and Ikenberry, "Political Formation"; Irons, *New Deal Lawyers;* Harris, "Snares of Liberalism?"; Clarke A. Chambers, "Social Security," in *Roosevelt New Deal,* 145–59; Leuchtenburg, *Roosevelt and New Deal,* 143–66.

20. Thurman Arnold, *The Folklore of Capitalism* (New Haven, Conn.: Yale University Press, 1937); James M. Landis, *The Administrative Process* (New Haven, Conn.: Yale University Press, 1938). The Landis book had initially been presented in 1937 as the Storrs Lectures on Jurisprudence at Yale University.

21. Otis L. Graham, Jr., "The State in America, 1945–1980s" (Paper presented at Symposium on Growth of American Government, Menlo Park, California, 1986).

22. Mark Leff, *The Limits of Symbolic Reform* (New York: Cambridge University Press, 1984); Grace Adams, *Workers on Relief* (New Haven, Conn.: Yale University Press, 1939); Hawley, *New Deal and Monopoly,* 192–94, 205–69, 312–18, 333–37, 344–56.

23. See Graham, *Toward a Planned Society,* 51–55; Philip J. Funigiello, *Toward a National Power Policy* (Pittsburgh: University of Pittsburgh Press, 1973); Thomas K. McCraw, *TVA and the Power Fight* (New York: J. B. Lippincott, 1971); Patrick Reagan, "The Architects of Modern American National Planning" (Ph.D. diss., Ohio State University, 1982), 306–19.

24. See especially Karl, *Uneasy State,* 149–81, and Karl, "In Search of National Planning: The Case for a Third New Deal" (Paper presented at meeting of Organization of American Historians, April 1983).

25. Arnold, *Making Managerial Presidency,* 91–108, quotations on pp. 96, 104, and 101. See also Richard Polenberg, *Reorganizing Roosevelt's Government* (Cambridge, Mass.: Harvard University Press, 1966), and Barry D. Karl, *Executive Reorganization and Reform in the New Deal* (Cambridge, Mass.: Harvard University Press, 1963).

26. Karl, "In Search of National Planning"; Graham, *Toward a Planned Society,* 64–65.

27. Karl, "In Search of National Planning"; Hawley, *New Deal and Monopoly,* 392–441; Leuchtenburg, *Roosevelt and New Deal,* 254–65; Hawley, "Corporate Ideal as Liberal Policy," 95–97; David L. Porter, *Congress and the Waning of the New Deal* (Port Arthur, N.Y.: Kennikat Press, 1980).

28. Karl, "In Search of National Planning," 26.

John A. Rohr

Constitutional Legitimacy and the Administrative State: A Reading of the Brownlow Commission Report

> Men are not corrupted by the exercise of power or debased by the habit of obedience, but by the exercise of power which they believe to be illegitimate, and by obedience to a rule which they consider to be usurped and oppressive.
>
> Alexis de Tocqueville

The administrative state is the political order that came into its own during the New Deal and still dominates our politics. Its hallmark is the expert agency tasked with important governing functions through loosely drawn statutes that empower unelected officials to undertake such important matters as preventing "unfair competition," granting licenses as "the public interest, convenience or necessity" will indicate, and maintaining a "fair and orderly market." The administrative state is not confined to regulating industry. Its writ runs to defense contracting and procurement, military and diplomatic policy, and the institutions of mass justice that manage programs in public assistance, public housing, public education, public health, disability benefits, veterans' benefits, and food stamps. In a word, the administrative state is the welfare/warfare state we know so well. I shall try to offer a "general consideration" of the New Deal legacy by emphasizing the legacy the New Dealers received from their predecessors rather than the legacy they have left for us. Specifically, I shall compare the principles of government the New Dealers relied on in establishing the administrative state with the principles of the founders of the Republic.[1] I shall present the establishment of the administrative state as in some sense a reenactment of the founding of the Republic. I say "in some sense." To draw comparisons between the 1780s and the 1930s, one needs a good deal of imagination and a high tolerance for ambiguity. I say "reenactment" because I intend to stress the continuities between these two periods rather than the discontinuities. I do not ignore the discontinuities; they are an important part of the story. Nevertheless, I maintain that, on balance, the continuities outweigh the discontinuities and that the New Deal stands for a reenactment, not a rejection, of the founding. The New Deal reenacted the founding because, to a considerable extent, the New Dealers spoke the lines they learned from the scripts written by the Federalists and the Anti-Federalists. I do not mean that they did this self-consciously, although some of them certainly did. They simply spoke as the thoughtful Americans they were. In founding the Republic the Federalists and the Anti-Federalists structured the American public argument from their day down to ours. For the most part, the New Dealers and their opponents carried on their arguments within the bounds of the original argument of 1787–88. In presenting the founding of the Republic as an argument, I follow Herbert Storing's lead in maintaining that the Anti-Federalists were founders along with the Federalists.[2] They were not "framers" of the Constitution, but they were founders of the Republic because the founding took place in public argument, as is fitting for a free society.[3] The precise focus of this paper is on two important state papers of the New Deal era: the Brownlow Report and the Report of the Attorney General's Committee on Administrative Procedure. These papers capture the spirit that informed the administrative state of the New Dealers. My purpose is to compare the principled arguments for administrative reform in these papers with the founding principles of the Republic. Despite my emphasis on continuities, I must acknowledge some startling departures from the founding principles in these documents. This is especially true of the Brownlow Report. To a considerable extent, the attorney general's report serves as a wholesome corrective to some notable excesses in the Brownlow Report.

THE BROWNLOW REPORT

The formal title of the Brownlow Report is the "Report of the President's Committee on Administrative Management." President Roosevelt's adviser Louis Brownlow chaired the committee. The other members were Charles Merriam and Luther Gulick. The report was submitted to Congress in January of 1937 with a strong letter of endorsement from the president.[4] Relying on fashionable principles of scientific management, the Brownlow Report condemned the absence of planning in the federal government, its archaic personnel system, and its chaotic fiscal management. In addition, the report issued a clarion call for exclusive presidential control of government reorganization. Rowland Egger, a distinguished political scientist, maintained that the Brownlow Report "was the first comprehensive reconsideration of the presidency and the president's control of the executive branch since 1787, and is probably the most important constitutional document of our time."[5] If one allows that constitutional documents can issue from institutions other than courts, Egger is surely correct. Most of the Brownlow proposals were at first rejected by Congress. They were casualties of the Court-packing fight. New Deal opponents successfully linked the two issues in the public mind and hung the "dictator bill" label on the legislative effort to enact the Brownlow recommendations into law.

Eventually, however, and quite incrementally, Congress gave the President much of what the Brownlow committee had called for. No less important than its legislative offspring was the impact of the Brownlow Report on popular and academic thought about the presidency. The Brownlow Report prepared us to accept President Truman's description of his office—"the buck stops here." Before Brownlow we might have thought the genius of American government lay in the fact that the buck stops nowhere. We might have said it floats freely among such competing institutions as the Senate, the House, the courts, the presidency, the bureaucracy, the states, our allies, our enemies, and a host of private organizations blessed with either fat coffers or righteous fervor or both. As disciples of Brownlow, we came to believe that the buck should stop with the president until Richard Nixon put the buck in his pocket. Then we knew something had gone wrong. President Roosevelt was aware of the constitutional significance of the Brownlow Committee. Committee member Luther Gulick tells of a committee meeting with the president just after Roosevelt's landslide reelection in 1936. Riding the crest of overwhelming popular support, Roosevelt was ready to institutionalize his political advantage. According to Gulick's notes, at the November 14 meeting the president said "that since the election he had received a great many suggestions that he move for a constitutional convention for the United States and observed that there was no way of keeping such an affair from getting out of hand what with Coughlin and other crackpots about. 'But,' he said, 'there is more than one way of killing a cat, just as in this job I assigned you.' "[6] Thus, according to one of the committee members, the president saw the committee as doing the sort of work one might associate with a constitutional convention. This is a remarkable statement. So remarkable is it that Brownlow prudently omitted it from the lengthy discussion of this meeting in his autobiography, *Passion for Anonymity*. Historian Barry Karl reports that the Gulick memorandum appeared in a manuscript version of the Brownlow autobiography, but was omitted from the printed text.[7] The constitutional significance of the committee's work did not escape Brownlow. Witness his description of an important meeting of the president, the committee, and key congressional leaders just before the release of the report:

Here, that Sunday afternoon in the White House [10 January 1937], for the first time in the history of the great American Republic, a President of the United States, deeming himself in fact as well as in name the head of the executive branch of the government, had come to close grips with the leaders of the legislative branch, who from the beginning of the government had considered themselves responsible for the control, confinement, bridling, and ultimate determination of the organization of all branches of the government.[8]

The scholarly judgment of Rowland Egger, the startling comments attributed to FDR, and the prudent omission of these comments by Brownlow and Brownlow's own sense of history in the making conspire with the later development of the presidency to suggest that the Brownlow Report was indeed a constitutional statement of considerable significance. I shall compare this document's constitutional arguments with the founding period under three headings: (1) the managerial presidency, (2) president and Congress, and (3) fundamental principles.

Managerial Presidency

The formal designation of the Brownlow committee as "the President's Committee on Administrative Management" made clear to all a change in administrative thought that had been recognized by the initiated for several decades. No longer would it suffice to think of efficiency in government in terms of cost-cutting alone. A positive state demanded the effective delivery of promised services. This change was captured in the committee's definition of the term administrative management: "organization for performance of the duties imposed upon the President in exercising the executive power vested in him by the Constitution of the United States."[9] Applying the principles of scientific management, the committee drew a sharp distinction between policy and administration. This distinction found its institutional embodiment in Congress, where policy was made, and in the executive branch, where it was carried out. Thus the budget would serve as "the means of control of the general policy of the Government by the Legislative Branch and of the details of administration by the Executive." This tidy arrangement whereby policy was assigned to Congress and administration to the executive was central to the committee's strategy. By describing virtually every governmental activity as some kind of administrative management—personnel management, fiscal management, planning management, or administrative reorganization—the committee asserted the president's power over the government as a whole.

The committee's broad understanding of administration sprung from vigorous Federalist roots. In *The Federalist*, No. 72, Publius offered two definitions of administration. "In its largest sense," the word "comprehends all the operations of the body politic, whether legislative, executive, or judiciary"; but a more modest meaning of administration restricts the term to "executive details." These "details," however, are rather impressive in their scope: "the actual conduct of foreign negotiations, the preparatory plans of finance, the application and disbursement of the public monies, in conformity to the general appropriations of the legislature, the arrangement of the army and navy, the direction of operations of war; these and other matters of a like nature constitute what seems to be most popularly understood by the administration of government."

Publius would have approved the Brownlow committee's broad understanding of administration. His own definition of even the modest version of administration was broad enough to support the "Administrative Republic" he had in mind.[10]

What would have puzzled him, however, is the committee's distinction between politics and administration. Publius assigned to administration a political task of the highest order; it was through sound administration that the loyalties of the people would gradually be transferred from the states to the federal government.[11] For the authors of the Brownlow Report, the sharp distinction between politics and administration provided rhetorical cover for the far-reaching changes they envisioned for the United States.

Perhaps the most startling statement of the Brownlow committee was its contention that government reorganization was an administrative matter and therefore should be under the exclusive control of the executive. In his message to Congress urging support of the Brownlow committee's recommendations, the president commented favorably on the proposition that "reorganization should be a continuing duty and authority of the Chief Executive on the basis of standards set by Congress."[12]

As the text of the document unfolds, however, it becomes quite clear that the "standards set by Congress" will be quite narrow indeed. For example, the committee calls for the addition of a Department of Social Welfare and a Department of Public Works to be added to the ten executive departments then in existence. Congress's task is simply to create the new departments and name them. Having discharged these responsibilities, Congress is then to "authorize the President to determine the appropriate assignment to twelve executive agencies of all operating administrative agencies and fix upon the Executive continuing responsibility and power for the maintenance of the effective division of duties among the departments."[13]

Lest anyone miss the point of the division of labor the committee has in mind, the report recommends that "two new departments be set up by law to cover these two fields [public welfare and public works], and that there be assigned to these departments by the president not only the appropriate new activities in these fields but also the old activities closely related thereto."[14] Thus Congress will establish the departments and then graciously step aside while the president, in accordance with the principles of scientific management, assigns them their activities.

The conceptual support for this breath-taking view of a managerial presidency was rooted in the committee's constitutional theory of executive power. The principle of separation of powers, the committee announced, "places in the President, and in the President alone, the whole executive power of the Government of the United States."[15] It would be hard to find such a doctrine in the framers of the Constitution. Hamilton's most exuberant defense of executive power appears in his first essay as *Pacificus*. This essay is remarkable for the *extent* of executive power it envisions, that is, the types of things the president can do on his own. Nowhere, however, in this essay does Hamilton claim exclusive executive power for the president. This doctrine finds its origins not in the framers of the Constitution, but in the presidency of Andrew Jackson. Its fulfillment comes in the presidency of Richard Nixon. At the heart of the doctrine is a fundamental error that transforms the President from chief executive officer into sole executive officer.

It is textually demonstrable from the Constitution itself that the *whole* executive power is not vested in the president. The Senate's executive role in treaties and appointments is spelled out in terms in Article II. Both houses of Congress share executive functions in their constitutional powers to declare war, to make rules for the armed forces, to create offices, to prescribe the discipline for the state militias, to grant letters of marque and reprisal, and to vest the power to appoint inferior officers in the heads of the executive departments or in the courts of law.

The explicit constitutional recognition of heads of executive departments negates the notion of the president as *sole* possessor of executive power. In the letter President Roosevelt wrote to accompany the Brownlow Report, he described the presidency as the "Chief Executive Office," but in so doing undercut his committee's position that the Constitution "places in the President, and in the President *alone,* the *whole* executive power of the Government of the United States" (emphasis added). If the president is the government's chief executive officer, he cannot be at the same time its sole executive officer. "Chief," as a hierarchical term, necessarily implies that subordinates possess, to a lesser degree, the power that is the chief's in the fullest, but not exclusive, sense.

The underpinnings of the committee's position on presidential power can be found in its democratic view of the office of the president. We shall examine this point in some detail below. Here it will suffice to note that the managerial view of the president, with its strict control of subordinates, was justified on the grounds that it is "of the essence of democratic government that these offices be selected by the Administration in office." In the name of democracy the issue of executive control was linked to the committee's call for the abolition of multimember administrative boards for administrative purposes in favor of single-headed agencies that would transmit presidential directives efficiently throughout the entire executive establishment.[16]

The committee's call for single-headed agencies in the name of executive efficiency was faithful to Publius's fondness for "unity, vigor, and dispatch" in the executive branch of government. Less faithful to Publius, however, was the committee's support for giving the president a free hand in picking his high-ranking subordinates. In *The Federalist,* No. 77, Publius maintained that the president would need the consent of the Senate to *remove* officers as well as to appoint them. Aside from the impeachment clauses, the Constitution is silent on the matter of a removal power; its directives concern only how to get people into office, not how to get them out. Thus Publius's musings on removal from office were purely speculative. As a matter of fact, events did not support his musings. The first Congress vested the removal power in the president alone. Nevertheless, Publius's opinion is important for our purposes because it gives a good indication of how he saw the relationship between the president and high-ranking executive officers. The first paragraph of *The Federalist*, No. 77, is worth quoting in full:

It has been mentioned as one of the advantages to be expected from the co-operation of the senate, in the business of appointments, that it would contribute to the stability of the administration. The consent of that body would be necessary to displace as well as to appoint. A change of the chief magistrate therefore would not occasion so violent or so general a revolution in the officers of the government, as might be expected if he were the sole disposer of offices. Where a man in any station had given satisfactory evidence of his fitness for it, a new president would be restrained from attempting a change, in favor of a person more agreeable to him, by the apprehension that the discountenance of the senate might frustrate the attempt, and bring some degree of discredit upon himself. Those who can best estimate the value of a steady administration will be most disposed to prize a provision, which connects the official existence of public men with the appro-bation or disapprobation of that body, which from the greater permanency of its own composition will in all probability be less subject to inconstancy, than any other members of the government.

Nothing in this passage indicates that Publius would quarrel with the Brownlow committee's insistence that the president control his subordinates. He would have some reservations, however, about the freedom the committee would give the president in picking his subordinates—or his "team," as we are wont to say today. Publius wants a stable administration and turns to the Senate, that stablest of constitutional bodies, to protect high-ranking officials from the postelection ravages of an incoming president. He seems to call for something akin to a merit system at the very top of the executive establishment and is pleased to report that the "official existence of public men" will be linked to senatorial approval instead of being simply at the whim of a newly chosen president.

So serious is Publius on this matter of administrative stability that in *The Federalist*, No. 72, he defends the reeligibility of the president on the grounds that a frequent turnover of presidents "could not fail to occasion a disgraceful and ruinous mutability in the administration of the government." Thus an im-portant constitutional principle, the indefinite reeligibility (until the Twenty-second Amendment) of the president, was justified by Publius on administrative grounds. If Publius would applaud the Brownlow committee's endorsement of presidential control of the executive branch of government, he would surely reject its effort to distinguish politics from administration. The stable adminis-tration Publius prized—even to the extent of protecting it from presidential whim—was part of his general strategy of winning popular support of the new government through sound administration. For Publius, stable administration was high politics.[17]

The final point on the committee's advocacy of a managerial presidency con-cerns the call for the heads of the twelve proposed executive departments to work together collectively as an executive council or "council of state" to advise the president.[18] The committee follows the framers' plan in looking on the heads of the executive departments as assistants to the president, but the recommendation that they render their assistance collectively is somewhat problematic. At the Constitutional Convention in 1787 the issue of an executive council was hotly debated. A vestigial remain of that debate appears in the second section of Article II, where we find that the president "may *require* the Opinion, in writing, of the principal Officer in each of the executive Departments, upon any Subject relating to the Duties of their respective Offices." The fact that the president may require written opinions only on subjects pertinent to each officer's specific responsibilities suggests a decisive rejection of the idea of an executive council. Presidents, of course, are free to discuss anything they please with their department heads as a group—as presidents have done with their cabinets since the earliest days of the Republic. This practice is not what the Brownlow committee had in mind. The committee was not interested in reinforcing the status quo. The council of state it envisioned was more formal and ambitious than the American cabinet, which is neither a cabinet in a parliamentary sense nor an executive council in any sense.

What is interesting about the Brownlow committee's recommendation is that the executive council was a favorite idea of the Anti-Federalists, and especially of those Anti-Federalists who thought that the president had too much power. During the convention George Mason was the most forceful advocate of an executive council. The failure of the convention to accommodate his wishes in this matter was one of the major reasons he gave for refusing to sign the Constitution he had labored on so diligently for nearly four months.[19] It is ironic that the Brownlow committee would call for an executive council as a means of strengthening the president's power, while Mason had favored a similar institution for the opposite reason.[20]

President and Congress

The Brownlow committee had a ready answer for the anticipated objection that its recommendations would distort the constitutional balance by giving excessive powers to the president. The answer was that it was only by centralizing executive power that the president could be truly accountable to Congress. Thus whatever fears might have been aroused at the thought of a managerial presidency would be quickly allayed by the assurance that these powers would have the happy result of "restoring to the Congress effective legislative control over the executive."[21]

The strategy of the committee was to justify exclusive presidential control over the executive branch as merely a means of making the president accountable to Congress. This argument pervades the committee's report. President Roosevelt agreed that the reforms called for in the report would be helpful "for making the Executive more strictly accountable to the Congress."[22] The point of the argument was that it was only by centralizing executive power in the hands of the president that Congress could actually hold him accountable.

The committee had little to say about just what Congress might do if it should find that its centralized executive had not acted responsibly. And for good reason; short of impeachment, there is little Congress could do. It could reduce or eliminate appropriations for programs favored by the president, but such actions are simply part of the ordinary operation of the principle of separation of powers. They are appropriate actions between equals who try to influence one another's behavior. They are not relevant to the issue of enforcing responsibility. The language of responsibility and accountability suggests superior and subordinate, not separate and equal, institutions. One who is accountable to another can be removed from office or at least have his decision reversed by the superior on appeal. This is why the executive accountability argument is a ruse. The framers of the Constitution made the president accountable to Congress only in the sense that both houses of Congress, acting in concert, could remove him from office; but the Brownlow committee is not concerned with impeachable offenses.

Lest there be any doubt that the committee's concern for executive accountability to Congress is disingenuous, consider the way it interprets the president's constitutional duty to recommend to Congress "such measures as he shall judge necessary and expedient" (Article II, Section 3). From this clause and the clause empowering the president to require written opinions from the heads of executive departments on matters under their jurisdiction, the committee concludes that "it is the duty of the executive departments to supply the Congress with information and advice concerning the laws which they administer."[23] To carry out this duty to provide Congress with the information it needs to legislate, the committee calls for an elaborate clearance system within the executive branch so that Congress will not be confused by differences that might happen to exist among departments. The Bureau of the Budget should provide the clearance before bills are submitted to Congress. Thus, from the president's constitutional duty to recommend legislation, the committee deduces a further duty to *keep* from Congress any information and proposals the executive does not want Congress to have. This is executive accountability to Congress—Brownlow style.

The text of the committee report betrays the disingenuousness of the frequent calls for presidential responsibility to Congress. This is clear at the very beginning of the document. In its introduction the committee states forthrightly that "the President is a political leader—leader of a party, leader of the Congress, leader of a people."[24] A president who leads Congress is the sort of president the committee had in mind. This position contrasts sharply with that of the framers of the Constitution; the rise of such a president was one of their great fears. One of the reasons for the intricate system of presidential selection through the electoral college was to safeguard against the choice of a "leader." In *The Federalist* "leadership" is used pejoratively; it is closely associated with "favorite" or "demagogue." As Robert Eden has noted, the only time Publius uses "leader" favorably is when he discusses the Revolution.[25] This is a clear indication of the antinomian character of the word. A leader is a blessing in times of revolution when legally constituted offices are often irrelevant; but a duly authorized constitutional order has no need for "leaders." Officers and representatives are quite enough. The Brownlow committee's description of the president as a leader in a threefold sense was an important departure from the language of the framers. It captured the frustration that FDR, like Theodore Roosevelt and Woodrow Wilson before him, must have felt from the constitutional constraints of the office the framers had designed.

The most telling expression of the committee's real position on the relationship between president and Congress appeared in a section of the report titled (significantly) "Accountability of the Executive to the Congress." The first paragraph of this section reads as follows:

Under the American system the Executive power is balanced and made safe by freedom of speech, by elections, by the protection of civil rights under an independent judiciary, by the making of laws which determine policies including especially appropriations and tax measures, by an independent elective Congress, and by the establishment of Executive accountability.[26]

For the Brownlow committee, "the Executive Power is balanced and made safe . . . by an independent elective Congress." Strange language this. At the founding of the Republic the framers were careful to provide for a method of selecting the president that would assure his independence from Congress. They feared that the "legislative vortex" would swallow up the other two branches. Legislative power was divided between two houses of Congress to weaken the legislature and to offset the natural advantage it enjoyed. The founders of the administrative state substitute an executive vortex for the legislative vortex of the framers. They look to Congress and the courts to balance and limit the executive, which now plays the lead role in the constitutional drama. Instead of dividing executive power in order to weaken it, as the framers had done to legislative power, the Brownlow committee argues vigorously for its unification under the managerial control of the president.

If one ignores the committee's misleading language on executive accountability to Congress, one finds in the Brownlow Report both an adherence to and a departure from the thought of the framers. The committee follows the framers in maintaining the principle of three separate, equal, and independent branches of government. Also, like the framers, the committee recognizes that one of the three is likely to overwhelm the other two and needs to be balanced and limited by them. Unlike the framers, however, the committee makes no effort to tilt the system against what they see as the dominant branch. On the contrary, the committee looks for ways to reinforce executive dominance.

Fundamental Principles

The Brownlow Report has been taken seriously for the past half century because it is one of the few statements in public administration literature that attempts to ground the teachings of scientific management in constitutional theory and fundamental principles of American government. In this section we shall examine how the report both affirmed and departed from the fundamental principles of 1787. The most striking similarity is the committee's thematic argument that effective government is instrumental for higher ends. Here there is a striking resemblance to the argument of *The Federalist*.

At the founding of the Republic there was a solid consensus that the primary purpose of government is the protection of individual rights. One of the major disputes between Federalists and Anti-Federalists was over the best means to achieve this end. The Anti-Federalists tended to see in the Constitution a government so powerful that it would threaten individual rights. Publius met this argument head on by boldly contending that it was only a strong government that could protect rights effectively. Publius would use power in defense of individual rights.

The Brownlow committee joins Publius in defending powerful government as instrumental for higher ends.[27] It departs from him and from the founding generation, however, in its articulation of those higher ends. In the Brownlow Report democracy replaces individual rights. The Brownlow Report was written at a time when democracy was subject to severe doubts at home and severe attacks abroad. In his message to Congress in support of the Brownlow Report, President Roosevelt noted that just as "our forefathers" struggled against tyranny and "against government by birth, wealth, or class," Americans of 1937 must struggle against confusion, ineffectiveness, waste, and inefficiency. "This battle, too, must be won, unless it is to be said that in our generation national self-government broke down and was frittered away in bad management."[28] Will it be said, the president asked, that "democracy was a great dream, but it could not do the job?"[29]

It is not surprising that the Brownlow Report should have grounded its case in an appeal to democracy that would sound quite strange to the framers of the Constitution. The Brownlow committee was faithfully reciting appropriate norms for an American society that had become far more democratic than the sort of society envisioned by the men of the late eighteenth century. What is surprising, however, is the absence of a serious discussion of the protection of individual rights as government's primary purpose. Twentieth-century Americans would reject the idea that their commitment to democracy had weakened their commitment to individual rights, despite the warning of their forefathers that they could not have it both ways. Twentieth-century Americans would be inclined to say that they can have democracy in addition to, not instead of, individual rights. If the Brownlow committee's virtual silence on rights can be interpreted as indifference to what the framers saw as the primary purpose of government, the committee's report and the administrative state it envisioned would represent a drastic departure from the founding principles of the Republic.

In defense of the Brownlow committee, one might note that *The Federalist* had little to say explicitly about individual rights because the matter was not in dispute. Like the Brownlow Report, *The Federalist* was a political document intended to persuade people to take a certain action. There was no need to discuss what everyone took for granted. The fact that Publius does not have much to say about individual rights does not mean that he was indifferent to them. It means only that the opponents of the Constitution needed no instruction in this matter.

Can the same argument be made in defense of the Brownlow committee? I do not think so—for three reasons.

First, there is, as we have seen, the pattern in the document of incessantly reminding the reader of the contribution the committee's proposal would make to democratic government. The most important readers of this document were the congressmen and senators who were being asked to enact its provisions into law. If members of Congress did not need to be reminded of the importance of individual rights, why should they be reminded of the importance of democracy? Fair-minded congressmen might legitimately worry about the threat the managerial presidency presented to democratic government; but surely they would worry no less about the threat to individual rights. If the committee were concerned about *both* democracy and individual rights, why was it so eloquent on the former and virtually silent on the latter?

Second, the only explicit mention of individual rights in the entire report appears in a list of "aims and activities" undertaken by the government. Individual rights and liberties are but one of several such aims and activities, along with "the frame of our national and community life, our economic system, . . . a democracy that has survived for a century and one-half."[30]

In fairness to the Brownlow committee, I should note that this list appears in the first paragraph of the report. Thus, even though the expression "individual rights" appears only once in the entire report, it appears in a prominent place. Further, I should note that the preamble of the Constitution lists securing the "blessings of liberty to ourselves and our posterity" as but one of six purposes for which the Constitution was ordained and established. Nevertheless, I would support my position that the committee is indifferent to rights by contrasting subsequent development of the democracy theme with the subsequent disregard of individual rights. It is democracy that supports the idea of the president as "leader of the people," which in turn supports the committee's effort to centralize executive power in his hands. Individual rights are marginal to the committee's grand strategy.

The marginality of individual rights is underscored by my third and strongest argument—the explicit mention of the purpose of government as something other than the protection of individual rights. In discussing governmental reorganization the committee emphasizes its managerial focus when it insists that the "whole basis of reorganization must not be superficial appearance but the integrity of the social services underneath, *which are the end of government*" (emphasis added).[31] One would like to think that this was a slip of the pen. In the American constitutional tradition social services are not the end of government. As it stands, the sentence is a textbook example of the triumph of administrative means over liberal ends.

At the beginning of the report the committee gave a fuller statement of the purpose of American government in a self-conscious language that was surely no slip of the pen. Our goal as a nation is nothing less than "the constant raising of the level of the happiness and dignity of human life, the steady sharing of the gains of our Nation, whether material or spiritual, among those who make the Nation what it is."[32]

It is surely significant that the same paragraph that provides this high language of the positive state does not shrink from proclaiming that "our American Government rests on the truth that the general interest is superior to and has priority over any special or private interest." Thomas Jefferson thought that the government rested on a different set of truths.

The Brownlow Report is vulnerable in its treatment of individual rights. This is probably because many of the successful attacks against the New Deal and its programs were packaged in terms of rights. Indeed, among New Dealers the expression "private rights" tended to be used as a code for business interests and is often used pejoratively. An approach to American government that ignores individual rights signals a serious departure from the intent of the framers. The Brownlow committee's treatment of individual rights demanded a corrective that was not long in coming. The attorney general's report of 1941 provided the corrective. It offered what the Brownlow committee failed to provide—a serious discussion of individual rights *within the framework of the administrative state*. Just as the Anti-Federalists corrected the excesses and defects of the Federalists, the attorney general's report would do the same for the Brownlow Report. In both cases the act of founding was in the public argument.

THE ATTORNEY GENERAL'S REPORT

The purpose of the Attorney General's Report on Administrative Procedure (AGR) is stated in its lengthy, formal title: "Report of the Committee on Administrative Procedure, Appointed by the Attorney General, at the Request of the President, to Investigate the Need for Procedural Reform in Various Administrative Tribunals and to Suggest Improvements Therein."[33] The immediate origin of the report was Attorney General Homer Cummings' letter of December 14, 1938, to President Roosevelt suggesting the creation of such a committee. In his letter the attorney general stressed the need for "proper safeguards for the protection of substantive rights and adequate, but not extravagant, judicial review."[34] In his reply of February 16, 1939, the president authorized the attorney general to establish a committee to investigate the reform of administrative procedure, but interestingly, he omitted any reference to rights or judicial review. Instead, the president stressed the likelihood that administrative reform would make the Justice Department more effective "in endeavoring to uphold actions of administrative agencies of the Government, when the validity of their decisions is challenged in the courts."[35] Thus the correspondence initiating the AGR presaged its two dominant themes—protection of rights and effective administration. Not surprisingly, the tension between these goals was never entirely resolved in the report; but just as the report originated in a concern over rights, so its final version clearly leaned in that direction as well.

The members of the committee were appointed by Attorney General Frank Murphy, Cummings's successor. The report was finally presented to Murphy's successor, Robert H. Jackson, on January 22, 1941. Two days later Attorney General Jackson submitted the report to the Senate.

AGR was at the center of a long struggle over administrative reform that began in the spring of 1933 when the American Bar Association appointed a "Special Committee on Administrative Law" and ended—at least for a while—with the passage of the Administrative Procedure Act in 1946. World War II accounted for the struggle's dragging on into the mid–1940s. The best and most serious arguments over administrative reform were developed in the crucial period from 1935 to 1941. While the attorney general's committee was conducting its exhaustive research on administrative practices, congressional critics of the New Deal, overriding the strenuous objections of Chairman Cellar of the House Judiciary Committee, seized the initiative by passing the Walter-Logan Act in 1940. This act was vetoed by President Roosevelt with an unusually stern message to Congress. One of the reasons FDR gave for vetoing Walter Logan—one of his milder reasons—was that he was awaiting the AGR, which was released a month after the president's veto. AGR itself was accompanied by a strong minority report that had a profound impact on the legislation that finally emerged from Congress (after the hiatus of World War II) as the Administrative Procedure Act of 1946 (APA). Thus, during the 1939–41 period, there were five important documents on administrative procedure: (1) the Walter-Logan Act accompanied by supporting statements from Senator Logan and Congressman Walter; (2) Congressman Cellar's Minority Report from the Judiciary Committee on the Walter-Logan Bill; (3) President Roosevelt's veto message on the Walter-Logan Act; (4) the AGR; and (5) the Minority Report of the AGR.

The centerpiece of these documents was the AGR. It was anticipated throughout the debate over Walter-Logan and was, of course, the target of its own minority report. Together with its minority report, it adumbrated the APA. These documents are mentioned at the outset to introduce the "cast of characters" in the discussion that follows. The discussion itself addresses three important themes in the AGR: (1) the adjudication of individual rights, (2) uniformity in administrative procedure, and (3) the scope of judicial review of administrative action.

Individual Rights and Adjudication

Questions on adjudication within the administrative process and judicial review of such adjudication provide the substance of four of the AGR's nine chapters. The central issue in these chapters is the protection of rights. This heavy emphasis on rights provides a welcome corrective to the critical disregard of this topic in the Brownlow Report and leads the New Deal argument back to the founding period.

On the subject of rights the AGR and the Walter-Logan Act were at one in insisting on their protection within the administrative process. Where these two documents differed sharply, however, was on the problem of how rights could be protected without jeopardizing the integrity of the administrative process. In the Walter-Logan Act the integrity of the public administration was not a serious issue. This act would surely have gone a long way toward protecting rights, but it would have dismantled the New Deal administrative apparatus in the process. For example, under Walter-Logan any individual or corporation "substantially interested in the effects of any administrative rule" could file a petition with the U.S. Court of Appeals for the District of Columbia to have that court "hear and determine whether any such rule is in conflict with the Constitution of the United States or the statute under which [it was] issued."[36] This litigation would take place *before* the rule went into effect, and while the litigation was in progress the rule could not be enforced.[37] This could impose serious delays in the execution of agency policy. Further, as Attorney General Jackson noted, there was nothing in the Walter-Logan Act "to prevent a succession of litigations by different individuals about the same rule."[38] Thus litigation could delay enforcement indefinitely. Finally, the Walter-Logan Act provided that even if the rule is upheld by the Court of Appeals *before* it goes into effect, it could be challenged anew in another court *after* it had gone into effect. The upshot of the Walter-Logan Act was that it would have "put new and advantageous weapons in the hands of those whose animus is strong enough and whose purse is long enough to wage unrestricted warfare on the administration of the laws."[39]

In contrast to Walter-Logan, the AGR made a self-conscious effort to safeguard the integrity of the administrative process along with its protection of individual rights. The best example of this twofold effort is the committee's careful attention to the use of "informal methods of adjudication," the title of the third chapter of AGR. Grounding its position in a solid empirical base that established the salience of informal adjudication, the AGR concludes that even where formal procedures are available, "informal procedures constitute the vast bulk of administrative adjudication and are truly the lifeblood of the administrative process."[40] The "informal process-as-lifeblood" metaphor is an expression that Kenneth C. Davis, a member of the committee's staff, has never tired of calling to the attention of students of administrative law.[41] It is the crucial element in the overall argument of the AGR because the expression is used in both a descriptive and prescriptive sense. Informal adjudication is the primary way in which rights are protected in the administrative state and this is the way it ought to be.

The discussion of informal procedure in AGR precedes the treatment of formal procedure and judicial review, which come into play only in those relatively few cases when the informal procedure fails to solve a problem satisfactorily. By stressing the *exceptional* nature of formal procedure and judicial review, the AGR invited Congress and an informed public to look to the activities of the agencies themselves and not just to judicial utterances about these agencies for realistic protection of individual rights.

The AGR puts considerable emphasis on the need for agencies to police themselves and to adopt voluntarily the sorts of administrative procedures that will guarantee both fair play and mission effectiveness. This approach contrasts sharply with the Walter-Logan Act and, to a lesser extent, the AGR minority report, which place much more faith in the capacity of courts to discipline the agencies. The AGR's willingness to make a moral appeal to the agencies' sense of decency and fairness explains its frequent references to the character of significant actors within the administrative process.[42] This concern with the character of administrators was quite common among New Dealers who favored administrative reform and helped to keep the argument over reform in line with the public argument of the founding period.[43]

Both the Federalists and Anti-Federalists had much to say about character and civic virtue. A main theme in Anti-Federalist thought was that it was only the small homogeneous republic that could promote civic virtue; this was the reason—and an important reason at that—the proposed Constitution was dangerous. The Federalists had a variety of responses to this position. Most of them ignored it, some denied it, and a few misunderstood it. The most serious response came, of course, in the famous argument in *The Federalist* in which self-interest is called on to do the work of virtue.[44] Although this is a major line of argument in *The Federalist,* Publius is careful not to press the logic of his position. There are *many* references in *The Federalist* to the need for civic virtue and good character, even though these references are not solidly integrated into the overall argument, which decisively favors interest over virtue.[45]

The 1939–41 debate on character lacked the depth of its illustrious predecessor of 1787–88. The sponsors of the Walter-Logan Act supported their call for vigorous judicial intervention in the administrative process with inflammatory references to career civil servants as persons ''attempting to control all the processes of government for their selfish ends.'' Career civil servants were described as ''employees who tend in some cases to become contemptuous of both Congress and the courts.''[46] They are ''disregardful of the rights of the governed.''[47] This mistrust of the civil service was quite consistent with Walter-Logan's intention to subject the public administration to rigid judicial control.[48] This position was just the opposite of AGR's reliance on the character of civil servants to buttress its commitment to informal administrative procedure as the first and most important bulwark in support of individual rights.

The main difference between the character arguments of 1787 and 1941 was not in the presence of name-calling in the latter. The Anti-Federalists were not reticent in such matters, especially when it came to describing the likely denizens of the proposed "federal city," which would some day become the nation's capital.[49]

What was missing in 1941 was serious attention to what was meant by good character, and, more important, how it is produced and sustained. The New Dealers frequently sounded a high-minded call for "reasoned decision making" and a sense of fair play on the part of administrators.[50] The context suggests that what they meant was the sort of attitude one might expect from men who were steeped in the tradition of American constitutional law. To get such decisions from such men would be no small accomplishment in an imperfect world. It certainly would satisfy Montesquieu, who once wrote: "At the birth of societies, the rulers of republics establish institutions; and afterwards the institutions mould the rulers."[51]

It is not surprising that at the founding of the Republic, the question of virtue and the proposed Constitution could be examined more clearheadedly than it could be some 150 years later. In the later period the people had learned to equate the Constitution with virtue itself without looking too closely at the self-interest that undergirds constitutional principle. One might doubt whether interest could do the work of virtue, but there was little doubt in administrative reform circles that constitutional principles were virtue's surrogate. It was too late in the day to wonder with Mercy Warren, the superb chronicler of Anti-Federalist sentiment, whether the Constitution, with its exaltation of self-interest, had led to the situation in which most of the inhabitants of America were "too proud for monarchy, yet too poor for nobility, and it is to be feared, too selfish and avaricious for a virtuous republic."[52]

The AGR presented its own case for reform without attacking the Walter-Logan Act directly. The official attack on Walter-Logan came in FDR's veto message, which was supplemented by an extensive academic literature harshly critical of the vetoed act.[53] The intemperate tone of FDR's veto message, which at times amounted to an indictment of the legal profession, made the more deliberate academic articles welcome additions to the cause of administrative reform from within the New Deal camp.

One of the most serious defects in FDR's veto message was his defense of the administrative process against judicial usurpation on the grounds of the large quantity of decisions that had to be made in modern government. "The judicial process requires to be supplemented by the administrative tribunal wherever there is a necessity for deciding issues on a quantity production basis."[54] This line of reasoning suggests that administrative adjudication is simply a necessary evil that, unfortunately, must be called on to do what judges could do much better if they had the time. It sets aside the excellence of administrative agencies and their superiority to courts in rendering certain types of decisions regardless of their quantity. Such decisions are best made initially by administrative agencies even if individual rights are concerned.

The academic literature was helpful in turning the New Deal case for administrative reform away from the shoals of a view of administration that rested on nothing more than a grudging concession to the inevitable. The academic authors understood that such a shallow position would only play into the hands of Walter-Logan supporters, who wanted judges to substitute their own judgments for those of administrators and wanted the Supreme Court to prescribe uniform rules of practice and procedure for quasi-judicial proceedings in administrative agencies.[55]

A common tactic in challenging the Walter-Logan effort to protect rights by denigrating the administrative process was to meet the rights argument head-on with the assertion that the judicial process protects only the rights of the few who are rich, whereas administrative tribunals defend everyone's rights. Charles Grove Haines presented a particularly persuasive version of this argument in his 1939 presidential address to the American Political Science Association. There he questioned the motives of lawyers whose commitment to rights does not go beyond "the presentation of the rights of clients that have ample funds to engage in the slow and tortuous process of expensive litigation."[56] This was a useful line of argument for New Deal purposes because it linked the Brownlow Report's concern for democracy to a populist notion of rights.

And yet at a deeper level the argument is wanting. What it ignores is that in the administrative state, the government often relieves the individual of the burden of initiating litigation. The citizen's initiative begins and ends with a complaint to an administrative investigator, who sets in motion the process that could eventually lead to the Interstate Commerce Commission's or the National Labor Relations Board's (NLRB) representing the public's interest in court. Such a procedure is a remarkably effective way of vindicating the rights of a middle-class or indigent plaintiff who cannot afford an expensive lawsuit.

What is missing, however, is the individual's active role in the lawsuit, which, before the days of the administrative state, was a practical way of enabling a citizen to act like a citizen—to take his or her turn at ordering public affairs. Alexis de Tocqueville grows lyric in the possibilities for civic activism he sees in the civil lawsuit.[57]

The administrative state tends to push the possibility for such citizen involvement rather high up on the economic scale. To the extent that administrative agencies bring the possibilities of initiating a lawsuit within the economic range of the poor and the middle class, such agencies democratize the defense of rights at the price of civic activism. Some might say that this is a small price to pay because, absent the administrative state, such persons would not be very active anyway. By protecting individual rights on a mass scale—and, despite the paradox, that's what the administrative state does—the administrative state would seem to be a faithful servant of the original covenant by which we do the bidding of Hobbes and Locke and enter civil society to secure the protection of our individual rights. All of us do this; not just the rich. So far, so good for the administrative state and the founding principle of initiating governments to protect rights. The only problem is that in the common law tradition, protection is what the *subject* expects from his king.[58] It is not what the citizen expects from a republic. Citizenship means activism, taking one's turn at ruling and being ruled.[59] The administrative state can protect rights en masse, but can it nourish citizens en masse?[60]

Uniformity in Administrative Procedure

A major point of contention between the AGR and the Walter-Logan Act was the need for a uniform administrative procedure. The AGR, which was based on exhaustive study and observation of actual administrative practice, stressed the diversity of administrative agencies and opposed any statutory effort to order a uniform procedure across the administrative board. Instead, the AGR recommended the creation of an "Office of Federal Administrative Procedure" that would examine the agencies on an ongoing basis and make recommendations for coordinating administrative procedures wherever practical. The director of the office would also make such legislative recommendations to Congress as he "may deem appropriate."[61]

The Walter-Logan Act favored a rigid procedure with exceptions for certain named agencies (e.g., Internal Revenue, Customs, Comptroller of the Currency, the military and naval establishments). Critics of Walter-Logan found the distinction between included and excluded agencies arbitrary. One critic suggested that the only common element among the agencies held to Walter-Logan's rigid procedure was that they were frequent targets of the foes of the New Deal.[62]

The minority report of the AGR favored a uniformity that was less rigid than Walter-Logan's. Eschewing any effort to place all the agencies in a "rigid mold," the minority thought that uniformity could be achieved on such fundamental matters as whether there should be notice in adjudication; whether a litigant should see the evidence and know the witnesses against him; and whether consideration of cases should be confined to the record. With such matters mandated by statute for all agencies, each agency would then develop its own particular additional procedures. Significantly, however, the minority tempered its enthusiasm for uniformity by permitting the president "to suspend the operation of any provisions as to any type of function or proceeding of any agency whenever he finds it impracticable or unworkable."[63]

The majority of the attorney general's committee rejected the idea of a code of administrative procedure with a provision for presidential exceptions. Citing the complexity and diversity of the administrative process, the majority wondered how the president can make "findings" on which agencies should be exempt from the code and under what circumstances. This is precisely what had eluded the committee after two years of exhaustive study. How could the president be expected to make serious findings on practicability on an ad hoc basis?

The debate over uniformity in the administrative state recalls the argument at the time of the founding over the failure of the unamended Constitution to provide for jury trials in civil cases. Article III, Section 2 provides:

The trial of all crimes, except in cases of impeachment, shall be by jury; and such Trial shall be held in the State where the said Crimes shall have been committed; but when not committed within any State, the Trial shall be at such Place or Places as the Congress may by Law direct.

Thus the Constitution guarantees a trial by jury in criminal cases but is silent on juries in civil suits. This silence alarmed the Anti-Federalists and gave them one of their main arguments against the Constitution.[64] So strong was their argument that the Federalists eventually agreed to the adoption of the Seventh Amendment, which provided for jury trials "in suits at common law, where the value in controversy shall exceed twenty dollars."

The main line of the Anti-Federalists' argument was the straightforward assertion that the new Constitution would deprive Americans of a cherished fundamental right. Occasionally this point was embellished with references to the history of Sweden, Rome, Sparta, and Carthage to show that liberty is doomed where jury trials are either unknown or abandoned.[65] James Wilson of Pennsylvania took the lead in fashioning the Federalist reply to this charge. Events forced leadership in this matter on him because the Pennsylvania Ratifying Convention—one of the earliest of such conventions—had almost come to blows over it.[66] Wilson defended the absence of jury trials in civil cases on the same grounds that the AGR defended the absence of uniformity in administrative procedure; the legal practices in the several states were simply too diverse to warrant a constitutional mandate for juries in civil cases. In New York there were juries in civil cases at common law but not in probate, admiralty, or chancery. In New Jersey there were no courts of admiralty or probate. Such actions were heard in courts of common law, where juries were the rule. Thus an admiralty case that would be decided without a jury in New York would come before a jury in a common law proceeding in New Jersey. Given this diversity, the Federalists argued, how could the Constitution guarantee juries in civil cases without committing Congress to selecting a procedure that would inevitably seem to favor one state's practice over another's?[67]

The AGR continuously refers to the diversity of administrative practices to ward off the movement for uniform administrative procedures.[68] The most succinct statement of this concern can be found in a letter from Attorney General Jackson, over whose name the AGR was issued, to President Roosevelt recommending a veto of Walter-Logan:

This bill abandons all account of underlying diversities and imposes the same procedures upon agencies as different in structure and function as the Veterans Administration, the Bureau of Reclamation, the Pure Food and Drug Administration, and the Office of Education. It is as if we should average the sizes of all men's feet and then buy shoes of only that size for the Army.[69]

The Federalists of 1787 and the New Dealers of 1941, having agreed on the folly of uniform procedures for substantive diversity, conclude by recommending that whatever uniformity might be needed in the future is best left to Congress.[70] On this point neither the Federalists nor the AGR prevailed. The Seventh Amendment was an explicit rejection of the position of James Wilson and the Federalists. The APA imposed far more uniformity than the AGR had in mind. Despite these failures, however, the founders of new political arrangements in 1787 and 1941 were at one in trying to resist the imposition of procedural rigidities on their new institutions of government.[71]

Scope of Review

Another issue in administrative reform that recalled the founding debate was the question of "scope of review." The expression refers to the scope or extent of a court's review of administrative action. For example, one statute might direct the courts to uphold an agency's decision if it is supported by "substantial evidence." Another statute might say that the agency's action should be overturned only if it can be shown to be "arbitrary and capricious." The arbitrary and capricious standard gives a court a *narrower* scope of review than the substantial evidence standard. That is, it is easier for an agency to pass judicial scrutiny if it need show only that it did *not* act in an arbitrary and capricious manner. If the court's scope of review is confined to that narrow issue, the agency will win its case once it satisfies the court that its action was not arbitrary and capricious. The agency does not have to show that its action was supported by *substantial* evidence. *Any* evidence—a "mere scintilla" as critics were wont to say—will suffice.

Scope of review is an extremely difficult question in administrative law. If the court applies a stringent test—for example, preponderance of evidence— there is a danger that the court will end up substituting its own judgment for that of the expert judgment of the agency. This is a particularly serious problem in questions involving complex scientific and technical matters in which judges have no particular competence. On the other hand, if the scope of review is quite relaxed (arbitrary and capricious), there rises the specter of government by arrogant technocrats.

In its simplest form the question of scope of review is reduced to the distinction between questions of law (in which courts would exercise an extensive review) and questions of fact (in which they would tend to defer to administrative expertise). The problem with the law/fact distinction is that experts seldom agree on where the line should be drawn in all but the simplest cases. Consider the following example. The National Labor Relations Act gives the NLRB jurisdiction over certain types of relations between employers and employees. The NLRB decides that it has jurisdiction over a dispute between a newspaper publisher and the newsboys who distribute the paper on the streets. The agency bases its decision on the "fact" that the newsboys are employees. The publisher says that they are not. Has the agency decided a question of law or of fact?[72]

The AGR gave considerable attention to scope of review in a discussion that even today would serve as a splendid introduction to this important topic. The marginal value of the law/fact distinction was recognized with the shrewd observation that "the knife of policy alone effects an artificial cleavage at the point where the court chooses to draw the line."[73] Relying on its stress on diversity in administration, the AGR thinks it unwise to impose anything resembling a fixed formula for scope of review. Instead, it favors letting the courts define their own role on a case-by-case basis, as they had been doing in the years immediately preceding the AGR. Only if Congress is dissatisfied with the relation between courts and agencies in a specific area should the scope of review be regulated by legislation.[74] The AGR's friendly outlook on the court is somewhat remarkable when one recalls FDR's titanic struggle with the judiciary in 1937. The AGR is a New Deal document, but it is the product of the late New Deal, a time when the Supreme Court of the United States had become "the Roosevelt Court." The irenic tone of AGR vis-à-vis the judiciary is somewhat amusing when one recalls that the attorney general over whose name the report was issued was Robert H. Jackson. In the same year in which AGR appeared Jackson's book, *The Struggle for Judicial Supremacy,* was published. The book was an unrelenting and bitter attack on the Supreme Court that had so frustrated FDR and the New Dealers. The AGR's willingness to trust the courts had a very different court in mind from Jackson's target in *The Struggle for Judicial Supremacy.*[75]

The AGR's reluctance to call for statutory mandates on scope of review contrasted sharply with the Walter-Logan Act, which would have imposed on the courts a standard of review that would have led to "independent judicial determination of the facts."[76] This fit the pattern of principled division between AGR and Walter-Logan, with AGR trying to curb administrative agencies without destroying the integrity of the administrative process. The Walter-Logan Act did not worry about making administrative agencies wards of the courts.

The dispute over scope of review could trace its ancestry to the founding period. Article III, Section 2 establishes the jurisdiction of the federal judiciary. The first paragraph of section 2 lists a long string of cases and controversies to which "the judicial power shall extend," for example, "all cases, in Law and Equity, arising under this Constitution, the Laws of the United States, and Treaties made, or which shall be made, under their authority." The second paragraph reads:

In all cases affecting Ambassadors, other public Ministers and Consuls, and those in which a State shall be Party, the Supreme Court shall have original Jurisdiction. In all other cases before mentioned, the Supreme Court shall have appellate Jurisdiction, *both as to Law and Fact,* with such exception, and under such Regulations as the Congress shall make [emphasis added].

The Anti-Federalists attacked the provision in this section that gives the Supreme Court appellate jurisdiction over questions of fact as well as questions of

law. Even in the eighteenth century there was some difficulty about the differences between questions of law and questions of fact.[77] The distinction was clear
enough for the Anti-Federalists, however, to know that they did not approve of
an appellate court having jurisdiction over a question of fact. This meant that a
distant court in an (as yet) unnamed "federal city" could overturn any finding
of fact by a jury in criminal cases—and in civil cases as well if Congress should
ever be pleased to allow juries in such cases. Such a prospect is startling enough
to contemporary opinion, but it was absolutely appalling to eighteenth-century
Americans. This is because the jury was looked on as a central political institution. It was prized less for its capacity to decide correctly than for its function
as a limit on governmental power. It was a bulwark of civil liberties.

The appellate provision in the Constitution was the eighteenth-century version
of scope of review. So broad was the scope of the Supreme Court's review that
it threatened the integrity and independence of the jury. This was similar to the
fears of the AGR a century and a half later. An excessive scope of judicial
review of agency actions threatened to undermine the public administration by
enabling judges to substitute their judgment for the expert judgment of the
administrator. In the case of the eighteenth-century jury, the expertise was not
technical, but political. The "twelve good men and true" were expected to
monitor their government by making decisions that were, at least in some sense,
final. This finality is what Article III threatened.

The Anti-Federalists had a good issue and they knew it. The Federal Farmer
argued that the logic of allowing an appeal on questions of fact was to replace
common law with European civil law because the finality of jury decisions on
factual matters was an essential element in common law jurisprudence.[78] Luther
Martin said that the appeal on both questions of law and fact would render the
jury useless—"a needless expense." For if "the general government is not
satisfied with the verdict of the jury, its officer may remove the prosecution to
the supreme court, and *there the verdict of the jury is to be of no effect,* but the
judges of this court are to decide upon the fact as well as the law" [emphasis
in original].[79]

An army of Anti-Federalists joined the chorus.[80] The Federalist response was
weak and unconvincing. Not even the "fertile genius" of James Wilson was
equal to the task.[81] Wilson's efforts in Pennsylvania were embarrassed by his
fellow Pennsylvania Federalist Judge McKean, whose imprudent remarks were
interpreted (perhaps correctly) as an attack on the jury system itself.[82] Even the
indomitable Publius seemed to have met his match. The best he could do was
to suggest rather lamely that the Supreme Court might make use of a second
jury in hearing questions of fact on appeal.[83] His argument then trailed off in
querulous comments about the difficulty of separating questions of law from
questions of fact. It was an embarrassing issue for the friends of the Constitution.
Surely they were relieved when the Seventh Amendment removed the issue from
the public argument with the words: "and no fact tried by a jury, shall be

otherwise re-examined in any Court of the United States, than according to the rules of the common law.''

The APA's solution to the scope of review debate of 1941 was not as neat and decisive as that of the Seventh Amendment. It achieved a brief truce in a battle that goes on to the present day, a battle that traces its origins to the founding of the Republic.

CONCLUSION

In looking for parallels between the respective public arguments of the founding and New Deal periods, one is inclined to see in the Brownlow Report a reincarnation of *The Federalist* and in the AGR a born-again Anti-Federalist rejoinder. Unfortunately the parallel is not that neat. In its cavalier treatment of rights the Brownlow committee departs from both Federalists and Anti-Federalists and, indeed, from the American political tradition as a whole. It is "Federalist" in its admiration of vigorous and effective government but not in its understanding of the ends of such government. The AGR departs from the Anti-Federalists in its unflagging defense of the new administrative order. Unlike Anti-Federalist literature, the AGR does not offer a principled argument *against a proposed* innovation. Instead, it offers a principled argument in *support* of a recently *established* innovation. Its concern with rights and procedures recalls sound Anti-Federalist sentiment, but its purpose is to rescue the new administrative state from its likely defects. Many Anti-Federalists may well have had similar intentions vis-à-vis the Constitution. Certainly many of them are on record, not as opposing the Constitution outright, but as insisting on certain amendments as a precondition of approval. Nevertheless, one must not put too fine a point on exact parallels between 1787 and the New Deal. The fact that the Bill of Rights emerged from the ratification debate and the APA from the 1939 to 1941 debate over administrative reform certainly is worthy of comment. APA is akin to a Bill of Rights in the administrative state. The more important point, however, is that the AGR, with its emphasis on rights and procedures, helped to integrate the public argument over the administrative state into the perennial American public argument.

Why is it important to integrate the argument over today's administrative state into the founding argument? Tocqueville has answered that question for us: "Men are not corrupted by the exercise of power or debased by the habit of obedience, but by the exercise of power which they believe to be illegitimate, and by obedience to a rule which they consider to be usurped and oppressive.''[84]

We live in an administrative state and for the foreseeable future we shall continue to do so. George Will put it nicely when he said, "I will do many things for my country, but I will not pretend that the careers of, say, Ronald Reagan and Franklin Roosevelt involve serious philosophical differences.''[85] As the end of the Reagan presidency drew near, it was quite clear that the administrative state of the New Dealers would emerge intact. It is important that

American citizens accept the legitimacy of a well-established political order that has governed them for the past half century and promises to continue to do so in the future. If the administrative state is seen as illegitimate, we must face the hard issue Tocqueville raises. We must then look on those who govern us as corrupt and on ourselves as debased. This is not a happy prospect. Serious people who see the administrative state as both illegitimate and inevitable are likely to become revolutionaries. They will have in mind not the frivolous revolution David Stockman writes about but the real thing.

It is the part of wisdom to continue the effort to legitimate the administrative state. To do this the administrative state must be grounded in the great legitimating symbol of the American political tradition—the public argument that gave us our Constitution. If we learn to integrate administrative institutions into our constitutional heritage, we will make progress in curbing the excesses of the administrative state. To legitimate is to tame, to civilize.

NOTES

1. For a self-conscious effort to link the New Deal to the founding period, see Robert L. Stern, "That Commerce Which Concerns More States Than One," *Harvard Law Review* 47 (1934): 1335ff.

2. Herbert J. Storing, *What the Anti-Federalists Were For* (Chicago: University of Chicago Press, 1983).

3. George Mason, Edmund Randolph, Luther Martin, Elbridge Gerry, Robert Yates, and John Lansing might well be considered both framers of the Constitution and Anti-Federalists. After participating in the Philadelphia Convention, they refused to sign the Constitution.

4. "Report of the President's Committee on Administrative Management," 74th Cong., 2nd Sess. (Washington, D.C.: Government Printing Office, 1937). Hereafter cited as Brownlow Report.

5. Rowland Egger, "The Period of Crisis: 1933 to 1945" in *American Public Administration: Past, Present, Future*, ed. Frederick C. Mosher (University: University of Alabama Press, 1975), 71.

6. Quoted in Barry D. Karl, *Executive Reorganization and Reform in the New Deal* (Chicago: University of Chicago Press, 1964), 27.

7. Ibid., 270.

8. Louis Brownlow, *A Passion for Anonymity: The Autobiography of Louis Brownlow,* second half (Chicago: University of Chicago Press, 1958), 392.

9. Brownlow Report, 2.

10. The expression "Administrative Republic" is taken from Harvey Flaumenhaft, "Hamilton's Administrative Republic and the American Presidency" in *The Presidency in the Constitutional Order*, ed. Joseph M. Bessette and Jeffrey Tulis (Baton Rouge: Louisiana State University Press, 1981), 65–112.

11. *The Federalist* 17, 27, and 46.

12. Brownlow Report, v.

13. Ibid., 33.

14. Ibid., 34.

15. Ibid., 31.

16. Ibid., 46.

17. See *The Federalist* 17, 27, and 46.

18. Brownlow Report, 47.

19. Herbert J. Storing, ed., *The Complete Anti-Federalist,* 7 vols. (Chicago: University of Chicago Press, 1981). Richard Henry Lee's proposal can be found in volume V, 117 (5.6.5 in Storing's reference system); the minority of the Convention of Pennsylvania appears in III, 162 (3.11.45); the Maryland Minority appears in V, 97 (5.4.7); George Mason's position appears in II, 12 (2.2.6); Cato's position appears in II, 115 (2.6.26); Federal Farmer's position appears in II, 306 (2.8.170); a Federal Republican's position appears in III, 82 (3.6.40); Charles C. Tansill, ed., "Debates in the Federal Convention of 1787 as Reported by James Madison," in *Documents Illustrative of the Formation of the Union of the American States* (Washington, D.C.: Government Printing Office, 1927), 686.

20. Storing, ed., *Complete Anti-Federalist,* II, p. 12. (2.2.6).

21. Brownlow Report, 33.

22. Ibid., v.

23. Ibid., 20.

24. Ibid., 2.

25. James Ceaser, *Presidential Selection: Theory and Development* (Princeton, N.J.: Princeton University Press, 1979), 52–61. In his discussion of "leader" in *The Federalist,* Ceasar follows Robert Eden. See Eden's discussion in *Political Leadership and Nihilism: A Study of Weber and Nietzsche* (Gainesville: University Presses of Florida, 1983), 3–6. Eden compares the Federalist's use of "leader" to the German *Verführer,* "tempter," "seducer," "deceiver." For examples of the pejorative use of "leader" or "leading individual," see *The Federalist* 10, 62, and 66. Benign reference to leaders of the Revolution appear in *The Federalist* 14 and 49.

26. Brownlow Report, 49.

27. The theme is pervasive. It is stated at the beginning (p. iii), at the end (p. 53), and throughout the document.

28. Brownlow Report, iii.

29. Ibid.

30. Ibid., 1.

31. Ibid., 38.

32. Ibid., 1.

33. Senate Document No. 8., 77th Congr., 1st Sess. (Washington, D.C.: Government Printing Office, 1941). An abridged version of the report has been reprinted under the title *Administrative Procedure in Government Agencies* (Charlottesville: University Press of Virginia, 1967), with a preface by Charles K. Woltz. The unabridged version is hereafter cited as AGR.

34. AGR, Appendix A, 251–52.

35. Ibid., 253.

36. Section 3 of the Walter-Logan Act. The full title of Walter-Logan is "An Act to provide for the more expeditious settlements of disputes with the United States, and for other purposes." H.R. 6324, 7th Congr., 3rd Sess., 1940.

37. Statement of Chairman Cellar of the House Committee on the Judiciary to accompany H.R. 6324, 76th Congr., 3rd Sess., Report 1149, Pt. 2, p. 3.

38. Jackson's comments were included in President Roosevelt's message, "Message from the President of the United States Returning Without Approval H.R. 6324." 7th Congr., 3rd Sess., December 18, 1940, p. 7. Hereafter cited as Walter-Logan veto message.

39. Ibid.

40. AGR, 35.

41. Kenneth C. Davis, *Discretionary Justice: A Preliminary Inquiry* (Baton Rouge: Louisiana State University Press, 1969), 21–22; Kenneth C. Davis, *Administrative Law and Government* (St. Paul: West Publishing Co., 1975), 215–17.

42. AGR, 46–50, 62, 68, 123, and ch. 8, passim.

43. A strong emphasis on the character of administrators appears in Walter Gellhorn, *Federal Administrative Proceedings* (Baltimore: Johns Hopkins University Press, 1941). The same is true of James M. Landis, *The Administrative Process* (Westport, Conn.: Greenwood Press, 1974). This book was originally published by Yale University Press in 1938. A good discussion of Landis's important contribution to regulatory theory can be found in Thomas K. McCraw, *Prophets of Regulation* (Cambridge, Mass.: Harvard University Press, 1984), 153–221.

44. *The Federalist* 51.

45. See, for example, *The Federalist* 29, 31, 49, 55, 63, and 76.

46. Statement of Mr. Walter of the House Committee on the Judiciary to accompany H.R. 6324. 76th Congr., 3rd Sess. Report 1149, p. 2.

47. Ibid.

48. Charles G. Haines, "The Adaptation of Administrative Law and Procedure to Constitutional Theories and Principles," *American Political Science Review* 34 (February 1940): 14.

49. See Storing, ed., *Complete Anti-Federalist,* 4.28.8, where "A Columbian Patriot" maintains that the people "wish for no federal city whose 'cloud cap't towers' may screen the state culprit from the hands of justice; while its exclusive jurisdiction may protect the riot of armies encamped within its limits." See also the satirical letter of Aristocratis to "his serenity the right respectable, most honorable highly renowned J[ame]s W[ilso]n, political hackney writer to the most lucrative order of the bank." Aristocratis goes on: "I would entreat you, dear sir, that when you arrive at the summit of your desires, you would deign to look back to your former condition, and make some provision for the relief of your insolvent brethren in time to come: that you would procure congress to constitute the ten miles square into a Sanctum-Sanctorum, a place of refuge for well born bankrupts, to shelter themselves and property from the rapacity of their persecuting creditors." Storing, ed., *Complete Anti-Federalist,* 3.16.2.

50. Gellhorn, *Federal Administration Proceedings,* 26–29, 35–37, 57, 70, 73, 97; Landis, *Administrative Process,* 28–29, 62. 98–99. New Dealers continued to stress reasoned decision-making and fair play even after they had been appointed to the Supreme Court. See the opinions of Justice Frankfurter in *SEC v. Chenery Corp.,* 318 U.S. 80 (1943), and Justice Jackson in *Wong Yang Sung v. McGrath,* 339 U.S. 33 (1950).

51. Montesquieu, *Considerations on the Causes of the Greatness of the Romans and Their Decline,* translated with Notes and Introduction by David Lowenthal (Ithaca, N.Y.: Cornell University Press, 1965), 25. I have translated *chefs* as "chiefs." Lowenthal has "leaders."

52. Storing, ed., *Complete Anti-Federalist,* VI, 216 (6.14.27).

53. Haines, "Adaptation of Administrative Law," 14; James Landis, "Crucial Issues

in Administrative Law: The Walter-Logan Bill,'' *Harvard Law Review* 52 (May 1940): 1077–102; Charles M. Wiltes, ''The Representative Function of Bureaucracy,'' *American Political Science Review* 35 (June 1941): 510–16; Louis L. Jaffe, ''The Report of the Attorney General's Committee on Administrative Procedure,'' *University of Chicago Law Review* 8 (April 1941): 401–40.

54. Walter-Logan veto message, 2.

55. Landis, ''Crucial Issues in Administrative Law,'' 1093.

56. Haines, ''Adaption of Administrative Law,'' 19.

57. Alexis de Tocqueville, *Democracy in America*, 2 vols. (New York: Randoom House, 1945), I: 295–96.

58. James H. Kettner, *The Development of American Citizenship: 1608–1870* (Chapel Hill: University of North Carolina Press, 1978), pt. I.

59. Aristotle, *Politics*, Bk. III.

60. For a further discussion of this point, see John A. Rohr, ''Civil Servants and Second Class Citizens,'' *Public Administration Review* 44 (March 1984): 135–40.

61. AGR, 194; Franklin D. Roosevelt, *Public Papers and Addresses*, ed. Samuel I. Rosenman, 13 vols. (New York: Random House, 1938–50): 7.

62. Landis, ''Crucial Issues in Administrative Law,'' 1093.

63. AGR, 216.

64. Storing, *What the Anti-Federalists Were For*, 64.

65. Storing, ed., *Complete Anti-Federalist*, IV, 212 (4.17.22); II, 149 (2.7.44).

66. John B. McMaster and Frederick D. Stone, *Pennsylvania and the Federal Constitution 1787–1788*, 2 vols. (New York: Da Capo Press, 1970), I; 356–61.

67. In addition to James Wilson's arguments, see *The Federalist* 83.

68. AGR, 104, 108.

69. Walter-Logan veto message, 8.

70. AGR, 92; *The Federalist* 83.

71. It is ironic that administrative agencies are continually accused of thwarting efficiency through excessive ''red tape.'' Red tape is the underside of the coin of procedural regularity. The New Dealers who wrote AGR were partial to administrative discretion and informal procedure. Red tape was imposed on the administrative process by the critics, not the friends, of the administrative state. They did so to preserve individual rights, just as the Anti-Federalists imposed the red tape of a jury trial in civil cases on the new government they had criticized. For a recent example of the close connection between red tape and civil liberties, see *Larkin v. Grendel's Den, Inc.*, 103 S.Ct. 505 (1982).

72. The Supreme Court held that NLRB's decision settled a question of fact; but the publisher's argument that NLRB had simply rendered a legal interpretation of the statutory word ''employee'' was surely not without merit. See *Hearst Publishing Co. v. NLRB*, 322 U.S. 111 (1984).

73. AGR, 88; citing John Dickinson, *Administrative Supremacy* (New York: Alfred A. Knopf, 1941).

74. AGR, 92.

75. Robert H. Jackson, *The Struggle for Administrative Supremacy* (New York: Alfred A. Knopf, 1941).

76. Landis, ''Crucial Issues in Administrative Law,'' 1093.

77. *The Federalist* 81. See also William E. Nelson, *Americanization of the Common*

Law: The Impact of Legal Change on Massachusetts Society Mass.: Harvard University Press, 1975), 165–71.

78. Storing, ed., *Complete Anti-Federalist*, 2.8.194.

79. Ibid., II, 70 (2.4.92).

80. Ibid., 2.7.25; 2.9.175; 3.2.7; 3.5.6; 3.11.38–39.

81. McMaster and Stone, *Pennsylvania and the Federal Constitution,* 359.

82. Ibid., 377.

83. *The Federalist* 81.

84. Tocqueville, Alexis de, *Democracy in America*, trans. George Lawrence, ed. J. P. Mayer (Garden City, N.Y.: Doubleday, 1966), 14.

85. George F. Will, *Statecraft As Soulcraft: What Government Does* (New York: Simon & Schuster, 1983), 23.

6   *Sidney M. Milkis*

New Deal Party Politics, Administrative Reform, and the Transformation of the American Constitution

More than a half century after the election of Franklin D. Roosevelt to the presidency the New Deal remains central to understanding past and current patterns of American politics. The reforms carried out during the 1930s, although moderate in many respects, led to a fundamental reappraisal of American values. As FDR put it in his 1932 campaign speech at The Commonwealth Club in San Francisco, the time had come for traditional rights, founded in pursuance of a commitment to limited government, to give way to "an economic declaration of rights," grounded in a commitment to guaranteeing a decent level of welfare for the American people.[1] This commitment to securing an "economic constitutional order" required that the political process be reconstituted in order to infuse the traditional institutions of constitutional government with the capacity for action. Thus the advent of Democratic liberalism, which led to the expansion of the national government's policy responsibilities, was inextricably linked with a program to reform the political process. Indeed, in important respects the "institutional" legacy of the New Deal has been as enduring and pervasive as the extension of social welfare programs that is the most recognized element of our inheritance from the political changes of the 1930s.

The institutional transformation of republican government as a result of the advent of the New Deal is the central focus of this chapter. In particular, it tries to explain the influence of the New Deal on the American party system. In particular, it tries to explain the influence of the New Deal on the American party system. In seeking to understand this influence it is important to recognize that the party politics of the Roosevelt administration was a primary ingredient in the endeavor to reevaluate traditional constitutional principles and institutions. In effect, Roosevelt viewed the American party system as a flawed political institution, which reinforced what he considered outmoded constitutional understandings and mechanisms. In this connection FDR continued and extended the political influence of the progressive tradition in American politics. The American party system was forged on the anvil of Jeffersonian principles, dedicated to establishing "a wall of separation" between the national government and society. As a result, it was from its inception in the early 1800s wedded to constitutional mechanisms, such as the separation of powers and federalism, that were designed to constrain state action. Beginning with Woodrow Wilson, therefore, twentieth-century reformers criticized American political parties as an obstacle to the development of a significant progressive program.[2]

In this respect the New Deal represented the culmination of efforts, which began in the Progressive era, to loosen the grip of partisan politics on the councils of power, with a view to shoring up the administrative capacities and extending the programmatic commitments of American government. The origins and organizing principles of the American party system had established it as a political force against the creation of a modern state. The New Deal commitment to building such a state meant that party politics had to be either reconstituted or eliminated.

Paradoxically, Roosevelt's party leadership and the New Deal both reconstituted and weakened partisanship in American politics. On the one hand, Roosevelt's effort to infuse the Democratic party with a commitment to "militant liberalism" established the foundation for the emergence of a more national and programmatic party system.[3] On the other hand, the New Deal facilitated the development of a "modern" presidency and administrative apparatus that displaced party politics, and collective responsibility, with executive administration. Because of this twofold strategy there has been considerable scholarly debate about FDR's goals and accomplishments as party leader. To some, Roosevelt's leadership of the Democratic party reinvigorated partisan politics and facilitated a realignment that addressed more clearly the fundamental political issues of the twentieth century, that is, those related to industrial conflicts in the United States.[4] Others, however, construe Roosevelt's actions as a party leader as a failure in the sense that he emphasized a personalized presidential politics more than partisanship. His presidency, therefore, was one of "broker leadership," which failed ultimately to bring about a truly reformed party system; that is to say, the New Deal electoral realignment did not bring forth a partisan politics structured by strongly organized and ideologically committed party organizations.[5]

Roosevelt was, in fact, both very serious and somewhat unsure in his efforts to alter the basis of the American party system. Although FDR wanted to change the character of the Democratic party, and thereby also influence a change in the American party system, ultimately he concluded that the public good and practical politics demanded that partisan politics be de-emphasized rather than restructured. In particular, once the presidency and executive department were "modernized," then some of the burden of party loyalty would be alleviated, freeing the chief executive, as leader of the whole people, to effect more directly the development of society and economy.

In this respect New Dealers used the Democratic party as a temporary way station on the road to administrative government, that is, a more centralized democracy, which would depend more heavily on the president and executive agencies for government action than had hitherto been the case in American politics. Perhaps this suggests why the "shadow of FDR" continued to influence presidential action, even while the commitment to the New Deal program has faded.[6] Lyndon Johnson relied heavily on—and strengthened further—executive institutions fashioned as a part of the creation of the New Deal, although he envisioned significant departures from New Deal policies. Even Republican presidents, such as Nixon and Reagan, who in many ways have posed fundamental challenges to New Deal principles and policies, have relied heavily on the institutional formula of the New Deal. As a result, the politics and governing institutions of the modern presidency have been extensively disassociated from party politics.

In certain respects this development has created a more prominent and powerful presidency, which has extensive autonomous domestic power, through rule-making and implementation, as well as autonomous power in international affairs.[7] Yet, as this chapter concludes, the emergence of the modern presidency has come at the cost of weakening certain valuable institutions such as political parties that traditionally have been critical agents of popular rule. In the end this has strengthened the national purpose while enervating certain foundational principles and institutions of republican government.

NEW DEAL PARTY POLITICS AND EXECUTIVE REFORM: MAKING PARTY GOVERNMENT LESS NECESSARY[8]

Party Responsibility and the New Deal

In the Introduction to the 1938 volume of his presidential papers and addresses, written in 1941, Roosevelt explained that his efforts to modify the Democratic party were undertaken to strengthen party responsibility to the electorate and to commit more fully his party to progressive reform:

I believe it to be my sworn duty, as President, to take all steps necessary to insure the continuance of liberalism in our government. I believe, at the same time, that it is my duty as head of the Democratic party to see to it that my party remains the truly liberal party in the political life of America.

There have been many periods in American history, unfortunately, when one major political party was no different than the other major party—except only in name. In a system of party government such as ours, however, elections become meaningless when the two major parties have no differences other than their labels. For such elections do not give the people of the United States an opportunity to decide upon the type of government which they prefer for themselves for the next two or the next four years, as the case may be. . . .

Generally speaking, in a representative form of government, there are usually two general schools of political belief—liberal and conservative. The system of party responsibility in America requires that one of its parties be the liberal party and the other be the conservative party.[9]

Roosevelt's party politics, then, were based on constitutional and policy concerns. FDR believed that democratic government required a more meaningful policy link between the councils of government and the electorate; furthermore, he reasoned that the clarification of political choice and centralization of authority would establish more advantageous conditions to bring about meaningful policy reform in the political system.

In this understanding Roosevelt no doubt was influenced by the thought and actions of Woodrow Wilson, who is recognized as the first American writer to advance the doctrine of responsible party government.[10] According to Wilson, the major flaw of American political parties was that, as loose confederations of state and local organizations, they were all too compatible with the decentralization of power built into the Constitution. The decentralized structure of parties had served the country well during the nineteenth century, providing a useful context for the facilitation of consensus and the coordination of limited national purpose in government action. Yet Wilson felt that further progress in American society required the development of party organizations that could be the vessels of a stronger and more permanent expression of national purpose.

Party organization is no longer needed for the mere rudimentary task of holding the machinery together or giving it to the sustenance of some common object, some single cooperative motive. The time is at hand when we can safely maximize the network of party in its detail and change its structure without imperilling its strength. This thing that has served us so well might now master us if we left it irresponsible. We must see to it that it is made responsible.[11]

According to Wilson, the reform of parties depended on extending the influence of the presidency. The limits on partisanship in American constitutional government notwithstanding, the president represented his party's "vital link of connection" with the nation. This place of the executive within the political system imposed an "extraordinary isolation" on the president, an isolation which, if used effectively enough, would enable the president to control programs within the party councils: "He can dominate his party by being spokesman for the real sentiment and purpose of the country, by giving the country at once the information and statements of policy which will enable it to form its judgments alike of parties and men."[12]

The presidency of Franklin D. Roosevelt represents the first concerted effort to translate this understanding of party politics into practice. The administration of Woodrow Wilson was an important precursor to such an attempt; but like all presidents after 1800, Wilson, in the end, reconciled himself to the strong fissures within his party.[13] In part this "compromise" with the disparate character of the Democratic party reflected Wilson's commitment to partisan politics; thus, as Arthur Link has pointed out, "he decided to work through and within his party in Congress, rather than to govern by a coalition of progressives as he might have done."[14] Moreover, Wilson's reconciliation with the traditional Democratic party was a matter of practical exigency. In his use of patronage, particularly, Wilson avoided a "bold frontal assault" on the localistic character of traditional partisan practices, lest he undermine the party unity required to get his policies enacted into law. As he was more intent on getting his program passed than reforming his party, Wilson made little effort to strengthen the Democratic party's organization or its fundamental commitment to progressive principles.[15]

Roosevelt, however, was less committed to working through partisan channels than was Wilson, and more important, the New Deal represented a more fundamental departure than did progressivism from traditional Democratic policies. Until the 1930s the "patron saint" of the Democratic party was Thomas Jefferson, and it was widely understood that this implied a commitment to individual autonomy, states' rights, and a limited role for the national government.[16] In fact, although Alexis de Tocqueville believed that equality generally required centralization of authority, American democracy and party politics had been allied to decentralization until the New Deal. This alliance, as Tocqueville observed, owed much to the extraordinary commitment in the United States to "provincial liberties."[17] That commitment was supported by the understanding of ardent defenders of popular rule, such as Jefferson, that decentralization of power was necessary to make government understandable and accessible to the people and, thereby, to nurture an active and competent citizenry.

Thus, before the New Deal, Democrats viewed centralization of authority as inimical to popular rule. American liberalism was associated with its Jeffersonian origins, which identified positive government with conservative efforts, beginning with Hamilton's economic policy, to advantage unjustly business enterprise. Even Woodrow Wilson's program of extending the role of the national government remained in its essentials committed to decentralization of power. Herbert Croly and Theodore Roosevelt expressed an alternative progressive understanding, one that envisioned a "new nationalism" and the possibility of resurrecting Hamiltonian nationalism as "the steward of public welfare."[18] As Croly wrote in *The Promise of American Life*, the aim of progressive reform was "to give democratic meaning and purpose to the Hamiltonian tradition and method."[19] Yet it was Wilson's progressive vision, one more closely tied to "Jeffersonianism," that triumphed in the election of 1912. The victory of Wilson over Theodore Roosevelt in that campaign, in which the latter as the standard bearer of the Progressive party was the only candidate to advocate "the substitution of frank social policy for the individualism of the past," ensured the triumph, Croly lamented, of "a higher conservatism over progressive democracy."[20]

The more decisive break with the American tradition of limited government anticipated by the Progressive party's campaign in 1912 came at the hands of Franklin Roosevelt during the 1930s. Roosevelt's triumph was greatly aided, of

course, by the economic exigencies created by the depression. Yet the advent
of the New Deal as an enduring reform program would not have been possible
without Roosevelt's deft reinterpretation of the "liberal" tradition in American
politics. The emergence of "modern" liberalism as the public philosophy of the
New Deal developed from a significant rethinking of the meaning of natural
rights in American politics. Although the progressive tradition anticipated many
elements of this understanding of government, FDR was the first advocate of
an active federal government to "appropriate" the term liberalism and make it
part of the common political vocabulary.[21] Whereas liberalism in American
politics hitherto was associated with Jeffersonian principles, which followed the
natural rights tradition of limited government, Roosevelt pronounced a "new
liberalism," which called for a radical reinterpretation of that tradition. Constitutional government and the natural rights tradition were not to be abandoned,
but the time had come for a very different understanding of rights. As FDR put
it in the aforementioned Commonwealth Club Address, "faith in America, faith
in our tradition of personal responsibility, faith in our institutions, faith in ourselves demand that we recognize the new terms of the old social contract."[22]

The defense of progressive reform in terms of extending the rights of the
Constitution was a critical development in the advent of a positive understanding
of government responsibility in the United States. The distinction between progressives and nonprogressives, as most boldly pronounced by Herbert Croly, all
too visibly placed reformers in opposition to constitutional government and the
self-interested basis of American politics. The national community anticipated
by the more visionary progressives was a direct challenge to the Jeffersonian
and Hamiltonian traditions, both of which rejected the concept of a national
democracy. Roosevelt's concept of liberalism, however, deftly linked the Hamiltonian and Jeffersonian traditions by asserting the connection between energetic
nationalism and rights, albeit rights that looked well beyond the purposes of
nationalism as defined by Hamiltonian principles. The use of the term liberalism
by Roosevelt gave legitimacy to progressive principles by imbedding them in
the parlance of constitutionalism and interpreting them as an expansion, rather
than a transcendence, of the natural rights tradition.[23]

In particular, the New Deal called for "an economic constitutional order,"
grounded in a commitment to guaranteeing a decent level of economic welfare
for the American people. The expansion of rights, according to New Dealers,
was made necessary by the ruthless and unjust turn natural rights liberalism
underwent during the later part of the nineteenth century. By that time the closing
of the Western frontiers and the growth of industrial combinations to the point
of "uncontrolled" and "irresponsible" units within the political system signaled
the turning of the tide. The new conditions of the political economy indicated
that constitutional principles were no longer served by a reliance on individual
initiative. The realization of the dream of the industrial revolution—to raise the
standard of living of everyone—may at one time have required the "use of
talents of men of tremendous will and tremendous ambition, since by no other

force could the problem of financing and engineering of new developments be brought to a consummation."[24] But with the decline of conditions favoring an expansion of the economic sector, the day of the "financial titan" was over. The impetus for the national welfare would now have to shift from the shoulders of the productive private citizen to the government; the guarantee of equal opportunity now required that individual initiative be restrained and directed by benign administration:

Our task now is not the discovery or exploitation of natural resources, or necessarily producing new goods. It is the soberer, less dramatic business of administering resources and plants already in hand, of seeking to reestablish foreign markets for our surplus production, of meeting the problem of under consumption, of adjusting production to consumption, of distributing wealth and products more equitably, of adopting existing economic organizations to the service of the people. The day of enlightened administration has come.[25]

The concerns expressed in Roosevelt's reappraisal of American political values represent an important guide to understanding the New Deal and its impact on the Democratic party. Under the leadership of Roosevelt the Democratic party became the instrument of greater national purpose. In the last analysis, however, this purpose was directed to the creation of an administrative state that would displace partisan politics with "enlightened administration." In part such an attempt to *transcend*, rather than *reform,* the American party system was symptomatic of the limited prospects for establishing party government in American politics. Moreover, and more fundamentally, New Dealers did not view the welfare state as a partisan issue. The reform program of the 1930s was defined as a "constitutional" matter, which required eliminating partisanship about the national government's obligation to provide economic security for the American people. Yet, ironically, this displacement of partisanship would require a major partisan effort in the short run to generate popular support for an economic constitutional order. It was necessary, therefore, to remake the Democratic party as an instrument to free the councils of government, particularly the President and bureaucracy, from the restraints of traditional party politics and constitutional understandings.

As Roosevelt was less diffident than Wilson about overcoming the limits of constitutional government, he was more intent on transforming the principles and organization of the Democratic party. Thus, as president-elect, he prepared to modify the partisan practices of previous administrations. Soon after he was elected president, for example, Roosevelt began to evaluate the personnel policy of Woodrow Wilson with a view to committing his own administration to more progressive appointments. Josephus Daniels, who was Wilson's secretary of navy, while FDR served as assistant secretary, wrote a letter to Roosevelt in December 1932 that included a quote from President-elect Wilson promising to "nominate progressives—and only progressives." The "pity" was, complained

Daniels, that Wilson adhered to traditional patronage practices and "appointed some who wouldn't recognize a Progressive principle if he met it in the road."[26] Roosevelt liked the Wilson quote, and wrote Wilson's biographer, Ray Stannard Baker, asking him to authenticate the quotation Daniels sent him.[27] A few weeks later FDR expressed to his attorney general, Homer Cummings, the desire to avoid Wilson's betrayal of the pledge to appoint reformers to the executive department. According to Cummings's diary, Roosevelt was determined to proceed along different lines, primarily with the view "to building upon a national organization rather than allowing patronage to be used merely to build Senatorial and Congressional machines."[28]

Although FDR generally followed traditional partisan politics during his first term, allowing Democratic Chairman James Farley to coordinate appointments in response to local organizations and Democratic senators, the recommendations of organization people were not followed so closely after 1936. Beginning in 1938, especially, when Roosevelt's partisan actions became more aggressive, patronage practices circumvented the traditional organization. As Ed Flynn, who became Democratic chairman in 1940, wrote in his memoirs:

The President turned more and more frequently to the so-called New Dealers. . . . In a sense, this short-circuited the National Committee over which Farley presided. As a result, many of the appointments in Washington went to men who were supporters of the President and believed in what he was trying to do, but who were not Democrats in many instances, and in all instances were not organization Democrats.[29]

Moreover, whereas Woodrow Wilson was careful in associating himself with legislative party leaders in the development of his policy program, Roosevelt relegated the party in Congress to a decidedly subordinated status. He offended legislators by his use of press conferences to announce important decisions before he communicated them to a coordinate branch of government. And Roosevelt, unlike Wilson, eschewed the use of the party caucus. He rejected as impractical, for example, the suggestion of Congressman Alfred Phillips, Jr., "that those sharing the burden of responsibility of party government should regularly and often be called into caucus and that such caucuses should evolve party policies and choice of party leaders."[30] In Roosevelt's second administration, as in that of Woodrow Wilson, Congress was chaffing at its subordinate position. The legislature, however, was treated far more sensitively by Wilson, who attempted to use the instrument of party, than it was by Roosevelt, who was far less willing to cultivate the support of the traditional party apparatus.[31]

The most dramatic aspect of Roosevelt's effort to remake the Democratic party was his intervention in several congressional primary campaigns in 1938. This action involved Roosevelt's interceding in a dozen states in an effort to unseat entrenched conservative incumbents within his own party. Such intervention was not unprecedented; in particular, William Howard Taft and Woodrow Wilson had made limited efforts to cleanse their parties of recalcitrant members in this way. Yet FDR's campaign against those who did not support his program took place on an unprecedentedly large scale and, unlike previous efforts, made no attempt to work through the regular party organization.[32] The degree to which this action was viewed as a shocking departure from precedents in American politics is indicated by the fact that the press soon labeled Roosevelt's 1938 primary campaigns as "the purge," a term that became notorious with Adolph Hilter's attempt to weed out dissension in the German Nazi party and Joseph Stalin's elimination of "disloyal" party members in the Soviet Communist party.

After the 1938 purge campaign columnist Raymond Clapper noted that "no President ever has gone as far as Mr. Roosevelt in striving to stamp his policies upon his party."[33] This massive partisan effort, as James Farley has suggested, may have been partly caused by Roosevelt's thirst for personal power.[34] FDR's actions to establish a personal party, however, must also be understood as part of an effort to alter the protractive character of constitutional government in the United States. He believed that the extension of presidential power over the party was the only effective way in which the reform program he envisioned could be translated into government action. In the last analysis Roosevelt believed that a more principled party politics could only come through the subordination of the national committee's role in presidential politics and the congressional leadership's influence on the development of party policy.

In part Roosevelt's party leadership began a process whereby the party system was transformed. The critical realignment of the 1930s gave impetus to the transcendence of traditional party politics and the nationalization of the political system, paving the way for the evolution of national and programmatic party organizations. This change did not occur overnight, but significant developments took place during the 1930s that signaled a shift in the locus of party politics from the state and local levels to the nation's capital.

One indication of such change was that the organization of the Democratic National Committee was modified to reflect the New Deal's emphasis on enhancing the role of the national government in ameliorating social and economic inequality. For example, at the urging of Pennsylvania senator Joseph Guffey, who columnists Alsop and Kintor called "the first of the liberal bosses," the Democratic National Committee (DNC) during Roosevelt's initial term established the first effective Negro Division a Democratic campaign committee ever had. Although the New Deal did not address the race issue directly, Guffey believed that blacks could be persuaded to give up their traditional loyalties to the Republicans as a result of support for New Deal economic programs. When he learned that Robert L. Vann, owner-editor of the *Pittsburg Courier* (the state's largest Negro journal), had indicted the Republicans for "indolently draw[ing] checks against the debt of the Civil War, without troubling themselves further with the lot of the colored people," Guffey prevailed on a reluctant James Farley to appoint Vann chief of a newly established "Colored Voter Division." Vann's first speech as a DNC spokesman began: "My friends, go turn Lincoln's picture to the wall. That debt has been paid in full." This message and Vann's organizational efforts helped to bring about the dramatic switch between 1932 and 1936 in black party loyalties from Republican to Democratic.[35]

The mobilization of black elites into the Democratic party's national organization and the effort by that organization to mobilize black voters was one of several institutional developments during the 1930s that began a process whereby the national organization of the Democratic party was institutionalized and strengthened. To be sure, the Democratic party did not become, nor did Roosevelt have any intention of making it, a social democratic party. But the New Deal did initiate a change in the party so that it came to represent more decisively than had heretofore been the case in American party politics the aspirations of disadvantaged groups most in need of government succor.

Another important development in this regard was the strong link forged between the Democratic party and labor. This was no easy task, given the sharp rifts within the labor movement during the 1930s. Nevertheless, all of the leading labor organizations were united behind FDR's reelection campaign of 1936. The strong labor effort on behalf of Roosevelt was skillfully orchestrated by Daniel Tobin, president of the Teamster's Union, who, as chairman of the labor division of the Democratic party during the 1932, 1936, and 1940 campaigns, skillfully negotiated the split between the American Federation of Labor and the Committee for Industrial Organization. As a result, Tobin facilitated a remarkably harmonious labor effort on behalf of Roosevelt, and carved out an important role for organized labor within the councils of the Democratic party.[36]

Perhaps the most significant change in the Democratic party, marking its initial transformation into a more national and programmatic organization, occurred in 1936 with the Roosevelt administration's successful push for the abolition of the two-thirds rule. This rule for Democratic national conventions required support from two-thirds of the delegates for the nomination of president and vice president. Although such a rule gave a united minority the power to prevent a decision, it had been defended in the past because it guarded the most loyal Democratic section—the South—against the imposition of an unwanted ticket by the less habitually Democratic North, East, and West.[37] The elimination of this rule, therefore, weakened the influence of Southern Democracy, widely considered, as journalist Thomas Stokes put it, "the ball and chain which hobbled the Party's forward march," and facilitated the adoption of a national reform program.[38]

These changes in the Democratic party initiated developments that came to a head with the purge campaign of 1938. As noted, this campaign, which focused especially on the South, was undertaken by Roosevelt not only to overcome the obstacle conservative Democrats posed to the completion of the New Deal, but also to galvanize a fundamental restructuring of the American party system. FDR believed that the elections of 1932 and 1936 had led to a definite, albeit inchoate, division in the country into liberal and conservative parties.[39] His march against conservative incumbents in the 1938 primary campaigns represented an effort to ratify this new party alignment, which presupposed a major reorganization of the relationship between the president and Congress. The development of a more national and programmatic party politics would necessarily greatly enhance the president's role within the party counsels. In a revamped party structure the chief executive, as the only national representative, would necessarily become, as Woodrow Wilson put it, "the vital link between party and nation." In the last analysis, however, the attempt to subordinate party deliberations to executive action weakened rather than reconstituted parties.

EXECUTIVE ACTION, ADMINISTRATIVE REFORM, AND THE DISPLACEMENT OF PARTY POLITICS

At the same time the New Deal initiated the formation of a more national and programmatic party politics, it made partisanship less important. Roosevelt's partisan leadership, although it did influence important changes in the Democratic party organization, more fundamentally envisioned a direct link with the public that would better enable him to make use of his position as head of the *whole nation* rather than as merely head of a *party* governing the nation.[40] Accordingly, Roosevelt, in all but one of the 1938 primary campaigns in which he personally participated, chose to make a direct appeal to public opinion rather than attempt to work through or reform the regular party apparatus.[41] The undertaking of a large-scale appeal to the nation was encouraged by Progressive reforms, especially the direct primary, which had begun to weaken greatly the grip of party organization on the voters. For example, William H. Meier, Democratic county chairman from Nebraska, wrote James Farley in 1938 that his state's direct primary law had "created a situation that has made candidates too independent of the party."[42]

Roosevelt, following Wilson, supported the direct primary. In his fireside chat initiating the purge campaign on June 24, 1938, Roosevelt said:

Fifty years ago party nominations were generally made in conventions—a system typified in the public imagination by a little group in a smoke filled room who made out the party slates. The direct primary was invented to make the nominating process a more democratic one—to give party voters themselves a chance to pick their candidates.[43]

The primary gave the president the opportunity to make a direct appeal to the people over the heads of congressional candidates and local party leaders. Thereby it provided an attractive vehicle for an attack on traditional party politics, which Roosevelt saw as an obstacle to his policy goals. Furthermore, radio broadcasting had made the opportunity to appeal directly to large audiences even more enticing. This was bound to be especially so in the case of an extremely popular president with as fine a radio presence as Roosevelt's. Woodrow Wilson argued that the "extraordinary isolation" of the executive office, when used effectively, enabled the president to "stand a little outside party and insist as if it were upon the general opinion."[44] Having established such a direct link with the nation, Wilson argued, the president's party could hardly resist him. No one utilized this potential of presidential leadership better than Roosevelt. Close associates such as Felix Frankfurter were constantly urging the president, when in the midst of political controversy, to use the radio—to "take the country to school," giving the people a "full dress exposition and analysis," as only he was capable.[45] This was a role Roosevelt relished. After Frankfurter urged him to go to the country in August 1937 to explain the issues that gave rise to the bitter Court-"packing" controversy, FDR, perhaps in anticipation of the purge campaign, responded: "You are absolutely right about the radio. I feel like saying to the country—'You will hear from me soon and often. This is not a threat but a promise.' "[46]

In the last analysis the "benign dictatorship" Roosevelt sought to impose on the Democratic party was not conducive to reforming the American party system. It tended instead to displace collective responsibility, and establish a strengthened presidency as an alternative to party government. Executive responsibility would seem to be a limited method of establishing party responsibility, for its success would depend heavily on the political ability and character of the incumbent. Moreover, Woodrow Wilson's prescription for party reform established a serious, if not intractable, dilemma: on the one hand, the decentralized character of politics in the United States can be modified only by strong presidential leadership; on the other hand, a president determined to alter fundamentally the connection between the executive and his party will eventually shatter party unity. In this light fellow Progressive Herbert Croly criticized Wilson's concept of presidential party leadership:

At the final test the responsibility is his rather than that of his party. The party that submits to such a dictatorship, however benevolent, cannot play its own proper part in a system of partisan government. It will either cease to have any independent life or its independence will eventually assume the form of revolt.[47]

Roosevelt was well aware of the limited extent to which his purposes could be achieved by party government in the American context. In fact it is useful to consider further Croly's criticism of Wilson's concept of party leadership, because, as FDR was sensitive to this criticism, it represents an important bridge between Progressivism and the New Deal. According to Croly, a critical flaw in Wilson's institutional understanding was in not confronting the limits of partisanship. At the same time, Wilson's false hope for partisanship caused him to underestimate the degree to which progressive democracy required "administrative aggrandizement," that is, the development of executive agencies as the principal instruments of democratic life. For Croly, progressive democracy's commitment to expanding the programmatic responsibilities of the national government "particularly [needed] an increase of administrative authority and efficiency."[48]

Wilson believed that it was possible in enhancing the capacities of the state to strengthen parties and administration, so that a reformed bureaucracy would "professionally" carry out the programmatic commitments stemming from a government organized effectively by a majority political party.[49] Yet, as Croly noted, the American party system, forged on principles dedicated to limiting state power, was established as an institution to weaken administrative authority. Consequently "under American conditions a strong responsible and efficient administration of the law and public business would be fatal to partisan responsibility."[50] Owing to its origins and development, the party system in the United States was sustained by patronage and administrative decentralization, which party leaders, especially those in Congress, tenaciously embraced. According to Croly, therefore, the central character of the party system could not be dislodged without a transcendence of partisan politics itself. Wilson's notion that the president could facilitate a transformation of the practices that sustained parties was unrealistic:

The executive has not the power to make an effective fight against the system, because public opinion, on which he depends for his weapons, still fails to understand its real importance. In cleaving to it party leaders in Congress are cleaving to the strongest and most necessary prop of the party system, but by so doing they are making the destruction of that system an indispensable condition of the success of progressive democracy.[51]

In the end perhaps Wilson's commitment to working within the party system reflected his ambivalence about expanding the programmatic responsibilities of the national government. In Croly's view, Theodore Roosevelt's embrace of a "new nationalism" necessarily required, as the bolt of Progressives from the Republican ranks in 1912 foreshadowed, the disintegration of the American party system. In many respects, therefore, as historian Barry Karl notes, the Progressive party of 1912 was an "attack on the whole concept of political parties."[52]

The disagreement within the Progressive tradition concerning the appropriate role of party is a critical precursor to New Deal party politics. In effect, FDR consciously patterned his leadership after that of Woodrow Wilson and Theodore Roosevelt, seeking to reconcile the strengths of these leaders. This concern to build on the Progressive movement is indicated in a correspondence FDR carried on with Ray Stannard Baker, Wilson's biographer and ardent advocate of reform. One of their more interesting exchanges occurred in March 1935, which Baker initiated by expressing a concern about the New Deal's pragmatic character:

While the defense and exposition of your policies has often been able and courageous in detail, it has seemed to me to lack the power of a unifying vision. There is such a vision beyond and above the confusing multiplicity of things which you are trying to do. If I did not believe it, if I did not myself feel it and see it, I should no longer support you.[53]

Baker went on to suggest that FDR follow Wilson in appealing "to the profoundest moral and social convictions" in the American people.

FDR's response to Baker represents a rather penetrating analysis of reform leadership, which belies his reputation as a shallow thinker. This response shows that he sought to combine principled rhetoric and instrumental policy achievement:

Theodore Roosevelt lacked Woodrow Wilson's appeal to the fundamental and failed to stir, as Wilson did, the truly profound moral and social convictions. Wilson, on the other hand, failed where Theodore Roosevelt succeeded, in stirring people to enthusiasm about specific individual events, even though these specific events may have been superficial in comparison with the fundamentals.[54]

This intent to link principles with specifics reflected FDR's plan to combine the democratic vision of Woodrow Wilson with the programmatic concerns of Herbert Croly and Theodore Roosevelt. The working out of that combination was resolved not only in a principled defense of social welfare programs, but also in an articulation of a public philosophy that would support the strengthening of the national government's administrative capacities. According to Roosevelt, the linking of principled rhetoric and the particulars of public management was the keystone of responsible democratic leadership:

You are so absolutely right about the response that this country gives to vision and profound moral purposes that I can only assure you of my hearty concurrence and my constant desire to make the appeal. I know at the same time that you will be sympathetic to the point of view that the public psychology and, for that matter, individual psychology, cannot, because of human weakness, be attuned for long periods to a constant repetition of the highest note on the scale.[55]

FDR indicated that the time would soon be ripe for a more fervent commitment to principle, and assured Baker that the reform vision expressed during the early days of his administration would be renewed. Anticipating the militant liberalism that would inspire the program of late 1935 and the reelection campaign of 1936, he ended: "I am inclined to think that in view of the unfolding of the domestic scene and now of the foreign scene, you are right in your thought that the time is at hand for a new stimulation of united American action. I am proposing that sort of thing before the year is out."[56]

Critics of Roosevelt's party leadership have argued that the ultimate failure to transform the Democratic party into a strong liberal party owed to his broker style of leadership, as well as to the fact that the New Deal was essentially a series of ad hoc responses to the political and economic exigencies created by the Depression. Yet apparently the pragmatism of FDR was not simply improvisation. It also reflected his understanding that a commitment to a purer form of liberal doctrine and politics would result in outright rejection by the American people, or would allow more extreme political actors, such as Huey Long and Father Coughlin, to, as Roosevelt put it to Baker, turn "the eyes of the audience away from the main drama itself." Thus New Deal pragmatism was connected to a rather well thought out plan to reshape the working of American democracy.

In the end a reconstituted party system was not considered the appropriate path to bring about such a change. Unlike Croly, Roosevelt was not willing to abandon partisanship. He believed that party leadership, at least for the time being, was necessary to organize public opinion into a governing coalition. Roosevelt, however, was persuaded, as was Croly, that the tradition of party politics in the United States dictated that a strengthening of the state required the demise of partisan politics. This helps to explain why the purge campaign was limited to a few Senate and congressional seats, for the most part in the South, rather than conducted as a more systematic nationwide attempt to elect New Dealers.[57] According to FDR, the traditional party apparatus was, for the most part, beyond repair, so wedded was it to the fragmented institutions of American politics. For example, when Ray Stannard Baker wrote to FDR in September 1936 complaining of the Curley machine in Massachusetts, and expressing the necessity to "clean out the Democratic organization" of that state, Roosevelt's response was one of sympathetic resignation: "There is, I fear, much too much in what you say—but what is a poor fellow to do about it: I wish I knew."[58]

The incorrigible character of the party system did not, to be sure, simply reflect its decrepitude. In fact its institutional fragmentation and ideological promiscuity were symptomatic of the obstacles to party government deeply ingrained in the U.S. Constitution. Just as New Dealers chose to circumvent or reappraise fundamental constitutional principles and mechanisms rather than assault them directly, so the Roosevelt administration's party politics avoided a full-scale challenge to the traditional pattern of partisan practices. The enormity of the failure of the purge campaign only reinforced this disinclination to seek a fundamental strengthening of the party system. Of the dozen states within which the President acted in the capacity against entrenched incumbents, he was successful in only two of them—Oregon and New York. Moreover the purge campaign galvanized opposition throughout the nation, apparently contributing to the heavy losses the Democrats sustained in the 1938 general elections.[59] E. E. Schattschneider calls the purge campaign "one of the greatest experimental tests of the nature of the American party system ever made."[60] Yet this experiment seemed to indicate the recalcitrance of traditional party politics. Former Wisconsin Governor Philip La Follete wrote after the 1938 election, in which he and many other Progressives were defeated in the wake of FDR's attempt to strengthen discipline within the party councils: "The result of the so-called purge by President Roosevelt showed that the fight to make the Democratic party liberal is a hopeless one."[61] Roosevelt himself told his attorney general, Homer Cummings, in December of 1938, that his attitude toward recalcitrant Democrats had "become all milk and honey."[62] Apparently FDR had come to the firm conclusion that the decentralization character of American politics recommended against strong partisan action as a means to achieve designed policy.

The Roosevelt administration's rejection of party government developed not only from practicality, but also from principle. As noted, New Dealers did not view the welfare state as a partisan issue, but as a constitutional one. The reform program of the 1930s was conceived as an economic bill of rights, which should be established as much as possible as permanent programs beyond the vagaries of public opinion and elections. This view of Democratic liberalism, first declared in the 1932 Commonwealth Club speech, was repeatedly reaffirmed throughout the Roosevelt presidency. One such occasion was an address delivered on September 17, 1937, which marked the sesquicentennial celebration of the Constitution. This was also the time, of course, when Roosevelt was engaged in a battle with the Supreme Court regarding the appropriate scope of legitimate government action. While expressing a reverence for the Constitution in his remarks, FDR made clear that the survival of constitutionalism depended on its being reshaped to accommodate an expansive supervisory role for government:

In our generation, a new idea has come to dominate thought about government, the idea that the resources of the nation can be made to produce a far higher standard of living for the masses of the people, if only government is intelligent and energetic in giving the right direction to economic life.

That idea—or more properly that ideal—is wholly justified by the facts. It cannot be thrust aside by those who want to go back to the condition of ten years ago or even preserve the conditions of today. It puts all forms of government to their proof. That ideal makes understandable the demands of labor for a more stable income, the demands of the great majority of businessmen for relief from disruptive trade practices, the demands of all for the end of that kind of license, often mistermed "liberty," which permits a handful of the population to take far more than its tolerable share from the rest of the people.[63]

Although the New Deal vision of a good society was never fully codified, it inspired significant efforts to revamp American political institutions. Ostensibly these changes were a modern adaptation of natural rights liberalism. Yet at the same time Roosevelt conserved the framework of the U.S. Constitution, he established an institutional legacy that would increasingly chip away at it. The genius of Roosevelt was that he transformed the American regime without seeming to do so. This transformation is so difficult to discern because of the pragmatism so central to FDR's statesmanship. Yet pragmatism was not simply a method of masterful indirection; it also represented a distinctly American philosophy that rose to prominence during the late nineteenth century and had an important influence on Progressives such as Herbert Croly. The principles of pragmatism guided John Dewey in his reinterpretation of the philosophy of liberalism in the early 1930s, and as historian Kenneth Davis points out, "the Dewey impact upon the overall mind" of the New Deal was "substantial." These principles grew out of a tradition committed to "planning as the technique for developing rational solutions to social and economic problems." Among the more zealous New Dealers, such a commitment emphasized benign administration as an antidote for the inherent weaknesses of the U.S. constitutional system. As such, the efforts to strengthen the state during the New Deal period were not truly an adaptation of constitutional principles and mechanisms, but a repudiation of them.[64]

Roosevelt was far too dedicated to "political" life to commit himself fully to the philosophical principles of pragmatism. He supported making public administration the center of government activity and strengthening the planning capacities of the American state. Nevertheless, although he rejected the administrative practices of traditional partisanship, FDR did not go so far as to commit himself to basing administration on scientific principles. He believed that reform of American politics required not only the linking of politics and administration by extending presidential control over bureaucratic agencies, but also avoiding the formation of a professional bureaucracy that would be fully insulated from the commitments and rhythms of political life.[65]

Thus, while advocates of national planning supported administrative reform that would establish a line between politics and administration, Roosevelt preferred to center political activity in a reformed executive department. This led to the emergence of a politics of administration, which entailed a shift of more and more government action from the regular political process to the executive department. Although the merger of politics and administration has often been viewed as evidence of the compatibility between the Constitution and the administrative state, this development has in fact led to a fundamental change in the traditional character of American politics. As we shall see, the mixing of politics and administration took place in such a way that the affairs of state came to *reflect* rather than *shape* public administration. The instrument of this change was an administrative reform program, which, along with the Court-"packing" bill, became a leading legislative priority for the Roosevelt administration during its second term. As a result, New Deal party politics became linked with a program that placed the affairs of state considerably beyond the scope of partisan politics.

In effect, beginning in 1937, Roosevelt sought administrative reforms that were intended to help him govern in the *absence* of party government. This program, as embodied in the 1937 Executive Reorganization Bill, would have greatly extended presidential authority over the executive department, including the independent regulatory commissions. Whereas a reconstituted party system would have established stronger linkages between the executive and legislature, the administrative program of the New Deal would combine executive action and public policy so that the President and executive agencies would be delegated authority to govern, making unnecessary the constant cooperation of party members in Congress. In a sense this would institutionalize the direct link between the presidency and the public presupposed by Roosevelt's style of partisan leadership. As the *Report of the President's Committee on Administrative Management* put it, with administrative reform, the "brief exultant commitment" to progressive government as expressed in the elections of 1932 and, especially,

1936 now would be more firmly established in "persistent, determined, competent, day by day administration."[66]

Interestingly, the administrative reform program, which was directed to making party politics less necessary, became, at Roosevelt's urging, a major focus of party responsibility. So strongly did the President favor this legislation that House Majority Leader Sam Rayburn appealed for party leadership in regard to the Executive Reorganization Bill, arguing that the defeat of this legislation would indicate a "vote of no confidence" in Roosevelt.[67] The defeat of this legislation in April 1938 had an important influence on Roosevelt's decision to purge the Democratic party; and he continued to push for administrative reform in the Seventy-sixth Congress, even though this effort required a tremendous expenditure of political capital. Consequently Roosevelt managed to keep administrative reform sufficiently prominent in the party councils so that a compromise measure passed in 1939. Although considerably weaker than Roosevelt's original proposal, the 1939 Executive Reorganization Act was a significant measure, which provided authority for the creation of the White House Office and the Executive Office of the President, and enhanced the chief executive's control over bureaucratic agencies. As such, the 1939 administrative reform program represents the genesis of the institutional presidency, which was better equipped to govern independently of the constraints imposed by the regular political process. This initiated a dynamic whereby executive administration, coupled with the enhanced personal responsibility of the president advanced by FDR's political leadership and the emergence of the mass media, displaced in important ways collective responsibility.

The intricate relationship between party politics and administrative reform during the creation of the New Deal suggests that Roosevelt strengthened party politics in the short run so as to free the president from partisan constraints in the long run. Roosevelt did not eschew party politics because he recognized that some sort of political organization would be necessary to sustain popular support for his programs. Yet at the same time Roosevelt believed that the strengthening of the state required the eventual demise of partisanship. Owing to the reforms of the Progressive era, such a development was already well under way by the 1930s, a situation Roosevelt hoped the New Deal would significantly extend. Ironically, he chose a partisan event to herald the promise of a less partisan future for American politics. In his Jackson Day speech of 1940 he pointed to both the limited and declining significance of party politics in the United States.

I do believe in party organization, but only in proportion to its proper place in government. I believe party organization is a sound and necessary part of our American system, and that, effectively organized nationally and by states and localities, parties are good instruments for the purpose of presenting and explaining issues, of drumming up interests and elections, and, incidentally, of improving the breed of candidates for public office.

But the future lies with those wise political leaders who realize the great public is interested more in government than in politics, that the independent vote in this country has been steadily on the increase, at least for the past generation, that the vast number of people consider themselves normally adherents of one party and still feel perfectly free to vote for one or more candidates of another party, come election day, and on the other hand, sometimes uphold party principles, even when precinct captains decide ''to take a walk.''

The growing independence of voters, after all, has been proven by the votes in every presidential election since my childhood—and the tendency frankly is on the increase. I am too modest, of course, to refer to certain recent elections. Party regulars who want to win must hold their allies and supporters among those independent voters. And do not let us forget it![68]

Roosevelt recognized during the 1930s realignment period that party influence might be waning, thereby anticipating the ''decline of party'' literature that began to appear during the 1960s. Thus FDR perhaps believed that the resurgence of party politics during the New Deal was temporary. In part his realization may be attributable to the disappointment of the purge, but more fundamentally Roosevelt believed that such a development was growing out of the need for more comprehensive government direction of social and economic processes. The expanded role of the national government would lead to the evolution of the professional welfare state, largely insulated from the fluctuations of party politics. That the Roosevelt administration expected party politics to become less important as the welfare state grew is further suggested by the instructions of Joseph Harris, director of the research staff of the President's Committee on Administrative Management, in an initial planning session in May 1936:

We must consider a planning structure in light of expansions of functions occurring in collectivist periods like the present and in periods of reaction during contracting phases marked by the dominance of rugged individualistic views. We must assume, however, that these contradictions will always be less in fact than in profession. We may assume the nature of the problems of American life are such as not to permit any political party for any length of time to abandon most of the collectivist functions which are now being exercised. This is true even though the details of policy programs may differ and even though the old slogans of opposition to governmental activity will survive long after their meaning has been sucked out.[69]

In important respects, then, the program of administrative reform pushed on the Democratic party by Roosevelt prepared his party to end all parties. *Fortune* magazine noted the threat such a program posed for party competition in 1937:

Whether or not he [Roosevelt] was right is not here important. What is important is that the kind of government for which he asked the popular endorsement was government for the people in which policy was formulated not by the mass of people nor by the representatives of the masses of the people but by the people's President. Precisely where that ... leaves the loyal opposition theory of Republican policy is all too clear. It leaves it nowhere. A useful opposition can function only in a country in which the vital decisions are made in the Legislature.[70]

Thus, because of Roosevelt's leadership and the administrative reform program of the New Deal, the Democratic party became, during the 1930s, a temporary way station on the road to administrative government. As the presidency gradually developed into a ubiquitous institution, it preempted party leaders in many of their limited, but significant duties: providing a link to interest groups, staffing the executive department, contributing to policy development, and organizing campaign support.[71] Moreover New Deal administrative reform was not directed to presidential government per se, but to imbedding progressive principles, considered tantamount to political rights, in a bureaucratic structure that would insulate reform and reformers from electoral change.

The civil service reform carried out by the Roosevelt administration demonstrates particularly the effort to displace partisan politics with executive administration. Unlike most of the elements of administrative reform that would strengthen the President per se, the extension of the merit system "upward, outward and downward" cast an especially New Deal hue on government machinery. This entailed extending merit protection after 1938 over the personnel appointed by the Roosevelt administration during his first term, four-fifths of whom were brought into government outside of regular merit channels.[72] Administrative reform, therefore, did not replace *politics* with *administration*; rather, it transformed the political character of public administration.

The merging of politics and administration took an interesting course as a result of the passage of the Hatch Act of 1939. Until the passage of this bill the Roosevelt administration was developing the expanding Executive Department into an inchoate national political machine. In fact, the use of federal workers in local and state political activity, including some of the purge campaigns, led to concern that FDR was putting together a modern Tammany, one that would operate on a national scale, independently of state and local governments.[73]

The Hatch Act, however, which in many respects was passed in reaction to the purge campaigns, made the full development of a presidential political machine less likely.[74] It removed the influence of all federal administrative officials who made policies of nationwide application from elections or nominating efforts for president, vice president, or members of Congress. The Hatch Act also reduced presidential control over nominating conventions by precluding the participation of federal administrative officers. At the 1936 Democratic convention about half of the delegates were federal job holders. With the passage of the Hatch Act only cabinet officers, congressmen, and a few top-ranking policy officers of the Roosevelt regime could be delegates in 1940. In effect, therefore, the Hatch Act demolished the national Roosevelt political machine as distinct from the regular Democratic organization.[75]

Accordingly, many New Dealers urged the President to veto this legislation, fearing that it would undermine what they viewed as a felicitous union of politics and administration. In their view, the task was not to take politics out of administration, but to infuse the expanding federal apparatus with the principles and commitment of the New Deal. Charles M. Shreve, executive secretary of the

Young Democrats of America, argued this point in a letter sent to Roosevelt as the President was considering whether or not to sign the Hatch Bill. Indicating to Thomas Corcoran, through whom this communication to the president was sent, that "it [was] impossible to exaggerate the importance of this matter," Shreve wrote:

We cannot encourage public service and enact a law as sweeping as this. Democracy will receive a great setback and the calibre of our public servants will drop drastically, if it becomes law. There is no justification for making political eunuchs of the future statesmen and leaders of our Democracy. It should suffice to point out that every Republican member of the House present for the vote voted for the Hatch Bill, together with every avowed Democratic enemy of the New Deal. Many members of both branches of Congress have admitted to our leaders that they voted for this Bill because they felt it would prevent your controlling the next Democratic National Convention. . . . We believe a veto . . . castigating the attempt to term all political activity by the Federal employees as "pernicious," will be approved by the American people and by well over one-third of Congress, while at the same time it will do more to preserve the New Deal from enemies within and without our party than any single thing that could be done.[76]

But the Hatch Bill was not so clearly a political defeat for President Roosevelt. He was more interested in orienting the Executive Department for the formation of public policy than he was in developing a national political machine, and the insulation of federal officials from party politics was not incompatible with such a task. This explains why, after much consideration, the President, though he fought passage of this legislation, decided to sign the Hatch Bill. Not only would such a veto have split his supporters irretrievably, but it also would have worked against the achievement of Roosevelt's reform program. The liberal and zealously nonpartisan senator from Nebraska George Norris wrote Roosevelt on getting wind of a possible presidential veto:

I cannot conceive of your opposition to legislation of this kind. I know that many politicians, in fact most politicians, in both political parties, are bitterly opposed to such a law but I have assumed all the time that you were one hundred percent for it. . . .
    I believe this bill is a great step towards the purification of politics and government. . . . To veto it would be the greatest mistake of your career—the full effects of which you could never overcome. You stand in the minds of millions of our best people as one who believes in pure politics, in the upbuilding and purification of everything that stands for better government, and more happiness for the rank and file of the people who want a better and cleaner government. You are their idol but, if you veto this bill, you will shatter their hopes, their aspirations and drive them into a bewilderment of desperation and sorrow.[77]

In order to obviate the debate between traditional partisans and nonpartisan reformers, the administration prepared a veto message that called for an alternative bill that would reform rather than transcend partisan politics. This message criticized the Hatch Bill not only for not covering state and local officials, an oversight that would greatly advance the power of "political machines," but also for not adopting campaign finance reform that might strengthen the national character of the party system. The draft veto message contained a proposal to prohibit all private contributions and appropriate public funds for the use of political parties, which might "free . . . political parties from the domination or influence of sinister elements and yield unexpected returns in the elevation of the whole tone of our political life."[78]

In the end, however, Roosevelt chose to sign the Hatch Bill on the last day before this measure would have become law without his signature. The message to the Congress that accompanied FDR's signature comported with concerns to overcome partisan politics. Although Roosevelt asked Congress to extend the act to state and local officials in the future, he made no mention of restructuring the American party system.[79] Apparently a push for responsible party government was deemed impractical in favor of a final push for the transcendence of partisan politics. The second Hatch Act, passed in 1940, extended these restrictions to state and local employees whose principal employment was in connection with any activity that was financed in whole or in part by the federal government. This concluded a compromise with the Congress that went a long way toward strengthening the nonpartisan character of the New Deal. The complex web of American constitutional government shaped progressive reform in the 1930s so that Roosevelt's great party leadership was, in the long run—or at least for a long time—to render party politics remarkably obsolete.

The New Deal Inheritance and the Extension of Democratic Liberalism

Although the New Deal strengthened partisanship in the short term, it led to institutional changes that set the tone for a less partisan future. The emphasis on executive rather than party responsibility during the New Deal established the conditions for the post–1950 resumption of party decline by preparing the executive department to be a government unto itself. Yet administrative reform was not conceived as a program to strengthen the presidency for its own sake. The modern presidency that emerged from the New Deal was created to chart the course for and direct the voyage to a more liberal America. Roosevelt envisioned the completion of this task in his 1944 State of the Union Address. In that speech, which Roosevelt, in a letter to Henry Wallace, called his "blast,"[80] FDR became the first president to call for a war on poverty:

It is our duty now to begin to lay the plans and determine the strategy for winning a lasting peace and the establishment of an American standard of living higher than ever before known. We cannot be content, no matter how high that general standard of living may be, if some fraction of our people—whether it be one-third, one-fifth, or one-tenth— is ill-fed, ill-clothed, ill-housed, or insecure. In our day these economic truths have become accepted as self-evident. We have accepted, so to speak, a Second Bill of Rights under which a new basis of security and prosperity can be established for all—regardless of station, race, or creed.

In the declaration of a Second Bill of Rights the government needed to provide, among other things, the right to a useful and remunerative job, the right to adequate medical care, the right to a decent home, and the right to a good education.[81]

Appropriately, given the institutional path chosen by the Roosevelt administration, this proposal for a new era of security was not the product of careful deliberations within the party councils, but a plan worked out within the newly established Executive Office. The program for a new Bill of Rights was developed by the National Resources Planning Board (NRPB), a planning agency formed by FDR in pursuance of the 1939 Executive Reorganization Act.

The particulars of the President's State of the Union Address were adopted from a report prepared by the NRPB that was made public in March 1943. Hailed by the press as "more revolutionary in some aspects than Britain's Beveridge Report," this blueprint for America's future also presented plans for a much greater government role in business.[82] Because the anti–New Deal Democrats and Republicans formed a majority in Congress, however, the report of the NRPB received little serious consideration. Moreover, this conservative coalition successfully led a movement to liquidate the NRPB in 1943, striking a significant blow to administrative government. Yet this action by Congress did not reassert a commitment to statutory law and limited government in American politics. The push for activist government and positive planning was sufficiently strong as a result of Roosevelt's leadership that the decentralized legislative branch was soon forced to accept once again presidential dominance of public policy. While Congress achieved some power in postwar planning after the NRPB was eliminated, Roosevelt transformed many of the board's functions to the Bureau of the Budget, which became the center of positive government planning under the very capable leadership of Harold D. Smith.[83]

Thus, although the New Deal program was never completed, the advent of the president and executive agencies as the center of government action was secured. The broad phrasing of the Constitution, especially Article II, simplified the transition to an administrative state, which represents a fundamental challenge to the traditional principles and institutions of American government. More than any other reform leader, FDR, through his political program, raised the question of just how far the American system of government could support not only the right to life, liberty, and the pursuit of happiness, but economic security as well. More fundamentally, however, New Deal liberalism raised the question of how far republican principles could be nurtured by public administration.

In a sense this is a question as old as the American Republic. In fact the concern to strengthen the administrative capacities of the national government during the 1930s was reminiscent of Hamilton's view that the American constitutional system provided a "frail" institutional design, and that its survival depended on enhancing its capacity for action. In a letter to James A. Bayard, dated April 6, 1802, he voiced support for efforts to strengthen the presidency, and thereby the federal government, urging that there be a "systematic and persevering endeavor to establish the future of a great empire on foundations much firmer than have yet been devised." Hamilton expressed approval in this regard of a proposal before the House of Representatives to reform the electoral college, providing for the discrimination between candidates for the presidency and vice presidency, as well as having electors chosen by the people in districts under the direction of Congress. Hamilton supported the popular selection of electors, for he regarded as "sound principle, to let the Federal Government rest as much as possible on the shoulders of the people, and as little as possible on those of the State Legislatures."[84] In Hamilton's view, a strong presidency, linked directly to the support of the people, could become the linchpin of an "administrative republic." The dominance of executive leadership in the formulation of policy and a strong administrative role in carrying out that policy were essential to resist the deterioration of republican government.[85]

Such a view, however, was considered mischievous by the more ardent defenders of popular rule among the founders, such as Jefferson and Madison, who felt that the primacy of the more decentralizing institutions—Congress and the state governments—was required to sustain an active and competent citizenry. In effect, Jefferson and Madison chose to defend a strict interpretation of the national government's powers because a program based on an elastic interpretation of the Constitution would invariably give rise to an administrative power that would undermine public deliberation and choice. By the early 1790s, then, Jefferson and Madison became committed to a program of political decentralization, which renewed the conflicts that had divided the Federalists and Anti-Federalists and, consequently, gave birth to the American party system.[86]

Ostensibly the advent of modern liberalism and the New Deal Democratic party represented a reconciliation between Jeffersonian and Hamiltonian principles. The New Deal involved a Hamiltonian celebration of administrative power, long believed to be incompatible with public deliberation and choice, yet sought to use this power to serve Jeffersonian purposes, that is unfailing commitment to popular rule and rough equality. Thus, in his Commonwealth Club Address, Roosevelt called for an end to Jeffersonian individualism, while, at the same time, claiming Jefferson would have supported the New Deal commitment to provide "a refuge and a help" to citizens against the abusive and excessive exercise of property rights.[87]

In fact, however, the playing out of New Deal liberalism led to the triumph of Hamiltonian principles. During the Roosevelt and Johnson presidencies the Democratic party became a party of administration, which slowly eroded the vitality of the more decentralizing and democratic institutions. Thus the New Deal brought valuable and probably necessary social and economic reforms, but at the cost of undermining valued institutions traditionally relied on in the American political experience to nurture and make effective popular rule. As historian Barry Karl has noted, "local government and community control," supported by mechanisms such as federalism and the decentralized structure of American party politics, "remain at the heart of the most intuitive conceptions of American democracy, even though they may also represent political corruption and locally condoned injustice." Thus the transfer of the locus of power during the New Deal to the federal government and the concomitant delegation of power to the executive department "threatened our sense of ourselves as citizens."[88]

If the New Deal undermined constitutional principles and forms, then, it did not do so by facilitating the advent of direct—or "pure"—democracy. Rather, New Deal liberalism weakened the republican character of the Constitution by bestowing an institutional legacy that excessively "refined" the working of popular sovereignty. It is not "democratic distemper" that afflicts our polity, but the absence of citizenship itself. In the last analysis such an inheritance of the New Deal cannot be attributed to any liberal conspiracy to pervert democracy.[89] It is the result instead of a misplaced faith in the democratic character of the New Deal administrative process, of a failed attempt to turn Hamilton on his head. Whereas Hamilton desired an energetic executive to withstand ardent republicanism, progressive administration looked to the presidency as the leading agent of egalitarian reform; and whereas Hamilton saw the presidency, along with courts, as a major protector of liberty against the demands of equality, progressive administration envisioned an executive branch that could direct a benign administration of policy toward greater equality at the expense of what was considered excessive individualism. Yet the attempt to so reconstitute the purpose of public administration presupposes that there can be a democratic variant of Hamiltonian nationalism, that it is in fact possible to turn Hamilton on his head. Even reformulated executive processes, however, may not be hospitable to public deliberation. Representative democracy is essentially fostered by public speech, by the deliberation that most effectively occurs in the legislature and local community. Civic involvement is enervated by a political process dominated by executive action, which can strengthen and lead, but not replace, the decentralizing institutions as the home of representative government. The benefit of a strong executive, as Hamilton noted in *The Federalist*, No. 70, is "promptitude of decision," which does not allow for the "difference of opinion and the jarring of parties" that promote popular rule.[90] Consequently the advent of progressive democracy strengthened the national purpose, but deliberation and legislative authorization, activities that are the essence of popular rule, were displaced by executive administration as the center of government activity.

The creation of the modern presidency, of course, did not lead to a complete centralization of administrative power. The discretion of the executive and administrative agencies has been greatly reduced by legislative and judicial action, since the excesses of the modern presidency became drastically apparent during the Johnson and Nixon administrations. Yet the renewal of congressional and judicial activism has not really restored legislation and adjudication; rather, the reforms designed to curb the modern presidency have involved Congress and the courts in the details of administration.[91] As a result, the pluralism celebrated by James Madison in *The Federalist*, No. 10, envisioning a multitude of political interests acting as a system of mutual restraints, has been supplanted by a labyrinthine administrative politics that has insulated the affairs of state from the regular channels of American politics, as well as the understanding and control of the rank and file citizenry.

Within such a political setting it remains to be seen how far the recent challenges to liberal reform, challenges that have been issued from the left and right of the New Deal, can bring about still another rendezvous with the American political destiny. In the past political parties have been critical agents of major reform, providing a focal point during periods of great national need for the usually separated branches of the Constitution to combine and "find their vital contact with the people."[92] Yet the displacement of party politics by executive administration during the 1930s created the condition for the end of parties, unless, or until, an anti-administration party would spring up, and the Republican party has slouched toward providing such loyal opposition to the New Deal since Roosevelt's second term. Indeed, given that the New Deal was based on a party strategy to replace traditional party politics with administration, it is not surprising that the challenge to liberal reform has entailed the development of a conservative "administrative presidency," which has retarded the revival of partisan politics.

In fact both the Nixon and Reagan presidencies, which in some respects departed from the political paradigm of the past fifty years, have extended still further and perhaps accelerated the demise of the pre–New Deal principles and institutions. The political programs of the Nixon and Reagan administrations have been based on the possibility that the modern presidency is a double-edged sword that can cut in a conservative as well as in a liberal direction. The fact that the challenge to welfare state politics has thus far been primarily confined to the presidency has reinforced this emphasis on strengthening executive power as a means of advancing conservative ends. Ironically, the attempt to bring about changes in public policy with administrative tools that were created, for the most part, during democratic administrations, especially in the Roosevelt and Johnson years, was considered especially useful by "minority" Republican presidents facing a hostile Congress and bureaucracy intent on preserving the programs of those administrations. Consequently "conservative" presidencies have deepened the commitment in the political system to an administrative constitution, by demonstrating (or attempting to demonstrate) that centralization of power can serve the purposes of those who are opposed to the welfare state. In the wake of such a development neither the Democrats nor the Republicans respect principles that might revive those institutions that have traditionally served as the primary instruments of popular rule in the American political system.

The opposition to liberal reform, then, might end, not in a challenge to the administrative state, but in a battle for its services. Such a possibility reflects a failure to reconsider seriously the legacy of the New Deal. Tocqueville observed that administrative centralization "can contribute wonderfully to the ephemeral greatness of one man but not to the permanent prosperity of the people."[93] In the end this imposes on statesmen, as well as on scholars, the obligation to recognize the limits of executive power, and any assessment of our inheritance from the New Deal should begin with a reconsideration of these limits.

NOTES

1. Franklin D. Roosevelt, *Public Papers and Addresses,* ed. Samuel I. Rosenman, 13 vols. 1 (New York: Random House, 1938–50), 1: 742–56.

2. On the party system and the Constitution, see Woodrow Wilson, *Constitutional Government in the United States* (New York: Columbia University Press, 1908); E. E. Schattschneider, *Party Government* (New York: Rinehart & Winston, 1942); Richard Hofstadter, *The Idea of a Party System* (Berkeley: University of California Press, 1969); Harry Jaffa, "A Phoenix from the Ashes: The Death of James Madison's Constitution (killed by James Madison) and the Birth of American Party Government" (Paper prepared for the Annual Meeting of the American Political Science Association, Washington, D.C., September 1977); James Ceaser, *Presidential Selection: Theory and Development* (Princeton, N.J.: Princeton University Press, 1979).

3. Roosevelt, *Public Papers and Addresses,* 7, xxxi.

4. Schattschneider, *Party Government,* 163–69; John Edward Hopper, "The Purge: Franklin D. Roosevelt and the 1938 Democratic Nominations" (Ph.D. diss., University of Chicago, 1966), 220–21.

5. James MacGregor Burns, *The Lion and the Fox* (New York: Harcourt, Brace & World, 1956), 376–80.

6. William E. Leuchtenburg, *In the Shadow of FDR: from Harry Truman to Ronald Reagan,* rev. ed. (Ithaca, N.Y.: Cornell University Press, 1983).

7. On the development of the modern presidency, see Fred I. Greenstein, "Nine Presidents in Search of a Modern Presidency," in *The New American Political System,* 2d ed., ed. Anthony King (Washington, D.C.: American Enterprise Institute, forthcoming).

8. For a more detailed discussion of the arguments presented in this section, see Sidney M. Milkis, "Franklin D. Roosevelt and the Transcendence of Partisan Politics," *Political Science Quarterly* 100 (Fall 1985): 479–504; Milkis, "The New Deal, Administrative Reform, and the Transcendence of Partisan Politics," *Administration and Society* 18 (February 1987): 433–72.

9. Roosevelt, *Public Papers and Addresses,* 7: xxvii–xxix.

10. On party responsibility and the presidency, see Wilson, *Constitutional Government,* especially chs. 3 and 8.

11. Ibid., 220.

12. Ibid., 68–69.

13. Arthur S. Link, "Woodrow Wilson and the Democratic Party," *Review of Politics* 18 (April 1956): 146–56.

14. Arthur S. Link, *Woodrow Wilson and the Progressive Era* (New York: Harper & Bros., 1954), 34.

15. Link, "Woodrow Wilson and the Democratic Party."

16. Leuchtenburg, *In the Shadow of FDR,* 253; Merrill D. Peterson, *The Jefferson Image in the American Mind* (New York: Oxford University Press, 1960), 355–76.

150 Sidney M. Milkis

17. Alexis de Tocqueville, *Democracy in America,* ed. J. P. Mayer (New York: Doubleday, 1966), 87–99.

18. Theodore Roosevelt made the first of a number of speeches on the New Nationalism at Osawatomie, Kansas, in August 1910, printed in Theodore Roosevelt, *Works of Theodore Roosevelt,* vol. 9 (New York: Da Capo Press, 1923–26), 10–30.

19. Herbert Croly, *The Promise of American Life* (New York: E. P. Dutton, 1963), 169.

20. Herbert Croly, *Progressive Democracy* (New York: Macmillan, 1914), 15.

21. James Ceaser, "The Theory of Governance in the Reagan Administration," in *The Reagan Presidency and the Governing of America,* ed. Lester Salamon and Michael S. Lund (Washington, D.C.: Urban Institute, 1985), 69.

22. Roosevelt, *Public Papers and Addresses,* 1: 756.

23. Samuel H. Beer, "In Search of a New Public Philosophy," in *The New American Political System,* ed. Anthony King (Washington, D.C.: American Enterprise Institute, 1978); Ceaser, "Theory of Governance"; David K. Nichols, "Progressivism and the American Political Tradition" (Paper prepared for the Annual Meeting of the American Political Science Association, Chicago, Illinois, September 1983).

24. Roosevelt, *Public Papers and Addresses,* 1: 747.

25. Ibid., 751–52.

26. Josephus Daniels to FDR, December 15, 1932, Ray Stannard Baker Collection, Franklin D. Roosevelt File, Princeton University Library, Princeton, New Jersey.

27. FDR to Baker, December 21, 1932; Baker to FDR, December 23, 1932, President's Personal File, 2332, Roosevelt Papers, Franklin D. Roosevelt Library, Hyde Park, New York.

28. Personal and Political Diary of Homer Cummings, January 5, 1933, Box 234, Number 2, Page 90, Homer Cummings Papers (#9973), Manuscripts Department, University of Virginia Library, Charlottesville, Virginia.

29. Edward J. Flynn, *You're the Boss* (New York: Viking Press, 1947), 153.

30. Alfred Phillips, Jr., to FDR, June 9, 1937; Roosevelt to Phillips, June 16, 1937. President's Personal File, 2666, Roosevelt Papers.

31. Lindsay Rogers, "Reorganization: Post-Mortem Notes," *Political Science Quarterly* 53 (June 1938): 170.

32. For a discussion of presidential efforts to further party discipline by intervening in primary elections, see Sidney M. Milkis, "Presidents and Party Purges: With Special Emphasis on the Lessons of 1938," in *Presidents and Their Parties: Leadership or Neglect?* Robert Harmel ed. (New York: Praeger, 1984).

33. Raymond Clapper, "Roosevelt Tries the Primaries," *Current History* (October 1938), 16.

34. James Farley, *Jim Farley's Story* (New York: McGraw-Hill, 1948), 120.

35. Joseph Alsop and Robert Kintner, "The Guffey-Biography of a Boss, New Style," *Saturday Evening Post* 210 (March 26, 1939): 5–7, 98–102; Nancy J. Weiss, *Farewell to the Party of Lincoln: Black Politics in the Age of FDR* (Princeton, N.J.: Princeton University Press, 1983), 14–15.

36. Tobin generally supported FDR's goal of making labor a principal, albeit not dominant, constituent of the Democratic party. At a Teamsters' convention on September 9, 1935, he successfully led the fight to defeat a resolution that would have prevented the executive board of the Teamsters from making contributions to partisan political campaign funds. Yet, while defending the principle that American labor get more involved

in partisan politics, he was careful to point out, "Don't misunderstand me, I am not in favor now of the establishment of a Labor Party, but it may come to that. I have been opposed to it in every convention and gathering of laboring men for the last thirty-five years." Report of the Committee on Resolutions, President's Personal File, 1180, Roosevelt Papers. For a description of Tobin's efforts to coordinate the labor support for FDR in the 1936 campaign, see Tobin to Marvin McIntyre, November 9, 1936, Official File, 4046, Roosevelt Papers.

37. Franklin Clarkin, "Two-thirds Rule Facing Abolition," *New York Times*, January 5, 1936, sec. 4, 10.

38. Thomas Stokes, *Chip Off My Shoulder* (Princeton, N.J.: Princeton University Press, 1940), 503.

39. Ann O'Hare McCormick, "Next Four Years," *New York Times Magazine*, November 18, 1936, 26.

40. Morton Frisch, *Franklin D. Roosevelt: The Contribution of the New Deal to American Political Thought and Practice* (Boston: St. Wayne, 1975), 79.

41. In retrospect this may have been an unfortunate strategy to follow. Edward Flynn, political boss of the Bronx during the time of the purge, noted with interest that the most important victory Roosevelt obtained in the purge was the one Flynn engineered in New York against House Rules Committee Chairman John J. O'Connor (Flynn, *You're the Boss*, 503). Given Roosevelt's interest in strengthening the national government and the presidency, however, his attempt to go over the heads of the local party leaders and influence the people directly is not surprising.

42. William H. Meier to James Farley, December 23, 1938, Official File, 300 (Democratic National Committee), Roosevelt Papers.

43. Roosevelt, *Public Papers and Addresses,* 7: 397–98.

44. Wilson, *Constitutional Government in the United States,* 69.

45. Felix Frankfurter to FDR, February 2, 1937, Box 198, The Papers of Thomas G. Corcoran, Manuscript Division, Library of Congress, Washington, D.C.

46. Frankfurter to FDR, August 9, 1937, Box 210, The Papers of Thomas G. Corcoran; FDR to Frankfurter, August 12, 1937, microfilm reel 60, Felix Frankfurter Papers, Manuscript Division, Library of Congress.

47. Croly, *Progressive Democracy,* 346.

48. Ibid., 347.

49. Woodrow Wilson, "The Study of Administration," *Political Science Quarterly* 2 (June, 1887): 197–222.

50. Croly, *Progressive Democracy,* 347.

51. Ibid., 348.

52. Barry Karl, *The Uneasy State: The United States from 1915–1945* (Chicago: University of Chicago Press, 1983), 234.

53. Baker to FDR, March 6, 1935, President's Personal File, 1820, Roosevelt Papers.

54. FDR to Baker, March 20, 1935, President's Personal File, 2332, Roosevelt Papers.

55. Ibid.

56. Ibid.

57. Several members of the so-called Elimination Committee, which helped Roosevelt to plan the purge, wanted to make 100 percent "followship" of presidential measures the criterion, with support of the Court-"packing" bill as the acid test. Roosevelt, however, had a much less inclusive "black list," choosing to make a few examples of

the most extreme recalcitrants in the Democratic party. See Turner Catledge, "New Deal Councils Split over Choice of Foes for Purge," *New York Times,* June 29, 1938, 1, 6.

58. Baker to FDR, September 26, 1936; FDR to Baker, September 30, 1936, President's Personal File, 2332, Roosevelt Papers.

59. James Farley wrote several party leaders throughout the country after the 1938 election, asking for an evaluation of the Democratic losses. Many of those who responded, including many from non-Southern states, mentioned unfavorable reaction to the purge. For example, Illinois Congressman James A. Meeks wrote to Farley in February 1939: "The so-called effort to purge from the party certain Congressmen and Senators met with unfavorable reaction. You readily understand that." Meeks to Farley, February 1, 1939, Official File, 300 (Democratic National Committee), Roosevelt Papers.

60. Schattschneider, *Party Government,* 163–69.

61. Philip F. La Follete et al., "Why We Lost," *The Nation,* December 3, 1938, 586–87.

62. Homer Cummings Diary, December 30, 1938, Box 235, Number 8, Page 270, Cummings Papers.

63. Roosevelt, *Public Papers and Addresses,* 6: 360–61.

64. John Dewey, "The Future of Liberalism," *Journal of Philosophy* 32 (April 25, 1935): 225–30; Kenneth S. Davis, *FDR: The New Deal Years, 1933–1937* (New York: Random House, 1986), 236; Donald Brand, "Corporatism and the Rule of Law: The End of Liberalism Revisited" (Paper prepared for delivery at the Annual Meeting of the American Political Science Association, September 1985, New Orleans, Louisiana).

65. In a memo to his budget director, Harold Smith, written in 1940, Roosevelt expressed his opposition to a bill that would give the citizens of the District of Columbia a right to select political delegates to national party conventions on the grounds that it was desirable to avoid the creation of an insular administrative apparatus:

The organic law and the whole history of the past century and a half make it clear that the District of Columbia was set up solely as a seat of government—a very small physical territory intended to be occupied primarily by government employees. These Government employees would obviously come from other states, implying that there was no intention of such employees losing their residence and voting rights in their places of origin.

In later years the Civil Service laws confirmed that by setting up the principle of quotas on employees based on the population of the several states.

Furthermore, it has been the policy of the government to keep the District as a residential area for those employees and to prevent as far as possible the establishment of industries within the District.

Government employees working in Washington should still retain their original residences in the several states and it is very important to prevent the building up of an inherited bureaucracy here. (Memorandum for the Director of the Budget, May 22, 1940, Office File, 51 Roosevelt Papers)

66. *Report of the President's Commission on Administrative Management* (Washington, D.C.: Government Printing Office, 1937), 53. The President's Committee on Administrative Management, headed by Louis Brownlow, played a central role in the planning and politics of executive reorganization from 1936 to 1940. For a full analysis of the background and impact of this commission, see Barry Karl, *Executive Reorganization and Reform in the New Deal* (Cambridge, Mass.: Harvard University Press, 1963).

67. Congressional Record, 75th Cong., 3rd Sess., April 8, 1938, 5121.

68. Roosevelt, *Public Papers and Addresses,* 9: 28.

69. "Outline for a New York Conference," May 9, 10, 1936. Papers of the President's Committee on Administrative Management, Franklin D. Roosevelt Library.

70. *Fortune,* February 1937, 70–71.

71. Although the literature on party development has generally neglected the importance of presidential leadership and the evolution of the presidency as an institution, there are a few important exceptions. See, especially, Lester Seligman, "The Presidential Office and the President as Party Leader (with a postscript on the Kennedy-Nixon era)," in *Parties and Elections in an Anti-Party Age,* ed. Jeff Fishel (Bloomington: Indiana University Press, 1978); Harold Bass, "The President and the National Party Organization," in *Presidents and Their Parties*; Theodore Lowi, *The Personal President: Power Invested, Promise Unfulfilled* (Ithaca, N.Y.: Cornell University Press, 1985), chs. 3 and 4.

72. Richard Polenberg, *Reorganizing Roosevelt's Government* (Cambridge, Mass.: Harvard University Press, 1966), 23, 184; Civil Service Commission, Statement Regarding Executive Order of June 24, 1938, extending the merit system, Papers of the President's Committee on Administrative Management.

73. On the use of federal employees in the 1938 primaries, see Special Committee to Investigate Senatorial Campaign Expenditures and the Use of Government Funds of 1938, *Investigation of Senatorial Campaign Expenditures,* Senate Report, 76th Cong., 1st Sess., No. 10288; Hopper, "The Purge," 107; Albert Jay Nock, "WPA, the Modern Tammany," *American Mercury,* (October 1938): 215–19.

74. *New York Times,* August 6, 1939, sec. 4, 3.

75. *New York Times,* July 30, 1939, sec. 4, 7; *Time,* July 30, 1939, 7–11.

76. Charles H. Shreve to Thomas Corcoran, and attached letter to FDR, July 24, 1939, Box 253, Corcoran Papers.

77. Norris to FDR, July 26, 1939, President's Secretary File, 152, Roosevelt Papers.

78. "Draft Speech on Returning Hatch Bill," July 29, 1939, President's Secretary File, 152, Roosevelt Papers.

79. "Message to Congress on the Signing of the Hatch Bill," August 2, 1939, President's Secretary File, 152, Roosevelt Papers.

80. FDR to Wallace, January 10, 1944, Presidents Personal File, 41, Roosevelt Papers.

81. Roosevelt, *Public Papers and Addresses,* 13: 40. Roosevelt also made the Second Bill of Rights the theme of his October 28, 1944, speech in Chicago, which climaxed his reelection campaign (vol. 13, 369–78).

82. *New York Times,* March 11, 1943, 1, 12.

83. In 1939, with authority granted by the Executive Reorganization Act, Roosevelt transferred the Bureau of the Budget from the Treasury Department to the Executive Office of the President, where it could become the personal tool of the President in coordinating the budgeting process. Moreover, the staff of the Bureau was increased and the director relieved of many of the routine duties heretofore required, so that it could potentially become a major instrument of fiscal policy and planning. This potential was greatly realized under the effective stewardship of Smith, who convinced Roosevelt to make the Bureau the center of government planning after the demise of the NRPB. The Bureau's immediate task was to draft a plan on full employment that was proposed by Roosevelt in his State of the Union Address of 1945. This speech proclaimed the right of employment "the most fundamental" of the "economic bill of rights." Memorandum, Harold Smith to Judge Rosenman, December 23, 1944, and attached draft of remarks

on full employment, Harold Smith Papers, Franklin D. Roosevelt Library; Roosevelt, *Public Papers and Addresses,* 13: 503.

84. Alexander Hamilton to James A. Bayard, April 6, 1802, *The Papers of Alexander Hamilton,* 25 (New York: Columbia University Press, 1977): 587–89. The author thanks Robert Eden for bringing this letter to his attention

85. See Harvey Flaumenhaft, "Hamilton's Administrative Republic and the American Presidency," in *The Presidency in the Constitutional Order,* ed. Joseph M. Bessette and Jeffrey Tulis (Baton Rouge: Louisiana State University Press, 1981), 65–112.

86. For an excellent account of the conflict between the Federalist and Republican parties and the relationship of the American party system to the Constitution, see James Piereson, "Party Government," *Political Science Reviewer,* 12 (1982): 2–53.

87. Roosevelt, *Public Papers and Addresses,* 1: 745; Leuchtenburg, *In the Shadow of FDR,* 253.

88. Karl, *Uneasy State,* 236, 239.

89. Samuel Huntington argues that the institutional legacy of liberal reform stems from "a dramatic upsurge of democratic fervor" during the 1960s. See "The Democratic Distemper," in *The American Commonwealth,* ed. Nathan Glazer and Irving Kristol (New York: Basic Books, 1976), 9–38. On the view that liberal reform came under the influence of an elitist "new class" during the 1960s, a class hostile to the "common appetites, preferences, and aspirations of the common people," see Irving Kristol, *Two Cheers for Capitalism* (New York: New American Library, 1978), esp. 23–27. The burden of my argument has been to suggest that many of the constitutional and political problems of liberal reform have their origin in the New Deal, although clearly (as Robert Eden's contribution to this volume shows persuasively), there was an expansion and radicalization of the New Deal during the 1960s and 1970s.

90. Alexander Hamilton, James Madison, and John Jay, *The Federalist Papers* (New York: New American Library, 1961), 426–27.

91. On this point, see Alan Schick, "Congress and the 'Details of Administration,' " *Public Administration Review* 36 (September/October 1976): 516–28; Jeremy Rabkin, "The Judiciary in the Administrative State," *The Public Interest* 71 (Spring 1983): 62–84.

92. Jaffa, "Phoenix from the Ashes," 43.

93. Tocqueville, *Democracy in America,* 88.

The Public Philosophy of the
New Freedom and the New Deal

The "public philosophy" is one of those strange and discordant terms that occasionally prove irresistible to journalists and politicians—rather like "Lebanese government," or "Democratic deficit reduction plan." The public does not philosophize, and philosophers (the genuine article) do not seek out the glare of publicity. Nevertheless, the term public philosophy points to the fact that political science as the crude study of political behavior or of the naked pursuit of power is not enough, indeed is wrong-headed. Politics is not simply concerned with power, influence, or even policies; it concerns opinions about what ought to be done and why, about what is good and why. For that reason, as anyone who has been around politicians knows, politics is a lot of talk. It is never just talk, but it is in an important sense mainly talk, since even the most jarring political events—wars and revolutions—must be explained by the participants to one another, who must be persuaded to undertake them in the first place. So although my approach to the study of the New Deal and the New Freedom may strike some as naive, I hope that you will see why it is at least presumptively reasonable. What I shall do is to look at how the New Freedom and the New Deal were justified by their originators, by Woodrow Wilson and Franklin D. Roosevelt; and more particularly at how their justifications square with the founding principles of American politics, as contained especially in the Declaration of Independence and the Constitution.

Woodrow Wilson was elected president in 1912 on the basis of a program that he called the New Freedom, in conscious or unconscious distinction from the "new birth of freedom" called for by Abraham Lincoln at Gettysburg in 1863. The "new birth of freedom" was a spiritual reawakening and baptism that every generation of Americans was called to undergo; it was a rededication to the principles that our forefathers had brought forth in 1776. Wilson's New Freedom, by contrast, was the dictate of a completely new age, the declaration of a break with the past so far-reaching that, as he put it on the campaign trail in 1912, "a new nation seems to have been created which the old formulas do not fit."[1] The New Freedom corresponded to the conditions of a new age, conditions that could not have been foreseen by the men of the Revolution, whose writings, Wilson did not hesitate to say, "read now like documents taken out of a forgotten age."[2]

What had so transformed the social and political landscape was the powerful cataracts of unchecked and unregulated capitalism, together with their attendant streams of technological innovation and public enlightenment. Steam and electricity had made possible industrialization on a scale and at a velocity that no one could have imagined; and the captains of industry, making the most of their opportunities, Wilson claimed, had built up giant trusts and monopolies that held the common man in thrall. But all of these transformations were summed up in the radical change in ideas that more than anything else separated the world of the twentieth century from the world of the founders. The fathers of the republic had constructed the national government "under the dominion of the Newtonian theory," Wilson explained in both his theoretical and political writings, whereas his generation had witnessed the setting of Newtonianism and the rising of a bright new star, Darwinism.[3] The founders had operated under "the Whig theory of political dynamics"—the political science version of Newtonian physics— according to which politics was a variety of mechanics, government a machine that could avail itself of the "nice poise and balance of forces" in the universe. And so the framers spoke of the "symmetry and perfect adjustment" of the Constitution as if it were a miniature solar system, everything being held in its proper orbit by the unvarying laws of gravity. "They constructed a government as they would have constructed an orrery," Wilson said, "to display the laws of nature."[4] But a century and a half later thinking men knew that government is not a machine, but an organism, a living thing, and hence accountable not to Newton, but to Darwin. Government is "modified by its environment, necessitated by its tasks, shaped to its functions by the sheer pressure of life," Wilson wrote in *Constitutional Government*.[5] "Living political constitutions must be Darwinian in structure and in practice."[6] To put it simply, if society is an organism, "it must develop."

Wilson's career, both as a professor and as a politician, was devoted to reforming the structure and practice of American government—to opening it to the salutary influence of progress. His constancy of purpose is by no means gainsaid by the fact that he started out life as a dyed-in-the-wool Burkean and states' rights Democrat, and ended it as a crusading reformer not only of the nation but also of the world. He was a student and admirer of Edmund Burke, and an enemy of Rousseau and of anyone else who would try to impose an abstract theory on society, all his life. But Burkeanism and progressivism were to Wilson, as they have proved to be for so many others, not in the slightest incompatible. "There is nothing so conservative of life as growth," he explained in an address on the occasion of Princeton's sesquicentennial.[7] "Progress is life, for the body politic as for the body natural. To stand still is to court death. Here, then, if you will but look, you have the law of conservatism disclosed: it is a law of progress."[8]

Wilson's career was dedicated to changing a government built "to display the laws of nature" into one changing and adapting in a constant display of the law of progress. His indictment of the government designed by the framers can be easily summarized: the spirit of the Constitution is the spirit of checks and balances, whether expressed in the separation of powers or in the committee system within Congress; this spirit results in the balancing of selfish interests (not their overcoming) within the state and the checking of all progressive legislation; therefore our politics lags hopelessly, inevitably behind the pace of our social and economic development. At the root of the mess, then, is not so much the Constitution as the eighteenth-century spirit that the Framers had infused into it. It is the spirit of checks and balances, which arises only to protect the natural rights of man against the encroaching power of government, that is to blame; and thus Wilson had to extend his critique to the very ground of limited government, to the idea of natural or unalienable rights.

To this task he applied his favorite, Burke. " 'If anyone asks me what a free government is,' he quoted Burke as saying, "I reply, it is what the people think so.' "[9] "The Declaration of Independence," Wilson continued, "speaks to the same effect. We think of it as a highly theoretical document, but except for its assertion that all men are equal it is not."[10] That is to say, except for the self-evident truth that lies at the heart of the Declaration, the truth that is the foundation of the whole argument of the Declaration, it is not a very theoretical document. Wilson denatures the rights proclaimed in the Declaration, removing their foundation in nature by separating them from the truth that nature and nature's God have made men equal. Deprived of their connection to creation and the Creator, human rights become mere positive or prescriptive rights, the creation or inheritance of men, who receive no guidance concerning the rightful use of their rights from nature or anything above man himself. As Wilson explained, the Declaration "expressly leaves to each generation of men the determination of what they will do with their lives, what they will prefer as the form and object of their liberty, in what they will seek their happiness."[11] The reason for this is that "the ideals of liberty cannot be fixed from generation to generation; only its conception can be, the large image of what it is. Liberty fixed in unalterable law would be no liberty at all."[12] The most unalterable of laws is, of course, the natural law, obedience to which would be, in Wilson's view, "no liberty at all." Whereas the Founders had understood man's freedom to be grounded in and directed toward the natural law, Wilson in effect proclaimed such liberty to be indistinguishable from slavery.

The single permanent feature of liberty is its "conception" or "large image," which turns out to mean the principle of "the freest right and opportunity of adjustment."[13] Political liberty is purely procedural; it is the right of the governed to strike the balance that suits them between "the power of the government and the privilege of the individual."[14] Far from securing the unchanging and unalienable rights of man, the Constitution is a changing and evolving balance between power and privilege, a balance that receives no guidance or only historical guidance from the Declaration, and that is not checked by any principle or authority extrinsic to the will of the parties. As Wilson declared, anticipating Justice Holmes and, perversely, even the new conservative Chief Justice William Rehnquist, "the Constitution contains no theories," either moral or political or economic. The only thing it does contain is history, its own and that of all preceding constitutional development from Magna Charta.[15] Wilson's theory (if I may use the proscribed term) of constitutional development is part of the comparative and historical approach to the study of politics that he (as well as others in the first generations of modern, i.e., academic, American political science, for instance, John W. Burgess and Westel W. Willoughby) imported from the universities of Germany. The German study of the state (*Staatswissenschaft*), whose roots lay in Hegel and to some extent in Kant, tended to reject the study of forms of government in favor of the study of the development of political systems from primitive to advanced stages of constitutionalism. Wilson's political science similarly elevated the biology, the evolutionary biology, of government over its morphology.[16]

Constitutional government exists, according to Wilson, to secure "the freest possible play of individual forces" in society, to preserve the greatest possible social variety by protecting "the best and fullest opportunities" for "complete self-development."[17] It is not rights, talents, or virtues that government ought to serve, but rather these "individual forces" that make for open-ended "self-development." But political liberty involves power as well as privilege, so the government must see to it that the great variety of developing "selves" conform with "symmetrical national development." In other words, development must touch all classes equally, not just the few, and it must proceed at the same pace in economy, society, and politics. But if political life is itself developing, how is politics to oversee or harmonize the development of society? The answer is leadership, a new word in American politics that Wilson helped to define and popularize.

Leadership is a kind of interpretation—not the imaginative and singular interpretation of the "man of thought," but the sympathetic interpretation of the common thought that characterizes the "man of action." The leader, through his extraordinary sympathy with the people (i.e., with the predominant forces of development within the mass of the people), achieves an insight into the historical destiny of the nation. The leader tests, "very circumspectly, the preparation of the nation for the next move in the progress of politics" by interpreting "the direction of the nation's permanent forces."[18] He makes explicit what the people perceive only inchoately; he gives sight to the blind forces of public opinion. In short, the leader is the herald of the overcoming of his own times, proclaiming at once the preservation, abolition, and transcendence of his age. Yet there is in his leadership no hint of "original origination" or willful creativity:

he concentrates and projects the consciousness of his people; he does not invent it.

Opening government to progress, therefore, entails opening it to the people. Leadership is connected to the people through what Wilson calls "common counsel," which produces the "community" that is the basis of constitutional government. "Common counsel" means listening to the voices of the people through the mechanism of the political party, summing up the general interest in the person of the President as the preeminent party and national leader.[19] To effect common counsel—to create the conditions of party leadership—it is necessary to eliminate all obstacles between the leader and the people, to level the mediating institutions and practices. This was the strategic objective of Wilson's and the progressive movement's political platform: the attack on political machines; the call for direct primaries; direct popular election of senators; the initiative, referendum, and recall; and the appeal over legislators' heads directly to the people. These are all means of circumventing or dismantling checks and balances that were built into our political system. Taken together, they point to an overall democratization of American political life by bringing the national government closer to "the prevailing popular thought and need."[20]

Leadership and party government are designed to serve the variety of interests in society by transcending them, by absorbing them into political ideals. The party and its leadership articulate these ideals and fashion electoral majorities around them. What results from this overcoming of the Hobbesian war of factions and interests is, to put it briefly, the New Freedom, which at its most radical is a freedom from all attachment to interests or to nature-bound considerations for the sake of the historical development of all human faculties. Concretely, the New Freedom means government, as Wilson expresses it, through the people rather than of, for, and by the people—government expressing the spirit of the age, rather than embodying the people's attempt to govern themselves in the light of certain self-evident truths.

FDR described memorably his relation to Woodrow Wilson at the beginning of the 1932 campaign, in his Acceptance Speech at the Democratic convention. Calling for the resumption of the nation's "interrupted march along the path of real progress," Roosevelt acknowledged that "our indomitable leader in that interrupted march is no longer with us, but there still survives today his spirit. ... Let us feel that in everything we do there still lives with us ... the great indomitable, unquenchable, progressive soul of our Commander-in-chief, Woodrow Wilson."[21] Roosevelt went on to explain that the task Wilson had set for himself was left unfinished, mostly because international affairs had pressed in on him, preventing his devoting two full terms to domestic reform. By Roosevelt's own admission, the incompleteness of the New Freedom was the starting point, indeed the raison d'être, of the New Deal, which would have two full terms more or less free to devote to domestic reforms, though the war in Asia and in Europe would eventually come to dominate Roosevelt's attention as World War I had dominated Wilson's. By virtue of his four elections and the peculiar distress caused by the Depression, President Roosevelt's immediate political legacy would be more striking and long lasting than Wilson's. But as we shall see, in a sense Wilson's influence was greater and deeper, inasmuch as his theoretical and practical achievements made the New Deal thinkable.

Now the term New Deal is itself interesting. It could mean either a new shuffle of the cards, with the rules and the game remaining the same; or a wholly new arrangement, a partnership on different terms, a fresh adjustment of interests and principles. In the event it meant and was exploited to mean both, although I will argue that the latter, more radical definition comes closer to the truth about it. It happens that there is a speech of Roosevelt's that is singularly apt for our purposes, as it is probably the most philosophical address that he ever gave, and one that meditates on the meaning of the Declaration, to boot. In what follows I shall therefore draw mainly on the Commonwealth Club Address of September 23, 1932, titled in his collected papers the "Campaign Address on Progressive Government," but known in an early draft as "Individualism, Romantic and Realistic."[22]

Before turning to Roosevelt's words, however, it is necessary to raise an objection to this whole procedure. It is well known that FDR's speeches were written for him by others, and that many of the policy measures advanced in the New Deal were improvisations. Can Roosevelt be properly said to have a political thought, then? According to many historians, the answer is doubtful. In Richard Hofstadter's words, FDR was an "opportunist" who groped and stumbled his way through eight years of reform, experimenting liberally but without an end or overall purpose in mind. "At the heart of the New Deal there was not a philosophy but a temperament."[23] This dictum of Hofstadter's has been echoed by others—for instance, James MacGregor Burns: "Roosevelt was no theorist. It is doubtful that he chose this course as a result of a well-defined political philosophy. It simply emerged."[24] Lately it has degenerated to the point of damning by faint praise. Although "not an intellectual," Paul Conkin writes, "Roosevelt was neither an anti-intellectual nor a pseudointellectual. He had no pretensions as a thinker."[25]

Despite the fact that his speeches were drafted by advisers, FDR demanded rewrites until he got what he wanted, often edited the final drafts himself, and, in effect, made the words his own through his masterly delivery. In any case, his speeches come closer to articulating the *public* philosophy of the New Deal than do any of his brains-trusters' books. Now, it is true that FDR once said, in a speech at Oglethorpe University: "The country needs and, unless I mistake its temper, the country demands bold, persistent experimentation. It is common sense to take a method and try it: If it fails, admit it frankly and try another. But above all, try something."[26] The three historians I have mentioned each make a point of quoting this remark, but no one seems to have noticed its context. Two paragraphs before, in the same speech, Roosevelt declared, "Let us not confuse objectives with methods."[27] A paragraph before that he warned that "few will disagree that the goal [of greater economic security and wider prosperity] is desirable,'' but many, ''sitting tightly on the roof-tops in the flood,'' will disagree as to the means of getting there. If disagreement leads to doing nothing, then ''agreement may come too late.''[28] Clearly he is calling for experimentation in means, not in ends (if such a thing were possible). In the general introduction and the introduction to the first volume of his collected public writings and speeches, he admitted that those who seek inconsistencies will find them, but he distinguished ''inconsistencies of methods'' from ''a consistency and continuity of objectives.''[29] Whatever inconsistencies may be found are, he insisted, the result of not knowing how to achieve a consistent, fixed goal. In his view, after all, the Great Depression presented a crisis for which there were no precedents.

The seriousness of the Commonwealth Club Address is apparent from the beginning. ''I want to speak,'' Roosevelt declared, ''not of politics but of Government. I want to speak not of parties, but of universal principles.'' After some preliminary remarks he launches directly into the problem:

The issue of Government has always been whether individual men and women will have to serve some system of Government or economics, or whether a system of Government and economics exists to serve individual men and women. This question has persistently dominated the discussion of Government for many generations. On questions relating to these things men have differed, and for time immemorial it is probable that honest men will continue to differ.

The puzzling thing about this statement is the conclusion, that ''the final word belongs to no man.''[30] If all men are created equal and are endowed with unalienable rights, governments being instituted to secure these rights, then the issue would seem to be settled once and for all. Governments—and economies— are designed to serve man, not the other way around. But if ''the final word belongs to no man,'' then it cannot belong to Jefferson or to the Declaration of Independence. Roosevelt silently questions the authority of the Declaration and prepares the way for his modification of it by indirectly doubting the truthfulness or the naturalness of the rights there proclaimed.

Perhaps unalienable rights are dubious, ''yet we can still believe in change and in progress,'' Roosevelt asserts. We are thus alerted to the possibility that because ''no man'' can have the final word—because, that is, human nature and reason are unable to pronounce conclusively—the question of government will have to be decided by history. Recognizing that he needs a new ground for democracy if it is not based on natural rights, Roosevelt immediately redefines it as ''a quest, a never-ending seeking for better things.'' He thereby identifies democracy with America (which was earlier said to be ''in the process of change and development''), and both with change or progress. While this emphasizes the country's ability to move itself out of the Depression, it does so only at the cost of unmooring America from its founding principles—from any permanent standard. How are we to distinguish ''better'' things from worse, mere ''change'' from salutary "progress"? The answer comes at the end of his speech, in his renovation of the Declaration of Independence.

But first he reviews some prominent episodes in American and European history to illustrate this "never-ending seeking for better things" in action. Only his last example need concern us here. With the coming of the industrial revolution and the modern industrial plant, the "dream" was born, Roosevelt says, of releasing everyone from the heaviest manual toil—of raising universally the standard of living to the degree that luxury was within the reach of the humblest citizen. To realize the dream, however, it was necessary to use the talents of "men of tremendous will and tremendous ambition" whom Roosevelt calls "financial Titans." Their methods were "not scrutinized with too much care," he explains, for it was thought that no price was too high to pay for the advantages of having "a finished industrial system." The United States "fearlessly, cheerfully, and, I think, rightly, accepted the bitter with the sweet."[31] As he explains it: "The financiers who pushed the railroads to the Pacific were always ruthless, often wasteful, and frequently corrupt; but they did build railroads, and we have them today."[32] It is as if morality were impossible in those days; the necessity of having a railroad and industrial system was so great that no other considerations could be afforded. One recalls that the Titans were the pre-Olympian gods who ruled the world before being overthrown by more powerful and intelligent deities. The world seems ripe for a new revelation or dispensation, which is not long in coming.

"Our industrial plant is built . . . ," Roosevelt declares bluntly. "Our last frontier has long since been reached."[33] Borrowing a page from Frederick Jackson Turner, he announces, "There is no safety valve in the form of a Western prairie" where the unemployed of the East may migrate for a "new start." "Equality of opportunity as we have known it no longer exists." This sentence, pregnant with notions of affirmative action and the new equality, echoes a prominent theme of Wilson's in his 1912 campaign.[34] Whereas Wilson had advocated breaking up monopolies in order to restore and radicalize equality of opportunity, however, Roosevelt emphasizes rather the concentration of governmental power necessary to confirm and broaden this new equality by a combination of measures ranging from the National Recovery Administration to Social Security. But this is a shift in tactics, not in objectives. Both Wilson and FDR agree that "the day of the great promoter or financial Titan, to whom we granted anything if only he would build, or develop, is over." Economic morality is now possible because America is free of the necessity of building its industrial plant. The task now is "not . . . necessarily producing more goods," but "administering resources and plants already in hand" and "adjusting production to consumption."[35]

In retrospect, this is an embarrassing claim, inasmuch as a tremendous increase in America's industrial base would shortly be undertaken during the war, not to mention the many transmutations that America's economy has gone through since—plastics, transistors, microchips, and so forth. But the logic of FDR's reasoning—which, incidentally, is borrowed from certain tenets of German historical economics, the chain of influence on this side of the Atlantic running backward roughly from Adolf Berle and Rexford Tugwell to Simon Patten and then to Richard Ely—the logic of this reasoning points unmistakably to Roosevelt's conclusion. Once a plentiful supply of "better things" has been produced, a supply that is self-renewing, in effect, and for all intents and purposes inexhaustible, then it is possible to start discussing the administration of these goods. After that point seeking after better things means attending to their consumption, not production. "The day of enlightened administration has come."[36] The consumer society and the welfare state have arrived.

To be sure, without some minimal attention production would probably decline, and the consumer society and the welfare state would progress à outrance. But a concern with consumption or distribution as the primary goal is the hallmark of the welfare state as such. What is required, then, is for government to exert its authority over the "highly centralized economic system" that the Titans have built up, in order to keep its "irresponsibility and greed" from reducing millions to "starvation and penury." The depression is, from this point of view, a blessing in disguise, inasmuch as it creates a coincidence of justice and interest that enables government and business (which is suffering too) to cooperate in applying "the earlier concepts of American government to the conditions of today." "The common task of statesman and businessman," he avers, is to develop "an economic declaration of rights, an economic constitutional order" that would be the minimum requirement of a "more permanently safe order of things."[37] Appealing to the principles of Jefferson as brought up to date by Wilson and Theodore Roosevelt, FDR now launches into his reinterpretation of the Declaration.

According to the Declaration, he says, government is a contract by which the people consented to lodge power in certain rulers on consideration that they, the people, be accorded certain rights. "The task of statesmanship," he asserts, "has always been the re-definition of these rights in terms of a changing and growing social order."[38] Here Roosevelt adopts Wilson's theory of the Constitution wholesale: not only does the implied contract among the people to set up a government come off as a contract between the people and their rulers, but the terms of the agreement, far from resting on unchanging and unalienable rights, are offered up as negotiable and renegotiable. The Declaration admits that prudence indeed will dictate concerning the application of unalienable rights in concrete political situations; but it hardly suggests that these rights are in need of "re-definition" to keep pace with social change.

Thus the rights proclaimed in the Declaration are "as old as the republic, and as new as the new economic order."[39] They are not, one observes, eternal. Specifically, "every man has a right to life," Roosevelt explains, "and this means that he also has a right to a comfortable living."[40] A right to a comfortable living presupposes that there is enough comfort to go around, that the fundamental problem of acquisition has been solved, that there exists, in FDR's word, a "plenty." Of all this he is confident. "We have no actual famine or dearth; our industrial and agricultural mechanism can produce enough and to spare." "Our government, formal and informal, political and economic, owes to everyone an avenue to possess himself of a portion of that plenty sufficient for his needs, through his own work."[41] Private economic power becomes a public trust, on the grounds that, as he says elsewhere (and often), "necessitous men are not free men." In other words, man cannot really be free until he leaves the realm of necessity behind him and enters the welfare state, the state of true civil society. As he put it in his 1932 Acceptance Speech, "we must lay hold of the fact that economic laws are not made by nature. They are made by human beings."[42]

Roosevelt continues to spell out the terms of the new contract. "Every man has a right to his own property; which means a right to be assured, to the fullest extent attainable, in the safety of his savings." The right to life implies the right to labor and make a comfortable living; the right to property implies the right to secure the fruits of one's labor and to be secure when one cannot labor (childhood, sickness, old age). "The final term of the high contract was for liberty and the pursuit of happiness." These rights mean nothing, he declares, unless they are so ordered that "one man's meat is not another man's poison"; freedom and opportunity should not be, to quote from a later speech, "a license to climb upwards by pushing other people down."[43]

In particular, what Roosevelt calls (following Thomas Paine) the "rights of personal competency"—the right "to read, to think, to speak, to choose and live a mode of life"—are inviolable, their restriction being "outside the protection of any contract." But if the statesman's task is to redefine the rights of the social contract in terms of "a changing and growing social order," why is it that these rights are specially exempted? If "new conditions" were to arise that would impose "new requirements" on government, say, that would require restrictions on free speech, why would it be improper for government to "redefine" free speech in line with new social needs? A defense of these rights would ultimately have to rely on man's unalienable or natural rights, yet Roosevelt has gone out of his way to avoid the idea of natural rights throughout his long discussion of the Declaration. There are at least two reasons for his silence. First, he is wary of the natural right to property, lest it snare him in the toils of reaction or of unbreakable economic laws. Second, to call the "right to make a comfortable living" or any of his other reformulations "natural" would call attention to the fact that they are precisely not natural in the ordinary sense of the term: they presuppose the accumulation of a civilized plenty, hence the incentives and virtues of accumulation, hence the spur of necessity and the stimulus of honor.

But for Roosevelt, "necessitous men are not free men." His reading of the Declaration presupposes that necessity has been beaten, that the struggle for existence has been won, that the search for a good existence, for the good life, can now be conducted without reference to the constraints of nature. In the idea of the welfare state that the New Deal helped to popularize, the realm of necessity is not abolished or entirely left behind, as in Marxism; rather, the government assumes responsibility for it, allowing individuals to enter the realm of freedom, to "choose and live a mode of life." The "self" turns from its own preservation and interest to the creation and affirmation of its own ends—to self-expression, as we call it today.

The New Deal's reabsorption of economics into politics—FDR's assertion of the primacy of politics, of the fact, as he puts it at the beginning of the speech, that "nothing in all of human life is foreign to the science of politics"—in the end collapses into a kind of economic determinism because he, following Woodrow Wilson, anchors political science in history. Wilson's historicism remained in inspiration and analysis idealistic (much closer to Kant and Hegel than to Marx), whereas FDR's substituted pragmatic experimentalism and economic realism as its exploratory categories (and so edged closer to Marx via John Dewey). For this he reaped great and immediate political success, though at what cost, particularly in the long run, to the idealism of the New Deal, to the soundness of the American political tradition, and to the health of America we are only now beginning to gauge.

NOTES

1. Woodrow Wilson, *The New Freedom* (New York: Doubleday, Page, 1913), 5.
2. Ibid., 4.
3. Woodrow Wilson, "Character of Democracy in the United States," in Wilson, *An Old Master and Other Political Essays* (New York: Harper & Bros., 1893), 90–97, 108, 112; Wilson, *Constitutional Government in the United States* (New York: Columbia University Press, 1908), 46–48, 54–57; Wilson, *New Freedom*, 45–48.
4. Wilson, *Constitutional Government*, 55; Wilson, *New Freedom*, 46–47.
5. Wilson, *Constitutional Government*, 56.
6. Ibid., 57.
7. *The Papers of Woodrow Wilson*, ed. Arthur S. Link, 43 vols. (Princeton, N.J.: Princeton University Press, 1966–83), 10:22.
8. *Papers of Woodrow Wilson*, 10:22–23.
9. Wilson, *Constitutional Government*, 4. On the spirit of the Constitution and the problems it causes, see Wilson, *Congressional Government: A Study in American Politics* (Baltimore: Johns Hopkins University Press, 1981; orig. ed., 1885), chs. 1, 6; Wilson, *Constitutional Government*, 54–60, 198–204; Wilson, *New Freedom*, 33–48.
10. Wilson, *Constitutional Government*, 4.
11. Ibid., 4–5, 22–23; Wilson, *New Freedom*, 48–50.
12. Wilson, *Constitutional Government*, 4. Cf. Wilson, *The State* (Boston: D.C. Heath, 1889), secs. 18, 1218–19.
13. Wilson, *Constitutional Government*, 4–6.
14. Ibid., 5; Wilson, *New Freedom*, 281–84.
15. Wilson, *Constitutional Government*, 25–53, 59–60; cf. 198–204.
16. See, in general, Wilson, *State*, chs. 1–2, 13–16; *Papers of Woodrow Wilson*, 5: 54ff; Wilson, *Constitutional Government*, ch. 2–3, 8.

17. Wilson, *State*, secs. 1273–74.

18. "Leaders of Men," in *Papers of Woodrow Wilson*, 6:644–71. For a commentary, see Charles R. Kesler, "Woodrow Wilson and the Statesmanship of Progress," in *Natural Right and Political Right: Essays in Honor of Harry V. Jaffa*, ed. Thomas B. Silver and Peter W. Schramm (Durham, N.C.: Carolina Academic Press, 1984), 103–27.

19. Wilson, *Constitutional Government*, 25–27, 204–22.

20. See, for example, Wilson, *New Freedom*, 100–17, 123–32, 229–42. For a discussion of Wilson's democratization of American politics, see Paul Eidelberg, *A Discourse on Statesmanship* (Urbana: University of Illinois Press, 1974), ch. 9.

21. Franklin Delano Roosevelt, *Public Papers and Addresses*, ed. Samuel I. Rosenman, 13 vols. (New York: Random House, 1938–50), 1: 648.

22. The speech is printed in *Public Papers and Addresses*, vol. 1, 742–56. According to Rexford Tugwell, it was drafted by Robert K. Straus and John Dalton, with later drafts by Adolf Berle and the three jointly. FDR made his final alterations on the joint version. See Tugwell, *In Search of Roosevelt* (Cambridge, Mass.: Harvard University Press, 1972), 172–80.

23. Richard Hofstadter, *The American Political Tradition* (New York: Alfred A. Knopf, 1967; orig. ed., 1948), 311, 379.

24. James MacGregor Burns, *The Lion and the Fox* (New York: Harcourt Brace Jovanovich, 1956), 198; cf. 144.

25. Paul K. Conkin, *The New Deal* (New York: Thomas Crowell, 1967), 13.

26. Roosevelt, *Public Papers and Addresses*, 1:646.

27. Ibid.

28. Ibid.

29. Ibid., xiii, 6; cf. 8–9. Cf. also Arthur Ekirch, Jr., *Ideologies and Utopias: The Impact of the New Deal on American Thought* (Chicago: Quadrangle, 1969), ch. 2.

30. Roosevelt, *Public Papers and Addresses*, 1:742–44.

31. Ibid., 743–44, 747.

32. Ibid., 747.

33. Ibid., 750.

34. Ibid. Cf. Wilson, *New Freedom*, 5–24, 283–84.

35. Roosevelt, *Public Papers and Addresses*, 1:751–52.

36. Ibid., 752.

37. Ibid., 749, 752–53.

38. Ibid., 753.

39. Ibid., 754.

40. Ibid.

41. Ibid.

42. Ibid., 657. "Necessitous men are not free men," a quotation attributed to "an old English judge," figures prominently in FDR's Acceptance Speech at the Democratic National Convention, June 27, 1936. See *Public Papers and Addresses*, 5:233.

43. Ibid., 1:755; 4:341.

8   *Arthur Shenfield*

The New Deal and the Supreme Court

Of all the effects of the legacy of the New Deal, the most baleful has almost
certainly been its subversion of the Supreme Court. Without this effect the other
destructive effects of the New Deal might not have survived long after the trauma
of the Great Depression and the fresh memory of it had passed away.

From the time of Chief Justice Marshall's magisterial statement in *Marbury
v. Madison*,[1] it has been a fundamental article of legal and political doctrine that
the Supreme Court is the supreme interpreter of the U.S. Constitution and the
ultimate authority for its application and enforcement. In effect, this means that
it was such ab initio (i.e., from 1787, not from 1803), though Marshall's three
predecessors did not say so, and at least Jefferson, of the early Presidents, did
not agree with it (though it was already implied in some of Hamilton's observations in *The Federalist*).[2] Statewise, it had already been explicitly accepted
by eight of the seventeen states to which the Union had grown by 1803.

Let us notice here that the Court was properly conceived to be the authority
for the enforcement of the Constitution, but not the actual enforcer (remember
Andrew Jackson's taunt in the case of the Georgia Indians, "John Marshall has
made his judgment. Now let him enforce it").[3] This point is relevant to our
times when federal judges have taken it on themselves to supervise the administration of schools, prisons, and state electoral reapportionment programs, thus
in my opinion contumaciously usurping the functions of the executive branch.
What Marshall's splendid intellect and wisdom did was not to give birth to the
doctrine of the judicial guardianship of the Constitution, but to give it clear and
compelling expression, for which generations of Americans must be deep in his
debt.

What the New Deal and the ideas and influences behind it and nurtured by it have done has been to produce "Government by Judiciary," as Professor Raoul Berger has aptly described it.[4] Thus Supreme Court justices have tended to erect their predilections above the tenets of the Constitution, and then to call them the Constitution. It is only in recent years, nearly forty years after the famous "switch in time to save nine" of 1937, that the Court has slowly and still almost minimally begun to return to something like the pre–New Deal interpretation of the Constitution.

At this point I must hasten to note that the so-called old Court, that is, the Court that for some forty years had resisted the ideas from which the New Deal sprang, and the New Deal Court itself until 1937, has also been accused, in my opinion mistakenly, of government by judiciary. Berger himself has explictly done so. And not he alone. Other respectable authorities have done so. Thus Judge Robert Bork, a legal scholar of high distinction, has written the following about Justice Frankfurter: "For years prior to his appointment to the Supreme Court, he denounced the bad old Court that imposed its political will by striking down State and Federal economic regulation. He knew that the Constitution did not compel or even guide the majority in its course."[5]

I have the highest respect for Judge Bork, but in answer I say that Frankfurter did not know this. He could not because it was not true. Further, mirabile dictu, Chief Justice Rehnquist expressed the view in 1972, when he was an associate justice, in *Weber v. Aetna*, that the liberty and property protected by the Fourteenth Amendment did not embody freedom of contract as a fundamental right.[6] Stranger still, he gave warm approval to the demise administered to the freedom of contract doctrine by *West Coast Hotel v. Parrish*, the case that ended the Supreme Court's opposition to the doctrines of the New Deal and opened the way to what I have described as the subversion of the Court (see below).[7]

To import the right of freedom of contract into the terms liberty and property is no error. Not only was it so understood by the Founding Fathers, devotees as they were of Locke and Blackstone, but liberty and property cannot be given significant meaning without it.[8] Of course to say that freedom of contract is a fundamental element in liberty and property does not mean that it may not be properly subject to some legal curbs and restraints. Only anarchists would challenge this position. The "old" Court's justices knew very well that freedom of contract had its proper limits, as do other freedoms, and their judgments showed this clearly. They were, like men from Missouri, required to be shown, and shown compellingly, that legislative limits to freedom of contract, whether imposed by Congress or the states, had a just, compelling, and constitutional foundation.

THE NEW DEAL'S ECONOMIC AGENDA AND THE COURT

The New Deal's essential purposes were economically *dirigiste*. Although President Roosevelt became the hero of the poor and huddled masses, of blacks and Hispanics, and of various other apparent or supposed victims of the Great Depression, he cared little for what came to be known as the civil rights movement. In World War II, during Roosevelt's third and fourth terms, the U.S. Army was segregated. Anti-Semitic and other racial jokes came easily and frequently to him, as indeed they did in those days to many upper-class Americans in their segregated clubs. In the South, Jim Crow was prevalent, and FDR lifted not a finger against it. However, though the concern of his New Deal was with economic programs, the ideas from which it sprang inevitably spilled over to wider social issues, as happened with some of the post-Rooseveltian Supreme Courts. I doubt that FDR would have cared very much for the *Miranda*[9] decision, or for *Griswold v. Connecticut*,[10] or *Roe v. Wade*,[11] and I am sure that he would have fumed at the Court's position on the publication by the *New York Times* of the Pentagon Papers.[12] I am also sure that he would have had no time for the reapportionment of state electoral constituencies,[13] at least as long as the existing disposition of voting units favored his friends and cronies in governors' mansions and state legislatures. Thus he would probably have agreed with President Eisenhower that the appointment of Governor Warren to the Supreme Court was "the biggest damn fool mistake I ever made." For Warren considered reapportionment to be his greatest achievement (despite the principled and lofty dissent of Justice Frankfurter). Yet, in the last analysis, these developments have been part of the broader changes in law and society wrought by the New Deal and the ideology behind it. The association of economic dirigisme with these other changes wrought by the ideology of the New Deal is ironic. The contradiction between them was, and still is, deeply rooted in the ideas popular in the quasi-intellectual circles that promoted the New Deal. On the one hand, the rights of property (and the liberty essential to those rights) were to be severely curtailed and the power of government expanded. On the other hand, the rights broadly embodied in the First Amendment (freedom of speech and of the press), the Fourth Amendment (against unreasonable searches and seizures), and the Eighth Amendment (against cruel and unusual punishments) were to be expanded, and reinforced by a new right of privacy nowhere mentioned in the Constitution, so that in these cases it was the power of government to provide protection against a wide range of evils that was to be curtailed. Whether the "old" Court was right or wrong in its view of the Fifth and Fourteenth Amendment property rights, we can say with certainty that, for about a century and a half from the birth of the Union, the Supreme Court would have been sorely dismayed by these undue, perhaps preposterous, expansions of the First, Fourth, and Eighth Amendment rights.

In its first century the Supreme Court did not have occasion to work out a clear construction of the rights of property or of economic liberty. The problems presented by economic activity in a complex modern industrial economy could not come urgently to the fore until well after the Civil War. On the whole, in the nineteenth century, the Court was not thoroughly antagonistic to a modern free-market approach, but it did make occasional significant attacks, arguably in *Munn v. Illinois*,[14] and certainly in the *Slaughterhouse* cases.[15] But at the end of the century the Court worked out a clear and sustainable line in its construction of substantive due process, derided by its critics as the Allgeyer-Lochner-Adair-Coppage doctrine.

The death knoll of the "old" Court's construction of substantive due process was sounded in 1937 and after, but let us be clear that the principle of substantive due process has never been buried. It has simply been shifted from economic rights to other true or imaginary rights. Justice Douglas, as hostile a critic of economic due process as any, himself said in *Poe v. Ullman*,[16] "The error of the old Court, as I see it, was not in entertaining enquiries concerning the constitutionality of social legislation, but in applying the standards that it did." In the Allgeyer-Lochner-Adair-Coppage cases the Court struck down statutes forbidding (a) freedom of contract in the purchase of insurance from out-of-state sources not licensed by the state (*Allgeyer v. Louisiana*)[17]; (b) freedom of contract for bakers to work more than a prescribed number of daily hours (*Lochner v. New York*)[18]; and (c) freedom of contract for employers to require employees to accept a "yellow dog" contract (*Adair v. U.S.*, and *Coppage v. Kansas*).[19] Continuing in a similar line the Court struck down (a) a state statute ousting the freedom to engage in the manufacture or sale of ice without a license, that is, a so-called certificate of public convenience and necessity (*New State Ice Co. v. Liebmann*)[20]; (b) the famed National Industrial Recovery Act (NIRA), which was at first the very heart of the New Deal, authorizing the federal government to control, regulate, or direct a large part of business and industry[21] (remember General Hugh Johnson and his fatuous "We Do Our Part" buttons); (c) the first Agricultural Adjustment Act, providing for the federal control and subsidization of agriculture[22]; (d) acts establishing minimum wages for women and minors in various industries (*Adkins v. Children's Hospital* and *Morehead v. New York*).[23] In an important case that arose in the early days of the New Deal, the determined champions of economic due process were temporarily overborne in a 5 to 4 decision. This was *Nebbia v. New York*,[24] which concerned a state law enforcing minimum prices for milk sold at retail. It was a typical example of the application of the confused notion, generalized in the NIRA, that a depression could be cured by the enforced raising of prices, without reference to other matters such as monetary policy. Apart from the question of liberty and property rights, the position of the minority of four was clearly persuasive by any test of economic analysis, and the case proved to be merely a temporary aberration in the "old" Court's anti–New Deal line of decisions.

The "switch in time to save nine" took effect in 1937 in *West Coast Hotel v. Parrish*, which upheld by 5 to 4 a state law imposing minimum wages for women. The facts in this case were hardly distinguishable from those of *Morehead v. New York*, but Justice Roberts, who had decided there against a minimum wage, now switched into its favor. It was widely believed that Chief Justice Hughes persuaded him to do so in order to forestall FDR's move to pack the Court by capitulating to him. Though both Hughes and Roberts denied this, grounds remain for the belief that it was not without substance.

In the same year *Adair* and *Coppage* were reversed in *Virginia Railway v. System Federation* and *NLRB v. Jones and Laughlin Steel Corporation*.[25] Thereafter the complexion of the Court was radically changed by retirements and new appointments, and economic due process was rapidly buried. The Fair Labor Standards Act, 1938, which applied national minimum wages across the board, and which extended and reinforced the already inordinately powerful pro–labor union Wagner Act, 1935, passed muster. *U.S. v. Carolene Products*[26] approved on remarkably flimsy grounds a prohibition against the sale of filled milk (i.e., skim milk with added fat). *Phelps Dodge v. NLRB*[27] swept away an employer's right to refuse to employ union members. *Williamson v. Lee Optical*[28] approved a truly ludicrous state law forbidding the fitting of lenses into new spectacle frames without a licensed optometrist's prescription. *Ferguson v. Skrupa*[29] approved a state law forbiding any person to engage in the business of debt adjusting except as an incident in the practice of law (an obvious act of promotion of the sectional interest of lawyers, who of course were and are prominent in state legislatures). *New Orleans v. Dukes*[30] allowed a city to deprive a street seller of her livelihood, not because it was against street selling (which it substantially allowed), but because she was a new entrant.

These cases are just a sample of a series that fundamentally changed the Court's attitude to property and economic liberty. Whereas the "old" Court had required to be shown a compelling state interest if it were to approve abridgement of economic freedom, especially centered on freedom of contract, the new Court required only a rational interest. But in practice a rational interest proved to be anything that was not completely nonsensical. It has been said with justice that after "the switch in time," the Court would strike down a law of a *dirigiste* economic character only if Congress or a state legislature had passed it in a patent state of lunacy. Indeed, where the legislators had presented no rational interest, the Court was ready to think it up for them, as, for example, Justice Douglas did in *Williamson v. Lee Optical*. Perhaps the most egregious feature of the attitude of the post–1937 Court was a penchant for occupational licensing of almost all and sundry. Walter Gellhorn has written that the Founding Fathers would be aghast to learn that in many states, aspiring beekeepers, embalmers, lightning rod salesmen, septic-tank cleaners, and taxidermists must obtain official approval before seeking the public's patronage. He said that in at least one state, about the only people who remain unlicensed are the clergy and university professors, presumably because they are not taken seriously.[31] As an Englishman, I was first surprised and then amused to find that American barbers have to be licensed. That is one piece of nonsense that our British socialist busybodies have never imposed on us. Naturally, quite apart from the normal difference in wage rates, a haircut costs much more in America than in England.

A SOCIAL AGENDA TOO

I have referred above to the development of the Court's view on First, Fourth, and Eighth Amendment rights arising from notions associated with New Deal ideology. Worse still in principle have been various other tendencies in the Court, especially in dealing with the problems of minorities. The splendid American principle that all persons are equal before the law, a principle arising from centuries of development of English law and capped and perfected in the U.S. Constitution, with its amendments, has been turned on its head to mean that they are distinctly unequal. Indeed, it has been in construing the Civil Rights Act, 1964, itself, which forbade the use of racial distinctions in the determination of rights, that the Court approved and endorsed the intrusion of racial discrimination. In the *De Funis* case[32] it avoided a determination on the ground that the case had become moot, a supine posture from which Justice Douglas, to his credit, demurred. In the *Bakke* case[33] the Court managed to sit on three separate stools, with a result of mixed merit and demerit. In *Griggs v. Duke Power*[34] the Court rejected an employment test, based properly on the qualifications for the relevant job, on the ground that it produced higher failure rates for blacks than for others. In *Fullilove v. Klutznick*[35] it approved quotas for minority businessmen for public works contracts. In the *Weber* case[36] the denial of seniority rights to a white worker because he was white was approved.

THE MEN BEHIND THE JUDGMENTS

Let me now return to the record of the "old" Court, which for forty years and more American law students have been taught was perverse, retrograde, and lamentable in every respect. First, consider the treatment of the so-called Four Horsemen of the Apocalypse—Justices Butler, McReynolds, Sutherland, and Van Devanter. These were the judges who metaphorically caused President Roosevelt to bite the carpet in enmity and rage, and were the target of his Court-packing plan. The Four Horsemen have been described by many an academic writer as legal primitives, rednecks, or Neanderthals. This is a disgraceful calumny, and it is time that their reputation was restored to their merited level. I invite you to read McReynolds's judgments in *Nebbia*, in the gold clause cases,[37] in *Meyer v. Nebraska*,[38] and in *Pierce v. Society of Sisters*,[39] and Sutherland's judgment in *New State Ice* and his dissent in *West Coast Hotel*, and see whether calumny is not too strong a word for the treatment meted out to them. The truth is that they stood for ideas, in my submission correctly rooted in the Constitution, which had become highly unpopular among academics and quasi-intellectuals, who responded with the venom often characteristic of such people. Now we have had half a century of experience of the economic dirigisme favored in such circles, and more and more of us have learned that the old, apparently discredited, ideas were right, without knowing in most cases that they were the bedrock of the Four Horsemen's judgments.

Consider *Lochner v. New York*.[40] This case perhaps more than any other has been treated as characteristic of the perversity of the "old" Court, especially because in his famous dissenting judgment Justice Holmes is supposed to have torn the majority's judgment to shreds, eloquently, pithily, and magisterially,

as only that great lawyer and man of high culture could do. I shall submit that
it was Holmes's judgment that was perverse; that indeed it was a piece of high-
class flippancy, which might have come well from the pen of an H. L. Mencken
or a Dorothy Parker, but not from a serious and eminent Supreme Court Justice.

I have written elsewhere that the question at issue was whether a New York
statute fixing maximum hours of work for bakers was within the proper limits
of the exercise of police power. If it was not, then it would be in conflict with
the Fourteenth Amendment protection of liberty and property; liberty because
that comprehended freedom of contract, and property because the right to bargain
freely for the use of one's labor was a species of property.

It is to be noted that there was no flexibility in the maxima laid down. The
work was to be limited to ten hours per day and sixty hours per week even in
emergencies, and of course even if the workers freely wanted to work longer.
It is also to be noted that the statute contained provisions for sanitary and health
arrangements that were not in issue because all members of the Court found
them to be proper, and hence within the exercise of the policy power. This is
important because the proponents of the statute argued inter alia that the limitation
of hours of work was necessary for health as well as for other reasons. It is to
be noted further that the Court had previously upheld a state statute in *Holden
v. Hardy*[41] that limited hours of work (in metal mining and smelting, and so on
in Utah), and other statutes that clearly infringed freedom of contract and other
personal freedoms in non-labor cases (e.g., *Mugler v. Kansas*[42] and *Jacobson v.
Massachusetts*[43]). However, in *Holden v. Hardy* the Utah statute did provide
for flexibility in emergencies, while cogent evidence was presented to show that
long hours in metal mining and smelting did have harmful effects on the workers'
health.

Justice Peckham, speaking for the majority of the Court in *Lochner*, found
that the New York statute did fall outside the proper limits of the police power
and was, therefore, unconstitutional. There can surely be no doubt that Peckham
was right in viewing the question of the limits of police power as the central
issue in the case. Whether, as he found, there was insufficient evidence to
distinguish baking from many other occupations that could be said to impinge
on workers' health but yet no one would propose to regulate was no doubt
debatable; as was the view advanced by Justice Harlan in dissent that if there
was doubt, the statute should be given the benefit of it. But he was surely right
in taking note of the well-known fact that laws of this character were often passed
on the colorable plea that they protected the public health or safety, when in
fact they were inspired by other motives.

In his famous dissent Holmes referred to the previous cases that could be held
to support the constitutionality of the statute, so that in his view there was ample
precedent for it. Had he contented himself with this he would have offered a
respectable case for the majority to answer (which, however, in the view taken
here, they did answer). But he added his famous statements that "the Fourteenth
Amendment does not enact Herbert Spencer's *Social Statics*," and that "general

propositions do not decide concrete cases. The decision will depend on a judgment or intuition more subtle than any articulate major premise.'' The reference to Spencer was gratuitous, for Peckham neither mentioned Spencer nor rested his argument simply on ideological dogma (unless the belief that there were limits to the police power were called dogma, in which case it was dogma that no one would challenge). In any case, was Holmes right? As so often, less than half right. In any detail, it is true that the Fourteenth Amendment did not enact Spencer's *Social Statics*. But in spirit they were in fair measure akin. The essence of Spencer's doctrine was laissez-faire. But laissez-faire does not mean anarchy. It means the maximum freedom for each citizen, subject to his not infringing on the freedom of others. Hence it requires a state to protect each and all against force and fraud—that and no more, which means a severely limited government. Subject to differences of detail, which admittedly could be important, what was that if not the essence of the aims of the Founding Fathers? Among them were men who were thoroughly familiar with, and approved, the liberal political doctrines of the Enlightenment. Their greatest inspiration was in Locke. They knew their Blackstone, and by the time the Bill of Rights was projected, they also knew their Adam Smith, whose *Wealth of Nations* was published in 1776.

The fact is that, to classical liberals, and the Founding Fathers were the most distinguished practitioners of classical liberalism in action that the world has seen, there are no distinctions between economic freedom and other freedoms (say, of speech and religion). All are fundamental, and indeed linked to one another. If they had had to set up a hierarchy of liberties, the Founding Fathers might well have given the primacy to economic liberty (expressed in the idea of private property) because unless a man were secure in his private property and protected from arbitrary seizure, life itself and other liberties were insecure. Therefore, they clearly approved of Locke's famous dictum, ''The great and chief end . . . of men putting themselves under government is the preservation of their property.'' Hence if they had lived to read Spencer, they might, like Holmes, have found his style unattractive and they might have demurred at some of his abrasive observations, but they would have agreed with the main thrust of his exposition. Thus, pace Holmes, the Constitution did enact the main substance of *Social Statics*. Of course the Fourteenth Amendment lay in the future when the Bill of Rights was adopted, but on the footing that it extended the Fifth Amendment to the states, the Fourteenth Amendment also enacted Spencer.

Thus the view that the Constitution was neutral as between various economic theories or policies is fundamentally false. This becomes obvious when we contemplate communism or any other totalitarian system. Communism would be incompatible with the Constitution not merely because of its political doctrine, for its economic doctrine is an essential part of its political doctrine. Hence the Constitution cannot be neutral in this case. Why, then, must it be neutral in other cases? Clearly neutrality must be limited to those economic doctrines that fall within the constraints of the Constitution. Therefore, ''what the crowd wants'' may have to be proscribed; and Holmes's dictum ''a constitution is not intended to embody a particular economic theory. . . . It is made for people of fundamentally differing views'' is dangerously misleading, if it means that the choice between theories is subject to no constitutional constraints. In short, Holmes's famous statement on Spencer's *Social Statics* was as misleading, perhaps as mischievous, as it was unworthy of the mountains of praise that have been heaped on it.[44]

The sad truth about Holmes is that, great legal scholar though he was, he had become a legal agnostic or skeptic. That is why he said that ''the prophecies of what the Courts will do and nothing more pretentious are what I mean by law,'' and why he was so skeptical of the goodness or badness of laws that he had no practical guide except what the crowd wanted. Personally he would bet that the crowd, if it knew more, would not want what it did.

Of course there is a sense in which what the courts will do determines the law, as every practicing lawyer knows. But the true question is why the courts do what they do, and that requires an examination of the nature and principles of the law. As for his obeisance to the wishes of the crowd, this would have been folly for any American, lawyer or not, but was utterly deplorable from the most distinguished jurist of the day. The U.S. Constitution is the very opposite of a pure democratic document. Its fundamental principle is and always has been that all political power, whether of the president, Congress, Court, or the democratic crowd itself, must be strictly constrained by law. For otherwise, as the Founding Fathers well knew and made absolutely clear, the result would be tyranny. And of all tyrannies, that of the crowd is often the worst and almost always the most capricious. Holmes was not entitled to let the crowd do what it wanted. Nor was the Court that his talents could, and sometimes did, adorn.

NOTES

1. 1 Cranch 137 (1803).
2. Papers 78 et seq.
3. Cherokee Nation v. Georgia. 30 U.S. 5 Peters 1 (1831).
4. Raoul Berger, *Government by Judiciary* (Cambridge, Mass.: Harvard University Press, 1977).
5. H. N. Hirsch, quoted in a review of his book *The Enigma of Felix Frankfurter*, *The Public Interest* 65 (Fall 1981): 110.
6. 406 U.S. 164 (1972).
7. 300 U.S. 379 (1937).
8. Bernard Bailyn, *Ideological Origins of the American Revolution* (Cambridge: Harvard University Press, 1967).
9. 384 U.S. 436 (1966).
10. 381 U.S. 479 (1965).
11. 410 U.S. 113 (1973).
12. New York Times v. USA. 403 U.S. 713 (1971).
13. Baker v. Carr. 369 U.S. 186 (1962): Reynolds v. Sims. 377 U.S. 533 (1964); et al.

14. 94 U.S. 113 (1877).
15. 83 U.S. 16 Wall 36 (1872).
16. 367 U.S. 497 (1961).
17. 165 U.S. 578 (1897).
18. 198 U.S. 45 (1905).
19. 208 U.S. 161 (1908); 236 U.S. 1 (1915).
20. 285 U.S. 262 (1932).
21. USA v. Schechter. 295 U.S. 495 (1935).
22. USA v. Butler. 297 U.S. 1 (1936).
23. 261 U.S. 525 (1923); 298 U.S. 587 (1936).
24. 291 U.S. 502 (1934).
25. 300 U.S. 315 (1937); 301 U.S. 1 (1937).
26. 304 U.S. 144 (1938).
27. 313 U.S. 177 (1941).
28. 348 U.S. 483 (1955).
29. 372 U.S. 726 (1963).
30. 427 U.S. 297 (1976).
31. See "The Abuse of Occupational Licensing," *University of Chicago Law Review* 44 (1976): 11–18. Quoted by Bernard Siegan in *Economic Liberties and the Constitution* (Chicago: University of Chicago Press, 1980), 200.
32. 414 U.S. 1038 (1974); 416 U.S. 315 (1974).
33. 438 U.S. 265 (1978).
34. 401 U.S. 424 (1971).
35. 100 S.Ct. 2758 (1980).
36. 443 U.S. 193 (1979).
37. 294 U.S. 240 (1935); 294 U.S. 317 (1935); 294 U.S. 330 (1935).
38. 262 U.S. 390 (1923).
39. 268 U.S. 510 (1925).
40. For a masterly and exhaustive analysis of *Lochner v. New York*, see Bernard Siegan, *Economic Liberties and the Constitution* (Chicago: University of Chicago Press, 1980). Professor Siegan's analysis is a most persuasive vindication of the Court's majority, and an exposure of much of the sophistry in Holmes's dissenting judgment.
41. 169 U.S. 366 (1898).
42. 123 U.S. 623 (1887).
43. 197 U.S. 11 (1904).
44. Arthur Shenfield, "The Influence of Holmes and Brandeis on Labor Law," *Government Union Review*, Summer 1982, 42–45.

Hiram Caton

Progressivism and Conservatism During the New Deal: A Reinterpretation of American Political Traditions

Three landslide defeats of the Roosevelt electoral combination, two of them administered by an avowed conservative, have prompted speculation that the nation may be in the process of a realignment that will set a political agenda for another long period.

Had these presidential victories been accompanied by comparable victories or merely Republican majorities in Congress, realignment would not be so much a possibility as a fact. But as things stand, the American public have declined to deliver a mandate for conservative politics, so that public life is stuck between a conservative rhetoric setting the tone from the executive branch and an ancien régime that is still vigorous in Congress, the courts, and the bureaucracy. Stalemate is the result. Budget deficits continue on their upward course in sovereign disregard of good intentions. Bureaucracies, regulations, and social services continue to grow, with some areas, notably medical care, undergoing spectacular growth in the past decade. Things are no different with the conservative moral agenda. The pro-life and anti-pornography crusades enjoy support in high echelons of government, but the private rights doctrine that legitimated abortion and pornography has not been repudiated. On the contrary, under the slogans of "euthanasia" and "helping to die" it is being extended to sanction the destruction of many people. If we consider an issue frequently identified by conservatives as constitutionally critical, and hence a benchmark of their position—affirmative action—we find the presidential voice restrained by its estimate of public sentiment favoring this distinctive intepretation of the obligations of government.

Considerations of this kind document the current hesitation of the American polity before alternative paths. One method that students of realignment use to interpret these complexities is to describe, as best they can, the changes in institutions and public opinion imparted to the polity by the ancien régime that conservatives are attempting to supercede. The ancien régime is identified as the welfare state, whose institutions were introduced as the New Deal. My task is to describe the conservative response to New Deal politics. Let me commence by reviewing some of the literature on this subject.

In his outstanding study, *The Conservative Intellectual Movement in America*, George Nash declared that "in 1945, no articulate, coordinated, self-consciously conservative intellectual force existed in the United States."[1] There were only scattered voices of protest, which in the next decade developed into a fledgling conservative movement linking libertarians, Burkean traditionalists, laissez-faire liberals, and the upmarket conservatism emanating from the newly emerged *National Review*. Nash states that the first self-consciously American conservative tract was Russell Kirk's *The Conservative Mind* (1953). Consulting the most recent edition (1978) of that landmark for further indications, we are given to understand that American conservatism is Burkean and that its exponents have been largely British. Kirk's slender catch of Americans includes John Adams and (halfheartedly) Alexander Hamilton, both men of the eighteenth century. No political parties, no founding documents, and no great Presidents earn Kirk's seal of approval. There is little in Kirk's study to contest the assessment argued by Louis Hartz, in *The Liberal Tradition in America* (1955), that conservatism is alien to American politics. In this survey Hartz purported to show that the institutions, manifestos, and parties of American politics were liberal from the beginning. Hartz's opinion was endorsed by Leo Strauss, who found that American politics was thoroughly shaped by the Lockean or liberal branch of modern political thought. Born of revolution, founded in contract theory, American politics proved to be dynamic and expansive beyond all expectation: one might say that America was the platonic idea of the unconservative regime.

Finally, and at the risk of overdrawing the point, let it be noted that the thinkers to whom postwar conservatives looked for instruction were not native born and did not situate their thought within the American political tradition. Eric Voegelin described the conservative-liberal contestation as a local episode in the epochal drama of the gospel and its perversion by fallen man. Voegelin finds that American politics and political mythology are heavily under Gnostic influence; for example, the concept of America as the incorrupt redeeming nation, whose liberty would be the light to the world. For Leo Strauss, the liberal-conservative contest was a contemporary episode in the epochal revolt of the Moderns against the restraining wisdom of the Ancients. The conservative residue that he detected in the nation's constitutional documents owed its presence to the freshness of the memory of the classical tradition that the Founders rejected. Friedrich von Hayek, whose *The Road to Serfdom* was a landmark of postwar conservatism, situated his polemic against socialism in the terrain occupied by nineteenth-century European liberals doing battle with conservatives, who arose in Europe, but not in America, in the aftermath of the French Revolution.

Our review seems to lead to the conclusion that the current topic fails for want of an object. This is a paradox for the historian, who detects a clear oppositional voice in New Deal politics and dubs it "conservative" without further ado. This difference between empirically minded historians and the classifications of theorists will subsequently require our attention. For the moment, however, let us examine the men and doctrine who composed the New Deal opposition so that we may relate them to the liberal tradition that we are authoritatively informed is the exclusive American political inheritance.

NEW DEAL CONSERVATISM

The cognomens of politics around 1935 were, on the one side, New Dealers, 100 percent New Dealers, Democrats, liberals—names preferred by Franklin Roosevelt—but in addition radicals, Communists, negrophiles, and dictators. The opposition were known as Republicans, conservative Democrats, the coalition, conservatives, Tories, oligarchs, reactionaries, irreconcilables, fascists, and copperheads. The terms liberal and conservative did not leap into the political idiom in 1932. They began to trickle in sometime around 1900, as Americans compared domestic political change with overseas events. Their immediate provenance is British, although these parties existed throughout Europe. We find Woodrow Wilson, first as political scientist and later as President, adopting this nomenclature to clarify the direction of change then in train. Some conservative leaders of the New Deal opposition did much the same thing, but they were not particularly keen to paint the conservative label on their position. Not so Roosevelt. Believing that an ideological and electoral realignment was in the making, he labeled the Democrats "liberals" and repeatedly invited the irreconcilable Democrats to cross over to the Republicans. When they declined the invitation, he attempted, unsuccessfully, to purge them through primary challenges.

The conservative opposition crossed party and geographical lines. The elections of 1932, 1934, and 1936 left the Republicans too weak to provide the leadership. They contented themselves with letting the Democrats do the talking on the floor of Congress. The election of 1938 substantially increased Republican representation as well as the number of conservatives of both parties, but leadership remained, as it had been, bipartisan. The opposition was known as "the coalition" because primary loyalties were to party and because it operated on an issue-by-issue basis. Because principle was nearly always engaged in New Deal legislation, the criterion for the selection of fighting issues was opportunity. For this reason the composition of the coalition was variable, but from 1937 its core in the Senate numbered about 35 and in the House about 180. After Joe Martin became the House Whip in 1939, House Republicans were a disciplined conservative phalanx. In 1937 an attempt was made, behind closed doors, to formalize the coalition into a party realignment, even as Roosevelt desired. The attempt foundered on the obduracy of party loyalty at the grass roots: at the end of the day would-be new party conservatives could not find the language to present their doctrine in a manner acceptable to local voters. Democrats, especially Southern Democrats, could not repair to the Republican banner, for that was to make a pact with the devil. The Jeffersonian name was bandied about but did not take. Nevertheless, the exercise did produce a statement of principles that summarized the positions defended by the five Democratic irreconcilables from the earliest days of the New Deal. These men were Senators Byrd and Glass of Virginia, Tydings of Maryland, Bailey of North Carolina, and Gore of Oklahoma. Let me review the headings of their position by reference to the coalition's statement of principles.

—The New Deal interpreted democracy to mean approximating social and economic equality through the instrumentality of government. This was bedrock FDR doctrine; Woodrow Wilson's doctrine of the New Freedom was claimed as its predecessor. Opponents said that the doctrine deflected American government fundamentally from the original aims of securing political liberty and political equality. Social equality was not thought to be an achievable goal. It could be attempted, critics said, only by those prepared to use despotic means. The vast enlargement of the ends of government implied by the new interpretation of the equality doctrine was said to imply rejection of the proposition, axiomatic in the American tradition, that liberty could be maintained only when the scope and powers of government were limited.

—The New Deal linked expansion of administrative agencies to economic recovery. The multiplication of such agencies, including bureaus established to create jobs, was intended to restore broadly based wealth. Opponents deemed this concept to be economically perverse. Their doctrine was that governments consume but do not produce wealth. All government expenditures are a charge on the public who must pay, directly or indirectly, from their productivity. Expenditures for public works and the like may facilitate production. But such expenditures are questionable, and on a large scale are definitely unsound, because market demand will call such enterprises into being when they are in fact facilitative, for then they will be profitable. The lesson is that small, frugal government serves every citizen's interest. Government has no business intervening in business.

—New Dealers dismissed this thinking as obsolete classical economics, lately superceded by the Keynesian dispensation. Their doctrine was that productive capacities were large enough or even too large; the problem of the Depression was underconsumption and unemployment. The remedy is the use of government as an interloper stimulating consumption and employment by schemes of redistribution of wealth and creation of employment. The basic mechanism of redistribution is government deficits and borrowing. These interventions were held to restore business confidence, thereby bringing hoarded capital back into circulation and lifting the economy out of its trough. Against all this, conservative critics made free-market rejoinders to the effect that the wealth created by deficit was a swindle that must, in the end, lead to inflation, to the removal of budgetary discipline, and finally to a collapse of credit.

—The introduction of novel aims of government backed by an economic apology for debt was believed to be closely linked to the New Dealers' contempt for the constitutional structure of political institutions, particularly the delimitation and separation of powers. In those days the Supreme Court was the repository of this sentiment and also its chief guardian, since Roosevelt's immense popularity effectively annexed the power of congressional decision to the Oval office. Roosevelt's attempt to subdue the Court's obstinacy by packing the bench was, for conservatives, the ineffaceable symbol of the New Deal's spirit of reckless innovation, and it was, therefore, a watershed for the stiffening of conservative resistance in Congress. But in 1937 Roosevelt got his way with the Court through the normal avenue of appointments. It was then that Hugo Black went to the bench from his Senate seat after acrimonious Judiciary Committee hearings, and things have not been the same since.

—The ethos of the New Deal was also the subject of much criticism. The welfare concept as such was obnoxious. The velvet glove of paternalism was believed to disguise the double threat of bureaucratic despotism and corruption of the citizen's sense of liberty. The dole and Social Security were two of the many legislative proposals that excited severe strictures. Republican Herbert Hoover and Democrat Senator Gore gave utterance to the sentiment when they rejected the dole as likely to corrupt the industry of the people. In Gore's laconic rime: "The dole spoils the soul." It was a sentiment widely shared in pre-Depression America, whose ethos was predominantly that of the small town. Youth were brought up to believe that you did your job, saved in order to buy and promptly paid your debts, looked after the family, made a good neighbor, went to church, and were honest in all things. Businessmen enjoyed high prestige and set the tone of goodwill through participation in churches and civic clubs. Ill manners were corrected, and everyone knew the difference between right and wrong. The courts dealt in justice rather than in arbitration; plea bargaining was unknown. Ex-nuptial births and divorce were stigmatized, often severely. Homosexuality was rigidly confined to the closet, and abortion was something that might happen amid the general corruption of cities. There was no television or plastic credit or rock music or domestic security systems. Drugs were not obtainable in towns, let alone in the schools. Such was the discipline, simplicity, and moderation of a people who regarded charity as a last resort and the dole as an indignity. That is the credo of small government, economic liberty, and simple manners that the conservative coalition opposed to the New Deal. Its provenance and career in American politics are readily described. It is the credo of Thomas Jefferson's First Inaugural Address. Its constitutional doctrines were elaborated by James Madison from the floor of the House and by John Marshall as chief justice. The credo was renewed by Andrew Jackson, who stamped it into the political ethos of the frontier states and made it the bulwark of American politics that it remained until the Depression. Americans had recently endorsed it by giving Harding and Coolidge huge electoral victories. Such was the tenor of things that Democratic chieftains intended to make Hoover's spending extravagance an election issue.

Roosevelt did indeed talk of fiscal responsibility in his first presidential campaign, but the party bosses had not detected a change in public sentiment and, above all, they had not reckoned with Roosevelt's persuasive powers. Recognizing the mandate that the overwhelming victory of 1932 gave him, Roosevelt, in his inaugural address, likened the depression to a war emergency, and sought extraordinary powers to deal with it. The Seventy-third Congress complied with dizzying alacrity; often it gave more than the President had sought. Even Senator Arthur Vandenberg, a vintage conservative Republican, declared that the nation required a dictator in its hour of travail. And the heartland of Jeffersonian democracy, rural America, unhesitatingly opted for the system of subsidies and price supports that have remained a permanent feature of agricultural economics. It may be said, then, that the welfare state did not slip in by stealth, subversion, or presidential strong-arm tactics. The American electorate, tutored by President Roosevelt, demanded it. At the end of the 100 Days its legitimacy was established; henceforth, government would be a partner in securing the general welfare. Let us examine a little more closely the terms of the new social contract.

The welfare state involved more than doctrine and programs; it also had its ethos and style. As we have seen, detractors tagged it as the spirit of dependency. This is not what the public saw coming from the White House. They saw a whirl of action conducted with good cheer, confidence, and seemingly unconquerable strength. Probably no President has enjoyed greater credibility for honorable, patriotic, and benevolent intentions. This reservoir of trust enabled Roosevelt to justify extraordinary innovations by merely taunting the opposition that they wanted to "take the country back to the horse and buggy days." In the hour of need it did not matter that progress was being made by discarding the Jeffersonian legacy. New Dealers communicated an infectious spirit of irreverence toward the past and pride in breaking new ground. The very word "change" became a shibboleth. This positive and enterprising attitude toward the future touched a chord of the national ethos, valorized by Jefferson himself when he declared the right of each generation to renegotiate the social contract, if necessary by a little armed rebellion now and again. The prevailing attitudes among coalition conservatives were in marked contrast. As opponents of a massive electoral mandate, the legitimacy that accrues to the big winner in democratic politics was against them. The men who witnessed congressional compliance during the 100 Days knew full well that the Leviathan abhorred in their doctrine was the new dispensation. The scope of action available to them was determined by this circumstance. They could only react as damage controllers, compelling compromise here or defeating a bill there, or even, as in 1937, bottling up an entire session of Congress. But the spirit of reaction—of dogged determination to stick to an agenda no longer honored by the American majority—hung heavily on them. The measure of their defeat may be assessed from the fact that even the irreconcilables voted for 50 percent of New Deal legislation, while the mean approval rate for the opposition was about 80 percent. No wonder that by 1945 their doctrine was obscure even to themselves. Roosevelt contributed to their confusion by ostentatiously annexing the Jeffersonian tradition to the New Deal in the annual Jefferson-Jackson Day dinners. This was a great effrontery. In doctrine, the New Deal gave the coup de grace to Jeffersonian principles. A more accurate genealogy of the New Deal leads to the Jeffersonians' ancient enemies, the Federalists, via the Bull Moose Progressives and Abraham Lincoln. Here, at this juncture, we encounter what may be the fundamental obstacle to sorting out the sense of "liberal" and "conservative" in the American political tradition. To underscore the confusion of these terms by the rhetorics of the New Deal, let me add to the evidence of Roosevelt's pretended Jeffersonianism the statement of that irreconcilable, Senator Josiah Bailey of North Carolina, who in 1935 wrote:

We must make the choice between the policy of liberty and the policy of control. I have made my choice and it is based on religious as well as political convictions. Being a Baptist, I am a liberal, and believe in liberty. Being a Democrat, I am a liberal and believe in liberty. Once we abandon the voluntary principles, we run squarely into Communism . . . there can be no half-way control.

To unravel this perplexing tangle requires that we understand how it was that in 1800 the American electorate endorsed Jeffersonian democracy as liberal and repudiated Federalism as oligarchic, whereas in 1932 these positions were exactly reversed. Can it be that liberal doctrine and conservative doctrine are fundamental to the American polity, and that the public endorses whichever suits its mood at a particular time? Is it conceivable that FDR, the champion of change and the scourge of reactionaries, was a conservative President? Is it conceivable that the so-called conservative coalition espoused vintage American liberalism, which became reactionary through opposition to a conservative, that is, Federalist, dispensation whose time had finally come? To play a little with these paradoxes might usefully jostle some dogmatic slumbers.

THE WELFARE STATE AS FEDERALIST LEGACY

Two doctrines, one economic, the other political, link the New Deal with Federalism. First, in economics New Dealers and Federalists affirmed what is known as political economy; that is, they construed the fiscal and legislative powers of government as a distinct force supervening on the market. They accordingly deemed it a legitimate and necessary task of government to direct this force toward the achievement of specific economic and political ends. To affirm political economy is to reject the notion of the insulation of the market from government intervention, which Adam Smith made the core doctrine of classic economics. If we are to understand how laissez-faire acquired its status in America as a great democratic doctrine, we must grasp the political motives that inspired Smith. Free enterprise, he believed, tends to diffuse wealth and liberty broadly. He argued that legislative restraints on trade attempt, by artificial means, to direct the market into channels in which it would not flow, left to itself. These channels are the mercantile and financial institutions of great wealth, which achieve preponderance through the instrumentalities of government favor (e.g., monopolies, licenses, privileges, exemptions, and bounties). The beneficiaries of favor, Smith argued, constitute a class whose superior social position is due entirely to regulative artifice. The removal of artificial restraints on trade and production, which was what was meant by laissez-faire, was, accordingly, a formula for popular democracy. Such was the doctrine that Jefferson espoused against Federalist schemes for the concentration of wealth and political power. Because the schemes were copied from British experience, that provenance made them, in America, automatically Tory. Jeffersonians took full electoral advantage of this circumstance. But the British system, which was the model throughout mercantile Europe, was put in place by the Junto Whigs who consolidated the Revolution of 1688 by creating a national debt. That debt became the bone of contention between Court and Country Whigs. In America the Federalists embraced the Court Whig interpretation of free government, whereas the Jeffersonians espoused the Country Whig doctrine, newly updated by Adam Smith.[2]

The second proposition linking the New Deal and the Federalists is a political maxim: that the fiscal preponderance of the federal treasury is a crucial tool for the consolidation of political power. Franklin Roosevelt gave this arch-Federalist concept effect, and in so doing he fundamentally altered the flow charts of power in American government. The President became what Jefferson, without hesitation, would have styled a "monocrat." By 1945 the New Deal had realized Jefferson's worst fears for America's future. Roosevelt had engaged the nation in a great war, with all the predictable consequences for the consolidation of power. The nation's largest concentrations of private capital were small potatoes compared with the concentration of capital achieved by extension of the powers of expenditure and taxation. And social welfare programs were creating vast webs of dependency on the largesse of the dictator in the White House. As contemporary Jeffersonians such as M. E. Bradford are helping us to appreciate, the Lincoln presidency was a watershed for the growth of government into the Federalist mold. The great political issue of the Civil War, union versus state sovereignty, was a replay of the Federalist versus Anti-Federalist argument of the ratification days, as well as a replay of the 1800 election issue. The great ethical question at stake, whether blacks had a claim under America's equality doctrine, also echoes the young republic. Federalists were often abolitionists. The two northern authors of *The Federalist*, Hamilton and Jay, were officers of the New York State Abolitionist Society. Federalists recognized that standing firm on slavery was equivalent to abandoning federation. They accordingly agreed to the policy of silence that was meant to remove the issue from political contention. The political cost associated with its removal was that it gave slave-owning patricians a free hand to stigmatize Federalists as enemies of equality. Lincoln as standard-bearer of Jefferson's party engrafted the Federalist political commitment onto it.

Theodore Roosevelt as progressive Republican put the axe to Adam Smith's political argument for laissez-faire in adopting the Federalist commitment to political economy. The argument here concerns the "New Nationalism." Although Roosevelt did not declare the doctrine until 1910, his Osawatomie speech summarized a line of thought and action that lay at the core of the Progressive movement. The argument acknowledges that laissez-faire approximated the intended democratic outcome in a nation of farmers. Yet the outcome depended on a once-only capitalizing source, the abundance of virgin land. Jefferson had envisioned that there was land enough for 1,000 generations; but by 1900 all was under ownership. Moreover, laissez-faire did not prevent the concentration of manufacturing, financial, and mercantile capital, as Smith believed it would. The vanishing of the frontier, and the growth of urban populations under the auspices of great financial and manufacturing capital, meant that the independent agrarian citizen who kept his musket above the mantel was giving way to landless urban employees incapable of comprehending or affecting the gargantuan economic institutions that influenced so much of their lives. The welfare of the common man, to which Jefferson's party was committed, could, therefore, be served only by abandoning small government and reliance on the independent individual. Roosevelt was a critic of this legacy of the Republican party. Government, he believed, had to attend to the welfare of citizens whose individual power bore no proportion to the power of great capital. It became the task of democratic government to ensure compatibility between great capital and the citizenry; and this objective endowed government with a responsibility for broad paternalistic intervention. It became the obligation of government to provide a stable economic and social order in which justice and "equality of opportunity, and of reward for equally good service," could be achieved. The nation should have the power to regulate property "to whatever degree the public welfare may require," and the President was to be the "steward of the public welfare."

Roosevelt also attempted to mold the ethos of pioneers, whose vigor and enterprise he cherished, into a new ethos that corresponded to changed conditions. It was the notion of the citizen as nationalist. By attaching his affections and loyalty to the nation, the citizen threatened with impotence and obscurity would acquire stature by partaking of the greatness of the nation as it embarked on its new course as a great power in global politics. Roosevelt's low esteem for Jefferson was accompanied by high regard for Federalists, Hamilton particularly. Not only had Hamilton attempted to prepare the nation for empire by building a credit system, a military establishment, a transport system, and manufactures, but he had also invoked the general welfare clause of the constitution to justify such projects—to the dismay of Jefferson. To cap our thumbnail history of the transformation of the nation's ethos and institutions into the Federalist mold, let it be noted that Theodore Roosevelt also recognized the Lincoln presidency as a landmark in the consolidation of federal power for the public good.

RETHINKING LIBERALS AND CONSERVATIVES

These observations suggest some alternative ways of thinking about the baffling inconsistencies in current interpretations of liberal and conservative. The identification of the New Deal as a corruption of the principles of liberty and as a baneful transformation of the American polity occurs on the ground of Jeffersonian republicanism, if one is an American; and on the ground of classical economics, if one is European. But from the Federalist perspective, the political structures and aims of the welfare state appear as the delayed fulfillment of a manifest destiny. The endurance of the Jeffersonian tradition, or, alternatively, the late arrival of the welfare state, is due to the plenty of land that formed the Jeffersonian experience in the colonial period; six generations were able to repeat that experience. Eventually land had to be exhausted, metropolises had to form, and the nation had to become an empire; in other words, it was manifest destiny that youthful, agrarian America would become a mature, urban nation. (Jefferson understood this as well; it was indeed his anxiety.) All mature nations are welfare states. Until the advent of democracy, welfare redistribution flowed through the institutions of aristocratic monarchies. These were the parish church and county sheriff, poor relief, religious orders dedicated to specific care, kinship exchange, the obligations of service, and patronage. When the French Revolution abolished the ancien régime, it merely substituted the salaried clerk for the priest, and the civil servant for the noblesse de robe. The fundamental concept of entitlements attaching to social status was retained under new interpretations entrenched legally as rights. This pattern was repeated by every modernizing European nation, including Prussia and the Soviet Union. The advent of the welfare state posed a fundamental legitimacy question in America because the young, land-rich nation had departed drastically from European models of social and government structure. In 1800 social structure scarcely rose above the level of rural district and town. Social status was the product of local ethos. The only welfare entitlements were those volunteered by Christian charity. Otherwise, there were political rights, which made no distinction among persons. As population grew, vocations diversified and wealth accumulated, the inequalities that invariably accompany status differentiations and entitlements began to develop. The welfare state in its Square Deal prototype and New Deal version came to terms with inequality by settling an order of status and entitlements. Critics as well as advocates of the welfare state often say that it was and remains a great leveler. The suggestion here, however, is to the opposite effect. In Europe the welfare state modernized the ancient system of status by detaching it from inherited privilege. In America it legitimated, through legislative enactments and new idioms, a social stratification unacknowledged in law or administration. The welfare state became the means by which indigenous ideals of justice, freedom, and equality found expression in a mature, complex society marked by enormous inequalities of wealth, power, privilege, and opportunity.

From this perspective we may perhaps throw some light on the difference between American and European conservatives. If Burke's *Reflections on the Revolution in France* be taken as the first testament of European conservatism, then its essence is the defense of class—the valorization of the aristocratic ethos against leveling, social planning, and tumultuous change, including changes of manners induced by consumerism. But because mature polities are necessarily hierarchical, leveling is episodic only. The enduring problem for European conservatives has been to find the avenues for perpetuating the aristocratic ideal, inclusive of its religious component, among elites composed of individuals recruited from all social strata. European conservatives have not typically experienced difficulties coming to terms with the governmental "intervention" characteristic of the welfare state. In England, France, and Germany they were at odds with the liberals about laissez-faire; and as "Tory socialists," they often took the lead in framing protective legislation. In America the problem was to create, from a geographically dispersed, socially undifferentiated, highly individualistic mass, cadres of public-spirited elites. This was the problem posed in *The Federalist* and explored with great subtletly by Tocqueville. The obstacles were Jefferson, and Madison after his defection from Federalism. The solution proved to be time, Lincoln, and the two Roosevelts. After the 100 Days, American and European conservatism were on a converging course.

It will be seen that I have delivered on my initial suggestion that FDR was a conservative. It is the ineluctable conclusion of the identification of the New Deal opposition as Jeffersonians. The conclusion nevertheless bears the marks of paradox, for the good reason that it was obtained by abstracting, in the manner of *The Federalist*, from all considerations except the requisites of political order for a free people. This abstraction has enabled me to attend to the permanent features of political order. To complete my task, I will discuss New Deal radicalism, which I view as a specific interpretation of the welfare state.

NEW DEAL RADICALISM: THE TRANSFORMATION OF PROGRESSIVISM

Although Franklin Roosevelt eschewed exotic doctrines and discouraged the idea of a New Deal philosophy, his presidency occurred at a time of great ferment of ideas. Advocates of these ideas attached themselves to the New Deal as senior administrators or as spokesmen, and imposed a visionary interpretation on the welfare state. They stated this interpretation so forcefully and frequently that many conservatives came to believe that the visionary intentions ascribed to the welfare state were part and parcel of its substance. I refer to the utopian concept that the instrumentalities of the modern state, when directed by correct theory, are the means for the replacement of pain, squalor, and oppression by the realization of human potential. I style this concept visionary because it is at odds with the very structure of politically organized society. Hence it is inconsistent with the actual performance of welfare states, and accordingly the public good under its radical interpretation is an endless quest. Conservatives who do not recognize that New Deal radicalism was only a visionary interpretation of permanent political structures engaged in the futile exercise of opposing the substance of the welfare state when their proper object was its style and interpretation. The radical interpretation of the welfare state during the New

Deal may be parsimoniously described as Deweyite with a supporting cast of miscellaneous socialists; its universal apostle and oracle was Margaret Mead.

John Dewey stated in American idioms the doctrine of Social Man issuing from nineteenth-century sociological systems purporting to be the science of society. Social Man is the negation of the robust individualism that fascinated the fin de siècle. "The world wants men great, strong, harsh, brutal—men with purpose who let nothing, nothing, nothing stand in their way.'' So wrote novelist Frank Norris, characterizing in these muscular words the sentiment that many reformers believed lived in the hearts of the new men of empire. Social Man is the legendary negation of the legendary entrepreneur. He finds his whole pleasure in compliant interaction with others. Because he thinks of himself only in his relations to others, he is incapable of anti-social behavior and cannot hold an independent opinion. Thanks to the new pedagogy, his inner and private self has been washed out, and with it, the springs of untrammeled competition and conflict have dried up. Gone with them are the springs of honor, veneration, and love. This is the other-directed "ultimate man," the corporate team player, and—at the outer reaches of the legend—the eusocial humanoid of Brave New World.

Yet the pedagogy and conditioning meant to produce Social Man also chartered the extreme indulgence of whim and sentiment that came to be called the "autonomous personality" obtained through permissive education. Inspecting the apparent contradiction of these two models of human conduct, we find that Dewey and the social progressives did not reject the intoxicating fin de siècle individualism for which "everything is permitted." Instead, they attempted to domesticate it by relocating individual liberty in a socioeconomic context that redirected energies from private economic aggrandizement to private self-realization. To express this in native political idiom: the progressive interpretation of the New Deal attempted to combine extreme Federalism with extreme Jeffersonian liberty.

This paradoxical combination is at the heart of the reform liberalism extending from the Wilson administration to the present day. Its characteristic politics is to launch successive waves of liberation on the pathos of a newly discovered repression. The remedy is to transfer wealth to victims through tax measures, and to impose government regimentation to prevent the continuance of the currently fashionable victimization.

Because classic economics lacks the conceptual wherewithal to measure the economic effects of political competition and policy, this major process went undescribed until the recent advent of public choice theory. It is now recognized that the sundry social welfare interest groups and professional organizations may be represented as entrepreneurial associations competing, by means of persuasion, for shares of public monies. The oppression-and-liberation message, in other words, is a commodity that, when purchased by votes and other political means, entails tangible resource gains for some and intangible self-esteem rewards for others. From this perspective the truth content of the message is immaterial; one is concerned with it merely as a mechanism by which identifiable groups transfer increments of wealth and power from others to themselves.

This process presents few novelties. It is powerfully described in *The Federalist* and other basic studies of politics. The novelty lies, rather, in the kinds of liberation that have been pursued, as well as in the concept that imparts to apparently disparate liberations their sense and direction.

What have these liberations been? New Deal intellectuals struck out in many directions, but the theme that has proved to be of enduring importance is sexuality. They did not of course discover sexuality as an object of scientific research and social or therapeutic manipulation. This was achieved by Europeans a generation previous. But they did give it a wide currency before the war; from the sixties it burgeoned into what is sometimes called the sexual revolution. This new wave of liberation comprises elements that heretofore have been almost universally regarded as social poison—promiscuity, pornography, homosexuality, abortion, the single-parent family, sexual equality, high-tech reproduction, and the convenient death (euthanasia). These far-reaching changes were, to no small degree, market-driven. The contraceptive pill became a money-spinner without the services of Madison Avenue. Pornography was a lucrative industry before its legal tolerance. Abortion clinics performed 600,000 illegal procedures annually before *Roe v. Wade*. But they were not merely market-driven. These innovative choices, illegal or criminal in 1950, shed their formerly stigmatized status, thanks to well-directed propaganda that endowed them with the sanctions of justice, social responsibility, and free choice. This was done, and could only be done, by stigmatizing pre-existing moral judgments and legal opinion as obsolete, repressive, irresponsible, and inhumane. There is no precedent for so rapid a transformation of deep values.

CONCLUSION

This brief sketch of New Deal radicalism and its aftermath is meant to indicate that its connection with the structures of the welfare state is adventitious—a chance encounter in the course of history. The essential connection is with science as the endless quest of discovery and manipulation. Science as an element of politics has been extensively studied, but it is not well known because we lack a theory able to relate its institutional embodiment (where we find politics as usual) to its intellectual penetration, which is unique among human activities. Institutional science has perfected the synthesis of open recruitment and earned status with hierarchy, favoritism, and resource concentration. It has all the marks of bureaucratic conservatism. But its conceptions and undertakings are the truly radical force at large today. Mere political radicalisms are no match for it; by comparison they are repetitive and dull. The message for political theorists is that the laboratory has superceded the public stage as the primary theater of action for human weal and woe. The new task, then, is to describe and understand the rule of the experts.

NOTES

1. George H. Nash, *The Conservative Intellectual Movement in America Since 1945* (New York: Basic Books, 1979).

2. Accurate description of the interplay between economic and political thought in America depends on recognizing that *The Wealth of Nations* was an apology for agrarian, not industrial, capitalism, which is neither discussed nor anticipated in that work. This is why the Southern agrarians could embrace Smith's vision of the benign effects of small government and the free market. See Joyce Appleby, *Capitalism and a New Social Order: The Republican Visions of the 1790s* (New York: New York University Press, 1984); Hiram Caton, "The Preindustrial Economics of Adam Smith," *Journal of Economic History* 45 (1985): 833–53; Caton, "The Second American Revolution," *The Eighteenth Century* 28 (1987): 69–82; Caton, *The Politics of Progress: The Origins and Development of the Commercial Republic, 1600–1835* (Gainesville: University Presses of Florida, 1988), 473–92, 504–11.

An Appraisal of Roosevelt's Legacy: How the Moderate Welfare State Transcended the Tension Between Progressivism and Socialism

> "A moderate welfare state does not quarrel with inequalities *per se*, but with entrenched economic disparaties which threaten to crush those of ability and effort. (This is what FDR meant by 'economic royalism.') The moderate welfare state, like the action of 'equal opportunity' itself... does not deny—indeed, it presupposes—that public policy should promote equal chances to achieve unequal things, and to reap the fruits thereof... It neither questions the reality of distinctions or merit, nor doubts that those are *ipso facto* distinctions of worth."
>
> Clifford Orwin, "Welfare and the New Dignity,"
> *The Public Interest* 71 (Spring 1983)

Roosevelt's New Deal has been described by some as "the prologue to Communism in America," and in order to substantiate that view, his critics have emphasized that he was fomenting class war by talking about the great industrial and financial interests as money changers and economic royalists. As a matter of fact, Roosevelt leveled the charge of money changers against big industry and finance in his First Inaugural Address, and complained about economic royalists in his second presidential campaign, giving the impression of a conspiracy on their part. His rhetoric clearly exaggerated the existing state of the danger, at least from them, but his intention was to expose the threat to capitalism by exaggerating it. That he wanted to appeal to popular prejudice is not at all surprising, considering the resistance of powerful moneyed interests to his programs and policies, but there is no suggestion here that Roosevelt ever intended to undermine the tradition. He surely reinterpreted the tradition profoundly, for there is no doubt that the welfare state goes well beyond anything the framers of the Constitution might have envisioned. But Roosevelt, the statesman who introduced the welfare principle, did not consider it to be a radical change; that is, it was not a change that went to the root of the system.

THE AIMS OF FDR: THE NEW DEAL

FDR managed political life in America more effectively than any other twentieth-century political leader, for more than anyone else he came to grips with the problem of the class struggle, arguing that economic freedom is an essential part of political freedom. The masses were disaffected by great dislocations in the economy, and he used the rhetoric of the class struggle in order to persuade them that his was a sympathetic ear. But he rejected the radical egalitarianism of the Marxist doctrine. Roosevelt's New Deal did not want to place property at the mercy of the propertyless or make freedom the preserve of the propertied. The New Deal attempted, rather, to achieve the right mean by integrating restraints over the processes of the economy and the freedoms of the individual into a regime that could provide for the greatest good of the greatest number.

On the occasion of the Supreme Court's invalidation of the National Recovery Administration, an editorial in the *New Republic* stated: "Either the nation must put up with the confusions and miseries of an essentially unregulated capitalism, or it must prepare to supersede capitalism with socialism. There is no longer a feasible middle course."[1] The fact is that the New Deal involved a considerable interference with private property. It operated on the assumption that government is entitled to interfere with property, and, to some extent, redistribute property. Roosevelt was in favor of private property, but he was not opposed to government interference with property that he conceived to be in the public interest or the common good. In other words, the emphasis was on private property, but not necessarily on private property wholly at the disposal of the individual or individual corporation. Roosevelt understood that an essentially unregulated capitalism leads to concentrated economic power, to the nakedness and violence of the class struggle, and, ultimately, to socialism. As he stated to the Congress in 1938: "Capital is essential; reasonable earnings on capital are essential; but the misuse of the powers of capital or selfish suspension of the employment of capital must be ended, or the capitalistic system will destroy itself through its own abuses."[2] And this is precisely why Marxism teaches that capitalism, simply speaking, leads inevitably to socialism by its own logic. What has evolved in America is a semifree or controlled capitalism, that is, an economic system that the government regulates, but does not operate. But the radical advocates of free private enterprise have never understood that government regulation is not socialism, and if properly guided, it prevents socialism.

FDR's conservative critics have helped to promote the false notion that the public concern for the economic interests of the many is the preserve of Marxism, but FDR rejected the notion of the inevitability of class divisions and the tendency of labor and capital to conflict. The particular resolution the New Deal achieved, which aimed at redistributing benefits between the various groups and interests in the society, had a powerful moderating effect on that portion of the society most susceptible to the attractions of a class orientation. The New Deal consciously nourished the expansion of the middle class, which constituted a stabilizing and moderating force in American life, for it tended to blur all distinctions of class without blurring distinctions between interests.

Roosevelt's New Deal constituted a profound modification of the traditional American democracy, a modification arrived at through a break with the earlier liberalism. We can see most clearly what that break effected by the New Deal means when examining the establishment of the welfare state. The question naturally arises as to whether we should understand the changes effected by the New Deal (that is, the coming-into-being of the welfare state) as a regime change or as a continuation of the existing regime. The great task for FDR was that of recreating democratic political institutions (how the American democracy could be improved without being fundamentally changed), which was tantamount to the introduction of a new quality into the regime. But the introduction of that new quality was done in such a way as to preserve the essential nature of the regime, that is, its liberal democratic character.

It seems that the accepted interpretations of the New Deal do not pay sufficient attention to the distinctive character of its innovations, and furthermore, the accepted interpretations are based on what amounts to a depreciation of the welfare state as a departure from the earlier liberalism. Owing to the collapse of the earlier liberalism, it became necessary to reexamine liberalism with a view to the question of whether the traditional understanding of the relationship between the government and the economy was adequate. The central errors of the earlier liberalism, Roosevelt maintained, were its unrestricted individualism, its policy of encouraging smallness and discouraging economic concentration (that is, its anti-trust approach of breaking down and destroying concentrated economic power), and its narrow and inflexible view of the functions of government. The Great Depression thrust on the government the responsibility for the general performance of the economy. FDR's New Deal rejected the notion that an economic system such as that of the United States would regulate itself automatically by the uncontrolled competition of private enterprise, and therefore it imposed regulations and controls on the economy as a whole. The view that the happiness and well-being of the greatest number should be provided for by government is, in modern terms, a welfare-state view, and it emerged in this country in the period of the Great Depression.

The earlier liberalism and the New Dealers shared the view that the concentration of economic power provides a threat to democracy, but the earlier liberalism had similar fears about the concentration of governmental power. Accordingly, the earlier liberalism sought to decentralize concentrations of economic power, whereas the New Dealers were more inclined, with some exceptions, to use regulatory legislation (i.e., governmental power) to control such concentrations. The New Dealers, in contradistinction to the earlier liberalism, envisioned a cooperation, not a conflict, between governmental power and private economic power, that is, between politics and private property, but with the political as the controlling element.

The earlier liberalism could be characterized as follows. The more fundamental issue of political reconstruction is almost entirely subordinated to the restoration of the old competitive system, that is, improving private competition or freedom of competition, which would require only a limited government. That liberalism called for the destruction of monopolies and trusts, not their regulation. There was an ill-defined recognition that some regulation was needed, but no principle was stated. In the New Deal, on the other hand, there was a principle stated that government must undertake responsibility for the maintenance and health of the economy as a whole to the point of rearranging that economy, if necessary, and redistributing its benefits. This moves away from an emphasis on the conditions of happiness toward the enjoyment or possession of happiness understood as material happiness or well-being. The welfare state is a society in which material happiness or well-being is no longer merely privately pursued, but now becomes a matter of governmental concern. The question arises, therefore, as to whether one should understand this shift as a qualitative shift in American politics as opposed, say, to a mere acceleration of political actions.

NEW DEAL POLICIES

Basil Rauch, a New Deal historian, asks whether the great series of New Deal measures, which included the National Labor Relations Act, the Social Security Act, and the Fair Labor Standards Act, represents a "new departure" in American political thought and practice. His answer is that the sheer quantity of governmental reformist activity initiated by the New Deal produced a "qualitative change" in American government—what is called positive government or the welfare state. Something new enters the tradition, Rauch admits, but it must be understood as derivative from the sheer quantity of reformist activity.[3] The quantitative change, from a certain moment on, becomes a qualitative change, and therefore the New Deal can be reduced to a series of legislative acts initiated by the Roosevelt administration. This interpretation of the New Deal leads to the consequence that there was no change, strictly speaking, and that all the fuss raised by the opposition was merely a reaction to the speed with which the series of New Deal legislative acts unfolded.

In Rauch one sees reflections of the notion that the New Deal did unthinkingly what it was driven to do, and that the driving force was the boiling up of events and not the grasp of the significance of those events by FDR or the direction given them by New Deal legislation. For to say that the qualitative change that had come about did so by the sheer force of the multiplicity of ad hoc responses to immediate problems is simply to say that the New Deal did not know what it was doing. FDR did not know the deepest roots of, nor could he foresee, the fullest consequences of his political actions. But he did act, and he did know, in principle, the character of the changes his actions were bringing about. Hence we may conclude that the principle was the directing force of the several legislative acts that made up the New Deal, no matter how clumsy some of those acts might have been. It is no small evidence of this that FDR gave a name to the whole before any of its parts were cast, for he introduced the term New Deal in his acceptance speech for the presidential nomination in July 1932. "I have . . . described the spirit of my program as a 'new deal,' which is plain English for a *changed* concept of the duty and responsibility of Government toward economic life."[4]

To understand the welfare state means to understand it in its relation to the Lockean-Jeffersonian tradition. The Declaration of Independence defines the function of government in terms of a certain understanding of the relation between happiness and the conditions of happiness. According to that understanding, life, liberty, and the pursuit of happiness constitute the conditions of happiness, and it is the function of government to guarantee those conditions, but not happiness itself. FDR, on the other hand, believed the function of government to be that of achieving the greater happiness of the greater number. He seemed to consider happiness as well-being, and he defined his own understanding of the change in terms of the movement from political to economic rights. It is this fundamental change in emphasis that gives the New Deal its distinctive character as a political movement, for from then on government furnished not only the conditions of happiness, but also, to a considerable extent, the enjoyment or possession of material happiness, which might properly be called well-being. Well-being or welfare is a kind of in-between concept, in between the conditions of happiness and happiness itself. It seems clear that Roosevelt was able to articulate what was happening more successfully than any other individual of that period.

THE NEW DEAL AS A CORRECTIVE, NOT A REVOLUTION

As a result of the climactic experience of the Great Depression, and the manner in which that depression was understood, the earlier liberalism became seriously threatened. The contribution that the New Deal made to the American political tradition consisted in correcting the earlier liberal view to the extent of correcting its narrow understanding of the functions of government (or of the relationship between government and the economy), and only in this light can we see the character of the New Deal in its full dimensions. Fundamental to the welfare-state position was Roosevelt's contention that "government has the final responsibility for the well-being of its citizenship," that is, for securing the material happiness or well-being of its citizens.[5]

The specific New Deal thesis was that government has the responsibility to provide not merely for the conditions of happiness but also for something approaching happiness itself or what we may call well-being or welfare. The difference between the welfare state and the Lockean-Jeffersonian liberalism would then seem to be rooted in the fundamental difference between happiness or well-being and the pursuit of happiness as the end or aim of the state. The essential failure of the earlier liberalism consisted in a one-sided and oversimplified concentration on individualism and all that this implies for politics and government. The correction of that view involves a realization that the function of government is more than a mere matter of guaranteeing life, liberty, and the pursuit of happiness, as has been so often supposed in our earlier political thought. FDR transcended some of the limitations of liberal democracy and even enlarged its horizons by teaching that a democratic society requires for its preservation the promotion of equality of opportunity through governmental provision for well-being or welfare.

, Surely the crucial difference between the earlier liberalism and the welfare state had something to do with the terms of the relationship between the government and the economic system. In the Progressive movement at the turn of the twentieth century, governmental regulation found a place. Theodore Roosevelt, William Howard Taft, and Woodrow Wilson all presided over the country during the introduction of some regulatory measures. But that regulation was not based on solid reflection on the relation between politics and the economy. The governmental regulation of progressivism did not reexamine the doctrines of nineteenth-century economic liberalism, according to which the happiness of the individual, understood in terms of economic well-being, was thought to be beyond the reach of governmental provision. There was, as it were, a tendency in nineteenth-century liberalism to reduce politics to formalism. The New Deal, driven by its motive force—the mind of Franklin D. Roosevelt—saw politics aimed at some substantive good for the individual. The subordination of the economy to the government that the New Deal sought to accomplish through regulation integrates economic well-being, or welfare, into the purposes of government and, in doing so, points beyond the prior formalism.

In what is apparently the generally accepted understanding, the New Deal was constituted essentially by the multiplicity of ad hoc responses to immediate problems, and that understanding is therefore incapable of taking very seriously the statesmanship of FDR. But according to our understanding, any adequate explanation of the New Deal must take into account the dimensions of the Roosevelt revolution, for implicit in that revolution was a conscious and deliberate attempt, on the part of FDR, to effect a fundamental change in orientation of government in its relationship to economic life—the coming into being of the welfare state, with its regulated or controlled economy. Accordingly, that fundamental change in orientation accomplished by the New Deal depended on the solution of a theoretical question: What is the purpose of liberal democratic government? Is it to provide merely for the conditions of happiness, or must it supply something of happiness itself, understood as well-being or welfare? It is only in the context of these considerations that one can make an appraisal of Roosevelt's legacy.

The welfare state surely differs from socialism precisely in that it does not abandon the principles of liberal democracy that call for the establishment of and respect for individual rights, including the right to property. But FDR did not seem to realize that, in constantly seeking to strengthen economic equality, the human personality could in fact become submerged in the interest of a better-regulated economic life, with its emphasis on health, welfare, and freedom from want. FDR may not have foreseen it, but the human passion for welfarism could result in what Tocqueville referred to as a soft despotism that

makes the exercise of free choice less useful and rarer, restricts the activity of free will within a narrower compass, and little by little robs each citizen of the proper use of his faculties. . . . It does not break a man's will, but it softens, bends, and guides it; it is not at all tyrannical, but it hinders, restrains, enervates, stifles, and stultifies so much that in the end each nation is not more than a flock of timid and hardworking animals with the government as its shepherd.[6]

FDR did not perceive that the claims of the welfare principle, pushed steadily toward their utmost extreme, could be fatal to the development of the human faculties.

When viewed from the perspective of the great crises in American history, the American experiment in self-government was faced in the 1930s with what was perhaps its greatest test for, although in the crises of the eighteenth and nineteenth centuries America was to be regarded as test case for liberal democracy, in the crisis of the twentieth century America is not the mere example, but the very citadel of liberal democracy. In that difficult and most critical period Roosevelt won the allegiance of a restive democratic nation, and at the same time his statesmanship added a new dimension to American political thought, for in the tension between progressivism and socialism he and, through him, the country rose above those alternatives. One could almost say that FDR insinuated his version of liberalism into the American political mind, which, as such, provided a viable alternative to the ideologies of progressivism and socialism. For, in a very emphatic sense, the coming into being of the welfare state required the emergence of a higher plane of thought regarding American ends than that which informed the Progressive movement.

Indeed, it would be no exaggeration to say that Roosevelt so completely set the tone for the politics of succeeding generations that we still think and act largely within the broad lines of the liberal doctrines that he articulated during the New Deal period. But in any attempt to secure that necessary balance between stability and social change in a political democracy, there is nothing more needed than the continuous confrontation of liberal and conservative principles and, as a result of their action and reaction to one another, the producing of orderly change, that is, reform rather than revolution. Surely part of the reason for the complacent character of present-day liberalism is the absence of a respectable alternative to that liberalism, for in the place of a healthy conservatism, with sound and generous principles and with eloquent spokesmen, there exists only a shadow that can be easily dismissed as mere reaction or mere selfishness. The liberalism that exists today seldom rises above simpleminded libertarianism. The cracker-barrel conservatism, which is a reaction to that liberalism, is largely compounded of a merely older liberalism, on the one hand, and sheer mean-spiritedness on the other.

NOTES

1. "Social Control vs. the Constitution," *New Republic*, June 12, 1935, 118.

2. Franklin D. Roosevelt, "Annual Message to Congress, January 3, 1938," in *The Public Papers and Addresses of Franklin D. Roosevelt*, ed. Samuel I. Rosenman, 13 vols. (New York, Random House, 1938–50), 7:9–10. Hereafter cited as *Public Papers and Addresses*.

3. Basil Rauch, *The History of the New Deal* (New York, 1963), ix, x.

4. Roosevelt, "Address to the Business and Professional Men's League, October 6, 1932," *Public Papers and Addresses*, 1:782.

5. Roosevelt, "Annual Message to Congress, January 3, 1938," *Public Papers and Addresses*, 7:14.

6. Alexis de Tocqueville, *Democracy in America*, ed. J. P. Mayer (New York: Doubleday, 1969), vol. 2, pt. 4, ch. 6, pp. 692–93.

John A. Wettergreen

The Regulatory Policy
of the New Deal

My topic may properly be described as the regulatory policy of Franklin D. Roosevelt. For I believe, apparently unlike many others, that Franklin Roosevelt was decisive for whatever success the New Deal had in the regulation of commerce. Now the regulation of commerce may not seem to be an exciting topic, and it is sometimes treated as a technical problem, as a problem for experts, as an economic problem, as a problem of administration. It is not my intention to treat it in that way. Let me begin by pointing out how difficult it is for Presidents to have an influence on the regulation of the economy.

Presidents have trouble even regulating their own families, as the following story ought to indicate. There was one black sheep in Franklin Roosevelt's family, Johnny. Johnny Roosevelt registered as a Republican, and the story of how he became one is instructive. Johnny wanted to go dancing at the Mayflower one night. His father said, "That's fine, but remember you must be in by one o'clock because after one o'clock they lock the gates of the White House and you're out." Well, Johnny stayed out late and didn't get back in time. When he came to the gate it was locked, so he went to the guard and said, "Let me in, I'm the son of the President." Of course the guard had heard many such stories and replied, "Sorry, buddy, you'll have to stay out. You can get in tomorrow with the rest of the folks." Johnny Roosevelt spent the night on the streets and he certainly didn't like it; he thought he deserved better. So the next morning he went out and registered Republican, saying, "What good was it to be a Democrat, if you couldn't even get into the White House."

Now, to appreciate how difficult Roosevelt's problem was, that story ought to be compared with a parallel story that took place almost exactly ten years earlier. The son of Calvin Coolidge spent the summer of 1924 hoeing cotton in South Carolina—of course he couldn't get to the Mayflower from there—and hoeing cotton is hard work. As they went down one row and turned back up another row hoeing cotton, the man who was working with young Coolidge said to him, "If my father were in the White House, I wouldn't be hoeing cotton." And young Coolidge said to him, "If your father were my father, you would be."

You can see how much more difficult it was to regulate even fairly docile young people in that one decade. It is hard for us to appreciate how difficult the situation was at the time of the New Deal. I think students of the New Deal ought to reconsider the question from the viewpoint of a democratic politician subject to the demands of the day.

The following anecdote from a recent biography of Franklin Roosevelt is illuminating. Shortly after Roosevelt took office, a friend told him that if he succeeded in the task that he had set for himself, he would go down in history as the greatest American president; but if he failed, he would be condemned as the worst. Roosevelt replied quietly, "If I fail, I shall be the last." I think that is what Roosevelt thought was at stake. Every student has to decide whether that was so or not. Roosevelt, of course, was thinking of the grave economic, political, and social conditions in the country. It was not hyperbole to say that a third of the nation was economically in dire straits. But beyond this, Roosevelt had foreign policy in mind. Already in 1933 he discerned the grim outlines of the global conflict that became World War II. Grave threats to democracy from abroad were as much his concern as the grave threats at home. And these together were redoubtable challenges for a president who meant to do the job.

Today when we look back at the New Deal we have great difficulty imagining these conditions, and even more difficulty assigning them their proper weight. We have no experience that would make serious men wonder whether this President would be the last. This conference demonstrates just how differently we think. Currently, our debate does not touch this possibility; instead scholars debate whether the New Deal was inevitable or not, whether it gave rise to an authentic administrative state, whether it was the beginning of the bureaucratization of America. Of course the American Left thinks that it was the first hesitant, unsuccessful experiment with centralized planning and administration of the economy, the first step toward a socialist regime. And although the American Right deplores the growth of the administrative state, or creeping socialism, it generally agrees with this assessment of the significance of the New Deal. For the American Left, the important thing about the New Deal was that it introduced Keynesian economics, the first attempts, however feeble and experimental, in the direction of a socialist economy. The American Right deplores this as the source of today's irresponsible politics of tax, tax, spend, spend, elect, elect. So that is the perspective in which we commonly see the New Deal. There are reasons, which other chapters in this book have ably expounded, for looking at the New Deal from this angle.

There is some truth to those claims. But the New Dealers did not understand the New Deal in this way; and above all, Franklin Roosevelt saw it in a different way. The New Dealers generally saw it as a problem of the preservation of free government in the face of grave internal and external threats. Can this be dismissed as mere rhetoric? Charles R. Kesler characterized these claims of the New Dealers as "Democratic boiler plate." In other words, just mere campaign rhetoric designed to rally the troops against Republicans and to discredit the Republicans, but not with any genuine meaning. Is it the case that there were no grave threats to free government in the 1930s? Professor Kesler usually takes speeches very seriously. When he comes to this claim in one of Roosevelt's utterances, however, he dismisses it as "boiler plate." Has he forgotten that what a boiler plate does is keep the boiler from exploding? In my judgment, this boiler plate was essential. All New Dealers, no matter what their disposition on other issues might be, understood the situation to be this serious, and the rhetoric had to be repeated in order to concert effort. As a practical matter, these would have been grave circumstances, simply because the whole spectrum of American opinion thought that they were grave. In my judgment, the opinion corresponded to realities that were very grave. Russell Kirk is probably right that Americans would not respond with Jacobin or Bolshevik revolution to these circumstances, but polities go to pieces in other ways as well.

In particular, the New Dealers were confronted with a conflict that might erupt into a violent struggle between what they called labor and what they called capital, between business interests—people who owned some means of production and people who had nothing (or so the theory goes) but their labor to sell. One did not have to read the Socialist papers to consider this a serious threat. Since the time of Thomas Jefferson the Democratic party had worried that an industrial society might be incapable of free government. When the Great Depression came traditional Democrats who read nothing but Jefferson saw industrial conflict as a potential nemesis for free government. This Jeffersonian apprehension was not mistaken. The Depression in fact did strike a fatal blow against the bulwark of Jeffersonian democracy, the middle class—that is, the small-business men and small farmers who had been assumed by politicians of all types to be the backbone of the nation. One should not be complacent about this; the Great Depression, together with World War II, left us what we have been ever since, a nation of wage workers; 95 percent of us are without independent means of subsistence in the Jeffersonian (and Aristotelian) sense. If the American experiment in republican self-government requires an economically independent middle class, as Jefferson and Aristotle thought, the Depression had to be viewed as a profound crisis. There was thus a core of truth in the Democratic fear that the struggle between capital and labor might bring the American experiment to an end.

They thought that certain important lessons from history could be applied to their problem. The first and one of the most interesting was that they realized, as Ellis Hawley points out in his chapter, that bureaucratic solutions to government's problems were not likely to succeed. They had learned from the experience of the Progressives and of Woodrow Wilson that you could not expect to set up an agency to manage economic problems. Recall what happened during the

Wilson administration. Two agencies were set up—two important ones for our purposes. One, the Federal Trade Commission, was intended to prevent all commercial unfairness—it is practically laughable that a single federal agency should be given this immense task, but that was its assignment and professed aim. The second was the Federal Reserve Board, which still exercises considerable influence on our economy. But at the beginning of the New Deal everyone knew that it had been a factor in the failure of the economy in 1928–29. Even the Democrats had to admit that the Federal Reserve Board had been an important cause of the depths of the Depression. So the New Dealers had to recognize that the kinds of agencies that had been tried by the Progressives to prevent a crisis like the Great Depression had failed.[1]

Recall that there had nearly been a Great Depression in 1907. Teddy Roosevelt did not create an agency to avert that threat; he worked together with the Morgan banking interests to keep the panic from precipitating a depression. To be sure, when Morgan later took conspicuous credit for stopping the panic of '07, the Progressives became angry at that and did what they could to prevent any capitalist interest from claiming such responsibility. They set up the Federal Reserve Board. The Federal Reserve Board subsequently contributed to the depths of the Depression in important ways. The lesson of this debacle was not lost on FDR. The New Dealers knew that direct, commanding, bureaucratic control was unlikely to succeed.

The second lesson that had been learned was especially clear in the case of Franklin Roosevelt. Unlike Woodrow Wilson, FDR understood that it was essential to have a large productive, corporate economy. Roosevelt knew that the economic progress and political health of this nation depended on having giant business corporations. This was something that the Progressives could not face; the exception, of course, was Theodore Roosevelt. FDR understood that we could not hold our own in military power—we could not hold our own in a war with a totalitarian regime armed by modern technology—unless we had that kind of economy. And Franklin Roosevelt also learned from Theodore Roosevelt that such wars were likely to be the fate of the twentieth century. He was right and so was Teddy. That is what the New Dealers had learned from the failure of progressivism—you must resign yourself to the kind of economy that Thomas Jefferson found abhorrent.

Furthermore, the New Dealers had a very different attitude toward the regulation of commerce than is usual today. We are now taught to think that there are two forms of economic life in the universe. One is laissez-faire capitalism, the other is socialism. And we are said to have a mixed economy today, that is, a mixture of laissez-faire capitalism and of socialism. The notion of the mixed economy rests on the premise that the two elemental forms are capitalism and socialism. I do not think that this understanding of the nature of our political economy is correct, and it most certainly cannot reflect the original understanding of these matters during the founding era because the Constitution says that Congress has the power to regulate commerce. Surely no one wants to say that the the framers of the Constitution didn't favor a free economy, or that they favored socialism, however adulterated by freedom. They thought, on the contrary, that a regulated commerce was perfectly consistent with a free economy. On our current assumptions, this is paradoxical. How can we understand it?

Both the American laissez-faire capitalists and American socialists deny that a free economy can also be a regulated economy. Both presuppose a theory of political economy according to which individual or private interests are categorically opposed to the common interests of society. This is the assumption that the New Deal did not make. Instead, it tried to develop a program in which private goods would not radically oppose the public good. As an ideology, capitalism asserts the primacy of private or individual goods over against the public good. Socialism, on the other hand, asserts the primacy of social goods, of the public good, or common good over against "individualism" as though every individual's good were simply the product of society's efforts. But the founders' notion of the constitutional regulation of commerce asserts that there is a possible harmony of private interests with one another and that regulation is what produces that harmony. I am going to try to show you how that is possible. But the basic idea of regulation as we see it in the Constitution is that commerce has a purpose—producing wealth—and other kinds of associations in this society have purposes too. For example, the Army has a purpose: winning wars. And the church has a purpose: getting you into heaven. And so on. In any free society there will be a number of associations, each of which will have a purpose that is specific to it and each of which ought, if it is a free society, to be able to govern itself to achieve that purpose. So if corporations govern themselves well, we'll be wealthy. If churches govern themselves well, you will go to heaven; when armies are governed well by the government we win wars. And so on. But of course the production of wealth can go haywire, as in the Great Depression, and in that case it might well threaten the other ends of the various associations that compose American society. A capitalist may think he has a right to sell his products to the Soviet Union for his own benefit, but this compromises the social purpose of the army: victory. Given the variety of aims that such diverse social organizations will pursue, government must regulate commerce. It must do so in order to make sure that the production of wealth is harmonious with the other ends that any free society has to pursue. Franklin Roosevelt understood this. It is no longer understood by leading circles today, as I shall indicate toward the end of this essay.

THE CONSTITUTIONAL PURPOSE OF THE SECURITIES AND EXCHANGE COMMISSION AND THE NATIONAL LABOR RELATIONS BOARD

Let us consider how the New Dealers handled these various interests. The speeches about the two basic regulatory agencies that were created by the New Deal must sound strange to our ears. These two agencies were the Securities and Exchange Commission (SEC) and the National Labor Relations Board (NLRB). If you read the speeches, for example, about the SEC, you will see that New Dealers believed that the causes of the Great Depression were not economic problems, or problems of administration (breakdowns of bureaucracy, for example), or even political problems. They thought of the fundamental causes of the Depression as moral causes.

To put it very simply, the depression was seen as a punishment for sin. George Anastoplo has argued that Americans were in dire straits in the depression but did not think that they deserved it. This is not quite accurate. I would put it this way: They were in dire straits and they didn't know what they had done to deserve it. And one of the things that the New Deal tried to do was to offer a moral interpretation of the depression.

Now it might seem strange—to repeat—that what looks like an economic collapse would have more than merely economic causes. But that is what the New Dealers thought. Representative Lea of California, who favored the Securities Exchange Act, stated:

If I undertook to try to fix the responsibility for the debacle that came to the stock market in 1929, I would not attempt to place my fingers on the exchanges and blame them alone. I would recognize another culprit—Mr. American Citizen who wants to get something for nothing. He had a large part in reference to the stock speculation. Now for this reason, the object of the Securities Exchange Act is not merely to regulate exchanges. That is only incidental to its purpose.[2]

According to Congressman Lea, the regulation of the securities exchanges, of the stock market, was only incidental to the purpose of the legislation establishing the SEC. And Franklin Roosevelt concurred with this view. Here is his account: "The merchandizing of securities, stocks and bonds, and so forth, is really traffic in the social welfare of people, not just the economic welfare, but the general welfare, economic as well as in other respects."[3] According to the President, "the Securities Act of 1933" was "a program to restore some old-fashioned standards of rectitude to securities trading." Without an ethical foundation, Franklin Roosevelt always insisted, economic well-being cannot be achieved.

What, then, was the sin that caused the Great Depression, according to the New Dealers? The sin was something they called speculation. We are bound to be amazed at this because today these transactions are entirely normal; they are well regulated; they are even, in a way, quite useful tools of the market as it currently stands. For example, Roosevelt, his allies in Congress, and the most radical of the New Dealers believed that the short selling of stock was a sin. Bizarre as it seems, selling at less than market price on a stock to be delivered at some future date was held to be sinful. Moreover, it was the kind of sin that brought about the Great Depression. This sounded strange when I first read it. I thought, as I suppose others have, that they were just blowing smoke. But what did they have in mind? The train of thought was something like this. If you sell short, you are betting that the stock is going to go down. That means you are betting on failure. You are not expecting success. You put your money into a trade, hoping that the enterprise would fail, in which case a mere trade of this stock would win you money. So that even when the company failed, you would profit.

They viewed this in moral terms: it was not just wrong, it was sinful. So at first the Securities Act and the Securities Exchange Act absolutely forbade all short sales. From one standpoint, this was nonsense. A commercial man of any experience knows that short sales are extremely useful as commercial devices. And I am sure that if I can understand that, Franklin Roosevelt understood it quite well. Nevertheless, he denounced short selling as somehow a moral failing. Why?

Not surprisingly, the answer is politics. To Roosevelt's left there were people like Sam Rayburn and Adolph Berle, who regarded business corporations as inherently vicious and wrong. For them, stock was not really even property. They said it was nothing but a piece of paper. Most of us would be happy to own some of that paper property, but for Berle and Rayburn, it was not real property. For Rayburn, real property meant land; property is a house, crops in the field, not just some piece of paper that says you own a factory. You don't really own it. You can't go there and walk through it and make sure they are producing what they say they are producing. So Rayburn and the others thought that the corporation itself was a corrupting influence on morality, and thereby a threat to political democracy.

Franklin Roosevelt needed the support of Rayburn and Berle and their like. Most of us understand that what Rayburn said about the corporation is not true. The corporation is a wonderful device for encouraging the production of wealth. But these people, if they could have had their way, would have, at the very least, demanded national laws of incorporation. Franklin Roosevelt regarded this as sheer folly. He agreed with Theodore Roosevelt and Oliver Wendell Holmes, Jr., that this is an age of combination; we must expect and learn to live with great combinations both of capital and labor. Trying to prevent them is an exercise in futility or Ludditism.

This is one side of the equation. The idea of corporate enterprise was attacked from the extreme Left, and measures were advanced to suppress the corporation as a business form. Roosevelt had to contend with that. On the other hand, who was defending corporate enterprise? The spokesmen of capitalism were weak and demoralized. Take Richard Whitney, president of the New York Stock Exchange. You would think a man in his position would defend the interests of the stock exchange. What did Whitney say? "I claim that this country has been built by speculation and that further progress must be made in that line." That sounds like the overture to a defense. But when it came time to testify about the form of the SEC, Whitney said that he wanted the stock exchange to elect the majority of members to the SEC. Indeed, he demanded it as a matter of right. That would have made the SEC into a representative body, independent of the people's control. It would have given a publicly authorized, permanent voice to the securities exchanges in government. Usually that is what one calls socialism, when government corporations—in this case financial institutions— are official parts of the government. And that is what business was advocating at this time. What Whitney proposed was not unusual. It is what steel corporation executives looked for. It is what other big business interests looked for. Indeed, I think it would not be inaccurate to say that big business in this period was more inclined to socialism—that is, to centralized planning and administration of the economy—than was labor.

Roosevelt corrected this serious error by advancing a very careful distinction between what he called speculation and production. Speculation was wrong. What we needed, what was right, was production. If you try to understand that distinction, I think that you will see it does not really make sense as an account of commerce. As indicated earlier, some speculative transactions have to be made in order to further production. But it is not really advanced as an account of commerce. What Roosevelt had in mind was a standard of respectability or praise. Speculators ought not be the model for Americans; productive work ought to be. Roosevelt attempted to demote the speculator; his concern was that if speculators were lionized, most people would despair of work as a way to get wealthy. They would believe that the main way to get wealthy was by speculation. So the SEC was set up with the idea of breeding confidence in the securities markets as safe places, meaning places in which there was no speculation and in which the enterprises whose stocks were traded were genuinely productive. In what follows, I shall briefly explain how that was done.

For the moment let me take up the NLRB and the problems of labor. Labor was very different from capital because labor was badly divided against itself. There were two factions. One was the American Federation of Labor (AFofL); the other was the Congress of Industrial Organizations (CIO). The AFofL, led by William Green, wanted to organize workers by craft and by tools. The CIO, led by John L. Lewis, wanted to organize by industry. The question before the country was posed by these two factions. How should unions be organized? Should they be organized by the skill or the tools that a person uses? Or should they be organized according to the industry they are in? Apart from all the other difficulties we discover when we think the question through, the political question comes to this: the aim of the AFofL was to produce a nationally organized union that would be able to paralyze American industry with a general strike. In other words, if you organize by carpenters, what that means is that when carpenters go on strike, everyone stops work. Carpenters work in the auto industry, they work in steel, they work in the rubber mills, and so on. If carpenters went on strike it would, in effect, be a universal strike. William Green made no bones about it. He thought that labor's ultimate tactic was the universal strike. Labor would have ultimate power if it were able to close down the American economy at will. That is the kind of power William Green thought that labor should have.

Green did not want what he called the regimentation of labor. He dreaded what he had seen in Italy, Germany, and the Soviet Union, where there was no free labor movement. Unions were arms of the government and of the party, the totalitarian party. He feared that would be the fate of American labor. Therefore, he refused to take an active part in the reelection campaign of Franklin Roosevelt in 1936. Green was also opposed to the conservation corps and to other programs that had the odor of regimentation of labor.

The strength of Green's position should be clear. He wanted a free labor movement, a very good thing. But he also wanted to organize that movement with the idea of crippling the American economy whenever the movement saw fit. Roosevelt sought a way to prevent labor from acquiring such power.

On the other hand, there was the CIO, to be organized by industries. That would have resulted in a much weaker, that is, a less unified and economically powerful, labor movement. Politically, however, the CIO approach was more effective because labor could be organized more quickly; industrywide unions could be organized by the federal government. This is more or less what did happen. It is the counterpart of Whitney's policy for business; labor would become merely an organ of the central government. How did Roosevelt handle the danger this approach posed of a fusion of union and government? One should recall that John L. Lewis, the animating spirit of the CIO, thought that he could just buy the Democrats and, in particular, Franklin Roosevelt. He said openly that the United Mine Workers, his home union, and the CIO had paid "cash on the barrel head for every piece of legislation we have got."[4] So he thought he had bought a party and an administration. However, within a couple of years he was back in the Republican party—where he had been all during the 1920s— because Franklin Roosevelt would not give his union the apple of his eye, the organization of the smaller steel companies.

Roosevelt's aim in response was to keep labor divided against itself, preventing the AFofL and CIO from unifying into one union organized on one principle. At the same time, of course, he meant to secure firm labor support for the Democratic party, for free government, and for Franklin Roosevelt. He was successful in these aims. A tremendous price was paid for this policy of preserving both unions. The price was nearly two and a half years of what Roosevelt himself called industrial war. Of that bloody period Roosevelt said, it is "a short time in the education of a nation." Roosevelt had to teach the nation how to organize a free labor movement; in other words, the government was going to organize unions. But he intended that the unions would be cut free from the tutelage of the federal government; otherwise, they would become merely tools of the government, as William Green feared.

Roosevelt's way of handling this problem may be clearly seen in the design of the NLRB. It was designed not to settle the issue between the two kinds of labor unions. The crucial section 9B of the Act says:

The National Labor Relations Board shall decide in each case whether, in order to insure to employees the full benefit of their rights to self organization and to collective bargaining and otherwise to effectuate the policy of this act. The unit [meaning the organization or the union] appropriate for the purposes of collective bargaining shall be the employer unit, the craft unit, the plant unit, or the subdivision thereof.

That meant "We won't take any stand in the law between what the AFofL wants and what the CIO wants." So the NLRB would not be legally empowered to unify the national labor movement. It would instead allow the various labor organizations to fight it out among themselves. The touchy political issue of the proper principle of union organization, which would have threatened labor support for the New Deal however it was decided, would be for the new agency to decide case by case. In the early days of the NLRB it was set up to favor the CIO. That is, people were appointed to it who were favorably disposed to the CIO. Furthermore, the CIO was better organized and so, in the short run, they were more successful—not because of what government had officially done for them, but because of their own organizing efforts. In other words, the CIO would be grateful, but not too grateful, to the NLRB and the Democrats who were its framers.

In form, the NLRB and the SEC were different. But their purposes were remarkably similar. The NLRB sanctioned unions as being freely organized; the Securities Exchange Commission sanctioned corporations as being freely organized.

What perspective do these examples suggest about the regulatory policy of the New Deal? Much is made of periods in New Deal historiography. Scholars claim that there are two or three or four New Deals. For Roosevelt, I would say that there was only one New Deal and the cause of it was liberalism. The word liberalism really came into our political vocabulary with Franklin Roosevelt. He made it what it has become by using it to describe a certain partisan position. Roosevelt was the first to use it in its current sense. What did it mean? Almost invariably, liberals meant people who supported the New Deal. However, Roosevelt said that it meant something more than that. He said that the New Deal's programs were a means to liberalism's end. In this sense, what he meant by liberalism was "the broad movement of the modern western world toward free government." Indeed, this is a definition that he consistently gives: "The cause of free government in the West."[5]

He thought, and I think generally speaking the New Deal thought, that at the time there were two basic challenges to liberalism—that is, to free government. On the one hand, there was the problem already mentioned, the demoralization or the proletarianization of the citizenry, the destruction of the middle class. We have forgotten what was taken for granted before the New Deal—that wage workers were thought to be incapable of free government, incapable of ruling themselves and so of ruling the nation. And this opinion was very strong, especially in the Democratic party. In particular, this anti-democratic sentiment was strong among liberals at the time. For example, Walter Lipman, a journalist who was practically the paragon of liberal opinion for forty years, said in 1934 that the New Deal was an anti-democratic movement that had set itself up to counter the irrational desires of the masses. He approved of that. He thought that was good. And so liberalism had become, much to Roosevelt's dismay, anti-democratic. Many elements within liberalism even had the smell of totalitarianism.

Roosevelt intended to do his best to stop that. He tried to mold the crowd, what Walter Lipmann called the individualistic crowd, to become a self-governing majority.[6]

The SEC and NLRB must be seen in this context. The SEC was a way of restoring confidence that work could work, that you could succeed by working. The way to wealth was open to the industrious and not only to speculators or stocktraders. The NLRB was designed to encourage people to organize freely into unions through which they could act effectually for their own interests.

The other problem to which the New Deal's regulatory policy was addressed was a problem of scale. What Ellis Hawley says on this score is most instructive. The New Deal was highly suspicious of the collusion between big government, big business, and big labor. The Progressives had seen that problem, and the reason for the danger to free government is clear. Once the middle class is destroyed, nothing can prevent such collusion. No political force exists to oppose it effectively. How did the liberals of the day think they could handle this problem—that is, the collusion of big business, big government, and big labor?

There were some people, for example, Louis Brandeis, who said that the whole thing ought to just be dismantled: Big is bad. Brandeis declaimed, "If the Lord had intended things to be big, he would have made man bigger—in brains, and character."[7] Brandeis meant that the Lord didn't intend for there to be big business, big labor, and big government; somehow things had gone haywire. But Brandeis was an exception along these lines. Most liberals didn't hold this view. Liberal Democrats favored the outlawing of certain commercial practices as the way to handle this problem. In other words, they wanted a system of what we would call economic crimes. If people do certain things, put them in jail. Liberal Democrats wanted this in the context of the New Deal. We have a lot of that now: when Congress has to start arming Environmental Protection agents, then we have what amount to economic crimes. But that was not the approach of the New Deal (except in the way that I indicated respecting short sales).

This liberal Democratic approach was based on the premise that bigness was bad. Generally speaking, the Democrats thought that regulation was going to be ineffective because the regulatory agencies would be taken over by the interests they regulated. So, they thought, "Let's just make laws against certain commercial practices we don't like. If somebody does it, we'll throw him in jail."

On the other hand, the liberal Republicans favored regulation. They didn't want to just make certain economic acts criminal, but held, for example, that if labor unions freely organized, and if a class of public-spirited civil servants could be created, then collusion could be avoided.

Liberal opinion was deeply divided and didn't know what to do. Roosevelt's aim was always to get the friends of free government together and keep them united long enough to beat the Nazis. Incidentally, this is why I think it is proper to say he was an experimentalist. And his other goals must always be taken with that great political goal in mind: A war is coming, a great war is coming, and the friends of free government must be united to win it.

Moreover, FDR knew that there were enemies here. There were friends of the Nazis in the United States. They were not the people you might think. Roosevelt had to do things in order to discredit these people and get them out of public life—one of them was Joseph Kennedy. Concerning this part of his battle for the liberal mind, he said, "If the Congress knew I was doing these things, they would impeach me."[8] From the time he was elected he had in view the real possibility that he would have to fight such a war. He wanted the friends of liberalism as much as possible to be united against that eventuality.

His way of handling this problem, as I have indicated, was to interpret the New Deal to the American people as a moral crisis. He made it a crisis of what he called individualism. Roosevelt did not, like the socialists, simply reject individualism. Nor did he, like the capitalists, just assert what is known as "rugged individualism." He always refused to oppose these against one another, that is, to oppose individualism to the interests of a free society. He always thought that they could be harmonized. Here, for example, is a passage from his message to the Congress in 1938 that expresses Roosevelt's position quite clearly: "The ownership of vast properties or the organization of thousands of workers creates a heavy obligation of public service. The power should not be sought or sanctioned unless the responsibility is accepted as well."[9]

In other words, the people who set up corporations or the people who organized labor unions, both of them, should not assume such power unless they are willing to accept a public responsibility for their actions.

Nor should government sanction those activities, neither those of corporate financiers, nor those of labor union organizers, unless it is satisfied that they are acting with awareness of their obligation of public service. Roosevelt continued: "The man who seeks freedom from such responsibility in the name of individual liberty, is either fooling himself or trying to cheat his fellow man. He wants to eat the fruits of orderly society without paying for them."

To summarize, Roosevelt sought to have government sanction the free organization of corporations or of labor unions without allowing corporations or labor unions to become mere arms of the government. The country needs corporations that are profitable and productive, and you want to encourage Americans to form them. You want unions of the same description. How can you get them and not have them become mere lackeys of some bureaucracy or agency? The answer was the SEC and the NLRB.

The SEC certifies that this corporation was freely organized. Its organizers did not lie about what their assets were. They did not commit any fraud in getting organized. Similarly, the NLRB says, "This union is sanctioned." That is to say, it is legitimate (or, as I like to say, sanctified). So the blessing of the government, in a way, is put on it. The idea of New Deal regulation is that government will sanction unions and corporations as free associations. Government will not enter into the actual operation of these free associations: so the New Deal insisted that the SEC not incorporate; there would be no national law of incorporation.

The New Dealers did not want the government to be in the business of saying, "This is a legitimate investment." Or, even worse, "This is a good investment." Of course, that is what business wanted. Business wanted national laws of incorporation. They wanted the federal government to put seals of approval on their stock. Many congressmen were happy to go along with that, especially the left wing of the Democratic party, but Roosevelt said, in effect, "No, that would mean government would be colluding with business."

And similarly with labor. What John L. Lewis wanted was a collusion government. Roosevelt rejected that option.

So both in the case of raising capital and in the case of organizing workers, the New Deal pursued the same principle. The principle is that the choice of the citizen, whether in buying stock or in joining a union, whether to join a CIO union or an AFofL union, whether to purchase this or that corporation's stock— that choice ought to be a free choice. It ought not be a choice that was swayed by force or fraud. And the two agencies were designed to secure this freedom from force and fraud.

What is the legacy of the New Deal respecting these matters? Many things could be learned from this story, but above all, the New Deal should instruct us regarding the critical importance of the moral and political dimensions of economic life. The politicians of the New Deal were much more sensitive to these issues than we are today. We tend to think of economic problems as merely technical problems that are susceptible to economic solutions. Of course I would not want to deny that there are technical solutions, but that is not the whole story. No doubt the New Dealers erred, when they erred, in the other direction— they tended to view economic problems as merely moral problems that were susceptible to moral solutions. But it seems to me that if they erred, they erred more on the right side than we do.

The New Deal also was wary of the danger of government as an organizer of interest groups. One might almost say that the principle of the current regime is that the main function of government is to organize interest groups, supply them with the citizens' treasures, and be solicitous of their interests at every turn. The New Deal certainly did these things, as Ellis Hawley remarked. But it was mindful not to let unions and corporations become mere agents of the government. This was true above all in these crucial regulatory agencies, the SEC and the NLRB, which still exist today and perform their functions well. Unfortunately what both American liberals and conservatives seek today is to reduce business or labor to dependence. Conservatives are tempted to say, "Why don't we just have a national law of incorporation? It would be simple, it would be efficient and predictable." Ralph Nader agrees. Nader doesn't care about simplicity or efficiency, but he does want power to be located in one place.[10]

There is thus a corrective to be found in the original policy. The New Dealers were much more aware of the danger of collusion. They were also much more realistic about the prospects for free government in the modern world than contemporary politicians and intellectuals. Today I think people are inclined to suppose that "the system works"; we will probably never have to fight a war, or, if we do, we'll all be fried. But winning the next war was always on Roosevelt's mind.

In these respects I greatly admire the New Deal. Not that I think it was a success in the decisive respect. In fact it failed to solve the central problem. It did not repair the economy in such a way as to bring about a rebirth of the middle class. The legitimate aim of Americans for genuine economic independence was abandoned. I would like to see that aim return as an objective of public policy. I think it is still really possible. But the New Deal did succeed despite this failure because it preserved the spirit of the middle class, even down to this day.

NOTES

1. On the failure of Progressive regulation, see, e.g., *Operation of the National and Federal Reserve Banking Systems*, Hearings before a Subcommittee of the Committee on Banking and Currency, U.S. Senate, 71st Cong., 3rd sess., pt. 1, January 19–30, 1931, 3, 53 56, 65, 69–70, 128, 147; *Banking Act of 1935*, Hearings before the Subcommittee on Monetary Policy, Banking, and Deposit Insurance of the Committee on Banking and Currency, U.S. Senate, 74th Congress, 1st sess., April 19, 1935–June 3, 1935, 439ff; Caroline Whitney, *Experiments in Credit Control: The Federal Reserve System* (New York: Columbia University Press, 1934); Lloyd W. Mints. *A History of Banking Theory in Great Britain and the United States* (Chicago: University of Chicago Press, 1945), 262ff; G. Cullom Davis, "The Transformation of the Federal Trade Commission," *Mississippi Valley Historical Review* 49 (1962): 278ff; William E. Leuchtenburg, "The Case of the Contentious Commissioner: Humphrey's Executor vs. U.S.," in *Freedom and Reform: Essays in Honor of Henry Steele Commager*, ed. Harold M. Hyman and Leonard W. Levy (New York: Harper & Row, 1967), 278ff.

2. Quoted in Bernard Schwartz, ed., *Economic Regulation of Business and Industry: A Legislative History of U.S. Regulatory Agencies* (New York: Chelsea House, 1973), 3:2776.

3. *Public Papers and Addresses of Franklin D. Roosevelt*, ed. Samuel I. Rosenman, 13 vols. (New York: Random House, 1938–50), 7:41 (#5, 1938).

4. Saul Alinsky, *John L. Lewis* (New York: SUNY, 1947), 177.

5. See, e.g., *Public Papers*, "Address at Jefferson Day Dinner (St. Paul, Minn.)" 1: 630 (#129, 3/18/32). Cf. Theodore Roosevelt, "The Romanov Scylla and the Bolshevist Charybdis," in *The Roosevelt Policy* (New York: Current Literature Publishing: 1919), 3:1037.

6. See Lipmann's *Method of Freedom* (New York: Macmillan, 1934) as quoted with approval by Arthur Schlesinger, *Age of Roosevelt: The Politics of Upheaval* (Boston: Houghton Mifflin, 1957), 3:400.

7. *Letters of Louis D. Brandeis* (Albany: State University of New York Press, 1978), 5:527.

8. See William Stevenson, *A Man Called Intrepid* (New York: Harcourt Brace Jovanovich, 1976), 86–90, 159–163.

9. *Public Papers*, 7:10 (#1, 1938).

10. See Ralph Nader, Mark Green, and Joe Seligman, *Taming the Giant Corporation* New York: W. W. Norton, 1976), 15–61.

The Democratic Party: Honoring and Dishonoring the New Deal

When liberals hear that Hillsdale College is holding a conference on the legacy of the New Deal, they do not race for front row seats. This is not surprising. Hillsdale has a conservative reputation. Burying the New Deal, discrediting the legacy of Franklin Roosevelt, was what conservatives ardently desired for many decades. Reviving the spirit of the New Deal, honoring and imitating Franklin Roosevelt, meant preaching "the liberal gospel." Therefore, you may be surprised, even appalled, to read what serious and deeply thoughtful conservatives like John Wettergreen have written in defense of Franklin Roosevelt and his New Deal. This chapter is a kind of commentary on this amazing development (for it is worth pondering): that it now falls to conservatives to do justice and honor to Franklin Roosevelt and the New Deal.

What has the Democratic party done with the legacy of the New Deal? To understand what it has done, we must recollect a dimension of the New Deal and of Roosevelt's politics that is generally ignored: that the fighting was about the American idea of honor. Since roughly 1970 the Democratic party has radicalized the New Deal attack on the traditional Jeffersonian idea of honor. But it has not continued Roosevelt's attempt to reconstitute, refine, and reinvigorate a shared conception of honor. To anticipate my critique: for almost two decades the Democratic party has been doing its level best to dishonor the legacy of the New Deal by gutting Roosevelt's conception of democratic honor.

This may sound odd because the Democratic party claims to be the guardian of the New Deal legacy. One would think that the Democrats would have a great stake in defending what Roosevelt stood for, would make it a point of honor to defend him because their own honor is at stake. They no longer see the matter in that light. The task has fallen to conservatives, not because conservatives agree with Franklin Roosevelt, but because Roosevelt, more than any public man in living memory, stands for the United States. This is, in great measure, his accomplishment and legacy, for Roosevelt understood that Americans use parties and partisan leaders like himself to stand up for what they honor. What Americans expect from government is inseparable from what they expect of themselves, what they honor in themselves. As Roosevelt explained:

Most people, who are not on the actual firing line of the moment, have come to attach major importance only to the motives behind the leaders of the past. To them it matters, on the whole, very little what party label American statesmen bore, or what mistakes they made in the smaller things, so long as they did the big job that their times demanded to be done.[1]

In order to do justice to Roosevelt's legacy we must understand what the big job was. In this same speech he gave a classic formulation, which remains the way Americans think about Roosevelt: "Behind us lies accomplished a really big job. It was the creation out of the pure unadulterated funk of the early thirties, of a new spirit with which we can now face the forties."[2] We think of the Great Depression as an economic catastrophe, a big technical job of getting the economy working. But a funk is a moral condition or a state of the soul in which one shrinks from facing difficulties, or shirks responsibility. It is a dispirited condition in which one's faculties are not fully active, fully engaged in fighting back. To be without spirit, without pluck, not to stand up and fight back is dishonorable. Americans expect more of themselves. The "big job" of pulling oneself out of a funk is a job of reasserting one's spirit, showing that one is spirited. But Roosevelt speaks of creating a new spirit with which we can now face the forties. It was not simply a matter of recovering one's spiritedness and reasserting oneself. People had persisted in the "pure unadulterated funk of the early thirties," Roosevelt argued, because they were honoring the wrong virtues. A standard of praise and blame, a moral standard or a code of honor, was the cause of the funk. Roosevelt's big job was to challenge that standard of honor and modify it significantly.

After I indicate how Roosevelt undertook to do this, I shall briefly recount the story of how the Democratic party turned away from the big job, set about dishonoring the most important legacy of the New Deal, and became the cause of a prolonged funk—a depression of spirit—from which we have yet to recover.

DEMOCRATIC HONOR IN CONTENTION

The reader will need a provisional account of honor in American society, for the idea has gone out of fashion. I shall be arguing that the most important legacy of the New Deal was the new notion of democratic honor that Roosevelt introduced, and that the partisan heritage of the New Deal was a disposition to wage war against the conception of American democratic honor that enjoyed its apogee in the 1920s. Tocqueville's account of American honor may serve as a summary of this conception. For although Abraham Lincoln and Theodore Roosevelt had modified American traditions decisively by the 1920s, from a partisan standpoint theirs was, in the first instance, a Republican tradition that FDR had to handle with care, rather than a Democratic tradition he could confidently assert. And as a Democratic president, he was in a position to work more directly on the notion of honor for which the Democratic party had spoken since Andrew Jackson, and to uproot it more permanently or transform it more thoroughly. Although Tocqueville's account requires quotation at unusual length, his is perhaps the most succinct and clearly etched portrait of this notion:

I have shown that the Americans form an almost exclusively industrial and commercial association, the principal object of which is to exploit an immense new country. . . . All the peaceable virtues that tend to give a semblance of order to the social body and to favor trade should therefore be especially honored among this people, and to neglect those virtues will be to incur public contempt.

All the turbulent virtues, which may bring a society *éclat,* but more often bring it trouble, occupy on the contrary a subaltern rank in the opinion of this same people. One can neglect such virtues without losing the esteem of one's fellow citizens, and one risks losing esteem by acquiring them.

The Americans make a no less arbitrary distinction among vices. . . .

To clear, till, and transform this vast uninhabited continent that is his domain, the American needs the daily support of an energetic passion. That passion can be no other than love of wealth. The passion of wealth is therefore not stigmatized in America, and provided that it does not overreach the limits that public order assigns it, it is honored. . . .

In the United States, fortunes are lost and regained without difficulty. The country is boundless and full of inexhaustible resources. The nation has all the needs and appetites of a growing being, and for all its efforts, it is always surrounded by more goods than it is capable of grasping. What is to be feared by such a people is not the ruin of some individuals, which may be soon repaired, but the inactivity and indolence of all. Audacity in industrial enterprises is the primary cause of its rapid progress, its force, its grandeur. Industry is for it like a vast lottery where a small number lose each day, but where the state gains continuously. Such a people ought thus to honor and look with favor on audacity in industrial pursuits. Now, every audacious enterprise endangers the fortune of the entrepreneur and of all those who put their trust in him. The Americans, who make of commercial temerity a kind of virtue, have no right to brand those who practice it with disgrace. . . .

In America all the vices that corrupt the purity of morals and destroy the conjugal bond are treated with a severity unknown in the rest of the world. Public opinion in the United States only mildly reproaches love of wealth, which serves the industrial greatness and prosperity of the nation; and it particularly condemns bad morals, which distract the human spirit from the pursuit of well-being and trouble the domestic order of the family, which is so necessary for business success. To be esteemed by their peers, Americans are thus constrained to bend themselves to regular habits. In this sense one can say that they make it a matter of honor to live chastely.

American honor accords with the ancient honor of Europe on one point: it places courage at the head of the virtues, and makes it the greatest of moral necessities for a man; but it does not picture courage in the same way.

Martial valor is little prized in the United States. The courage they know best and esteem most emboldens a man to defy the fury of the ocean to arrive sooner in port, bear without complaint the miseries of the desert, and of solitude, crueler than all miseries. It is the courage that makes one almost insensible to the sudden loss of a fortune painfully won, and instantly prompts fresh exertions to build a new one. Courage of this kind is primarily necessary for the sustenance and prosperity of the American association, and is particularly honored and glorified by it. One cannot betray want of such courage without dishonor.[3]

What became of this code of honor during the New Deal? To answer this question, let us begin with FDR's effect on his party. Roosevelt reshaped the Democratic party by identifying entrepreneurial individualism with economic royalism: because the new kings were in command of great concentrations of economic power, the party of Jefferson had to choose once and for all between hatred of arbitrary executives and love for free and solitary enterprise: it had to choose against the old Jeffersonian public philosophy and for the New Deal.[4] In foreign affairs Roosevelt did not have to transform the party of Woodrow Wilson altogether in order to make it the party of open diplomacy and disarmament; but he did have to persuade the electorate that a party hostile to the tough realism and imperial activism of William McKinley and Theodore Roosevelt could be entrusted with the direction of American foreign policy.[5] He had to make the Democratic party the standard-bearer of an American ruling ethos and the guardian of American democratic honor.[6]

Roosevelt attempted to turn the electorate against the Republican ruling ethos by beginning at the top, identifying the devastation of the Crash and the depression with the ethos that previous presidents had embodied.[7] He turned plebiscites on the economic crisis into critical elections that sealed the political fate of Herbert Hoover's conception of administrative excellence and Calvin Coolidge's ideal of limited government.[8] These revaluations not only distinguished his presidency, making Roosevelt the focus of new expectations. They signaled a much broader changing of the guard. For they announced that public honors, and a high place in public counsels, could now be won by types of men and women who had never been in the running before. Roosevelt encouraged new patterns of recruitment to civil service and political office, patterns that often circumvented party channels.[9] Washington suddenly became a magnet for social activists, for a new breed of political lawyer and administrator-politician.

In challenging the majority party's ruling ethos, and in bringing a sudden influx of new actors into national politics, Roosevelt set an example that Eugene McCarthy, George McGovern, and Jimmy Carter may be said to have imitated: the sudden influx of the "amateurs" into Democratic party politics after 1970 can be viewed as a second wave imitating the first wave that broke into Democratic politics during the early days of the New Deal.[10]

Roosevelt may also have set several precedents by losing battles in order to win the war for a new ruling ethos. Two of his most memorable defeats fall into this pattern. The Court-packing plan was a setback for Roosevelt's assertion of presidential prerogative. Events shortly gave him several appointments to the Court, so insofar as its aim was to bring the judiciary to accept the constitutionality of New Deal legislation, packing the Court proved to be unnecessary, and trying it only made things worse.[11] But Roosevelt had another purpose that could not be achieved by an effortless transition through timely retirements. He required an occasion to challenge the ideal of judgment and the ruling ethos that the hostile Court had upheld.[12] His brazen affront to the judiciary signaled to the legal fraternity what Roosevelt admired and how much he was willing to suffer to get it. It dramatized the choice that aspiring judges would henceforth face, a partisan choice between the tradition of Justice McReynolds and the liberal jurisprudence of Holmes and Brandeis, or, more broadly, between the old rights industry and the new.[13] Roosevelt's very defeat was dramatic proof of how seriously he regarded the choice between these traditions; the fact that an unusually astute, politically circumspect President was willing to risk serious political losses in order to redirect the legal profession was a political education not likely to be lost on ambitious lawyers.[14]

Roosevelt's attempt in the off-year elections of 1938 to purge the Democratic party and remake it in a more liberal image was similarly a failure on the battlefield but a success in clarifying the nature of the political war and carrying it to the enemy. As a practical initiative it failed of its purpose and taught future presidents not to meddle in the congressional primaries of their own party.[15] Roosevelt was rebuffed in his choice of means, but his purpose, of purging the majority party in order to make it a more effective vehicle of liberalism and social change, was pregnant with the future. The transformation of a political party is a long work for many hands; party loyalty and solidarity raise powerful obstacles against it. By means of his attempted purge, Roosevelt made it a test of honor for liberals to challenge party solidarity and party conceptions of democratic honor. He set an example of principled disloyalty by his willingness to attempt a purge, and thus sharpened and clarified the choice that future liberal Democrats might have to make. This lesson the McGovern Democrats embraced with a vengeance; by comparison to Roosevelt's efforts in 1938, the 1970 insurgency (described more fully below) was a spectacularly successful purge.[16]

The New Deal also set precedent by asserting a ruling ethos that was newly inclusive, granting legitimacy and respectability to types of social leaders who had not previously been honored. Union organizing, social work, ethnic group leadership, legal defense of minority rights—all these vocations acquired a more serious claim to public esteem during the New Deal. It was not merely that Democratic administrations were eager to work with a new coalition of interest groups. Roosevelt understood that he was engaged in a comprehensive struggle over standards of honor; he saw that the ruling ethos of a commercial society cuts across the line between private and public or between social and governmental leadership. The attack on laissez-faire individualism meant lowering the prestige of successful financial and industrial entrepreneurs; but since prestige is always relative, the New Deal revaluation necessarily entailed raising the prestige of other types of social leadership.

Roosevelt thus initiated a many-pronged attack on an established ruling ethos, on that standard of virtue and democratic honor that had prevailed during the era of laissez-faire and had provided much of the poetry of everyday American life before the depression. Although it would be foolhardy to say that he was entirely circumspect or foresaw defeat in the cases I have cited, it is not unreasonable to say that Roosevelt was occasionally willing to wage his war about standards of democratic honor by losing battles, and even willing to risk the weakening or decline of the Democratic party for the sake of such clarity.[17]

Moreover, Roosevelt grasped the importance of organizational rules and regulatory regimes in the war over democratic honors: rules can redefine the game so as to give a decided advantage to certain players. He perceived that changing the rules could put a generation of public officers out to pasture, and smooth the way to advancement for new cadres of political activists.[18] In all these respects, the legacy of the New Deal was a heritage of waging war against the conception of American democratic honor that enjoyed its apogee in the 1920s.

Roosevelt transformed this deeply rooted conception of democratic honor in at least three ways. First, he articulated and set an example of a courage that was neither martial valor nor entrepreneurial guts. Roosevelt's epithet for Al Smith, "the happy warrior," is a sobriquet that came to stand for Roosevelt himself. It conveyed something more than the panache, combativeness, and confidence that Teddy Roosevelt had brought into presidential politics.[19] Because Franklin Roosevelt was too crippled for fisticuffs and had chosen a collectivizing task, there was nothing individualistic in either the happiness or the combativeness of "the happy warrior." The alternatives for which it came to stand were rather between undertaking collective enterprises joyfully and conducting them with élan (FDR), or leaving them to grim technicians (Hoover) and modest nightwatchmen (Coolidge) who would do them stoically, minimally, and unobtrusively. Out of such caricatures our familiars come.[20] Roosevelt's civil or social courage in guiding complex collective enterprises was not entirely new to the American political tradition, but his gay demeanor made such courage more fetching and infectious than did Lincoln's tragic melancholy, and thus perhaps more social.[21]

Second, Roosevelt reinterpreted the task of subduing nature as a cooperative task in which the main actors were not individual entrepreneurs, but organized groups. The corporatist side of the New Deal welfare state and its strategy of distributing governmental tasks to business, labor, and agriculture need to be understood in this light. For these delegations of power habituated Americans to think of the Baconian conquest of nature as a civilized and social work. As Tocqueville argued, democracies are like other societies in making virtues out of the most necessary vices: democratic honor substitutes the subjugation of nature through science, technology, and hard work, for the domination of a subject class; but like aristocratic honor, its standard of praise and blame is decidedly social.[22] Under Roosevelt and his successors the vices of large organizations and of those who make them work—not merely the occasional entrepreneur-founder or robber-baron—came to be excused and praised as virtues because they were qualities of character that made America great. The war against want, or, more broadly, the campaign against nature for the relief of man's estate, became a war in which Americans shared not so much through lonely efforts whose only effective reward was wealth, but through collective efforts in which honors and other social incentives, such as professional prestige, played a constant part. This revaluing of the typical vices of organizational leaders meant that party politicians, union officials, farm association representatives, as well as corporate executives began to see themselves, and garner recognition, as major actors in the continuing American conquest of nature.

Third, Roosevelt sought to make the president, both as party leader and as chief executive, the guardian and the embodiment of American democratic honor. In Tocqueville's portrait, which is, in this respect, true to the earlier American tradition, the presidency plays no role. When Americans thought of democracy, of the needs of society as a whole, they did not envision their association as having a head in the presidency: Hamilton had lost to Jefferson on this point of honor.[23] Roosevelt worked assiduously to change this persuasion. Following Woodrow Wilson and Theodore Roosevelt, he agreed that only the presidency could overcome the centrifugal tendencies of American federalism and the separation of powers. He found a more effective strategy for enhancing the office than his predecessors had imagined. They had advocated making the presidency the spokesman for the majority, appealing to the electorate over the heads of congressmen and governors. FDR greatly expanded the rhetorical presidency, but he managed as well to bind the organized electorate to the national government directly, through their interests in the presidency as the source of programmatic action. Instead of merely appealing to the electorate over the heads of Congress, he brought the organized electorate to their congressmen with new demands that required executive cooperation and leadership. In sum, Roosevelt deflected the American notion of democratic honor from its established path, advancing a new image of courage while identifying the prosperity of the country and American greatness with the presidency and with collaborative organizational leadership in business, labor, and agriculture.

The New Deal legacy was thus both a rejection and a rebirth of American democratic honor. On the one hand, it broached an attack on an established and deeply rooted ruling ethos. On the other hand, by modifying and redirecting the American conception of democratic honor, it revitalized and refined it, arguably making it immeasurably stronger by linking it to great concentrations of organizational power, above all the national government. The New Deal brought about a transformation in the American notion of democratic honor by means of critical elections in 1932 and 1936. Roosevelt's reinterpretation of democratic

honor carried the nation, and like the "American notion of honor" that Tocqueville described, it came to be identified with the moral authority of "the
American association" as a whole.[24]

REDRESSING THE NEW DEAL LEGACY

New Clarity in Foreign Affairs

The new regime within the Democratic party began in a falling out over foreign
policy during the Vietnam War.[25] The power of Lyndon Johnson rested on two
foundations that the new Democrats tried subsequently to undermine: the institutional powers of the presidency and the disciplinary resources of the majority
party leader.[26] As president, Johnson capitalized on the postwar tradition of
bipartisanship in foreign policy to prosecute the war in Indochina.[27] But although
he abhorred Woodrow Wilson's fate and sought to avoid anything like Wilson's
public conflict with Lodge over the League of Nations Treaty,[28] Johnson failed
to prevent Senator William Fulbright from restoring the Senate Foreign Relations
Committee to prominence as a center of public criticism.[29] One purpose of the
McGovern insurgency was to consolidate and perpetuate such adversarial relationships between Congress and the Executive in order to make future Vietnams
impracticable.[30] The congressional reforms of the early 1970s did so. The aban-
donment of the seniority system prevented full committee chairman from controlling appointments to subcommittees, and this left subcommittee chairmen
free to focus public attention on their preferred criticisms of the executive, or
to impede the implementation of foreign policy.[31] Congress thereby became a
copartner in the formulation of policy as well as overseer of its implementation.
By multiplying formal procedures whereby policy could be challenged before
and during its execution, these initiatives multiplied the occasions for debate
and conflict between Congress and the executive in foreign policy.[32] These
congressional reforms followed on the reforms in the Democratic party and helped
to realize their purpose: in one aspect party reform looked promising to the
insurgents because it was a way to put an end to bipartisan foreign policy as a
check on congressional dissent. They sought permanent institutional barriers to
reinforce adversarial practices that had initially been seized on as emergency
measures. Had the Democratic party remained as it was, these crisis tactics might
well have receded from view as exceptional departures from anti-partisan norms
and practices governing the legislature's role in foreign policy, which had been
cultivated by both major parties for a generation.[33] The insurgents concluded
that new and permanent adversarial norms for foreign policy debate were necessary, in addition to new or revived institutional barriers, in order to check the
freedom of maneuver that President Johnson had enjoyed, and to deny future
presidents that range of discretion.[34] Restraints on criticism from within the
administration party were to be removed. Foreign policy would henceforth be
conducted under continuous public scrutiny of a new kind.[35]

This relaxation of anti-partisan norms and the elevation of an adversarial code transformed informal practices as dramatically as they strengthened Congress's formal role in foreign policy making. In the quest for clarity, or under the aegis of the public's right to know, "leaks" and even more serious breaches of confidentiality in the executive branch would be revalued, and converted from shocking emergency tactics into standard operating procedure.[36] Pressure was similarly exerted on the courts to make adversarial legal proceedings in foreign policy cases a matter of routine.[37]

Clarity in foreign policy was a fitting objective for party reform (in the first instance) because the task was not merely to give a new thrust to the separation of powers or renewed weight to the checks and balances of the formal constitution. The goal was also to create a new informal "working constitution" by changing the routines of party and the constraints on politicians affiliated with the parties, especially the majority party.[38] The combined effect of the formal and informal innovations was to institutionalize highly public and dramatic dissent competing for centerstage with the President in foreign policy—in part by removing the obstacles of party loyalty and previous established foreign policy, and in part by giving old institutional obstacles to executive action new vitality.[39]

In these respects, the reforms had the look of liberalism, relying on institutions and procedures to shape public conduct. This familiar look disarmed many Democrats, who mistook the reforms for just another set of impartial rules. But the Fraser Commission proposals were more substantive than they at first appeared; they constituted a system for advancing a new type of foreign policy activist to prominence within the Democratic party.[40] The McGovern reforms reflected a preceding struggle between the modern plebiscitarian presidency, on the one hand, and a challenging opinion leadership, on the other.[41] Under the new regulations Democratic party institutions were remade to give more scope to independent opinion leaders and the public interest organizations that they led.[42] The reformers sought to give oppositional opinion leadership many new institutional footholds within the majority party, and subsequently within all branches of government.[43] They made such footholds easier to secure by making it hard for party leaders to discourage the foreign policy initiatives of independent opinion leaders loosely affiliated with the Democratic party.[44] Thus the toleration recently accorded Jesse Jackson's sallies into public diplomacy by other Democratic candidates and party leaders, throughout the 1984 primary season and the presidential campaign, was, in a sense, the logical outcome of the reformers' determination to permanently diminish the role of party in constraining open partisan conflict over foreign policy.[45]

This blurring of the line between party leaders and affiliated but independent opinion leaders helps to explain why changing the norms of the majority party had wider consequences in loosening the restraints on opinion leadership in the media. Political parties stand on the borderline between formal or constitutional orders of representative government and more informal modes of representation. Like the parties, the media can advance a claim to "represent" the people, unofficially or informally; but the claim of the long-established parties was more deeply rooted, of longer standing, and on the whole more credible because parties were largely composed of candidates accountable to the people at short electoral intervals.[46] By reshaping the norms of the Democratic party to give greater scope and respectability to independent opinion leaders, treating their spokesmanship as informal representation roughly on a par with party representation, the reformers deliberately closed the previously visible gap between political parties collectively accountable to the electorate, on the one hand, and unelected opinion leaders, in the media and in the public interest lobbies, on the other. An expanded role for both public interest lobbies and the media in American foreign policy was thus a pronounced and distinctive feature of the pursuit of clarity by the reformed Democrats.[47]

Taken as a whole, these new dispositions meant that foreign policy would be kept in the public eye by adversarial proceedings. They inaugurated a new relation between the legislature and the executive, between the two major parties, and between elected representatives and independent opinion leadership in the media and in public interest organizations.[48] They introduced a new formal and informal "constitutionalism," in which private and public bureaucracies were to collaborate on new terms in providing (or not) for the common defense.[49]

The reforms seemed to reflect the theory that programmatic competition between parties would produce better conduct in foreign policy (just as it was said to produce better government in domestic policy) by keeping clear alternatives before the electorate and fostering a more informed and more critical public. In the new dispensation this was not, however, a theory that the electorate could refute by turning away from McGovern, Carter, or Mondale at the polls. The reformers do not seem to have entertained the possibility that the best informed and most critical public might well prefer to judge both parties by impartial or bipartisan norms, especially as regards performance in foreign policy. That preference had been grounded at least since *The Federalist* in the argument or observation that rationality in public deliberations on foreign affairs seldom, if ever, results from a liberation of entrepreneurial partisans and independent opinion leaders.[50] It was not this kind of rational clarity that the reform Democrats sought, however, but rather the rhetorical clarity that principled or committed opposition promotes, regardless of its rational content.

Keeping fundamental foreign policy alternatives intransigently and outspokenly before the electorate required the reform Democrats to transform the electorate's standards of judgment by weaning them away from impartial bipartisan or antipartisan norms in the domain of foreign policy. Given this objective, the insurgents had to be willing to go down to defeat in presidential elections in order to reach their goal. For the habits of a large electorate are always slow to change.[51]

Clarity and Racial Justice

The McGovern reforms brought new personnel into the Washington community, and prominence to members of the foreign policy establishment who advocated a new U.S. posture and new constraints on the executive; it thus imparted some of the impetus of the anti-war movement to the making of American foreign policy.[52] Similarly, in domestic policy, the success of the insurgents reinvigorated the civil rights movement and institutionalized it, both within the Democratic party and in all branches of government.[53] Perhaps the most important result for domestic policy was that the majority party officially moved away from the national consensus embodied in the 1964 Civil Rights Act and the 1965 Voting Rights Act, a consensus based on the doctrine of equal opportunity secured by a color-blind constitution.[54] In its place the reformers advocated a new doctrine of equality featuring group compensation for past injustices committed by the white majority against "discrete and insular minorities."[55]

Informed readers may balk at my suggestion that this policy was adopted in order to clarify American politics on the issue of racial justice, since the constitutional and moral basis of affirmative action remains murky and candor has hardly characterized the implementation of the new equality of compensatory privilege.[56] But clarity in democratic politics is always partial: public attention is limited to a few issues at a time, and politics is a partisan affair. The reform strategy was designed to bring one peculiar kind of clarity into American politics by making at least one of the two major parties keep the issue of racial justice at the center of its program and, even more significantly, in the administrative actions of its adherents.[57]

In foreign policy open opposition by the new politics liberals, in Congress and in the media, was primarily designed to influence the government and professional politicians. Influencing the electorate was only necessary, as I have suggested, insofar as a change in their expectations about partisanship in foreign policy debate was required.[58] But things were different in the role opinion leaders sought for themselves (and then for government or administration) in the sphere of race relations.

Here the task of opinion leaders was primarily to influence or restrain the electoral majority while advancing the causes of minorities. Only in this way, it was thought, could the cause of civil rights be prosecuted effectively in the North—that is, in circumstances in which government action was not what kept blacks in a state of second-class citizenship.[59] The McGovern reforms in effect compelled the majority party to identify itself as closely as possible with the aspirations of politically organized racial and sexual minorities. The point of the racial and sexual quotas in state party delegations that the McGovern rules mandated was not to seat token members of minority groups, to make the party's nominating convention a microcosm of the country.[60] The objective of the policy of affirmative action the new Democrats adopted was rather to speed up the momentum of social change by putting opinion leaders, the movers and shakers, where they could get the most attention from Congress, the judiciary, and executive agencies—where they could put their views forward with the greatest political effect and thereby stymie the counter-efforts of spokesmen for the (racially and sexually prejudiced) majority.

Group compensation and quotas make tortured constitutional doctrine and in this respect do nothing to promote clarity about racial justice. But they have undoubtedly kept race relations near the center of regional and national attention. Since the New Deal, Democrats had commonly understood social change in terms of quantifiable economic goods, and affirmative action seemed to be in this tradition because it focused attention on such goods. But to understand the novelty of the new Democratic policy one must appreciate that affirmative action was intended to use such goods, and the debate over the distribution of goods, to reshape the habits and prejudices of the governed.[61] To be sure, it was a kind of party patronage to secure congressional seats, administrative positions, entrance to careers, and lucrative contracts for members of minority groups. But the new Democrats expected, and on the whole received, something other than gratitude for being so patronizing. They saw quite correctly that organized minorities and their leaders had a stake in political clarity of a kind, that their raison d'être was to keep the concerns of their constituencies in the forefront of public attention. Beyond securing jobs and tangible benefits, their task was to speak out against damaging prejudices and for more advantageous beliefs. By embracing group compensation and the new equality, the new Democrats sought to make the party a vehicle for reshaping racial prejudices and habits through partisan politics and partisan administration. So necessary was prejudice for the causes of opinion leaders that where it did not exist it would have to be invented.[62]

Under the New Deal party system civil rights policy had been governed by norms of consensus comparable to the norms of bipartisanship that had limited the scope of partisan initiatives in foreign policy. The leadership of the Democratic party from Harry Truman to Lyndon Johnson had been committed to bipartisanship in foreign policy with all it entailed; and to equality of opportunity under the protection of a color-blind constitution. Despite the accomplishments that this policy could show by 1968, tension between the civil rights leadership and the professional politicians produced bitter objections similar to those we have noted in the anti-war movement.[63] The rules produced by the Fraser and Hughes commissions were intended to break the power of party professionals like Lyndon Johnson, George Meany, and Richard Daley; to produce a new alliance with the civil rights leadership and womens' organizations; and thereby to institutionalize adversarial confrontation between branches of government and between the parties over compensation to disadvantaged minorities. They succeeded in attaining all these objectives.

THE NEW DEMOCRATIC DEPRESSION

I have tried in this sketch to delineate some of the major elements of the comprehensive change in public policy—in the institutional forms and norms of public conduct—that the reform Democrats have tried to bring about since 1968. The war they were trying to win was a struggle to introduce a new kind of clarity into American politics, featuring sharp conflict in which committed opposition spokesmen, always a minority, would have new resources, new powers, and a new position of legitimacy on offense as well as on defense. The reforms ostensibly meant that candidates who could never in the past have contended for the presidency could now be nominated by the majority party. To what degree they have had this result remains disputable.[64] The presidential nomination was not, however, the real prize. The presidency was rather the symbolic focus of a struggle to redefine the scope of acceptable partisanship and the kinds of citizens who could be considered respectable contenders for public honors. The long-term aim was to establish that the convention was not a rabble of rousers, but an assembling of the new presidential elite.[65] The effect of the rules on the state party organizations and Congress was arguably more profound than on the presidential contest because taken together with the new Democratic program, the rules very nearly removed the Democrats from contention, as we have argued. The presidency ceased to be the end of party politics and became a means of redefining what kind of candidate for public office was respectable or tolerable: as I have tried to explain, the real war was over the democratic standard of public honors or the ruling ethos of the American polity.

If the New Deal set a precedent for the McGovernite purge in the Democratic party, it was also very much the target of that purge. For from the viewpoint of the reformers, the ultimate cause of American involvement in Vietnam was precisely the New Deal legacy of American greatness and democratic honor; the imperial presidency as the embodiment of majority will and a majoritarian ruling ethos was a formidable obstacle to minority progress and minority will. The reformers made it their business to dismantle this obstacle.

If we look again at Tocqueville's account, we can see that the reformed Democratic party has become, with increasing consistency, the antithesis of what Tocqueville termed "the American idea of honor in our day." It is hard to locate a common interest or much shared ground on which the new Democrats can stand together, but such unity as they have is provided by common enmity and the determination to keep this American notion of democratic honor on the defensive or uproot it altogether. From their viewpoint, Roosevelt not only compromised with this insufferable and misguided conception of democratic honor: his politics fortified it with knowledge and organizational skill, making it a magnet for the best and the brightest, and therefore more resourceful and dangerous. Political science should not abandon the New Deal as a paradigm in this respect, for it is a cardinal fact of political realignments in American politics that they define a new consensus and a new common horizon for comprehensive public deliberations. They do not merely raise an argument about the democratic ethos and democratic honor: they settle the argument as a political matter and consolidate the resolution in practice.[66]

The pursuit of clarity by the reform Democrats, by contrast, institutionalized an attack on the New Deal legacy of democratic honor and sought to put that legacy on the defensive in the routine conduct of every branch of government. The new politics made it respectable and legitimate to oppose any possible majoritarian consensus on democratic honor, in the name of minority honor, dignity, or rights. It thus decreased the authority of democratic honor generally, without replacing the New Deal consensus on standards of honor with any comparable majoritarian standard. In matters of honor the United States became a pandemonium. By making routine a challenge that Roosevelt had framed as a momentous and extraordinary decision to be resolved by the American people almost at one stroke, the McGovernites' pursuit of routine and continuous conflict over democratic honor and the American ruling ethos had the effect of indefinitely postponing any practical resolution of the argument between contending notions of honor. To articulate the implications of this suspension of judgment, I shall conclude with some reflections suggested by Tocqueville's chapter on honor.[67]

Democratic honor is both positively and negatively significant for Tocqueville. Positively, it is the necessary, though not sufficient, condition for common action: without shared standards of honor or the same opinions about virtue and vice, citizens cannot act in concert.[68] Honor is a matter of morals and manners, and today we think of these matters as a function of arbitrary choice by adopting the language of "values."[69] Tocqueville rejects that perspective on principle and advances an argument against it: he demonstrates that neither aristocratic nor democratic honor is arbitrary or bizarre—that is, neither is merely a medley of invidious discriminations and vanities.[70] Tocqueville argues that the moral habit made possible by shared opinions concerning democratic honor is the habit of judging the actions and speech of others by a standard of the common good, of evaluating their virtues and vices in the perspective of the needs of "the association" as a whole.[71] Thus even the entrepreneurial ethos that Tocqueville describes was, at base, not simply individualistic: it was a highly social notion of honor that taught democratic citizens how to think about the connection between their virtues and the accomplishment of the common good. It did not lead them into metaphysics about invisible hands, but focused their energies on the highly visible work of their own hands.

By sanctioning the infinite multiplication of competing standards of democratic honor and by promoting rivalry and contestation between deeply opposed claims to honor, the Democratic party since 1970 has, from this perspective, undermined the conditions for cooperative action on a national scale. Its policy is one that suppresses the habit of judging oneself and others by any comprehensive standard for "the association as a whole." American parties are the main associations for common action and a partisan approximation of "the association as a whole." They are not the whole, but before 1970 they never lost touch with the whole for long. Roosevelt attempted to make the Democratic party a party to end all parties in the sense that it would eliminate partisanship about certain paramount issues.[72] The McGovern insurgency made the Democratic party a party to end all parties in the very different sense that it would work to erode the foundation of common action by undermining any shareable standard of democratic honor. The reform Democrats have curiously made it a point of honor to convert their party into a machine for effacing the habits of judging that make political parties, but also liberal polities, possible.

The negative side of honor, for Tocqueville, is that it provides a powerful alternative, and hence opposition, to the police or to administrative supervision. As we would say, a standard of honor is nothing if it is not "internalized," meaning that we identify it as our own and defend it as a matter of honor. A code of honor is a moral substitute for external supervision. More precisely, when one is on one's honor one is alone and then submits to the approbation or disapproval of society. And knowing the standard of honor, one can ignore many possible objections and grounds for blame. As Tocqueville notes, every particular society is distinctive, though not arbitrary, in what it sanctions and what it singles out for praise. In principle, then, its solid citizens are always vulnerable to moral objections based on a comprehensive understanding of what is good for man as man, rather than on a parochial knowledge of what is good for the citizens of a given polity. The moral authority of the association secures its honorable men by suppressing those inconvenient objections. A self-respecting democracy is not, then, altogether respectful of the universal opinion of mankind or of the universal standards by which man as man is to be judged. Instead, its authority supports every citizen who lives by the democratic honor code, refusing to dishonor them for certain vices and ensuring that they will be honored for certain virtues. This authority can buttress our own civil courage or spiritedness in defending our right to act on our honor, that is, without direct supervision by the police, the courts, or government agencies. It thus creates a powerful moral obstacle to the expansion of administrative supervision over the details of every citizen's life.

But the effect of dividing Americans into opposed troops with rival conceptions of democratic honor is not only to make citizens unfit for common action on behalf of the common good and to remove a formidable obstacle to the expansion of administrative meddling in every sphere of life. It also sweeps away trust and confidence in other citizens' self-restraint. If we do not share roughly the same notion of democratic honor, it hardly makes sense for you to try to influence my conduct by appealing to my sense of honor. On the contrary, if you are convinced beforehand that my sense of honor is not democratic, you have no alternative but to hound me with the courts, the police, or an administrative agency. Thus not only is an obstacle removed: a powerful incentive for the expansion of administrative and judicial supervision is created. Worse yet, when contending groups of citizens are thrown back on their own resources to defend themselves against such intrusive supervision, the inevitable result is to divert their political energies into highly focused interest groups and single-issue or-ganizations.[73] The urgent need to defend oneself through such limited associations reinforces our narrowest interests and leaves less time for citizens to associate in political parties or to act and deliberate with "the association as a whole" in view.[74]

Thus the deeper reason that it has fallen to conservatives to do justice to the New Deal and to Franklin Roosevelt is that the moral and political depression of the past two decades has been a liberal funk. The big job of working out of it, the task of recovering our poise and high spirits, was a task conservatives had to undertake because no one else would think through and act on a standard of democratic honor to which all Americans could hold themselves and their representatives. That is why American conservatives have the difficult responsibility of honoring and emulating Roosevelt's undertaking by making it their own.

NOTES

1. Address at Jackson Day dinner, January 8, 1940, in Franklin D. Roosevelt, *Public Papers and Addresses,* ed. Samuel I. Rosenman, 13 vols. (New York: Random House, 1938–50), 1940 vol., 29.

2. Ibid., 33.

3. Alexis de Tocqueville, *Democracy in America,* vol. 2, bk. 3, ch. 18. See the translation by George Lawrence, edited by J. P. Mayer (Garden City: Doubleday, 1969), 621–23. The translation here is my own and more literal than Lawrence's.

4. Elliot A. Rosen, *Hoover, Roosevelt, and the Brains Trust: From Depression to New Deal* (New York: Columbia University Press, 1977), esp. 38–65; Alan Brinkley, *Voices of Protest: Huey Long, Father Coughlin, and the Great Depression* (New York: Alfred A. Knopf, 1982).

5. Rosen, *Hoover, Roosevelt, and the Brains Trust,* 95–114. Roosevelt had to steer a course between the internationalist legacy of Progressivism, exemplified in his chief rival for the nomination for 1932, Newton D. Baker, and the isolationist faction headed by Hearst. He was able to do so successfully not because he was a trimmer, but because he sought to combine the best of Woodrow Wilson and Theodore Roosevelt in his foreign policy. See Alonzo L. Hamby, *Liberalism and its Challengers: FDR to Reagan* (New York: Oxford University Press, 1985), 12–51; John Milton Cooper, Jr., *The Warrior and the Priest: Woodrow Wilson and Theodore Roosevelt* (Cambridge, Mass.: Harvard University Press, 1983).

6. The documentary sources differ widely in their sensitivity to this issue. I have relied heavily on *Roosevelt and Frankfurter: Their Correspondence 1928–1945,* annotated by Max Freedman (Boston: Little, Brown, 1967), because Frankfurter appears to have been a perceptive observer of Roosevelt, and contributor to his outlook, on the question of officeholding and public honors. This work hereafter cited as *RFC.*

7. See Frankfurter to Walter Lippmann, May 31, 1932: "The behavior of those who determined the standards of society during the mad years preceding the October crash was bound to be followed by the long course of wreckage through which we are now living. Seeing life, as I do, so largely through the effects of men and measures upon the minds of generous, able and ambitious youth, I could see, as though it were a visible object, the directions in which they were pushed by those who set directions for them— those who are conventionally recognized and esteemed as the most successful in our society. 'We live by symbols,' says Holmes. The symbols for these lads here during the post-war period were the Coolidges and the Mellons, the Hoovers and the Hugheses, the Youngs and Bakers. And I ask you in all sadness of heart what directions and standards did these men set for the young? What examples of courage in speech and action did these men set before them, what criteria of 'success' did they represent?" *RFC,* 63–64.

8. It should be emphasized that Hoover's unpopularity, and the economic crisis, led many Democrats to the conclusion that a normal campaign would defeat him. Hoover

was initially delighted at the nomination of Roosevelt, regarding him as the weakest of the Democratic contenders. That there would be a critical election and a realignment in 1932 was by no means predetermined. It was the result of a conscious gamble that Roosevelt and his advisers chose. A realignment of political parties was proposed by Raymond Moley on May 19, 1932. Moley recognized what Kristi Andersen has documented, that the Democratic party could become a majority party by including a previously ignored electorate: "Constant references in the 'Forgotten Man' speech, the memoranda and drafts of the St. Paul Address, and again in the Moley memo . . . to the nation's 'economic infantry' cannot be dismissed as a cliché. As Al Smith had discerned, Roosevelt was determined to shift the party's orientation to the laboring class, the farmer, and the small businessman." Rosen, *Hoover, Roosevelt and the Brains Trust,* 141. Indeed, the scope was even wider than Rosen suggests. See Kristi Andersen, *The Creation of a Democratic Majority, 1928–1936* (Chicago: University of Chicago Press, 1979); James E. Campbell, "Sources of the New Deal Realignment: The Contributions of Conversion and Mobilization to Partisan Change," *Western Political Quarterly* (October, 1985): pp. 357–76.

9. Rosen, *Hoover, Roosevelt and the Brains Trust;* Katie Louchheim, ed., *The Making of the New Deal: The Insiders Speak* (Cambridge, Mass.: Harvard University Press, 1983); Nancy J. Weiss, "The Black Cabinet," in *Farewell to the Party of Lincoln: Black Politics in the Age of FDR* (Princeton, N.J.: Princeton University Press, 1983), 136–56; Sidney M. Milkis, "Franklin D. Roosevelt and the Transcendence of Partisan Politics," *Political Science Quarterly* 100 (Fall 1985): 479–504; Milkis, "The New Deal, Administrative Reform, and the Transcendence of Partisan Politics," *Administration and Society* 18 (February 1987) 433–72. See also Frankfurter to Roosevelt, January 18, 1937: "How to build up a passionate, devoted, capable, fighting personnel for national administration has been the one subject about which I have been continuously thinking for thirty years. I hope, therefore, there will be a chance of talking with you about all this in your good time," in *RCF*, 378; Jerold S. Auerbach, "Lawyers and Social Change in the Depression Decade," in *The New Deal,* ed. John Braeman, Robert H. Bremner, and David Brody (Columbus: Ohio State University Press, 1975), 1:133–69; John A. Salmond, "Aubrey Williams: Atypical New Dealer?" in the same volume, 218–45. Southern politicians were particularly incensed by this side of the New Deal. Compare Robert A. Garson, *The Democratic Party and the Politics of Sectionalism, 1941–1948* (Baton Rouge: Louisiana State University Press; London School of Economics, 1974).

10. Jerold S. Auerbach, "New Deal, Old Deal, or Raw Deal: Some Thoughts on New Left Historiography," *Journal of Southern History* 35 (1969): 17–30; See Katie Louchheim, ed., *The Making of the New Deal: The Insiders Speak* (Cambridge, Mass.: Harvard University Press, 1983), xi–xviii; Byron E. Shafer, *Quiet Revolution: The Struggle for the Democratic Party and the Shaping of Post-Reform Politics* (New York: Russell Sage Foundation, 1983), passim.

11. William E. Leuchtenburg, "Franklin D. Roosevelt's Court 'Packing' Plan," in *Essays on The New Deal,* ed. Harold M. Hollingsworth and William F. Holmes (Austin: University of Texas Press, 1969), 69–115, esp. 109–15.

12. Consider Frankfurter's reasoning for backing Roosevelt's shock tactics: "It was clear that some major operation was necessary. Any major action to the body politic, no less than to the body physical, involves some shock. But I have, as you know, deep faith in your instinct to make the wise choice—the choice that will carry intact the motley

aggregation that constitutes the progressive army toward the goal of present-day needs.
. . . I have a deep conviction that the problem is essentially an educational one—to make
the country understand what the real function of the Supreme Court is and how, for a
long stretch of years, it has been exercising it," *RFC,* 383.

13. Decisive evidence on this point is FDR's reasoning for going ahead without accepting compromise, after it had become clear that he might suffer a serious defeat. C. C.
Burlingham wrote urging a compromise. Roosevelt replied that

I do not in the least object to what you have written but may I put it this way: *I think you are looking
a day or a week or a year ahead, while I am trying to look a generation ahead.*

For exactly thirty years I have been watching, as a lawyer, the processes of American justice. I
have attended Bar Association meetings of many kinds. I have read Law Journals and Reviews. I
have met, liked and *given honor* to many great lawyers and many great judges. But the net result
is this—neither the American Bar nor the American Bench in that whole period have been responsible
for any major improvement in the processes of justice. And on the other side of the picture, the
American Bar and the American Bench have encouraged bad morals and bad ethics on the part of
American non-lawyer citizens. It is, therefore, not to be wondered that a large majority of the lawyers
and judges of the country would prefer to see nothing done in regard to reforming the Federal
Courts—to say nothing of state and local courts. (*RFC,* 400 [May 27, 1937], my emphasis)

I draw the term rights industry from Richard E. Morgan, *Disabling America: The "Rights
Industry" in Our Time* (New York: Basic Books, 1984).

14. Precisely because he sought to frame such a character-forming political choice,
Roosevelt was dismayed when Brandeis refused his support. Leuchtenburg repeats the
judgment of contemporary journalists that Senator Robinson's death was the end of the
fight for Roosevelt. See Joseph Alsop and Turner Catledge, *The 168 Days* (Garden City,
N.Y.: Doubleday, 1938), 274–76; Leuchtenburg, "Franklin D. Roosevelt's Court 'Packing' Plan," 105–7. To Max Freedman, it appears rather that Roosevelt was determined
to continue the fight. What ended it was the desertion of one of his principal spokesmen
and supporters, Governor Herbert Lehman of New York. See *RFC,* 403–4. Frankfurter
proposed that FDR quote Theodore Roosevelt to frame this choice: "For the peaceful
progress of our people during the twentieth century we shall owe most to those judges
who hold to a twentieth century economic and social philosophy, and not to a long
outgrown philosophy, which was itself the product of primitive economic conditions,"
RCF, 384.

15. See Sidney M. Milkis, "Presidents and Party Purges: With Special Emphasis on
the Lessons of 1938," in *Presidents and Their Parties: Leadership or Neglect?* ed. Robert
Harmel (New York: Praeger, 1984), 151–75; Garson, *Democratic Party.*

16. Shafer, *Quiet Revolution,* 523–39. David Vogel, "The Public Interest Movement
and the American Reform Tradition," *Political Science Quarterly,* (Winter 1980–81):
607–28.

17. See Milkis, "Franklin D. Roosevelt and the Decline of Political Parties."

18. Most obviously, Roosevelt initiated the change to a simple majority rule for
presidential nomination in the Democratic National Convention, breaking the veto power
that the two-thirds requirement had given the South. See Garson, *Democratic Party,* 1–
31. See Milkis, "Party Leadership." The substantive effect of procedural changes is a
major theme of Shafer's *Quiet Revolution.*

19. Franklin D. Roosevelt, *The Happy Warrior, Alfred E. Smith: A Study of a Public
Servant* (Boston: Houghton Mifflin, 1928).

20. Compare note 7 above, and consider Frankfurter's remarks to Walter Lippmann, June 22, 1930:

You perform an important educational task in making clear once again that government is not business, that government is quite an art in itself. Hoover may unwittingly render a great service in driving home that truth by his very failures. For, as you point out, there was a peculiarly favorable conjunction of man and circumstances in putting the engineering and business theory of politics to the test through Hoover's presidency. The professionalism of politics was one of my themes in one of the Dodge lectures and I am very much delighted to have your own illuminating analysis of the matter. Reiteration is the essence of political education. (*RCF*, 45)

Frankfurter framed a statement of Roosevelt's made just before he took the oath of office on March 4, 1933: "The quality of National politics, viewed as a science which is capable of affecting for the better the lives of the average man and woman in America, is the concern of National leadership" (*RFC*, 37).

21. One of Frankfurter's anecdotes sums up well the peculiarly infectious character of Roosevelt's courage:

From the time he was a boy, according to his mother, he had the self-sufficiency and strength that come from a reserved inner life. Thus, while to outward view he was usually debonair and had a gaiety at times easily taken for jauntiness, he had a will of steel well-sheathed by a captivating smile. For too many people optimism is an evasion, a Micawber's hope that something will turn up. In Roosevelt, optimism was not an anodyne, it was an energy—an energy to spur his resourcefulness, a force that gave creative energy to others. An official not given to idolatry was once heard to say, "After talking with the President for an hour, I could eat bricks for lunch." (*RFC*, 748)

22. Tocqueville, *Democracy in America*, 616–26.

23. Forrest McDonald, *Alexander Hamilton: A Biography* (New York: W. W. Norton, 1979).

24. Tocqueville, *Democracy in America*, 621. (Lawrence translates "association" as "community.")

25. What follows is in part a reflection on Shafer's fine political history of this episode, *Quiet Revolution*. To my knowledge, there is no single study that undertakes to deal with the comprehensive change in policy the new Democrats have attempted to bring about; Shafer devotes his last chapter (523–39) to a very tentative account. His caveats (603, n. 6) about the difficulty of moving from an account of the party reform to later developments apply to my attempt here. The closest approximation of an account of the comprehensive change I have in view is Ole R. Holsti and James N. Rosenau, *American Leadership in World Affairs: Vietnam and the Breakdown of Consensus* (Boston: Allen & Unwin, 1984). Their findings suggest the scope of the change that has come about, but they abstract from how it happened:

Discussion of the processes whereby the values and beliefs of leaders are aggregated—through public pressures, lobbying, polls, leadership interactions, policy-making processes and the like—and thereby transformed into the broader patterns and institutions through which foreign policy is framed and executed, is deferred for another time. (xiv)

26. In certain respects the rules change of 1970 can be considered a countercoup because Lyndon Johnson was an outsider to the *presidential* Democratic party: he probably could not have been nominated under the old primary system, as his hapless run against John Kennedy in 1960 demonstrated. Once in the presidency, however, Johnson was a formidable incumbent indeed, precisely for the reasons that made him unpalatable to the

presidential selection party: he was a master of the ways of Capitol Hill as a former leader of the legislative majority in the Senate. He was able to deliver to all the constituencies of the Democratic party through national legislation, and was potentially in a far stronger position than Kennedy had been to restore the party leadership role of the president to what it had been under Roosevelt and Truman. See Hamby, *Liberalism and Its Challengers*, 231–81.

27. See Leslie H. Gelb, "Vietnam: The System Worked," originally in *Foreign Policy* 3 (Summer 1971), reprinted in Robert W. Tucker and William Watts, *Beyond Containment: U.S. Foreign Policy in Transition* (Washington, D.C.: Potomac Associates, 1973), 48–49; Seyom Brown, "The Disintegration of the Foreign Policy Consensus," in Brown, *The Faces of Power: Constancy and Change in United States Foreign Policy from Truman to Reagan* (New York: Columbia University Press, 1983), 306–17.

28. Lyndon Baines Johnson, *The Vantage Point: Perspectives of the Presidency 1963– 69* (New York: Holt, Rinehart & Winston, 1971), 152, 323, and esp. 531:

Throughout those years of crucial decisions I was sustained by the memory of my predecessors who had also borne the most painful duty of a President—to lead our country in a time of war. I recalled often the words of one of those men, Woodrow Wilson, who in the dark days of 1917 said: "It is a fearful thing to lead this great peaceful people into war. . . . But the right is more precious than peace."

Doris Kearns describes Johnson's morbid fear of Wilson's fate in *Lyndon Johnson and the American Dream* (New York: Harper & Row, 1976).

29. See the account of the meetings before the Gulf of Tonkin Resolution, Johnson, *Vantage Point*, 116–19, 55. Relations with the Senate Foreign Relations Committee were strained by U.S. intervention in the Dominican Republic nine months later (April 29, 1965); Fulbright in particular was highly critical of the Johnson administration policy. Johnson's gathering of the bipartisan precedents for his policy in Vietnam was not retrospective rationale, but rather a recrimination against the opposition for breaking faith with previous norms: see Johnson, *The Vantage Point*, 48–62, and note the substantial concurrence of Gelb, "Vietnam."

30. See the debates in Richard M. Pfeffer, ed., *No More Vietnams? The War and the Future of American Foreign Policy* (New York: Harper & Row, 1968). One shortcoming of Shafer's study is his tendency to ignore foreign policy considerations as a driving motive of the insurgency, as in the following argument:

During the days when the Hughes Commission was being created, the major actors in what was to become a reform movement were individuals who had acquired their formative political experiences in civil rights struggles or in poverty politics over the previous decade. As a result, they had explicit— and often quite radical—*policy* goals for reform politics. . . . When the Party Structure Commission was finally appointed, however, the key individuals with ties to this alternative coalition were of a noticeably different character. *Their* formative experiences in politics, almost without exception, were the insurgent nomination campaigns of 1968. If they saluted, vaguely, an additional range of policy goals, they were focused overwhelmingly on the issue of party reform—as an end in itself. (Shafer, *Quiet Revolution*, 76)

Since Nixon continued the Vietnam War after 1968, and this remained the foremost issue that had brought these key individuals into the 1968 campaigns, Shafer seems to be overlooking what was so obvious it did not even require mention.

31. Roger H. Davidson, "Two Avenues of Change: House and Senate Committee Reorganization," in *Congress Reconsidered*, ed. Lawrence C. Dodd and Bruce I. Op-

penheimer (Washington, D.C.: Congressional Quarterly Press, 1982), 107–33; Roger H. Davidson, "Subcommittee Government: New Channels for Policy Making," 99–133, and Charles O. Jones, "Congress and the Presidency," 134–77, in *The New Congress,* ed. Thomas E. Mann and Norman J. Ornstein (Washington, D.C.: American Enterprise Institute, 1981).

32. Edward A. Kolodziej, "Formulating Foreign Policy," in *The Power to Govern: Assessing Reform in the United States,* ed. Richard M. Pious (New York: Academy of Political Science, 1981), 174–89; I. M. Destler, "Executive-Congressional Conflict in Foreign Policy: Explaining It; Coping with it," in *Congress Reconsidered,* 296–316.

33. This point will be controversial because there were many factors working against the continuation of these older norms and practices. I am aware that this is so.

34. Pfeffer, ed., *No More Vietnams?* Joshua Muravchik, "Why the Democrats Lost," *Commentary* 79 (January 1985): 15–26; Carl Gershman, "The Rise and Fall of the New Foreign Policy Establishment," *Commentary* 70 (July 1980): 13–24.

35. See I. M. Destler, Leslie H. Gelb, and Anthony Lake, *Our Own Worst Enemy: The Unmaking of American Foreign Policy* (New York: Simon & Schuster, 1984), esp. 129–62.

36. After McNamara's resignation from the Johnson administration, and Daniel Ellsberg's releasing of the Pentagon Papers, arguments for dramatic public defection from official positions as a legitimate and routine measure began to appear.

37. "The public constitution is the arrangement of rule which appears to the public and is taught in the schools; the private constitution is the way in which the regime 'really works' behind the scenes." Harvey C. Mansfield, Jr., *Statesmanship and Party Government* (Chicago: University of Chicago Press, 1965), 3.

38. Destler, Gelb, and Lake, *Our Own Worst Enemy,* 127–62; Holsti and Rosenau, *American Leadership in World Affairs.*

39. That the reforms were substantive and intended to advance a new type of activist is Shafer's main theme, but he is reserved about the foreign policy dimension. *Quiet Revolution,* 3–10, 74–75, 128–30, 235–36, 425–27, 503–4, 523–29. See the brief paragraph on foreign policy attitudes, 536. One needs to trace out where the activists went. Gary Hart's track and subsequent foreign policy stance are easy to document; see Muravchik, "Why the Democrats Lost." Others went into congressional committee staffs. More subtly, as George Armstrong Kelly observed,

the Vietnam protest began with the defection of those intellectuals whose links with the establishment were cursory. But from early 1968 it was fed by another kind of intellectual—technocrats, managers, and leaders of the dominant interest, many of whom, despite their original allegiance, became the most vocal. . . . There was stern self-reprobation in these *volte-faces.* But there was also a quotient of machiavellianism, or stay-on-topness. The Nixon victory could not have served the managerial intellectuals better, for it furnished an air-tight excuse for their desertion. (Kelly, "A Strange Death for Liberal America?" originally published in *Foreign Policy* 6 (Spring 1972), reprinted in Tucker and Watts, *Beyond Containment,* 83)

See also Godfrey Hodgson, "The Establishment," originally in *Foreign Policy* 10 (Spring 1973), reprinted in Tucker and Watts, *Beyond Containment,* 130–61.

40. The terms plebiscitary leader democracy and opinion leadership are explained in more detail in Joseph M. Bessette, Jeffrey Tulis, Glenn Thurow, and James W. Ceaser, "The Rise of the Rhetorical Presidency," *Presidential Studies Quarterly* 11 (Summer 1981): 158–71; Jeffrey Tulis, "Public Policy and the Rhetorical Presidency" (Paper

presented to the Annual Meeting of the American Political Science Association, New York City, September 1981); Robert Eden, "Opinion Leadership and the Liberal Cause," in *Political Leadership and Nihilism: A Study of Weber and Nietzsche* (Gainesville: University Presses of Florida, 1984), 1–35; James W. Ceaser, *Presidential Selection: Theory and Development* (Princeton, N.J.: Princeton University Press, 1979).

41. Shafer, *Quiet Revolution,* 74–75, 131, 317–18, 523–39.

42. See Jeffrey M. Berry, *The Interest Group Society* (Boston: Little, Brown, 1984), esp. 51–53; Hugh Heclo, "Issue Networks and the Executive Establishment," in *The New American Political System,* ed. Anthony King (Washington, D.C.: American Enterprise Institute, 1976), 87–124.

43. Shafer, *Quiet Revolution,* 524–25; Destler, Gelb, and Lake, *Our Own Worst Enemy.*

44. See Muravchik, "Why the Democrats Lost."

45. Harvey C. Mansfield, Jr., "The Media World and Democratic Representation," *Government and Opposition* 16 (Summer 1982): 318–34.

46. One effect of the change described by Destler, Gelb, and Lake (*Our Own Worst Enemy,* 91–126, 129–62), in "Establishment" to "Professional Elite," is that in addition to two foreign policy establishments identified with the major parties, we now have a wide array of organized professional factions: every persuasion of opinion leaders has its associated cadre of experts to put before the media and congressional committees.

47. In addition to the works cited above, see Leslie H. Gelb, "Domestic Change and National Security Policy," in *The Next Phase in Foreign Policy,* ed. Henry Owen (Washington, D.C.: Brookings Institution, 1973), 249–80.

48. I. M. Destler, "The Constitution and Foreign Affairs," *News for Teachers of Political Science* 45 (Spring 1985): 14–16, 23. This is curiously reserved in contrast to Destler, Gelb, and Lake's *Our Own Worst Enemy,* and oddly silent about the crisis outlined in that work. Cf. Berry's remark on the tremendous change since the second edition of Raymond A. Bauer, Ithiel de Sola Pool, and Lewis Anthony Dexter's *American Business and Public Policy,* in Berry, *Interest Group Society,* 44–45. On the formal constitutional side, see Robert Scigliano, "The War Powers Resolution and the War Powers," in Joseph M. Bessette and Jeffrey Tulis, *The Presidency in the Constitutional Order* (Baton Rouge: Louisiana State University Press, 1981), 115–53, and in the same volume, Gary J. Schmitt, "Executive Privilege: Presidential Power to Withhold Information from Congress," 154–94.

49. That modern liberalism inherited a new esteem for opinion leadership from Woodrow Wilson, and that *The Federalist* viewed such leadership with suspicion is argued in Eden, *Political Leadership,* 1–15. See also Harvey C. Mansfield, Jr., "Rationality and Representation in Burke's 'Bristol Speech,' " in *Nomos VII: Rational Decision,* ed. C. J. Friedrich (New York: Prentice-Hall, 1964), 197–216. The bearing of such arguments on American foreign policy, as an alternative to the current state of deliberations between Congress and the Executive, is perhaps best brought out by Hadley Arkes, *Bureaucracy, The Marshall Plan, and the National Interest* (Princeton, N.J.: Princeton University Press, 1972).

50. One evil of the arduous plebiscitary selection procedure now in place is that no candidate who entertains doubts about winning can stay the course. The reforms have exacted a high spiritual price for aspiring to the presidency, as one must bring a sacrifice of the intellect beyond what was formerly required of other politicians. Thus it is unlikely that Democratic campaigners will admit to themselves that their party has dealt itself and

them out of the presidential game. Perhaps it is only fair that to balance accounts, Democratic party candidates should make similar demands on the electorate.

51. Muravchik, "Why the Democrats Lost," 15–26; Gershman, "Rise and Fall of the New Foreign Policy Establishment," 13–24.

52. Berry, *Interest Group Society,* 26–28; William J. Crotty, *Decision for the Democrats: Reforming the Party Structure* (Baltimore: Johns Hopkins University Press, 1968), 136–37. Shafer emphasizes the contradiction between the ideology of participatory democracy that moved many of the reformers, and the quota policy that the new rules imposed; his evidence supports the view that it was not civil rights groups or elected black leaders who pressed the quota policy, but rather the representatives of the women's movement. Shafer, *Quiet Revolution,* 119–20, 129–30, 169–75, 206–7, 462–70, 532. Although he recognizes that the rules broke the hold of the party regulars, and gave new scope for groups like the NAACP, Shafer is perhaps more sure than the civil rights leaders were that the regular or orthodox coalition provided adequate scope for them. For a partial corrective, see Alonzo L. Hamby, "Martin Luther King, Jr.," in his *Liberalism and its Challengers,* 139–82. Compare also Muravchik, "Why the Democrats Lost," 15–26.

53. The consensus also found expression in the Immigration Act of 1965. Its passage, as Nathan Glazer says, "marked the disappearance from Federal law of crucial distinctions on the basis of race and national origin. The nation agreed with this act that there would be no effort to control the future ethnic and racial character of the American population and rejected the claim that some racial and ethnic groups were more suited to be Americans than others." Glazer, *Affirmative Discrimination: Ethnic Inequality and Public Policy* (New York: Basic Books, 1975), 4. On the new racial justice, see Herman Belz, *Affirmative Action from Kennedy to Reagan: Redefining American Equality* (Washington, D.C.: Washington Legal Foundation, 1984); Terry Eastland and William J. Bennett, *Counting by Race: Equality from the Founding Fathers to Bakke and Weber* (New York: Basic Books, 1979).

54. Edward J. Erler, "Equal Protection and Personal Rights: The Regime of the 'Discrete and Insular Minority,' " *Georgia Law Review* 16 (Winter 1982): 407–44. On the importance of white guilt in the later thought of Martin Luther King, see Hamby, *Liberalism and its Challengers:* 139–82.

55. Harvey C. Mansfield, Jr., "The Underhandedness of Affirmative Action," *National Review,* May 4, 1984, 26–32, 61.

56. See the discussion of administration in John A. Wettergreen, "Constitutional Problems of American Bureaucracy in *I.N.S. v. Chadha*" (Paper prepared for presentation at the Annual Meeting of the American Political Science Association, New Orleans, Louisiana, September 1985).

57. The underlying difficulty in speaking of nonpartisanship is that a foreign policy consensus is always partial to some definite notion of the common good of one country, to a regime and enduring national interests. Patriotism is partisanship. Substantively, the bipartisan consensus had been anti-communist. As Joel Sokolsky reminds me, Democratic administrations before Vietnam were threatened with a breakdown of the bipartisan norms on the right by advocates of rollback rather than containment. Substantively, the insurgents did want to replace containment with detente; but when Nixon initiated detente they did not give his administration bipartisan support. Instead, they permanently abandoned the norms of consensus in foreign policy.

58. See Allen J. Matusow, *The Unraveling of America: A History of Liberalism in the 1960s* (New York: Harper & Row, 1984), 180–216.

59. Crotty, *Decision for the Democrats*, 284, n. 4; Shafer, *Quiet Revolution*, 206–7; Muravchik, "Why the Democrats Lost."

60. To remind oneself of the magnitude of this change, compare Nancy J. Weiss, "Why Blacks Became Democrats," in *Farewell to the Party of Lincoln*, 209–35, with Matusow, *Unraveling of America*: 180–216.

61. The term institutional racism was devised as a way of establishing the existence of racism without the existence of racists, allowing administrators and opinion leaders to wage war on prejudice without having to relieve anyone of it.

62. Before the civil and voting rights legislation of 1964 and 1965 and their vigorous enforcement, civil rights leaders had grounds for doubting that this commitment was substantial. Johnson's legislation made it clear that equal opportunity could be made law with teeth in it. See James C. Harvey, *Black Civil Rights During the Johnson Administration* (Jackson: University and College Press of Mississippi, 1973), for an assessment of the strengths and weaknesses of Johnson's commitment by the old criterion. By 1970, when the Democratic party rewrote its rules, commitment to equal opportunity had been rejected as insufficient; compensation for past injustice became the test of the liberalism of public policy.

In arguing that enforcement was wanting under Johnson, Matusow misses the main thrust of the movement away from equality of opportunity toward affirmative action after 1964 within the civil rights movement itself. Matusow, *Unraveling of America,* 214–16.

63. The pattern described by Keech and Matthews still describes recent presidential nominations remarkably well for the cases of Carter in 1980 and Mondale in 1984, although in Mondale's case it is probably because he adopted the strategy of success appropriate to the new primary system, as modeled by Aldritch. It is true that Carter would not have been the Democratic nominee in 1976 under the old rules. See Shafer, *Quiet Revolution*, 523ff., and compare William R. Keech and Donald R. Matthews, *The Party's Choice* (Washington, D.C.: Brookings Institution, 1976), with John H. Aldritch, *Before the Convention: A Theory of Presidential Nominating Campaigns* (Chicago: University of Chicago Press, 1980).

64. Jeanne J. Kirkpatrick, *The New Presidential Elite* (New York: Russell Sage Foundation and Twentieth Century Fund, 1976). See Shafer, *Quiet Revolution:* "The continuing result was nothing less than the transformation of the elite stratum in presidential politics, that collection of specialized political actors who mount campaigns and who staff the presidential administrations which follow" (533). However, had the election of Jimmy Carter not given them presidential appointments, the reformers would still have succeeded in establishing a new definition of what constituted acceptable partisanship in American politics.

65. If one inquires why liberal political science has such difficulty in taking the study of public honors or ruling ethos seriously, one is led back to the classic works of liberal political philosophy. Montesquieu, for example, accepted Hobbes's view of honor as something essentially conventional and arbitrary. It is beyond the scope of this essay to explore Tocqueville's rejection of previous liberal thought on this topic.

66. These reflections were set in motion by Delba Winthrop, "Rights: A Point of Honor" (Paper presented at the Claremont Institute Conference, *Tocqueville Observes the New Order,* January 24–26, 1985), and by William Kristol, "Liberty, Equality, Honor," *Social Philosophy and Policy* 2 (Autumn 1984): 125–140.

67. This is inferred by joining the chapter on honor with ch. 2, bk. 1, vol. 2 of Tocqueville, *Democracy in America.*

68. Tocqueville, *Democracy in America,* vol. 2, 433–34.

69. See Allan Bloom, *The Closing of the American Mind* (New York: Simon & Schuster, 1987), 194–216.

70. Tocqueville, *Democracy in America,* vol. 2, 616: "I think that [honor] can be explained by reasons other than the caprice of particular individuals or nations, which has been the reason given hitherto."

71. "It is chiefly courage of this sort which is needed to maintain the American association and make it prosper, and it is held by them in particular esteem and honor. To betray a lack of it brings certain shame." Ibid., 622.

72. Milkis, "Franklin D. Roosevelt and the Decline of Political Parties."

73. Berry, *Interest Group Society,* 26–41.

74. Ibid., 46–66; see Wettergreen, "Constitutional Problems of American Bureaucracy."

Bibliography

Adams, Grace. *Workers on Relief*. New Haven, Conn.: Yale University Press, 1939.

Aldritch, John H. *Before the Convention: A Theory of Presidential Nominating Campaigns*. Chicago: University of Chicago Press, 1980.

Alsop, Joseph, and Turner Catledge. *The 168 Days*. Garden City, N.Y.: Doubleday, 1938.

Alsop, Joseph, and Robert Kintner. "The Guffey-Biography of a Boss, New Style." *Saturday Evening Post* 210 (March 26, 1939): 5–7, 98–102.

Amenta, Edwin, and Theda Skocpol. "States and Social Policies." *Annual Review of Sociology* 12 (1986): 131–57.

Andersen, Kristi. *The Creation of a Democratic Majority, 1928–1936*. Chicago: University of Chicago Press, 1979.

Arnold, Peri E. *Making the Managerial Presidency*. Princeton, N.J.: Princeton University Press, 1986.

Arnold, Thurman. *The Folklore of Capitalism*. New Haven, Conn.: Yale University Press, 1937.

Auerbach, Jerold S. "Lawyers and Social Change in the Depression Decade." In *The New Deal*, edited by John Braeman, Robert H. Bremner, and David Brody. Vol. 1. Columbus: Ohio State University Press, 1975, 133–69.

———. "New Deal, Old Deal, or Raw Deal: Some Thoughts on New Left Historiography." *Journal of Southern History* 35 (1969): 17–30.

Axelrod, Robert. "Where the Votes Come From: An Analysis of Electoral Coalitions, 1952–1968." *American Political Science Review* 66 (March 1972): 11–20.

Beard, Charles A., and George H. E. Smith. *The Future Comes: A Study of the New Deal*. New York: Macmillan, 1933.

Beer, Samuel H. "In Search of a New Public Philosophy." In *The New American Political System,* edited by Anthony King. Washington, D.C.: American Enterprise Institute, 1978.

Belz, Herman. "The Constitution in the Gilded Age: The Beginnings of Constitutional Realism in American Scholarship." *American Journal of Legal History* 13 (1969): 110–25.

———. "The Realist Critique of Constitutionalism in the Era of Reform." *American Journal of Legal History* 15 (1971): 288–306.

———. "Changing Conceptions of Constitutionalism in the Era of World War Two and the Cold War." *Journal of American History* 59 (December 1972): 640–69.

———. "New Left Reverberations in the Academy: The Antipluralist Critique of Constitutionalism." *Review of Politics* 36 (April 1974): 265–83.

———. *Affirmative Action from Kennedy to Reagan: Redefining American Equality.* Washington, D.C.: Washington Legal Foundation, 1984.

Benjamin, Roger, and Stephen Elkins, eds. *The Democratic State.* Lawrence: University Press of Kansas, 1985.

Berkowitz, Edward, and Kim McQuaid. "Businessman and Bureaucrat: The Evolution of the American Welfare System, 1900–1940." *Journal of Economic History* 38 (March 1978).

Berle, Beatrice Biship, and Travis Beal Jacobs, eds. *Navigating the Rapids 1918–1970: From the Papers of Adolf A. Berle.* New York: Harcourt Brace Jovanovich, 1973.

Berry, Jeffrey M. *The Interest Group Society.* Boston: Little, Brown, 1984.

Bessette, Joseph M., and Jeffrey Tulis. *The Presidency in the Constitutional Order.* Baton Rouge: Louisiana State University Press, 1981.

Bessette, Joseph M., Jeffrey Tulis, Glenn Thurow, and James W. Ceaser. "The Rise of the Rhetorical Presidency." *Presidential Studies Quarterly* 11 (Summer 1981): 158–71.

Braeman, John, Robert H. Bremner, and David Brody, eds. *The New Deal.* 2 vols. Columbus: Ohio State University Press, 1975.

Brand, Donald. "Corporatism and the Rule of Law: *The End of Liberalism* Revisited." Paper presented at the Annual Meeting of the American Political Science Association, September 1985, New Orleans, Louisiana.

———. *Corporatism and the Rule of Law: The National Recovery Administration.* Ithaca, N.Y.: Cornell University Press, 1988.

Bright, Charles C. "The State in the United States During the Nineteenth Century." In *State-Making and Social Movements,* edited by Charles Bright and Susan Harding. Ann Arbor: University of Michigan, 1984, 121–58.

Bright, Charles, and Susan Harding, eds. *State-Making and Social Movements.* Ann Arbor: University of Michigan Press, 1984.

Brinkley, Alan. *Voices of Protest.* New York: Alfred A. Knopf, 1982.

Brownlow, Louis. *A Passion for Anonymity: The Autobiography of Louis Brownlow,* second half. Chicago: University of Chicago Press, 1958.

Buffa, Dudley W. *Union Power and American Democracy: The UAW and the Democratic Party, 1935–72.* Ann Arbor: University of Michigan Press, 1984.

———. *Union Power and American Democracy: The UAW and the Democratic Party, 1972–83.* Ann Arbor: University of Michigan Press, 1984.

Burnham, Walter Dean. *Critical Elections and the Mainsprings of American Politics.* New York: W. W. Norton, 1970.

———. "The System of 1896: An Analysis." In *The Evolution of American Electoral*

Systems, edited by Paul Kleppner, Walter Dean Burnham, Ronald P. Formisano et al. Westport, Conn.: Greenwood Press, 1981, 147–202.

———. *The Current Crisis in American Politics.* New York: Oxford University Press, 1982.

Burns, James MacGregor. *The Lion and the Fox.* New York: Harcourt, Brace & World, 1956.

Calef, Wesley. *Private Grazing and Public Lands.* Chicago: University of Chicago Press, 1960.

Campbell, James E. "Sources of the New Deal Realignment: The Contributions of Conversion and Mobilization to Partisan Change." *Western Political Quarterly* 38 (September 1985): 357–76.

Caton, Hiram. *The Politics of Progress: The Origins and Development of the Commercial Republic, 1600–1835.* Gainesville: University Presses of Florida, 1988.

Ceaser, James W. *Presidential Selection: Theory and Development.* Princeton, N.J.: Princeton University Press, 1979.

———. *Reforming the Reforms.* Cambridge, Mass.: Ballinger, 1982.

———. "The Theory of Governance in the Reagan Administration." In *The Reagan Presidency and the Governing of America,* edited by Lester Salamon and Michael S. Lund. Washington, D.C.: Urban Institute, 1985.

Chambers, John W. *The Tyranny of Change.* New York: St. Martin's Press, 1980.

Chambers, W. N., and W. D. Burnham. *The American Party Systems.* New York: Oxford University Press, 1967.

Chandler, Alfred D., Jr. *The Visible Hand: The Managerial Revolution in American Business.* Cambridge, Mass.: Harvard University Press, 1977.

Chubb, John E., and Paul E. Peterson, eds. *The New Direction in American Politics.* Washington, D.C.: Brookings Institution, 1985.

Clubb, Jerome M., et al. *Partisan Realignment: Voters, Parties, and Government in American History.* Beverly Hills, Calif.: Sage Publications, 1980.

Cohen, Wilbur J., ed. *The Roosevelt New Deal: A Program Assessment Fifty Years After.* Austin, Tex.: Lyndon B. Johnson School of Public Affairs, 1986.

Coleman, Peter J. *Progressivism and the World of Reform: New Zealand and the Origins of the American Welfare State.* Lawrence: University Press of Kansas, 1987.

Collins, Robert M. "David Potter's *People of Plenty* and the Recycling of Consensus History." *Reviews in American History* 16 (June 1988): 321–35.

Cook, Paul B. *Academicians in Government from Roosevelt to Roosevelt.* New York: Garland, 1982.

Cooper, John Milton, Jr. *The Warrior and the Priest: Woodrow Wilson and Theodore Roosevelt.* Cambridge, Mass.: Harvard University Press, 1983.

Croly, Herbert. *Progressive Democracy.* New York: Macmillan, 1914.

———. *The Promise of American Life.* New York: E. P. Dutton, 1963.

Crotty, William J. *Decision for the Democrats: Reforming the Party Structure.* Baltimore: Johns Hopkins University Press, 1968.

———. *Party Reform.* New York: Longman, 1983.

Crotty, William J., and Gary C. Jacobson. *American Parties in Decline.* Boston: Little, Brown, 1980.

Crundon, Robert M. *Ministers of Reform: The Progressive Achievement in American Civilization 1889–1920.* New York: Basic Books, 1982.

Dallek, Robert. *Franklin D. Roosevelt and American Foreign Policy, 1932–1945*. New York: Oxford University Press, 1979.

Dalton, Russell J., Scott C. Flanagan, and Paul Allen Beck, eds. *Electoral Change in Advanced Industrial Democracies: Realignment or Dealignment?* Princeton, N.J.: Princeton University Press, 1984.

Davis, Kenneth C. *Discretionary Justice: A Preliminary Inquiry*. Baton Rouge: Louisiana State University Press, 1969.

———. *Administrative Law and Government*. 2d ed. St. Paul: West Publishing Co., 1975.

———. *FDR: The New Deal Years, 1933–1937*. New York: Random House, 1986.

Dewey, John. "The Future of Liberalism." *Journal of Philosophy* 32 (April 25, 1935): 225–30.

Dickinson, John. *Administrative Supremacy*. New York: Alfred A. Knopf, 1941.

Dodd, Lawrence C., and Bruce I. Oppenheimer, eds. *Congress Reconsidered*. (Washington, D.C.: Congressional Quarterly Press, 1982.

Eastland, Terry, and William J. Bennett. *Counting by Race: Equality from the Founding Fathers to Bakke and Weber*. New York: Basic Books, 1979.

Eden, Robert. *Political Leadership and Nihilism: A Study of Weber and Nietzsche*. Gainesville: University Presses of Florida, 1984.

———. "Tocqueville on Political Realignment and Constitutional Forms." *Review of Politics* 48 (Summer 1986): 348–72.

———. "Partisanship and the Constitutional Revolution: The Founders' View Is Newly Problematic." In *Constitutionalism in Perspective: The Constitution in Twentieth Century Politics*, edited by Sarah Baumgartner Thurow. Landham, Md.: University Press of America, 1988, 51–65.

Egger, Rowland. "The Period of Crisis: 1933 to 1945." In *The American Public Administration: Past, Present, Future*, edited by Frederick C. Mosher. University: University of Alabama Press, 1975, 49–96.

Elliott, Ward E. Y. *The Rise of Guardian Democracy: The Supreme Court's Role in Voting Rights Disputes, 1845–1969*. Cambridge, Mass.: Harvard University Press, 1974.

Engeman, Thomas S. "Presidential Statesmanship and the Constitution: The Limits of Presidential Studies." *Review of Politics* 44 (Spring 1982): 266–81.

Epstein, David F. *The Political Theory of* The Federalist. Chicago: University of Chicago Press, 1984.

Epstein, Leon D. *Political Parties in the American Mold*. Madison: University of Wisconsin Press, 1986.

Erler, Edward J. "Equal Protection and Personal Rights: The Regime of the 'Discrete and Insular Minority.' " *Georgia Law Review* 16 (Winter 1982): 407–44.

———. "The Fourteenth Amendment and the Protection of Minority Rights." *Brigham Young University Law Review* 3 (1987): 977–1001.

Elkins, Ann, ed. *The Democratic State*. Lawrence: University Press of Kansas, 1985.

Evans, Peter, et al., eds. *Bringing the State Back In*. New York: Cambridge University Press, 1985.

Farley, James. *Jim Farley's Story*. New York: McGraw-Hill, 1948.

Fiorina, Morris P. "The Decline of Collective Responsibility in American Politics." *Daedalus* 109 (1980): 44.

Flaumenhaft, Harvey. "Hamilton's Administrative Republic and the American Presidency." In *The Presidency in the Constitutional Order,* edited by Joseph M. Bessette and Jeffrey Tulis. Baton Rouge: Louisiana State University Press, 1981, 65–112.

Flynn, Edward J. *You're the Boss.* New York: Viking Press, 1947.

Franck, Thomas M., ed. *The Tethered Presidency: Congressional Restraints on Executive Power.* New York: New York University Press, 1981.

Frederick, J. G. *Readings in Economic Planning.* New York: Business Bourse, 1932.

Freedman, Max, ed. *Roosevelt and Frankfurter: Their Correspondence 1928–1945,* annot. Max Freedman. Boston: Little, Brown, 1967.

Frisch, Morton J. "Roosevelt the Conservator: A Rejoinder to Hofstadter." *Journal of Politics* 25 (1963): 361–72.

———. *Franklin D. Roosevelt: The Contribution of the New Deal to American Political Thought and Practice.* Boston: Twayne Publishers, 1975.

Frisch, Morton J., and Richard A. Stevens. *American Political Thought: The Philosophical Dimension of American Statesmanship.* New York: Charles Scribner's Sons, 1971.

Funigiello, Philip J. *Toward a National Power Policy.* Pittsburgh: University of Pittsburgh Press, 1973.

Furniss, Norman, and Timothy Tilton. *The Case for the Welfare State.* Bloomington: Indiana University Press, 1977.

Gellhorn, Walter. *Federal Administrative Proceedings.* Baltimore: Johns Hopkins University Press, 1941.

Gilman, Bradley. *Roosevelt: The Happy Warrior.* Boston: Little, Brown, 1923.

Ginsberg, Benjamin. "Critical Elections and the Substance of Party Conflict, 1844–1968." *Midwestern Journal of Political Science* 16 (November 1972): 603–25.

Glazer, Nathan. *Affirmative Discrimination: Ethnic Inequality and Public Policy.* New York: Basic Books, 1975.

———. *Ethnic Dilemmas 1964–1982.* Cambridge, Mass.: Harvard University Press, 1983.

Goldwin, Robert A., ed. *Political Parties in the Eighties.* Washington, D.C.: American Enterprise Institute, 1980.

Graebner, William. *A History of Retirement.* New Haven, Conn.: Yale University Press, 1980.

Graham, Otis L., Jr. *Toward a Planned Society.* New York: Oxford University Press, 1976.

———. "The State in America, 1945–1980s." Paper presented at Symposium on Growth of American Government, Menlo Park, California, 1986.

Haines, Charles G. "The Adaptation of Administrative Law and Procedure to Constitutional Theories and Principles." *American Political Science Review* 34 (February 1940).

Hamby, Alonzo L. *Liberalism and Its Challengers: FDR to Reagan.* New York: Oxford University Press, 1985.

Hamilton, Alexander, James Madison, and John Jay. *The Federalist,* ed. Benjamin F. Wright. Cambridge, Mass.: Harvard University Press, 1966.

Hansen, Susan B. *The Politics of Taxation: Revenue Without Representation.* New York: Praeger, 1983.

Harmel, Robert, ed. *Presidents and Their Parties: Leadership or Neglect?* New York: Praeger, 1984.

Harris, Howell J. "The Snares of Liberalism? Politicians, Bureaucrats, and the Shaping of Federal Labor Policy in the United States." In *Shop Floor Bargaining and the State,* edited by S. Tolliday and J. Zeitlin. New York: Cambridge University Press, 1985, 143–66.

Harris, Howell J. "The Snares of Liberalism? Politicians, Bureaucrats, and the Shaping of Federal Labor Policy in the United States." In *Shop Floor Bargaining and the State,* edited by S. Tolliday and J. Zeitlin. New York: Cambridge University Press, 1985, 143–66.

Harris, Richard A,. and Sidney M. Milkis, eds. *Remaking American Politics.* Boulder, Colo.: Westview Press, Spring 1988.

———. "The New Deal and Business." In *The New Deal,* edited by John Braeman, Robert H. Bremner, and David Brody. Vol. 1. Columbus: Ohio State University Press, 1975, 50–82.

———. "The Corporate Ideal as Liberal Philosophy in the New Deal." In *The Roosevelt New Deal: A Program Assessment Fifty Years After,* edited by Wilbur J. Cohen. Austin, Tex.: Lyndon B. Johnson School of Public Affairs, 1986, 51–103.

Heclo, Hugh, and Lester M. Salamon. *The Illusion of Presidential Government.* Boulder, Colo.: Westview Press, 1981.

Hirschfield, Charles. "National Progressivism and World War I." *Mid-America* 65 (1963): 139–56.

Hofstadter, Richard A. *The American Political Tradition and the Men Who Made It.* New York: Vintage Books, 1955.

———. *The Idea of a Party System.* Berkeley: University of California Press, 1969.

Hollingsworth, Harold M., and William F. Holmes, eds. *Essays on the New Deal.* Austin: University of Texas Press, 1969.

Holsti, Ole R., and James N. Rosenau. *American Leadership in World Affairs: Vietnam and the Breakdown of Consensus.* Boston: Allen & Unwin, 1984.

Holt, James. "The New Deal and the American Anti-Statist Tradition." In *The New Deal,* edited by John Braeman, Robert H. Bremner, and David Brody. Vol. 1. Columbus: Ohio State University Press, 1975, 31.

Hopper, John Edward. "The Purge: Franklin D. Roosevelt and the 1938 Democratic Nominations." Ph.D. diss., University of Chicago, 1966.

Horowitz, David A. "Visions of Harmonious Abundance." Ph.D. diss., University of Minnesota, 1971.

Huntington, Samuel P. "The Democratic Distemper." In *The American Commonwealth,* edited by Nathan Glazer and Irving Kristol. New York: Basic Books, 1976, 9–38.

———. "The Visions of the Democratic Party." *The Public Interest,* Spring 1985, 63–78.

Huthmacher, J. Joseph, and Warren I. Susman, eds. *Herbert Hoover and the Crisis of American Capitalism.* Cambridge, Mass.: Schenkman, 1973.

Irons, Peter H. *The New Deal Lawyers.* Princeton, N.J.: Princeton University Press, 1982.

Jackson, Robert H. *The Struggle for Administrative Supremacy.* New York: Alfred A. Knopf, 1941.

Jaffe, Louis L. "The Report of the Attorney General's Committee on Administrative Procedure." *University of Chicago Law Review* 8 (April 1941): 401–40.

Jensen, Pamela K. "The Moral Foundations of the American Republic." *Interpretation* 15 (January 1987): 97–128.

Jones, Gordon S., and John Marini, eds. *The Imperial Congress: Crisis in the Separation of Powers*. New York: Pharos Books, 1988.

Karl, Barry D. *Executive Reorganization and Reform in the New Deal*. Cambridge, Mass.: Harvard University Press, 1963.

———. *The Uneasy State: The United States from 1915–1945*. Chicago: University of Chicago Press, 1983.

———. "In Search of National Planning: The Case for a Third New Deal." Paper presented at meeting of Organization of American Historians, April 1983.

Kearns, Doris. *Lyndon Johnson and the American Dream*. New York: Harper & Row, 1976.

Keech, William R., and Donald R. Matthews. *The Party's Choice*. Washington, D.C.: Brookings Institution, 1976.

Keeter, Scott, and Cliff Zukin. *Uninformed Choice: The Failure of the New Presidential Nominating System*. New York: Praeger, 1983.

Kelly, George Armstrong. *Idealism, Politics and History: Sources of Hegelian Thought*. Cambridge, Eng.: Cambridge University Press, 1969).

Kelly, George Armstrong. *Politics and Religious Consciousness in America*. New Brunswick, N.J.: Transaction Books, 1984.

Kemble, Penn. "A New Direction for the Democrats?" *Commentary* 74 (October 1982): 31–38.

Kesler, Charles R. "Woodrow Wilson and the Statesmanship of Progress." In *Natural Right and Political Right: Essays in Honor of Harry V. Jaffa*, edited by Thomas B. Silver and Peter W. Schramm. Durham, N.C.: Carolina Academic Press, 1984, 103–27.

———, ed. *Saving the Revolution:* The Federalist Papers *and the American Founding*. Glencoe, Ill.: The Free Press, 1987.

———. "The Reagan Revolution and the Legacy of the New Deal: Obstacles to Party Realignment." In *The 1984 Election and the Future of American Politics*, edited by Dennis J. Mahoney and Peter W. Schramm. Durham, N.C.: Carolina Academic Press, 1987, 245–64.

———. "Introduction." In *Keeping the Tablets: American Conservative Political Thought,* edited by William F. Buckley and Charles R. Kesler. New York: Harper & Row, 1988.

Kettner, James H. *The Development of American Citizenship: 1608–1870*. Chapel Hill: University of North Carolina Press, 1978.

Key, V. O., Jr. *Southern Politics in State and Nation*. New York: Alfred A. Knopf, 1949.

———. "A Theory of Critical Elections." *Journal of Politics* 17 (February 1955): 1–15.

———. "Secular Realignment and the Party System." *Journal of Politics* 21 (1959): 198–210.

King, Anthony, ed. *The New American Political System*. Washington, D.C.: American Enterprise Institute, 1976.

———, ed. *Both Ends of the Avenue: The Presidency, the Executive Branch, and Congress in the 1980s*. Washington, D.C.: American Enterprise Institute, 1983.

Kirwan, Kent A. "The Crisis of Identity in the Study of Public Administration: Woodrow Wilson." *Polity*, Spring 1977, 321–43.

———. "Historicism and Statesmanship in the Reform Argument of Woodrow Wilson." *Interpretation* 9 (September 1981): 339–51.

Kleppner, Paul. *The Third Electoral System, 1853–1892: Parties, Voters, and Political Cultures*. Chapel Hill: University of North Carolina Press, 1979.

———. *Who Voted: The Dynamics of Electoral Turnout 1870–1980*. New York: Praeger, 1982.

Kleppner, Paul, et al. *The Evolution of American Electoral Systems*. Westport, Conn.: Greenwood Press, 1981.

Kolson, Kenneth. "Party, Opposition, and Political Development." *Review of Politics* 40 (1978): 163–82.

Kristol, Irving. *Two Cheers for Democracy*. New York: New American Library, 1978.

Ladd, Everett Carl, with Charles D. Hadley. *Transformations of the American Party System*. New York: W. W. Norton, 1975.

Landis, James M. *The Administrative Process*. Westport, Conn.: Greenwood Press, 1974. Originally published by Yale University Press in 1938.

———. "Crucial Issues in Administrative Law: The Walter-Logan Bill." *Harvard Law Review* 52 (May 1940): 1077–1102.

Landy, Marc. "Forging the New Deal Democratic Party: From Coalition to Institution." Paper presented to the annual meeting of the American Political Science Association, Washington, D.C., September 1, 1984.

Lash, Joseph P. *Dealers and Dreamers: A New Look at the New Deal*. New York: Doubleday, 1988.

Latham, Earl. *The Politics of Railroad Coordination, 1933–1936*. Cambridge, Mass.: Harvard University Press, 1959.

Lazarus, Simon. *The Genteel Populists*. New York: McGraw-Hill, 1976.

Johnson, Lyndon Baines. *The Vantage Point: Perspectives of the Presidency 1963–1969*. New York: Holt, Rinehart & Winston, 1971.

Leff, Mark Hugh. *The Limits of Symbolic Reform: The New Deal and Taxation, 1933–1939*. New York: Cambridge University Press, 1984.

Leuchtenburg, William E. *Franklin D. Roosevelt and the New Deal*. New York: Harper & Row, 1963.

———. "The New Deal and the Analogue of War." In *Change and Continuity in Twentieth-Century America*, edited by John Braeman, Robert H. Bremner, and Everett Walters. Columbus: Ohio State University Press, 1964, 80–143.

———. "Franklin D. Roosevelt's Court 'Packing' Plan." In *Essays on The New Deal*, edited by Harold M. Hollingsworth and William F. Holmes. Austin: University of Texas Press, 1969, 69–115.

———. *In the Shadow of FDR: From Harry Truman to Ronald Reagan*. Ithaca, N.Y.: Cornell University Press, 1982.

Levy, Leonard W., and Daniel J. Mahoney, eds. *The Framing and the Ratification of the Constitution*. New York: Macmillan, 1987.

Link, Arthur S. *Woodrow Wilson and the Progressive Era*. New York: Harper & Bros. 1954.

———. "Woodrow Wilson and the Democratic Party." *Review of Politics* 18 (April 1956): 146–56.

Lorwin, Lewis L., and A. Ford Hinrichs. *National Economic and Social Planning*. Washington, D.C.: Government Printing Office, 1935.

Louchheim, Katie, ed. *The Making of the New Deal: The Insiders Speak*. Cambridge, Mass.: Harvard University Press, 1983.

Lowi, Theodore. "The Public Philosophy: Interest-Group Liberalism." *American Political Science Review* 41 (March 1967): 5–24.

———. *The End of Liberalism: The Second Republic of the United States*. New York: W. W. Norton, 1979.

———. *The Personal President: Power Invested, Promise Unfulfilled*. Ithaca, N.Y.: Cornell University Press, 1985.

Lustig, R. Jeffrey. *Corporate Liberalism: The Origins of Modern American Political Theory, 1890–1920*. Berkeley: University of California Press, 1982.

Lyon, Leverett S., et al. *The National Recovery Administration*. Washington, D.C.: Brookings Institution, 1935.

McConnell, Grant. *Private Power and American Democracy*. New York: Vintage Books, 1966.

McConnell, Scott. "Vietnam and the 60's Generation: A Memoir." *Commentary* 79 (June 1985): 40–46.

McCraw, Thomas K. *TVA and the Power Fight*. New York: J. B. Lippincott, 1971.

———. *Prophets of Regulation*. Cambridge, Mass.: Harvard University Press, 1984, 153–221.

———, ed. *Regulation in Perspective: Historical Essays*. Cambridge, Mass.: Harvard University Press, 1981.

McGerr, Michael E. *The Decline of Popular Politics: The American North, 1865–1928*. New York: Oxford University Press, 1986.

MacMaster, John B., and Frederick D. Stone. *Pennsylvania and the Federal Constitution 1787–1788*. 2 vols. New York: Da Capo Press, 1970.

McQuaid, Kim. "Corporate Liberalism in the American Business Community." *Business History Review* 12 (August 1978): 342–68.

———. "The Frustration of Corporate Revival During the Early New Deal." *Historian* 41 (August 1979): 682–700.

McWilliams, Wilson C. "Parties as Civic Associations." In *Party Renewal in America*, edited by Gerald M. Pomper. New York: Praeger, 1980, 55–60.

Mahoney, Dennis J., and Peter W. Schramm, eds. *The 1984 Election and the Future of American Politics*. Durham, N.C.: Carolina Academic Press, 1987.

Malbin, Michael J. *Unelected Representatives*. New York: Basic Books, 1980.

Mann, Thomas E., and Norman J. Ornstein, eds. *The New Congress*. Washington, D.C.: American Enterprise Institute, 1981.

Mansfield, Harvey C., Jr. *The Spirit of Liberalism*. Cambridge, Mass.: Harvard University Press, 1979.

———. "The American Election: Entitlements Versus Opportunity." *Government and Opposition*, Winter 1985, 3–17.

———. *Taming the Prince: The Necessary Contradictions of Executive Power*. New York: Free Press, 1989.

Marini, John. "Administrative Decentralization and Regulation." Paper presented to the Annual Meeting of the American Political Science Association, Denver, Colorado, September 2–5, 1982.

———. "Administrative Centralization and the Legislature: Why Congress Cannot Gov-

ern.'' Paper presented at the Annual Meeting of the American Political Science
    Association, Washington, D.C., August 31, 1986.

Matusow, Allen J. *The Unraveling of America: A History of Liberalism in the 1960s.*
    New York: Harper & Row, 1984.

Melnick, R. Shep. "The Politics of Partisanship." Occasional Paper No. 83–84, Center
    for American Political Studies, John F. Kennedy School of Government, Harvard
    University, Cambridge, Massachusetts.

Milkis, Sidney M. "Presidents and Party Purges: With Special Emphasis on the Lessons
    of 1938." In *Presidents and Their Parties: Leadership or Neglect?* edited by
    Robert Harmel. New York: Praeger, 1984.

———. "Franklin D. Roosevelt and the Transcendence of Partisan Politics." *Political
    Science Quarterly* 100 (Fall 1985): 479–504.

———. "The New Deal, Administrative Reform, and the Transcendence of Partisan
    Politics." *Administration and Society* 18 (February 1987): 433–72.

Moley, Raymond. *The First New Deal.* New York: Harcourt, Brace & World, 1966.

Nash, Gerald. "Experiments in Industrial Mobilization, WIB and NRA." *Mid-America*
    45 (July 1963): 157–74.

New Deal Legacy and the Constitution: A Half-Century Retrospect, 1933–1983 Pro-
    ceedings of a Conference at Boalt Hall School of Law, University of California,
    Berkeley, April 16, 1983.

Nichols, David K. "Progressivism and the American Political Tradition." Presented to
    the Annual Meeting of the American Political Science Association, Chicago,
    Illinois, September 1983.

Nock, Albert Jay. "WPA, the Modern Tammany." *American Mercury,* October 1938,
    215–19.

Nourse, Edwin G., et al. *Three Years of the Agricultural Adjustment Administration.*
    Washington, D.C.: Brookings Institution, 1937.

Oakeshott, Michael, *On Human Conduct.* Oxford: Clarendon Press, 1975.

Oakeshott, Michael, *Rationalism in Politics and Other Essays.* N.Y.: Oxford University
    Press, 1981.

Orloff, Anna, and Theda Skocpol. "Why Not Equal Protection?" *American Sociological
    Review* 49 (December 1984): 726–50.

Ornstein, Norman J., ed. *The Role of the Legislature in Western Democracies.* Wash-
    ington, D.C.: American Enterprise Institute, 1981.

Orwin, Clifford. "Welfare and the New Dignity." *The Public Interest* 71 (Spring 1983):
    85–95.

Parrish, Michael E. *Securities Regulation and the New Deal.* New Haven, Conn.: Yale
    University Press, 1970.

Perna, Francis. "The National Recovery Administration: The Interest Group Approach
    to Economics." Ph.D. diss., Cornell University, 1981.

Peterson, Merrill D. *The Jefferson Image in the American Mind.* New York: Oxford
    University Press, 1960.

Petrocik, John R. "The Post-New Deal Party Coalitions and the Election of 1984." Paper
    presented to the Annual Meeting of the American Political Science Association,
    New Orleans, September 1, 1985.

Piereson, James. "Party Government." *The Political Science Reviewer* 12 (1982): 2–53.

Pious, Richard M., ed. *The Power to Govern: Assessing Reform in the United States.* New York: Academy of Political Science, 1981.

Polenberg, Richard. *Reorganizing Roosevelt's Government: The Controversy over Executive Reorganization, 1936–1939.* Cambridge, Mass.: Harvard University Press, 1966.

Pomper, Gerald M. "The Decline of Party in American Elections." *Political Science Quarterly* 92 (Spring 1977): 21–41.

———, ed. *Party Renewal in America.* New York: Praeger, 1980.

Porter, David L. *Congress and the Waning of the New Deal.* Port Arthur, N.Y.: Kennikat Press, 1980.

Potter, David M. *People of Plenty: Economic Abundance and the American Character.* Chicago: University of Chicago Press, 1954.

Rabin, Jack, and James S. Bowman, eds. *Politics and Administration: Woodrow Wilson and American Public Administration.* New York: Marcel Dekker, 1984.

Rabkin, Jeremy. "The Judiciary in the Administrative State." *The Public Interest* 71 (Spring 1983): 62–84.

Reagan, Patrick. "The Architects of Modern American National Planning." Ph.D. diss., Ohio State University, 1982.

Reich, Robert B. *The Next American Frontier.* New York: Times Books, 1983.

Reiter, Howard. *Selecting the President: The Nominating Process in Transition.* Philadelphia: University of Pennsylvania Press, 1987.

Report of the President's Commission on Administrative Management. Washington, D.C.: Government Printing Office, 1937.

Riesman, David. *The Lonely Crowd: A Study of the Changing American Character.* New Haven, Conn.: Yale University Press, 1950.

———. *Individualism Reconsidered, and Other Essays.* New York: The Free Press, 1954.

Robinson, Edgar Eugene. *The Roosevelt Leadership, 1933–1945.* Philadelphia: J. B. Lippincott, 1955.

Rodgers, Daniel T. "In Search of Progressivism." *Reviews in American History* 10 (December 1982): 113–32.

Rogers, Lindsay. "Reorganization: Post-Mortem Notes." *Political Science Quarterly* 53 (June 1938): 170.

Rohr, John A. "Civil Servants and Second Class Citizens." *Public Administration Review* 44 (March 1984): 135–40.

———. *To Run a Constitution: The Legitimacy of the Administrative State.* Lawrence: University Press of Kansas, 1986.

Romasco, Albert U. *The Politics of Recovery: Roosevelt's New Deal.* New York: Oxford University Press, 1983.

Roos, Charles F. *NRA Economic Planning.* Bloomington, Ind.: Principia, 1937.

Roosevelt, Franklin D. *The Happy Warrior: A Study of a Public Servant.* Boston: Houghton Mifflin, 1928.

———. *Public Papers and Addresses.* Edited by Samuel I. Rosenman. 13 vols. New York: Random House, 1938–50.

Roosevelt, Theodore. *Works of Theodore Roosevelt.* New York: Da Capo Press, 1923–26.

Rosen, Elliot A. *Hoover, Roosevelt, and the Brains Trust: From Depression to New Deal*. New York: Columbia University Press, 1977.

Rosenof, Theodore. *Dogma, The Depression, and the New Deal: The Debate of Political Leaders over Economic Recovery*. Port Washington, N.Y.: Kennikat Press, 1975.

Sanders, Elizabeth. "Business, Bureaucracy and the Bourgeoisie: The New Deal Legacy." In *The Political Economy of Public Policy*, edited by Alan Stone and Edward J. Harpham. Beverly Hills, Calif.: Sage Publications, 1982, 115–40.

Schattschneider, E. E. *Party Government*. New York: Rinehart & Winston, 1942.

Scheingold, Stuart A. *The Politics of Rights: Lawyers, Public Policy and Political Change*. New Haven, Conn.: Yale University Press, 1974.

Schick, Alan. "Congress and the 'Details of Administration.' " *Public Administration Review* 36 (September/October 1976): 516–28.

Schlesinger, Arthur M., Jr. *The Crisis of the Old Order*. Boston: Houghton Mifflin, 1957.

———. *The Politics of Upheaval*. Boston: Houghton Mifflin, 1960.

———. *The Coming to Power: Critical Elections in American History*. New York: Chelsea House, 1971.

Seligman, Lester. "The Presidential Office and the President as Party Leader (with a post-script on the Kennedy-Nixon era)." In *Parties and Elections in an Anti-Party Age,* edited by Jeff Fishel. Bloomington: Indiana University Press, 1978.

Shafer, Byron E. "Anti-Party Politics." *The Public Interest* 63 (Spring 1981): 95–110.

———. *Quiet Revolution: The Struggle for the Democratic Party and the Shaping of Post-Reform Politics*. New York: Russell Sage Foundation, 1983.

Sheppard, Burton. *Rethinking Congressional Reform: The Reform Roots of the Special Interest Congress*. Cambridge, Mass.: Schenkman, 1985.

Silbey, Joel H., Allan C. Bogue, and William H. Flanigan, eds. *The History of American Electoral Behavior*. Princeton, N.J.: Princeton University Press, 1978.

Silver, Thomas B., and Peter W. Schramm, eds. *Natural Right and Political Right: Essays in Honor of Harry V. Jaffa*. Durham, N.C.: Carolina Academic Press, 1984.

Sitkoff, Harvard, ed. *Fifty Years Later: The New Deal Evaluated*. Philadelphia: Temple University Press, 1985.

Skocpol, Theda. "Political Response to Capitalist Crisis." *Politics and Society* 10 (1980): 167–201.

Skocpol, Theda, and John Ikenberry. "The Political Formation of the American Welfare State in Historical and Comparative Perspective." *Comparative Social Research* 6 (1983): 87–148.

Skowronek, Stephen. *Building a New American State: The Expansion of National Administrative Capacities, 1877–1920*. Cambridge, Eng.: Cambridge University Press, 1982.

Special Committee to Investigate Senatorial Campaign Expenditures and the Use of Government Funds of 1938, Investigation of Senatorial Campaign Expenditures. Senate Report, 76th Congress, 1st Session, Number 10288.

Stern, Robert L. "That Commerce Which Concerns More States Than One." *Harvard Law Review* 47 (1934): 1335ff.

———. "The Commerce Clause and the National Economy, 1933–1946." *Harvard Law Review* 59 (1946): 645ff.

Stokes, Thomas. *Chip Off My Shoulder*. Princeton, N.J.: Princeton University Press, 1940.

Storing, Herbert J., ed. *The Complete Anti-Federalist*. 7 vols. Chicago: University of Chicago Press, 1981.

————. *What the Anti-Federalists Were For*. Chicago: University of Chicago Press, 1983.

Sundquist, James L. *Dynamics of the Party System: Alignment and Realignment of Political Parties in the United States*. Washington, D.C.: Brookings Institution, 1973.

————. "Whither the American Party System Revisited." *Political Science Quarterly* 98 (Winter 1983–84): 573–94.

Tansill, Charles C., ed. "Debates in the Federal Convention of 1787 as Reported by James Madison." In *Documents Illustrative of the Formation of the Union of the American States*. Washington, D.C.: Government Printing Office, 1927.

Thernstrom, Abigail M. *Whose Votes Count? Affirmative Action and Minority Voting Rights*. Cambridge, Mass.: Harvard University Press, 1987.

Thurow, Sarah Baumgartner, ed. *Constitutionalism in Perspective: The U.S. Constitution in 20th Century Politics*. Vol. 3 of Constitutionalism in America. (Lanham, Md.: University Press of America, 1988.

Tocqueville, Alexis de. *Democracy in America*, ed. J. P. Mayer. New York: Doubleday, 1969.

Trilling, Richard J., and Bruce A. Campbell. "Toward a Theory of Realignment." In the volume edited by them, *Realignment in American Politics: Toward a Theory*. Austin: University of Texas Press, 1980.

Truman, David B. "Party Reform, Party Atrophy, and Constitutional Change: Some Reflections." *Political Science Quarterly* 99 (Winter 1984–85): 637–56.

Tulis, Jeffrey K. *The Rhetorical Presidency*. Princeton, N.J.: Princeton University Press, 1987.

Turner, James. "Understanding the Populists," *Journal of American History* 67 (September 1980): 354–73.

U.S. Treasury Department. *The Reports of Alexander Hamilton*. Edited by Jacob E. Cooke. New York: Harper & Row, 1964.

Vogel, David. "The Public Interest Movement and the American Reform Tradition." *Political Science Quarterly* (Winter 1980–81): 607–28.

Walton, Hanes, Jr. *Black Political Parties: An Historical and Political Analysis*. New York: Free Press, 1972.

Wattenberg, Martin P. *The Decline of American Political Parties, 1952–1980*. Cambridge, Mass.: Harvard University Press, 1984.

Weinstein, James. *The Corporate Ideal in the Liberal State*. Boston: Beacon Press, 1968.

Weiss, Nancy J. *Farewell to the Party of Lincoln: Black Politics in the Age of FDR*. Princeton, N.J. Princeton University Press, 1983.

Wettergreen, John A. "The American Voter and His Surveyors." *The Political Science Reviewer* 7(Fall 1977): 181–227.

————. "Constitutional Problems of American Bureaucracy in *I.N.S. v. Chadha*." Paper prepared for presentation at the Annual Meeting of the American Political Science Association, New Orleans, Louisianna, September 1, 1985.

————. "Origin of Affirmative Action." Paper prepared for the Annual Meeting of the American Political Science Association, Chicago, Illinois, September 1987.

White, Theodore H. *America in Search of Itself: The Making of the President 1956–1980*. New York: Harper & Row, 1982.

Whiting, Theodore. *Final Report of the Federal Emergency Relief Administration*. Washington: Government Printing Office, 1942.

Will, George F. *Statecraft as Soulcraft: What Government Does*. New York: Simon Schuster, 1983.

Wilson, Woodrow. *Constitutional Government in the United States*. New York: Columbia University Press, 1908.

———. "The Study of Administration." *Political Science Quarterly* 2 (June 1987): 197–222.

Wiltse, Charles M. "The Representative Function of Bureaucracy." *American Political Science Review* 35 (June 1941): 510–16.

Witcover, Jules. *Marathon: The Pursuit of the Presidency 1972–1976*. New York: Viking Press, 1977.

Wolfe, Christopher. *The Rise of Modern Judicial Review*. New York: Basic Books, 1986.

Zuckert, Michael P. "Selt-Evident Truth and the Declaration of Independence." *The Review of Politics* 49 (Summer 1987): 319–39.

Index

Index

About the Contributors

HIRAM CATON is currently a professor in the School of Humanities at Griffith University in Brisbane, Australia, and Director of the Bonhoeffer Institute. His books include *The Origins of Subjectivity: An Essay on Descartes* and *The Politics of Progress: The Origins and Development of the Commercial Republic, 1600–1835*.

PETER J. COLEMAN has served as Professor of History at the University of Illinois at Chicago and as Fellow of the Stout Research Centre at Victoria University in Wellington, New Zealand. His most recent book is *Progressivism and the World of Reform: New Zealand and the Origins of the American Welfare State*.

ROBERT EDEN is Professor of Political Science at Hillsdale College in Michigan and the author of *Political Leadership and Nihilism: A Study of Weber and Nietzsche*. He is completing a book on constitutionalism and realignment in the United States.

MORTON J. FRISCH is Professor of Political Science at Northern Illinois University. He is the author of *Franklin D. Roosevelt: The Contribution of the New Deal to American Political Thought and Practice* and coeditor, with Richard A. Stevens, of *American Political Thought: The Philosophical Dimension of American Statesmanship*. He is the editor of *The Selected Writings and Speeches of Alexander Hamilton*.

ELLIS W. HAWLEY is Professor of History at the University of Iowa. His publications include *The New Deal and the Problem of Monopoly* and *The Great*

War and the Search for a Modern Order, 1917–1933. He is the editor of *The Public Papers of Herbert Hoover* and *Herbert Hoover as Secretary of Commerce,* and coauthor of *Hoover and the Crisis of American Capitalism.*

CHARLES R. KESLER is Assistant Professor of Government and Associate Director of the Henry Salvatori Center at Claremont McKenna College. He is the editor of *Saving the Revolution:* The Federalist Papers *and the American Founding* and, with William F. Buckley, of *Keeping the Tablets: American Conservative Political Thought.* He is currently completing a book on *Cicero and the Natural Law.*

SIDNEY M. MILKIS is Assistant Professor of Politics at Brandeis University. He is the author, with Richard A. Harris, of *Social Regulation and The Reagan Revolution: A Tale of Two Agencies* and coeditor with him of *Remaking American Politics.* He is at work on a study of presidential leadership from FDR to Ronald Reagan, *Party Leadership and the Development of the Modern Presidency.*

DON PAARLBERG is Professor Emeritus in Agricultural Economics at Purdue University. He has held appointments from three Presidents—Eisenhower, Nixon, and Ford—having been a special assistant to the President, coordinator of the Food for Peace program, Assistant Secretary of Agriculture, and Director of the Agricultural Economics program. He has also served as economic adviser to four secretaries of agriculture: Benson, Hardin, Butz, and Knebel. He is the author of *Farmers of Five Continents, Farm and Food Policy: Issues of the 1980s, Great Myths of Economics,* and *American Farm Policy.*

JOHN A. ROHR is a professor at the Center for Public Administration and Policy at Virginia Polytechnic Institute and State University. He is the author of *To Run a Constitution: The Legitimacy of the Administrative State, Ethics for Bureaucrats: An Essay on Law and Values,* and *Prophets Without Honor: Public Policy and the Selective Conscientious Objector.*

ARTHUR SHENFIELD is an economist and barrister at law in Great Britain. His nine books include works on taxation, the European Economic Community, socialism, and economic policy. He was the economic director of the Confederation of British Industry from 1955 to 1967, the director of the London Industrial Policy Group from 1967 to 1969, and the director of London's International Institute for Economic Research from 1971 to 1973. From 1972 to 1974 he was president of the Mont Pelerin Society.

JOHN A. WETTERGREEN is Professor of Political Science at San Jose State University. From 1984 to 1985 he was the project director for the Office of the

Bicentennial of the Constitution of the United States. He has just completed a study of the transformation of the New Deal state since the 1950s, *Total Regulation: The New Bureaucracy in America*. He is also the author of a forthcoming book on the political philosophy of James Harrington.

What People Are Saying
about the Left Behind Series

"This is the most successful Christian-fiction series ever."
—Publishers Weekly

"Tim LaHaye and Jerry B. Jenkins . . . are doing for
Christian fiction what John Grisham did for courtroom
thrillers."
—TIME

"The authors' style continues to be thoroughly captivating
and keeps the reader glued to the book, wondering what
will happen next. And it leaves the reader hungry for
more."
—Christian Retailing

"Combines Tom Clancy–like suspense with touches of
romance, high-tech flash and Biblical references."
—The New York Times

"It's not your mama's Christian fiction anymore."
—The Dallas Morning News

"Wildly popular—and highly controversial."
—USA Today

"Bible teacher LaHaye and master storyteller Jenkins have
created a believable story of what could happen after the
Rapture. They present the gospel clearly without being
preachy, the characters have depth, and the plot keeps
the reader turning pages."
—Moody Magazine

"Christian thriller. Prophecy-based fiction. Juiced-up
morality tale. Call it what you like, the Left Behind
series . . . now has a label its creators could never have
predicted: blockbuster success."
—Entertainment Weekly

Tyndale House books by
Tim LaHaye and Jerry B. Jenkins

The Left Behind series
Left Behind®
Tribulation Force
Nicolae
Soul Harvest
Apollyon
Assassins
The Indwelling
The Mark
Book 9—available fall 2001

Left Behind®: The Kids
#1: The Vanishings
#2: Second Chance
#3: Through the Flames
#4: Facing the Future
#5: Nicolae High
#6: The Underground
#7: Busted!
#8: Death Strike
#9: The Search
#10: On the Run
#11: Into the Storm
#12: Earthquake!
#13: The Showdown
#14: Judgment Day
#15: Battling the Commander
#16: Fire from Heaven

Tyndale House books by Tim LaHaye
Are We Living in the End Times?
How to Be Happy Though Married
Spirit-Controlled Temperament
Transformed Temperaments
Why You Act the Way You Do

Tyndale House books by Jerry B. Jenkins
And Then Came You
As You Leave Home
Still the One

LEFT

A NOVEL OF THE EARTH'S LAST DAYS

BEHIND®

LARGE PRINT EDITION

TIM LaHAYE
JERRY B. JENKINS

Tyndale House Publishers, Inc.
WHEATON, ILLINOIS

Visit Tyndale's exciting Web site at www.tyndale.com

For the latest Left Behind news, visit the Left Behind Web site at www.leftbehind.com

Published in association with the literary agency of Alive Communications, Inc., 7680 Goddard Street, Suite 200, Colorado Springs, CO 80920.

Left Behind series designed by Catherine Bergstrom

Left Behind is a registered trademark of Tyndale House Publishers, Inc.

ISBN 0-8423-5420-4

Library of Congress Cataloging-in-Publication Data

LaHaye, Tim F.
    Left Behind : a novel / Tim LaHaye and Jerry B. Jenkins.
        p. cm.
    ISBN 0-8423-2911-0 (hardcover)
    ISBN 0-8423-2912-9 (softcover)
    ISBN 0-8423-5420-4 (large print ed.)
    I. Jenkins, Jerry B. II. Title
PS3562.A315L44   1995
813'.54—dc20   95-19132

Printed in the United States of America

07 06 05 04 03 02 01
10 9 8 7 6 5 4 3 2 1

ONE

RAYFORD Steele's mind was on a woman he had never touched. With his fully loaded 747 on autopilot above the Atlantic en route to a 6 A.M. landing at Heathrow, Rayford had pushed from his mind thoughts of his family.

Over spring break he would spend time with his wife and twelve-year-old son. Their daughter would be home from college, too. But for now, with his first officer dozing, Rayford imagined Hattie Durham's smile and looked forward to their next meeting.

Hattie was Rayford's senior flight attendant. He hadn't seen her in more than an hour.

Rayford used to look forward to getting home to his wife. Irene was attractive and vivacious enough, even at forty. But lately he had found himself repelled by her obsession with religion. It was all she could talk about.

God was OK with Rayford Steele. Rayford even enjoyed church occasionally. But since Irene had hooked up with a smaller congregation and was into weekly Bible studies and church every Sunday, Rayford had become uncomfortable. Hers was not a church where people gave you the benefit of the doubt, assumed the best about you, and let you be. People there had actually asked him, to his face, what God was doing in his life.

"Blessing my socks off" had become the smiling response that seemed to satisfy them, but he found more and more excuses to be busy on Sundays.

Rayford tried to tell himself it was his wife's devotion to a divine suitor that caused his mind to wander. But he knew the real reason was his own libido.

Besides, Hattie Durham was drop-dead gorgeous. No one could argue that. What he enjoyed most was that she was a toucher. Nothing inappropriate, nothing showy. She simply touched his arm as she brushed past or rested her hand gently on his shoulder when she stood behind his seat in the cockpit.

It wasn't her touch alone that made Rayford enjoy her company. He could tell from her expressions, her demeanor, her eye contact that she at least admired and respected him. Whether she was interested in anything more, he could only guess. And so he did.

They had spent time together, chatting for hours over drinks or dinner, sometimes with coworkers, sometimes not. He had not returned so much as one brush of a finger, but his eyes had held her gaze, and he could only assume his smile had made its point.

Maybe today. Maybe this morning, if her coded tap on the door didn't rouse his first officer, he would reach and cover the hand on his shoulder—in a friendly way he hoped she would recognize as a step, a first from his side, toward a relationship.

And a first it would be. He was no prude, but Rayford had never been unfaithful to Irene. He'd had plenty of opportunities. He had long felt guilty about a private necking session he enjoyed at a company Christmas party more than twelve years before. Irene had stayed home, uncomfortably past her ninth month carrying their surprise tagalong son, Ray Jr.

Though under the influence, Rayford had known enough to leave the party early. It was clear Irene noticed he was slightly drunk, but she couldn't have suspected anything else, not from her straight-arrow captain. He was the pilot who had once consumed two martinis during a snowy shutdown at O'Hare and then voluntarily grounded himself when the weather cleared. He offered to pay for bringing in a relief pilot, but Pan-Continental was so impressed that instead they made an example of his self-discipline and wisdom.

In a couple of hours Rayford would be the first to see hints of the sun, a teasing palette of pastels that would signal the reluctant dawn over the continent. Until then, the blackness through the window seemed miles thick. His groggy or sleeping passengers had window shades down, pillows and blankets in place. For now the plane was a dark, humming sleep chamber for all but a few wanderers, the attendants, and one or two responders to nature's call.

The question of the darkest hour before dawn, then, was whether Rayford Steele should risk a new, exciting relationship with Hattie Durham. He suppressed a smile. Was he kidding himself? Would someone with his reputation ever do anything but dream about a beautiful woman fifteen years his junior? He wasn't so sure anymore. If only Irene hadn't gone off on this new kick.

Would it fade, her preoccupation with the end of the world, with the love of Jesus, with the salvation of souls? Lately she had been reading everything she could get her hands on about the rapture of the church. "Can you imagine, Rafe," she exulted, "Jesus coming back to get us before we die?"

"Yeah, boy," he said, peeking over the top of his newspaper, "that would kill me."

She was not amused. "If I didn't know what would happen to me," she said, "I wouldn't be glib about it."

"I *do* know what would happen to me," he insisted. "I'd be dead, gone, *finis*. But you, of course, would fly right up to heaven."

He hadn't meant to offend her. He was just having fun. When she turned away he rose and pursued her. He spun her around and tried to kiss her, but she was cold. "Come on, Irene," he said. "Tell me thousands wouldn't just keel over if they saw Jesus coming back for all the good people."

She had pulled away in tears. "I've told you and told you. Saved people aren't good people, they're—"

"Just forgiven, yeah, I know," he said, feeling rejected and vulnerable in his own living room. He returned to his chair and his paper. "If it makes you feel any better, I'm happy for you that you can be so cocksure."

"I only believe what the Bible says," Irene said.

Rayford shrugged. He wanted to say, "Good for you," but he didn't want to make a bad situation worse. In a way he had envied her confidence, but in truth he wrote it off to her being a more emotional, more feelings-oriented person. He didn't want to articulate it, but the fact was, he was brighter—yes, more intelligent. He believed in rules, systems, laws, patterns, things you could see and feel and hear and touch.

If God was part of all that, OK. A higher power, a loving being, a force behind the laws of nature, fine. Let's sing about it, pray about it, feel good about our ability to be kind to others, and go about our business. Rayford's greatest fear was that this religious fixation would not fade like Irene's Amway days, her Tupperware phase, and her aerobics spell. He could just see her ringing doorbells and asking if she could read people a verse or two. Surely she knew better than to dream of his tagging along.

Irene had become a full-fledged religious fanatic, and somehow that freed Rayford to daydream without guilt about Hattie Durham. Maybe he would say something, suggest something, hint at something as he and Hattie strode through Heathrow toward the cab line. Maybe earlier. Dare he assert himself even now, hours before touchdown?

Next to a window in first class, a writer sat hunched over his laptop. He shut down the machine, vowing to get back to his journal later. At thirty, Cameron Williams was the youngest ever senior writer for the prestigious *Global Weekly*. The envy of the rest of the veteran staff, he either scooped them on or was assigned to the best stories in the world. Both admirers and detractors at the magazine called him Buck, because they said he was always bucking tradition and authority. Buck believed he lived a charmed life, having been eyewitness to some of the most pivotal events in history.

A year and two months earlier, his January 1 cover story had taken him to Israel to interview Chaim Rosenzweig and had resulted in the most bizarre event he had ever experienced.

The elderly Rosenzweig had been the only unanimous choice for Newsmaker of the Year in the history of *Global Weekly*. Its staff had customarily steered clear of anyone who would be an obvious pick as *Time*'s Man of the Year. But Rosenzweig was an automatic. Cameron Williams had gone into the staff meeting prepared to argue for Rosenzweig and against whatever media star the others would typically champion.

He was pleasantly surprised when executive editor Steve Plank opened with, "Anybody want to nominate someone stupid, such as anyone other than the Nobel prizewinner in chemistry?"

The senior staff members looked at each other, shook their heads, and pretended to begin leaving. "Put the chairs on the wagon—the meetin' is over," Buck said. "Steve, I'm not angling for it, but you know I know the guy and he trusts me."

"Not so fast, Cowboy," a rival said, then appealed to Plank. "You letting Buck assign himself now?"

"I might," Steve said. "And what if I do?"

"I just think this is a technical piece, a science story," Buck's detractor muttered. "I'd put the science writer on it."

"And you'd put the reader to sleep," Plank said. "C'mon, you know the writer for showcase pieces comes from this group. And this is not a science piece any more than the first one Buck did on him. This has to be told so the reader gets to know the man and understands the significance of his achievement."

"Like that isn't obvious. It only changed the course of history."

"I'll make the assignment today," the executive editor said. "Thanks for your willingness, Buck. I assume everyone else is willing as well." Expressions of eagerness filled the room, but Buck also heard grumbled predictions that the fair-haired boy would get the nod. Which he did.

Such confidence from his boss and competition from his peers made him all the more determined to outdo himself with every assignment. In Israel, Buck stayed in a military compound and met with Rosenzweig in the same kibbutz on the outskirts of Haifa where he had interviewed him a year earlier.

Rosenzweig was fascinating, of course, but it was his discovery, or invention—no one knew quite how to categorize it— that was truly the "newsmaker of the year." The humble man called himself a botanist, but he was in truth a chemical engineer who had concocted a synthetic fertilizer that caused the desert sands of Israel to bloom like a greenhouse.

"Irrigation has not been a problem for decades," the old man said. "But all that did was make the sand wet. My formula, added to the water, fertilizes the sand."

Buck was not a scientist, but he knew enough to shake his head at that simple statement. Rosenzweig's formula was fast making Israel the richest nation on earth, far more profitable than its oil-laden neighbors. Every inch of ground blossomed with flowers and grains, including produce never before conceivable in Israel. The Holy Land became an export capital, the envy of the world, with virtually zero unemployment. Everyone prospered.

The prosperity brought about by the miracle formula changed the course of history for Israel.

Flush with cash and resources, Israel made peace with her neighbors. Free trade and liberal passage allowed all who loved the nation to have access to it. What they did not have access to, however, was the formula.

Buck had not even asked the old man to reveal the formula or the complicated security process that protected it from any potential enemy. The very fact that Buck was housed by the military evidenced the importance of security. Maintaining that secret ensured the power and independence of the state of Israel. Never had Israel enjoyed such tranquility. The walled city of Jerusalem was only a symbol now, welcoming everyone who embraced peace. The old guard believed God had rewarded them and compensated them for centuries of persecution.

Chaim Rosenzweig was honored throughout the world and revered in his own country. Global leaders sought him out, and he was protected by security systems as complex as those that protected heads of state. As heady as Israel became with newfound glory, the nation's leaders were not stupid. A kidnapped and tortured Rosenzweig could be forced to reveal a secret that would similarly revolutionize any nation in the world.

Imagine what the formula might do if modified to work on the vast tundra of Russia! Could

regions bloom, though snow covered most of
the year? Was this the key to resurrecting that
massive nation following the shattering of the
Union of Soviet Socialist Republics?

Russia had become a great brooding giant with
a devastated economy and regressed technology.
All the nation had was military might, every
spare mark going into weaponry. And the switch
from rubles to marks had not been a smooth
transition for the struggling nation. Streamlining
world finance to three major currencies had taken
years, but once the change was made, most were
happy with it. All of Europe and Russia dealt
exclusively in marks. Asia, Africa, and the Middle
East traded in yen. North and South America and
Australia dealt in dollars. A move was afoot to
go to one global currency, but those nations that
had reluctantly switched once were loath to do it
again.

Frustrated at their inability to profit from Israel's
fortune and determined to dominate and occupy
the Holy Land, the Russians had launched an
attack against Israel in the middle of the night.
The assault became known as the Russian Pearl
Harbor, and because of his interview with Rosenzweig, Buck Williams was in Haifa when it
happened. The Russians sent intercontinental
ballistic missiles and nuclear-equipped MiG
fighter-bombers into the region. The number of

aircraft and warheads made it clear their mission was annihilation.

To say the Israelis were caught off guard, Cameron Williams had written, was like saying the Great Wall of China was long. When Israeli radar picked up the Russian planes, they were nearly overhead. Israel's frantic plea for support from her immediate neighbors and the United States was simultaneous with her demand to know the intentions of the invaders of her airspace. By the time Israel and her allies could have mounted anything close to a defense, it was obvious the Russians would have her outnumbered a hundred to one.

They had only moments before the destruction would begin. There would be no more negotiating, no more pleas for a sharing of the wealth with the hordes of the north. If the Russians meant only to intimidate and bully, they would not have filled the sky with missiles. Planes could turn back, but the missiles were armed and targeted.

So this was no grandstand play designed to bring Israel to her knees. There was no message for the victims. Receiving no explanation for war machines crossing her borders and descending upon her, Israel was forced to defend herself, knowing full well that the first volley would bring about her virtual disappearance from the face of the earth.

With warning sirens screaming and radio and television sending the doomed for what flimsy cover they might find, Israel defended herself for what would surely be the last time in history. The first battery of Israeli surface-to-air missiles hit their marks, and the sky was lit with orange-and-yellow balls of fire that would certainly do little to slow a Russian offensive for which there could be no defense.

Those who knew the odds and what the radar screens foretold interpreted the deafening explosions in the sky as the Russian onslaught. Every military leader who knew what was coming expected to be put out of his misery in seconds when the fusillade reached the ground and covered the nation.

From what he heard and saw in the military compound, Buck Williams knew the end was near. There was no escape. But as the night shone like day and the horrific, deafening explosions continued, nothing on the ground suffered. The building shook and rattled and rumbled. And yet it was not hit.

Outside, warplanes slammed to the ground, digging craters and sending burning debris flying. Yet lines of communication stayed open. No other command posts had been hit. No reports of casualties. Nothing destroyed yet.

Was this some sort of a cruel joke? Sure, the

first Israeli missiles had taken out Russian fighters and caused missiles to explode too high to cause more than fire damage on the ground. But what had happened to the rest of the Russian air corps? Radar showed they had clearly sent nearly every plane they had, leaving hardly anything in reserve for defense. Thousands of planes swooped down on the tiny country's most populated cities.

The roar and the cacophony continued, the explosions so horrifying that veteran military leaders buried their faces and screamed in terror. Buck had always wanted to be near the front lines, but his survival instinct was on full throttle. He knew beyond doubt that he would die, and he found himself thinking the strangest thoughts. Why had he never married? Would there be remnants of his body for his father and brother to identify? Was there a God? Would death be the end?

He crouched beneath a console, surprised by the urge to sob. This was not at all what he had expected war to sound like, to look like. He had imagined himself peeking at the action from a safe spot, recording in his mind the drama.

Several minutes into the holocaust, Buck realized he would be no more dead outside than in. He felt no bravado, only uniqueness. He would be the only person in this post who would see and know what killed him. He made his way to a door on rubbery legs. No one seemed to notice or care to warn him. It was as if they had all been sentenced to death.

He forced open the door against a furnace blast and had to shield his eyes from the whiteness of the blaze. The sky was afire. He still heard planes over the din and roar of the fire itself, and the occasional exploding missile sent new showers of flame into the air. He stood in stark terror and amazement as the great machines of war plummeted to the earth all over the city, crashing and burning. But they fell between buildings and in deserted streets and fields. Anything atomic and explosive erupted high in the atmosphere, and Buck stood there in the heat, his face blistering and his body pouring sweat. What in the world was happening?

Then came chunks of ice and hailstones big as golf balls, forcing Buck to cover his head with his jacket. The earth shook and resounded, throwing him to the ground. Facedown in the freezing shards, he felt rain wash over him. Suddenly the only sound was the fire in the sky, and it began to fade as it drifted lower. After ten minutes of thunderous roaring, the fire dissipated, and scattered balls of flame flickered on the ground. The firelight disappeared as quickly as it had come. Stillness settled over the land.

As clouds of smoke wafted away on a gentle

breeze, the night sky reappeared in its blue-
blackness and stars shone peacefully as if nothing
had gone awry.

Buck turned back to the building, his muddy
leather jacket in his fist. The doorknob was
still hot, and inside, military leaders wept and
shuddered. The radio was alive with reports
from Israeli pilots. They had not been able to
get airborne in time to do anything but watch
as the entire Russian air offensive seemed to
destroy itself.

Miraculously, not one casualty was reported
in all of Israel. Otherwise Buck might have
believed some mysterious malfunction had
caused missile and plane to destroy each other.
But witnesses reported that it had been a firestorm, along with rain and hail and an earthquake, that consumed the entire offensive effort.

Had it been a divinely appointed meteor
shower? Perhaps. But what accounted for
hundreds and thousands of chunks of burning,
twisted, molten steel smashing to the ground
in Haifa, Jerusalem, Tel Aviv, Jericho, even
Bethlehem—leveling ancient walls but not so
much as scratching one living creature? Daylight revealed the carnage and exposed Russia's
secret alliance with Middle Eastern nations,
primarily Ethiopia and Libya.

Among the ruins, the Israelis found combustible material that would serve as fuel and preserve their natural resources for more than six years. Special task forces competed with buzzards and vultures for the flesh of the enemy dead, trying to bury them before their bones were picked clean and disease threatened the nation.

Buck remembered it vividly, as if it were yesterday. Had he not been there and seen it himself, he would not have believed it. And it took more than he had in him to get any reader of *Global Weekly* to buy it either.

Editors and readers had their own explanations for the phenomenon, but Buck admitted, if only to himself, that he became a believer in God that day. Jewish scholars pointed out passages from the Bible that talked about God destroying Israel's enemies with a firestorm, earthquake, hail, and rain. Buck was stunned when he read Ezekiel 38 and 39 about a great enemy from the north invading Israel with the help of Persia, Libya, and Ethiopia. More stark was that the Scriptures foretold of weapons of war used as fire fuel and enemy soldiers eaten by birds or buried in a common grave.

Christian friends wanted Buck to take the next step and believe in Christ, now that he was so clearly spiritually attuned. He wasn't prepared to go that far, but he was certainly a different person and a different journalist from then on. To him, nothing was beyond belief.

Not sure whether he'd follow through with anything overt, Captain Rayford Steele felt an irresistible urge to see Hattie Durham right then. He unstrapped himself and squeezed his first officer's shoulder on the way out of the cockpit. "We're still on auto, Christopher," he said as the younger man roused and straightened his headphones. "I'm gonna make the sunup stroll."

Christopher squinted and licked his lips. "Doesn't look like sunup to me, Cap."

"Probably another hour or two. I'll see if anybody's stirring anyway."

"Roger. If they are, tell 'em Chris says, 'Hey.'"

Rayford snorted and nodded. As he opened the cockpit door, Hattie Durham nearly bowled him over.

"No need to knock," he said. "I'm coming."

The senior flight attendant pulled him into the galleyway, but there was no passion in her touch. Her fingers felt like talons on his forearm, and her body shuddered in the darkness.

"Hattie—"

She pressed him back against the cooking compartments, her face close to his. Had she not been clearly terrified, he might have enjoyed this and returned her embrace. Her knees buckled as she tried to speak, and her voice came in a whiny squeal.

"People are missing," she managed in a whisper, burying her head in his chest.

He took her shoulders and tried to push her back, but she fought to stay close. "What do you m—?"

She was sobbing now, her body out of control. "A whole bunch of people, just gone!"

"Hattie, this is a big plane. They've wandered to the lavs or—"

She pulled his head down so she could speak directly into his ear. Despite her weeping, she was plainly fighting to make herself understood. "I've been everywhere. I'm telling you, dozens of people are missing."

"Hattie, it's still dark. We'll find—"

"I'm not crazy! See for yourself! All over the plane, people have disappeared."

"It's a joke. They're hiding, trying to—"

"Ray! Their shoes, their socks, their clothes, everything was left behind. These people are gone!"

Hattie slipped from his grasp and knelt whimpering in the corner. Rayford wanted to comfort her, to enlist her help, or to get Chris to go with him through the plane. More than anything he wanted to believe the woman was crazy. She knew better than to put him on. It was obvious she really believed people had disappeared.

He had been daydreaming in the cockpit. Was he asleep now? He bit his lip hard and winced at the pain. So he was wide awake. He stepped into first class, where an elderly woman sat stunned in the predawn haze, her husband's sweater and trousers in her hands. "What in the world?" she said. "Harold?"

Rayford scanned the rest of first class. Most passengers were still asleep, including a young man by the window, his laptop computer on the tray table. But indeed several seats were empty. As Rayford's eyes grew accustomed to the low light, he strode quickly to the stairway. He started down, but the woman called to him.

"Sir, my husband—"

Rayford put a finger to his lips and whispered, "I know. We'll find him. I'll be right back."

What nonsense! he thought as he descended, aware of Hattie right behind him. *"We'll find him"?*

Hattie grabbed his shoulder and he slowed. "Should I turn on the cabin lights?"

"No," he whispered. "The less people know right now, the better."

Rayford wanted to be strong, to have answers, to be an example to his crew, to Hattie. But when he reached the lower level he knew the rest of the flight would be chaotic. He was as scared as anyone on board. As he scanned the seats, he nearly panicked. He backed into a secluded spot behind the bulkhead and slapped himself hard on the cheek.

This was no joke, no trick, no dream. Something was terribly wrong, and there was no place to run. There would be enough confusion and terror without his losing control. Nothing had prepared him for this, and he would be the one everybody would look to. But for what? What was he supposed to do?

First one, then another cried out when they realized their seatmates were missing but that their clothes were still there. They cried, they screamed, they leaped from their seats. Hattie grabbed Rayford from behind and wrapped her hands so tight around his chest that he could hardly breathe. "Rayford, what is this?"

He pulled her hands apart and turned to face her. "Hattie, listen. I don't know any more than you do. But we've got to calm these people and get on the ground. I'll make some kind of an announcement, and you and your people keep everybody in their seats. OK?"

She nodded but she didn't look OK at all. As he edged past her to hurry back to the cockpit, he heard her scream. *So much for calming the passengers,* he thought as he whirled to see her on her knees in the aisle. She lifted a blazer, shirt and tie still intact. Trousers lay at her feet. Hattie frantically turned the blazer to the low light and read the name tag. "Tony!" she wailed. "Tony's gone!"

Rayford snatched the clothes from her and tossed them behind the bulkhead. He lifted Hattie by her elbows and pulled her out of sight. "Hattie, we're hours from touchdown. We can't have a planeload of hysterical people. I'm going to make an announcement, but you have to do your job. Can you?"

She nodded, her eyes vacant. He forced her to look at him. "Will you?" he said.

She nodded again. "Rayford, are we going to die?"

"No," he said. "That I'm sure of."

But he wasn't sure of anything. How could he know? He'd rather have faced an engine fire or even an uncontrolled dive. A crash into the ocean had to be better than this. How would he keep people calm in such a nightmare?

By now keeping the cabin lights off was doing more harm than good, and he was glad to be able to give Hattie a specific assignment. "I don't know what I'm going to say," he said, "but get the lights on so we can make an accurate record of who's here and who's gone, and then get more of those foreign visitor declaration forms."

"For what?"

"Just do it. Have them ready."

Rayford didn't know if he had done the right thing by leaving Hattie in charge of the passengers and crew. As he raced up the stairs, he caught sight of another attendant backing out of a galleyway, screaming. By now poor Christopher in the cockpit was the only one on the plane unaware of what was happening. Worse, Rayford had told Hattie he didn't know what was happening any more than she did.

The terrifying truth was that he knew all too well. Irene had been right. He, and most of his passengers, had been left behind.

TWO

CAMERON Williams had roused when the old woman directly in front of him called out to the pilot. The pilot had shushed her, causing her to peek back at Buck. He dragged his fingers through his longish blond hair and forced a groggy smile. "Trouble, ma'am?"

"It's my Harold," she said.

Buck had helped the old man put his herringbone wool jacket and felt hat in the overhead bin when they boarded. Harold was a short, dapper gentleman in penny loafers, brown slacks, and a tan sweater vest over a shirt and tie. He was balding, and Buck assumed he would want the hat again later when the air-conditioning kicked in.

"Does he need something?"

"He's gone!"

"I'm sorry?"

"He's disappeared!"

"Well, I'm sure he slipped off to the washroom while you were sleeping."

"Would you mind checking for me? And take a blanket."

"Ma'am?"

"I'm afraid he's gone off naked. He's a religious person, and he'll be terribly embarrassed."

Buck suppressed a smile when he noticed the woman's pained expression. He climbed over the sleeping executive on the aisle, who had far exceeded his limit of free drinks, and leaned in to take a blanket from the old woman. Indeed, Harold's clothes were in a neat pile on his seat, his glasses and hearing aid on top. The pant legs still hung over the edge and led to his shoes and socks. *Bizarre,* Buck thought. *Why so fastidious?* He remembered a friend in high school who had a form of epilepsy that occasionally caused him to black out when he seemed perfectly conscious. He might remove his shoes and socks in public or come out of a washroom with his clothes open.

"Does your husband have a history of epilepsy?"

"No."

"Sleepwalking?"

"No."

"I'll be right back."

The first-class lavs were unoccupied, but as Buck headed for the stairs he found several other

passengers in the aisle. "Excuse me," he said,
"I'm looking for someone."

"Who isn't?" a woman said.

Buck pushed his way past several people and
found lines to the washrooms in business and
economy. The pilot brushed past him without
a word, and Buck was soon met by the senior
flight attendant. "Sir, I need to ask you to return
to your seat and fasten your belt."

"I'm looking for—"

"Everybody is looking for someone," she said.
"We hope to have some information for you in
a few minutes. Now, please." She steered him
back toward the stairs, then slipped past him
and took the steps two at a time.

Halfway up the stairs Buck turned and surveyed
the scene. It was the middle of the night, for
heaven's sake, and as the cabin lights came on,
he shuddered. All over the plane, people were
holding up clothes and gasping or shrieking that
someone was missing.

Somehow he knew this was no dream, and he
felt the same terror he had endured awaiting
his death in Israel. What was he going to tell
Harold's wife? *You're not the only one? Lots
of people left their clothes in their seats?*

As he hurried back to his seat, his mind
searched its memory banks for anything he had
ever read, seen, or heard of any technology that

could remove people from their clothes and make them disappear from a decidedly secure environment. Whoever did this, were they on the plane? Would they make demands? Would another wave of disappearances be next? Would he become a victim? Where would he find himself?

Fear seemed to pervade the cabin as he climbed over his sleeping seatmate again. He stood and leaned over the back of the chair ahead of him. "Apparently many people are missing," he told the old woman. She looked as puzzled and fearful as Buck himself felt.

He sat down as the intercom came on and the captain addressed the passengers. After instructing them to return to their assigned seats, the captain explained, "I'm going to ask the flight attendants to check the lavatories and be sure everybody is accounted for. Then I'll ask them to pass out foreign entry cards. If anyone in your party is missing, I would like you to fill out the card in his or her name and list every shred of detail you can think of, from date of birth to description.

"I'm sure you all realize that we have a very troubling situation. The cards will give us a count of those missing, and I'll have something to give authorities. My first officer, Mr. Smith, will now make a cursory count of empty seats. I will try to contact Pan-Continental. I must tell you, however, that our location makes it extremely difficult to communicate with the ground without long delays. Even in this satellite age, we're in a pretty remote area. As soon as I know anything, I'll convey it to you. In the meantime, I appreciate your cooperation and calm."

Buck watched as the first officer came rushing from the cockpit, hatless and flushed. He hurried down one aisle and up the other, eyes darting from seat to seat as the flight attendants passed out cards.

Buck's seatmate roused, drooling, when an attendant asked if anyone in his party was missing. "Missing? No. And there's nobody in this party but me." He curled up again and went back to sleep, unaware.

The first officer had been gone only a few minutes when Rayford heard his key in the cockpit door and it banged open. Christopher flopped into his chair, ignored the seat belt, and sat with his head in his hands.

"What's going on, Ray?" he said. "We got us more than a hundred people gone with nothing but their clothes left behind."

"That many?"

"Yeah, like it'd be better if it was only fifty? How the heck are we gonna explain landing with less passengers than we took off with?"

Rayford shook his head, still working the radio, trying to reach someone, anyone, in Greenland or an island in the middle of nowhere. But they were too remote even to pick up a radio station for news. Finally he connected with a Concorde several miles away heading the other direction. He nodded to Christopher to put on his own earphones.

"You got enough fuel to get back to the States, over?" the pilot asked Rayford.

He looked at Christopher, who nodded and whispered, "We're halfway."

"I could make Kennedy," Rayford said.

"Forget it," came the reply. "Nothing's landing in New York. Two runways still open in Chicago. That's where we're going."

"We came from Chicago. Can't I put down at Heathrow?"

"Negative. Closed."

"Paris?"

"Man, you've got to get back where you came from. We left Paris an hour ago, got the word what's happening, and were told to go straight to Chicago."

"What's happening, Concorde?"

"If you don't know, why'd you put out the Mayday?"

"I've got a situation here I don't even want to talk about."

"Hey, friend, it's all over the world, you know?"

"Negative, I don't know," Rayford said. "Talk to me."

"You're missing passengers, right?"

"Roger. More than a hundred."

"Whoa! We lost nearly fifty."

"What do you make of it, Concorde?"

"First thing I thought of was spontaneous combustion, but there would have been smoke, residue. These people materially disappeared. Only thing I can compare it to is the old *Star Trek* shows where people got dematerialized and rematerialized, beamed all over the place."

"I sure wish I could tell my people their loved ones were going to reappear just as quickly and completely as they disappeared," Rayford said.

"That's not the worst of it, Pan Heavy. People everywhere have disappeared. Orly lost air-traffic controllers and ground controllers. Some planes have lost flight crews. Where it's daylight there are car pileups, chaos everywhere. Planes down all over and at every major airport."

"So this was a spontaneous thing?"

"Everywhere at once, just a little under an hour ago."

"I was almost hoping it was something on this plane. Some gas, some malfunction."

"That it was selective, you mean, over?"

Rayford caught the sarcasm.

"I see what you mean, Concorde. Gotta admit this is somewhere we've never been before."

"And never want to be again. I keep telling myself it's a bad dream."

"A nightmare, over."

"Roger, but it's not, is it?"

"What are you going to tell your passengers, Concorde?"

"No clue. You, over?"

"The truth."

"Can't hurt now. But what's the truth? What do we know?"

"Not a blessed thing."

"Good choice of words, Pan Heavy. You know what some people are saying, over?"

"Roger," Rayford said. "Better it's people gone to heaven than some world power doing this with fancy rays."

"Word we get is that every country has been affected. See you in Chicago?"

"Roger."

Rayford Steele looked at Christopher, who began changing the settings to turn the monstrous wide-body around and get it headed back toward the States. "Ladies and gentlemen," Rayford said over the intercom, "we're not going to be able to land in Europe. We're headed back to Chicago. We're almost exactly halfway to our original destination, so we will not have a fuel problem.

I hope this puts your minds at ease somewhat. I will let you know when we are close enough to begin using the telephones. Until I do, you will do yourself a favor by not trying."

When the captain had come back on the intercom with the information about returning to the United States, Buck Williams was surprised to hear applause throughout the cabin. Shocked and terrified as everyone was, most were from the States and wanted at least to return to familiarity to sort this thing out. Buck nudged the businessman on his right. "I'm sorry, friend, but you're going to want to be awake for this."

The man peered at Buck with a disgusted look and slurred, "If we're not crashin', don't bother me."

When the Pan-Continental 747 was finally within satellite communications range of the United States, Captain Rayford Steele connected with an all-news radio outlet and learned the far-reaching effects of the disappearance of people from every continent. Communication lines were jammed. Medical, technical, and service people were among the missing all over the world. Every

civil service agency was on full emergency status,
trying to handle the unending tragedies. Rayford
remembered the El-train disaster in Chicago years
before and how the hospitals and fire and police
units brought everyone in to work. He could
imagine that now, multiplied thousands of times.

Even the newscasters' voices were terror filled, as
much as they tried to mask it. Every conceivable
explanation was proffered, but overshadowing all
such discussion and even coverage of the carnage
were the practical aspects. What people wanted
from the news was simple information on how to
get where they were going and how to contact
their loved ones to determine if they were still
around. Rayford was instructed to get in a multi-
state traffic pattern that would allow him to land
at O'Hare at a precise moment. Only two runways
were open, and every large plane in the country
seemed headed that way. Thousands were dead in
plane crashes and car pileups. Emergency crews
were trying to clear expressways and runways, all
the while grieving over loved ones and coworkers
who had disappeared. One report said that so
many cabbies had disappeared from the cab corral
at O'Hare that volunteers were being brought in
to move the cars that had been left running with
the former drivers' clothes still on the seats.

Cars driven by people who spontaneously
disappeared had careened out of control, of

course. The toughest chore for emergency personnel was to determine who had disappeared, who was killed, and who was injured, and then to communicate that to the survivors.

When Rayford was close enough to communicate to the tower at O'Hare, he asked if they would try to connect him by phone to his home. He was laughed off. "Sorry, Captain, but phone lines are so jammed and phone personnel so spotty that the only hope is to get a dial tone and use a phone with a redial button."

Rayford filled the passengers in on the extent of the phenomenon and pleaded with them to remain calm. "There is nothing we can do on this plane that will change the situation. My plan is to get you on the ground as quickly as possible in Chicago so you can have access to some answers and, I hope, some help."

The in-flight phone embedded in the back of the seat in front of Buck Williams was not assembled with external modular connections the way most phones were. Buck imagined that Pan-Con Airlines would soon be replacing these relics to avoid complaints from computer users. But Buck guessed that inside the phone the connection was standard and that if he could somehow get in there without damaging the phone, he could connect his computer's modem directly to the line. His own cellular phone was not cooperating at this altitude.

In front of him, Harold's wife rocked and whimpered, her face buried in her hands. The executive next to Buck snored. Before drinking himself into oblivion soon after takeoff, he had said something about a major meeting in Scotland. Would he be surprised by the view upon landing!

All around Buck, people cried, prayed, and talked. Flight attendants offered snacks and drinks, but few accepted. Having preferred an aisle seat for a little more legroom, Buck was now glad he was partially hidden near the window. He removed from his computer bag a tiny tool kit he had never expected to use and went to work on the phone.

Disappointed to find no modular connection even inside the housing, he decided to play amateur electrician. These phone lines always have the same color wires, he decided, so he opened his computer and cut the wire leading to the female connector. Inside the phone, he cut the wire and sliced off the protective rubber coating. Sure enough, the four inner wires from both computer and phone looked identical. In a few minutes, he had spliced them together.

Buck tapped out a quick message to his executive editor, Steve Plank, in New York, telling of his destination. "I will bang out all I know, and I'm sure this will be just one of many similar stories. But at least this will be up to the minute, as it happens. Whether it will be of any use, I don't know. The thought hits me, Steve, that you may be among the missing. How would I know? You know my computer address. Let me know you're still with us."

He stored the note and set up his modem to send it to New York in the background, while he was working on his own writing. At the top of the screen a status bar flashed every twenty seconds, informing him that the connection to his ramp on the information superhighway was busy. He kept working.

The senior flight attendant startled him several pages into his own reflections and feelings. "What in the world are you doing?" she said, leaning in to stare at the mess of wires leading from his laptop to the in-flight phone. "I can't let you do that."

He glanced at her name tag. "Listen, beautiful Hattie, are we or are we not looking at the end of the world as we know it?"

"Don't patronize me, sir. I can't let you sit here and vandalize airline property."

"I'm not vandalizing it. I'm adapting it in an emergency. With this I can hopefully make a connection where nothing else will work."

"I can't let you do it."

"Hattie, can I tell you something?"

"Only that you're going to put that phone back the way you found it."

"I will."

"Now."

"No, I won't do that."

"That's the only thing I want to hear."

"I understand that, but please listen."

The man next to Buck stared at him and then at Hattie. He swore, then used a pillow to cover his right ear, pressing his left against the seat back.

Hattie grabbed a computer printout from her pocket and located Buck's name. "Mr. Williams, I expect you to cooperate. I don't want to bother the pilot with this."

Buck reached for her hand. She stiffened but didn't pull away. "Can we talk for just a second?"

"I'm not going to change my mind, sir. Now please, I have a plane full of frightened people."

"Aren't you one of them?" He was still holding her hand.

She pursed her lips and nodded.

"Wouldn't you like to make contact with someone? If this works, I can reach people who can make phone calls for you, let your family know you're all right, even get a message back to you. I haven't destroyed anything, and I promise I can put it back the way I found it."

"You can?"

"I can."

"And you'd help me?"

"Anything. Give me some names and phone numbers. I'll send them in with what I'm trying to upload to New York, and I'll insist that someone make the calls for you and report back to me. I can't guarantee I'll get through or that if I do they'll get back to me, but I will try."

"I'd be grateful."

"And can you protect me from other overly zealous flight attendants?"

Hattie managed a smile. "They might all want your help."

"This is a long shot as it is. Just keep everybody away from me, and let me keep trying."

"Deal," she said, but she looked troubled.

"Hattie, you're doing the right thing," he said. "It's OK in a situation like this to think of yourself a little. That's what I'm doing."

"But everybody's in the same boat, sir. And I have responsibilities."

"You have to admit, when people disappear, some rules go out the window."

Rayford Steele sat ashen faced in the cockpit. Half an hour from touchdown in Chicago, he had told the passengers everything he knew. The

simultaneous disappearance of millions all over
the globe had resulted in chaos far beyond imagination. He complimented everyone on remaining
calm and avoiding hysterics, although he had
received reports of doctors on board who handed
out Valium like candy.

Rayford had been forthright, the only way he
knew to be. He realized he had told the people
more than he might have if he'd lost an engine or
his hydraulics or even his landing gear. He had
been frank with them that those who had not had
loved ones disappear might get home to discover
that they had been victims of the many tragedies
that had ensued.

He thought, but didn't say, how grateful he was
to have been in the air when this event had taken
place. What confusion must await them on the
ground! Here, in a literal sense, they were above
it all. They had been affected, of course. People
were missing from everywhere. But except for the
staff shortage caused by the disappearance of
three crew members, the passengers didn't suffer
the way they might have had they been in traffic
or if he and Christopher had been among those
who had disappeared.

As he settled into a holding pattern miles from
O'Hare, the full impact of the tragedy began to
come into view. Flights from all over the country
were being rerouted to Chicago. Planes were

reorganized based on their fuel supplies. Rayford needed to stay in priority position after flying across the eastern seaboard and then over the Atlantic before turning back. It was not Rayford's practice to communicate with ground control until after he landed, but now the air-traffic control tower was recommending it. He was informed that visibility was excellent, despite intermittent smoke from wreckages on the ground, but that landing would be risky and precarious because the two open runways were crowded with jets. They lined either side, all the way down the runway. Every gate was full, and none were backing out. Every mode of human transport was in use, busing passengers from the ends of the runways back to the terminal.

But, Rayford was told, he would likely find that his people—at least most of them—would have to walk all the way. All remaining personnel had been called in to serve, but they were busy directing planes to safe areas. The few buses and vans were reserved for the handicapped, elderly, and flight crews. Rayford passed the word along that his crew would be walking.

Passengers reported that they had been unable to get through on the in-flight phones. Hattie Durham told Rayford that one enterprising passenger in first class had somehow hooked up the phone to his computer, and while he composed messages it was automatically dialing and redialing New York. If a line opened, this would be the guy who got through.

By the time the plane began its descent into Chicago, Buck had been able to squeeze onto only one briefly freed-up line to his computer service, which prompted him to download his waiting mail. This came just as Hattie announced that all electronic devices must be turned off.

With an acumen he didn't realize he possessed, Buck speed-tapped the keys that retrieved and filed all his messages, downloaded them, and backed him out of the linkup in seconds. Just when his machine might have interfered with flight communications, he was off-line and would have to wait to search his files for news from friends, coworkers, relatives, anyone.

Before her last-minute preparations for landing, Hattie hurried to Buck. "Anything?" He shook his head apologetically. "Thanks for trying," she said. And she began to weep.

He reached for her wrist. "Hattie, we're all going to go home and cry today. But hang in there. Get your passengers off the plane, and you can at least feel good about that."

"Mr. Williams," she sobbed, "you know we lost several old people, but not all of them. And we lost several middle-aged people, but not all of them. And we lost several people your age and my age, but not all of them. We even lost some teenagers."

He stared at her. What was she driving at?

"Sir, we lost every child and baby on this plane."

"How many were there?"

"More than a dozen. But all of them! Not one was left."

The man next to Buck roused and squinted at the late-morning sun burning through the window. "What in blazes are you two talking about?" he said.

"We're about to land in Chicago," Hattie said. "I've got to run."

"Chicago?"

"You don't want to know," Buck said.

The man nearly sat in Buck's lap to get a look out the window, his boozy breath enveloping Buck. "What, are we at war? Riots? What?"

Having just cut through the cloud bank, the plane allowed passengers a view of the Chicago area. Smoke. Fire. Cars off the road and smashed into each other and guardrails. Planes in pieces on the ground. Emergency vehicles, lights flashing, picking their way around the debris.

As O'Hare came into view, it was clear no one was going anywhere soon. There were planes as far as the eye could see, some crashed and burning, the others gridlocked in line. People trudged through the grass and between vehicles toward the terminal. The expressways that led to the airport looked like they had during the great Chicago blizzards, only without the snow.

Cranes and wreckers were trying to clear a path through the front of the terminal so cars could get in and out, but that would take hours, if not days. A snake of humanity wended its way slowly out of the great terminal buildings, between the motionless cars, and onto the ramps. People walking, walking, walking, looking for a cab or a limo. Buck began plotting how he would beat the new system. Somehow, he had to get moving and get out of such a congested area. The problem was, his goal was to get to a worse one: New York.

"Ladies and gentlemen," Rayford announced, "I want to thank you again for your cooperation today. We've been asked to put down on the only runway that will take this size plane and then to taxi to an open area about two miles from the terminal. I'm afraid I'm going to have to ask you to use our inflatable emergency chutes, because we will not be able to hook up to any gateways. If you are unable to walk to the terminal, please stay with the plane, and we will send someone back for you."

There was no thanking them for choosing Pan-Continental, no "We hope you'll make us your choice next time you need air service." He did remind them to stay seated with their belts fastened until he turned off the seat belt sign, because privately he knew this would be his most difficult landing in years. He knew he could do it, but it had been a long time since he had had to land a plane among other aircraft.

Rayford envied whoever it was in first class who had the inside track on communicating by modem. He was desperate to call Irene, Chloe, and Ray Jr. On the other hand, he feared he might never talk to them again.

THREE

HATTIE Durham and what was left of her cabin crew encouraged passengers to study the safety cards in their seat pockets. Many feared they would be unable to jump and slide down the chutes, especially with their carry-on luggage. They were instructed to remove their shoes and to jump seatfirst onto the chute. Then crew members would toss them their shoes and bags. They were advised not to wait in the terminal for their checked baggage. That, they were promised, would eventually be delivered to their homes. No guarantees when.

Buck Williams gave Hattie his card and got her phone number, "just in case I get through to your people before you do."

"You're with *Global Weekly?*" she said. "I had no idea."

"And you were going to send me to my room for tampering with the phone."

She appeared to be trying to smile. "Sorry," Buck said, "not funny. I'll let you go."

Always a light traveler, Buck was grateful he had checked no baggage. Never did, not even on international flights. When he opened the bin to pull down his leather bag, he found the old man's hat and jacket still perched atop it. Harold's wife sat staring at Buck, her eyes full, jaw set. "Ma'am," he said quietly, "would you want these?"

The grieving woman gratefully gathered in the hat and coat, and crushed them against her chest as if she would never let them go. She said something Buck couldn't hear. He asked her to repeat it. "I can't jump out of any airplane," she said.

"Stay right here," he said. "They'll send someone for you."

"But will I still have to jump and slide down that thing?"

"No, ma'am. I'm sure they'll have a lift of some sort."

Buck carefully laid his laptop and case in among his clothes. With his bag zipped, he hurried to the front of the line, eager to show others how easy it was. He tossed his shoes down first, watching them bounce and skitter onto the runway. Then he clutched his bag across his chest, took a quick step and threw his feet out in front of him.

A bit enthusiastic, he landed not on his seat but on his shoulders, which threw his feet over the top of his head. He picked up speed and hit the bottom with his weight shifting forward. The buggy-whip centripetal force slammed his stockinged feet to the ground and brought his torso up and over in a somersault that barely missed planting his face on the concrete. At the last instant, still hanging on to his bag for dear life, he tucked his head under and took the abrasion on the back of his head rather than on his nose. He fought the urge to say, "No problem," but he couldn't keep from rubbing the back of his head, already matted with blood. It wasn't a serious problem, only a nuisance. He quickly retrieved his shoes and began jogging toward the terminal, as much from embarrassment as need.

He knew there would be no more hurrying once he hit the terminal.

Rayford, Christopher, and Hattie were the last three off the 747. Before disembarking, they had made sure all able-bodied people got down the chutes and that the elderly and infirm were transported by bus. The bus driver insisted that the crew ride with him and the last passengers, but Rayford refused. "I can't see passing my own passengers as they walk to the terminal," he said. "How would that look?"

Christopher said, "Suit yourself, Cap. You mind if I take him up on his offer?"

Rayford glared at him. "You're serious?"

"I don't get paid enough for this."

"Like this was the airline's fault. Chris, you don't mean it."

"The heck I don't. By the time you get up there, you'll wish you'd ridden, too."

"I should write you up for this."

"Millions of people disappear into thin air and I should worry about getting written up for riding instead of walking? Later, Steele."

Rayford shook his head and turned to Hattie. "Maybe I'll see you up there. If you can get out of the terminal, don't wait for me."

"Are you kidding? If you're walking, I'm walking."

"You don't need to do that."

"After that dressing-down you just gave Smith? I'm walking."

"He's first officer. We ought to be last off the ship and first to volunteer for emergency duty."

"Well, do me a favor and consider me part of your crew, too. Just because I can't fly the thing doesn't mean I don't feel some ownership. And don't treat me like a little woman."

"I would never do that. Got your stuff?"

Hattie pulled her bag on wheels and Rayford carried his navigator's leather box. It was a long walk, and several times they waved off offers of rides from units speeding out to pick up the nonambulatory. Along the way they passed other passengers from their flight. Many thanked Rayford; he wasn't sure for what. For not panicking, he guessed. But they looked as terrified and shell-shocked as he felt.

They shielded their ears from flights screaming in to land. Rayford tried to calculate how long it would be before this runway was shut down, too. He couldn't imagine the other open strip holding many more planes, either. Would some have to try to put down on highways or open fields? And how far away from the big cities would they have to look for open stretches of highway unencumbered by bridges? He shuddered at the thought.

All around were ambulances and other emergency vehicles trying to get to ugly wreckage scenes.

Finally in the terminal, Rayford found crowds standing in lines behind banks of phones. Most had angry people waiting, yelling at callers who shrugged and redialed. Airport snack bars and restaurants were already sold out of or low on food, and all newspapers and magazines were gone. In shops where staffers had disappeared, looters walked off with merchandise.

Rayford wanted more than anything to sit and talk with someone about what to make of this. But everybody he saw—friend, acquaintance, or stranger—was busy trying to make arrangements. O'Hare was like a massive prison with resources dwindling and gridlock growing. No one slept. Everyone scurried about, trying to find some link to the outside world, to contact their families, and to get out of the airport.

At the flight center in the bowels of the place, Rayford found much the same thing. Hattie said she would try making her calls from the lounge and would meet him later to see if they could share a ride to the suburbs. He knew they were unlikely to find any rides going anywhere, and he didn't relish walking twenty miles. But all hotels in the area were already full.

Finally a supervisor asked for the attention of the fliers in the underground center. "We have some secure lines, about five," he said. "Whether you can get through, we don't know, but it's your best chance. They do bypass the normal trunk lines out of here, so you won't be competing with all the pay phones in the terminal. Streamline your calls. Also, there are a limited number of helicopter rides available to suburban hospitals and police departments, but naturally you're secondary to medical emergencies. Get in line over here for phones and rides to the suburbs.

As of right now we have no word of the cancellation of any flights except for the remainder of today. It's your responsibility to be back here for your next flight or to call in and find out its status."

Rayford got in line, beginning to feel the tension of having flown too long and known too little. Worse was the knowledge that he had a better idea than most of what had happened. If he was right, if it were true, he would not be getting an answer when he dialed home. As he stood there, a TV monitor above him broadcast images of the chaos. From around the globe came wailing mothers, stoic families, reports of death and destruction. Dozens of stories included eyewitnesses who had seen loved ones and friends disappear before their eyes.

Most shocking to Rayford was a woman in labor, about to go into the delivery room, who was suddenly barren. Doctors delivered the placenta. Her husband had caught the disappearance of the fetus on tape. As he videotaped her great belly and sweaty face, he asked questions. How did she feel? "How do you think I feel, Earl? Turn that thing off." What was she hoping for? "That you'll get close enough for me to slug you." Did she realize that in a few moments they'd be parents? "In about a minute, you're going to be divorced."

Then came the scream and the dropping of the camera, terrified voices, running nurses, and the doctor. CNN reran the footage in superslow motion, showing the woman going from very pregnant to nearly flat stomached, as if she had instantaneously delivered. "Now, watch with us again," the newsman intoned, "and keep your eyes on the left edge of your screen, where a nurse appears to be reading a printout from the fetal heart monitor. There, see?" The action stopped as the pregnant woman's stomach deflated. "The nurse's uniform seems to still be standing as if an invisible person is wearing it. She's gone. Half a second later, watch." The tape moved ahead and stopped. "The uniform, stockings and all, are in a pile atop her shoes."

Local television stations from around the world reported bizarre occurrences, especially in time zones where the event had happened during the day or early evening. CNN showed via satellite the video of a groom disappearing while slipping the ring onto his bride's finger. A funeral home in Australia reported that nearly every mourner disappeared from one memorial service, including the corpse, while at another service at the same time, only a few disappeared and the corpse remained. Morgues also reported corpse disappearances. At a burial, three of six pallbearers stumbled and dropped a casket when the other three disappeared. When they picked up the casket, it too was empty.

Rayford was second in line for the phone, but what he saw next on the screen convinced him he would never see his wife again. At a Christian high school soccer game at a missionary headquarters in Indonesia, most of the spectators and all but one of the players disappeared in the middle of play, leaving their shoes and uniforms on the ground. The CNN reporter announced that, in his remorse, the surviving player took his own life.

But it was more than remorse, Rayford knew. Of all people, that player, a student at a Christian school, would have known the truth immediately. The Rapture had taken place. Jesus Christ had returned for his people, and that boy was not one of them. When Rayford sat at the phone, tears streamed down his face. Someone said, "You have four minutes," and he knew that would be more than he needed. His answering machine at home picked up immediately, and he was pierced to hear the cheerful voice of his wife. "Your call is important to us," she said. "Please leave a message after the beep."

Rayford punched a few buttons to check for messages. He ran through three or four mundane ones, then was startled to hear Chloe's voice. "Mom? Dad? Are you there? Have you seen

what's going on? Call me as soon as you can.
We've lost at least ten students and two profs,
and all the married students' kids disappeared.
Is Raymie all right? Call me!" Well, at least he
knew Chloe was still around. All he wanted
was to hold her.

Rayford redialed and left a message on his own
machine. "Irene? Ray? If you're there, pick up.
If you get this message, I'm at O'Hare and
trying to get home. It may take a while if I don't
get a copter ride. I sure hope you're there."

"Let's go, Cap," someone said. "Everybody's
got a call to make."

Rayford nodded and quickly dialed his daughter's dorm room at Stanford. He got the irritating
message that his call could not be completed as
dialed.

Rayford gathered his belongings and checked
his mail slot. Besides a pile of the usual junk, he
found a padded manila envelope from his home
address. Irene had taken to mailing him little
surprises lately, the result of a marriage book
she had been urging him to read. He slipped the
envelope into his case and went looking for
Hattie Durham. Funny, he had no emotional
attraction whatever to Hattie just now. But he
felt obligated to be sure she got home.

As he stood in a crowd by the elevator, he heard
the announcement that a helicopter was available

for no more than eight pilots and would make
a run to Mount Prospect, Arlington Heights,
and Des Plaines. Rayford hurried to the pad.
"Got room for one to Mount Prospect?"

"Yup."

"How about another to Des Plaines?"

"Maybe, if he gets here in about two minutes."

"It's not a he. She's a flight attendant."

"Pilots only. Sorry."

"What if you have room?"

"Well, maybe, but I don't see her."

"I'll have her paged."

"They're not paging anyone."

"Give me a second. Don't leave without me."

The chopper pilot looked at his watch. "Three
minutes," he said. "I'm leavin' at one."

Rayford left his bag on the ground, hoping it
would hold the helicopter pilot in case he was a
little late. He charged up the stairs and into the
corridor. Finding Hattie would be impossible.
He grabbed a courtesy phone. "I'm sorry, we're
unable to page anyone just now."

"This is an emergency and I am a Pan-Continental
captain."

"What is it?"

"Have Hattie Durham meet her party at K-17."

"I'll try."

"Do it!"

Rayford stood on tiptoe to see Hattie coming,

yet still somehow she surprised him. "I was fourth in line for the phone in the lounge," she said, appearing at his side. "Got a better deal?"

"Got us a helicopter ride if we hurry," he said.

As they skipped down the stairs she said, "Wasn't it awful about Chris?"

"What about him?"

"You really don't know?"

Rayford wanted to stop and tell her to quit making him work so hard. That frustrated him about people her age. They enjoyed a volleying conversation game. He liked to get to the point. "Just tell me!" he said, sounding more exasperated than he intended.

As they burst through the door and onto the tarmac, the chopper blades whipped their hair and deafened them. Rayford's bag had already been put on board, and only one seat remained. The pilot pointed at Hattie and shook his head. Rayford grabbed her elbow and pulled her aboard as he climbed in. "Only way she's not coming is if you can't handle the weight!"

"What do you weigh, doll?" the pilot said.

"One-fifteen!"

"I can handle the weight!" he told Rayford. "But if she's not buckled in, I'm not responsible!"

"Let's go!" Rayford shouted.

He buckled himself in and Hattie sat in his lap. He wrapped his arms around her waist and clasped his wrists together. He thought how ironic it was that he had been dreaming of this for weeks, and now there was no joy, no excitement in it, nothing sensual whatever. He was miserable. Glad to be able to help her out, but miserable.

Hattie looked embarrassed and uncomfortable, and Rayford noticed she took a sheepish peek at the other seven pilots in the copter. None seemed to return her gaze. This disaster was still too fresh and there were too many unknowns. Rayford thought he heard or lip-read one of them saying, "Christopher Smith," but there was no way he could hear inside the raucous craft. He put his mouth next to Hattie's ear.

"Now what about Chris?" he said.

She turned and spoke into his ear. "They wheeled him past us while I was going into the lounge. Blood all over!"

"What happened?"

"I don't know, but, Rayford, he didn't look good!"

"How bad?"

"I think he was dead! I mean, they were working on him, but I'd be surprised if he made it."

Rayford shook his head. What next? "Did he get hit or something? Did that bus crash?" Wouldn't that be ironic!

"I don't know," she said. "The blood seemed

like it was coming from his hand or his waist or both."

Rayford tapped the pilot on the shoulder. "Do you know anything about First Officer Christopher Smith?"

"He with Pan-Con?" the pilot said.

"Yes!"

"Was he the suicide?"

Rayford recoiled. "I don't think so! Was there a suicide?"

"Lots of 'em, I guess, but mostly passengers. Only crew member I heard about was a Smith from Pan. Slit his wrists."

Rayford quickly scanned the others in the chopper to see if he recognized anyone. He didn't, but one was nodding sadly, having overheard the pilot's shouting. He leaned forward. "Chris Smith! You know him?"

"My first officer!"

"Sorry."

"What'd you hear?"

"Don't know how reliable this is, but the rumor is he found out his boys had disappeared and his wife was killed in a wreck!"

For the first time the enormity of the situation became personal for Rayford. He didn't know Smith well. He vaguely remembered Chris had two sons. Seemed they were young teenagers, very close in age. He had never met the wife.

But suicide! Was that an option for Rayford? No, not with Chloe still there. But what if he had discovered that Irene and young Ray were gone and Chloe had been killed? What would he have to live for?

He hadn't been living for them anyway, certainly not the last several months. He had been playing around on the edges of his mind with the girl in his lap, though he had never gone so far as touching her, even when she often touched him. Would he want to live if Hattie Durham were the only person he cared about? And why did he care about her? She was beautiful and sexy and smart, but only for her age. They had little in common. Was it only because he was convinced Irene was gone that he now longed to hold his own wife?

There was no affection in his embrace of Hattie Durham just now, nor in hers. Both were scared to death, and flirting was the last thing on their minds. The irony was not lost on him. He recalled that the last thing he daydreamed about—before Hattie's announcement—was finally making a move on her. How could he have known she would be in his lap hours later and that he would have no more interest in her than in a stranger?

The first stop was the Des Plaines Police Department, where Hattie disembarked. Rayford advised her to ask for a ride home with the police

if a squad car was available. Most had been
pressed into service in more congested areas, so
that was unlikely. "I'm only about a mile from
here anyway!" Hattie shouted above the roar
as Rayford helped her from the chopper. "I can
walk!" She wrapped her arms around his neck
in a fierce embrace, and he felt her quiver in fear.
"I hope everyone's OK at your place!" she said.
"Call me and let me know, OK?"

He nodded.

"OK?" she insisted.

"OK!"

As they lifted off he watched her survey the
parking lot. Spotting no squad cars, she turned
and hurried off, pulling her suitcase on wheels.
By the time the helicopter began to swing toward
Mount Prospect, Hattie was trotting toward her
condominium.

Buck Williams had been the first passenger from
his flight to reach the terminal at O'Hare. He
found a mess. No one waiting in line for a phone
would put up with his trying to plug his modem
into it, and he couldn't get his cellular phone to
work, so he made his way to the exclusive Pan-
Con Club. It, too, was jammed, but despite a
loss of personnel, including the disappearance
of several employees while on the job, some

semblance of order prevailed. Even here people waited in line for the phones, but as each became available, it was understood that some might try faxing or connecting directly by modem. While Buck waited, he went to work again on his computer, reattaching the inside modem cord to the female connector. Then he called up the messages that he had quickly downloaded before landing.

The first was from Steve Plank, his executive editor, addressed to all field personnel:

Stay put. Do not try to come to New York. Impossible here. Call when you can. Check your voice mail and your E-mail regularly. Keep in touch as possible. We have enough staff to remain on schedule, and we want personal accounts, on-the-scene stuff, as much as you can transmit. Not sure of transportation and communications lines between us and our printers, nor their employee levels. If possible, we'll print on time.

Just a note: Begin thinking about the causes. Military? Cosmic? Scientific? Spiritual? But so far we're dealing mainly with what happened.

Take care, and keep in touch.

The second message was also from Steve and was for Buck's eyes only.

Buck, ignore general staff memo. Get to New York as soon as you can at any expense. Take care of family matters, of course, and file any personal experience or reflections, just like everyone else. But you're going to head up this effort to get at what's behind the phenomenon. Ideas are like egos—everybody's got one.

Whether we'll come to any conclusions, I don't know, but at the very least we'll catalog the reasonable possibilities. You may wonder why we need you here to do this; I do have an ulterior motive. Sometimes I think because of the position I'm in, I'm the only one who knows these things; but three different department editors have turned in story ideas on various international groups meeting in New York this month. Political editor wants to cover a Jewish Nationalist conference in Manhattan that has something to do with a new world order government. What they care about that, I don't know and the political editor doesn't either. Religion editor has something in my in box about a conference of Orthodox Jews also coming for a meeting. These are not just from Israel but apparently all over, and they are no longer haggling over the Dead Sea Scrolls. They're still giddy over the destruction of Russia and her allies—

which I know you still think was supernatural, but hey, I love you anyway. Religion
editor thinks they're looking for help in
rebuilding the temple. That may be no big
deal or have anything to do with anything
other than the religion department, but I
was struck by the timing—with the other
Jewish group meeting at pretty much the
same time and at the same place about something entirely political. The other religious
conference in town is among leaders of all
the major religions, from the standard ones
to the New Agers, also talking about a one-
world religious order. They ought to get
together with the Jewish Nationalists, huh?
Need your brain on this. Don't know what
to make of it, if anything.

I know all anybody cares about is the
disappearances. But we need to keep an
eye on the rest of the world. You know
the United Nations has that international
monetarist confab coming up, trying to gauge
how we're all doing with the three-currency
thing. Personally I like it, but I'm a little
skittish about going to one currency unless
it's dollars. Can you imagine trading in yen
or marks here? Guess I'm still provincial.

Everybody's pretty enamored with this
Carpathia guy from Romania who so

impressed your friend Rosenzweig. He's
got everybody in a bind in the upper house
in his own country because he's been invited
to speak at the U.N. in a couple of weeks.
Nobody knows how he wangled an invitation, but his international popularity reminds
me a lot of Walesa or even Gorbachev.
Remember them? Ha!

Hey, friend, get word to me you didn't
disappear. As far as I know right now, I lost
a niece and two nephews, a sister-in-law I
didn't like, and possibly a couple of other
distant relatives. You think they'll be back?
Well, save that till we get rolling on what's
behind this. If I had to guess, I'm anticipating
some God-awful ransom demand. I mean,
it's not like these people who disappeared
are dead. What in the world is going to
happen to the life insurance industry? I'm
not ready to start believing the tabloids.
You just know they're going to be saying
the space aliens finally got us.

Get in here, Buck.

FOUR

Buck kept pressing a handkerchief soaked with cold water onto the back of his head. His wound had stopped bleeding, but it stung. He found another message in his E-mail in box and was about to call it up when he was tapped on the shoulder.

"I'm a doctor. Let me dress your wound."

"Oh, it's all right, and I—"

"Just let me do this, pal. I'm going crazy here with nothing to do, and I have my bag. I'm workin' free today. Call it a Rapture Special."

"A what?"

"Well, what would you call what happened?" the doctor said, removing a bottle and gauze from his bag. "This is gonna be pretty rudimentary, but we will be sterile. AIDS?"

"I'm sorry?"

"C'mon, you know the routine." He snapped

on rubber gloves. "Have you got HIV or anything fun like that?"

"No. And, hey, I appreciate this." At that instant the doctor splashed a heavy dose of disinfectant on the gauze and held it against Buck's scraped head. "Yow! Take it easy!"

"Be a big boy there, stud. This'll hurt less than the infection you'd get otherwise." He roughly scraped the wound, cleansing it and causing it to ooze blood again. "Listen, I'm going to do a little shave job so I can get a bandage to hold. All right with you?"

Buck's eyes were watering. "Yeah, sure, but what was that you said about rapture?"

"Is there any other explanation that makes sense?" the doctor said, using a scalpel to tear into Buck's hair. A club attendant came by and asked if they could move the operation into one of the washrooms.

"I promise to clean up, hon," the doctor said. "Almost done here."

"Well, this can't be sanitary, and we do have other members to think about."

"Why don't you just give them their drinks and nuts, all right? You'll find this just isn't going to upset them that much on a day like this."

"I don't appreciate being spoken to that way."

The doctor sighed as he worked. "You're right. What's your name?"

"Suzie."

"Listen, Suzie, I've been rude and I apologize. OK? Now let me finish this, and I promise not to perform any more surgery right out here in public." Suzie left, shaking her head.

"Doc," Buck said, "leave me your card so I can properly thank you."

"No need," the doctor said, putting his stuff away.

"Now give me your take on this. What did you mean about the Rapture?"

"Another time. Your turn for the phone."

Buck was torn, but he couldn't pass up the chance to communicate with New York. He tried dialing direct but couldn't get through. He hooked his modem up to the phone and initiated repeat dialing while he looked at the message from Steve Plank's secretary, the matronly Marge Potter.

Buck, you scoundrel! Like I don't have enough to do and worry about today, I've got to check on your girlfriends' families? Where'd you meet this Hattie Durham? You can tell her I reached her mother out west, but that was before a flood or storm or something knocked phone lines out again. She's perfectly healthy but rattled, and she was very grateful to know her daughter hadn't disappeared. The two sisters are OK, too, according to Mom.

You are a dear for helping people like this, Buck. Steve says you're going to try to come in. It'll be good to see you. This is so awful. So far we know of several staffers who disappeared, several more we haven't heard from, including some in Chicago. Everybody from the senior staff is accounted for, now that we've heard from you. I hoped and prayed you'd be all right. Have you noticed it seems to have struck the innocents? Everyone we know who's gone is either a child or a very nice person. On the other hand, some truly wonderful people are still here. I'm glad you're one of them, and so is Steve. Call us.

No word whether she had been able to reach Buck's widowed father or married brother. Buck wondered if that was on purpose or if she simply had no news yet. His niece and nephew had to be gone if it was true that no children had survived. Buck gave up trying to reach the office directly but again successfully connected with his on-line service. He uploaded his files and a few hastily batted out messages of his whereabouts. That way, by the time the telephone system once again took on some semblance of normalcy, *Global Weekly* would have already gotten a head start on his stuff.

He hung up and disconnected to the grateful look of the next in line, then went looking for that doctor. No luck. Marge had referred to the innocents. The doctor assumed it was the Rapture. Steve had pooh-poohed space aliens. But how could you rule out anything at this point? His mind was already whirring with ideas for the story behind the disappearances. Talk about the assignment of a lifetime!

Buck got in line at the service desk, knowing his odds of getting to New York by conventional means were slim. While he waited he tried to remember what it was Chaim Rosenzweig, the Newsmaker of the Year, had told him about the young Nicolae Carpathia of Romania. Buck had told only Steve Plank about it, and Steve agreed it wasn't worth putting in the already tight story. Rosenzweig had been impressed with Carpathia, that was true. But why?

Buck sat on the floor in line and moved when he had to. He called up his archived files on the Rosenzweig interview and did a word search on Carpathia. He recalled having been embarrassed to admit to Rosenzweig that he had never heard of the man. As the taped interview transcripts scrolled past, he hit the pause button and read.

When he noticed his low battery light flashing, he fished an extension cord out of his bag and plugged the computer into a socket along the wall. "Watch the cord," he called out occasionally as people passed. One of the women behind the counter hollered at him that he'd have to unplug.

He smiled at her. "And if I don't, are you going to have me thrown out? Arrested? Cut me some slack today, of all days!" Hardly anyone took note of the crazy man on the floor yelling at the counter woman. Such rarely happened in the Pan-Con Club, but nothing surprised anyone today.

Rayford Steele disembarked on the helipad at Northwest Community Hospital in Arlington Heights, where the pilots had to get off and make room so a patient could be flown to Milwaukee. The other pilots hung around the entrance, hoping to share a cab, but Rayford had a better idea. He began walking.

He was about five miles from home, and he was betting he could hitch a ride easier than finding a cab. He hoped his captain's uniform and his clean-cut appearance would set someone's mind at ease about giving him a ride.

As he trudged along, his trenchcoat over his arm and his bag in his hand, he had an empty, despairing feeling. By now Hattie would be getting to her condo, checking her messages, trying to get calls through to her family. If he was right that Irene and Ray Jr. were gone, where would they have been when it happened? Would he find evidence that they had disappeared rather than being killed in some related accident?

Rayford calculated that the disappearances would have taken place late evening, perhaps around 11 P.M. central time. Would anything have taken them away from home at that hour? He couldn't imagine what, and he doubted it.

A woman of about forty stopped for Rayford on Algonquin Road. When he thanked her and told her where he lived, she said she knew the area. "A friend of mine lives there. Well, lived there. Li Ng, the Asian girl on Channel 7 news?"

"I know her and her husband," Rayford said. "They still live on our street."

"Not anymore. They dedicated the noon newscast to her today. The whole family is gone."

Rayford exhaled loudly. "This is unbelievable. Have you lost people?"

"'Fraid so," she said, her voice quavery. "About a dozen nieces and nephews."

"Wow."

"You?"

"I don't know yet. I'm just getting back from a flight, and I haven't been able to reach anybody."

"Do you want me to wait for you?"

"No. I have a car. If I need to go anywhere, I'll be all right."

"O'Hare's closed, you know," she said.

"Really? Since when?"

"They just announced it on the radio. Runways are full of planes, terminals full of people, roads full of cars."

"Tell me about it."

As the woman drove, sniffling, into Mount Prospect, Rayford felt fatigue he had never endured before. Every few houses had driveways jammed with cars, people milling about. It appeared everyone everywhere had lost someone. He knew he would soon be counted among them.

"Can I offer you anything?" he asked the woman as she pulled into his driveway.

She shook her head. "I'm just glad to have been able to help. You could pray for me, if you think of it. I don't know if I can endure this."

"I'm not much for praying," Rayford admitted.

"You will be," she said. "I never was before either, but I am now."

"Then you can pray for me," he said.

"I will. Count on it."

Rayford stood in the driveway and waved to the woman till she was out of sight. The yard and the walk were spotless as usual, and the huge home, his trophy house, was sepulchral. He unlocked the front door. From the newspaper on the stoop to the closed drapes in the picture window to the bitter smell of burned coffee when he opened the door, everything pointed to what he dreaded.

Irene was a fastidious housekeeper. Her morning routine included the coffeepot on a timer kicking on at six, percolating her special blend of decaf with an egg. The radio was set to come on at 6:30, tuned to the local Christian station. The first thing Irene did when she came downstairs was open the drapes at the front and back of the house.

With a lump in his throat Rayford tossed the newspaper into the kitchen and took his time hanging up his coat and sliding his bag into the closet. He remembered the package Irene had mailed him at O'Hare and put it in his wide uniform pocket. He would carry it with him as he searched for evidence that she had disappeared. If she was gone, he sure hoped she had been right. He wanted above all else for her to have seen her dream realized, for her to have been taken away by Jesus in the twinkling of an eye—a thrilling, painless journey to his side in heaven, as she always loved to say. She deserved that if anybody did.

And Raymie. Where would he be? With her? Of course. He went with her to church, even when Rayford didn't go. He seemed to like it, to get into it. He even read his Bible and studied it.

Rayford unplugged the coffeepot that had been turning itself off and then back on for seven hours and had ruined the brew. He dumped the mess and left the pot in the sink. He flicked off the radio, which was piping the Christian station's network news hookup into the air, droning on about the tragedy and mayhem that had resulted from the disappearances.

He looked about the living room, dining room, and kitchen, expecting to see nothing but the usual neatness of Irene's home. His eyes filling with tears, he opened the drapes as she would have. Was it possible she had gone somewhere? Visited someone? Left him a message? But if she had and he did find her, what would that say about her own faith? Would that prove this was not the Rapture she believed in? Or would it mean she was lost, just like he was? For her sake, if this was the Rapture, he hoped she *was* gone. But the ache and the emptiness were already overwhelming.

He switched on the answering machine and heard all the same messages he had heard when he had gotten through from O'Hare, plus the message he had left. His own voice sounded strange to him. He detected in it a fatalism, as if he knew he was not leaving a message for his wife and son, but only pretending to.

He dreaded going upstairs. He moseyed through

the family room to the garage exit. If only one of the cars was missing. And one was! Maybe she had gone somewhere! But as soon as he thought of it, Rayford slumped onto the step just inside the garage. It was his own BMW that was gone. The one he had driven to O'Hare the day before. It would be waiting for him when the traffic cleared.

The other two cars were there, Irene's and the one Chloe used when she was home. And all those memories of Raymie were there, too. His four-wheeler, his snowmobile, his bike. Rayford hated himself for his broken promises to spend more time with Raymie. He'd have plenty of time to regret that.

Rayford stood and heard the rattle of the envelope in his pocket. It was time to go upstairs.

It was nearly Buck Williams's turn at the head of the line at the Pan-Con Club counter when he found the material he had been looking for on disk. At some point during their several days of taping, Buck had raised the issue of every other country trying to curry favor with Dr. Rosenzweig and hoping to gain access to his formula for its own gain.

"This has been an interesting aspect," Rosenzweig had allowed, his eyes twinkling. "I was

most amused by a visit from the vice president
of the United States himself. He wanted to honor
me, to bring me to the president, to have a
parade, to confer a degree, all that. He diplomati-
cally said nothing about my owing him anything
in return, but I would owe him everything, would
I not? Much was said about what a friend of
Israel the United States has been over the decades.
And this has been true, no? How could I argue?

"But I pretended to see the awards and kind-
nesses as all for my own benefit, and I humbly
turned them down. Because you see, young man,
I am most humble, am I not?" The old man had
laughed uproariously at himself and relayed
several other stories of visiting dignitaries who
worked at charming him.

"Was anyone sincere?" Buck had asked. "Did
anyone impress you?"

"Yes!" Rosenzweig had said without hesitation.
"From the most perplexing and surprising corner
of the world—Romania. I do not know if he was
sent or came on his own, but I suspect the latter
because I believe he is the lowest-ranking official
I entertained following the award. That is one of
the reasons I wanted to see him. He asked for the
audience himself. He did not go through typical
political and protocol channels."

"And he was . . . ?"

"Nicolae Carpathia."

"Carpathia like the—?"

"Yes, like the Carpathian Mountains. A melodic name, you must admit. I found him most charming and humble. Not unlike myself!" Again he had laughed.

"I've not heard of him."

"You will! You will."

Buck had tried to lead the old man. "Because he's . . ."

"Impressive, that's all I can say."

"And he's some sort of a low-level diplomat at this point?"

"He is a member of the lower house of Romanian government."

"In the senate?"

"No, the senate is the upper house."

"Of course."

"Don't feel bad that you don't know, even though you are an international journalist. This is something only Romanians and amateur political scientists like me know. That is something I like to study."

"In your spare time."

"Precisely. But even I had not known of this man. I mean, I knew someone in the House of Deputies—that's what they call the lower house in Romania—was a peacemaker and leading a movement toward disarmament. But I did not know his name. I believe his goal is global disarmament, which we Israelis have come to distrust. But of course he must first bring about disarmament in his own country, which not even you will see in your lifetime. This man is about your age, by the way. Blond and blue eyed, like the original Romanians, who came from Rome, before the Mongols affected their race."

"What did you like so much about him?"

"Let me count," Rosenzweig had said. "He knew my language as well as his own. And he speaks fluent English. Several others also, they tell me. Well educated but also widely self-taught. And I just like him as a person. Very bright. Very honest. Very open."

"What did he want from you?"

"That was what I liked the best. Because I found him so open and honest, I asked him outright that question. He insisted I call him Nicolae, and so I said, 'Nicolae' (this is after an hour of pleasantries), 'what do you want from me?' Do you know what he said, young man? He said, 'Dr. Rosenzweig, I seek only your goodwill.' What could I say? I said, 'Nicolae, you have it.' I am a bit of a pacifist myself, you know. Not unrealistically. I did not tell him this. I merely told him he had my goodwill. Which is something you also have."

"I suspect that is not something you bestow easily."

"That is why I like you and why you have it. One day you must meet Carpathia. You would like each other. His goals and dreams may never be realized even in his own country, but he is a man of high ideals. If he should emerge, you will hear of him. And as you are emerging in your own orbit, he will likely hear of you, or from you, am I right?"

"I hope you are."

Suddenly it was Buck's turn at the counter. He gathered up his extension cord and thanked the young woman for bearing with him. "Sorry about that," he said, pausing briefly for forgiveness that was not forthcoming. "It's just that today, of all days, well, you understand."

Apparently she did not understand. She'd had a rough day, too. She looked at him tolerantly and said, "What can I not do for you?"

"Oh, you mean because I did not do something you asked?"

"No," she said. "I'm saying that to everybody. It's my little joke because there's really nothing I can do for anybody. No flights are scheduled today. The airport is going to close any minute. Who knows how long it will take to clear all the wreckage and get any kind of traffic moving again? I mean, I'll take your request and every-thing, but I can't get your luggage, book you a flight, get you a phone, book you a hotel room, anything we love to do for our members. You are a member, aren't you?"

"Am I a member!"

"Gold or platinum?"

"Lady, I'm, like, a kryptonite member."

He flashed his card, showing that he was among the top 3 percent of air travelers in the world. If any flight had one seat in the cheapest section, it had to be given to him and upgraded to first class at no charge.

"Oh, my gosh," she said, "tell me you're not the Cameron Williams from that magazine."

"I am."

"*Time?* Honest?"

"Don't blaspheme. I'm from the competition."

"Oh, I knew that. The reason I know is that I wanted to get into journalism. I studied it in college. I just read about you, didn't I? Youngest award winner or most cover stories by someone under twelve?"

"Funny."

"Or something."

"I can't believe we're joking on a day like this," he said.

She suddenly clouded over. "I don't even want to think about it. So what could I do for you if I could do anything?"

"Here's the thing," Buck said. "I have to get to

New York. Now don't give me that look. I know
it's the worst place to try to get to right now. But
you know people. You know pilots who fly on
the side, charter stuff. You know what airports
they would fly out of. Let's say I had unlimited
resources and could pay whatever I needed to.
Who would you send me to?"

She stared at him. "I can't believe you asked
me that."

"Why?"

"Because I do know someone. He flies these
little jets out of like Waukegan and Palwaukee
airports. He's expensive and he's the type who
would charge double during a crisis, especially
if he knew who you were and how desperate."

"There won't be any hiding that. Give me the
info."

Hearing it on the radio or seeing it on television
was one thing. Encountering it for yourself was
something else again. Rayford Steele had no idea
how it would feel to find evidence that his own
wife and son had vanished from the face of the
earth.

At the top of the stairs he paused by the family
photos. Irene, always one for order, had hung
them chronologically, beginning with his and her
great-grandparents. Old, cracked black and

whites of stern-faced, rawboned men and women of the Midwest. Then came the faded color shots of their grandparents on their fiftieth wedding anniversaries. Then their parents, their siblings, and themselves. How long had it been since he had studied their wedding photo, her with her flip hairstyle and him with his hair over his ears and muttonchops?

And those family pictures with Chloe eight years old, holding the baby! How grateful he was that Chloe was still here and that somehow he would connect with her! But what did this all say about the two of them? They were lost. He didn't know what to hope and pray for. That Irene and Raymie were still here and that this was not what it appeared?

He could wait no longer. Raymie's door was open a crack. His alarm was beeping. Rayford turned it off. On the bed was a book Raymie had been reading. Rayford slowly pulled the blankets back to reveal Raymie's Bulls pajama top, his underpants, and his socks. He sat on the bed and wept, nearly smiling at Irene's harping about Raymie's not wearing socks to bed.

He laid the clothes in a neat pile and noticed a picture of himself on the bed table. He stood smiling inside the terminal, his cap tucked under his arm, a 747 outside the window in the background. The picture was signed, "To Raymie with love, Dad." Under that he had written, "Rayford Steele, Captain, Pan-Continental Airlines, O'Hare." He shook his head. What kind of a dad autographs a picture for his own son?

Rayford's body felt like lead. It was all he could do to force himself to stand. And then he was dizzy, realizing he hadn't eaten in hours. He slowly made his way out of Raymie's room without looking back, and he shut the door.

At the end of the hall he paused before the French doors that led to the master suite. What a beautiful, frilly place Irene had made it, decorated with needlepoint and country knickknacks. Had he ever told her he appreciated it? *Had* he ever appreciated it?

There was no alarm to turn off here. The smell of coffee had always roused Irene. Another picture of the two of them, him looking confidently at the camera, her gazing at him. He did not deserve her. He deserved this, he knew, to be mocked by his own self-centeredness and to be stripped of the most important person in his life.

He approached the bed, knowing what he would find. The indented pillow, the wrinkled covers. He could smell her, though he knew the bed would be cold. He carefully peeled back the blankets and sheet to reveal her locket, which carried a picture of him. Her flannel nightgown, the one he always kidded her about and which she wore only when he was not home, evidenced her now departed form.

His throat tight, his eyes full, he noticed her wedding ring near the pillow, where she always supported her cheek with her hand. It was too much to bear, and he broke down. He gathered the ring into his palm and sat on the edge of the bed, his body racked with fatigue and grief. He put the ring in his jacket pocket and noticed the package she had mailed. Tearing it open, he found two of his favorite homemade cookies with hearts drawn on the top in chocolate.

What a sweet, sweet woman! he thought. *I never deserved her, never loved her enough!* He set the cookies on the bedside table, their essence filling the air. With wooden fingers he removed his clothes and let them fall to the floor. He climbed into the bed and lay facedown, gathering Irene's nightgown in his arms so he could smell her and imagine her close to him.

And Rayford cried himself to sleep.

FIVE

BUCK Williams ducked into a stall in the Pan-Con Club men's room to double-check his inventory. Tucked in a special pouch inside his jeans, he carried thousands of dollars' worth of traveler's checks, redeemable in dollars, marks, or yen. His one leather bag contained two changes of clothes, his laptop, cellular phone, tape recorder, accessories, toiletries, and some serious, insulated winter gear.

He had packed for a ten-day trip to Britain when he left New York three days before the apocalyptic disappearances. His practice overseas was to do his own laundry in the sink and let it dry a whole day while wearing one outfit and having one more in reserve. That way he was never burdened with lots of luggage.

Buck had gone out of his way to stop in Chicago first to mend fences with the *Global Weekly*'s bureau chief there, a fiftyish black woman named Lucinda Washington. He had gotten crossways with her—what else was new?—when he scooped her staff on, of all things, a sports story that was right under their noses. An aging Bears legend had finally found enough partners to help him buy a professional football team, and Buck had somehow sniffed it out, tracked him down, gotten the story, and run with it.

"I admire you, Cameron," Lucinda Washington had said, characteristically refusing to use his nickname. "I always have, as irritating as you can be. But the very least you should have done was let me know."

"And let you assign somebody who should have been on top of this anyway?"

"Sports isn't even your gig, Cameron. After doing the Newsmaker of the Year and covering the defeat of Russia by Israel, or I should say by God himself, how can you even get interested in penny-ante stuff like this? You Ivy League types aren't supposed to like anything but lacrosse and rugby, are you?"

"This was bigger than a sports story, Lucy, and—"

"Hey!"

"Sorry, *Lucinda*. And wasn't that just a bit of stereotyping? Lacrosse and rugby?"

They had shared a laugh.

"I'm not even saying you should have told me you were in town," she had said. "All I'm saying is, at least let me know before the piece runs in the *Weekly*. My people and I were embarrassed enough to get beat like that, especially by the legendary Cameron Williams, but for it to be a, well—"

"That's why you squealed on me?"

Lucinda had laughed again. "That's why I told Plank it would take a face-to-face to get you back in my good graces."

"And what made you think I'd care about that?"

"Because you love me," she had said. "You can't help yourself." Buck had smiled. "But, Cameron, if I catch you in my town again, on my beat without my knowledge, I'm gonna whip your tail."

"Well, I'll tell you what, Lucinda. Let me give you a lead I don't have time to follow up on. I happen to know the NFL franchise purchase is not going to go through after all. The money was shaky and the league's gonna reject the offer. Your local legend is going to be embarrassed."

Lucinda had begun scribbling furiously. "You're not serious," she had said, reaching for her phone.

"No, I'm not, but it was sure fun to see you swing into action."

"You creep," she had said. "Anybody else I'd be throwing out of here on his can."

"But you love me. You can't help yourself."

"That wasn't even Christian," she had said.

"Don't start with that again."

"Come on, Cameron. You know you got your mind right when you saw what God did for Israel."

"Granted, but don't start calling me a Christian. Deist is as much as I'll cop to."

"Stay in town long enough to come to my church, and God'll getcha."

"He's already got me, Lucinda. But Jesus is another thing. The Israelis hate Jesus, but look what God did for them."

"The Lord works in—"

"—mysterious ways, yeah, I know. Anyway, I'm going to London Monday. Working on a hot tip from a friend there."

"Yeah? What?"

"Not on your life. We don't know each other that well yet."

She had laughed, and they had parted with a friendly embrace. That had been three days ago.

Buck had boarded the ill-fated flight to London prepared for anything. He was following a tip from a former Princeton classmate, a Welshman who had been working in the London financial district since graduate school. Dirk Burton had been a reliable source in the past, tipping off Buck about secret high-level meetings among international financiers. For years Buck had been slightly amused at Dirk's tendency to buy into conspiracy theories. "Let me get this straight," Buck had asked him once, "you think these guys are the real world leaders, right?"

"I wouldn't go that far, Cam," Dirk had said. "All I know is, they're big, they're private, and after they meet, major things happen."

"So you think they get world leaders elected, handpick dictators, that kind of a thing?"

"I don't belong to the conspiracy book club, if that's what you mean."

"Then where do you get this stuff, Dirk? Come on, you're a relatively sophisticated guy. Power brokers behind the scenes? Movers and shakers who control the money?"

"All I know is, the London Exchange, the Tokyo Exchange, the New York Exchange—we all basically drift until these guys meet. Then things happen."

"You mean like when the New York Stock Exchange has a blip because of some presidential decision or some vote of Congress, it's really because of your secret group?"

"No, but that's a perfect example. If there's a blip in your market because of your president's health, imagine what it does to world markets when the real money people get together."

"But how does the market know they're meeting? I thought you were the only one who knew."

"Cam, be serious. OK, not a lot of people agree with me, but then I don't say this to just anyone. One of our muckety-mucks is part of this group. When they have a meeting, no, nothing happens right away. But a few days later, a week, changes occur."

"Like what?"

"You're going to call me crazy, but a friend of mine is related to a girl who works for the secretary of our guy in this group, and—"

"Whoa! Hold it! What's the trail here?"

"OK, maybe the connection is a little remote, but you know the old guy's secretary is not going to say anything. Anyway, the scuttlebutt is that this guy is real hot on getting the whole world onto one currency. You know half our time is spent on exchange rates and all that. Takes computers forever to constantly readjust every day, based on the whims of the markets."

Buck was not convinced. "One global currency? Never happen," he had said.

"How can you flatly say that?"

"Too bizarre. Too impractical. Look what happened in the States when they tried to bring in the metric system."

"Should have happened. You Yanks are such rubes."

"Metrics were only necessary for international trade. Not for how far it is to the outfield wall at Yankee Stadium or how many kilometers it is from Indianapolis to Atlanta."

"I know, Cam. Your people thought you'd be paving the way for the Communists to take over if you made maps and distance markers easy for them to read. And where are your Commies now?"

Buck had passed off most of Dirk Burton's ideas until a few years later when Dirk had called him in the middle of the night. "Cameron," he had said, unaware of the nickname bestowed by his friend's colleagues, "I can't talk long. You can pursue this or you can just watch it happen and wish it had been your story. But you remember that stuff I was saying about the one world currency?"

"Yeah. I'm still dubious."

"Fine, but I'm telling you the word here is that our guy pushed the idea at the last meeting of these secret financiers and something's brewing."

"What's brewing?"

"Well, there's going to be a major United Nations Monetary Conference, and the topic is going to be streamlining currency."

"Big deal."

"It *is* a big deal, Cameron. Our guy got shot down. He, of course, was pushing for world currency to become pounds sterling."

"What a surprise that that won't happen. Look at your economy."

"But listen, the big news, if you can believe any leak out of the secret meeting, is that they have it down to three currencies for the entire world, hoping to go to just one inside a decade."

"No way. Won't happen."

"Cameron, if my information is correct, the initial stage is a done deal. The U.N. conference is just window dressing."

"And the decision has already been made by your secret puppeteers."

"That's right."

"I don't know, Dirk. You're a buddy, but I think you would rather be doing what I'm doing."

"Who wouldn't?"

"Well, that's true. I sure wouldn't want to be doing what you're doing."

"But I'm not wrong, Cameron. Test my information."

"How?"

"I'll predict what's going to come out of the U.N. within two weeks, and if I'm right, you start treating me with a little deference, a little respect."

Buck realized that he and Dirk had been sparring the way everyone at Princeton had during weekend pizza and beer bashes in the dorms. "Dirk, listen. That sounds interesting, and I'm listening. But you do know, don't you, all kidding aside, that I wouldn't think any less of you even if you were way off base here?"

"Well, thanks, Cam. Really. That means a lot to me. And for that little tidbit, I'm going to give you a bonus. I'm not only going to tell you that the U.N. resolution is going to be for dollars, marks, and yen within five years, but I'm also going to tell you that the real power behind the power is an American."

"What do you mean, the power behind the power?"

"The mightiest of the secret group of international money men."

"This guy runs the group, in other words?"

"He's the one who shot down sterling as one of the currencies and has dollars in mind for the one world commodity in the end."

"I'm listening."

"Jonathan Stonagal."

Buck had hoped Dirk would name someone ludicrous so he could burst into laughter. But he had to admit, if only to himself, that if there was anything to this, Stonagal would be a logical choice. One of the richest men in the world and long known as an American power broker, Stonagal would have to be involved if serious global finance was being discussed. Though he was already in his eighties and appeared infirm in news photos, he not only owned the biggest banks and financial institutions in the United States, but he also owned or had huge interests in the same throughout the world.

Though Dirk was a friend, Buck had felt the need to play him along a bit, to keep him eager to provide information. "Dirk, I'm going back to bed. I appreciate all this and find it very interesting. I'm going to see what comes out of this U.N. deal, and I'm also going to see if I can trace the movements of Jonathan Stonagal. If it happens the way you think, you'll be my best informant. Meanwhile, see if you can find out for me how many are in this secret group and where they meet."

"That's easy," Dirk had said. "There are at least ten, though more than that sometimes come to the meetings, including some heads of state."

"U.S. presidents?"

"Occasionally, believe it or not."

"That's sort of one of the popular conspiracy theories here, Dirk."

"That doesn't mean it isn't true. And they usually meet in France. I don't know why. Some kind of private chalet or something there gives them a sense of security."

"But nothing escapes your friend of a friend

of a relative of a subordinate of a secretary, or whatever."

"Laugh all you want, Cam. Our guy in the group, Joshua Todd-Cothran, may just not be quite as buttoned-down as the rest."

"Todd-Cothran? Doesn't he run the London Exchange?"

"That's the guy."

"Not buttoned-down? How could he have that position and not be? Plus, who ever heard of a Brit who was not buttoned-down?"

"It happens."

"Good night, Dirk."

Of course, it had all proven correct. The U.N. made its resolution. Buck discovered that Jonathan Stonagal had lived in the Plaza Hotel in New York during the ten days of the confab. Mr. Todd-Cothran of London had been one of the more eloquent speakers, expressing such eagerness to see the matter through that he volunteered to carry the torch back to the prime minister regarding Great Britain moving to the mark from the pound.

Many Third World countries fought the change, but within a few years the three currencies had swept the globe. Buck had told only Steve Plank of his tip on the U.N. meetings, but he didn't say where he'd gotten the information, and neither he nor Plank felt it worth a speculative article. "Too risky," Steve had said. Soon they both wished they had run with it in advance. "You'd have become even more of a legend, Buck."

Dirk and Buck had become closer than ever, and it wasn't unusual for Buck to visit London on short notice. If Dirk had a serious lead, Buck packed and went. His trips had often turned into excursions into countries and climates that surprised him, thus he had packed the emergency gear. Now, it appeared, it was superfluous. He was stuck in Chicago after the most electrifying phenomenon in world history, trying to get to New York.

Despite the incredible capabilities of his laptop, there was still no substitute for the pocket notebook. Buck scribbled a list of things to do before setting off again:

> Call Ken Ritz, charter pilot
> Call Dad and Jeff
> Call Hattie Durham with news of family
> Call Lucinda Washington about local hotel
> Call Dirk Burton

The phone awakened Rayford Steele. He had not moved for hours. It was early evening and beginning to get dark. "Hello?" he said, unable to mask the sleepy huskiness in his voice.

"Captain Steele?" It was the frantic voice of Hattie Durham.

"Yes, Hattie. Are you all right?"

"I've been trying to reach you for hours! My phone was dead for the longest time, then everything was busy. I thought I was getting a ring on your phone, but you never answered. I don't know anything about my mother or my sisters. What about you?"

Rayford sat up, dizzy and disoriented. "I got a message from Chloe," he said.

"I knew that," she said. "You told me at O'Hare. Are your wife and son all right?"

"No."

"No?"

Rayford was silent. What else was there to say?

"Do you know anything for sure?" Hattie asked.

"I'm afraid I do," he said. "Their bedclothes are here."

"Oh, no! Rayford, I'm sorry! Is there anything I can do?"

"No, thanks."

"Do you want some company?"

"No, thanks."

"I'm scared."

"So am I, Hattie."

"What are you going to do?"

"Keep trying to get Chloe. Hope she can come home or I can get to her."

"Where is she?"

"Stanford. Palo Alto."

"My people are in California, too," Hattie said. "They've got all kinds of trouble out there, even worse than here."

"I imagine it's because of the time difference," Rayford said. "More people on the roads, that sort of thing."

"I'm scared to death of what's become of my family."

"Let me know what you find out, Hattie, OK?"

"I will, but you were supposed to call me. 'Course my phone was dead, and then I couldn't get through to you."

"I wish I could say I tried to call you, Hattie, but I didn't. This is hard for me."

"Let me know if you need me, Rayford. You know, just someone to talk to or be with."

"I will. And you let me know what you find out about your family."

He almost wished he hadn't added that. Losing his wife and child made him realize what a vapid relationship he had been pursuing with a twenty-seven-year-old woman. He hardly knew her, and he certainly didn't much care what happened to her family any more than he cared when he heard

about a remote tragedy on the news. He knew
Hattie was not a bad person. In fact, she was nice
and friendly. But that was not why he had been
interested in her. It had merely been a physical
attraction, something he had been smart enough
or lucky enough or naive enough not to have
acted upon. He felt guilty for having considered
it, and now his own grief would obliterate all but
the most common courtesy of simply caring for
a coworker.

"There's my call waiting," she said. "Can you
hold?"

"No, just go ahead and take it. I'll call you
later."

"I'll call you back, Rayford."

"Well, OK."

Buck Williams had gotten back in line and gained
access to a pay phone. This time he wasn't trying
to hook up his computer to it. He simply wanted
to see how many personal calls he could make.
He reached Ken Ritz's answering machine first.

"This is Ritz's Charter Service. Here's the deal
in light of the crisis: I've got Learjets at both Palwaukee and Waukegan, but I've lost my other
flyer. I can get to either airport, but right now
they're not lettin' anyone into any of the major
strips. Can't get into Milwaukee, O'Hare,

Kennedy, Logan, National, Dulles, Dallas, Atlanta. I can get into some of the smaller, outlying airports, but it's a seller's market. Sorry to be so opportunistic, but I'm asking two dollars a mile, cash up front. If I can find someone who wants to come back from where you're goin', I might be able to give you a little discount. I'm checkin' this tape tonight and will take off first thing in the morning. Longest trip with guaranteed cash gets me. If your stop is on the way, I'll try to squeeze you in. Leave me a message and I'll get back to you."

That was a laugh. How would Ken Ritz get hold of Buck? With his cellular phone unreliable, the only thing he could think of was to leave his New York voice-mail number. "Mr. Ritz, my name is Buck Williams, and I need to get as close to New York City as you can get me. I'll pay the full fare you're asking in traveler's checks, redeemable in whatever currency you want." Sometimes that was attractive to private contractors because they kept up with the differences in currency and could make a little margin on the exchange. "I'm at O'Hare and will try to find a place to stay in the suburbs. Just to save you time, let me just pick somewhere between here and Waukegan. If I get a new number in the meantime, I'll call it in. Meanwhile, you may leave a message for me at the following New York number."

Buck was still unable to get through to his office
directly, but his voice-mail number worked. He
retrieved his new messages, mostly from coworkers checking on him and lamenting the loss of
mutual friends. Then there was the welcome
message from Marge Potter, who was a genius
to think of leaving it there for him. "Buck, if you
get this, call your father in Tucson. He and your
brother are together, and I hate to tell you here,
but they're having trouble reaching Jeff's wife
and the kids. They should have news by the time
you call. Your father was most grateful to hear
that you were all right."

Buck's voice mail also noted that he still had
a saved message. That was the one from Dirk
Burton that had spurred his trip in the first place.
He would need to listen to it again when he had
time. Meanwhile, he left a message for Marge that
if she had time and an open line, she needed to let
Dirk know Buck's flight never made it to Heathrow. Of course, Dirk would know that by now,
but he needed to know Buck wasn't among the
missing and that he would get there in due time.

Buck hung up and dialed his father. The line
was busy, but it was not the same kind of a tone
that tells you the lines are down or that the whole
system is kaput. Neither was it that irritating
recording he'd grown so used to. He knew it
would be only a matter of time before he could

get through. Jeff must be beside himself not knowing about his wife, Sharon, and the kids. They'd had their differences and had even been separated before the children came along, but for several years the marriage had been better. Jeff's wife had proven forgiving and conciliatory. Jeff himself admitted he was puzzled that she would take him back. "Call me undeserving, but grateful," he once told Buck. Their son and daughter, who both looked like Jeff, were precious.

Buck pulled out the number the beautiful blonde flight attendant had given him and chastised himself for not trying again to reach her earlier. It took a while for her to answer.

"Hattie Durham, this is Buck Williams."

"Who?"

"Cameron Williams, from the *Global*—"

"Oh yes! Any news?"

"Yes, ma'am, good news."

"Oh, thank God! Tell me."

"Someone from my office tells me they reached your mother and that she and your sisters are fine."

"Oh, thank you, thank you, thank you! I wonder why they haven't called here? Maybe they've tried. My phone has been haywire."

"There are other problems in California, ma'am. Lines down, that kind of a thing. It may be a while before you can talk to them."

"I know. I heard. Well, I sure appreciate this. How about you? Have you been able to reach your family?"

"I got word that my dad and brother are OK. We still don't know about my sister-in-law and the kids."

"Oh. How old are the kids?"

"Can't remember. Both under ten, but I don't know exactly."

"Oh." Hattie sounded sad, guarded.

"Why?" Buck asked.

"Oh, nothing. It's just that—"

"What?"

"You can't go by what I say."

"Tell me, Miss Durham."

"Well, you remember what I told you on the plane. And on the news it looks like all children are gone, even unborn ones."

"Yeah."

"I'm not saying that means your brother's children are—"

"I know."

"I'm sorry I brought that up."

"No, it's OK. This is too strange, isn't it?"

"Yeah. I just got off the phone with the captain who piloted the flight you were on. He lost his wife and son, but his daughter is OK. She's in California, too."

"How old is she?"

"About twenty, I guess. She's at Stanford."

"Oh."

"Mr. Williams, what did you call yourself?"

"Buck. It's a nickname."

"Well, Buck, I know better than to say what I said about your niece and nephew. I hope there are exceptions and that yours are OK." She began to cry.

"Miss Durham, it's OK. You have to admit, no one is thinking straight right now."

"You can call me Hattie."

That struck him as humorous under the circumstances. She had been apologizing for being inappropriate, yet she didn't want to be too formal. If he was Buck, she was Hattie.

"I suppose I shouldn't tie up this line," he said. "I just wanted to get the news to you. I thought maybe by now you already knew."

"No, and thanks again. Would you mind calling me again sometime, if you think of it? You seem like a nice person, and I appreciate what you did for me. It would be nice to hear from you again. This is kind of a scary, lonely time."

He couldn't argue with that understatement. Funny, her request had sounded like anything but a come-on. She seemed wholly sincere, and he was sure she was. A nice, scared, lonely woman whose world had been skewed, just like his and everyone's he knew.

When Buck got off the phone, he saw the young woman at the counter flagging him down. "Listen," she whispered, "they don't want me making an announcement that would start a stampede, but we just heard something interesting. The livery companies have gotten together and moved their communications center out to a median strip near the Mannheim Road interchange."

"Where's that?"

"Just outside the airport. There's no traffic coming into the terminals anyway. Total gridlock. But if you can walk as far as that interchange, supposedly you'll find all those guys with walkie-talkies trying to get limos in and out from there."

"I can imagine the prices."

"No, you probably can't."

"I can imagine the wait."

"Like standing in line for a rental car in Orlando," she said.

Buck had never done that, but he could imagine that, too. And she was right. After he had hiked, with a crowd, to the Mannheim interchange, he found a mob surrounding the dispatchers. Intermittent announcements got everyone's attention.

"We're filling every car. A hundred bucks a head to any suburb. Cash only. Nothing's going to Chicago."

"No cards?" someone shouted.

"I'll say it again," the dispatcher said. "Cash only. If you know you've got cash or a check-book at home, you can plead with the driver to trust you till you get there." He called out a list-ing of which companies were heading which directions. Passengers ran to fill the cars as they lined up on the shoulder of the expressway.

Buck handed a hundred-dollar traveler's check to the dispatcher for the northern suburbs. An hour and a half later, he joined several others in a limo. After checking his cellular phone again to no avail, he offered the driver fifty dollars to use his phone. "No guarantees," the driver said. "Sometimes I get through, some-times I don't."

Buck checked the phone log in his laptop for Lucinda Washington's home number and dialed. A teenage boy answered, "Washingtons."

"Cameron Williams of *Global Weekly* calling for Lucinda."

"My mom's not here," the young man said.

"Is she still at the office? I need a recommenda-tion where to stay near Waukegan."

"She's nowhere," the boy said. "I'm the only one left. Mama, Daddy, everybody else is gone. Disappeared."

"Are you sure?"

"Their clothes are here, right where they were

sitting. My daddy's contact lenses are still on top of his bathrobe."

"Oh, man! I'm sorry, son."

"That's all right. I know where they are, and I can't even say I'm surprised."

"You know where they are?"

"If you know my mama, you know where she is, too. She's in heaven."

"Yeah, well, are you all right? Is there someone to look after you?"

"My uncle's here. And a guy from our church. Probably the only one who's still around."

"You're all right then?"

"I'm all right."

Cameron folded the phone and handed it back to the driver. "Any idea where I should stay if I'm trying to fly out of Waukegan in the morning?"

"The chain hotels are probably full, but there's a couple of fleabags on Washington you might sneak into. You'd be close enough to the airport. You'd be my last drop-off."

"Fair enough. They got phones in those dives?"

"More likely a phone and a TV than running water."

SIX

IT HAD been ages since Rayford Steele had been drunk. Irene had never been much of a drinker, and she had become a teetotaler during the last few years. She insisted he hide any hard stuff if he had to have it in the house at all. She didn't want Raymie even knowing his daddy still drank.

"That's dishonest," Rayford had countered.

"It's prudent," she said. "He doesn't know everything, and he doesn't have to know everything."

"How does that jibe with your insistence that we be totally truthful?"

"Telling the whole truth doesn't always mean telling everything you know. You tell your crew you're taking a bathroom break, but you don't go into detail about what you're doing in there, do you?"

"Irene!"

"I'm just saying you don't have to make it obvious to your preteen son that you drink hard liquor."

He had found her point hard to argue, and he had kept his bourbon stashed high and out of sight. If ever there was a moment that called for a stiff drink, this was it. He reached behind the empty cake cover in the highest cabinet over the sink and pulled down a half-finished fifth of whiskey. His inclination, knowing no one he cared about would ever see, was to tip it straight up and guzzle. But even at a time like this there were conventions and manners. Guzzling booze from the bottle was simply not his style.

Rayford poured three inches into a wide crystal glass and threw it back like a veteran. That was about as out of character as he could find comfortable. The stuff hit the back of his throat and burned all the way down, giving him a chill that made him shudder and groan. *What an idiot!* he thought. *And on an empty stomach, too.*

He was already getting a buzz when he replaced the bottle, then thought better of it. He slipped it into the garbage under the sink. Would this be a nice memorial to Irene, giving up even the occasional hard drink? There would be no benefit to Raymie now, but he didn't feel right about drinking alone anyway. Did he have the capacity to become a closet drunk? *Who doesn't?* he wondered. Regardless, he wasn't going to cash in his maturity because of what had happened.

Rayford's sleep had been deep but not long enough. He had few immediate chores. First he had to connect with Chloe. Second he had to find out what Pan-Con wanted from him in the next week. Normal regulations would have grounded him after an overly long flight and a rerouted emergency landing. But who knew what was going on now?

How many pilots had they lost? When would runways be cleared? Flights scheduled? If he knew anything about the airlines, it would all be about dollars. As soon as they could get those machines airborne, they could start being profitable again. Well, Pan-Con had been good to him. He would hang in there and do his part. But what was he supposed to do about this grief, this despair, this empty ache?

Finally he understood the bereaved who complained when their loved one was too mangled to see or whose body had been destroyed. They often complained that there was no sense of closure and that the grieving process was more difficult because they had a hard time imagining their loved one actually dead.

That had always seemed strange to him. Who would want to see a wife or child stretched out and made up for a funeral? Wouldn't you want to remember them alive and happy as they were? But he knew better now. He had no doubt that his wife and son were gone as surely as if they had died, as his own parents had years before. Irene and Ray would not be coming back, and he didn't know if he would ever see them again, because he didn't know if there were second chances on this heaven thing.

He longed to be able to see their bodies, at least—in bed, in a casket, anywhere. He would have given anything for one last glimpse. It wouldn't have made them any less dead to him, but maybe he wouldn't feel so abandoned, so empty.

Rayford knew there would not likely be phone connections between Illinois and California for hours, maybe days. Yet he had to try. He dialed Stanford, the main administration number, and didn't even get a busy signal or a recorded message. He dialed Chloe's room. Still nothing. Every half hour or so he hit the redial button. He refused to hope she would answer; if she did, it would be a wonderful surprise.

Rayford found himself ravenous and knew he'd better get something in his stomach before the few ounces of booze did a number on him. He mounted the stairs again, stopping in Raymie's room to pick up the little pile of clothes by which he would remember the boy. He put them in a cardboard gift box he found in Irene's closet, then placed her nightgown, locket, and ring in another.

He took the boxes downstairs, along with the two cookies she had mailed him. The rest of that batch of cookies had to be around somewhere. He found them in a Tupperware bowl in the cupboard. He was grateful that their smell and taste would remind him of her until they were gone.

Rayford added a couple to the two he had brought down, put them on a paper plate, and poured himself a glass of milk. He sat at the kitchen table next to the phone but couldn't force himself to eat. He felt paralyzed. To busy himself, he erased the calls on the answering machine and added a new outgoing message. He said, "This is Rayford Steele. If you must, please leave a very brief message. I am trying to leave this line open for my daughter. Chloe, if it's you, I'm either sleeping or close by, so give me a chance to pick up. If we don't connect for some reason, do whatever you have to, to get home. Any airline can charge it to me. I love you."

And with that he slowly ate his cookies, the smell and taste bringing images to him of Irene in the kitchen, and the milk making him long for his boy. This was going to be hard, so hard.

He was exhausted, and yet he couldn't bring himself to go upstairs again. He knew he would have to force himself to sleep in his own bedroom that night. For now he would stretch out on the couch in the living room and hope Chloe would get through. He idly pushed the redial button again, and this time he got the quick busy signal that told him something was happening. At the very least, lines were being worked on. That was progress. He knew she was thinking of him while he was thinking of her. But she had no idea what might have happened to her mother or her brother. Would he have to tell her by phone? He feared he would. She would surely ask.

He lumbered to the couch and lay down, a sob in his throat but no more tears to accompany it. If only Chloe would somehow get his message and get started home, he could at least tell her face-to-face.

Rayford lay there grieving, knowing the television would be full of scenes he didn't want to see, dedicated around the clock to the tragedy and mayhem all over the world. And then it hit him. He sat up, staring out the window in the darkness. He owed it to Chloe not to fail her. He loved her and she was all he had left. He had to find out how they had missed everything Irene had been trying to tell them, why it had been so hard to accept and believe. Above all, he had to study, to learn, to be prepared for whatever happened next.

If the disappearances were of God, if they had been his doing, was this the end of it? The Christians, the real believers, get taken away, and the rest are left to grieve and mourn and realize their error? Maybe so. Maybe that was the price. *But then what happens when* we *die?* he thought. *If heaven is real, if the Rapture was a fact, what does that say about hell and judgment? Is that our fate? We go through this hell of regret and remorse, and then we literally go to hell, too?*

Irene had always talked of a loving God, but even God's love and mercy had to have limits. Had everyone who denied the truth pushed God to his limit? Was there no more mercy, no second chance? Maybe there wasn't, and if that was so, that was so.

But if there were options, if there was still a way to find the truth and believe or accept or whatever it was Irene said one was supposed to do, Rayford was going to find it. Would it mean admitting that he didn't know everything? That he had relied on himself and that now he felt stupid and weak and worthless? He could admit that. After a lifetime of achieving, of excelling, of being better than most and the best in most circles, he had been as humbled as was possible in one stroke.

There was so much he didn't know, so much he didn't understand. But if the answers were still there, he would find them. He didn't know whom to ask or where to start, but this was something he and Chloe could do together. They'd always gotten along all right. She'd gone through the typical teenage independence, but she had never done anything stupid or irreparable as far as he knew. In fact, they had probably been too close; she was too much like him.

It wasn't simply Raymie's age and innocence that had allowed his mother's influence to affect him so. It was his spirit. He didn't have the killer instinct, the "me first" attitude Rayford thought he would need to succeed in the real world. He wasn't effeminate, but Rayford had worried that he might be a mama's boy—too compassionate, too sensitive, too caring. He was always looking out for someone else when Rayford thought he should be looking out for number one.

How grateful he was now that Raymie took after his mother more than he took after his father. And how he wished there had been some of that in Chloe. She was competitive, a driver, someone who had to be convinced and persuaded. She could be kind and generous when it suited her purpose, but she was like her dad. She took care of herself.

Good job, big shot, Rayford told himself. *The*

girl you were so proud of because she was so much like you is in your same predicament.

That, he decided, would have to change. As soon as they reconnected, that *would* change. They would be on a mission, a quest for truth. If he was already too late, he would have to accept and deal with that. He'd always been one who went for a goal and accepted the consequences. Only these consequences were eternal. He hoped against all hope that there was another chance at truth and knowledge out there somewhere. The only problem was that the ones who knew were gone.

The Midpoint Motel on Washington Street, a few miles from the tiny Waukegan Airport, was tacky enough that there wasn't a waiting list. Buck Williams was pleasantly surprised they had not even raised their rates for the crisis. When he saw the room, he knew why, and he wondered what two places in the world this dive was midpoint *between.* Whatever they were, either had to be better. There was a phone, however, and a shower, a bed, and a TV. Run-down as it was, it would suffice. First Buck called his voice mail in New York. Nothing from this Ritz character or anything else new, so he listened to his saved message from Dirk Burton, which reminded him why he had felt it so important to get to London. Buck tapped it into his laptop as he listened:

Cameron, you always tell me this message center is confidential, and I hope you're right. I'm not even going to identify myself, but you know who it is. Let me tell you something major and encourage you to come here as quickly as possible. The big man, your compatriot, the one I call the supreme power broker internationally, met here the other day with the one I call our muckety-muck. You know who I mean. There was a third party at the meeting. All I know is that he's from Europe, probably Eastern Europe. I don't know what their plans are for him, but apparently something on a huge scale.

My sources say your man has met with each of his key people and this same European in different locations. He introduced him to people in China, the Vatican, Israel, France, Germany, here, and the States. Something is cooking, and I don't even want to suggest what it is other than in person. Visit me as soon as you can. In case that's not possible, let me just encourage this: Watch the news for the installation of a new leader in Europe. If you say, as I did, that no elections are scheduled and no changes of power are imminent, you'll get my drift. Come soon, friend.

Buck called Ken Ritz's machine to tell him where he was. Then he tried calling west once again and finally got through. Buck was surprised at what a relief it was to hear his father's voice, though he sounded tired, discouraged, and not a little panicky.

"Everybody OK out there, Dad?"

"Well, not everybody. Jeff was here with me, but he's taken the four-wheel drive to see if he can get to the accident site where Sharon was last seen."

"Accident?"

"She was pickin' up the kids at a retreat or something, something to do with her church. She doesn't go with us anymore, you know. Story is, she never got there. Car flipped over. No trace of her, 'cept her clothes, and you know what that means."

"She's gone?"

"Looks that way. Jeff can't accept it. He's takin' it hard. Wants to see for himself. Trouble is, the kids are gone, too, all of 'em. All their friends, everybody at that retreat thing in the mountains. State police found all the kids' clothes, about a hundred sets of them, and some kind of a late-night snack burning on the stove."

"Whew, boy! Tell Jeff I'm thinking of him. If he wants to talk, I'm here."

"I can't imagine he'll want to talk, Cameron, unless you have some answers."

"That's one thing I haven't got, Dad. I don't know who does. I have this feeling that whoever had the answers is gone."

"This is awful, Cam. I wish you were out here with us."

"Yeah, I'll bet."

"You bein' sarcastic?"

"Just expressing the truth, Dad. If you wanted me out there, it'd be the first time."

"Well, this is the kind of time when maybe we change our minds."

"About me? I doubt it."

"Cameron, let's not get into this, huh? For once, think of somebody other than yourself. You lost a sister-in-law and a niece and a nephew yesterday, and your brother'll probably never get over it."

Buck bit his tongue. Why did he always have to do this, and especially right now? His dad was right. If only Buck could admit that, maybe they could move on. He had been resented by the family ever since he'd gone on to college, following his academic prowess to the Ivy League. Where he came from, the kids were supposed to follow their parents into the business. His dad's

was trucking fuel into the state, mostly from
Oklahoma and Texas. It was a tough business
with local people thinking the resources ought to
all come from their own state. Jeff had worked
his way up in the little business, starting in the
office, then driving a truck, now running the
day-to-day operations.

There had been a lot of bad blood, especially
since Cameron was away at school when his
mother fell ill. She had insisted he stay in school,
but when he missed coming home for Christmas
due to money problems, his dad and brother never
really forgave him. His mother died while he was
away, and he got the cold shoulder even at her
funeral.

Some healing had occurred over the years,
mostly because his family loved to claim him
and brag about him once he became known as
a journalistic prodigy. He had let bygones be
bygones but resented that he was now welcome
because he was somebody. And so he rarely went
home. There was too much baggage to reconcile
completely, but he was still angry with himself
for opening old wounds when his family was
suffering.

"If there's some kind of memorial service or
something, I'll try to make it, Dad. All right?"

"You'll *try?*"

"That's all I can promise. You can imagine how

busy things are at *Global* right now. Needless
to say, this is the story of the century."

"Will you be writing the cover story?"

"I'll have a lot to do with the coverage, yeah."

"But the cover?"

Buck sighed, suddenly tired. It was no wonder.
He'd been awake nearly twenty-four hours.
"I don't know, Dad. I've already filed a lot of
stuff. My guess is this next issue will be a huge
special with lots of stuff from all over. It's
unlikely my piece would be the sole cover article.
It looks like I do have the assignment for a pretty
major treatment two weeks from now."

He hoped that would satisfy his dad. He
wanted to get off and get some sleep. But it
didn't.

"What's that mean? What's the story?"

"Oh, I'll be pulling together several writers'
pieces on the theories behind what's happened."

"That'll be a big job. Everybody I talk to has a
different idea. You know your brother is afraid it
was like the last judgment of God or something."

"He does?"

"Yeah. But I don't think so."

"Why not, Dad?" He didn't really want to get
into a lengthy discussion, but this surprised him.

"Because I asked our pastor. He said if it was
Jesus Christ taking people to heaven, he and I and
you and Jeff would be gone, too. Makes sense."

"Does it? I've never claimed any devotion to the faith."

"The heck you haven't. You always get into this liberal, East Coast baloney. You know good and well we had you in church and Sunday school from the time you were a baby. You're as much a Christian as any one of us."

Cameron wanted to say, "Precisely my point." But he didn't. It was the lack of any connection between his family's church attendance and their daily lives that made him quit going to church altogether the day it became his choice.

"Yeah, well, tell Jeff I'm thinking about him, huh? And if I can work it out at all, I'll get back there for whatever he's going to do about Sharon and the kids."

Buck was grateful the Midpoint at least had plenty of hot water for a long shower. He had forgotten about the nagging throb at the back of his head until the water hit it and loosened the bandage. He didn't have anything to redress it, so he just let it bleed awhile, then found some ice. In the morning he would find a bandage, just for looks. For now, he had had it. He was bone weary.

There was no remote control for the TV and no way he would get up once he stretched out. He turned CNN on low so it wouldn't interrupt his sleep, and he watched the world roundup before dozing off. Images from around the globe were almost more than he could take, but news was his business. He remembered the many earthquakes and wars of the last decade and the nightly coverage that was so moving. Now here was a thousand times more of the same, all on the same day. Never in history had more people been killed in one day than those who disappeared all at once. Had they been killed? Were they dead? Would they be back?

Buck couldn't take his eyes, heavy as they were, off the screen as image after image showed disappearances caught on home videotape. From some countries came professional tapes of live television shows in progress, a host's microphone landing atop his empty clothes, bouncing off his shoes, and making a racket as it rolled across the floor. The audience screamed. One of the cameras panned the crowd, which had been at capacity a moment before. Now several seats were empty, clothes draped across them.

Nothing could have been scripted like this, Buck thought, blinking slowly. If somebody tried to sell a screenplay about millions of people disappearing, leaving everything but their bodies behind, it would be laughed off.

Buck was not aware that he was asleep until the cheap phone jangled so loudly it sounded as if it would rattle itself off the table. He groped for it.

"Sorry to bother you, Mr. Williams, but I just noticed you was off the phone there. While you was talkin', you got a call. Guy name of Ritz. Says you can call him or you can just be waitin' for him outside at six in the mornin'."

"OK. Thanks."

"What're you gonna do? Call him or meet him?"

"Why do you need to know?"

"Oh, I ain't bein' nosy or nothin'. It's just that if you're leavin' here at six, I gotta get payment in advance. You got the long-distance call and all. And I don't get up till seven."

"I'll tell you what, uh, what was your name?"

"Mack."

"I'll tell you what, Mack. I left you my charge card number, so you know I'm not going to sneak out on you. But in the morning I'm going to leave a traveler's check in the room for you, covering the price of the room and a lot more than enough for the phone call. You get my meaning?"

"A tip?"

"Yes, sir."

"That would be nice."

"What I need for you to do for me is slip a bandage under my door."

"I got one. You need it right now? You all right?"

"I'm fine. Not now. When you turn in. Nice

and quiet like. And turn off my phone, OK, just in case? If I have to get up that early, I've got to do some serious sleeping right now. Can you handle that for me, Mack?"

"I sure can. I'll turn it off right now. You want a wake-up call?"

"No, thanks," Buck said, and he smiled when he realized the phone was dead in his hand. Mack was as good as his word. If he found that bandage in the morning, he would leave Mack a good tip. Buck forced himself to get up and shut off the TV set and the light. He was the type who could look at his watch before retiring and wake up precisely when he told himself to. It was nearly midnight. He would be up at five-thirty.

By the time he hit the mattress, he was out. When he awoke five and a half hours later, he had not moved a muscle.

Rayford felt as if he were sleepwalking as he padded through the kitchen to head upstairs. He couldn't believe how tired he still was after his long nap and his fitful dozing on the couch. The newspaper was still rolled up and rubber-banded on a chair where he had tossed it. If he had any trouble sleeping upstairs, maybe he would glance at the paper. It should be interesting to read the meaningless news of a world that didn't realize it

was going to suffer the worst trauma in its
history just after the paper had been set in type.

Rayford punched the redial button on the
phone and walked slowly toward the stairs, only
half listening. What was that? The dial tone had
been interrupted, and the phone in Chloe's dorm
room was ringing. He hurried to the phone as a
girl answered.

"Chloe?"

"No. Mr. Steele?"

"Yes!"

"This is Amy. Chloe's trying to find a way back
there. She'll try to call you along the way, sometime tomorrow. If she can't get through, she'll call
you when she gets there or she'll get a cab home."

"She's on her way?"

"Yeah. She didn't want to wait. She tried calling
and calling, but—"

"Yeah, I know. Thanks, Amy. Are you all
right?"

"Scared to death, like everybody else."

"I can imagine. Did you lose anyone?"

"No, and I feel kinda guilty about that. Seems
like everyone I know lost somebody. I mean I
lost a few friends, but nobody close, no family."

Rayford didn't know whether to express
congratulations or remorse. If this was what he
now believed it had been, this poor child hardly
knew anyone who'd been taken to heaven.

"Well," he said, "I'm glad you're all right."

"How about you?" she said. "Chloe's mom and brother?"

"I'm afraid they're gone, Amy."

"Oh, no!"

"But I would appreciate your letting me tell Chloe, just in case she reaches you before she reaches me."

"Oh, don't worry. I don't think I could tell her even if you wanted me to."

Rayford lay in bed several minutes, then idly thumbed through the first section of the paper. Hmm. A surprise move in Romania.

> Democratic elections became passé when, with the seeming unanimous consensus of the people and both the upper and lower houses of government, a popular young businessman/politician assumed the role of president of the country. Nicolae Carpathia, a 33-year-old born in Cluj, had in recent months taken the nation by storm with his popular, persuasive speaking, charming the populace, friend and foe alike. Reforms he proposed for the country saw him swept to prominence and power.

Rayford glanced at the photo of the young Carpathia, a strikingly handsome blond who looked not unlike a young Robert Redford. *Wonder if he would've wanted the job had he known what was about to happen?* Rayford thought. *Whatever he has to offer won't amount to a hill of beans now.*

SEVEN

KEN Ritz roared up to the Midpoint precisely at six, rolled down his window, and said, "You Williams?"

"I'm your man," Buck said. He climbed into the late model four-wheel drive with his one bag. Fingering his freshly bandaged head, Buck smiled at the thought of Mack enjoying his extra twenty bucks.

Ritz was tall and lean with a weathered face and a shock of salt-and-pepper hair. "Let's get down to business," he said. "It's 740 miles from O'Hare to JFK and 746 from Milwaukee to JFK. I'm gonna get you as close to JFK as I can, and we're about equidistant between O'Hare and Milwaukee, so let's call it 743 air miles. Multiply that by two bucks, you're talkin' fourteen hundred and eighty-six. Round it off to fifteen hundred for the taxi service, and we got us a deal."

"Deal," Buck said, pulling out his checks and starting to sign. "Pretty expensive taxi."

Ritz laughed. "Especially for a guy coming out of the Midpoint."

"It was lovely."

Ritz parked in a metal Quonset hut at the Waukegan airport and chatted while running through preflight procedures. "No crashes here," he said. "There were two at Palwaukee. They lost a couple of staff people here though. Weirder than weird, wasn't it?"

Buck and Ritz shared stories of lost relatives, where they were when it happened, and exactly who they were. "Never flew a writer before," Ken said. "Charter, I mean. Must've flown a bunch of your types when I was commercial."

"Better money on your own?"

"Yeah, but I didn't know that when I switched. It wasn't my choice."

They were climbing into the Lear. Buck shot him a double take. "You were grounded?"

"Don't worry, partner," the pilot said. "I'll get you there."

"You owe it to me to tell me if you were grounded."

"I was fired. There's a difference."

"Depends on what you were fired for, doesn't it?"

"True enough. This ought to make you feel

real good. I was fired for bein' too careful. Beat that."

"Talk to me," Buck said.

"You remember a lot of years ago when there was all that flak about puddle jumpers goin' down in icy weather?"

"Yeah, until they made some adjustments or something."

"Right. Well, you remember that one pilot refused to fly even after he was told to and the public was assured everything up to that point was explainable or a fluke?"

"Uh-huh."

"And you remember that there was another crash right after that, which proved the pilot right?"

"Vaguely."

"Well, I remember it plain as day, because you're lookin' at him."

"I do feel better."

"You know how many of those same model puddle jumpers are in the air today? Not a one. When you're right, you're right. But was I reinstated? No. Once a troublemaker, always a troublemaker. Lots of my colleagues were grateful though. And some pilots' widows were pretty angry that I got ignored and then canned, too late for their husbands."

"Ouch."

As the jet screamed east, Ritz wanted to know what Buck thought of the disappearances. "Funny you should ask," Buck said. "I've got to start working on that in earnest today. What's your read of it? And do you mind if I flip on a tape recorder?"

"Fine," Ritz said. "Dangedest thing I've ever seen. 'Course, that doesn't make me unique. I have to say, though, I've always believed in UFOs."

"You're kidding! A levelheaded, safety-conscious pilot?"

Ritz nodded. "I'm not talking about little green men or space aliens who kidnap people. I'm talking about some of the more documentable stuff, like some astronauts have seen, and some pilots."

"You ever see anything?"

"Nope. Well, a couple of unexplainable things. Some lights or mirages. Once I thought I was flying too close to a squad of helicopters. Not too far from here either. Glenview Naval Air Station. I radioed a warning, then lost sight of them. I suppose that's explainable. I could have been going faster than I realized and not been as close as I thought. But I never got an answer, no acknowledgment that they were even airborne. Glenview wouldn't confirm it. I shrugged it off, but a few weeks later, close to the same spot, my instruments went wacky on me. Dials spinning, meters sticking, that kind of thing."

"What did you make of that?"

"Magnetic field or some force like that. Could be explainable, too. You know there's no sense reporting strange occurrences or sightings near a military base, because they just reject 'em out of hand. They don't even take seriously anything strange within several miles of a commercial airport. That's why you never hear stories of UFOs near O'Hare. Not even considered."

"So, you don't buy the kidnapping space aliens, but you connect the disappearances with UFOs?"

"I'm just sayin' it's not like *E.T.*, with creatures and all that. I think our ideas of what space people would look like are way too simple and rudimentary. If there is intelligent life out there, and there has to be just because of the sheer odds—"

"What do you mean?"

"The vastness of space."

"Oh, so many stars and so much area that something has to be out there somewhere."

"Exactly. And I agree with people who think those beings are more intelligent than we are. Otherwise, they wouldn't have made it here, if they are here. And if they are, I'm thinking they're sophisticated and advanced enough that they can do things to us we've never dreamed of."

"Like making people disappear right out of their clothes."

"Sounded pretty silly until the other night, didn't it?"

Buck nodded.

"I've always laughed about people assuming these beings could read our thoughts or get into our heads and stuff," Ritz continued. "But look who's missing. Everybody I've read about or heard about or knew who's now gone was either under twelve years old or was an unusual personality."

"With all the people who disappeared, you think they had something in common?"

"Well, they've got something in common now, wouldn't you say?"

"But something set them apart, made them easier to snatch?" Buck asked.

"That's what I think."

"So we're still here because we were strong enough to resist, or maybe we weren't worth the trouble."

Ritz nodded. "Something like that. It's almost like some force or power was able to read the level of resistance or weakness, and once that force got sunk in, it was able to rip those people right off the earth. They disappeared in an instant, so they had to be dematerialized. The question is whether they were destroyed in the process or could be reassembled."

"What do you think, Mr. Ritz?"

"At first I would have said no. But a week ago I would have told you that millions of people all over the world disappearing into thin air sounds like a B movie. When I allow for the fact that it actually happened, I have to allow for the next logical step. Maybe they're somewhere specific in some form, and maybe they can return."

"That's a comforting thought," Buck said. "But is it more than wishful thinking?"

"Hardly. That idea and fifty cents would be worth half a dollar. I fly planes for money. I haven't got a clue. I'm still as much in shock as the next guy, and I don't mind tellin' you, I'm scared."

"Of?"

"That it might happen again. If it was anything like I think it was, maybe all this force needs to do now is crank up the power somehow and they can get older people, smarter people, people with more resistance that they ignored the first time around."

Buck shrugged and sat in silence for a few minutes. Finally he said, "There's a little hole in your argument. I know of some people who are missing who seem as strong as anyone."

"I wasn't talking physical strength."

"Neither was I." Buck thought about Lucinda Washington. "I lost a friend and coworker who was bright, healthy, happy, strong, and a forceful personality."

"Well, I'm not saying I know everything or even anything. You wanted my theory, there it is."

Rayford Steele lay on his back, staring at the ceiling. Sleep had come hard and intermittently, and he hated the logy feeling. He didn't want to watch the news. He didn't want to read the paper, even knowing a new one had flopped up onto the porch before dawn. All he wanted was for Chloe to get home so they could grieve together. There was nothing, he decided, more lonely than grief.

He and his daughter would have work to do, too. He wanted to investigate, to learn, to know, to act. He started by searching for a Bible, not the family Bible that had collected dust on his shelf for years, but Irene's. Hers would have notes in it, maybe something that would point him in the right direction.

It wasn't hard to find. It was usually within arm's reach of where she slept. He found it on the floor, next to the bed. Would there be some guide? An index? Something that referred to the Rapture or the judgment or something? If not, maybe he'd start at the end. If *genesis* meant "beginning," maybe *revelation* had something to do with the end, even though it didn't mean that. The only Bible verse Rayford could quote by heart was Genesis 1:1: "In the beginning God created the heavens and the earth." He hoped there'd be some corresponding verse at the end of the Bible that said something like, "In the end God took all his people to heaven and gave everybody else one more chance."

But no such luck. The very last verse in the Bible meant nothing to him. It said, "The grace of the Lord Jesus be with you all. Amen." And it sounded like the religious mumbo jumbo he had heard in church. He backed up a verse and read, "He who testifies to these things says, 'Yes, I am coming quickly.' Amen. Come, Lord Jesus."

Now he was getting somewhere. Who was this who testified of these things, and what were these things? The quoted words were in red. What did that mean? He looked through the Bible and then noticed on the spine, "Words of Christ in red." So Jesus said he was coming quickly. Had he come? And if the Bible was as old as it seemed, what did "quickly" mean? It must not have meant soon, unless it was from the perspective of someone with a long view of history. Maybe Jesus meant that when he came, he would do it quickly. Was that what this was all about? Rayford glanced at the last chapter as a whole. Three

other verses had red letters, and two of those
repeated the business about coming quickly.

Rayford could make no sense of the text of the
chapter. It seemed old and formal. But near the
end of the chapter was a verse that ended with
words that had a strange impact on him. Without
a hint of their meaning, he read, "Let the one
who is thirsty come; let the one who wishes take
the water of life without cost."

Jesus wouldn't have been the one who was
thirsty. He would not have been the one who
wished to take the water of life. That, Rayford
assumed, referred to the reader. It struck him
that he was thirsty, soul thirsty. But what was
the water of life? He had already paid a terrible
cost for missing it. Whatever it was, it had been
in this book for hundreds of years.

Rayford idly leafed through the Bible to other
passages, none of which made sense to him. They
discouraged him because they didn't seem to flow
together, to refer to each other, to have a direction. Language and concepts foreign to him were
not helping.

Here and there he saw notes in the margins
in Irene's delicate handwriting. Sometimes she
simply wrote, "Precious." He was determined
to study and find someone who could explain
those passages to him. He was tempted to write,
"precious," next to that verse in Revelation about

taking the water of life without cost. It sounded precious to him, though he couldn't yet make it compute.

Worst of all, he feared he was reading the Bible too late. Clearly he was too late to have gone to heaven with his wife and son. But was he too late, period?

In the front flyleaf was last Sunday's church bulletin. What was this, Wednesday morning? Three days ago he had been where? In the garage. Raymie had begged him to go with them to church. He promised he would next Sunday. "That's what you said last week," Raymie had said.

"Do you want me to fix this four-wheeler for you or not? I don't have all the time in the world."

Raymie was not one for pushing a guilt trip. He just repeated, "Next Sunday?"

"For sure," Rayford had said. And now he wished next Sunday were here. He wished even more that Raymie were there to go with him because he *would* go. Or would he? Would he be off work that day? And would there be church? Was anyone left in that congregation? He pulled the bulletin from Irene's Bible and circled the phone number. Later that day, after he checked in with Pan-Continental, he would call the church office and see if anything was going on.

He was about to set the Bible on the bed table

when he grew curious and opened the front flyleaf again. On the first white-papered page he saw the inscription. He had given this Bible to Irene on their first wedding anniversary. How could he have forgotten, and what had he been thinking? She was no more devout than he back then, but she talked about wanting to get serious about church attendance before the children came along. He had been angling for something or trying to impress her. Maybe he thought she would think him spiritual if he gave her a gift like that. Maybe he was hoping she would let him off the hook and go to church by herself if he proved his spiritual sensitivity with this gift.

For years he had tolerated church. They had gone to one that demanded little and offered a lot. They made many friends and had found their doctor, dentist, insurance man, and even country club entrée in that church. Rayford was revered, proudly introduced as a 747 captain to newcomers and guests, and even served on the church board for several years.

When Irene discovered the Christian radio station and what she called "real preaching and teaching," she grew disenchanted with their church and began searching for a new one. That gave Rayford the opportunity to quit going at all, telling her that when she found one she really liked, he would start going again. She found one, and he tried it occasionally, but it was a little too literal and personal and challenging for him. He was not revered. He felt like a project. And he pretty much stayed away.

Rayford noticed another bit of Irene's handwriting. It was labeled her prayer list, and he was at the top. She had written, "Rafe, for his salvation and that I be a loving wife to him. Chloe, that she come to Christ and live in purity. Ray Jr., that he never stray from his strong, childlike faith." Then she had listed her pastor, political leaders, missionaries, world conflict, and several friends and other relatives.

"For his salvation," Rayford whispered. "Salvation." Another ten-dollar church word that had never really impressed him. He knew Irene's new church was interested in the salvation of souls, something he'd never heard in the previous church. But the closer he had gotten to the concept, the more he had been repelled. Didn't salvation have something to do with confirmation, baptism, testifying, getting religion, being holy? He hadn't wanted to deal with it, whatever it was. And now he was desperate to know exactly what it meant.

Ken Ritz radioed ahead to airports in suburban New York, finally getting clearance to touch down at Easton, Pennsylvania. "You know," Ritz said, "these are the old stompin' grounds of Larry Holmes, once the heavyweight champion of the world."

"The guy that beat Ali?"

"One and the same. If he was still around, whoever was takin' people might've got a knock on the noggin from ol' Larry. You can bet on that."

The pilot asked personnel in Easton if they could arrange a ride to New York City for his passenger.

"You're joking, right, Lear?"

"Didn't mean to, over."

"We got a guy can get him to within a couple of miles of the subway. No cars in or out of the city yet, and even the trains have some kind of a complicated route that takes them around bad sites."

"Bad sites?" Buck repeated.

"Say again," Ritz radioed.

"Haven't you been watching the news? Some of the worst disasters in the city were the result of disappearing motormen and dispatchers. Six trains were involved in head-ons with lots of deaths. Several trains ran up the back of other ones. It'll be days before they clear all the tracks and replace cars. You sure your man wants to get into midtown?"

"Roger. Seems like the type who can handle it."

"Hope he's got good hiking boots, over."

It cost Buck another premium for a ride close enough to the train that he could walk the rest of the way. His driver had not even been a cabbie, nor the vehicle a cab. But it might as well have been. It was just as decrepit and unsafe.

A two-mile walk got him to the train platform at about noon, where he waited more than forty minutes with a mass of humanity, only to find himself among the last half who had to wait another half an hour for the next train. The zigzag ride took two hours to get to Manhattan, and all during the trip Buck tapped at the keys on his laptop or stared out the window at the grid-lock that went on for miles. He knew many of his locally based colleagues would have already filed similar reports, so his only hope of scoring with Steve Plank and having this see publication was if his were more powerfully or eloquently written. He was in such awe of the scene that he doubted he could pull it off. At the very least he was adding drama to his own memoirs. New York City was at a standstill, and the biggest surprise was that they were letting people in at all. No doubt many of these, like him, lived here and needed to get to their homes and apartments.

The train lurched to a stop, far short of where he had been told it would reach. The garbled announcement, the best he could make out, informed passengers that this was the new last stop. Their next jog would have put them in the middle of a crane site where cars were being lifted off the track. Buck calculated about a fifteen-mile walk to his office and another five to his apartment.

Fortunately, Buck was in great shape. He put everything into his bag and shortened the strap so he could carry it close to his body without it swinging. He set off at what he guessed was a four-mile-per-hour pace, and three hours later he was hurting. He was sure he had blisters, and his neck and shoulders were tired from the bag and strap. He was sweating through his clothes, and there was no way he was going to get to his apartment before stopping in at the office.

"Oh, God, help me," Buck breathed, more exasperated than praying. But if there was a God, he decided, God had a sense of humor. Leaning against a brick wall in an alley in plain sight was a yellow bicycle with a cardboard sign clipped to it. It read, "Borrow this bike. Take it where you like. Leave it for someone else in need. No charge."

Only in New York, he thought. *Nobody steals something that's free.*

He thought about breathing a prayer of thanks, but somehow the world he was looking at didn't show any other evidence of a benevolent Creator. He mounted the bike, realized how long it had been since he had been aboard one, and wobbled off till he found his balance. It wasn't long before he cruised into midtown between the snarl of wreckage and wreckers. Only a few other people were traveling as efficiently as he was—couriers on bikes, two others on yellow bikes just like his, and cops on horseback.

Security was tight at the *Global Weekly* building, which somehow didn't surprise him. After identifying himself to a new desk clerk, he rode to the twenty-seventh floor, stopped in the public washroom to freshen up, and finally entered the main suites of the magazine. The receptionist immediately buzzed Steve Plank's office, and both Steve and Marge Potter hurried out to embrace and welcome him.

Buck Williams was hit with a strange, new emotion. He nearly wept. He realized he, along with everyone else, was enduring a hideous trauma and that he had no doubt been running on adrenaline. But somehow, getting back to familiar territory—especially with the expense and effort it had taken— made him feel as if he had come home. He was with people who cared about him. This was his family. He was really, really glad to see them, and it appeared the feeling was mutual.

He bit his lip to keep from clouding up, and as he followed Steve and Marge down the hall past his tiny, cluttered office and into Steve's spacious office/conference room, he asked if they had heard about Lucinda Washington.

Marge stopped in the corridor, bringing her hands to her face. "Yes," she managed, "and I wasn't going to do this again. We've lost several. Where does the grieving start and end?"

With that, Buck lost it. He couldn't pretend any longer, though he was as surprised as anyone at his own sensitivity. Steve put an arm around his secretary and guided her and Buck into his office, where others from the senior staff waited.

They cheered when they saw Buck. These people, the ones he had worked with, fought with, feuded with, irritated, and scooped, now seemed genuinely glad to see him. They could have no idea how he felt. "Boy, it's good to be back here," he said, then sat and buried his head in his hands. His body began to shake, and he could fight the tears no longer. He began to sob, right there in front of his colleagues and competitors.

He tried to wipe the tears away and compose himself, but when he looked up, forcing an embarrassed smile, he noticed everyone else was emotional, too. "It's all right, Bucky," one said. "If this is your first cry, you'll discover it won't be your last. We're all just as scared and stunned and grief stricken as you are."

"Yeah," another said, "but his personal account will no doubt be more compelling." Which made everyone laugh and cry all the more.

Rayford talked himself into calling the Pan-Con Flight Center early in the afternoon. He learned that he was to report in for a Friday flight two days later. "Really?" he said.

"Don't count on actually flying it," he was told. "Not too many flights are expected to be lifting off by then. Certainly none till late tomorrow, and maybe not even then."

"There's a chance I'll get called off before I leave home?"

"More than a chance, but that's your assignment for now."

"What's the route?"

"ORD to BOS to JFK."

"Hmm. Chicago, Boston, New York. Home when?"

"Saturday night."

"Good."

"Why? Got a date?"

"Not funny."

"Oh, gosh, I'm sorry, Captain. I forgot who I was talking to."

"You know about my family?"

"Everybody here knows, sir. We're sorry.
We heard it from the senior flight attendant
on your aborted Heathrow run. You got the
word on your first officer on that flight, didn't
you?"

"I heard something but never got any official
word."

"What'd you hear?"

"Suicide."

"Right. Awful."

"Can you check on something for me?"

"If it's in my power, Captain."

"My daughter is trying to get back this way
from California."

"Unlikely."

"I know, but she's on her way. Trying anyway.
She'll more than likely try to fly Pan. Can you
check and see if she's on any of the manifests
coming east?"

"Shouldn't be too hard. There are precious few,
and you know none of them will be landing
here."

"How about Milwaukee?"

"Don't think so." He was tapping computer
keys. "Where would she originate?"

"Somewhere near Palo Alto."

"Not good."

"Why?"

"Hardly anything coming out of there. Let me check."

Rayford could hear the man talking to himself, trying things, suggesting options. "Air California to Utah. Hey! Found her! Name Chloe with your last name?"

"That's her!"

"She checked in at Palo Alto. Pan put her on a bus to some outlying strip. Flew her to Salt Lake City on Air California. First time out of the state for that plane, I'll bet. She got on a Pan-Con plane, oh, an oldie, and they took her to, um, oh brother. Enid, Oklahoma."

"Enid? That's never been on our routes."

"No kidding. They were overrun with Dallas's spillover, too. Anyway, she's flying Ozark to Springfield, Illinois."

"Ozark!"

"I just work here, Cap."

"Well, somebody's trying to make it work, aren't they?"

"Yeah, the good news is, we've got a turboprop or two down there that can get her up into the area, but it doesn't say where she might land. It might not even come up on this screen because they won't know till they get close."

"How will I know where to pick her up?"

"You may not. I'm sure she'll call you when she lands. Who knows? Maybe she'll just show up."

"That would be nice."

"Well, I'm sorry for what you're going through, sir, but you can be grateful your daughter didn't get on Pan-Con directly out of Palo Alto. The last one out of there went down last night. No survivors."

"And this was after the disappearances?"

"Just last night. Totally unrelated."

"Wouldn't that have been a kick in the teeth?" Rayford said.

"Indeed."

EIGHT

WHEN the other senior writers and editors drifted back to their offices, Steve Plank insisted Buck Williams go home and rest before coming back for an eight o'clock meeting that evening.

"I'd rather get done now and go home for the night."

"I know," the executive editor said, "but we've got a lot to do and I want you sharp."

Still, Buck was reluctant. "How soon can I get to London?"

"What have you got there?"

Buck filled Steve in on his tip about a major U.S. financier meeting with international colleagues and introducing a rising European politico. "Oh, man, Buck," Steve said, "we're all over that. You mean Carpathia."

Buck was stunned. "I do?"

"He was the guy Rosenzweig was so impressed with."

"Yeah, but you think he's the one my informant is—"

"Man, you *have* been out of touch," Steve said. "It's not that big a deal. The financier has to be Jonathan Stonagal, who seems to be sponsoring him. I told you Carpathia was coming to address the U.N., didn't I?"

"So he's the new Romanian ambassador to the U.N.?" Buck said.

"Hardly."

"What then?"

"President of the country."

"Didn't they just elect a leader, what, eighteen months ago?" Buck said, remembering Dirk's tip that a new leader would seem out of place and time.

"Big shake-up there," Steve said. "Better check it out."

"I will."

"I don't mean you. I really don't think there's much of a story. The guy is young and dashing and all that, charming and persuasive as I understand it. He had been a meteoric business star, making a killing when Romanian markets opened to the West years ago. But as of last week he wasn't even in their senate yet. He was only in the lower house."

"The House of Deputies," Buck said.

"How did you know that?"

Buck grinned. "Rosenzweig educated me."

"For a minute there I thought you really did know everything. That's what you get accused of around here, you know."

"What a crime."

"But you play it with such humility."

"That's me. So, Steve, why don't you think it's important that a guy like Carpathia comes from nowhere to unseat the president of Romania?"

"He didn't exactly come from nowhere. His businesses were built on Stonagal financing. And Carpathia has been a disarmament crusader, very popular with his colleagues and the people."

"But disarmament doesn't fit with Stonagal. Isn't he a closet hawk?"

Plank nodded.

"So there are mysteries."

"Some, but, Buck, what could be bigger than the story you're on? You haven't got time to fool with a guy who becomes president of a nonstrategic country."

"There's something there, though, Steve. My guy in London tips me off. Carpathia's tied in with the most influential nonpolitician in the world. He goes from lower house to president without a popular election."

"And—"

"There's more? Which side of this argument are you on? Did he have the sitting president killed or something?"

"Interesting you should say that, because the only wrinkle in Carpathia's history is some rumors that he was ruthless with his business competition years ago."

"How ruthless?"

"People took dirt naps."

"Ooh, Steve, you talk just like a mobster."

"And listen, the previous president stepped down for Carpathia. Insisted on his installation."

"And you say there's no story here?"

"This is like the old South American coups, Buck. A new one every week. Big deal. So Carpathia's beholden to Stonagal. All that means is that Stonagal will have free rein in the financial world of an Eastern European country that thinks the best thing that ever happened to it was the destruction of Russia."

"But, Steve, this is like a freshman congressman becoming president of the United States in an off-election year, no vote, president steps aside, and everybody's happy."

"No, no, no, big difference. We're talking Romania here, Buck. *Romania.* Nonstrategic, scant gross national product, never invaded anybody, never anyone's strategic ally. There's nothing there but low-level internal politics."

"It still smells major to me," Buck said. "Rosenzweig was high on this guy, and he's an astute observer. Now Carpathia's coming to speak at the U.N. What next?"

"You forget he was coming to the U.N. *before* he became president of Romania."

"That's another puzzle. He was a nobody."

"He's a new name and face in disarmament. He gets his season in the sun, his fifteen minutes of fame. Trust me, you're not going to hear of him again."

"Stonagal had to be behind the U.N. gig, too," Buck said. "You know Diamond John is a personal friend of our ambassador."

"Stonagal is a personal friend of every elected official from the president to the mayors of most medium-sized cities, Buck. So what? He knows how to play the game. He reminds me of old Joe Kennedy or one of the Rockefellers, all right? What's your point?"

"Just that Carpathia is speaking at the U.N. on Stonagal's influence."

"Probably. So what?"

"He's up to something."

"Stonagal's always up to something, keeping the skids greased for one of his projects. OK, so he gets a businessman into Romanian politics, maybe even gets him installed as president. Who knows, maybe he even got him his little audience with Rosenzweig, which never amounted to anything. Now he gets Carpathia a little international exposure. That happens all the time because of guys like Stonagal. Would you rather chase this nonstory than tie together a cover piece that tries to make sense of the most monumental and tragic phenomenon in the history of the world?"

"Hmm, let me think about that," Buck said, smiling, as Plank punched him.

"Man, you can sure chase rabbit trails," the executive editor said.

"You used to like my instincts."

"I still do, but you're a little sleep-deprived right now."

"I'm definitely not going to London? Because I've got to tell my guy."

"Marge tried to reach the guy who was supposed to meet your plane. She can tell you how to get through and all that. But be back here by eight. I'm bringing in the department editors interested in the various international meetings coming here this month. You're going to be tying that coverage together, so—"

"So they can all hate me in the same meeting?" Buck said.

"They'll feel important."

"But *is* it important? You want me to ignore Carpathia, but you're going to complicate my life with, what was it, an ecumenical religious convention and a one-world-currency confab?"

"You *are* short on sleep, aren't you, Buck? This is why I'm still your boss. Don't you get it? Yes, I want coordination and I want a well-written piece. But think about it. This gives you automatic entrée to all these dignitaries. We're talking Jewish Nationalist leaders interested in one world government—"

"Unlikely and hardly compelling."

"—Orthodox Jews from all over the world looking at rebuilding the temple, or some such—"

"I'm being overrun by Jews."

"—international monetarists setting the stage for one world currency—"

"Also unlikely."

"But this will let you keep an eye on your favorite power broker—"

"Stonagal."

"Right, and heads of various religious groups looking to cooperate internationally."

"Bore me to death, why don't you? These people are discussing impossibilities. Since when have religious groups been able to get along?"

"You're still not getting it, Buck. You're going to have access to all these people—religious, monied, political—while trying to write a piece about what happened and why it happened. You can get the thinking of the greatest minds from the most diverse viewpoints."

Buck shrugged in surrender. "You've got a point. I still say our department editors are going to resent me."

"There's something to be said for consistency."

"I still want to try to get to Carpathia."

"That won't be hard. He's already a media darling in Europe. Eager to talk."

"And Stonagal."

"You know he never talks to the press, Buck."

"I like a challenge."

"Go home and take a load off. See you at eight."

Marge Potter was preparing to leave as Buck approached. "Oh yes," Marge said, setting down her stuff and flipping through her notebook. "I tried Dirk Burton several times. Got through once to his voice mail and left him your message. Received no confirmation. OK?"

"Thanks."

Buck wasn't sure he'd be able to rest at home with everything flying through his brain. He was pleasantly surprised when he reached street level to find that representatives of various cab companies were posted outside office buildings, directing people to cabs that could reach certain areas via circuitous routes. For premium fares, of course. For thirty dollars, in a shared cab, Buck

was let off two blocks from his apartment. In
three hours he would have to be back at the
office, so he made arrangements with the cabbie
to meet him at the same spot at seven forty-five.
That, he decided, would be a miracle. With all
the cabs in New York, he had never before had to
make such an arrangement, and to his knowledge
had never even seen the same cabbie twice.

Rayford was pacing, miserable. He came to the
painful realization that this was the worst season
of his life. He had never even come close before.
His parents had been older than those of his
peers. When they had died within two years of
each other, it had been a relief. They were not
well, not lucid. He loved them and they were no
burden, but they had virtually died to him years
before, due to strokes and other ailments. When
they did pass, Rayford had grieved in a way, but
mostly he was just sentimental about them. He
had good memories, he appreciated the kindness
and sympathy he received at their funerals, and
he got on with his life. Whatever tears he shed
were not from remorse or heartache. He felt
primarily nostalgic and melancholy.

The rest of his life had been without complication or pain. Becoming a pilot was akin to rising
to any other highly paid professional level. You

had to be intelligent and disciplined, accomplished. He came through the ranks in the usual way—military-reserve duty, small planes, then bigger ones, then jets and fighters. Finally he had reached the pinnacle.

He had met Irene in Reserve Officer Training Corps in college. She had been an army brat who had never rebelled. Many of her chums had turned their backs on military life and didn't even want to own up to it. Her father had been killed in battle and her mother married another military man, so Irene had seen or lived on nearly every army base in the United States.

They were married when Rayford was a senior in college and Irene a sophomore. She dropped out when he went into the military, and everything had been on schedule since. They had Chloe during their first year of marriage but, due to complications, waited another eight years for Ray Jr. Rayford was thrilled with both children, but he had to admit he had longed for a namesake boy.

Unfortunately, Raymie came along during a bleak period for Rayford. He was thirty and feeling older, and he didn't enjoy having a pregnant wife. Many people thought, because of his premature but not unattractive gray hair, that he was older, and so he endured the jokes about being an old father. It was a particularly difficult pregnancy for Irene, and Raymie was a couple of weeks late. Chloe was a spirited eight-year-old, so Rayford disengaged as much as possible.

Irene, he believed, slipped into at least some mild depression during that time and was short tempered with him and weepy. At work Rayford was in charge, listened to, and admired. He had been rated for the biggest, latest, and most sophisticated planes in the Pan-Continental stable. His work life was going swimmingly; he didn't enjoy going home.

He had drunk more during that period than ever before or since, and the marriage had gone through its most trying time. He was frequently late getting home and at times even fibbed about his schedule so he could leave a day early or come back a day late. Irene accused him of all manner of affairs, and because she was wrong, he denied them with great vigor and, he felt, justified anger.

The truth was, he was hoping for and angling for just what she was charging. What frustrated him so was that, despite his looks and bearing, it just wasn't in him to pull it off. He didn't have the moves, the patter, the style. A flight attendant had once called him a hunk, but he felt like a geek, an egghead. Sure, he had access to any woman with a price, but that was beneath him. While he toyed with and hoped for an old-fashioned affair, he somehow couldn't bring

himself to stoop to something as tawdry as
paying for sex.

Had Irene known how hard he was trying to
be unfaithful, she would have left him. As it was,
he had indulged in that make-out session at the
Christmas party before Raymie was born, but he
was so inebriated he could hardly remember it.

The guilt and nearly spoiling his image straightened him up and made him cut down on his
drinking. Seeing Raymie born sobered him even
more. It was time to grow up and take as much
responsibility as a husband and father as he did
as a pilot.

But now, as Rayford ran all those memories
through his throbbing head, he felt the deepest
regret and remorse a man can feel. He felt like a
failure. He was so unworthy of Irene. Somehow
he knew now, though he had never allowed
himself to consider it before, that she couldn't in
any way have been as naive or stupid as he had
hoped and imagined. She had to have known
how vapid he was, how shallow, and yes, cheap.
And yet she had stayed by him, loved him, fought
to keep the marriage together.

He couldn't argue that she became a different
person after she switched churches and got serious about her faith. She preached at him at first,
sure. She was excited and wanted him to discover
what she had found. He ran. Eventually she

either gave up or resigned herself to the fact that he was not going to come around by her pleading or cajoling. Now he knew from seeing her list that she had never given up. She had simply taken to praying for him.

No wonder Rayford had never gotten that close to ultimately defiling his marriage with Hattie Durham. Hattie! How ashamed he was of that silly pursuit! For all he knew, Hattie was innocent. She had never bad-mouthed his wife or the fact that he was married. She had never suggested anything inappropriate, at least for her age. Young people were more touchy and flirtatious, and she claimed no moral or religious code. That Rayford had obsessed over the possibilities with Hattie, while she probably hardly knew it, made him feel all the more foolish.

Where was this guilt coming from? He had locked eyes with Hattie numerous times, and they had spent hours alone together over dinners in various cities. But she had never asked him to her room or tried to kiss him or even hold his hand. Maybe she would have responded had he been the aggressor, but maybe not. She might just as easily have been offended, insulted, disappointed.

Rayford shook his head. Not only was he guilty of lusting after a woman to whom he had no right, but he was still such a klutz he hadn't even known how to pursue her.

And now he faced the darkest hours of his soul.
He was nervous about Chloe. He wanted her
home and safe in the worst way, hoping that
having his own flesh and blood in the house
would somehow assuage his grief and pain. He
knew he should be hungry again, but nothing
appealed. Even the fragrant and tasty cookies
he thought he would have to ration had become
painful reminders of Irene. Maybe tomorrow.

Rayford switched on the television, not out
of interest in seeing more mayhem, but with
the hope of some news of order, traffic clearing,
people connecting. After a minute or two of the
same old same old, he turned it off again. He
rejected the idea of calling O'Hare about the likelihood of getting in to get his car, because he
didn't want to tie up the phone for even a minute
in case Chloe was trying to get through. It had
been hours since he'd heard she left Palo Alto.
How long would it take to make all those crazy
connections and finally get on an Ozark flight
from Springfield to the Chicago area? He remembered the oldest joke in the airline industry:
Ozark spelled backward is Krazo. Only it didn't
amuse him just then.

He leaped when the phone rang, but it was
not Chloe. "I'm sorry, Captain," Hattie said.
"I promised to call you back, but I fell asleep after
the call I took and have been out ever since."

"That's quite all right, Hattie. In fact, I need to—"

"I mean, I didn't want to bother you anyway at a time like this."

"No, that's OK, I just—"

"Have you talked to Chloe?"

"I'm waiting for her to call right now, so I really have to get off!"

Rayford had been more curt than he intended and Hattie was, at first, silent. "Well, all right then. I'm sorry."

"I'll call you, Hattie. OK?"

"OK."

She had sounded hurt. He was sorry about that, but not sorry that he had gotten rid of her for the time being. He knew she was only trying to help and be kind, but she hadn't been listening. She was alone and afraid just like he was, and no doubt by now she had found out about her family. Oh, no! He hadn't even asked about them! She would hate him, and why shouldn't she? *How selfish could I be?* he wondered.

Eager as he was to hear from Chloe, he had to risk a couple more minutes on the phone. He dialed Hattie, but her line was busy.

Buck tried calling Dirk Burton in London as soon as he got home, not wanting to wait longer with

the time difference overseas. He got a puzzling
response. Dirk's personal answering machine
ran through its usual message, but as soon as
the leave-a-message beep sounded, a longer tone
indicated that the tape was full. Strange. Dirk
was either sleeping through it all or—

Buck had not considered that Dirk could have
disappeared. Besides leaving Buck with a million
questions about Stonagal, Carpathia, Todd-
Cothran, and the whole phenomenon, Dirk
was one of his best friends from Princeton. *Oh,
please let this be a coincidence,* he thought. *Let
him be traveling.*

As soon as Buck hung up, his phone rang. Of
all people, it was Hattie Durham. She was crying.
"I'm sorry to bother you, Mr. Williams, and
I had promised myself I would never use your
home number—"

"That's all right, Hattie. What is it?"

"Well, it's silly really, but I just went through
something, and I don't have anybody to talk to
about it. I couldn't get through to my mother
and sisters, and well, I just thought maybe you'd
understand."

"Try me."

She told Buck about her call to Captain Steele
and brought him up to date on who Steele was,
that he had lost his wife and son, and that she
had been late calling him back after hearing her

good news from Buck. "And then he just brushed me off because he's waiting for a call from his daughter."

"I can understand that," Buck tried, rolling his eyes. How did he get into this lonely hearts club? Didn't she have any girlfriends to unload on?

"I can, too," she said. "That's just it. And I know he's grieving because it's like his wife and son are dead, but he knew I was on pins and needles about my family, and he never even asked."

"Well, I'm sure it is all just part of the tension of the moment, the grief, like you say, and—"

"Oh, I know it. I just wanted to talk to somebody, and I thought of you."

"Well, hey, anytime," Buck lied. *Oh, boy,* he thought. *My home number is definitely going to come off that next batch of business cards.* "Listen, I'd better let you go. I've got an evening meeting tonight myself, and—"

"Well, thanks for listening."

"I understand," he said, though he doubted he ever would. Maybe Hattie showed more depth and sense when she wasn't under stress. He hoped so.

Rayford was glad Hattie's line was busy, because he could tell her he had tried to call her right back, but he didn't have to tie up his phone any longer. A minute later, his phone rang again.

"Captain, it's me again. I'm sorry, I won't keep you long, but I thought you might have tried to call me, and I've been on the phone, so—"

"As a matter of fact, I did, Hattie. What have you found out about your family?"

"They're fine." She was crying.

"Oh, thank God," he said.

Rayford wondered what had gotten into him. He said he was happy for her, but he had come to the conclusion that those who had not disappeared had missed out on the greatest event of cosmic history. But what was he supposed to say—"Oh, I'm sorry your family was left behind, too"?

When he hung up, Rayford sat next to the phone with a nagging feeling that he had for sure missed Chloe's call this time. It made him mad. His stomach was growling and he knew he should eat, but he had decided he would hold off as long as possible, hoping to eat with Chloe when she arrived. Knowing her, she wouldn't have eaten a thing.

NINE

BUCK'S subconscious waking system failed him that evening, but by 8:45 P.M. he was back in Steve Plank's office, disheveled and apologetic. And he had been right. He felt the resentment from veteran department editors. Juan Ortiz, chief of the international politics section, was incensed that Buck should have anything to do with the summit conference Juan planned to cover in two weeks.

"The Jewish Nationalists are discussing an issue I have been following for years. Who would have believed they would consider warming to one world government? That they would even entertain the discussion is monumental. They're meeting here, rather than in Jerusalem or Tel Aviv, because their idea is so revolutionary. Most Israeli Nationalists think the Holy Land has gone too far with its bounty already. This is historic."

"Then what's your problem," Plank said, "with my adding our top guy to the coverage?"

"Because *I* am your top guy on this."

"I'm trying to make sense of all these meetings," Plank said.

Jimmy Borland, the religion editor, weighed in. "I understand Juan's objections, but I've got two meetings at the same time. I welcome the help."

"Now we're getting somewhere," Plank said.

"But I'll be frank, Buck," Borland added. "I want a say in the final piece."

"Of course," Plank said.

"Not so fast," Buck said. "I don't want to be treated like a pool reporter here. I'm going to have my own take on these meetings, and I'm not trying to horn in on your expert territories. I wouldn't want to do the coverages of the individual meetings themselves. I want to bring some coordination, find the meaning, the common denominators. Jimmy, your two groups—the religious Jews who want to rebuild the temple and the ecumenicalists who want some sort of one-world religious order—are they going to be at odds with each other? Will there be religious Jews—"

"Orthodox."

"OK, Orthodox Jews at the ecumenical meeting? Because that seems at cross purposes with rebuilding the temple."

"Well, at least you're thinking like a religion editor," Jimmy said. "That's encouraging."

"But what's your thought?"

"I don't know. That's what makes this so interesting. That they should meet at the same time in the same city is too good to be true."

Financial editor Barbara Donahue brought closure to the discussion. "I've dealt with you before on these kinds of efforts, Steve," she said. "And I appreciate the way you let everybody vent without threat. But we all know your mind is made up about Buck's involvement, so let's lick our wounds and get on with it. If we each get to put our own spin on the coverage in our departments and have some input on the overall piece that I assume goes in the main well, let's get on with it."

Even Ortiz nodded, though to Buck he seemed reluctant.

"Buck's the quarterback," Plank said, "so keep in touch with him. He'll report to me. You want to say anything, Buck?"

"Just thanks a lot," he said ruefully, causing everyone to chuckle. "Barbara, your monetarists are meeting right at the U.N., like they did when they went to the three-currency thing?"

She nodded. "Same place and pretty much the same people."

"How involved is Jonathan Stonagal?"

"Overtly, you mean?" she said.

"Well, everybody knows he's circumspect. But is there a Stonagal influence?"

"Does a duck have lips?"

Buck smiled and jotted a note. "I'll take that as a yes. I'd like to hang around that one, maybe try to get to Diamond John."

"Good luck. He probably won't show his face."

"But he'll be in town, won't he, Barbara? Wasn't he at the Plaza for the duration last time?"

"You do get around, don't you?" she said.

"Well, he only had each of the principals up to his suite every day."

Juan Ortiz raised a hand. "I'm going along with this, and I have nothing personal against you, Buck. But I don't believe there is a way to coordinate this story without inventing some tie-in. I mean, if you want to lead off a feature story by saying there were four important international meetings in town almost all at once, fine. But to make them interrelated would be stretching."

"If I find that they aren't interrelated, there won't be an overall story," Buck said. "Fair enough?"

Rayford Steele was nearly beside himself with worry, compounded by his grief. Where was Chloe? He had been inside all day, pacing, mourning, thinking. He felt stale and claustrophobic. He had called Pan-Continental and was told his car might be released by the time he got back from his weekend flight. The news on TV showed the amazing progress being made at clearing the road-ways and getting mass transportation rolling again. But the landscape would appear tacky for months. Cranes and wreckers had run out of junkyards, so the twisted wreckages remained in hazardous piles at the sides of roads and express-ways.

By the time Rayford got around to calling his wife's church, it was after hours, and he was grateful he wouldn't have to talk to anyone. As he hoped, a new message was on their answering machine, though it was communicated by a stunned-sounding male voice.

"You have reached New Hope Village Church. We are planning a weekly Bible study, but for the time being we will meet just once each Sunday at 10 A.M. While our entire staff, except me, and most of our congregation are gone, the few of us left are maintaining the building and distributing a videotape our senior pastor prepared for a time such as this. You may come by the church office anytime to pick up a free copy, and we look forward to seeing you Sunday morning."

Well, of course, Rayford thought, *that pastor had often spoken of the Rapture of the church.* That was why Irene was so enamored with it.

What a creative idea, to tape a message for those
who had been left behind! He and Chloe would
have to get one the next day. He hoped she
would be as interested as he was in discovering
the truth.

Rayford gazed out the front window in the
darkness, just in time to see Chloe, one big suitcase on the ground next to her, paying a cab-
driver. He ran from the house in his stocking feet
and gathered her into his arms. "Oh, Daddy!"
she wailed. "How's everybody?"

He shook his head.

"I don't want to hear this," she said, pulling
away from him and looking to the house as if
expecting her mother or brother to appear in the
doorway.

"It's just you and me, Chloe," Rayford said,
and they stood together in the darkness, crying.

It was Friday before Buck Williams was able
to track down Dirk Burton. He reached the supervisor in Dirk's area of the London Exchange.
"You must tell me precisely who you are and your
specific relationship to Mr. Burton before I am
allowed to inform you as to his disposition," Nigel
Leonard said. "I am also constrained to inform
you that this conversation shall be taped, beginning immediately."

"I'm sorry?"

"I'm taping our conversation, sir. If that is a problem for you, you may disconnect."

"I don't follow."

"What's to follow? You understand what a tape is, do you?"

"Of course, and I'm turning mine on now as well, if you don't mind."

"Well, I *do* mind, Mr. Williams. Why on earth would *you* be taping?"

"Why would *you?*"

"We are the ones with a most unfortunate situation, and we need to investigate all leads."

"What situation? Was Dirk among those who disappeared?"

"Nothing so tidy as that, I'm afraid."

"Tell me."

"First your reason for asking."

"I'm an old friend. We were college classmates."

"Where?"

"Princeton."

"Very well. When?"

Buck told him.

"Very well. The last time you spoke to him?"

"I don't recall, OK? We've been trading voice-mail messages."

"Your occupation?"

Buck hesitated. "Senior writer, *Global Weekly,* New York."

"Would your interest be journalistic in nature?"

"I won't preclude that," Buck said, trying not to let his anger seep through, "but I can't imagine that my friend, important as he is to me, is of interest to my readers."

"Mr. Williams," Nigel said carefully, "allow me to state categorically, on both our tapes apparently, that what I am about to say is strictly off the record. Do you understand?"

"I—"

"Because I am aware that both in your country and in the British Commonwealth, anything said following an assertion that we are off the record is protected."

"Granted," Buck said.

"Beg pardon?"

"You heard me. Granted. We're off the record. Now where is Dirk?"

"Mr. Burton's body was discovered in his flat this morning. He had suffered a bullet wound to the head. I'm sorry, as you were a friend, but suicide has been determined."

Buck was nearly speechless. "By whom?" he managed.

"The authorities."

"What authorities?"

"Scotland Yard and security personnel here at the exchange."

Scotland Yard? Buck thought. *We'll see about that.* "Why is the exchange involved?"

"We're protective of our information and our personnel, sir."

"Suicide is impossible, you know," Buck said.

"Do I?"

"If you are his supervisor, you know."

"There have been countless suicides since the disappearances, sir."

Buck was shaking his head as if Nigel could see him from across the Atlantic. "Dirk didn't kill himself, and you know it."

"Sir, I can appreciate your sentiments, but I don't know any more than you did what was in Mr. Burton's mind. I was partial to him, but I would not be in a position to question the conclusion of the medical examiner."

Buck slammed the phone down and marched into Steve Plank's office. He told Steve what he had heard.

"That's terrible," Steve said.

"I have a contact at Scotland Yard who knows Dirk, but I don't dare talk to him about it by phone. Can I have Marge book me on the next flight to London? I'll be back in time for all these summits, but I've got to go."

"If you can get a flight. I don't know that JFK is even open yet."

"How about La Guardia?"

"Ask Marge. You know Carpathia will be here tomorrow."

"You said yourself he was small potatoes. Maybe he'll still be here when I get back."

Rayford Steele hadn't been able to talk his grieving daughter into leaving the house. Chloe had spent hours in her little brother's room, and then in her parents' bedroom, picking through their personal effects to add to the boxes of memories her father had put together. Rayford felt so bad for her. He had secretly hoped she would be of comfort to him. He knew she would be eventually. But for now she needed time to face her own loss. Once she had cried herself out, she was ready to talk. And after she had reminisced to the point where Rayford didn't know if his heart could take any more, she finally changed the subject to the phenomenon of the disappearances themselves.

"Daddy, in California they're actually buying into the space invasion theory."

"You're kidding."

"No. Maybe it's because you were always so practical and skeptical about all that tabloid newspaper stuff, but I just can't get into it. I mean, it has to be something supernatural or otherworldly, but—"

"But what?"

"It just seems that if some alien life force was capable of doing this, they would also be capable of communicating to us. Wouldn't they want to take over now or demand ransom or get us to do something for them?"

"Who? Martians?"

"Daddy! I'm not saying I believe it. I'm saying I don't. But doesn't my reasoning make sense?"

"You don't have to convince me. I admit I wouldn't have dreamed any of this even possible a week ago, but my logic has been stretched to the breaking point."

Rayford hoped Chloe would ask his theory. He didn't want to start right in on a religious theme. She had always been antagonistic about that, having stopped going to church in high school when both he and Irene gave up fighting with her over it. She was a good kid, never in trouble. She made grades good enough to get her a partial academic scholarship, and though she occasionally stayed out too late and went through a boy-crazy period in high school, they had never had to bail her out of jail and there was never any evidence of drug use. He didn't take that lightly.

Rayford and Irene knew Chloe had come home from more than one party drunk enough to spend the night vomiting. The first time, he and Irene chose to ignore it, to act as if it didn't happen.

They believed she was levelheaded enough to know better the next time. When the next time came, Rayford had a chat with her.

"I know, I know, I know, OK, Dad? You don't need to start in on me."

"I'm not starting in on you. I want to make sure you know enough to not drive if you drink too much."

"Of course I do."

"And you know how stupid and dangerous it is to drink too much."

"I thought you weren't starting in on me."

"Just tell me you know."

"I think I already said that."

He had shaken his head and said nothing.

"Daddy, don't give up on me. Go ahead, give me both barrels. Prove you care."

"Don't make fun of me," he had said. "Someday you're going to have a child and you won't know what to say or do either. When you love somebody with all your heart and all you care about is her welfare—"

Rayford hadn't been able to continue. For the first time in his adult life, he had choked up. It had never happened during his arguments with Irene. He had always been too defensive, concerned too much about making his point to think about how much he cared for her. But with Chloe, he really wanted to say the right thing, to

protect her from herself. He wanted her to know
how much he loved her, and it was coming out
all wrong. It was as if he were punishing, lectur-
ing, reprimanding, condescending. That had
caused him to break.

Though he hadn't planned it, that involuntary
show of emotion got through to Chloe. For
months she had been drifting from him, from
both her parents. She had been sullen, cold,
independent, sarcastic, challenging. He knew it
was all part of growing up and becoming one's
own person, but it was a painful, scary time.

As he bit his lip and breathed deeply, hoping
to regain composure and not embarrass himself,
Chloe had come to him and wrapped her arms
around his neck, just as she had as a little girl.
"Oh, Daddy, don't cry," she had said. "I know
you love me. I know you care. Don't worry about
me. I learned my lesson and I won't be stupid
again, I promise."

He had dissolved into tears, and so had she.
They had bonded as never before. He didn't
recall ever having to discipline her again, and
though she had not come back to church, he had
started to drift by then himself. They had become
buddies, and she was growing up to be just like
him. Irene had kidded him that their children
each had their own favorite parent.

Now, just days after Irene and Raymie had

disappeared, Rayford hoped the relationship that
had really begun with an emotional moment
when Chloe was in high school would blossom
so they could talk. What was more important
than what had happened? He knew now what
her crazy college friends and the typical Califor-
nian believed. What else was new? He always
generalized that people on the West Coast
afforded the tabloids the same weight Midwest-
erners gave the *Chicago Tribune* or even the
New York Times.

Late in the day, Friday, Rayford and Chloe
reluctantly agreed they should eat, and they
worked together in the kitchen, rustling up a
healthy mixture of fruits and vegetables. There
was something calming and healing about working with her in silence. It was painful on the one
hand, because anything domestic reminded him
of Irene. And when they sat to eat, they automatically sat in their customary spots at either end of
the table—which made the other two open spots
that much more conspicuous.

Rayford noticed Chloe clouding up again, and
he knew she was feeling what he was. It hadn't
been that many years since they had enjoyed
three or four meals a week together as a family.
Irene had always sat on his left, Raymie on his
right, and Chloe directly across. The emptiness
and the silence were jarring.

Rayford was ravenous and finished a huge salad. Chloe stopped eating soon after she had begun and wept silently, her head down, tears falling in her lap. Her father took her hand, and she rose and sat in his lap, hiding her face and sobbing. His heart aching for her, Rayford rocked her until she was silent. "Where are they?" she whined at last.

"You want to know where I think they are?" he said. "Do you really want to know?"

"Of course!"

"I believe they are in heaven."

"Oh, Daddy! There were some religious nuts at school who were saying that, but if they knew so much about it, how come they didn't go?"

"Maybe they realized they had been wrong and had missed their opportunity."

"You think that's what we've done?" Chloe said, returning to her chair.

"I'm afraid so. Didn't your mother tell you she believed that Jesus could come back some day and take his people directly to heaven before they died?"

"Sure, but she was always more religious than the rest of us. I thought she was just getting a little carried away."

"Good choice of words."

"Hm?"

"She got carried away, Chloe. Raymie too."

"You don't really believe that, do you?"

"I do."

"That's about as crazy as the Martian invasion theory."

Rayford felt defensive. "So what's *your* theory?"

Chloe began to clear the table and spoke with her back to him. "I'm honest enough to admit I don't know."

"So now I'm not being honest?"

Chloe turned to face him, sympathy on her face. "Don't you see, Dad? You've gravitated to the least painful possibility. If we were voting, my first choice would be that my mom and my little brother are in heaven with God, sitting on clouds, playing their harps."

"So I'm deluding myself, is that what you're saying?"

"Daddy, I don't fault you. But you have to admit this is pretty far-fetched."

Now Rayford was angry. "What's more far-fetched than people disappearing right out of their clothes? Who else could have done that? Years ago we'd have blamed it on the Soviets, said they had developed some super new technology, some death ray that affected only human flesh and bone. But there's no Soviet threat anymore, and the Russians lost people, too. And how did this . . . this whatever it was—how did it choose who to take and who to leave?"

"You're saying the only logical explanation is God, that he took his own and left the rest of us?"

"That's what I'm saying."

"I don't want to hear this."

"Chloe, our own family is a perfect picture of what happened. If what I'm saying is right, the logical two people are gone and the logical two were left."

"You think I'm that much of a sinner?"

"Chloe, listen. Whatever you are, I am. I'm not judging you. If I'm right about this, we missed something. I always called myself a Christian, mostly because I was raised that way and I wasn't Jewish."

"Now you're saying you're not a Christian?"

"Chloe, I think the Christians are gone."

"So I'm not a Christian either?"

"You're my daughter and the only other member of my family still left; I love you more than anything on earth. But if the Christians are gone and everyone else is left, I don't think anyone is a Christian."

"Some kind of a super Christian, you mean."

"Yeah, a true Christian. Apparently those who were taken were recognized by God as truly his. How else can I say it?"

"Daddy, what does this make God? Some sick, sadistic dictator?"

"Careful, honey. You think I'm wrong, but what if I'm right?"

"Then God is spiteful, hateful, mean. Who wants to go to heaven with a God like that?"

"If that's where your mom and Raymie are, that's where I want to be."

"I want to be with them, too, Daddy! But tell me how this fits with a loving, merciful God. When I went to church, I got tired of hearing how loving God is. He never answered *my* prayers and I never felt like he knew me or cared about me. Now you're saying I was right. He didn't. I didn't qualify, so I got left behind? You'd better hope you're not right."

"But if I'm not right, who is right, Chloe? Where are they? Where is everybody?"

"See? You've latched onto this heaven thing because it makes you feel better. But it makes me feel worse. I don't buy it. I don't even want to consider it."

Rayford dropped the subject and went to watch television. Limited regular programming had resumed, but he was still able to find continuing news coverage. He was struck by the unusual name of the new Romanian president he had recently read about. Carpathia. He was scheduled to arrive at La Guardia in New York on Saturday and hold a press conference Monday morning before addressing the United Nations.

So La Guardia was open. That was where Rayford was supposed to fly later that evening with an oversold flight. He called Pan-Continental at O'Hare. "Glad you called," a supervisor said. "I was about to call you. Is your 757 rating up to date?"

"No. I used to fly them regularly, but I prefer the 747 and haven't been rated this year on the '57."

"That's all we're flying east this weekend. We'll have to get somebody else. And you need to get rated soon, just so we have flexibility."

"Duly noted. What's next for me?"

"You want a Monday run to Atlanta and back the same day?"

"On a . . . ?"

"'47."

"Sounds perfect. Can you tell me if there'll be room on that flight?"

"For?"

"A family member."

"Let me check." Rayford heard the computer keys and the distracted voice. "While I'm checking, ah, we got a request from a crew member to be assigned to your next flight, only I think she was thinking you'd be going on that run tonight, Logan to JFK and back."

"Who? Hattie Durham?"

"Let me see. Right."

"So is she assigned to Boston and New York?"

"Uh-huh."

"And I'm not, so that question is moot, right?"

"I guess so. You got any leanings one way or the other?"

"I'm sorry?"

"She's gonna ask again, is my guess. You have any objection to her being assigned to one of your upcoming flights?"

"Well, it won't be Atlanta, right? That's too soon."

"Right."

Rayford sighed. "No objections, I guess. No, wait. Let's just let it happen if it happens."

"I'm not following you, Captain."

"I'm just saying if she gets assigned in the normal course, I have no objection. But let's not go through any gymnastics to make it happen."

"Gotcha. And your flight to Atlanta looks like it could handle your freebie. Name?"

"Chloe Steele."

"I'll put her in first class, but if they sell out, you know I've got to bump her back."

When Rayford got off the phone, Chloe drifted into the room. "I'm not flying tonight," he said.

"Is that good news or bad news?"

"I'm relieved. I get to spend more time with you."

"After the way I talked to you? I figured you'd want me out of sight and out of mind."

"Chloe, we can talk frankly to each other. You're my family. I hate to think of being away from you at all. I've got a down-and-back flight to Atlanta Monday and have you booked in first class if you want to go."

"Sure."

"And I only wish you hadn't said one thing."

"Which?"

"That you don't even want to consider my theory. You've always liked my theories. I don't mind your saying you don't buy it. I don't know enough to articulate it in a way that makes any sense. But your mother talked about this. Once she even warned me that if I didn't know for sure I'd be going if Christ returned for his people, I shouldn't be flip about it."

"But you were?"

"I sure was. But never again."

"Well, Daddy, I'm not being flip about it. I just can't accept it, that's all."

"That's fair. But don't say you won't even consider it."

"Well, did you consider the space invaders theory?"

"As a matter of fact, I did."

"You're kidding."

"I considered everything. This was so far beyond

human experience, what were we supposed to think?"

"OK, so if I take back that I won't even consider it, what does that mean? We become religious fanatics all of a sudden, start going to church, what? And who says it's not too late? If you're right, maybe we missed our chance forever."

"That's what we have to find out, don't you think? Let's check this out, see if there's anything to it. If there is, we should want nothing more than to know if there's still a chance we can be with Mom and Raymie again someday."

Chloe sat shaking her head. "Gee, Dad. I don't know."

"Listen, I called the church your mom was going to."

"Oh, brother."

He told her about the recording and the offer of the tape.

"Dad! A tape for those left behind? Please!"

"You're coming at this as a skeptic, so sure it sounds ridiculous to you. I see no other logical explanation, so I can't wait to hear the tape."

"You're desperate."

"Of course I am! Aren't you?"

"I'm miserable and scared, but I'm not so desperate that I'm going to lose my faculties. Oh, Daddy, I'm sorry. Don't look at me like

that. I don't blame you for checking this out.
Go ahead, and don't worry about me."

"Will you go with me?"

"I'd rather not. But if you want me to . . ."

"You can wait in the car."

"It's not that. I'm not afraid of meeting someone I disagree with."

"We'll go over there tomorrow," Rayford said,
disappointed in her reaction but no less determined to follow through, for her sake as much
as his. If he was right, he did not want to fail his
own daughter.

TEN

CAMERON Williams convinced himself he should not call his and Dirk Burton's mutual friend at Scotland Yard before leaving New York. With communications as difficult as they had been for days and after the strange conversation with Dirk's supervisor, Buck didn't want to risk someone listening in. The last thing he wanted was to compromise his Scotland Yard contact's integrity.

Buck took both his real and his phony passport and visa—a customary safety precaution—caught a late flight to London out of La Guardia Friday night, and arrived at Heathrow Saturday morning. He checked into the Tavistock Hotel and slept until midafternoon. Then he set out to find the truth about Dirk's death.

He started by calling Scotland Yard and asking for his friend Alan Tompkins, a midlevel

operative. They were almost the same age, and
Tompkins was a thin, dark-haired, and slightly
rumpled investigator Buck had interviewed for
a story on British terrorism.

They had taken to each other and even enjoyed
an evening at a pub with Dirk. Dirk, Alan, and
Buck had become pals, and whenever Buck
visited, the three got together. Now, by phone,
he tried to communicate to Tompkins in such a
way that Alan would catch on quickly and not
give away that they were friends—in case the line
was tapped.

"Mr. Tompkins, you don't know me, but
my name is Cameron Williams of *Global
Weekly.*" Before Alan could laugh and greet
his friend, Buck quickly continued, "I'm here
in London to do a story preliminary to the international monetary conference at the United
Nations."

Alan sounded suddenly serious. "How can I
help you, sir? What does that have to do with
Scotland Yard?"

"I'm having trouble locating my interview
subject, and I suspect foul play."

"And your subject?"

"His name is Burton. Dirk Burton. He works
at the exchange."

"Let me do some checking and call you back."

A few minutes later, Buck's phone rang.

"Yes, Tompkins from the Yard. I wonder if you would be so kind as to come in and see me."

Early on Saturday morning in Mount Prospect, Illinois, Rayford Steele phoned the New Hope Village Church again. This time a man answered the phone. Rayford introduced himself as the husband of a former parishioner. "I know you, sir," the man said. "We've met. I'm Bruce Barnes, the visitation pastor."

"Oh, yes, hi."

"By former parishioner, I assume you're telling me that Irene is no longer with us?"

"That's right, and our son."

"Ray Jr., wasn't it?"

"Right."

"You also had an older daughter, did you not, a nonattender?"

"Chloe."

"And she—?"

"Is here with me. I was wondering what you all make of this—how many people have disappeared, are you still meeting, that kind of thing. I know you have a service on Sundays and that you're offering this tape."

"Well, you know just about everything then, Mr. Steele. Nearly every member and regular attender of this church is gone. I am the only

person on the staff who remains. I have asked
a few women to help out in the office. I have
no idea how many will show up Sunday, but
it would be a privilege to see you again."

"I'm very interested in that tape."

"I'd be happy to give you one in advance. It's
what I will be discussing Sunday morning."

"I don't know how to ask this, Mr. Barnes."

"Bruce."

"Bruce. You'll be teaching or preaching or
what?"

"Discussing. I will be playing the tape for
any who have not heard it, and then we will
discuss it."

"But you . . . I mean, how do you account
for the fact that you are still here?"

"Mr. Steele, there is only one explanation for
that, and I would prefer to discuss it with you
in person. If I know when you might come by
for the tape, I'll be sure to be here."

Rayford told him he and perhaps Chloe would
come by that afternoon.

Alan Tompkins waited just inside the vestibule at
Scotland Yard. When Buck arrived, Alan formally
shook his hand and led him to a rundown
compact, which he drove quickly to a dark pub a
few miles away. "Let's not talk till we get there,"

Alan said, continually checking his mirrors.
"I need to concentrate." Buck had never seen his
friend so agitated and, yes, scared.

The pair took pints of dark ale to a booth in
a secluded corner, but Alan never touched his.
Buck, who hadn't eaten since the flight, switched
his empty mug for Alan's full one and downed it,
too. When the waitress came for the mugs, Buck
ordered a sandwich. Alan declined and Buck,
knowing his limit, ordered a soda.

"I know this will be like pouring petrol on a
flame," Alan began, "but I need to tell you this
is a nasty business and that you want to stay as
far away from it as you can."

"Darn right you're fanning my flame," Buck
said. "What's going on?"

"Well, they say it's suicide, but—"

"But you and I both know that's nonsense.
What's the evidence? Have you been to the
scene?"

"I have. Shot through the temple, gun in his
hand. No note."

"Anything missing?"

"Didn't appear to be, but, Cameron, you know
what this is about."

"I don't!"

"Come, come, man. Dirk was a conspiracy
theorist, always sniffing around Todd-Cothran's
involvement with international moneymen, his

role in the three-currency conference, even his association with your Stonagal chap."

"Alan, there are books about this stuff. People make a hobby of ascribing all manner of evil to the Tri-Lateral Commission, the Illuminati, even the Freemasons, for goodness sake. Dirk thought Todd-Cothran and Stonagal were part of something he called the Council of Ten or the Council of Wise Men. So what? It's harmless."

"But when you have an employee, admittedly several levels removed from the head of the exchange, trying to connect his boss to conspiracy theories, he has a problem."

Buck sighed. "So he gets called on the carpet, maybe he gets fired. But tell me how he gets dead or pushed to suicide."

"I'm going to tell you something, Cameron," Alan said. "I know he was murdered."

"Well, I'm pretty sure he was, too, because I think I'd have had a clue if he was suicidal."

"They're trying to pin it on his remorse over losing people in the great disappearance, but it won't wash. He didn't lose anybody close as far as I know."

"But you *know* he was murdered? Pretty strong words for an investigator."

"I know because I knew him, not because I'm an investigator."

"That won't hold up," Buck said. "I can also say I knew him and that he couldn't have committed suicide, but I'm prejudiced."

"Cameron, this is so simple it would be a cliché if Dirk wasn't our friend. What did we always kid him about?"

"Lots of things. Why?"

"We kidded him about being such a klutz."

"Yeah. So?"

"If he was with us right now, where would he be sitting?"

It suddenly dawned on Buck what Alan was driving at. "He would be sitting to one of our lefts, and he was such a klutz because he was left-handed."

"He was shot through the right temple and the so-called suicide weapon was found in his right hand."

"So what did your bosses say when you told them he was left-handed and that this had to be murder?"

"You're the first person I've told."

"Alan! What are you saying?"

"I'm saying I love my family. My parents are still living and I have an older brother and sister. I have a former wife I'm still fond of. I wouldn't mind snuffing her myself, but I certainly wouldn't want anyone else harming her."

"What are you afraid of?"

"I'm afraid of whoever was behind Dirk's murder, of course."

"But you'd have all of Scotland Yard behind you, man! You call yourself a law-enforcement officer and you're going to let this slide?"

"Yes, and that's just what you're going to do!"

"I am not. I wouldn't be able to live with myself."

"Do something about this and you won't be alive at all."

Buck waved the barmaid over and asked for chips. She brought him a heaping, greasy mass. It was just what he wanted. The ale had worked on him and the sandwich had not been enough to counteract it. He felt light-headed, and he was afraid he might not be hungry again for a long time.

"I'm listening," he whispered. "What are you trying to tell me. Who's gotten to you?"

"If you believe me, you won't like it."

"I have no reason not to believe you and I already don't like it. Now spill."

"Dirk's death was ruled a suicide and that was that. Scene cleared, body cremated. I asked about an autopsy and was laughed off. My superior officer, Captain Sullivan, asked what I thought an autopsy would show. I told him abrasions, scrapes, signs of a struggle. He asked if I thought it made sense that a bloke would wrestle with himself before shooting himself. I kept the personal knowledge to myself."

"Why?"

"I smelled something."

"What if I put a story in an international magazine that pointed out the discrepancies? Something would have to happen."

"I have been told to tell you to go home and forget you ever heard about this suicide."

Buck squinted in disbelief. "Nobody knew I was coming."

"I think that's true, but somebody assumed you might show up. I wasn't surprised you came."

"Why should you be? My friend is dead, ostensibly by his own hand. I wasn't going to ignore that."

"You're going to ignore it now."

"You think I'm going to turn coward just because you did?"

"Cameron, you know me better than that."

"I wonder if I know you at all! I thought we were kindred spirits. We were justice freaks, Alan. Seekers of truth. I'm a journalist, you're an investigator. We're skeptics. What is this running from the truth, especially when it concerns our friend?"

"Did you hear me? I said I was told to call you off, if and when you showed up."

"Then why did you let me come to the Yard?"

"I'd have been in trouble if I had tipped you off."

"With whom?"

"I thought you'd never ask. I was visited by what you in America call a goon."

"A heavy?"

"Precisely."

"He threatened you?"

"He did. He said if I didn't want what had happened to my friend to happen to me or to my family, I would do as he said. I was afraid he was the same guy who had murdered Dirk."

"And he probably was. So, why didn't you report the threat?"

"I was going to. I started by trying to handle it myself. I told him he didn't have to worry about me. The next day I went to the exchange and asked for a meeting with Mr. Todd-Cothran."

"The big man himself?"

"In the flesh. I don't have an appointment, of course, but I insist it's Scotland Yard business, and he allows me in. His very office is intimidating. All mahogany and dark green draperies. Well, I get right down to business. I tell him, 'Sir, I believe you've had an employee murdered.' And just as calm as you like, he says, 'Tell you what, governor'—which is a term cockneys use on each other, not something people of his station usually call people of mine. Anyway, he says, 'Tell you what, governor, the next time somebody visits

your flat at ten o'clock at night, as a certain
gentleman did last night, greet him for me, won't
you?'"

"What did you say?"

"What could I say? I was stunned to silence!
I just looked at him and nodded. 'And let me tell
you something else,' he says. 'Tell your friend
Williams to keep out of this.' I say, 'Williams?'
like I don't know who he's talking about. He
ignores that because, of course, he knows better."

"Somebody listened to Dirk's voice mail."

"No question. And he says, 'If he needs
convincing, just tell him I'm as partial as he
is to Dad and Jeff.' That your brother?"

Buck nodded. "So you caved?"

"What was I supposed to do? I tried playing
Mr. Brave Boy. I said, 'I could be wired. I could
be recording this conversation.' Cool as can be,
he said, 'Metal detector would have picked it up.'
'I've got a good memory. I'll expose you,' I told
him. He said, 'At your own risk, governor.
Who's going to believe you over me? Marianne
wouldn't even believe you—of course, she might
not be healthy enough to understand.'"

"Marianne?"

"My sister. But that's not the half of it. As if
he needs to drive the point home, he called my
captain on his speakerphone. He said to him,
'Sullivan, if one of your men was to come to my

office and harass me about anything, what should I do?' And Sullivan, one of my idols, sounded like a little baby. He said, 'Mr. Todd-Cothran, sir, you do whatever you need to do.' And Todd-Cothran said, 'What if I was to kill him where he sits?' And Sullivan said, 'Sir, I'm sure it would be justifiable homicide.' Now get this. Todd-Cothran said, right over the phone to Scotland Yard, where you know they tape every incoming call, and Todd-Cothran knows it just as well, 'What if his name happened to be Alan Tompkins?' Just like that, plain as day. And Sullivan said, 'I'd come over there and dispose of the body myself.' Well, I got the picture."

"So you have no one to turn to."

"Nobody I can think of."

"And I'm supposed to just turn tail and run."

Alan nodded. "I have to report back to Todd-Cothran that I've delivered the message. He'll expect you on the next plane out."

"And if I'm not?"

"No guarantees, but I wouldn't push it."

Buck shoved the plates aside and pushed his chair back. "Alan, you don't know me well, but you have to know I'm not the type of guy who takes this stuff sitting down."

"That's what I was afraid of. I'm not either, but where do I turn? What do I do? You'd think someone somewhere can be trusted, but what can anyone do? If this proves Dirk was right, that he got too close to some clandestine thing Todd-Cothran was into, where does it end? Does it include your man Stonagal? And how about the others on the international team of financiers they meet with? Have you considered that they may own everybody? I grew up reading the stories about your Chicago mobsters who had paid off cops and judges and even politicians. No one could touch them."

Buck nodded. "No one could touch them except the ones who couldn't be bought."

"The Untouchables?"

"Those were my heroes," Buck said.

"Mine too," Alan said. "That's why I'm an investigator. But if the Yard is dirty, who do I turn to?"

Buck rested his chin in his hand. "Do you think you're being watched? Followed?"

"I've been looking for that. So far, no."

"Nobody knows where we are now?"

"I tried to keep an eye out for a tail. In my professional opinion, we're here unnoticed. What are you going to do, Cameron?"

"There's precious little I can do here, apparently. Maybe I'll head back right away under a different name and make it look, to whoever cares, like I'm being obstinate and staying here."

"What's the use?"

"I may be scared, Alan, but I will look for my angle. And somehow I will find the person with the clout to help. I don't know your country well enough to know whom to trust. Of course I trust you, but you've been incapacitated."

"Am I weak, Cameron? Do you see that I have a choice?"

Buck shook his head. "I feel for you," he said. "I can't say what I'd do in your place."

The barmaid was making some sort of an announcement, asking people a question at every other table or so. As she neared them, Buck and Alan fell silent to hear. "Anyone drivin' a light green sedan? Fella says the inside light is on."

"That's mine," Alan said. "I don't remember even having the inside light on."

"Me either," Buck said, "but it was light out when we got here. Maybe we didn't notice."

"I'll get it. Probably won't hurt anything, but that old beater's battery can't take much."

"Careful," Buck said. "Be sure no one was tampering with it."

"Unlikely. We're right in front, remember."

Buck leaned out of his chair and followed Alan with his eyes as the investigator strolled out. Sure enough, the car's inside light could be seen from inside the pub. Alan went around to the driver's side and reached in to turn the light off. When he came back he said, "Gettin' daft in my old age. Next I'll be leavin' the headlights on."

Buck was sad, thinking of his friend's predicament. What a spot, working at something you'd wanted all your life to do and knowing that your superiors were beholden to what amounted to an international thug. "I'm going to call the airport and see if I can get a flight tonight."

"Nothin's going your way this time of the evening," Alan said.

"I'll take something to Frankfurt and head back from there in the morning. I don't think I should test my luck here."

"There's a phone up by the door. I'll pay the girl."

"I insist," Buck said, sliding a fifty-mark bill across the table.

Buck was on the phone to Heathrow while Alan counted the change from the barmaid. Buck got a seat on a flight to Frankfurt forty-five minutes later that would allow him to catch a Sunday morning flight to JFK.

"Oh, Kennedy's open, is it?" he said.

"Just an hour ago," the woman said. "Limited flights, but your Pan-Continental out of Germany goes there in the morning. How many passengers?"

"One."

"Name?"

Buck peeked in his wallet to remind himself of
the name on his phony British passport.
"Pardon?" he said, stalling, as Alan approached.

"Name, sir."

"Oh, sorry. Oreskovich. George Oreskovich."

Alan mouthed that he would be in the car.
Buck nodded.

"All right, sir," the woman said. "You're all
set with a flight to Frankfurt this evening, continuing to JFK in New York tomorrow. Can I do
anything else for you?"

"No, thank you."

As Buck hung up, the door of the pub was
blown into the room and a blinding flash and
deafening crash sent patrons screaming to the
floor. As people crept to the door to see what
had happened, Buck stared in horror at the frame
and melted tires of what had been Alan's Scotland Yard–issue sedan. Windows had been blown
out all up and down the street and a siren was
already sounding. A leg and part of a torso lay
on the sidewalk—the remains of Alan Tompkins.

As the patrons surged out to get a look at the
burning wreckage, Buck elbowed his way
through them, pulling his real passport and
identification from his wallet. In the confusion he
flipped the documents near what was left of the
car and hoped they wouldn't get burned beyond
readability. Whoever wanted him dead could

assume him dead. Then he slipped through the crowd into the now-empty pub and sprinted to the back. But there was no back door, only a window. He raised it and crawled through, finding himself in a two-foot alleyway between buildings. Scraping his clothes on both sides as he hurried to a side street, he ran two blocks and hailed a cab. "The Tavistock," he said.

A few minutes later, when the cabbie was within three blocks of his hotel, Buck saw squad cars in front of the place and blocking traffic. "Just run me out to Heathrow, please," he said. He realized he had left his laptop among his things, but he had no choice. He had transferred the best stuff electronically already, but who knew who would have access to his material now?

"You don't need anything at the hotel then?" the cabbie said.

"No. I was just going to see someone."

"Very good, sir."

More authorities seemed to be combing Heathrow. "You wouldn't know where a fellow could get a hat like yours, would you?" Buck asked the cabbie as he paid.

"This old thing? I might be persuaded to part with it. I've got more than one other just like it. A souvenir, eh?"

"Will this do?" Buck said, pressing a large bill into his hand.

"It'll more than do, sir, and thank you kindly."
The driver removed his official London cabbie
pin and handed over the cap.

Buck pressed the too-large fisherman's style hat
down over his ears and hurried into the terminal.
He paid cash for his tickets in the name of
George Oreskovich, a naturalized Englishman
from Poland on his way to a holiday in the States,
via Frankfurt. He was in the air before the
authorities knew he was gone.

ELEVEN

RAYFORD was glad he could take Chloe out for a drive Saturday after having been cooped up with their grief. He was glad she had agreed to accompany him to the church.

Chloe had been sleepy and quiet all day. She had mentioned the idea of dropping out of the university for a semester and taking some classes locally. Rayford liked it. He was thinking of her. Then he realized she was thinking of him, and he was touched.

As they chatted on the short drive, he reminded her that after their day trip to Atlanta Monday they would have to drive home separately from O'Hare so he could get his car back. She smiled at him. "I think I can handle that, now that I'm twenty."

"I do treat you like a little girl sometimes, don't I?" he said.

"Not too much anymore," she said. "You can make up for it, though."

"I know what you're going to say."

"You don't either," she said. "Guess."

"You're going to say I can make up for treating you like a little girl by letting you have your own mind today, by not trying to talk you into anything."

"That goes without saying, I hope. But you're wrong, smart guy. I was going to say you could convince me you see me as a responsible adult by letting me drive *your* car back from the airport Monday."

"That's easy," Rayford said, suddenly switching to a babyish voice. "Would that make you feel like a big girl? OK, Daddy will do that."

She punched him and smiled, then quickly sobered. "It's amazing what amuses me these days," she said. "Good grief, I feel like an awful person."

Rayford let that comment hang in the air as he turned the corner and the tasteful little church came into view. "Don't make too much of what I just said," Chloe said. "I don't have to come in, do I?"

"No, but I'd appreciate it."

She pursed her lips and shook her head, but when he parked and got out, she followed.

Bruce Barnes was short and slightly pudgy, with

curly hair and wire-rimmed glasses. He dressed
casually but with class, and Rayford guessed him
to be in his early thirties. He emerged from the
sanctuary with a small vacuum in his hands.
"Sorry," he said. "You must be the Steeles. I'm
kind of the whole staff around here now, except
for Loretta."

"Hello," an older woman said from behind
Rayford and Chloe. She stood in the doorway of
the church offices sunken-eyed and disheveled,
as if she'd come through a war. After pleasantries
she retreated to a desk in the outer office.

"She's putting together a little program for
tomorrow," Barnes said. "Tough thing is, we
have no idea how many to expect. Will you
be here?"

"Not sure yet," Rayford said. "I probably will
be."

They both looked at Chloe. She smiled politely.
"I probably won't be," she said.

"Well, I've got the tape for you," Barnes said.
"But I'd like to ask for a few more minutes of
your time."

"I've got time," Rayford said.

"I'm with him," Chloe said resignedly.

Barnes led them to the senior pastor's office.
"I don't sit at his desk or use his library," the
younger man said, "but I do work in here at his
conference table. I don't know what's going to

happen to me or to the church, and I certainly
don't want to be presumptuous. I can't imagine
God would call me to take over this work, but
if he does, I want to be ready."

"And how will he call you?" Chloe said, a smile
playing at her mouth. "By phone?"

Barnes didn't respond in kind. "To tell you
the truth, it wouldn't surprise me. I don't know
about you, but he got my attention last week.
A phone call from heaven would have been less
traumatic."

Chloe raised her eyebrows, apparently in
surrender to his point.

"Folks, Loretta there looks like I feel. We're
shell-shocked and we're devastated, because we
know exactly what happened."

"Or you think you do," Chloe said. Rayford
tried to catch her eye to encourage her to back
off, but she seemed unwilling to look at him.
"There's every kind of theory you want on every
TV show in the country."

"I know that," Barnes said.

"And each is self-serving," she added. "The
tabloids say it was space invaders, which would
prove the stupid stories they've been running
for years. The government says it's some sort
of enemy, so we can spend more on high-tech
defense. You're going to say it was God so you
can start rebuilding your church."

Bruce Barnes sat back and looked at Chloe, then at her father. "I'm going to ask you something," he said, turning to her again. "Could you let me tell you my story briefly, without interrupting or saying anything, unless there's something you don't understand?"

Chloe stared at him without responding.

"I don't want to be rude, but I don't want you to be either. I asked for a few moments of your time. If I still have it, I want to try to make use of it. Then I'll leave you alone. You can do anything you want with what I tell you. Tell me I'm crazy, tell me I'm self-serving. Leave and never come back. That's up to you. But can I have the floor for a few minutes?"

Rayford thought Barnes was brilliant. He had put Chloe in her place, leaving her no smart remark. She merely waved a hand of permission, for which Barnes thanked her, and he began.

"May I call you by your first names?"

Rayford nodded. Chloe didn't respond.

"Ray, is it? And Chloe? I sit here before you a broken man. And Loretta? If anyone has a right to feel as bad as I do, it's Loretta. She's the only person in her whole clan who is still here. She had six living brothers and sisters, I don't know how many aunts and uncles and cousins and nieces and nephews. They had a wedding here last year and she must have had a hundred relatives alone. They're all gone, every one of them."

"That's awful," Chloe said. "We lost my mom and my little brother, you know. Oh, I'm sorry. I wasn't going to say anything."

"It's all right," Barnes said. "My situation is almost as bad as Loretta's, only on a smaller scale. Of course it's not small for me. Let me tell you my story." As soon as he began with seemingly innocuous details, his voice grew thick and quiet. "I was in bed with my wife. She was sleeping. I was reading. Our children had been down for a couple of hours. They were five, three, and one. The oldest was a girl, the other two boys. That was normal for us—me reading while my wife slept. She worked so hard with the kids and a part-time job that she was always knocked out by nine or so.

"I was reading a sports magazine, trying to turn the pages quietly, and every once in a while she would sigh. Once she even asked how much longer I would be. I knew I should go in the other room or just turn the light off and try to sleep myself. But I told her, 'Not long,' hoping she'd fall asleep and I could just read the whole magazine. I can usually tell by her breathing if she's sleeping soundly enough that my light doesn't bother her. And after a while I heard that deep breathing.

"I was glad. My plan was to read till midnight. I was propped up on an elbow with my back to her, using a pillow to shield the light a little. I don't know how much longer I had been reading when I felt the bed move and sensed she had gotten up. I assumed she was going to the bathroom and only hoped she didn't wake up to the point where she'd bug me about still having the light on when she got back. She's a tiny little thing, and it didn't hit me that I didn't hear her walk to the bathroom. But, like I say, I was engrossed in my reading.

"After a few more minutes I called out, 'Hon, you OK?' And I didn't hear anything. I began wondering, was it just my imagination that she had gotten up? I reached behind me and she was not there, so I called out again. I thought maybe she was checking on the kids, but usually she's such a sound sleeper that unless she's heard one of them she doesn't do that.

"Well, probably another minute or two went by before I turned over and noticed that she was not only gone, but that it also appeared she had pulled the sheet and covers back up toward her pillow. Now you can imagine what I thought. I thought she was so frustrated at me for still reading that she had given up waiting for me to turn off the light and decided to go sleep on the couch. I'm a fairly decent husband,

so I went out to apologize and bring her back
to bed.

"You know what happened. She wasn't out on
the couch. She wasn't in the bathroom. I poked
my head into each of the kids' rooms and whispered for her, thinking maybe she was rocking
one of them or sitting in there. Nothing. The
lights were off all over the house, except for my
bedside. I didn't want to wake the kids by yelling
for her, so I just turned on the hall light and
checked their rooms again.

"I'm ashamed to say I still didn't have a clue
until I noticed my oldest two kids weren't in their
beds. My first thought was that they had gone
into the baby's room, like they do sometimes, to
sleep on the floor. Then I thought my wife had
taken one or both of them to the kitchen for
something. Frankly I was just a little perturbed
that I didn't know what was going on in the
middle of the night.

"When the baby was not in his crib, I turned
the light on, stuck my head out the door and
called down the hall for my wife. No answer.
Then I noticed the baby's footie pajamas in the
crib, and I knew. I just knew. It hit me all of a
sudden. I ran from room to room, pulling back
the covers and finding the kids' pajamas. I didn't
want to, but I tore the cover back from my
wife's side of the bed and there was her night-

gown, her rings, and even her hair clips on the pillow."

Rayford was fighting the tears, remembering his own similar experience. Barnes took a deep breath and exhaled, wiping his eyes. "Well, I started phoning around," he said. "I started with the pastor, but of course I got his answering machine. A couple of other places I got answering machines, too, so I grabbed the church directory and started looking up older folks, the people I thought might not like answering machines and wouldn't have one. I let their phones ring off the hook. No answers.

"Of course I knew it was unlikely I'd find anybody. For some reason I ran out and jumped in my car and raced over here to the church. There was Loretta, sitting in her car in her robe, hair up in curlers, crying her eyes out. We came into the foyer and sat by the potted plants, crying and holding each other, knowing exactly what had happened. Within about half an hour, a few others showed up. We basically commiserated and wondered aloud what we were supposed to do next. Then somebody remembered Pastor's Rapture tape."

"His what?" Chloe asked.

"Our senior pastor loved to preach about the coming of Christ to rapture his church, to take believers, dead and alive, to heaven before a

period of tribulation on the earth. He was particularly inspired once a couple of years ago."

Rayford turned to Chloe. "You remember
your mother talking about that. She was so
enthusiastic about it."

"Oh yeah, I do."

"Well," Barnes said, "the pastor used that
sermon and had himself videotaped in this office
speaking directly to people who were left behind.
He put it in the church library with instructions
to get it out and play it if most everyone seemed
to have disappeared. We all watched it a couple
of times the other night. A few people wanted to
argue with God, trying to tell us that they really
had been believers and should have been taken
with the others, but we all knew the truth. We
had been phony. There wasn't a one of us who
didn't know what it meant to be a true Christian.
We knew we weren't and that we had been left
behind."

Rayford had trouble speaking, but he had to
ask. "Mr. Barnes, you were on the staff here."

"Right."

"How did you miss it?"

"I'm going to tell you, Ray, because I no longer
have anything to hide. I'm ashamed of myself,
and if I never really had the desire or the motiva-
tion to tell others about Christ before, I sure
have it now. I just feel awful that it took the

most cataclysmic event in history to reach me.
I was raised in the church. My parents and
brothers and sisters were all Christians.

"I loved church. It was my life, my culture. I
thought I believed everything there was to believe
in the Bible. The Bible says that if you believe in
Christ you have eternal life, so I assumed I was
covered.

"I especially liked the parts about God being
forgiving. I was a sinner, and I never changed.
I just kept getting forgiveness because I thought
God was bound to do that. He had to. Verses
that said if we confessed our sins he was faithful
and just to forgive us and to cleanse us. I knew
other verses said you had to believe *and* receive,
to trust and to abide, but to me that was sort of
theological mumbo jumbo. I wanted the bottom
line, the easiest route, the simplest path. I knew
other verses said that we are not to continue in
sin just because God shows grace.

"I thought I had a great life. I even went to
Bible college. In church and at school, I said
the right things and prayed in public and even
encouraged people in their Christian lives. But
I was still a sinner. I even said that. I told people
I wasn't perfect; I was forgiven."

"My wife said that," Rayford said.

"The difference is," Bruce said, "she was
sincere. I lied. I told my wife that we tithed to the

church, you know, that we gave ten percent of
our income. I hardly ever gave any, except when
the plate was passed I might drop in a few bills to
make it look good. Every week I would confess
that to God, promising to do better next time.

"I encouraged people to share their faith, to
tell other people how to become Christians. But
on my own I never did that. My job was to visit
people in their homes and nursing homes and
hospitals every day. I was good at it. I encouraged them, smiled at them, talked with them,
prayed with them, even read Scripture to them.
But I never did that on my own, privately.

"I was lazy. I cut corners. When people
thought I was out calling, I might be at a movie
in another town. I was also lustful. I read things
I shouldn't have read, looked at magazines that
fed my lusts."

Rayford winced. That hit too close to home.

"I had a real racket going," Barnes was saying,
"and I bought into it. Down deep, way down
deep, I knew better. I knew it was too good to be
true. I knew that true Christians were known by
what their lives produced and that I was producing nothing. But I comforted myself that there
were worse people around who called themselves
Christians.

"I wasn't a rapist or a child molester or an adul-
terer, though many times I felt unfaithful to my

wife because of my lusts. But I could always pray and confess and feel as though I was clean. It should have been obvious to me. When people found out I was on the pastoral staff at New Hope, I would tell them about the cool pastor and the neat church, but I was shy about telling them about Christ. If they challenged me and asked if New Hope was one of those churches that said Jesus was the only way to God, I did everything but deny it. I wanted them to think I was OK, that I was with it. I may be a Christian and even a pastor, but don't lump me with the weirdos. Above all, don't do that.

"I see now, of course, that God *is* a sin-forgiving God, because we're human and we need that. But we are to receive his gift, abide in Christ, and allow him to live through us. I used what I thought was my security as a license to do what I wanted. I could basically live in sin and pretend to be devout. I had a great family and a nice work environment. And as miserable as I was privately most of the time, I really believed I would go to heaven when I died.

"I hardly ever read my Bible except when preparing a talk or lesson. I didn't have the 'mind of Christ.' *Christian,* I knew vaguely, means 'Christ one' or 'one like Christ.' That sure wasn't me, and I found out in the worst way possible.

"Let me just say to you both—this is your

decision. These are your lives. But I know, and
Loretta knows, and a few others who were playing around the edges here at this church know
exactly what happened a few nights ago. Jesus
Christ returned for his true family, and the rest
of us were left behind."

Bruce looked Chloe in the eyes. "There is no
doubt in my mind that we have witnessed the
Rapture. My biggest fear, once I realized the
truth, was that there was no more hope for me.
I had missed it, I had been a phony, I had set up
my own brand of Christianity that may have
made for a life of freedom but had cost me my
soul. I had heard people say that when the
church was raptured, God's Spirit would be
gone from the earth. The logic was that when
Jesus went to heaven after his resurrection, the
Holy Spirit that God gave to the church was
embodied in believers. So when they were taken,
the Spirit would be gone, and there would be
no more hope for anyone left. You can't know
the relief when Pastor's tape showed me otherwise.

"We realize how stupid we were, but those
of us in this church—at least the ones who felt
drawn to this building the night everyone else
disappeared—are now as zealous as we can be.
No one who comes here will leave without knowing exactly what we believe and what we think

is necessary for them to have a relationship
with God."

Chloe stood and paced, her arms folded across
her chest. "That's a pretty interesting story," she
said. "What was the deal with Loretta? How did
she miss it if her whole extended family were true
Christians?"

"You should have her tell you sometime,"
Bruce said. "But she tells me it was pride and
embarrassment that kept her from Christ. She
was a middle child in a very religious family, and
she said she was in her late teens before she even
thought seriously about her personal faith. She
had just drifted along with the family to church
and all the related activities. As she grew up, got
married, became a mother and a grandmother,
she just let everyone assume she was a spiritual
giant. She was revered around here. Only she had
never believed and received Christ for herself."

"So," Chloe said, "this believing and receiving
stuff, this living for Christ or letting him live
through you, that's what my mother meant
when she talked about salvation, getting saved?"

Bruce nodded. "From sin and hell and judgment."

"Meantime, we're not saved from all that."

"That's right."

"You really believe this."

"I do."

"It's pretty freaky stuff, you have to admit."

"Not to me. Not anymore."

Rayford, always one for precision and order, asked, "So, what did you do? What did my wife do? What made her more of a Christian, or, ah . . . what, uh—"

"Saved her?" Bruce said.

"Yes," Rayford said. "That's exactly what I want to know. If you're right, and I've already told Chloe that I think I see this now, we need to know how it works. How it goes. How does a person get from one situation to the other? Obviously, we were not saved from being left, and we're here to face life without our loved ones who were true Christians. So, how do we become true Christians?"

"I'm going to walk you through that," Bruce said. "And I'm going to send you home with the tape. And I'm going to go through this all in detail tomorrow morning at ten for whoever shows up. I'll probably do the same lesson every Sunday morning for as long as people need to know. One thing I'm sure of, as important as all the other sermons and lessons are, nothing matters like this one."

While Chloe stood with her back to the wall, arms still folded, watching and listening, Bruce turned to Rayford. "It's really quite simple. God made it easy. That doesn't mean it's not a supernatural transaction or that we can pick and choose the good parts—as I tried to do. But if we see the truth and act on it, God won't withhold salvation from us.

"First, we have to see ourselves as God sees us. The Bible says all have sinned, that there is none righteous, no not one. It also says we can't save ourselves. Lots of people thought they could earn their way to God or to heaven by doing good things, but that's probably the biggest misconception ever. Ask anyone on the street what they think the Bible or the church says about getting to heaven, and nine of ten would say it has something to do with doing good and living right.

"We're to do that, of course, but not so we can earn our salvation. We're to do that in *response* to our salvation. The Bible says that it's not by works of righteousness that we have done, but by his mercy God saved us. It also says that we are saved by grace through Christ, not of ourselves, so we can't brag about our goodness.

"Jesus took our sins and paid the penalty for them so we wouldn't have to. The payment is death, and he died in our place because he loved us. When we tell Christ that we acknowledge ourselves as sinners and lost, and receive his gift of salvation, he saves us. A transaction takes place. We go from darkness to light, from lost to found; we're saved. The Bible says that to those who receive him, he gives the power to become sons of God. That's what Jesus is—the Son of God. When we become sons of God, we have what Jesus has: a relationship with God, eternal life, and because Jesus paid our penalty, we also have forgiveness for our sins."

Rayford sat stunned. He sneaked a peek at Chloe. She looked frozen, but she didn't appear antagonistic. Rayford felt he had found exactly what he was looking for. It was what he had suspected and had heard bits and pieces of over the years, but he had never put it all together. In spite of himself, he was still reserved enough to want to mull it over, to see and hear the tape, and to discuss it with Chloe.

"I have to ask you," Bruce said, "something I never wanted to ask people before. I want to know if you're ready to receive Christ right now. I would be happy to pray with you and lead you in how to talk to God about this."

"No," Chloe said quickly, looking at her dad as if afraid he was going to do something foolish.

"No?" Bruce was clearly surprised. "Need more time?"

"At least," Chloe said. "Surely this isn't something you rush into."

"Well, let me tell you," Bruce said. "It's something I wish I had rushed into. I believe God has forgiven me and that I have a job to do here. But

I don't know what's going to happen now, with the true Christians all gone. I'd sure rather have come to this point years ago than now, when it was nearly too late. You can imagine that I would much rather be in heaven with my family right now."

"But then who would tell us about this?" Rayford asked.

"Oh, I'm grateful for that opportunity," Bruce said. "But it has cost me dearly."

"I understand." Rayford could feel Bruce's eyes burning into him as if the young man knew Rayford was nearly ready to make a commitment. But he had never rushed into anything in his life. And while he didn't put this on the same scale as dealing with a salesman, he needed time to think, a cooling-off period. He was analytical, and while this suddenly made a world of sense to him and he didn't doubt at all Bruce's theory of the disappearances, he would not act immediately. "I'd appreciate the tape, and I can guarantee you, I will be back tomorrow."

Bruce looked at Chloe. "No guarantees from me," she said, "but I appreciate your time and I will watch the tape."

"That's all I can ask," Bruce said. "But let me leave you with one little reminder of urgency. You may have heard this off and on your whole lives, the way I did. Maybe you haven't. But I need to tell you that you don't have any guarantees. It's too late for you to disappear like your loved ones did a few days ago. But people die every day in car accidents, plane crashes—oh, sorry, I'm sure you're a good pilot—all kinds of tragedies. I'm not going to push you into something you're not ready for, but just let me encourage you that if God impresses upon you that this is true, don't put it off. What would be worse than finally finding God and then dying without him because you waited too long?"

TWELVE

BUCK checked into the Frankfurt Hilton at the airport under his phony name, knowing he had to call the States before his family and his colleagues heard he was dead. He started by finding a pay phone in the lobby and dialing his father's number in Arizona. With the time difference, it was shortly after noon on Saturday there.

"I'm really sorry about this, Dad, but you're going to hear I was killed in some sort of a car bombing, terrorist attack, that kind of thing."

"What the devil is going on, Cameron?"

"I can't get into it now, Dad. I just want you to know I'm all right. I'm calling from overseas, but I'd rather not say where. I'll be back tomorrow, but I'm going to have to lay low for a while."

"Your sister-in-law and niece and nephew's memorial services are tomorrow evening," Mr. Williams said.

"Oh, no. Dad, it would really be obvious if I showed up there. I'm sorry. Tell Jeff how really sorry I am."

"Well, do we have to play this charade out? I mean should we make it a memorial for you, too?"

"No, I'm not going to be able to play dead that long. Once the people at the *Global* find out I'm all right, the secret won't hold for long."

"Are you going to be in danger when whoever thinks they killed you finds out?"

"Probably, but Dad, I've got to get off now. Tell Jeff for me, huh?"

"I will. Be careful."

Buck switched to another phone and called the *Global.* Disguising his voice, he asked the receptionist to plug him into Steve Plank's after-hours voice mail. "Steve, you know who this is. No matter what you hear in the next twenty-four hours, I'm all right. I will call you tomorrow and we can meet. Let the others believe what they hear for now. I'm going to need to remain incognito until I can find someone who can really help. Talk to you soon, Steve."

Chloe was silent in the car. Rayford fought the urge to jabber. That was not his nature, but he felt the same urgency he had sensed in Bruce

Barnes. He wanted to remain sensible, yes, analytical. He wanted to study, to pray, to be sure. But wasn't that just insurance? Could he be more sure?

What had he done in his raising of Chloe that could make her so cautious, so careful, that she might look down her nose at what was so obvious to him? He had found the truth, and Bruce was right. They needed to act on it before anything happened to them.

The news was full of crime, looting, people taking advantage of the chaos. People were being shot, maimed, raped, killed. The roadways were more dangerous than ever. Emergency units were understaffed, fewer air- and ground-traffic controllers manned the airports, fewer qualified pilots and crews flew the planes.

People checked the graves of loved ones to see if their corpses had disappeared, and unscrupulous types pretended to do the same while looking for valuables that might have been buried with the wealthy. It had become an ugly world overnight, and Rayford was worried about his and Chloe's safety. He didn't want to go much longer without watching the tape and making good on the decision he had already made.

"Can we watch it together?" he suggested.

"I'd really rather not, Dad. I can see where you're going with this, and I'm not comfortable with it yet. This is very personal. It isn't a group or family thing."

"I'm not so sure about that."

"Well, don't push me. You deal with it on your own, and I will later."

"You know I'm just worried about you and that I love you and care about you, don't you?"

"Of course."

"Will you watch it before the church meeting tomorrow?"

"Daddy, please. You're going to push me away if you keep bugging me about it. I'm not sure I even want to go to that. I heard his pitch today and he said himself it's going to be the same thing tomorrow."

"Well, what if I decide to become a Christian tomorrow? I'd kind of like you there."

Chloe looked at him. "I don't know, Dad. It's not like graduation or something."

"Maybe it is. I feel like your mother and your brother got promoted and I didn't."

"Gross."

"I'm serious. They qualified for heaven. I didn't."

"I don't want to talk about this now."

"OK, but let me just say one more thing. If you don't go tomorrow, I wish you'd watch the tape while I'm gone."

"Oh, I—"

"Because I'd really like to have you settle this thing before our flight Monday. Air travel is becoming more dangerous, and you never know what might happen."

"Daddy, come on! All my life all I've heard you do is set people straight about how safe flying is. Every time there's a crash, someone asks if you aren't afraid or if you've ever had a close call, and you rattle off all these statistics about how flying is so many times safer than riding in a car. So don't start with that."

Rayford gave up. He would deal with his own soul and pray for his daughter, but clearly there would be no badgering her into the faith.

Chloe went to bed early Saturday night while Rayford settled in front of the television and popped in the video. "Hello," came the pleasant voice of the pastor Rayford had met several times. As he spoke he sat on the edge of the desk in the very office Rayford had just visited. "My name is Vernon Billings, and I'm pastor of the New Hope Village Church of Mount Prospect, Illinois. As you watch this tape, I can only imagine the fear and despair you face, for this is being recorded for viewing only after the disappearance of God's people from the earth.

"That you are watching indicates you have been left behind. You are no doubt stunned, shocked, afraid, and remorseful. I would like you to consider what I have to say here as instructions for life following Christ's rapture of his church. That is what has happened. Anyone you know or knew of who had placed his or her trust in Christ alone for salvation has been taken to heaven by Christ.

"Let me show you from the Bible exactly what has happened. You won't need this proof by now, because you will have experienced the most shocking event of history. But as this tape was made beforehand and I am confident that I will be gone, ask yourself, how did he know? Here's how, from 1 Corinthians 15:51-57."

The screen began to scroll with the passage of Scripture. Rayford hit the pause button and ran to get Irene's Bible. It took him a while to find 1 Corinthians, and though it was slightly different in her translation, the meaning was the same.

The pastor said, "Let me read to you what the great missionary evangelist, the apostle Paul, wrote to the Christians at the church in the city of Corinth:

"Behold, I tell you a mystery: We shall not all sleep, but we shall all be changed—in a moment, in the twinkling of an eye, at the last trumpet. For the trumpet will sound, and the dead will be raised incorruptible, and we shall be changed. For this corruptible must put on incorruption, and this mortal must put on immortality. So when this corruptible has put on incorruption, and this mortal has put on immortality, then shall be brought to pass the saying that is written: 'Death is swallowed up in victory. O Death, where is your sting? O Hades, where is your victory?' The sting of death is sin, and the strength of sin is the law. But thanks be to God, who gives us the victory through our Lord Jesus Christ."

Rayford was confused. He could follow some of that, but the rest was like gibberish to him. He let the tape roll. Pastor Billings continued, "Let me paraphrase some of that so you'll understand it clearly. When Paul says we shall not all sleep, he means that we shall not all die. And he's saying that this corruptible being must put on an incorruptible body which is to last for all of eternity. When these things have happened, when the Christians who have already died and those that are still living receive their immortal bodies, the Rapture of the church will have taken place.

"Every person who believed in and accepted the sacrificial death, burial, and resurrection of Jesus Christ anticipated his coming again for them. As you see this tape, all those will have already seen the fulfillment of the promise of

Christ when he said, 'I will come again and receive you unto Myself; that where I am, there you may be also.'

"I believe that all such people were literally taken from the earth, leaving everything material behind. If you have discovered that millions of people are missing and that babies and children have vanished, you know what I am saying is true. Up to a certain age, which is probably different for each individual, we believe God will not hold a child accountable for a decision that must be made with heart and mind, fully cognizant of the ramifications. You may also find that unborn children have disappeared from their mothers' wombs. I can only imagine the pain and heartache of a world without precious children, and the deep despair of parents who will miss them so.

"Paul's prophetic letter to the Corinthians said this would occur in the twinkling of an eye. You may have seen a loved one standing before you, and suddenly they were gone. I don't envy you that shock.

"The Bible says that men's hearts will fail them for fear. That means to me that there will be heart attacks due to shock, people will commit suicide in their despair, and you know better than I the chaos that will result from Christians disappearing from various modes of transportation, with the loss of firefighters and police officers and emergency workers of all sorts.

"Depending on when you're viewing this tape, you may have already found that martial law is in effect in many places, emergency measures trying to keep evil elements from looting and fighting over the spoils of what is left. Governments will tumble and there will be international disorder.

"You may wonder why this has happened. Some believe this is the judgment of God on an ungodly world. Actually, that is to come later. Strange as this may sound to you, this is God's final effort to get the attention of every person who has ignored or rejected him. He is allowing now a vast period of trial and tribulation to come to you who remain. He has removed his church from a corrupt world that seeks its own way, its own pleasures, its own ends.

"I believe God's purpose in this is to allow those who remain to take stock of themselves and leave their frantic search for pleasure and self-fulfillment, and turn to the Bible for truth and to Christ for salvation.

"Let me encourage you that your loved ones, your children and infants, your friends, and your acquaintances have not been snatched away by some evil force or some invasion from outer space. That will likely be a common explanation.

What sounded ludicrous to you before might
sound logical now, but it is not.

"Also, Scripture indicates that there will be a
great lie, announced with the help of the media
and perpetrated by a self-styled world leader.
Jesus himself prophesied about such a person.
He said, 'I have come in My Father's name, and
you do not receive Me; if another comes in his
own name, him you will receive.'

"Let me warn you personally to beware of
such a leader of humanity who may emerge from
Europe. He will turn out to be a great deceiver
who will step forward with signs and wonders
that will be so impressive that many will believe
he is of God. He will gain a great following
among those who are left, and many will believe
he is a miracle worker.

"The deceiver will promise strength and peace
and security, but the Bible says he will speak out
against the Most High and will wear down the
saints of the Most High. That's why I warn
you to beware now of a new leader with great
charisma trying to take over the world during
this terrible time of chaos and confusion. This
person is known in the Bible as Antichrist. He
will make many promises, but he will not keep
them. You must trust in the promises of God
Almighty through his Son, Jesus Christ.

"I believe the Bible teaches that the Rapture of

the church ushers in a seven-year period of trial and tribulation, during which terrible things will happen. If you have not received Christ as your Savior, your soul is in jeopardy. And because of the cataclysmic events that will take place during this period, your very life is in danger. If you turn to Christ, you may still have to die as a martyr."

Rayford paused the tape. He had been prepared for the salvation stuff. But tribulation and trial? Losing his loved ones, facing the pride and self-centeredness that had kept him out of heaven— wasn't that enough? There would be *more?*

And what of this "great deceiver" the pastor had talked about? Maybe he had taken this prophecy business too far. But this was no snake-oil salesman. This was a sincere, honest, trustworthy man—a man of God. If what the pastor said about the disappearances was true—and Rayford knew in his heart that it was—then the man deserved his attention, his respect.

It was time to move beyond being a critic, an analyst never satisfied with the evidence. The proof was before him: the empty chairs, the lonely bed, the hole in his heart. There was only one course of action. He punched the play button.

"It doesn't make any difference, at this point, why you're still on earth. You may have been too selfish or prideful or busy, or perhaps you simply didn't take the time to examine the claims of Christ for yourself. The point now is, you have another chance. Don't miss it.

"The disappearance of the saints and children, the chaos left behind, and the despairing of the heartbroken are evidence that what I'm saying is true. Pray that God will help you. Receive his salvation gift right now. And resist the lies and efforts of the Antichrist, who is sure to rise up soon. Remember, he will deceive many. Don't be counted among them.

"Nearly eight hundred years before Jesus came to earth the first time, Isaiah in the Old Testament prophesied that the kingdoms of nations will be in great conflict and their faces shall be as flames. To me, this portends World War III, a thermonuclear war that will wipe out millions.

"Bible prophecy is history written in advance. I urge you to find books on this subject or find people who may have been experts in this area but who for some reason did not receive Christ before and were left behind. Study so you'll know what is coming and you can be prepared.

"You'll find that government and religion will change, war and inflation will erupt, there will be widespread death and destruction, martyrdom of saints, and even a devastating earthquake. Be prepared.

"God wants to forgive you your sins and assure you of heaven. Listen to Ezekiel 33:11: 'I have no pleasure in the death of the wicked, but that the wicked turn from his way and live.'

"If you accept God's message of salvation, his Holy Spirit will come in unto you and make you spiritually born anew. You don't need to understand all this theologically. You can become a child of God by praying to him right now as I lead you—"

Rayford paused the tape again and saw the concern on the pastor's face, the compassion in his eyes. He knew friends and acquaintances would think him crazy, perhaps even his own daughter would. But this rang true with him. Rayford didn't understand about the seven years of tribulation and this new leader, the liar who was supposed to emerge. But he knew he needed Christ in his life. He needed forgiveness of sin and the assurance that one day he would join his wife and son in heaven.

Rayford sat with his head in his hands, his heart pounding. There was no sound from upstairs where Chloe rested. He was alone with his thoughts, alone with God, and he felt God's presence. Rayford slid to his knees on the carpet. He had never knelt in worship before, but he sensed the seriousness and the reverence of the moment. He pushed the play button and

tossed the remote control aside. He set his
hands palms down before him and rested his
forehead on them, his face on the floor. The
pastor said, "Pray after me," and Rayford did.
"Dear God, I admit that I'm a sinner. I am
sorry for my sins. Please forgive me and save
me. I ask this in the name of Jesus, who died
for me. I trust in him right now. I believe that
the sinless blood of Jesus is sufficient to pay the
price for my salvation. Thank you for hearing
me and receiving me. Thank you for saving my
soul."

As the pastor continued with words of assurance, quoting verses that promised that whoever
called upon the name of the Lord would be
saved and that God would not cast out anyone
who sought him, Rayford stayed where he was.
As the tape finished the pastor said, "If you
were genuine, you are saved, born again, a
child of God." Rayford wanted to talk to God
more. He wanted to be specific about his sin.
He knew he was forgiven, but in a childlike
way, he wanted God to know that he knew
what kind of a person he had been.

He confessed his pride. Pride in his intelligence.
Pride in his looks. Pride in his abilities. He
confessed his lusts, how he had neglected his
wife, how he had sought his own pleasure. How
he had worshiped money and things. When he

was through, he felt clean. The tape had scared
him, all that talk about the tough times ahead,
but he knew he would rather face them as a true
believer than in the state he had been.

His first prayer following that was for Chloe.
He would worry about her and pray for her
constantly until he was sure she had joined him
in this new life.

Buck arrived at JFK and immediately called
Steve Plank. "Stay right where you are, Buck,
you renegade. Do you know who wants to talk
with you?"

"I couldn't guess."

"Nicolae Carpathia himself."

"Yeah, right."

"I'm serious. He's here and he's got your old
friend Chaim Rosenzweig with him. Apparently
Chaim sang your praises, and with all the media
after him, he's asking for you. So I'll come get
you, you'll tell me what in the world you've
gotten yourself into, we'll get you undead, and
you can have that great interview you've been
looking for."

Buck hung up and clapped. *This is too good
to be true,* he thought. *If there's one guy who's
above these international terrorists and bullies
and even the dirt at the London Exchange and*

*Scotland Yard, it will be this Carpathia. If Rosen-
zweig likes him, he's got to be all right.*

Rayford couldn't wait to go to New Hope the
next morning. He began reading the New Testament, and he scrounged around the house for
any books or study guides Irene had collected.
Though much of it was still difficult to understand, he found himself so hungry and thirsty
for the story of the life of Christ that he read
through all four Gospels until it was late and
he fell asleep.

All Rayford could think of throughout the reading was that he was now part of this family that
included his wife and son. Though he was scared
of what the pastor had predicted on the tape
about all the bad things that would happen in the
world now that the church had been raptured,
he was also excited about his new faith. He knew
he would one day be with God and Christ, and
he wanted that for Chloe more than ever.

Rayford kept himself from bugging her. He
determined not to tell her what he had done
unless she asked. She didn't ask before he left
for church in the morning, but she apologized
for not going with him. "I will go with you
sometime," she said. "I promise. I'm not being
antagonistic. I'm just not ready."

Rayford fought the urge to warn her not to wait too long. He also wanted to plead with her to watch the tape, but she knew he had watched it and she asked him nothing about it. He had rewound it and left it in the VCR, hoping and praying she would watch it while he was gone.

Rayford got to the church just before ten o'clock and was shocked to have to park nearly three blocks away. The place was packed. Few were carrying Bibles, and hardly anyone was dressed up. These were scared, desperate people who filled every pew, including in the balcony. Rayford wound up standing in the back with nowhere to sit.

Right at ten o'clock, Bruce began, but he asked Loretta to stand by the door and make sure any latecomers were welcomed. Despite the crowd, he did not use the platform spotlights, nor did he stand in the pulpit. He had placed a single microphone stand in front of the first pew, and he simply talked to the people.

Bruce introduced himself and said, "I'm not in the pulpit because that is a place for people who are trained and called to it. I am in a place of leadership and teaching today by default. Normally we at this church would be thrilled to see a crowd like this," he said. "But I'm not about to tell you how great it is to see you here. I know you're here seeking to know what

happened to your children and loved ones, and
I believe I have the answer. Obviously, I didn't
have it before, or I too would be gone. We'll not
be singing or making any announcements, except
to tell you we have a Bible study scheduled for
Wednesday night at seven. We will not be taking
any offering, though we will have to start doing
that next week to meet our expenses. The church
has some money in the bank, but we do have a
mortgage and I have living expenses."

Bruce then told the same story he had told
Rayford and Chloe the day before, and his
voice was the only sound in the place. Many
wept. He showed the videotape, and more than
a hundred people prayed along with the pastor
at the end. Bruce urged them to begin coming
to New Hope.

He added, "I know many of you may still be
skeptical. You may believe what happened was
of God, but you still don't like it and you resent
him for it. If you would like to come back and
vent and ask questions this evening, I will be
here. But I choose not to offer that opportunity
this morning because so many here are brand-
new in their faith and I don't want to confuse
the issue. Rest assured we will be open to any
honest question.

"I do want to open the floor to anyone who
received Christ this morning and would like to

confess it before us. The Bible tells us to do that, to make known our decision and our stand. Feel free to come to the microphone."

Rayford was the first to move, but as he came down the aisle he sensed many falling in behind him. Dozens waited to tell their stories, to say where they'd been on their spiritual journey. Most were just like he was, having been on the edges of the truth through a loved one or friend, but never fully accepting the truth about Christ.

Their stories were moving and hardly anyone left, even when the clock swept past noon and forty or fifty more still stood in line. All seemed to need to tell of the ones who had left them. At two o'clock, when everyone was hungry and tired, Bruce said, "I'm going to have to bring this to a close. One thing I wasn't going to do today was anything traditionally churchy, including singing. But I feel we need to praise the Lord for what has happened here today. Let me teach you a simple chorus of adoration."

Bruce sang a brief song from Scripture, honoring God the Father, Jesus his Son, and the Holy Spirit. When the people joined in, quietly and reverently and heartfelt, Rayford was too choked up to sing. One by one people stopped singing and mouthed the words or hummed, they were so overcome. Rayford believed it was the most

moving moment of his life. How he longed to
share it with Irene and Raymie and Chloe.

People seemed reluctant to leave, even after
Bruce closed in prayer. Many stayed to get
acquainted, and it became obvious a new congregation had begun. The name of the church was
more appropriate than ever. New Hope. Bruce
shook hands with people as they left, and no
one ducked him or hurried past. When Rayford
shook his hand, Bruce asked, "Are you busy
this afternoon? Would you be able to join me
for a bite?"

"I'd want to call my daughter first, but sure."

Rayford let Chloe know where he'd be. She
didn't ask about the church meeting, except to
say, "It went long, huh? Lot of people there?"
And he simply told her yes on both counts. He
was committed to not saying more unless she
asked. He hoped and prayed her curiosity would
get the best of her, and if he then could do justice
to what had happened that day, maybe she would
wish she'd been in on it. At the very least, she
would have to recognize how it had affected him.

At a small restaurant in nearby Arlington
Heights, Bruce looked exhausted but happy. He
told Rayford he felt such a mix of emotions he
hardly knew what to make of them. "My grief
over the loss of my family is still so raw I can
hardly function. I still feel shame over my phoni-

ness. And yet since I repented of my sins and truly received Christ, in just a few days he has blessed me beyond anything I could have imagined. My house is lonely and cold and carries painful memories. And yet look what happened today. I've been given this new flock to shepherd, a reason for living."

Rayford merely nodded. He sensed Bruce simply needed someone to talk to.

"Ray," Bruce said, "churches are usually built by seminary-trained pastors and elders who have been Christians most of their lives. We don't have that luxury. I don't know what kind of leadership model we're going to have. It doesn't make sense to have elders when the interim pastor, which is all I can call myself, is himself a brand-new Christian and so is everybody else. But we're going to need a core of people who care about each other and are committed to the body. Loretta and a few of the people I met with the night of the Rapture are already part of that team, along with a couple of older men who were in the church for years but somehow missed the point as well.

"I know this is very new to you, but I feel as if I should ask you to join our little core group. We will be at the church for the Sunday morning meeting, the occasional Sunday evening meeting, the Wednesday night Bible study, and we will

meet at my home one other evening every week.
That's where we will pray for each other, keep
each other accountable, and study a little deeper
to stay ahead of the new congregation. Are you
willing?"

Rayford sat back. "Wow," he said. "I don't
know. I'm so new at this."

"We all are."

"Yeah, but you were raised in it, Bruce. You
know this stuff."

"I only missed the most important point."

"Well, I'll tell you what appeals to me about
it. I'm hungry for knowledge of the Bible. And
I need a friend."

"So do I," Bruce said. "That's the risk. We
could wind up grating on each other."

"I'm willing to take the risk if you are," Rayford said. "As long as I'm not expected to take
any leadership role."

"Deal," Barnes said, thrusting out his hand.
Rayford shook it. Neither smiled. Rayford had
the feeling this was the beginning of a relationship born of tragedy and need. He just hoped it
worked out. When Rayford finally arrived home,
Chloe was eager to hear all about it. She was
amazed at what her father told her and said she
was embarrassed to say she had not watched the
tape yet. "But I will now, Dad, before we go to
Atlanta. You're really into this, aren't you? It

sounds like something I want to check out, even
if I don't do anything about it."

Rayford had been home about twenty minutes
and had changed into his pajamas and robe to
relax for the rest of the evening when Chloe
called out to him. "Dad, I almost forgot. A
Hattie Durham called for you several times. She
sounded pretty agitated. Said she works with
you."

"Yeah," Rayford said. "She wanted to be
assigned to my next flight and I ducked her. She
probably found out and wants to know why."

"Why *did* you duck her?"

"It's a long story. I'll tell you sometime."

Rayford was reaching for the phone when it
rang. It was Bruce. "I forgot to confirm," he said.
"If you've agreed to be part of the core team, the
first responsibility is tonight's meeting with the
disenchanted and the skeptics."

"You *are* going to be a tough taskmaster, aren't
you?"

"I'll understand if you weren't planning on it."

"Bruce," Rayford said, "except for heaven,
there's no place I'd rather be. I wouldn't miss it.
I might even be able to get Chloe to come to this
one."

"What one?" Chloe asked when he hung up.

"In a minute," he said. "Let me call Hattie and
calm the waters."

Rayford was surprised that Hattie said nothing
about their flight assignments. "I just got some
disconcerting news," she said. "You remember
that writer from *Global Weekly* who was on our
flight, the one who had his computer hooked up
to the in-flight phone?"

"Vaguely."

"His name was Cameron Williams, and I talked
to him by phone a couple of times since the flight.
I tried calling him from the airport in New York
last night but couldn't get through."

"Uh-huh."

"I just heard on the news that he was killed
in England in a car bombing."

"You're kidding!"

"I'm not. Isn't that too bizarre? Rayford, sometimes I don't know how much of this I can take.
I hardly knew this guy, but I was so shocked
I just broke down when I heard. I'm sorry to
bother you with it, but I thought you might
remember him."

"No, that's all right, Hattie. And I know how
overwhelming this is for you because it has been
for me, too. I've got a lot to talk to you about,
actually."

"You do?"

"Could we get together sometime soon?"

"I've put in to work one of your flights," she
said. "Maybe if that works out."

"Maybe," he said. "And if it doesn't, maybe you could come over for dinner with Chloe and me."

"I'd like that, Rayford. I really would."

THIRTEEN

Buck Williams sat near an exit at JFK Airport reading his own obituary. "Magazine Writer Assumed Dead," the headline read.

Cameron Williams, 30, the youngest senior writer on the staff of any weekly newsmagazine, is feared dead after a mysterious car bombing outside a London pub Saturday night that took the life of a Scotland Yard investigator.

Williams, a five-year employee of *Global Weekly,* had won a Pulitzer as a reporter for the *Boston Globe* before joining the magazine as a staff reporter at 25. He quickly rose to the position of senior writer and has since written more than three dozen cover stories, four times assigned the *Weekly*'s Newsmaker of the Year story.

The journalist won the prestigious Ernest Hemingway Prize for war correspondence when he chronicled the destruction of the Russian air force over Israel 14 months ago. According to Steve Plank, executive editor of *Global Weekly,* the administration of the magazine is refusing to confirm the report of Williams's death "until we see hard evidence."

Williams's father and a married brother reside in Tucson, where Williams lost his sister-in-law, niece, and nephew in last week's disappearances.

Scotland Yard reports that the London bombing appeared to be the work of Northern Ireland terrorists and might have been a case of retribution. Captain Howard Sullivan called his 29-year-old subordinate, victim Alan Tompkins, "one of the finest men and brightest investigators it has been my privilege to work with."

Sullivan added that Williams and Tompkins had become friends after the writer had interviewed the investigator for an article on terrorism in England several years ago. The two had just emerged from the Armitage Arms Pub in London when a bomb exploded in Tompkins's Scotland Yard vehicle.

Tompkins's remains have been identified,

though only items of personal identification of Williams were recovered from the scene.

Rayford Steele had a plan. He had decided to be honest with Chloe about his attraction to Hattie Durham and how guilty he felt about it. He knew it would disappoint Chloe, even if it didn't shock her. He intended to talk about his new desire to share his faith with Hattie, hoping he could make some progress with Chloe without her feeling threatened. Chloe had gone with him to the church meeting for skeptics the night before, as she promised. But she had left a little over half-way through. She also fulfilled her promise to watch the video the former pastor had taped. They had discussed neither the meeting nor the video.

They wouldn't have much time together once they arrived at O'Hare, so Rayford broached the subject in the car as they gaped at the wreckage and debris lining the roadways. Between their house and the airport, they saw more than a dozen homes that had been gutted by fire. Rayford's theory was that families had disappeared, leaving something on the stove.

"And you think this was God's doing?" Chloe said, not disrespectfully.

"I do."

"I thought he was supposed to be a God of love and order," she said.

"I believe he is. This was his plan."

"There were plenty of tragedies and senseless deaths before this."

"I don't understand all that either," Rayford said. "But like Bruce said last night, we live in a fallen world. God left control of it pretty much to Satan."

"Oh, brother," she said. "Do you wonder why I walked out?"

"I figured it was because the questions and answers were hitting a little too close to home."

"Maybe they were, but all this stuff about Satan and the Fall and sin and all that . . ." She stopped and shook her head.

"I don't claim to understand it any better than you do, honey," Rayford said. "But I know I'm a sinner and that this world is full of them."

"And you consider me one."

"If you're part of everybody, then, yes, I do. Don't you?"

"Not on purpose."

"You're never selfish, greedy, jealous, petty, spiteful?"

"I try not to be, at least not at anyone else's expense."

"But you think you're exempt from what the

Bible says about everybody being a sinner, about there not being one righteous person anywhere, 'No not one'?"

"I don't know, Daddy. I just have no idea."

"You know what I'm worried about, of course."

"Yeah, I know. You think the time is short, that in this new dangerous world I'm going to wait too long to decide what I'm going to do, and then it'll be too late."

"I couldn't have said it better myself, Chloe. I just hope you know I'm thinking only of you, nothing else."

"You don't have to worry about that, Daddy."

"What did you think of the video? Did it make sense to you?"

"It made a lot of sense if you buy into all that. I mean, you have to start with that as a foundation. Then it all works neatly. But if you're not sure about God and the Bible and sin and heaven and hell, then you're still wondering what happened and why."

"And that's where you are?"

"I don't know where I am, Dad."

Rayford fought the urge to plead with her. If they had enough time over lunch in Atlanta, he would try the approach of telling her about Hattie. The plane was supposed to sit only

about forty-five minutes before the return to
O'Hare. Rayford wondered if it was fair to pray
for a delay.

"Nice cap," Steve Plank said as he hurried into
JFK and slapped Buck on the shoulder. "And
what's this? Two day's growth?"

"I was never too much for disguises," Buck
said.

"You're not famous enough to need to hide,"
Steve said. "You staying away from your apartment for a while?"

"Yeah, and probably yours. You sure you weren't
followed?"

"You're being a little paranoid, aren't you,
Buck?"

"I have a right," Buck said as they climbed into
a cab. "Central Park," he informed the driver.
Then he told Steve the entire story.

"What makes you think Carpathia is going to
help?" Plank asked later as they walked through
the park. "If the Yard and the exchange are
behind this, and you think Carpathia is linked to
Todd-Cothran and Stonagal, you might be asking
Carpathia to turn against his own angels."

They strolled under a bridge to elude the hot
spring sun. "I have a hunch about this guy,"
Buck said, his voice echoing off the cobblestone

walls. "It wouldn't surprise me to discover that he met with Stonagal and Todd-Cothran in London the other day. But I have to believe he's a pawn."

Steve pointed to a bench and they sat. "Well, I met Carpathia this morning at his press conference," Steve said, "and all I can say is that I hope you're right."

"Rosenzweig was impressed with him, and that's one insightful old scientist."

"Carpathia's impressive," Steve conceded. "He's handsome as a young Robert Redford, and this morning he spoke in nine languages, so fluently you'd have thought each was his native tongue. The media is eating him up."

"You say that as if you're not the media," Buck said.

Steve shrugged. "I'm proving my own point. I've learned to be a skeptic, to let *People* and the tabloids chase the personalities. But here's a guy with substance, with a brain, with something to say. I liked him. I mean, I saw him only in a press conference setting, but he seems to have a plan. You'll like him, and you're a bigger skeptic than I am. Plus he wants to see you."

"Tell me about that."

"I told you. He's got a little entourage of nobodies, with one exception."

"Rosenzweig."

"Right."

"What's Chaim's connection?"

"Nobody's sure yet, but Carpathia seems to attract experts and consultants who keep him up to speed on technology, politics, finances, and all that. And you know, Buck, he's not that much older than you are. I think they said this morning he's thirty-three."

"Nine languages?"

Plank nodded.

"Do you remember which ones?"

"Why would you ask that?"

"Just thinking."

Steve pulled a reporter's notebook from his side pocket. "You want 'em in alphabetical order?"

"Sure."

"Arabic, Chinese, English, French, German, Hungarian, Romanian, Russian, and Spanish."

"One more time," Buck said, thinking.

Steve repeated them. "What's on your mind?"

"This guy's the consummate politician."

"He is not. Trust me, this was no trick. He knew these languages well and used them effectively."

"But don't you see which languages they are, Steve? Think about it."

"Spare me the effort."

"The six languages of the United Nations, plus the three languages of his own country."

"No kidding?"

Buck nodded. "So am I gonna get to meet him soon?"

The flight to Atlanta was full and busy, and Rayford had to change altitudes continually to avoid choppy air. He got to see Chloe for only a few seconds while his first officer was in the cockpit and the plane was on autopilot. Rayford made a hurried walk-through but had no time to chat.

He got his wish in Atlanta. Another 747 had to be flown back to Chicago in the middle of the afternoon, and the only other pilot available had to be back earlier. Chicago coordinated with Atlanta, switched the two assignments, and found a seat for Chloe, too. That gave Rayford and Chloe more than two hours for lunch, enough time to get away from the airport.

Their cab driver, a young woman with a beautiful lilt to her voice, asked if they wanted to see "a truly unbelievable sight."

"If it's not out of the way."

"It's just a couple of blocks from where y'all are going," she said.

She maneuvered around several detours and construction horses, then through two streets manned by traffic cops. "Over yonder," she said, pointing, and she pulled into a sandy parking lot rimmed by three-foot concrete-block walls. "Can you see that parking garage 'cross the way?"

"What in the world?" Chloe said.

"Strange, isn't it?" the cabbie said.

"What happened?" Rayford asked.

"This has been going on since the vanishings," she said.

They peered at a six-story garage with cars seemingly jammed into each other at all angles in a gridlock so tight and convoluted that cranes worked to lift them out through the open sides of the structure.

"They were all in there after a late ballgame that night," she said. "The police say it was bad anyway, long lines of cars trying to get out, people taking turns merging and lots of 'em not taking turns at all. So some people who got tired of waiting just tried to edge in and make other people let 'em in, you know."

"Yeah."

"And then, poof, they say more than a third of the cars ain't got drivers, just like that. If they had room, they kept going till they hit other cars or the wall. If they didn't have room, they just pushed up against the car in front of 'em. The ones that were left couldn't go one way or the other. It was such a mess that people just left their cars and climbed over other cars and went looking for help. They started at dawn moving the cars on the ground levels with tow trucks, then they got them cranes in there by noon, and they been at it ever since."

Rayford and Chloe sat and watched, shaking their heads. Cranes normally used for hoisting beams up to new buildings were wrapping cables around cars, tugging, yanking, dragging them past each other and through openings in the concrete to clear the garage. It appeared it would take several more days.

"How about you?" Rayford asked the driver. "Did you lose people?"

"Yes, sir. My mama and my grandmama and two baby sisters. But I know where they are. They're in heaven, just like my mama always said."

"I believe you're right," Rayford said. "My wife and son are gone, too."

"Are you saved now?" the girl asked.

Rayford was shocked by her forthrightness, but he knew exactly what she meant. "I am," he said.

"I am, too. You got to be blind or somethin' to not see the light now."

Rayford wanted to peek at Chloe, but he did not. He tipped the young woman generously when they got to the restaurant. Over lunch he told Chloe of his history with Hattie, such as it was.

She was silent a long time, and when she spoke her voice was weak. "So you never actually acted on it?" she said.

"Thankfully, no. I never would have been able to live with myself."

"It would have broken Mom's heart, that's for sure."

He nodded miserably. "Sometimes I feel as bad as if I had been unfaithful to her. But I justified my considering it because your mom was so obsessed with her faith."

"I know. Funny thing, though. That kept me straighter at school than I might have been otherwise. I mean, I'm sure Mom would be disappointed to know a lot of the things I've said and done while I've been away—don't ask. But knowing how sincere and devout she was, and what high hopes and expectations she had for me, kept me from doing something really stupid. I knew she was praying for me. She told me every time she wrote."

"Did she also tell you about the end times, Chloe?"

"Sure. All the time."

"But you still don't buy it?"

"I want to, Dad. I really do. But I have to be intellectually honest with myself."

It was all Rayford could do to stay calm. Had he been this pseudosophisticated at that age? Of course he had. He had run everything through that maddening intellectual grid—until recently, when the supernatural came crashing through his academic pretense. But like the cabbie had said, you'd have to be blind not to see the light now, no matter how educated you thought you were.

"I'm going to invite Hattie to dinner with us this week," he said.

Chloe narrowed her eyes. "What, you feel like you're available now?"

Rayford was stunned at his own reaction. He had to keep himself from slapping his own daughter, something he had never done. He gritted his teeth. "How can you say that after all I've just told you?" he said. "That's insulting."

"So was what you were hoping for with this Hattie Durham, Dad. Do you think she was unaware of what was going on? How do you think she'll interpret this? She may come on like gangbusters."

"I'm going to make it clear what my intentions are, and they are totally honorable, more honorable than they ever could have been before, because I had nothing of worth to offer her."

"So, now you're going to switch from hitting on her to preaching at her."

He wanted to argue, but he couldn't. "I care about her as a person, and I want her to know the truth and be able to act on it."

"And what if she doesn't?"

"That's her choice. I can only do my part."

"Is that how you feel about me, too? If I don't act on it the way you want, you'll be satisfied that you've done your part?"

"I should, but obviously I care much more about you than I do Hattie."

"You should have thought of that before you risked everything to chase her."

Rayford was offended again, but he had brought this on himself and felt he deserved it. "Maybe that's why I never did anything about it," he said. "Ever think of that?"

"This is all news to me," she said. "I hope you restrained yourself because of your wife and kids."

"I almost didn't."

"So I gather. What if this strategy with Hattie just makes you all the more attractive to her? What's to keep you from being attracted to her, too? It's not like you're still married, if you're convinced Mom is in heaven."

Rayford ordered dessert and laid his napkin on the table. "Maybe I'm being naive, but your mother being in heaven is just like losing her to sudden death. The last thing on my mind is another woman, and certainly not Hattie. She's too young and immature, and I'm too disgusted with myself for having been tempted by her in the

first place. I want to be up front with her and see
what she says. It'll be instructive to know whether
all this was just in my mind."

"You mean for future reference?"

"Chloe, I love you, but you're being bratty."

"I know. I'm sorry. That was uncalled for.
But seriously, how will you know if she tells
you the truth? If you tell her you were interested
for the wrong reasons and that you aren't interested anymore, why should she be vulnerable
enough to admit she thought you two had
possibilities?"

Rayford shrugged. "You may be right. But
I have to be honest with her even if she's not
honest with me. I owe her that much. I want her
to take me seriously when I tell her what I think
she needs now."

"I don't know, Dad. I think it's a little too soon
to be pushing her toward God."

"How soon is too soon, Chloe? There are no
guarantees, not now."

Steve pulled from his breast pocket two sets of
press credentials, permitting the bearers to attend
Nicolae Carpathia's speech to the General Assem-
bly of the United Nations that very afternoon.
Buck's credentials were in the name of George
Oreskovich.

"Do I take care of you, or what?"

"Unbelievable," Buck said. "How much time do we have?"

"A little over an hour," Steve said, rising to hail a cab. "And like I said, he wants to meet you."

"He reads, doesn't he? He's got to think I'm dead."

"I suppose. But he'll remember me from this morning and I'll be able to assure him it will be just as valuable for him to be interviewed by George Oreskovich as by the legendary Cameron Williams."

"Yeah, but Steve, if he's like the other politicians I know, he's hung up on image, on high-profile journalists. Like it or not, that's what I've become. How are you going to get him to settle for an unknown?"

"I don't know. Maybe I'll tell him it's really you. Then, while you're with him, I'll release the report that your obit was wrong and that right now you're doing a cover-story interview with Carpathia."

"A cover story? You've come a long way from calling him a low-level bureaucrat from a non-strategic country."

"I was at the press conference, Buck. I met him. And I can at least gauge the competition. If we don't feature him prominently, we'll be the only national magazine that doesn't."

"Like I say, if he's like the typical politician—"

"You can put that out of your mind, Buck. You're going to find this guy the farthest thing you've ever seen from the typical politician. You're going to thank me for getting you the exclusive interview with him."

"I thought that was his idea because of my colossal name," Buck said, smiling.

"So? I could have turned him down."

"Yeah, and been the executive editor of the only national magazine that fails to cover the most exciting new face to visit the States."

"Believe me, Buck," Steve said during the ride to the U.N. building, "this is going to be a refreshing change from the doom and gloom we've been writing and reading for days."

The two used their press credentials to get in, but Buck hung back out of sight of his colleagues and the competition until all were seated in the General Assembly. Steve held a seat for him in the back, where he would not draw attention when he slipped in at the last minute. Meanwhile, Steve would use his cellular phone to call in the story of Buck's reappearance, so it would hit the news by the end of the day.

Carpathia entered the assembly in a dignified yet inauspicious manner, though he had an entourage of a half dozen, including Chaim Rosenzweig and a financial wizard from the

French government. Carpathia appeared an inch or two over six feet tall, broad shouldered, thick chested, trim, athletic, tanned, and blond. His thick shock of hair was trimmed neatly around the ears, sideburns, and neck, and his navy-on-navy pinstripe suit and matching tie were exquisitely conservative.

Even from a distance, the man seemed to carry himself with a sense of humility and purpose. His presence dominated the room, and yet he did not seem preoccupied or impressed with himself. His jewelry was understated. His jaw and nose were Roman and strong, his piercing blue eyes set deep under thick brows.

Buck was struck that Carpathia carried no notebook, and he assumed the man must have his speech notes in his breast pocket. Either that or they were being carried by an aide. Buck was wrong on both counts.

Secretary-General Mwangati Ngumo of Botswana announced that the assembly was privileged to hear briefly from the new president of the nation of Romania and that the formal introduction of their guest would be made by the Honorable Dr. Chaim Rosenzweig, with whom they were all familiar.

Rosenzweig hurried to the podium with a vigor that belied his age, and he initially received a more enthusiastic response than did Carpathia.

The popular Israeli statesman and scholar said simply that it gave him great pleasure to introduce "to this worthy and august body a young man I respect and admire as much as anyone I've ever met. Please welcome His Honor, President Nicolae Carpathia of Romania."

Carpathia rose, turned to the assembly, and nodded humbly, then shook hands warmly with Rosenzweig. With courtly manners he remained at the side of the lectern until the older man was seated, then stood relaxed and smiling before speaking extemporaneously. Not only did he not use notes, but he also never hesitated, misspoke, or took his eyes off his audience.

He spoke earnestly, with passion, with a frequent smile, and with occasional, appropriate humor. He mentioned respectfully that he was aware that it had not been a full week yet since the disappearance of millions all over the world, including many who would have been "in this very room." Carpathia spoke primarily in perfect English with only a hint of a Romanian accent. He used no contractions and enunciated every syllable of every word. Once again he employed all nine languages with which he was fluent, each time translating himself into English.

In one of the most touching scenes Buck had ever witnessed, Carpathia began by announcing that he was humbled and moved to visit "for the first time this historic site, where nation after nation has set its sights. One by one they have come from all over the globe on pilgrimages as sacred as any to the Holy Lands, exposing their faces to the heat of the rising sun. Here they have taken their stand for peace in a once-and-for-all, rock-solid commitment to putting behind them the insanity of war and bloodshed. These nations, great and small, have had their fill of the death and maiming of their most promising citizens in the prime of their youth.

"Our forebears were thinking globally long before I was born," Carpathia said. "In 1944, the year the International Monetary Fund and the World Bank were established, this great host nation, the United States of America, along with the British Commonwealth and the Union of Soviet Socialist Republics, met at the famous Dumbarton Oaks Conference to propose the birth of this body."

Displaying his grasp of history and his photographic memory of dates and places, Carpathia intoned, "From its official birth on October 24, 1945, and that first meeting of your General Assembly in London, January 10, 1946, to this day, tribes and nations have come together to pledge their wholehearted commitment to peace, brotherhood, and the global community."

He began in almost a whisper, "From lands

distant and near they have come: from Afghanistan, Albania, Algeria . . ." He continued, his voice rising and falling dramatically with the careful pronunciation of the name of each member country of the United Nations. Buck sensed a passion, a love for these countries and the ideals of the U.N. Carpathia was clearly moved as he plunged on, listing country after country, not droning but neither in any hurry.

A minute into his list, representatives noticed that with each name, someone from that country rose in dignity and stood erect, as if voting anew for peace among nations. Carpathia smiled and nodded at each as they rose, and nearly every country was represented. Because of the cosmic trauma the world had endured, they had come looking for answers, for help, for support. Now they had been given the opportunity to take their stand once again.

Buck was tired and felt grimy, wearing two-day-old clothes. But his worries were a distant memory as Carpathia moved along. By the time he got into the *S*s in his alphabetical listing, those standing had begun to quietly applaud each new country mentioned. It was a dignified, powerful thing, this show of respect and admiration, this re-welcome into the global village. The applause was not so loud that it kept anyone from hearing Carpathia, but it was so heartfelt and moving that Buck couldn't suppress the lump in his throat. Then he noticed something peculiar. The press representatives from various countries were standing with their ambassadors and delegations. Even the objectivity of the world press had temporarily vanished in what they might previously have written off as jingoism, superpatriotism, or sanctimony.

Buck found himself eager to stand as well, ruing the fact that his country was near the end of the alphabet, but feeling pride and anticipation welling up within him. As more and more countries were named and their people stood proudly, the applause grew louder, merely because of the increased numbers. Carpathia was up to the task, his voice growing more emotional and powerful with each new country name.

On and on he thundered as people stood and clapped. "Somalia! South Africa! Spain! Sri Lanka! Sudan! Suriname! Swaziland! Sweden! Syria!"

More than five minutes into the recitation, Carpathia had not missed a beat. He had never once hesitated, stammered, or mispronounced a syllable. Buck was on the edge of his seat as the speaker swept through the Ts and reached "Uganda! Ukraine! The United Arab Emirates! The United Kingdom! The United States of America!" And Buck leaped to his feet, Steve right

with him, along with dozens of other members
of the press.

Something had happened in the disappearances
of loved ones all over the globe. Journalism
might never be the same. Oh, there would be
skeptics and those who worshiped objectivity.
But what had happened to brotherly love? What
had become of depending on one another? What
had happened to the brotherhood of men and
nations?

It was back. And while no one expected that the
press might become the public-relations agency
for a new political star, Carpathia certainly had
them in his corner this afternoon. By the end of
his litany of nearly two hundred nations, young
Nicolae was at an emotional, fevered pitch. With
such electricity and power in the simple naming
of all the countries who had longed to be united
with each other, Carpathia had brought the entire
crowd to its feet in full voice and applause, press
and representative alike. Even the cynical Steve
Plank and Buck Williams continued to clap and
cheer, never once appearing embarrassed at their
loss of detached objectivity.

And there was more, as the Nicolae Carpathia
juggernaut sailed on. Over the next half hour he
displayed such an intimate knowledge of the
United Nations that it was as if he had invented
and developed the organization himself. For

someone who had never before set foot on American soil, let alone visited the United Nations, he displayed amazing understanding of its inner workings.

During his speech he casually worked in the name of every secretary-general from Trygve Lie of Norway to Ngumo and mentioned their terms of office not just by year but also by specific day and date of their installation and conclusion. He displayed awareness and understanding of each of the six principal organs of the U.N., their functions, their current members, and their particular challenges.

Then he swept through the eighteen U.N. agencies, mentioning every one, its current director, and its headquarters city. This was an amazing display, and suddenly it was no wonder this man had risen so quickly in his own nation, no wonder the previous leader had stepped aside. No wonder New York had already embraced him.

After this, Buck knew, Nicolae Carpathia would be embraced by all of America. And then the world.

FOURTEEN

RAYFORD'S plane touched down in Chicago during rush hour late Monday afternoon. By the time he and Chloe got to their cars, they had not had the opportunity to continue their conversation. "Remember, you promised to let me drive your car home," Chloe said.

"Is it that important to you?" he asked.

"Not really. I just like it. May I?"

"Sure. Just let me get my phone out of it. I want to see when Hattie can join us for dinner. That's all right with you, isn't it?"

"As long as you don't expect me to cook or something sexist and domestic like that."

"I hadn't even thought of it. She loves Chinese. We'll order some."

"She loves Chinese?" Chloe repeated. "You are familiar with this woman, aren't you?"

Rayford shook his head. "It's not like that. I

mean, yes, I probably know more about her than I should. But I can tell you the culinary preferences of a dozen crew members, and I hardly know anything else about them."

Rayford retrieved his phone from the BMW and turned the ignition switch far enough to read the gas gauge. "You picked the right car," he said. "It's almost full. You'll beat me home. Your mother's car is on empty. You going to be all right there by yourself for a few minutes? I think I'll pick up a few groceries while I'm out."

Chloe hesitated. "It's eerie in there when you're by yourself, isn't it?" she said.

"A little. But we've got to get used to it."

"You're right," she said quickly. "They're gone. And I don't believe in ghosts. I'll be fine. But don't be long."

At the post-U.N.-appearance press conference for Nicolae Carpathia of Romania, Buck briefly found himself the center of attention. Someone recognized him and expressed surprise and pleasure that he was alive. Buck tried to quiet everyone and tell them that it had all been a misunderstanding, but the furor continued as Chaim Rosenzweig saw him and hurried over, covering Buck's hand with both of his and pumping vigorously. "Oh, I am so glad to see you alive and well," he said. "I heard dreadful news about your demise. And President Carpathia was also disappointed to hear of it. He had so wanted to meet you and had agreed to an exclusive interview."

"Can we still do that?" Buck whispered, to the boos and catcalls of the competition.

"You'll do anything to get a scoop," someone groused. "Even have yourself blown up."

"It will probably not be possible until late tonight," Rosenzweig said. His hand swept the room, crowded with TV cameras, lights, microphones, and the press. "His schedule is full all day, and he has a photo shoot at *People* magazine early this evening. Perhaps following that. I'll speak to him."

"What's your connection?" Buck asked, but the old man put a finger to his lips and pulled away to return and sit near Carpathia as the press conference began.

The young Romanian was no less impressive and persuasive up close, beginning the session with his own statement before fielding questions. He conducted himself like an old pro, though Buck knew his press relations in Romania and the limited other areas of Europe he had visited would not have provided him this experience.

At one point or another, Buck noticed,

Carpathia met the eyes of every person in the
room, at least briefly. He never looked down,
never looked away, never looked up. It was as
if he had nothing to hide and nothing to fear.
He was in command of himself and seemingly
unaffected by the fuss and attention.

He seemed to have unusually good eyesight; it
was clear he could see people's name tags from
across the room. Anytime he spoke to a member
of the press, he referred to them by name as Mr.
or Ms. so-and-so. He insisted that people call
him by whatever name made them comfortable.
"Even Nick," he said, smiling. But no one did.
They followed his lead and called him "Mr.
President" or "Mr. Carpathia."

Carpathia spoke in the same impassioned and
articulate tones he had used in his speech. Buck
wondered if this was always the same, in public
or private. Whatever else he brought to the world
scene, he had a mastery of spoken communication second to none.

"Let me begin by saying what an honor it is for
me to be in this country and at this historic site.
It has been a dream of mine since I was a small
boy in Cluj to one day see this place."

The initial pleasantries over, Carpathia
launched into another minispeech, again showing
incredible knowledge and grasp of the U.N. and
its mission. "You will recall," he said, "that in

the previous century the U.N. seemed to be in decline. U.S. president Ronald Reagan escalated the East-West controversies, and the U.N. seemed a thing of the past with its emphasis on North-South conflicts. This organization was in trouble financially, with few members willing to pay their share. With the end of the Cold War in the 1990s, however, your next president, Mr. Bush, recognized what he called the 'new world order,' which resonated deep within my young heart. The original basis for the U.N. charter promised cooperation among the first fifty-one members, including the great powers."

Carpathia went on to discuss the various peace-keeping military actions the U.N. had taken since the Korean conflict of the 1950s. "As you know," he said, speaking again of things long before he was born, "the U.N. has its legacy in the League of Nations, which I believe was the first international peacekeeping body. It came about at the end of the First World War, but when it failed to prevent a second, it became anachronistic. Out of that failure came the United Nations, which must remain strong to prevent World War III, which would result in the end of life as we know it."

After Carpathia outlined his eagerness to support the U.N. in any way possible, someone interjected a question about the disappearances.

He became suddenly serious and unsmiling, and spoke with compassion and warmth.

"Many people in my country lost loved ones to this horrible phenomenon. I know that many people all over the world have theories, and I wish not to denigrate any one of them, the people or their ideas. I have asked Dr. Chaim Rosenzweig of Israel to work with a team to try to make sense of this great tragedy and allow us to take steps toward preventing anything similar from ever happening again.

"When the time is appropriate I will allow Dr. Rosenzweig to speak for himself, but for now I can tell you that the theory that makes the most sense to me is briefly as follows: The world has been stockpiling nuclear weapons for innumerable years. Since the United States dropped atomic bombs on Japan in 1945 and the Soviet Union first detonated its own devices September 23, 1949, the world has been at risk of nuclear holocaust. Dr. Rosenzweig and his team of renowned scholars is close to the discovery of an atmospheric phenomenon that may have caused the vanishing of so many people instantaneously."

"What kind of a phenomenon?" Buck asked.

Carpathia glanced briefly at his name tag and then into his eyes. "I do not want to be premature, Mr. Oreskovich," he said. Several members of the press snickered, but Carpathia never lost pace. "Or I should say, 'Mr. Cameron Williams of *Global Weekly.*'" This elicited amused applause throughout the room. Buck was stunned.

"Dr. Rosenzweig believes that some confluence of electromagnetism in the atmosphere, combined with as yet unknown or unexplained atomic ionization from the nuclear power and weaponry throughout the world, could have been ignited or triggered—perhaps by a natural cause like lightning, or even by an intelligent life-form that discovered this possibility before we did—and caused this instant action throughout the world."

"Sort of like someone striking a match in a room full of gasoline vapors?" a journalist suggested.

Carpathia nodded thoughtfully.

"How is that different from the idea of aliens from outer space zapping everybody?"

"It is not wholly different," Carpathia conceded, "but I am more inclined to believe in the natural theory, that lightning reacted with some subatomic field."

"Why would the disappearances be so random? Why some people and not others?"

"I do not know," Carpathia said. "And Dr. Rosenzweig tells me they have come to no conclusions on that either. At this point they are postulating that certain people's levels of electricity made them more likely to be affected. That would account for all the children and babies and even fetal material that vanished. Their electromagnetism was not developed to the point where it could resist whatever happened."

"What do you say to people who believe this was the work of God, that he raptured his church?"

Carpathia smiled compassionately. "Let me be careful to say that I do not and will not criticize any sincere person's belief system. That is the basis for true harmony and brotherhood, peace and respect among peoples. I do not accept that theory because I know many, many more people who should be gone if the righteous were taken to heaven. If there is a God, I respectfully submit that this is not the capricious way in which he would operate. By the same token, you will not hear me express any disrespect for those who disagree."

Buck was then astonished to hear Carpathia say that he had been invited to speak at the upcoming ecumenical religious confab scheduled that month in New York. "There I will discuss my views of millenarianism, eschatology, the Last Judgment, and the second coming of Christ. Dr. Rosenzweig was kind enough to arrange that invitation, and until then I think it would be best if I did not attempt to speak on those subjects informally."

"How long will you be in New York?"

"If the people of Romania will permit me, I may be here an entire month. I hate to be away from my people, but they understand that I am concerned for the greater global good, and with technology as it is today and the wonderful people in positions of influence in Romania, I feel confident I can keep in contact and that my nation will not suffer for my brief absence."

By the time of the evening network news, a new international star had been born. He even had a nickname: Saint Nick. More than sound bites had been taken from the floor of the U.N. and the press conference. Carpathia enjoyed several minutes on each telecast, rousing the U.N. audience with the recitation of countries, urgently calling for a recommitment to world peace.

He had carefully avoided specific talk of global disarmament. His was a message of love and peace and understanding and brotherhood, and to quit fighting seemed to go without saying. No doubt he would be back to hammer home that point, but in the meantime, Carpathia was on the charmed ride of his life.

Broadcast commentators urged that he be named an adjunct adviser to the U.N. secretary-general and that he visit each headquarters of the various U.N. agencies around the world. By late that evening, he was invited to make appearances at each of the international meetings coming up within the next few weeks.

He was seen in the company of Jonathan Stonagal, no surprise to Buck. And immediately following the press conference he was whisked away to other appointments. Dr. Rosenzweig found Buck. "I was able to get a commitment from him for late this evening," the old man said. "He has several interviews, mostly with the television people, and then he will be live on ABC's *Nightline* with Wallace Theodore. Following that, he will return to his hotel and will be happy to give you an uninterrupted half hour."

Buck told Steve he wanted to hurry home to his apartment, get freshened up, get his messages, run to the office and educate himself as quickly as possible from the files, and be totally prepared for the interview. Steve agreed to accompany him.

"But I'm still paranoid," Buck admitted. "If Stonagal is related in any way to Todd-Cothran, and we know he is, who knows what he thinks about what happened in London?"

"That's a long shot," Steve said. "Even if that dirt goes into the exchange and Scotland Yard, that doesn't mean Stonagal would have any interest in it. I would think he'd want to stay as far from it as possible."

"But, Steve, you have to agree it's likely that

Dirk Burton was murdered because he got too close to Todd-Cothran's secret connections with Stonagal's international group. If they wipe out people they see as their enemies—even friends of their enemies like Alan Tompkins and I were— where will they stop?"

"But you're assuming Stonagal was aware of what happened in London. He's bigger than that. Todd-Cothran or the guy at the Yard may have seen you as a threat, but Stonagal has probably never heard of you."

"You don't think he reads the *Weekly?*"

"Don't be hurt. You're like a gnat to him if he even knows your name."

"You know what a swat with a magazine can do to a gnat, Steve?"

"There's one big hole in your argument," Steve said later as they entered Buck's apartment. "If Stonagal *is* dangerous to you, what does that make Carpathia?"

"Like I said, Carpathia can be only a pawn."

"Buck! You just heard him. Did I overrate him?"

"No."

"Were you blown away?"

"Yes."

"Does he look like anybody's pawn?"

"No. So I can assume only that he knows nothing about this."

"You're pretty sure he met with Todd-Cothran and Stonagal in London before coming here?"

"That had to be business," Buck said. "Planning for the trip and his involvement with international advisers."

"You're taking a big risk," Steve said.

"I have no choice. Anyway, I'm willing. Until he proves otherwise, I'm going to trust Nicolae Carpathia."

"Hmph," Steve said.

"What?"

"It's just that usually you work the other way around. You distrust someone until they prove otherwise."

"Well, it's a new world, Steve. Nothing's the same as it was last week, is it?"

And Buck pushed the button on his answering machine while beginning to undress for his shower.

Rayford pulled into his driveway with a sack of groceries on the seat beside him. He had gotten a hold of Hattie Durham, who wanted to keep him on the phone talking until he begged off. She was delighted with the dinner invitation and said she could come three nights later, on Thursday.

Rayford guessed he was half an hour behind Chloe, and he was impressed that she had left the garage door open for him. When he found the door locked between the garage and the house, however, he was concerned. He knocked. No answer.

Rayford reopened the garage door to go around to the front, but just before shutting it on his way out, he stopped. Something was different in the garage. He flipped on the light to add to the single bulb of the door opener. All three cars were in their places, but—

Rayford walked around the Jeep at the end. Raymie's stuff was missing! His bike. His four-wheeler. What was this?

Rayford jogged to the front door. The window of the storm door was broken and the door hung on one hinge. The main door had been kicked in. No small feat, as the door was huge and heavy with a dead bolt. The entire frame had been obliterated and lay in pieces on the floor of the entryway. Rayford rushed in, calling for Chloe.

He ran from room to room, praying nothing had happened to the only family member he had left. Everything of immediate material value seemed to be gone. Radios, televisions, VCRs, jewelry, CD players, video games, the silver, even the china. To his relief there was no sign of blood or struggle.

Rayford was on the phone to the police when

his call waiting clicked. "I hate to put you on hold," he said, "but that may be my daughter."

It was. "Oh, Daddy!" she said, crying. "Are you all right? I came in through the garage and saw all that stuff missing. I thought maybe they'd come back, so I locked the door to the garage and was going to lock the front, but I saw the glass and wood and everything, so I ran out the back. I'm three doors down."

"They're not coming back, hon," he said. "I'll come get you."

"Mr. Anderson said he would walk me home."

A few minutes later Chloe sat rocking on the couch, her arms folded across her stomach. She told the police officer what she had told her father; then he took Rayford's statement. "You folks don't use your burglar alarm?"

Rayford shook his head. "That's my fault. We used it for years when we didn't need it, and I got tired of being awakened in the middle of the night with the false alarms and the . . . the, uh—"

"Calls from us, I know," the cop said. "That's what everybody says. But this time it would have been worth it, huh?"

"Hindsight and all that," Rayford said. "Never really thought we needed the security in this neighborhood."

"This kind of crime is up two hundred percent

here in the last week alone," the officer said. "The bad guys know we don't have the time or manpower to do a blessed thing about it."

"Well, will you put my daughter's mind at ease and tell her they aren't interested in hurting us and that they won't be back?"

"That's right, miss," he said. "Your dad should get this door boarded up till it can be fixed, and I would arm that security system. But I wouldn't expect a repeat visit, at least not by the same bunch. We talked to the people across the street. They saw some kind of a carpet-service minivan here for about half an hour this afternoon. They went in the front, came through, opened the garage door, backed into the empty space in there, and carted your stuff off almost under your noses."

"Nobody saw them break in the front?"

"Your neighbors don't have a clear view of your entrance. Nobody really does. Slick job."

"I'm just glad Chloe didn't walk in on them," Rayford said.

The cop nodded on his way out. "You can be grateful for that. I imagine your insurance will take care of a lot of this. I don't expect to be recovering any of it. We haven't had any luck with the other cases."

Rayford embraced Chloe, who was still shaking. "Can you do me a favor, Dad?" she said.

"Anything."

"I want another copy of that video, the one from the pastor."

"I'll call Bruce, and we'll pick one up tonight." Suddenly Chloe laughed.

"Now this is funny?" Rayford said.

"I just had a thought," she said, smiling through her tears. "What if the burglars watch that tape?"

FIFTEEN

ONE of the first messages on Buck's answering machine was from the flight attendant he had met the week before. "Mr. Williams, this is Hattie Durham," she said. "I'm in New York on another flight and thought I'd call to say hi and thanks again for helping me make contact with my family. I'll wait a second and keep jabbering here, in case you're screening your calls. It would be fun to get together for a drink or something, but don't feel obligated. Well, maybe another time."

"So who's that?" Steve called out as Buck hesitated near the bathroom door, waiting to hear all the messages before getting into the shower.

"Just a girl," he said.

"Nice?"

"Better than nice. Gorgeous."

"Better call her back."

"Don't worry."

Several other messages were unimportant. Then came two that had been left that very afternoon. The first was from Captain Howard Sullivan of Scotland Yard. "Ah yes, Mr. Williams. I hesitate to leave this message on your machine, but I would like to speak with you at your earliest convenience. As you know, two gentlemen with whom you were associated have met with untimely demises here in London. I would like to ask you a few questions. You may be hearing from other agencies, as you were seen with one of the victims just before his unfortunate end. Please call me." And he left the number.

The next message had come less than half an hour later and was from Georges Lafitte, an operative with Interpol, the international police organization headquartered in Lyons, France. "Mr. Williams," he said in a thick French accent, "as soon as you get this message, I would like you to call me from the nearest police station. They will know how to contact us directly, and they will have a printout of information on why we need to speak with you. For your own sake, I would urge you not to delay."

Buck leaned out to stare at Steve, who looked as puzzled as Buck was. "What are you now?" Steve asked. "A suspect?"

"I'd better not be. After what I heard from Alan about Sullivan and how he's in Todd-Cothran's pocket, there's no way I'm going to London and voluntarily put myself in their custody. These messages aren't binding, are they? I don't have to act on them just because I heard them, do I?"

Steve shrugged. "Nobody but me knows you heard them. Anyway, international agencies have no jurisdiction here."

"You think I might be extradited?"

"If they try to link you with either of those deaths."

Chloe didn't want to stay home alone that evening. She rode with her father to the church where Bruce Barnes met them and gave them another video. He shook his head when he heard about the break-in. "It's becoming epidemic," he said. "It's as if the inner city has moved to the suburbs. We're no safer here anymore."

It was all Rayford could do to keep from telling Bruce that replacing the stolen tape was Chloe's idea. He wanted to tell Bruce to keep praying, that she must still be thinking about things. Maybe the invasion of the house had made her feel vulnerable. Maybe she was getting the point that the world was much more dangerous now, that there were no guarantees, that her own time could be short. But Rayford also knew he could offend her, insult her, push her away if he used this situation to sic Bruce on her. She had enough information; he just had to let God work on her. Still, he was encouraged and wanted to let Bruce know what was going on. He supposed he would have to wait for a more opportune time.

While they were out, Rayford bought items that needed to be replaced right away, including a TV and VCR. He arranged to have the front door fixed and got the insurance paperwork started. Most important, he armed the security system. Still, he knew, neither he nor Chloe would sleep soundly that night.

They came home to a phone call from Hattie Durham. Rayford thought she sounded lonely. She didn't seem to have a real reason to call. She simply told him she was grateful for the dinner invitation and was looking forward to it. He told her what had happened at their home, and she sounded genuinely troubled.

"Things are getting so strange," she said. "You know I have a sister who works in a pregnancy clinic."

"Uh-huh," Rayford said. "You've mentioned it."

"They do family planning and counseling and referrals for terminating pregnancies."

"Right."

"And they're set up to do abortions right there."

Hattie seemed to be waiting for some signal of affirmation or acknowledgment that he was listening. Rayford grew impatient and remained silent.

"Anyway," she said, "I won't keep you. But my sister told me they have zero business."

"Well, that would make sense, given the disappearances of unborn babies."

"My sister didn't sound too happy about that."

"Hattie, I imagine everyone's horrified by that. Parents are grieving all over the world."

"But the women my sister and her people were counseling *wanted* abortions."

Rayford groped for a pertinent response. "Yes, so maybe those women are grateful they didn't have to go through the abortion itself."

"Maybe, but my sister and her bosses and the rest of the staff are out of work now until people start getting pregnant again."

"I get it. It's a money thing."

"They have to work. They have expenses and families."

"And aside from abortion counseling and abortions, they have nothing to do?"

"Nothing. Isn't that awful? I mean, whatever happened put my sister and a lot of people like her out of business, and nobody really knows yet whether anyone will be able to get pregnant again."

Rayford had to admit he had never found Hattie guilty of brilliance, but now he wished he could look into her eyes. "Hattie, um, I don't know how to ask this. But are you saying your sister is hoping women can get pregnant again so they'll need abortions and she can keep working?"

"Well, sure. What is she going to do otherwise? Counseling jobs in other fields are pretty hard to come by, you know."

He nodded, feeling stupid, knowing she couldn't see him. What kind of lunacy was this? He shouldn't waste his energy arguing with someone who clearly didn't have a clue, but he couldn't help himself.

"I guess I always thought clinics like the one where your sister works considered these unwanted pregnancies a nuisance. Shouldn't they be glad if such problems disappear, and even happier—except for the small complication that the human race will eventually cease to exist—if pregnancies never happen again?"

The irony was lost on her. "But, Rayford, that's her job. That's what the center is all about. It's sort of like owning a gas station and nobody needing gas or oil or tires anymore."

"Supply and demand."

"Exactly! See? They need unwanted pregnancies because that's their business."

"Sort of like doctors wanting people to be sick or injured so they have something to do?"

"Now you've got it, Rayford."

After Buck had shaved and showered, Steve told him, "I was paged a minute ago. New York City detectives are looking for you at the office. Unfortunately, someone told them you would be at the Plaza with Carpathia later."

"Brilliant!"

"I know. Maybe you ought to just face this."

"Not yet, Steve. Let me get the Carpathia interview and get that piece started. Then I can extricate myself from this mess."

"You're hoping Carpathia can help."

"Precisely."

"What if you can't get to him before somebody gets to you?"

"I've got to. I've still got my Oreskovich press credentials and identification. If the cops are waiting for me at the Plaza, maybe they won't recognize me at first."

"C'mon, Buck. You think they aren't on to your phony ID by now, after you slipped out of Europe with it? Let me switch with you. If they think I'm you trying to pass yourself off as Oreskovich, that may buy you enough time to get in to see Carpathia."

Buck shrugged. "Worth a try," he said. "I don't want to stay here, but I want to see Carpathia on *Nightline.*"

"Want to come to my place?"

"They'll probably look for me there before long."

"Let me call Marge. She and her husband don't live far away."

"Don't use my phone."

Steve grimaced. "You act like you're in a spy movie." Steve used his own cellular phone. Marge insisted they come over right away. She said her husband liked to watch his *M*A*S*H* rerun at that time of night but that she could talk him into taping it tonight.

Buck and Steve saw two unmarked squad cars pull up in front of Buck's apartment building as they climbed into a cab. "It *is* like a spy movie," Buck said.

Marge's husband was none too pleased to be displaced from his favorite spot and his favorite show, but even he was intrigued when *Nightline* began. Carpathia was either a natural or well-coached. He looked directly into the camera whenever possible and appeared to be speaking to individual viewers.

"Your speech at the United Nations," Wallace Theodore began, "which was sandwiched between two press conferences today, seems to have electrified New York, and because so much of it has been aired on both early evening and late night local newscasts, you've become a popular man in this country seemingly all at once."

Carpathia smiled. "Like anyone from Europe, particularly Eastern Europe, I am amazed at your technology. I—"

"But isn't it true, sir, that your roots are actually in Western Europe? Though you were born in Romania, are you not by heritage actually Italian?"

"That is true, as it is true of many native Romanians. Thus the name of our country. But as I was saying about your technology. It is amazing, but I confess I did not come to your country to become or to be made into a celebrity. I have a goal, a mission, a message, and it has nothing to do with my popularity or my personal—"

"But is it not true that you just came from a photo session with *People* magazine?"

"Yes, but I—"

"And is it not also true that they have already named you their newest Sexiest Man Alive?"

"I do not know what that means, really. I submitted to an interview that was mostly about my childhood and my business and political career, and I was under the impression that they do this sexy-man coverage in January each year, so it is too early for next year and too close to this year's."

"Yes, and I'm sure, Mr. Carpathia, that you were as thrilled as we were over the young singing star who was so named two months ago, but—"

"I regret to say I was not aware of the young man before I saw his photograph on the cover of the magazine."

"But, sir, are you saying you are not aware that *People* magazine is breaking tradition by, in effect, unseating their current sexiest man and installing you in his place with next week's issue?"

"I believe they tried to tell me that, but I do not understand. The young man did some damage to a hotel or some such thing, and so—"

"And so you were a convenient replacement for him."

"I know nothing about that, and to be perfectly honest, I might not have submitted to the interview under those circumstances. I do not consider myself sexy. I am on a crusade to see the peoples of the world come together. I do not seek a position of power or authority. I simply ask to be heard. I hope my message comes through in the article in the magazine as well."

"You already have a position of both power and authority, Mr. Carpathia."

"Well, our little country asked me to serve, and I was willing."

"How do you respond to those who say you skirted protocol and that your elevation to the presidency in Romania was partially effected by strong-arm tactics?"

"I would say that that is the perfect way to attack a pacifist, one who is committed to disarmament not only in Romania and the rest of Europe but also globally."

"So you deny having a business rival murdered seven years ago and using intimidation and powerful friends in America to usurp the president's authority in Romania?"

"The so-called murdered rival was one of my dearest friends, and I mourn him bitterly to this day. The few American friends I have may be influential here, but they could not have any bearing on Romanian politics. You must know that our former president asked me to replace him for personal reasons."

"But that completely ignores your constitution's procedure for succession to power."

"This was voted upon by the people and by the government and ratified with a huge majority."

"After the fact."

"In a way, yes. But in another way, had they not ratified it, both popularly and within the houses of government, I would have been the briefest reigning president in our nation's history."

Marge's husband growled, "This Roman kid is light on his feet."

"Romanian," Marge corrected.

"I heard him say he's a full-blood Eye-talian," her husband said. Marge winked at Steve and Buck.

Buck was amazed at Carpathia's thought processes and command of language. Theodore asked him, "Why the United Nations? Some would say you would have more impact and get more mileage out of an appearance before our Senate and House of Representatives."

"I would not even dream of such a privilege," Carpathia said. "But, you see, I was not looking for mileage. The U.N. was envisioned originally as a peacekeeping effort. It must return to that role."

"You hinted today, and I hear it in your voice even now, that you have a specific plan for the U.N. that would make it better and which would be of some help during this unusually horrific season in history."

"I do. I did not feel it was my place to suggest such changes when I was a guest; however, I have no hesitation in this context. I am a proponent of disarmament. That is no secret. While I am impressed with the wide-ranging capabilities,

plans, and programs of the United Nations, I do
believe, with a few minor adjustments and the
cooperation of its members, it can be all it was
meant to be. We can truly become a global
community."

"Can you briefly outline that in a few
seconds?"

Carpathia's laugh appeared deep and genuine.
"That is always dangerous," he said, "but I
will try. As you know, the Security Council
of the United Nations has five permanent
members: the United States, the Russian Federation, Britain, France, and China. There are also
ten temporary members, two each from five
different regions of the world, which serve for
two-year terms.

"I respect the proprietary nature of the original
five. I propose choosing another five, just one
each from the five different regions of the world.
Drop the temporary members. Then you would
have ten permanent members of the Security
Council, but the rest of my plan is revolutionary. Currently the five permanent members
have veto power. Votes on procedure require
a nine-vote majority; votes on substance require
a majority, including all five permanent members. I propose a tougher system. I propose
unanimity."

"I beg your pardon?"

"Select carefully the representative ten permanent members. They must get input and support from all the countries in their respective regions."

"It sounds like a nightmare."

"But it would work, and here is why. A nightmare is what happened to us last week. The time is right for the peoples of the world to rise up and insist that their governments disarm and destroy all but ten percent of their weapons. That ten percent would be, in effect, donated to the United Nations so it could return to its rightful place as a global peacekeeping body, with the authority and the power and the equipment to do the job."

Carpathia went on to educate the audience that it was in 1965 that the U.N. amended its original charter to increase the Security Council from 11 to 15. He said that the original veto power of the permanent members had hampered military peace efforts, such as in Korea and during the Cold War.

"Sir, where did you get your encyclopedic knowledge of the U.N. and world affairs?"

"We all find time to do what we really want to do. This is my passion."

"What is your personal goal? A leadership role in the European Common Market?"

"Romania is not even a member, as you know. But no, I have no personal goal of leadership, except as a voice. We must disarm, we must empower the United Nations, we must move to one currency, and we must become a global village."

Rayford and Chloe sat in silence before their new television, taken with the fresh face and encouraging ideas of Nicolae Carpathia. "What a guy!" Chloe said at last. "I haven't heard a politician with anything to say since I was a little girl, and I didn't understand half of it then."

"He is something," Rayford agreed. "It's especially nice to see somebody who doesn't seem to have a personal agenda."

Chloe smiled. "So you're not going to start comparing him with the liar the pastor's tape warned us of, somebody from Europe who tries to take over the world?"

"Hardly," Rayford said. "There's nothing evil or self-seeking about this guy. Something tells me the deceiver the pastor talked about would be a little more obvious."

"But," Chloe said, "if he's a deceiver, maybe he's a good one."

"Hey, which side of this argument are you on? Does this guy look like the Antichrist to you?"

She shook her head. "He looks like a breath

of fresh air to me. If he starts trying to weasel his
way into power, I might be suspicious, but a pacifist, content to be president of a small country?
His only influence is his wisdom, and his only
power is his sincerity and humility."

The phone rang. It was Hattie, eager to talk to
Rayford. She was nearly manic with praise for
Carpathia. "Did you see that guy? He's so handsome! I just have to meet him. Do you have any
flights scheduled to New York?"

"Wednesday I have a late morning flight and
come back the next morning. Then we're going
to see you for dinner that night, right?"

"Yeah, and that's great, but Rayford, would
you mind if I tried to work that flight? I heard on
the news that the death report on that magazine
writer was wrong and he's in New York. I'm
going to see if I can meet with him and get him
to introduce me to this Carpathia."

"You think he knows him?"

"Buck knows everybody. He does all these
big international stories. He's got to. Even if he
doesn't, I wouldn't mind seeing Buck."

That was a relief to Rayford. So Hattie wasn't
afraid to talk about two younger guys she was
clearly interested in seeing, or at least meeting.
He was sure she wasn't just saying it to test his
level of interest. Surely she knew he wasn't interested in anyone with his wife so recently gone.

Rayford wondered whether he should follow through on his plan to be honest with her about his past feelings for her. Maybe he should just jump right into urging that she watch the pastor's videotape.

"Well, good luck with it," Rayford said lamely.

"But can I apply for your flight?"

"Why don't you just see if it comes up that way on the schedule?"

"Rayford!"

"What?"

"You don't want me on your flight! Why? Have I said or done something?"

"Why do you think that?"

"You think I don't know you squashed my last request?"

"I didn't exactly squash it. I just said—"

"You might as well have."

"I said what I just told you. I'm not opposed to your working my flights, but why don't you just let them come as they come?"

"You know the odds of that! If I wait, the odds are against me. If I push for certain ones, with my seniority I can usually get them. Now what's the deal, Rayford?"

"Can we talk about this when you come for dinner?"

"Let's talk about it now."

Rayford paused, groping for words. "Look

what your special requests do to the schedules, Hattie. Everybody else has to slide to accommodate you."

"That's your reason? You're worried about everybody else?"

He didn't want to lie. "Partly," he said.

"That never bothered you before. You used to encourage me to request your flights and sometimes you checked with me to make sure I had done it."

"I know."

"So, what's changed?"

"Hattie, please. I don't want to discuss this by phone."

"Then meet me somewhere."

"I can't do that. I can't leave Chloe so soon after we've had a burglary."

"Then I'll come there."

"It's late."

"Rayford! Are you brushing me off?"

"If I was brushing you off, I wouldn't have invited you to dinner."

"With your daughter at your home? I think I'm getting set up for the royal brush."

"Hattie, what are you saying?"

"Only that you enjoyed running around with me in private, pretending like something was going on."

"I'll admit that."

"And I do feel bad about your wife, Rayford, I really do. You're probably feeling guilty, even though we never did anything to feel guilty about. But don't cast me aside before you have a chance to get over your loss and start living again."

"That's not it. Hattie, what's to cast aside? It's not like we had a relationship. If we did, why are you so interested in this magazine guy and the Romanian?"

"Everybody's interested in Carpathia," she said. "And Buck is the only way I know of to get to him. You can't think I have designs on him. Really! An international newsmaker? Come on, Rayford."

"I don't care if you do. I'm only saying, how does that jibe with whatever you thought we had going?"

"You want me to not go to New York and to forget about both of them?"

"Not at all. I'm hardly saying that."

"Because I will. If I had ever thought there was really a chance with you, I'd have pursued it, believe me."

Rayford was taken aback. His fears and assumptions were correct, but now he felt defensive. "You never thought there was a chance?"

"You hardly gave me any indication. For all

I knew you thought I was a cute kid, way too young, fun to be with, but don't touch."

"There's some truth to that."

"But you never once wished it was something more, Rayford?"

"That's something I would like to talk with you about, Hattie."

"You can answer it right now."

Rayford sighed. "Yes, there were times I wished it was something more."

"Well, glory be. I missed my guess. I had given up, figured you were an untouchable."

"I am."

"Now, sure. I can understand that. You're in pain and probably worse because you were considering someone besides your wife for a while. But does that mean I can't even fly with you, talk to you, have a drink with you? We could go back to the way things used to be, and except for what's in your mind there still wouldn't be anything wrong with it."

"It doesn't mean you can't talk with me or work with me when our schedules coincide. If I didn't want to have anything to do with you, I wouldn't have invited you over."

"I can see what that's all about, Rayford. You can't tell me I wasn't going to get the 'let's be friends' routine."

"Maybe that and a little more."

"Like what?"

"Just something I want to tell you about."

"What if I told you I'm not interested in that kind of socializing? I don't expect you to run to me now that your wife is gone, but I didn't expect to be ignored either."

"How is having you over for dinner ignoring you?"

"Why did you never have me over before?"

Rayford was silent.

"Well?"

"It would have been inappropriate," he muttered.

"And now it's inappropriate to meet any other way?"

"Frankly, yes. But I do want to talk to you, and it isn't about brushing you off."

"Is my curiosity supposed to force me to come now, Rayford? Because, I'll tell you what, I have to decline. I'm going to be busy. Accept my regrets. Something came up, unavoidable, you understand."

"Please. Hattie. We really want you to come. I want you to."

"Rayford, don't bother. There are plenty of flights to New York. I won't go through any gymnastics to get on yours. In fact, I'll make sure I stay away from them."

"You don't have to do that."

"Of course I do. No hard feelings. I would have liked to have met Chloe, but you probably would have felt obligated to tell her you once nearly fell for me."

"Hattie, will you listen to me for a second? Please."

"No."

"I want you to come over Thursday night, and I really have something important to talk to you about."

"Tell me what it is."

"Not on the phone."

"Then I'm not coming."

"If I tell you generally, will you?"

"Depends."

"Well, I know what the disappearances were all about, all right? I know what they meant, and I want to help you find the truth."

Hattie was dead silent for a long moment. "You haven't become some kind of a fanatic, have you?"

Rayford had to think about that one. The answer was yes, he most certainly had, but he wasn't going to say that. "You know me better than that."

"I thought I did."

"Trust me, this is worth your time."

"Give me the basics, and I'll tell you if I want to hear it."

"Absolutely not," Rayford said, surprising himself with his resolve. "That I will not do, except in person."

"Then I'm not coming."

"Hattie!"

"Good-bye, Rayford."

"Hat—"

She hung up.

SIXTEEN

"I WOULDN'T do this for just anybody," Steve
Plank said after he and Buck had thanked Marge
and headed to separate cabs. "I don't know how
long I can hold them off and convince them I'm
you pretending to be someone else, so don't be
far behind."

"Don't worry."

Steve took the first cab, Buck's George
Oreskovich press credentials on his chest. He
was to go directly to the Plaza Hotel, where he
would ask for his appointment with Carpathia.
Buck's hope was that Steve would be immediately intercepted, arrested as Buck, and clear
the way for Buck to get in. If Buck was accosted
by authorities, he would show his identity as
Steve Plank. Both knew the plan was flimsy,
but Buck was willing to try anything to keep
from being extradited and framed for Alan

Tompkins's murder, and possibly even Dirk Burton's.

Buck asked his cabbie to wait about a minute after Steve had left for the Plaza. He arrived at the hotel in the midst of flashing police lights, a paddy wagon, and several unmarked cars. As he threaded his way through onlookers, the police hustled Steve, hands cuffed behind his back, out the door and down the steps.

"I'm telling you," Steve said. "The name's Oreskovich!"

"We know who you are, Williams. Save your breath."

"That's not Cam Williams!" another reporter said, pointing and laughing. "You idiots! That's Steve Plank."

"Yeah, that's it," Plank joined in. "I'm Williams's boss from the *Weekly!*"

"Sure you are," a plainclothesman said, stuffing him into an unmarked car.

Buck ducked the reporter who had recognized Plank, but when he got inside and picked up a courtesy phone to call Rosenzweig's room, another press colleague, Eric Miller, whirled around and covered his own phone, whispering, "Williams, what's going on? The cops just shuttled your boss out of here, claiming he was you!"

"Do me a favor," Buck said. "Sit on this for at least half an hour. You owe me that."

"I owe you nothing, Williams," Miller said. "But you look scared enough. Give me your word you'll tell me first what's going on."

"All right. You'll be the first press guy I tell anyway. Can't promise I won't tell someone else."

"Who?"

"Nice try."

"If you're trying to call Carpathia, Cameron, you can forget it. We've been trying all night. He's not giving any more interviews tonight."

"Is he back?"

"He's back, but he's incommunicado."

Rosenzweig answered Buck's call. "Chaim, it's Cameron Williams. May I come up?"

Eric Miller slammed his phone down and moved close.

"Cameron!" Rosenzweig said. "I can't keep up with you. First you're dead, then you're alive. We just got a call that you had been arrested in the lobby and would be questioned about a murder in London."

Buck didn't want Miller to detect anything. "Chaim, I have to move quickly. I'll be using the name Plank, all right?"

"I'll arrange it with Nicolae and get him to my room somehow. You come." He told Buck the number.

Buck put a finger to his lips so Miller wouldn't ask, but he couldn't shake him. He jogged to the

elevator, but Eric stepped on with him. A couple
tried to join them. "I'm sorry, folks," Buck said.
"This car is malfunctioning." The couple left
but Miller stayed. Buck didn't want him to see
what floor he was going to, so he waited till the
doors shut, then turned the car off. He grabbed
Miller's shirt at the neck and pressed him against
the wall.

"Listen, Eric, I told you I'd call you first with
what's shakin' here, but if you try to horn in on
this or follow me, I'm gonna leave you dry."

Miller shook loose and straightened his clothes.
"All right, Williams! Geez! Lighten up!"

"Yeah, I lighten up and you come snooping
around."

"That's my job, man. Don't forget that."

"Mine too, Eric, but I don't follow other
people's leads. I make my own."

"You interviewing Carpathia? Just tell me
that."

"No, I'm risking my life to see if a movie star's
in the house."

"So it's Carpathia then, really?"

"I didn't say that."

"C'mon, man, let me in on it! I'll give you
anything!"

"You said Carpathia wasn't giving any more
interviews tonight," Buck said.

"And he's not giving any more to anybody

except the networks and national outlets, so I'll
never get to him."

"That's your problem."

"Williams!"

Buck reached for Miller's throat again. "I'm
going!" Eric said.

When Buck emerged at the VIP floor, he was
astounded to see that Miller had somehow beat
him there and was hurriedly introducing himself
to a uniformed guard as Steve Plank. "Mr. Rosenzweig is waiting for you, sir," the guard said.

"Wait a minute!" Buck shouted, showing
Steve's press credentials. "I'm Plank. Run this
impostor off."

The guard put a hand on each man. "You'll
both have to wait here while I call the house
detective."

Buck said, "Just call Rosenzweig and have him
come out here."

The guard shrugged and punched in the room
number on a portable phone. Miller leaned in,
saw the number, and sprinted toward the room.
Buck took off after him, the unarmed guard yelling and still trying to reach someone on the
phone.

Buck, younger and in better shape, overtook
Miller and tackled him in the hallway, causing
doors up and down the corridor to open. "Take
your brawl somewhere else," a woman shouted.

Buck yanked Miller to his feet and put him in a headlock. "You are a clown, Eric. You really think Rosenzweig would let a stranger into his room?"

"I can sweet-talk my way into anywhere, Buck, and you know you would do the same thing."

"Problem is, I already did. Now beat it."

The guard caught up with them. "Dr. Rosenzweig will be out in a minute."

"I have just one question for him," Miller said.

"No, you don't," Buck said. He turned to the guard. "He doesn't."

"Let the old man decide," the guard said, then just as suddenly stepped aside, pulling Buck and Miller with him to clear the hall. There, sweeping past them, were four men in dark suits, surrounding the unmistakable Nicolae Carpathia.

"Excuse me, gentlemen," Carpathia said. "Pardon me."

"Oh, Mr. Carpathia, sir. I mean President Carpathia," Miller called out.

"Sir?" Carpathia said, turning to face him. The bodyguards glowered. "Oh, hello, Mr. Williams," Carpathia said, noticing Buck. "Or should I say Mr. Oreskovich? Or should I say Mr. Plank?"

The interloper stepped forward. "Eric Miller from *Seaboard Monthly*."

"I know it well, Mr. Miller," Carpathia said,

"but I am late for an appointment. If you will call me tomorrow, I will talk to you by phone. Fair enough?"

Miller looked overwhelmed. He nodded and backed away. "I thought you said your name was Plank!" the guard said, causing everyone but Miller to smile.

"Come on in, Buck," Carpathia said, motioning him to follow. Buck was silent. "That is what they call you, is it not?"

"Yes, sir," Buck said, certain that not even Rosenzweig knew that.

Rayford felt terrible about Hattie Durham. Things couldn't have gone worse. Why hadn't he just let her work his flight? She'd have been none the wiser and he could have eased into his real reason for inviting her to dinner Thursday night. Now he had spoiled everything.

How would he get to Chloe now? His real motive, even for talking with Hattie, was to communicate to Chloe. Hadn't she seen enough yet? Shouldn't he be more encouraged by her insistence on replacing the stolen videotape? He asked if she wanted to go to New York with him for the overnight trip. She said she'd rather stay home and start looking into taking classes locally. He wanted to push, but he didn't dare.

After she had gone to bed, he called Bruce Barnes and told him his frustrations.

"You're trying too hard, Rayford," the younger man said. "I should think telling other people about our faith would be easier than ever now, but I've run into the same kind of resistance."

"It's really hard when it's your own daughter."

"I can imagine," Bruce said.

"No, you can't," Rayford said. "But it's all right."

Chaim Rosenzweig was in a beautiful suite of rooms. The bodyguards were posted out front, while Carpathia invited Rosenzweig and Buck into a private parlor for a meeting of just the three of them. Carpathia shed his coat and laid it carefully across the back of a couch. "Make yourselves comfortable, gentlemen," he said.

"I do not need to be here, Nicolae," Rosenzweig whispered.

"Oh, nonsense, Doctor!" Carpathia said. "You do not mind, do you, Buck?"

"Not at all."

"You do not mind my calling you Buck, do you?"

"No, sir, but usually it's just people at—"

"Your magazine, yes, I know. They call you

that because you buck the traditions and the trends and the conventions, am I right?"

"Yes, but how—"

"Buck, this has been the most incredible day of my life. I have felt so welcome here. And the people have seemed so receptive to my proposals. I am overwhelmed. I shall go back to my country a happy and satisfied man. But not soon. I have been asked to stay longer. Did you know that?"

"I heard."

"It is amazing, is it not, that all those different international meetings right here in New York over the next few weeks are all about the world-wide cooperation in which I am interested?"

"It is," Buck said. "And I've been assigned to cover them."

"Then we will be getting to know each other better."

"I look forward to that, sir. I was most moved at the U.N. today."

"Thank you."

"And Dr. Rosenzweig has told me so much about you."

"As he has told me much about you."

There was a knock at the door. Carpathia looked pained. "I had hoped we would not be disturbed." Rosenzweig rose slowly and shuffled to the door and a subdued conversation.

He slipped back to Buck. "We'll have to give

him a couple of minutes, Cameron," he whispered, "for an important phone call."

"Oh, no," Carpathia said. "I will take it later.
This meeting is a priority for me—"

"Sir," Rosenzweig said, "begging your
pardon . . . it is the president."

"The president?"

"Of the United States."

Buck rose quickly to leave with Rosenzweig,
but Carpathia insisted they stay. "I am not such
a dignitary that I would not share this honor
with my old friend and my new friend. Sit
down!"

They sat and he pushed the speaker button on
the phone. "This is Nicolae Carpathia speaking."

"Mr. Carpathia, this is Fitz. Gerald Fitzhugh."

"Mr. President, I am honored to hear from
you."

"Well, hey, it's good to have you here!"

"I appreciated your note of congratulations on
my presidency, sir, and your immediate recognition of my administration."

"Boy, that was a heckuva thing, how you
took over there. I wasn't sure what had
happened at first, but I don't suppose you
were either."

"That is exactly right. I am still getting used
to it."

"Well, take it from a guy who's been in the

saddle for six years. You don't ever get used to it. You just develop calluses in the right places, if you know what I mean."

"Yes, sir."

"Listen, the reason I called is this. I know you're gonna be here a little longer than you expected, so I want you to spend a night or two here with me and Wilma. Can you do that?"

"In Washington?"

"Right here at the White House."

"That would be such a privilege."

"We'll have somebody talk to your people about the right time, but it's got to be soon 'cause Congress is in session, and I know they'll want to hear from you."

Carpathia shook his head and Buck thought he seemed overcome emotionally. "I would be more than honored, sir."

"Speaking of something that was a heckuva thing, your speech today and your interview tonight—well, that was something. Look forward to meetin' ya."

"The feeling is mutual, sir."

Buck was only a little less overcome than Carpathia and Rosenzweig. He had long since lost his awe of U.S. presidents, especially this one, who insisted on being called Fitz. He had done a Newsmaker of the Year piece on Fitzhugh—Buck's first, Fitz's second. On the

other hand, it wasn't every day that the president called the room in which you sat.

The glow of the call seemed to stay with
Carpathia, but he quickly changed the subject.
"Buck, I want to answer all your questions and
give you whatever you need. You have been so
good to Chaim, and I am prepared to give you
a bit of a secret—you would call it a scoop.
But first, you are in deep trouble, my friend.
And I want to help you if I can."

Buck had no idea how Carpathia knew he
was in trouble. So he wouldn't even have to
bring him up to speed and ask for his help?
This was too good to be true. The question
was, what did Carpathia know, and what did
he need to know?

The Romanian sat forward and looked directly
into Buck's eyes. That gave Buck such a feeling
of peace and security that he felt free to tell him
everything. Everything. Even that his friend Dirk
had tipped him off about someone meeting with
Stonagal and Todd-Cothran, and Buck's assuming it was Carpathia.

"It *was* I," Carpathia said. "But let me make
this very clear. I know nothing of any conspiracy. I have never even heard of such a thing.
Mr. Stonagal felt it would be good for me to
meet some of his colleagues and men of international influence. I formed no opinions about

any of them, neither am I beholden to any of
them.

"I will tell you something, Mr. Williams. I
believe your story. I do not know you except
by your work and your reputation with people
I respect, such as Dr. Rosenzweig. But your
account has the ring of truth. I have been told
that you are wanted in London for the murder
of the Scotland Yard agent and that they have
several witnesses who will swear they saw you
distract Tompkins, plant the device, and activate
it from within the pub."

"That's crazy."

"Well, of course it is if you were mourning the
mysterious death of your mutual friend."

"That's exactly what we were doing, Mr.
Carpathia. That and trying to get to the bottom
of it."

Rosenzweig was called to the door again, then
he whispered in Carpathia's ear. "Buck, come
here," Carpathia said, rising and leading Buck
toward a window, away from Rosenzweig.
"Your plan to get in here while being pursued
was most ingenious, but your boss has been
identified and now they know you are here.
They would like to take you into custody and
extradite you to England."

"If that happens and Tompkins's theory is
right," Buck said, "I'm a dead man."

"You believe they will kill you?"

"They killed Burton and they killed Tompkins. I'm much more dangerous to them with my potential readership."

"If this plot is as you and your friends say it is, Cameron, writing about these people, exposing them, will not protect you."

"I know. Maybe I should do it anyway. I don't see any way out."

"I can make this go away for you."

Buck's mind was suddenly reeling. This was what he had wanted, but he had feared Carpathia could do nothing quickly enough to keep him from getting into Todd-Cothran's and Sullivan's hands. Was it possible Carpathia was in deeper with these people than he had let on?

"Sir, I need your help. But I am a journalist first. I can't be bought or bargained with."

"Oh, of course not. I would never ask such a thing. Let me tell you what I can do for you. I will arrange to have the London tragedies revisited and reevaluated, exonerating you."

"How will you do that?"

"Does it matter, if it is the truth?"

Buck thought a moment. "It *is* the truth."

"Of course."

"But how will you do that? You have maintained this innocence, Mr. Carpathia, this man-

from-nowhere persona. How can you affect what
has happened in London?"

Carpathia sighed. "Buck, I told you your friend
Dirk was wrong about a conspiracy. That is true.
I am not in bed with Todd-Cothran or Stonagal
or any of the other international leaders I have
been honored to meet recently. However, there
are important decisions and actions coming up
that will affect them, and it is my privilege to
have a say in those developments."

Buck asked Carpathia if he minded if they sat
down again. Carpathia signaled to Rosenzweig
to leave them for a few minutes. "Look," Buck
said when they were seated, "I'm a young man,
but I've been around the block. It feels to me
as if I'm about to find out just how deep into
this—well, if it's not a conspiracy, it's something
organized—how deep into this thing you are.
I can play along and save my life, or I can
refuse and you let me take my chances in
London."

Carpathia held up a hand and shook his
head. "Buck, let me reiterate that we are talking
politics and diplomacy, not skullduggery or
crime."

"I'm listening."

"First," Carpathia said, "a little background.
I believe in the power of money. Do you?"

"No."

"You will. I was a better-than-average businessman in Romania while still in secondary school.
I studied at night, many languages, the ones I
needed to succeed. During the day I ran my own
import-and-export businesses and made myself
wealthy. But what I thought was wealth was
paltry compared to what was possible. I needed
to learn that. I learned it the hard way. I borrowed millions from a European bank, then
found that someone in that bank informed my
major competitor what I was doing. I was
defeated at my own game, defaulted on my loan,
and was struggling. Then that same bank bailed
me out and ruined my rival. I didn't mean to or
want to hurt the rival. He was used by the bank
to lock me into a relationship."

"Was that bank owned by an influential
American?"

Carpathia ignored the question. "What I had
to learn, in just over a decade, is how much
money is out there."

"Out there?"

"In the banks of the world."

"Especially those owned by Jonathan Stonagal," Buck suggested.

Carpathia still wasn't biting. "That kind of
capital is power."

"This is the kind of thing I write against."

"It is about to save your life."

"I'm still listening."

"That kind of money gets a man's attention. He becomes willing to make concessions for it. He begins to see the wisdom of letting someone else, a younger man, someone with more enthusiasm and vigor and fresh vision, take over."

"That's what happened in Romania?"

"Buck, do not insult me. The former president of Romania asked me of his own free will to replace him, and the support for that move was unanimous within the government and almost totally favorable among the masses. Everyone is better off."

"The former president is out of power."

"He lives in luxury."

Buck could not breathe. What was Carpathia implying? Buck stared at him, unable to move, unable to respond. Carpathia continued. "Secretary-General Ngumo presides over a country that is starving. The world is ripe for my plan of ten members of the Security Council. These things will work together. The secretary-general must devote his time to the problems within Botswana. With the right incentive, he will do that. He will be a happy, prosperous man, with a happy and prosperous people. But first he will endorse my plan for the Security Council. The representatives from each of the ten will be an interesting mix, some current ambassadors, but mostly new people with good financial backgrounds and progressive ideas."

"Are you telling me you will become secretary-general of the U.N.?"

"I would never seek such a position, but how could I refuse such an honor? Who could turn his back on such an enormous responsibility?"

"How much say will you have about who represents each of the ten permanent members of the Security Council?"

"I will merely be there to provide servant leadership. Are you aware of that concept? One leads by serving, not by dictating."

"Let me take a wild guess," Buck said. "Todd-Cothran is in line for a role on your new Security Council."

Carpathia sat back, as if learning something. "Would that not be interesting?" he said. "A nonpolitician, a brilliant financial mind, one who was wise enough and kind enough and globally minded enough to allow the world to go to a three-currency system that did not include his own pounds sterling? He brings no baggage to such a role. The world would have a certain level of comfort with him, would they not?"

"I suppose they would," Buck said, his mind black with depression as if he were losing his soul before his very eyes. "Unless, that is, Todd-

Cothran were in the middle of a mysterious suicide, a car bombing, that sort of a thing."

Carpathia smiled. "I should think a man in a position of international potential like that would want a very clean house just now."

"And you could effect that?"

"Buck, you overestimate me. I am just saying that if you are right, I might try to stop what is clearly an unethical and illegal action against an innocent man—you. I cannot see how there is anything wrong with that."

Rayford Steele could not sleep. For some reason he was overcome anew with grief and remorse over the loss of his wife and son. He slid out of bed and onto his knees, burying his face in the sheet on the side where his wife used to sleep. He had been so tired, so tense, so worried about Chloe that he had pushed from his heart and mind and soul his terrible loss. He believed totally that his wife and son were in heaven, and he knew they were better off than they had ever been.

Rayford knew he had been forgiven for mocking his wife, for never really listening, for having ignored God for so many years. He was grateful he had been given a second chance and that he now had new friends and a place to learn the

Bible. But that didn't stop the aching emptiness in his heart, the longing to hold his wife and son, to kiss them and tell them how much he loved them. He prayed for the grief to lessen, but part of him wanted it, needed it, to remain.

In a way he felt he deserved this pain, though he knew better. He was beginning to understand the forgiveness of God, and Bruce had told him that he needn't continue to feel shame over sin that had been dealt with.

As Rayford knelt praying and weeping, a new anguish flooded over him. He felt hopeless about Chloe. Everything he had tried had failed. He knew it had been only days since the disappearance of her mother and brother, and even less time since his own conversion. What more could he say or do? Bruce had encouraged him just to pray, but he was not made that way. He would pray, of course, but he had always been a man of action.

Now, every action seemed to push her farther away. He felt that if he said or did anything more, he would be responsible for her deciding against Christ once and for all. Rayford had never felt more powerless and desperate. How he longed to have Irene and Raymie with him right then. And how he despaired over Chloe.

He had been praying silently, but the torment welled up within him, and despite himself he heard his own muffled cries, "Chloe! Oh, Chloe! Chloe!"

He wept bitterly in the darkness, suddenly jarred by a creak and footsteps. He turned quickly to see Chloe, the dim light from her room silhouetting her robed form in the doorway. He didn't know what she had heard.

"Are you all right, Dad?" she asked quietly.

"Yeah."

"Nightmare?"

"No. I'm sorry to disturb you."

"I miss them, too," she said, her voice quavery. Rayford turned and sat with his back to the bed. He held his arms open to her. She came and sat next to him, letting him hold her.

"I believe I'll see them again someday," he said.

"I know you do," she said, no disrespect in her voice. "I know you do."

SEVENTEEN

AFTER a few minutes, Chloe gave Rayford evidence that she had heard his cry. "Don't worry about me, Daddy, OK? I'm getting there."

Getting where? Did she mean that her decision was just a matter of time or simply that she was getting over her grief? He wanted so badly to tell her he was worried, but she knew that. Her very presence brought him comfort, but when she padded back to her room he felt desperately alone again.

He could not sleep. He tiptoed downstairs and turned on the new TV, tuning in CNN. From Israel came the strangest report. The screen showed a mob in front of the famous Wailing Wall, surrounding two men who seemed to be shouting.

"No one knows the two men," said the CNN reporter on the scene, "who refer to each other as

Eli and Moishe. They have stood here before the
Wailing Wall since just before dawn, preaching in
a style frankly reminiscent of the old American
evangelists. Of course the Orthodox Jews here
are in an uproar, charging the two with desecrating this holy place by proclaiming that Jesus
Christ of the New Testament is the fulfillment
of the Torah's prophecy of a messiah.

"Thus far there has been no violence, though
tempers are flaring, and authorities keep a watch-
ful eye. Israeli police and military personnel have
always been loath to enter this area, leaving religious zealots here to handle their own problems.
This is the most explosive situation in the Holy
Land since the destruction of the Russian air
force, and this newly prosperous nation has been
concerned almost primarily with outside threats.

"For CNN, this is Dan Bennett in Jerusalem."

Had it not been so late, Rayford would have
called Bruce Barnes. He sat there, feeling a part of
the family of believers to which the two men in
Jerusalem apparently belonged. This was exactly
what he had been learning, that Jesus was the
Messiah of the Old Testament. Bruce had told
him and the rest of the core group at New Hope
that there would soon spring up 144,000 Jews
who would believe in Christ and begin to evangelize around the world. Were these the first two?

The CNN anchorwoman turned to national

news. "New York is still abuzz following several appearances today by new Romanian president Nicolae Carpathia. The thirty-three-year-old leader wowed the media at a small press conference this morning, followed by a masterful speech to the United Nations General Assembly in which he had the entire crowd standing and cheering, including the press. He reportedly sat for a cover photo session with *People* magazine and will be their first ever Sexiest Man Alive to appear less than a year after the previous designate.

"Associates of Carpathia have announced that he has already extended his schedule to include addresses to several international meetings in New York over the next two weeks and that he has been invited by President Fitzhugh to speak to a joint session of Congress and spend a night at the White House.

"At a press conference this afternoon the president voiced support for the new leader."

The president's image filled the screen. "At this difficult hour in world history, it's crucial that lovers of peace and unity step forward to remind us that we're part of a global community. Any friend of peace is a friend of the United States, and Mr. Carpathia is a friend of peace."

CNN broadcast a question asked of the president. "Sir, what do you think of Carpathia's ideas for the U.N.?"

"Let me just say this: I don't believe I've ever
heard anybody, inside or outside the U.N., show
such a total grasp of the history and organization
and direction of the place. He's done his home-
work, and he has a plan. I was listening. I hope
the respective ambassadors and Secretary-General
Ngumo were, too. No one should see a fresh
vision as a threat. I'm sure every leader in the
world shares my view that we need all the help
we can get at this hour."

The anchorwoman continued: "Out of New
York late this evening comes a report that a
Global Weekly writer has been cleared of all
charges and suspicion in the death of a Scotland
Yard investigator. Cameron Williams, award-
winning senior writer at the *Weekly,* had been
feared dead in a car bombing that took the life
of the investigator Alan Tompkins, who was also
an acquaintance of Williams.

"Tompkins's remains had been identified and
Williams's passport and ID were found among
the rubble after the explosion. Williams's
assumed death was reported in newspapers
across the country, but he reappeared in New
York late this afternoon and was seen at the
United Nations press conference following
Nicolae Carpathia's speech.

"Earlier this evening, Williams was considered
an international fugitive, wanted by both Scot-

land Yard and Interpol for questioning in connection with the bombing death. Both agencies
have since announced he has been cleared of all
charges and is considered lucky to have escaped
unharmed.

"In sports news, Major League Baseball
teams in spring training face the daunting task
of replacing the dozens of players lost in the
cosmic disappearances. . . ."

Rayford still was not sleepy. He made himself
coffee, then phoned the twenty-four-hour line
that kept track of flight and crew assignments.
He had an idea. "Can you tell me whether I can
still get Hattie Durham assigned to my JFK run
Wednesday?" he asked.

"I'll see what I can do," came the response.
"Whoops, no. I guess you can't. She's going to
New York already. Yours is the 10 A.M. flight.
Hers is the 8 A.M."

Buck Williams had returned to his apartment
after midnight, assured by Nicolae Carpathia that
his worries were over. Carpathia had phoned
Jonathan Stonagal, put him on speakerphone,
and Stonagal had done the same as he made the
middle-of-the-night phone call to London that
cleared Williams. Buck heard Todd-Cothran's
husky-voiced agreement to call off the Yard and

Interpol. "But my package is secure?" Todd-Cothran asked.

"Guaranteed," Stonagal had said.

Most alarming to Buck was that Stonagal did his own dirty work, at least in this instance. Buck had looked accusingly at Carpathia, despite his relief and gratitude.

"Mr. Williams," Carpathia said, "I was confident Jonathan could handle this, but I am just as ignorant of the details as you are."

"But this just proves Dirk was right! Stonagal *is* conspiring with Todd-Cothran, and you knew it! And Stonagal promised him his package was secure, whatever that means."

"I assure you I knew nothing until you told me, Buck. I had no prior knowledge."

"But now you know. Can you still in good conscience allow Stonagal to help promote you in international politics?"

"Trust me, I will deal with them both."

"But there have to be many more! What about all the other so-called dignitaries you met?"

"Buck, just be assured there is no place around me for insincerity or injustice. I will deal with them in due time."

"And meanwhile?"

"What would you advise? It seems to me that I am in no position to do anything right now. They seem intent on elevating me, but until they do I can do nothing but what your media calls whistle-blowing. How far would I get with that, before I know how far their tentacles reach? Before recently, would you not have thought Scotland Yard would be a trustworthy place to start?"

Buck nodded miserably. "I know what you mean, but I hate this. They know that you know."

"That may work to my advantage. They may think I am with them, that this makes me even more dependent upon them."

"Doesn't it?"

"Only temporarily. You have my word. I *will* deal with this. For now I am glad to have extricated you from a most delicate situation."

"I'm glad, too, Mr. Carpathia. Is there anything I can do for you?"

The Romanian smiled. "Well, I need a press secretary."

"I was afraid you were going to say that. I'm not your man."

"Of course not. I would not have dreamed of asking."

As a joke, Buck suggested, "What about the man you met in the hall?"

Carpathia displayed his prodigious memory once more. "That Eric Miller fellow?"

"He's the one. You'd love him."

"And I already told him to call me tomorrow. May I say you recommended him?"

Buck shook his head. "I was kidding." He told Carpathia what had happened in the lobby, on the elevator, and in the hall before Miller introduced himself. Nicolae was not amused. "I'll rack my brain and see if I can think of another candidate for you," Buck said. "Now you promised me a scoop tonight, too."

"True. It is new information, but it must not be announced until I have the ability to effect it."

"I'm listening."

"Israel is particularly vulnerable, as they were before Russia tried to invade them. They were lucky that time, but the rest of the world resents their prosperity. They need protection. The U.N. can give it to them. In exchange for the chemical formula that makes the desert bloom, the world will be content to grant them peace. If the other nations disarm and surrender a tenth of their weapons to the U.N., only the U.N. will have to sign a peace accord with Israel. Their prime minister has given Dr. Rosenzweig the freedom to negotiate such an agreement because he is the true owner of the formula. They are, of course, insisting on guarantees of protection for no less than seven years."

Buck sat shaking his head. "You're going to get the Nobel Peace prize, *Time*'s Man of the Year, and our Newsmaker of the Year."

"Those certainly are not my goals."

Buck left Carpathia believing that as deeply as he had ever believed anything. Here was a man unaffected by the money that could buy lesser men.

At his apartment Buck discovered yet another phone message from Hattie Durham. He had to call that girl.

Bruce Barnes called the core group together for an emergency meeting at New Hope Village Church Tuesday afternoon. Rayford drove over, hoping it would be worth his time and that Chloe wouldn't mind being home alone for a while. They had both been edgy since the break-in.

Bruce gathered everyone around his desk in the office. He began by praying that he would be lucid and instructive in spite of his excitement and then had everyone turn to the book of Revelation.

Bruce's eyes were bright and his voice carried the same passion and emotion as when he had called. Rayford wondered what had him so excited. He had asked Bruce on the phone, but Bruce insisted on telling everyone in person.

"I don't want to keep you long," he said, "but I'm onto something deep here and wanted to share it. In a way, I want you all to be wary, to be wise as serpents and harmless as doves, as the Bible says.

"As you know, I've been studying Revelation and several commentaries about end-times events. Well, today in the pastor's files I ran across one of his sermons on the subject. I've been reading the Bible and the books on the subject, and here's what I've found."

Bruce pulled up the first blank sheet on a flip chart and showed a time line he had drawn. "I'll take the time to carefully teach you this over the next several weeks, but it looks to me, and to many of the experts who came before us, that this period of history we're in right now will last for seven years. The first twenty-one months encompass what the Bible calls the seven Seal Judgments, or the Judgments of the Seven-Sealed Scroll. Then comes another twenty-one-month period in which we will see the seven Trumpet Judgments. In the last forty-two months of this seven years of tribulation, if we have survived, we will endure the most severe tests, the seven Vial Judgments. That last half of the seven years is called the Great Tribulation, and if we are alive at the end of it, we will be rewarded by seeing the Glorious Appearing of Christ."

Loretta raised her hand. "Why do you keep saying 'if we survive'? What are these judgments?"

"They get progressively worse, and if I'm reading this right, they will be harder and harder to survive. If we die, we will be in heaven with Christ and our loved ones. But we may suffer horrible deaths. If we somehow make it through the seven terrible years, especially the last half, the Glorious Appearing will be all that more glorious. Christ will come back to set up his thousand-year reign on earth."

"The Millennium."

"Exactly. Now, that's a long time off, and of course we may be only days from the beginning of the first twenty-one-month period. Again, if I'm reading it right, the Antichrist will soon come to power, promising peace and trying to unite the world."

"What's wrong with uniting the world?" someone asked. "At a time like this it seems we need to come together."

"There might be nothing wrong with that, except that the Antichrist will be a great deceiver, and when his true goals are revealed, he will be opposed. This will result in a great war, probably World War III."

"How soon?"

"I fear it will be very soon. We need to watch for the new world leader."

"What about the young man from Europe who is so popular with the United Nations?"

"I'm impressed with him," Bruce said. "I will

have to be careful and study what he says and does. He seems too humble and self-effacing to fit the description of this one who would take over the world."

"But we're ripe for someone to do just that," one of the older men said. "I found myself wishing that guy was our president." Several others agreed.

"We need to keep an eye on him," Bruce said. "But for now, let me just briefly outline the Seven-Sealed Scroll from Revelation five, and then I'll let you go. On the one hand, I don't want to give you a spirit of fear, but we all know we're still here because we neglected salvation before the Rapture. I know we're all grateful for the second chance, but we cannot expect to escape the trials that are coming."

Bruce explained that the first four seals in the scroll were described as men on four horses: a white horse, a red horse, a black horse, and a pale horse. "The white horseman apparently is the Antichrist, who ushers in one to three months of diplomacy while getting organized and promising peace.

"The red horse signifies war. The Antichrist will be opposed by three rulers from the south, and millions will be killed."

"In World War III?"

"That's my assumption."

"That would mean within the next six months."

"I'm afraid so. And immediately following that, which will take only three to six months because of the nuclear weaponry available, the Bible predicts inflation and famine—the black horse. As the rich get richer, the poor starve to death. More millions will die that way."

"So if we survive the war, we need to stockpile food?"

Bruce nodded. "I would."

"We should work together."

"Good idea, because it gets worse. That killer famine could be as short as two or three months before the arrival of the fourth Seal Judgment, the fourth horseman on the pale horse—the symbol of death. Besides the postwar famine, a plague will sweep the entire world. Before the fifth Seal Judgment, a quarter of the world's current population will be dead."

"What's the fifth Seal Judgment?"

"Well," Bruce said, "you're going to recognize this one because we've talked about it before. Remember my telling you about the 144,000 Jewish witnesses who try to evangelize the world for Christ? Many of their converts, perhaps millions, will be martyred by the world leader and the harlot, which is the name for the one world religion that denies Christ."

Rayford was furiously taking notes. He wondered what he would have thought about such crazy talk just three weeks earlier. How could he have missed this? God had tried to warn his people by putting his Word in written form centuries before. For all Rayford's education and intelligence, he felt he had been a fool. Now he couldn't get enough of this information, though it was becoming clear that the odds were against a person living until the Glorious Appearing of Christ.

"The sixth Seal Judgment," Bruce continued, "is God pouring out his wrath against the killing of his saints. This will come in the form of a worldwide earthquake so devastating that no instruments would be able to measure it. It will be so bad that people will cry out for rocks to fall on them and put them out of their misery." Several in the room began to weep. "The seventh seal introduces the seven Trumpet Judgments, which will take place in the second quarter of this seven-year period."

"The second twenty-one months," Rayford clarified.

"Right. I don't want to get into those tonight, but I warn you they are progressively worse. I want to leave you with a little encouragement. You remember we talked briefly about the two witnesses, and I said I would study that more carefully? Revelation 11:3-14 makes it clear that God's two special witnesses, with supernatural power to work miracles, will prophesy one thousand two hundred and sixty days, clothed in sackcloth. Anyone who tries to harm them will be devoured. No rain will fall during the time that they prophesy. They will be able to turn water to blood and to strike the earth with plagues whenever they want.

"Satan will kill them at the end of three and a half years, and their bodies will lie in the street of the city where Christ was crucified. The people they have tormented will celebrate their deaths, not allowing their bodies to be buried. But after three and a half days, they will rise from the dead and ascend to heaven in a cloud while their enemies watch. God will send another great earthquake, a tenth of the city will fall, and seven thousand people will die. The rest will be terrified and give glory to God."

Rayford glanced around the office as people murmured among themselves. They had all seen it, the report of the two crazy men preaching about Jesus at the Wailing Wall in Jerusalem.

"Is that them?" someone asked.

"Who else could it be?" Bruce said. "It has not rained in Jerusalem since the disappearances.

These men came out of nowhere. They have the miraculous power of saints like Elijah and Moses, and they call each other Eli and Moishe. At this moment, the men are still preaching."

"The witnesses."

"Yes, the witnesses. If any one of us still harbored any doubts or fears, not sure what has been going on, these witnesses should allay them all. I believe these witnesses will see hundreds of thousands of converts, the 144,000, who will preach Christ to the world. We're on their side. We have to do our parts."

Buck reached Hattie Durham at her home number Tuesday night. "So, you're coming through New York?" he said.

"Yes," she said, "and I'd love to see you and maybe get to meet a VIP."

"You mean other than me?"

"Cute," she said. "Have you met Nicolae Carpathia yet?"

"Of course."

"I knew it! I was just telling someone the other day that I'd love to meet that man."

"No promises, but I'll see what I can do. Where should we meet?"

"My flight gets in there about eleven and I have a one o'clock appointment in the Pan-Con Club.

But if we don't get back in time for that, it's OK. I don't fly out till morning, and I didn't even tell the guy I would meet him at one."

"Another guy?" Buck said. "You've got some weekend planned."

"It's nothing like that," she said. "It's a pilot who wants to talk to me about something, and I'm not sure I even want to listen. If I'm back and have time, fine. But I haven't committed to it. Why don't we meet at the club and see where we want to go from there?"

"I'll try to arrange the meeting with Mr. Carpathia, probably at his hotel."

It was late Tuesday night when Chloe changed her mind and agreed to go to New York with her father. "I can see you're not ready to be out without me," she said, embracing him and smiling. "It's nice to be needed."

"To tell you the truth," he said, "I'm going to insist on a meeting with Hattie, and I want you there."

"For her protection or yours?"

"Not funny. I've left her a message insisting that she see me in the Pan-Con Club at JFK at one in the afternoon. Whether she will or not, I don't know. Either way, you and I will get some time together."

"Daddy, time together is all we've had. I'd think you'd be tired of me by now."

"That'll never happen, Chloe."

Early Wednesday morning Buck was summoned to the office of Stanton Bailey, publisher of *Global Weekly*. In all his years of award-winning work, he had been in there only twice, once to celebrate his Hemingway war correspondence award and once on a Christmas tour of what the employees enviously called Mahogany Row.

Buck ducked in to see Steve first, only to be told by Marge that he was in with the publisher already. Her eyes were red and puffy. "What's happening?" he said.

"You know I can't say anything," she said. "Just get in there."

Buck's imagination ran wild as he entered the suite of offices inhabited by the brass. He hadn't known Plank had been summoned, too. What could it mean? Were they in trouble for the shenanigans they had pulled Monday night? Had Mr. Bailey somehow found out the details of the London business and how Buck had escaped? And he certainly hoped this meeting would be over in time for his appointment with Hattie Durham.

Bailey's receptionist pointed him to the

Tim LaHaye & Jerry B. Jenkins 365

publisher's outer office, where his secretary raised one brow and waved him in. "You're not going to announce me?" he joked. She smirked and returned to her work.

Buck knocked quietly and carefully pushed open the door. Plank sat with his back to Buck and didn't turn. Bailey didn't rise but beckoned him in. "Sit right there next to your boss," Bailey said, which Buck thought an interesting choice of words. Of course, it was true, but that was not how Steve was usually addressed.

Buck sat and said, "Steve."

Steve nodded but kept looking at Bailey.

"Couple of things, Williams," Bailey began, "before I get down to business. You're cleared of everything overseas, right?"

Buck nodded. "Yes, sir. There should never have been any doubt."

"Well, 'course there shouldn't, but you were lucky. I guess it was smart to make it look like whoever was after you got you, but you made us think that for a while too, you know."

"Sorry. I'm afraid that was unavoidable."

"And you wound up giving them ammunition to use against you if they wanted to bust you for some reason."

"I know. That surprised me."

"But you got it taken care of."

"Right."

"How?"

"Sir?"

"What part of 'how' don't you understand? How did you extricate yourself? We got word there were witnesses who say you did it."

"There must have been enough others who knew the truth. Tompkins was a friend of mine. I had no reason to kill him, and I sure didn't have the means. I wouldn't have the slightest idea how to make a bomb or transport it or detonate it."

"You could have paid to have it done."

"But I didn't. I don't run in those circles, and if I did, I wouldn't have had Alan killed."

"Well, the news coverage is all vague enough that none of us look bad. Just looks like a misunderstanding."

"Which it was."

"Of course it was. Cameron, I asked to see you this morning because I have just accepted one of the least welcome resignations I have ever received."

Buck sat silent, his head spinning.

"Steve here tells me this will be news to you, so let me just drop it on you. He is resigning immediately to accept the position of international press secretary to Nicolae Carpathia. He's received an offer we can't come close to, and while I don't think it's wise or a good fit, he does, and it's his life. What do you think about that?"

Buck couldn't contain himself. "I think it stinks. Steve, what are you thinking of? You're going to move to Romania?"

"I'll be headquartered here, Buck. At the Plaza."

"Nice."

"I'll say."

"Steve, this isn't you. You're not a PR guy."

"Carpathia is no ordinary political leader. Tell me you weren't on your feet cheering Monday."

"I was, but—"

"But nothing. This is the opportunity of a lifetime. Nothing else would have lured me from this job."

Buck shook his head. "I can't believe it. I knew Carpathia was looking for somebody, but—"

Steve laughed. "Tell the truth, Buck. He offered it to you first, didn't he?"

"No."

"He as much as told me he did."

"Well, he didn't. Matter of fact, I recommended Miller from *Seaboard.*"

Plank recoiled and shot a glance at Bailey. "Really?"

"Yeah, why not? He's more the type."

"Buck," Steve said, "Eric Miller's body washed up on Staten Island last night. He fell off the ferry and drowned."

"Well," Bailey said summarily, "enough of that ugly business. Steve has recommended you to replace him."

Buck was still reeling from the news about Miller, but he heard the offer. "Oh, please," he said, "you're not serious."

"You wouldn't want the job?" Bailey asked. "Shape the magazine, determine the coverage, still write the top stories yourself? Sure you would. By policy it would almost double your salary, and if that's what it took to get you to agree, I'd guarantee it."

"That's not it," Buck said. "I'm too young for the job I've got now."

"You don't believe that or you wouldn't be as good at it as you are."

"Yeah, but that's the sentiment of the staff."

"What else is new?" Bailey roared. "They think I'm too old. They thought Steve was too laid-back. Others thought he was too pushy. They'd complain if we brought in the pope himself."

"I thought he was missing."

"You know what I mean. Now how about it?"

"I could never replace Steve, sir. I'm sorry. People may have complained, but they knew he was fair and in their corner."

"And so would you be."

"But they'd never give me the benefit of the

doubt. They'd be in here undermining me and complaining from day one."

"I wouldn't allow it. Now, Buck, this offer isn't going to sit on the table indefinitely. I want you to take it, and I want to be able to announce it immediately."

Buck shrugged and looked at the floor. "Can I have a day to think about it?"

"Twenty-four hours. Meantime, don't say a word to anybody. Plank, anybody else know about you?"

"Only Marge."

"We can trust her. She'll never tell a soul. I had a three-year affair with her and never worried about anybody finding out."

Steve and Buck flinched.

"Well," Bailey said, "you never knew, did you?"

"No," they said in unison.

"See how tight-lipped she is?" He waited a beat. "I'm kidding, boys. I'm kidding!"

He was still laughing as they left the office.

EIGHTEEN

BUCK followed Steve to his office. "Did you hear about those kooks at the Wailing Wall?" Steve said.

"Like I'm interested in that right now," Buck said. "Yeah, I saw them, and no, I don't want to cover that story. Now what is this?"

"This will be your office, Buck. Marge will be your secretary."

"You can't possibly think I would want your job. First off, we can't afford to lose you. You're the only sane person here."

"Including you?"

"Especially including me. You must have really run interference for me with Bailey if he thinks I would be anything but a powder keg in your job."

"*Your* job."

"You think I should take it."

"You bet I do. I suggested no one else and Bailey had no other candidates."

"He'd have all the candidates he wanted if he just announced the opening. Who wouldn't want this job, besides me?"

"If it's such a plum, why *don't* you want it?"

"I'd feel as if I were sitting in your chair."

"So order your own chair."

"You know what I mean, Steve. It won't be the same without you. This job isn't me."

"Look at it this way, Buck. If you don't take it, you have no say in who becomes your new boss. Anybody on this staff you want to work for?"

"Yeah, you."

"Too late. I'm gone tomorrow. Now seriously, you want to work for Juan?"

"You wouldn't recommend him."

"I'm not going to recommend anybody but you. You don't take it, you're on your own. You take your chances you'll wind up working for a colleague who already resents you. How many hot assignments you think you'll get then?"

"If I got dumped on, I'd threaten to go to *Time* or somewhere. Bailey wouldn't let that happen."

"You turn down a promotion, he might make it happen. Rejecting advancement is not a good career move."

"I just want to write."

"Tell me you haven't thought you could run

this editorial department better than I do at times."

"A lot of times."

"Here's your chance."

"Bailey would never stand for my assigning myself all the best stuff."

"Make that a condition of your acceptance. If he doesn't like it, it's his decision, not yours."

For the first time, Buck allowed a sliver of light to enter his head about the possibility of taking the executive editor job. "I still can't believe you'd leave to become a press secretary, Steve. Even for Nicolae Carpathia."

"Do you know what's in store for him, Buck?"

"A little."

"There's a sea of power and influence and money behind him that will propel him to world prominence so quick it'll make everyone's head spin."

"Listen to yourself. You're supposed to be a journalist."

"I hear myself, Buck. I wouldn't feel this way about anybody else. No U.S. president could turn my head like this, no U.N. secretary-general."

"You think he'll be bigger than that."

"The world is ready for Carpathia, Buck. You were there Monday. You saw it. You heard it. Have you ever met anyone like him?"

"No."

"You never will again, either. If you ask me, Romania is too small for him. Europe is too small for him. The U.N. is too small for him."

"What's he gonna be, Steve, king of the world?"

Steve laughed. "That won't be the title, but don't put it past him. The best part is, he's not even aware of his own presence. He doesn't seek these roles. They are thrust upon him because of his intellect, his power, his passion."

"You know, of course, that Stonagal is behind him."

"Of course. But he'll soon supersede Stonagal in influence because of his charisma. Stonagal can't be too visible, and so he will never have the masses behind him. When Nicolae comes to power, he'll in essence have jurisdiction over Stonagal."

"Wouldn't that be something?"

"I say it'll happen sooner than any of us can imagine, Buck."

"Except you, of course."

"That's exactly how I feel. You know I've always had good instincts. I'm sure I'm sitting on one of the greatest rises to power of anyone in history. Maybe *the* greatest. And I'll be right there helping it happen."

"What do you think of *my* instincts, Steve?"

Steve pressed his lips together. "Other than

your writing and reporting, your instincts are the things I most envy."

"Then rest easy. My gut feeling is the same as yours. And except that I could never be anybody's press secretary, I almost envy you. You *are* uniquely positioned to enjoy the ride of your life."

Steve smiled. "We'll keep in touch. You'll always have access, to me and to Nicolae."

"I can't ask for more than that."

Marge interrupted on the intercom without signaling first. "Hit your TV, Steve, or whoever's TV it is now."

Steve smiled at Buck and switched it on. CNN was broadcasting live from Jerusalem, where two men had tried to attack the preachers at the Wailing Wall. Dan Bennett was on the scene for CNN.

"It was an ugly and dangerous confrontation for what many here are calling the two heretical prophets, known only as Moishe and Eli," Bennett said. "We know these names only because they have referred to each other thus, but we have been unable to locate anyone who knows any more about them. We know of no last names, no cities of origin, no families or friends. They have been taking turns speaking—preaching, if you will—for hours and continuing to claim that Jesus Christ is the Messiah. They have

proclaimed over and over that the great worldwide disappearances last week, including many
here in Israel, evidenced Christ's rapture of his
church.

"A heckler asked why they had not disappeared, if they knew so much. The one called
Moishe answered, and I quote, 'Where we come
from and where we go, you cannot know.' His
companion, Eli, was quoted, 'In my Father's
house are many mansions,' apparently a New
Testament quotation attributed to Christ."

Steve and Buck exchanged glances.

"Surrounded by zealots most of the day, the
preachers were finally attacked just moments
ago by two men in their midtwenties. Watch the
tape as our cameras caught the action. You can
see the two at the back of the crowd, working
their way to the front. Both are wearing long,
hooded robes and are bearded. You can see that
they produce weapons as they emerge from the
crowd.

"One has an Uzi automatic weapon and the
other a bayonet-type knife that appears to have
come from an Israeli-issue military rifle. The one
wielding the knife surges forward first, displaying
his weapon to Moishe, who had been speaking.
Eli, behind him, immediately falls to his knees,
his face toward the sky. Moishe stops speaking
and merely looks at the man, who appears to

trip. He sprawls while the man with the Uzi points the weapon at the preachers and appears to pull the trigger.

"There is no sound of gunfire as the Uzi apparently jams, and the attacker seems to trip over his partner and both wind up on the ground. The group of onlookers has backed away and run for cover, but watch again closely as we rerun this. The one with the gun seems to fall of his own accord.

"As we speak, both attackers lie at the feet of the preachers, who continue to preach. Angry onlookers demand help for the attackers, and Moishe is speaking in Hebrew. Let's listen and we'll translate as we go.

"He's saying, 'Men of Zion, pick up your dead! Remove from before us these jackals who have no power over us!'

"A few from the crowd approach tentatively while Israeli soldiers gather at the entrance to the Wall. The zealots are waving them off. Eli is speaking.

"'You who aid the fallen are not in danger unless you come against the anointed ones of the Most High,' apparently referring to himself and his partner. The fallen attackers are being rolled onto their backs, and those attending them are weeping and shouting and backing away. 'Dead! Both dead!' they are saying, and now the crowd seems to want the soldiers to enter. They are clearing the way. The soldiers are, of course, heavily armed. Whether they will try to arrest the strangers, we don't know, but from what we saw, the two preachers neither attacked nor defended themselves against the men now on the ground.

"Moishe is speaking again: 'Carry off your dead, but do not come nigh to us, says the Lord God of Hosts!' This he has said with such volume and authority that the soldiers quickly have checked pulses and carried off the men. We will report any word we receive on the two who attempted to attack the preachers here at the Wailing Wall in Jerusalem. At this moment, the preachers have continued their shouting, proclaiming, 'Jesus of Nazareth, born in Bethlehem, King of the Jews, the chosen one, ruler of all nations.'

"In Israel, Dan Bennett for CNN."

Marge and a few others on the staff had drifted into Steve's office during the telecast. "If that doesn't beat all," one said. "What a couple of kooks."

"Which two?" Buck said. "You can't say the preachers, whoever they are, didn't warn 'em."

"What's going on over there?" someone else asked.

"All I know," Buck said, "is that things happen there that no one can explain."

Steve raised his eyebrows. "If you believe in the Virgin Birth, that's been true for centuries."

Buck rose. "I've got to get to JFK," he said.

"What are you gonna do about the job?"

"I've got twenty-four hours, remember?"

"Don't use them all. Answer too quick, you look eager; too slow, you look indecisive."

Buck knew Steve was right. He was going to have to accept the promotion just to protect himself from other pretenders. He didn't want to be obsessed with it all day. Buck was glad for the diversion of seeing Hattie Durham. His only question now was whether he would recognize her. They had met under most traumatic circumstances.

Rayford and Chloe arrived in New York just after noon on Wednesday and went directly to the Pan-Con Club to wait for Hattie Durham. "I'm guessing she won't show," Chloe said.

"Why?"

"Because I wouldn't if I were her."

"You're not her, thank God."

"Oh, don't put her down, Dad. What makes you any better?"

Rayford felt awful. Chloe was right. Why should he think less of Hattie just because she seemed dim at times? That hadn't bothered him when he had seen her only as a physical diversion. And now, just because she had been nasty with him on the phone and never acknowledged his last invitation to meet today, he had categorized her as less desirable or less deserving.

"I *am* no better," he conceded. "But why wouldn't you show up if you were her?"

"Because I'd have an idea of what you'd have in mind. You're going to tell her you no longer have feelings for her, but that now you care about her eternal soul."

"You make that sound cheap."

"Why should it impress her that you care about her soul when she thinks you used to be interested in her as a person?"

"That's just it, Chloe. I wasn't ever interested in her as a person."

"She doesn't know that. Because you were so circumspect and so careful, she thought you were better than most men, who would just come right out and hit on her. I'm sure she feels bad about Mom, and she probably understands that you're not in any state of mind to start a new relationship. But it can't make her day to be sent away like it was just as much her fault."

"It *was,* though."

"No, it wasn't, Dad. She was available. You

shouldn't have been, but you were giving signals like you were. In this day and age, that made you fair game."

He shook his head. "Maybe that was why I was never good at that game."

"I'm glad, for Mom's sake, that you weren't."

"So, you think I shouldn't what, let her down easy or tell her about God?"

"You've already let her down, Daddy. She guessed what you were going to say and you confirmed it. That's why I say she won't come. She's still hurt. Probably mad."

"Oh, she was mad, all right."

"Then what makes you think she's going to be receptive to your heaven pitch?"

"It's not a pitch! Anyway, doesn't it prove I care about her in a genuine way now?"

Chloe went and got a soft drink. When she returned and sat next to her father, she put a hand on his shoulder. "I don't want to sound like a know-it-all," she said. "I know you're more than twice my age, but let me give you an idea how a woman thinks, especially someone like Hattie. OK?"

"I'm all ears."

"Does she have any religious background?"

"I don't think so."

"You never asked? She never said?"

"Neither of us ever gave it much thought."

"You never complained to her about Mom's obsession, like you sometimes did with me?"

"Come to think of it, I did. Of course, I was trying to use that to prove that your mother and I were not communicating."

"But Hattie didn't say anything about her own thoughts about God?"

Rayford tried to remember. "You know, I think she did say something supportive, or maybe sympathetic, about your mom."

"That makes sense. Even if she had wanted to come between you, she might have wanted to be sure you were the one putting the wedge between yourself and Mom, not her."

"I'm not following."

"That's not my point anyway. What I'm getting at is that you can't expect someone who is not even a church person to give a rip about heaven and God and all that. I'm having trouble dealing with it, and I love you and know it's become the most important thing in your life. You can't assume she has any interest, especially if it comes to her as a sort of a consolation prize."

"For?"

"For losing your attention."

"But my attention is purer now, more genuine!"

"To you, maybe. To her this is going to be much less attractive than the possibility of having someone who might love her and be there for her."

"That's what God will do for her."

"Which sounds real good to you. I'm just telling you, Dad, it's not going to be something she wants to hear right now."

"So, what if she does show up? Should I not talk to her about it?"

"I don't know. If she shows, that might mean she's still hoping there's a chance with you. Is there?"

"No!"

"Then you owe it to her to make that clear. But don't be so emphatic, and don't choose that time to try to sell her on—"

"Stop talking about my faith as something I'm trying to sell or pitch."

"Sorry. I'm just trying to reflect how it's going to sound to her."

Rayford had no idea what to say or do about Hattie now. He feared his daughter was right, and that gave him a glimpse of where her mind was, too. Bruce Barnes had told him that most people are blind and deaf to the truth until they find it; then it makes all the sense in the world. How could he argue? That's what had happened to him.

Hattie had rushed up to Buck when he arrived at the club around eleven. His anticipation of any possibilities dissipated when the first thing out of her mouth was, "So, am I gonna get to meet Nicolae Carpathia?"

When Buck had originally promised to try to introduce her to Nicolae, he hadn't thought it through. Now, after hearing Steve rhapsodize about the prominence of Carpathia, he felt trivial calling to ask if he could introduce a friend, a fan. He called Dr. Rosenzweig. "Doc, I feel kinda stupid about this, and maybe you should just say no, that he's too busy. I know he's got a lot on his plate and this girl is no one he needs to meet."

"It's a girl?"

"Well, a young woman. She's a flight attendant."

"You want him to meet a flight attendant?"

Buck didn't know what to say. That reaction was exactly what he had feared. When he hesitated, he heard Rosenzweig cover the phone and call out for Carpathia. "Doc, no! Don't ask him!"

But he did. Rosenzweig came back on and said, "Nicolae says that any friend of yours is a friend of his. He has a few moments, but only a few moments, right now."

Buck and Hattie rushed to the Plaza in a cab. Buck realized immediately how awkward he felt and how much worse he was about to feel. Whatever reputation he enjoyed with Rosenzweig and Carpathia as an international journalist would forever be marred. He would be known as the hanger-on who dragged a groupie up to shake hands with Nicolae.

Buck couldn't hide his discomfort, and on the elevator he blurted, "He really has only a second, so we shouldn't stay long."

Hattie stared at him. "I know how to treat VIPs, you know," she said. "I often serve them on flights."

"Of course you do."

"I mean, if you're embarrassed by me or—"

"It's not that at all, Hattie."

"If you think I won't know how to act—"

"I'm sorry. I'm just thinking of his schedule."

"Well, right now we're on his schedule, aren't we?"

He sighed. "I guess we are."

Why, oh, why, do I get myself into these things?

In the hallway Hattie stopped by a mirror and checked her face. A bodyguard opened the door, nodded at Buck, and looked Hattie over from head to toe. She ignored him, craning her neck to find Carpathia. Dr. Rosenzweig emerged from the parlor. "Cameron," he said, "a moment please."

Buck excused himself from Hattie, who looked none too pleased. Rosenzweig pulled him aside and whispered, "He wonders if you could join him alone first?"

Here it comes, Buck thought, flashing Hattie an apologetic look and holding up a finger to indicate he would not be long. *Carpathia's gonna have my neck for wasting his time.*

He found Nicolae standing a few feet in front of the TV, watching CNN. His arms were crossed, his chin in his hand. He glanced Buck's way and waved him in. Buck shut the door behind him, feeling as if he had been sent to the principal's office. But Nicolae did not mention Hattie.

"Have you seen this business in Jerusalem?" he said. Buck said he had. "Strangest thing I have ever seen."

"Not me," Buck said.

"No?"

"I was in Tel Aviv when Russia attacked."

Carpathia kept his eyes on the screen as CNN played over and over the attack on the preachers and the collapsing of the would-be assassins. "Yes," he mumbled. "That would have been something akin to this. Something unexplainable. Heart attacks, they say."

"Pardon?"

"The attackers are dead of heart attacks."

"I hadn't heard that."

"Yes. And the Uzi did not jam. It is in perfect working order."

Nicolae seemed transfixed by the images. He continued to watch as he talked. "I wondered what you thought of my choice for press secretary."

"I was stunned."

"I thought you might be. Look at this. The preachers never touched either of them. What are the odds? Were they scared to death, was that it?"

The question was rhetorical. Buck didn't answer.

"Hm, hm, hm," Carpathia exclaimed, the least articulate Buck had ever heard him. "Strange indeed. There is no question Plank can do the job though, do you agree?"

"Of course. I hope you know you've crippled the *Weekly*."

"Ah! I have strengthened it. What better way to have the person I want at the top?"

Buck shuddered, relieved when Carpathia looked away from the TV at last. "This makes me feel just like Jonathan Stonagal, maneuvering people into positions." He laughed, and Buck was pleased to see that he was kidding.

"Did you hear what happened to Eric Miller?" Buck asked.

"Your friend from *Seaboard Monthly?* No. What?"

"Drowned last night."

Carpathia looked shocked. "You do not say! Dreadful!"

"Listen, Mr. Carpathia—"

"Buck, please! Call me Nicolae."

"I'm not sure I'll be comfortable doing that. I just wanted to apologize for bringing this girl up to meet you. She's just a flight attendant, and—"

"Nobody is just anything," he said, taking Buck's arm. "Everyone is of equal value, regardless of their station."

Carpathia led Buck to the door, insisting he be introduced. Hattie was appropriate and reserved, though she giggled when Carpathia kissed her on each cheek. He asked her about herself, her family, her job. Buck wondered if he had ever taken a Carnegie course on how to win friends and influence people.

"Cameron," Dr. Rosenzweig whispered. "Telephone."

Buck took it in the other room. It was Marge. "I hoped you'd be there," she said. "You just got a call from Carolyn Miller, Eric's wife. She's pretty shook up and really wants to talk to you."

"I can't call her from here, Marge."

"Well, get back to her as soon as you get a minute."

"What's it about?"

"I have no idea, but she sounded desperate. Here's her number."

When Buck reemerged, Carpathia was shaking hands with Hattie and then kissed her hand. "I am charmed," he said. "Thank you, Mr. Williams. And Miss Durham, it shall be my pleasure should our paths cross again."

Buck ushered her out and found her nearly overcome. "Some guy, huh?" he said.

"He gave me his number!" she said, nearly squealing.

"His number?"

Hattie showed Buck the business card Nicolae had handed her. It showed his title as president of the Republic of Romania, but his address was not Bucharest as one would expect. It was the Plaza Hotel, his suite number, phone number, and all. Buck was speechless. Carpathia had penciled in another phone number, not at the Plaza, but also in New York. Buck memorized it.

"We can eat at the Pan-Con Club," Hattie said. "I don't really want to see this pilot at one, but I think I will, just to brag about meeting Nicolae."

"Oh, now it's Nicolae, is it?" Buck managed, still shaken by Carpathia's business card. "Trying to make someone jealous?"

"Something like that," she said.

"Would you excuse me a second?" he said. "I need to make a call before we head back."

Hattie waited in the lobby while Buck ducked around the corner and dialed Carolyn Miller. She sounded horrible, as if she had been crying for hours and hadn't slept, which was no doubt true.

"Oh, Mr. Williams, I appreciate your calling."

"Of course, ma'am, and I am so sorry about your loss. I—"

"You remember that we've met?"

"I'm sorry, Mrs. Miller. Refresh me."

"On the presidential yacht two summers ago."

"Certainly! Forgive me."

"I just didn't want you to think we'd never met. Mr. Williams, my husband called me last night before heading for the ferry. He said he was tracking a big story at the Plaza and had run into you."

"True."

"He told me a crazy story about how you two had a wrestling match or something over an interview with this Romanian guy who spoke at—"

"Also true. It wasn't anything serious, ma'am. Just a disagreement. No hard feelings."

"That's how I took it. But that was the last conversation I'll ever have with him, and it's driving me crazy. Do you know how cold it was last night?"

"Nippy, as I recall," Buck said, puzzled at her abrupt change of subject.

"Cold, sir. Too cold to be standing outside on the ferry, wouldn't you say?"

"Yes, ma'am."

"And even if he was, he's a good swimmer. He was a champion in high school."

"All due respect, ma'am, but that had to be—what, thirty years ago?"

"But he's still a strong swimmer. Trust me. I know."

"What are you saying, Mrs. Miller?"

"I don't know!" she shouted, crying. "I just wondered if you could shed any light. I mean, he fell off the ferry and drowned? It doesn't make any sense!"

"It doesn't to me either, ma'am, and I wish I could help. But I can't."

"I know," she said. "I was just hoping."

"Ma'am, is someone with you, watching out for you?"

"Yes, I'm OK. I have family here."

"I'll be thinking of you."

"Thank you."

Buck could see Hattie in a reflection. She seemed patient enough. He called a friend at the telephone company. "Alex! Do me a favor. Can you still tell me who's listed if I give you a number?"

"Long as you don't tell anybody I'm doin' it."

"You know me, man."

"Go ahead."

Buck recited the number he had memorized

from the card Carpathia had given Hattie. Alex was back to him in seconds, reading off the information as it scrolled onto his computer screen. "New York, U.N., administrative offices, secretary-general's office, unlisted private line, bypasses switchboard, bypasses secretary. OK?"

"OK, Alex. I owe you."

Buck was lost. He couldn't make any of this compute. He jogged out to Hattie. "I'm gonna be another minute," he said. "Do you mind?"

"No. As long as we can get back by one. No telling how long that pilot will wait. He's got his daughter with him."

Buck turned back to the phones, glad he had no interest in competing with Carpathia or this pilot for Hattie Durham's affection. He called Steve. Marge answered and he was short with her. "Hey, it's me. I need Plank right away."

"Well, have a nice day yourself," she said and rang him through.

"Steve," he said quickly, "your boy just made his first mistake."

"What're you talking about, Buck?"

"Is your first job going to be announcing Carpathia as the new secretary-general?"

Silence.

"Steve? What's next?"

"You're a good reporter, Buck. The best. How did this get out?"

Buck told him about the business card.

"Whew! That doesn't sound like Nicolae. I can't imagine it was an oversight. Must have been on purpose."

"Maybe he's assuming this Durham woman is too ditzy to figure it out," Buck said, "or that she wouldn't show me. But how does he know she won't call the number too soon and ask for him there?"

"As long as she waits until tomorrow, Buck, he'll be all right."

"Tomorrow?"

"You can't use this, all right? Are we off the record?"

"Steve! Who do you think you're talking to? Are you working for Carpathia already? You're still my boss. You don't want me to run with something, you just tell me. Remember?"

"Well, I'm telling you. The Kalahari Desert makes up much of Botswana where Secretary-General Ngumo is from. He returns there tomorrow a hero, having become the first leader to gain access to the Israeli fertilizer formula."

"And how did he do that?"

"By his stellar diplomacy, of course."

"And he cannot be expected to handle the duties of both the U.N. and Botswana during this strategic moment in Botswana history, right, Steve?"

"And why should he, when someone is so perfectly suited to step right in? We were there Monday, Buck. Who's going to oppose this?"

"Don't you?"

"I think it's brilliant."

"You're going to be a perfect press secretary, Steve. And I've decided to accept your old job."

"Good for you! Now you'll sit on this till tomorrow, you got it?"

"Promise. But will you tell me one more thing?"

"If I can, Buck."

"What did Eric Miller get too close to? What lead was he tracking?"

Steve's voice became hollow, his tone flat. "All I know about Eric Miller," he said, "is that he got too close to the railing on the Staten Island Ferry."

NINETEEN

RAYFORD watched Chloe as she wandered around the Pan-Con Club, then stared out the window. He felt like a wimp. For days he had told himself not to push, not to badger her. He knew her. She was like him. She would run the other way if he pushed too hard. She had even talked him into backing off of Hattie Durham, should Hattie show up.

What was the matter with him? Nothing was as it was before or would ever be again. If Bruce Barnes was right, the disappearance of God's people was only the beginning of the most cataclysmic period in the history of the world. *And here I am,* Rayford thought, *worried about offending people. I'm liable to "not offend" my own daughter right into hell.*

Rayford also felt bad about his approach to Hattie. He had dealt with his own wrong in having pursued her, and he regretted having led her on. But he could no longer treat her with kid gloves, either. What scared him most was that it seemed, from what Bruce was teaching, that many people would be deceived during these days. Whoever came forward with proclamations of peace and unity had to be suspect. There would be no peace. There would be no unity. This was the beginning of the end, and all would be chaos from now on.

The chaos would make peacemakers and smooth talkers only more attractive. And to people who didn't want to admit that God had been behind the disappearances, any other explanation would salve their consciences. There was no more time for polite conversation, for gentle persuasion. Rayford had to direct people to the Bible, to the prophetic portions. He felt so limited in his understanding. He had always been an erudite reader, but this stuff from Revelation and Daniel and Ezekiel was new and strange to him. Frighteningly, it made sense. He had begun taking Irene's Bible with him everywhere he went, reading it whenever possible. While the first officer read magazines during his downtime, Rayford would pull out the Bible.

"What in the world?" he was asked more than once.

Unashamed, he said he was finding answers and direction he had never seen before. But with his own daughter and his friend? He had been too polite.

Rayford looked at his watch. Still a few minutes before one o'clock. He caught Chloe's eye and signaled that he was going to make a phone call. He dialed Bruce Barnes and told him what he had been thinking.

"You're right, Rayford. I went through a few days of that, worried what people would think of me, not wanting to turn anybody off. It just doesn't make sense anymore, does it?"

"No, it doesn't. Bruce, I need support. I'm going to start becoming obnoxious, I'm afraid. If Chloe wants to laugh or run the other way, I'm going to force her to make a decision. She'll have to know exactly what she's doing. She'll have to face what we've found in the Bible and deal with it. I mean, the two preachers in Israel alone are enough to give me the confidence that things are happening exactly the way the Bible said they would."

"Have you been watching this morning?"

"From a distance here in the terminal. They keep rerunning the attack."

"Rayford, get to a TV right now."

"What?"

"I'm hanging up, Ray. See what happened to

the attackers and see if that doesn't confirm everything we read about the two witnesses."

"Bruce—"

"Go, Rayford. And start witnessing yourself, with total confidence."

Bruce hung up on him. Rayford knew him well enough, despite their brief relationship, to be more intrigued than offended. He hurried to a TV monitor where he was stunned to hear the report of the deaths of the attackers. He dug out Irene's Bible and read the passage from Revelation Bruce had spoken from. The men in Jerusalem were the two witnesses, preaching Christ. They had been attacked, and they didn't even have to respond. The attackers had fallen dead and no harm had been done to the witnesses.

Now, on CNN, Rayford watched as crowds surged into the area in front of the Wailing Wall to listen to the witnesses. People knelt, weeping, some with their faces on the ground. These were people who had felt the preachers were desecrating the holy place. Now it appeared they were believing what the witnesses said. Or was it merely fear?

Rayford knew better. He knew that the first of the 144,000 Jewish evangelists were being converted to Christ before his eyes. Without taking his gaze from the screen, he prayed silently, *God, fill me with courage, with power, with whatever I need to be a witness. I don't want to be afraid anymore. I don't want to wait any longer. I don't want to worry about offending. Give me a persuasiveness rooted in the truth of your Word. I know it is your Spirit that draws people, but use me. I want to reach Chloe. I want to reach Hattie. Please, Lord. Help me.*

Buck Williams felt naked without his equipment bag. He would feel ready to work only when he had his cellular phone, his tape recorder, and his new laptop. He asked the cabbie to stop by the *Global Weekly* office so he could pick up the bag. Hattie waited in the cab, but she told him she was not going to be happy if she missed her appointment. Buck stood by the window of the cab. "I'll just be a minute," he said. "I thought you weren't sure whether you wanted to see this guy."

"Well, now I do, OK? Call it revenge or rubbing it in or whatever you want, but it's not often you get to tell a captain you've met someone he hasn't."

"You talking about Nicolae Carpathia or me?"

"Very funny. Anyway, he has met you."

"This is the captain from that flight where you and I met?"

"Yes—now hurry!"

"I might want to meet him."

"Go!"

Buck called Marge from the lobby. "Could you meet me at the elevator with my equipment bag? I've got a cab waiting here."

"I would," she said, "but both Steve and the old man are asking for you."

What now? he wondered. Buck checked his watch, wishing the elevator was faster. Such was life in the skyscrapers.

He grabbed his bag from Marge, breezed into Steve's office, and said, "What's up? I'm on the run."

"Boss wants to see us."

"What's it about?" Buck said as they headed down the hall.

"Eric Miller, I think. Maybe more. You know Bailey wasn't thrilled at my short notice. He only agreed to it thinking that you'd jump at the promotion, because you know where every-thing is and what's planned for the next couple of weeks."

In Bailey's office the boss got right to the point. "I'm gonna ask you two some pointed questions, and I want some quick and straight answers. A whole bunch of stuff is coming down right now, and we're gonna be on top of every bit of it. First off, Plank, rumors are flying that Mwangati Ngumo is calling a press conference for late this afternoon, and everybody thinks he's stepping down as secretary-general."

"Really?" Plank said.

"Don't play dumb with me," Bailey growled. "It doesn't take a genius to figure what's happening here. If he's stepping down, your guy knows about it. You forget I was in charge of the African bureau when Botswana became an associate member of the European Common Market. Jonathan Stonagal had his fingers all over that, and everybody knows he's one of this Carpathia guy's angels. What's the connection?"

Buck saw Steve pale. Bailey knew more than either of them expected. For the first time in years, Steve sounded nervous, almost panicky. "I'll tell you what I know," he said, but Buck guessed there was more he didn't say. "My first assignment tomorrow morning is to deny Carpathia's interest in the job. He's going to say he has too many revolutionary ideas and that he would insist on almost unanimous approval on the parts of the current members. They would have to agree to his ideas for reorganization, a change of emphasis, and a few other things."

"Like what?"

"I'm not at liberty to—"

Bailey rose, his face red. "Let me tell you something, Plank. I like you. You've been a superstar for me. I sold you to the rest of the brass when nobody else recognized you had what it takes. You sold me on this punk here, and he's made us all look good. But I paid you six figures long before you deserved it because I knew someday it would pay off. And it did. Now, I'm telling you that nothing you say here is gonna go past these walls, so I don't want you holdin' out on me.

"You brats think that because I'm two or three years from the pasture, I don't still have contacts, don't have my ear to the ground. Well, let me tell you, my phone's been ringing off the hook since you left here this morning, and I've got a gut feeling something big is coming down. Now what is it?"

"Who's been calling you, sir?" Plank said.

"Well, first off, I get a call from a guy who knows the vice president of Romania. Word over there is the guy has been asked to be prepared to run the day-to-day stuff indefinitely. He's not going to become the new president because they just got one, but that tells me Carpathia expects to be here awhile.

"Then, people I know in Africa tell me Ngumo has some inside track on the Israeli formula but that he's quietly not happy about the deal requiring him to step down from the U.N. He's going to do it, but there's going to be trouble if everything doesn't go as promised.

"Then, of all things, I get a call from the

publisher at *Seaboard Monthly* wanting to talk
to me about how you, Cameron, and his guy that
drowned last night were working the same angle
on Carpathia, and whether I think you're going
to mysteriously get dead, too. I told him that as
far as I knew, you were working on a general
cover story about the guy and that we were going
to be positive. He said his guy had intended to
take a slightly different approach—you know,
zig when everybody else is zagging. Miller was
doing a story on the meaning behind the disappearances, which I know you were planning for
an issue or two from now. How that ties in with
Carpathia, and why it might paint him in a dark
light, I don't know. Do you?"

Buck shook his head. "I see them as two totally
different pieces. I asked Carpathia what he made
of what happened, and everybody has heard that
answer. I didn't know that's what Miller was
working on, and I sure wouldn't have thought
he would somehow link Carpathia with the
disappearances."

Bailey sat back down. "To tell you the truth,
when I first took the call from the guy at *Seaboard,* I thought he was calling for a reference
on you, Cameron. I was thinking, if I lose both
these turkeys the same week, I'm taking early
retirement. Can we get that stuff out of the way,
before I make Plank tell me what else he knows?"

"What stuff?" Buck said.

"You looking to leave?"

"I'm not."

"You taking the promotion?"

"I am."

"Good! Now, Steve. What else is Carpathia gonna push for before he accepts the U.N. job?" Plank hesitated and looked as if he were considering whether he should tell what he knew. "I'm telling you, you owe me," Bailey said. "Now I don't intend to use this. I just want to know. Cameron and I have to decide which story we're going to push first. I want to get him onto the one that interests me most, the one about what was behind the disappearances. Sometimes I think we get too snooty as a newsmagazine and we forget that everyday people out there are scared to death, wanting to make some sense of all this. Now, Steve, you can trust me. I already told you I won't tell anyone or compromise you. Just run it down for me. What does Carpathia want, and is he going to take this job?"

Steve pursed his lips and began reluctantly. "He wants a new Security Council setup, which will include some of his own ideas for ambassadors."

"Like Todd-Cothran from England?" Buck said.

"Probably temporarily. He's not entirely pleased with that relationship, as you may know."

Buck suddenly realized that Steve knew everything.

"And?" Bailey pressed.

"He wants Ngumo personally to insist on him as his replacement, a large majority vote of the representatives, and two other things that, frankly, I don't think he'll get. Militarily, he wants a commitment to disarmament from member nations, the destruction of ninety percent of their weapons, and the donation of the other ten percent to the U.N."

"For peacekeeping purposes," Bailey said. "Naive, but logical sounding. You're right, he probably won't get that. What else?"

"Probably the most controversial and least likely. The logistics alone are incredible, the cost, the . . . everything."

"What?"

"He wants to move the U.N."

"Move it?"

Steve nodded.

"Where?"

"It sounds stupid."

"Everything sounds stupid these days," Bailey said.

"He wants to move it to Babylon."

"You're not serious."

"*He* is."

"I hear they've been renovating that city for

years. Millions of dollars invested in making it, what, New Babylon?"

"Billions."

"Think anyone will agree to that?"

"Depends how bad they want him." Steve chuckled. "He's on *The Tonight Show* tonight."

"He'll be more popular than ever!"

"He's meeting right now with the heads of all these international groups that are in town for unity meetings."

"What does he want with them?"

"We're still confidential here, right?" Steve asked.

"Of course."

"He's asking for resolutions supporting some of the things he wants to do. The seven-year peace treaty with Israel, in exchange for his ability to broker the desert-fertilizer formula. The move to New Babylon. The establishment of one religion for the world, probably head-quartered in Italy."

"He's not going to get far with the Jews on that one."

"They're an exception. He's going to help them rebuild their temple during the years of the peace treaty. He believes they deserve special treat-ment."

"And they do," Bailey said. "The man is bril-liant. Not only have I never seen someone with such revolutionary ideas, but I've also never seen anyone who moves so quickly."

"Aren't either of you the least bit shaky about this guy?" Buck said. "It looks to me like people who get too close wind up eliminated."

"Shaky?" Bailey said. "Well, I think he's a little naive, and I'll be very surprised if he gets everything he's asking for. But then he's a politician. He won't couch these as ultimatums, and he can still accept the position even if he doesn't get them. It sounds like he may have run roughshod over Ngumo, but I think he had Botswana's best interest in mind. Carpathia will be a better U.N. chief. And he's right. If what happened in Israel happens in Botswana, Ngumo needs to stay close to home and manage the prosperity. Shaky? No. I'm as impressed with the guy as you two are. He's what we need right now. Nothing wrong with unity and togetherness at a time of crisis."

"What about Eric Miller?"

"I think people are making too much of that. We don't know that his death wasn't just what it appeared and was only coincidental with his run-in with you and Carpathia. Anyway, Carpathia didn't know what Miller was after, did he?"

"Not that I know of," Buck said, but he noticed that Steve said nothing.

Marge buzzed in on the intercom. "Cameron has an urgent message from a Hattie Durham. Says she can't wait any longer."

"Oh, no," Buck said. "Marge, apologize all over the place for me. Tell her it was unavoidable and that I'll either call her or catch up with her later."

Bailey looked disgusted. "Is this what I can expect from you on work time, Cameron?"

"Actually, I introduced her to Carpathia this morning, and I want her to introduce me to an airline captain in town today for part of that story on what people think happened last week."

"I'll make no bones about it, Cameron," Bailey said. "Let's do the big Carpathia story next issue, then follow up with the theories behind the vanishings after that. If you ask me, that could be the most talked about story we've ever done. I thought we beat *Time* and everybody else on our coverage of the event itself. I liked your stuff, by the way. I don't know that we'll have anything terribly fresh or different about Carpathia, but we have to give it all we've got. Frankly, I love the idea of you running the point on this coverage of all the theories. You must have one of your own."

"I wish I did," Buck said. "I'm as in the dark as anybody. What I'm finding, though, is that the people who have a theory believe in it totally."

"Well, I've got mine," Bailey said. "And it's almost eerie how close it matches Carpathia's, or Rosenzweig's, or whoever. I've got relatives who believe the space alien stuff. I've got an uncle who thinks it was Jesus, but he also thinks Jesus forgot *him*. Ha! I think it was natural, some kind of a phenomenon where all our high-tech stuff interacted with the forces of nature and we really did a number on ourselves. Now come on, Cameron. Where are you on this?"

"I'm in the perfect position for my assignment," he said. "I haven't the foggiest."

"What are people saying?"

"The usual. A doctor at O'Hare told me he was sure it was the Rapture. Other people have said the same. You know our Chicago bureau chief—"

"Lucinda Washington? It's going to be your job to find a replacement for her, you know. You'll have to go there, get the lay of the land, get acquainted. But you were saying?"

"Her son believes she and the rest of the family were taken to heaven."

"So, how'd *he* get left behind?"

"I'm not sure what the deal is on that," Buck said. "Some Christians are better than others or something. That's one thing I'm going to find out before I finish this piece. This flight attendant who just called, I'm not sure what she thinks, but she said the captain she's meeting today thinks he has an idea."

"An airline captain," Bailey repeated. "That would be interesting. Unless his idea is the same as the other scientific types. Well, carry on. Steve, we're gonna announce this today. Good luck, and don't worry about anything you've said here finding its way into the magazine, unless we get it through other sources. We're agreed on that, aren't we, Williams?"

"Yes, sir," Buck said.

Steve didn't look so sure.

Buck ran to the elevator and called information for the number of the Pan-Con Club. He asked them to page Hattie, but when they couldn't locate her, he assumed she hadn't arrived yet or had gone out with her pilot friend. He left a message to have her call him on his cellular phone, then headed that way in a cab just in case.

His mind was whirring. He agreed with Stanton Bailey that the big story was what had been behind the disappearances, but he was also becoming suspicious of Nicolae Carpathia. Maybe he shouldn't be. Maybe he should focus on Jonathan Stonagal. Carpathia should be smart enough to see that his elevation could help Stonagal in ways that would be unfair to his competitors. But Carpathia had pledged that he would "deal with" both Stonagal and Todd-Cothran, knowing full well they were behind illegal deeds.

Did that make Carpathia innocent? Buck certainly hoped so. He had never in his life wanted to believe more in a person. In the days since the disappearances, he'd hardly had a second to think for himself. The loss of his sister-in-law and niece and nephew tugged at his heart almost constantly, and something made him wonder if there wasn't something to this Rapture thing. If anybody in his orbit would be taken to heaven, it would have been them.

But he knew better than that, didn't he? He was Ivy League educated. He had left the church when he left the claustrophobic family situation that threatened to drive him crazy as a young man. He had never considered himself religious, despite a prayer for help and deliverance once in a while. He had built his life around achievement, excitement, and—he couldn't deny it—attention. He loved the status that came with having his byline, his writing, his thinking in a national magazine. And yet there was a certain loneliness in his existence, especially now with Steve moving on. Buck had dated and had considered escalating a couple of serious relationships, but he had always been considered too mobile for a woman who wanted stability.

Since the clearly supernatural event he had witnessed in Israel with the destruction of the Russian air force, he had known the world was changing. Things would never again be as they had been. He wasn't buying the space alien theory of the disappearances, and while it very well could be attributed to some incredible cosmic energy reaction, who or what was behind that? The incident at the Wailing Wall was another unexplainable bit of the supernatural.

Buck found himself more intrigued by the "whys and wherefores" story, as he liked to think of it, than even the rise of Nicolae Carpathia. As taken as he was with the man, Buck hoped against hope that he wasn't just another slick politician. He was the best Buck had ever seen, but was it possible that Dirk's death, Alan's death, Eric's death, and Buck's predicament were totally independent of Carpathia?

He hoped so. He wanted to believe a person could come along once in a generation who could capture the imagination of the world. Could Carpathia be another Lincoln, a Roosevelt, or the embodiment of Camelot that Kennedy had appeared to some?

On impulse, as the cab crawled into the impossible traffic at JFK, Buck plugged his laptop modem into his cellular phone and brought up a news service on his screen. He quickly called up Eric Miller's major pieces for the last two years and was stunned to find he had written about the rebuilding and improvement in Babylon. The title of Miller's series was "New Babylon, Stonagal's Latest Dream." A quick scan of the article showed that the bulk of the financing came from Stonagal banks throughout the world. And of course there was a quote attributed to Stonagal: "Just coincidence. I have no idea the particulars of the financing undertaken by our various institutions."

Buck knew that the bottom line with Nicolae Carpathia would have nothing to do with Mwangati Ngumo or Israel or even the new Security Council. To Buck, the litmus test for Carpathia was what he did about Jonathan Stonagal once Carpathia was installed as secretary-general of the United Nations.

Because if the rest of the U.N. went along with Nicolae's conditions, he would become the most powerful leader in the world overnight. He would have the ability to enforce his wishes militarily if every member were disarmed and U.N. might were increased. The world would have to be desperate for a leader they trusted implicitly to agree to such an arrangement. And the only leader worth the mantle would be one with zero tolerance for a murderous, behind-the-scenes schemer like Jonathan Stonagal.

TWENTY

RAYFORD and Chloe Steele waited until one-thirty in the afternoon, then decided to head for their hotel. On their way out of the Pan-Con Club, Rayford stopped to leave a message for Hattie, in case she came in. "We just got another message for her," the girl at the counter said. "A secretary for a Cameron Williams said Mr. Williams would catch up with her here if she would call him when she got in."

"When did that message come?" Rayford asked.

"Just after one."

"Maybe we'll wait a few more minutes."

Rayford and Chloe were sitting near the entrance when Hattie rushed in. Rayford smiled at her, but she immediately seemed to slow, as if she had just happened to run into them. "Oh, hi," she said, showing her identification at the counter and taking her message. Rayford let her play her game. He deserved it.

"I really shouldn't have come to see you," she said, after being introduced to Chloe. "And now that I'm here, I should return this call. It's from the writer I told you about. He introduced me to Nicolae Carpathia this morning."

"You don't say."

Hattie nodded, smiling. "And Mr. Carpathia gave me his card. Did you know he's going to be named *People* magazine's Sexiest Man Alive?"

"I had heard that, yes. Well, I'm impressed. Quite a morning for you, wasn't it? And how is Mr. Williams?"

"Very nice, but very busy. I'd better call him. Excuse me."

Buck was on an escalator inside the terminal when his phone rang. "Well, hello yourself," Hattie said.

"I am so sorry, Miss Durham."

"Oh, please," she said. "Anybody who leaves me in midtown Manhattan in an expensive cab can call me by my first name. I insist."

"And I insist on paying for that cab."

"I'm just kidding, Buck. I'm going to meet with this captain and his daughter, so don't feel obligated to come over."

"Well, I'm already here," he said.

"Oh."

"But that's all right. I've got plenty to do. It was good to see you again, and next time you come through New York—"

"Buck, I don't want you to feel obligated to entertain me."

"I don't."

"Sure you do. You're a nice guy, but it's obvious we're not kindred spirits. Thanks for seeing me and especially for introducing me to Mr. Carpathia."

"Hattie, I could use a favor. Would it be possible to introduce me to this captain? I'd like to interview him. Is he staying overnight?"

"I'll ask him. You should meet his daughter anyway. She's a doll."

"Maybe I'll interview her, too."

"Yeah, good approach."

"Just ask him, Hattie, please."

Rayford wondered if Hattie had a date with Buck Williams that evening. The right thing to do would be to invite her to dinner at his and Chloe's hotel. Now she was waving him over to the pay phone.

"Rayford, Buck Williams wants to meet you. He's doing a story and wants to interview you."

"Really? Me?" he said. "About what?"

"I don't know. I didn't ask. I suppose about flying or the disappearances. You *were* in the air when it happened."

"Tell him sure, I'll see him. In fact, why don't you ask him to join the three of us for dinner tonight, if you're free." Hattie stared at Rayford as if she had been tricked into something. "Come on, Hattie. You and I will talk this afternoon, then we'll all get together for dinner at six at the Carlisle."

She turned back to the phone and told Buck. "Where are you now?" she asked. She paused. "You're not!" Hattie peeked around the corner, laughed, and waved. Covering the mouthpiece, she turned to Rayford. "That's him, right there on the portable phone!"

"Well, why don't you both hang up and you can make the introductions," Rayford said. Hattie and Buck hung up, and Buck tucked his phone away as he entered.

"He's with us," Rayford told the woman at the desk. He shook Buck's hand. "So you're the writer for *Global Weekly* who was on my plane."

"That's me," Buck said.

"What do you want to interview me about?"

"Your take on the disappearances. I'm doing a cover story on the theories behind what happened, and it would be good to get your perspective as a professional and as someone who was right in the middle of the turmoil when it happened."

What an opportunity! Rayford thought. "Happy to," he said. "You can join us for dinner then?"

"You bet," Buck said. "And this is your daughter?"

Buck was stunned. He loved Chloe's name, her eyes, her smile. She looked directly at him and gave a firm handshake, something he liked in a woman. So many women felt it was feminine to offer a limp hand. *What a beautiful girl!* he thought. He had been tempted to tell Captain Steele that, as of the next day, he would no longer be just a writer but would become executive editor. But he feared that would sound like bragging, not complaining, so he had said nothing.

"Look," Hattie said, "the captain and I need a few minutes, so why don't you two get acquainted and we'll all get back together later. Do you have time, Buck?"

I do now, he thought. "Sure," he said, looking at Chloe and her father. "Is that all right with you two?"

The captain seemed to hesitate, but his daughter looked at him expectantly. She was clearly old enough to make her own decisions, but apparently she didn't want to make things awkward for her dad.

"It's OK," Captain Steele said hesitantly. "We'll be in here."

"I'll stash my bag, and we'll just take a walk in the terminal," Buck said. "If you want to, Chloe."

She smiled and nodded.

It had been a long time since Buck had felt awkward and shy around a girl. As he and Chloe strolled and talked, he didn't know where to look and was self-conscious about where to put his hands. Should he keep them in his pockets or let them hang free? Let them swing? Would she rather sit down or people watch or window-shop?

He asked her about herself and where she went to college, what she was interested in. She told him about her mother and her brother, and he sympathized. Buck was impressed at how smart and articulate and mature she seemed. This was a girl he could be interested in, but she had to be at least ten years younger than he was.

She wanted to know about his life and career. He told her anything she asked but little more. Only when she asked if he had lost anybody in the vanishings did he tell her about his family in Tucson and his friends in England. Naturally,

he said nothing about the Stonagal or Todd-
Cothran connections.

When the conversation lulled, Chloe caught
him gazing at her, and he looked away. When
he looked back, she was looking at him. They
smiled shyly. *This is crazy,* he thought. He was
dying to know if she had a boyfriend, but he
wasn't about to ask.

Her questions were more along the lines of a
young person asking a veteran professional about
his career. She envied his travel and experience.
He pooh-poohed it, assuring her she would tire
of that kind of a life.

"Ever been married?" she asked.

He was glad she had asked. He was happy to
tell her no, that he had never really been serious
enough with anyone to be engaged. "How about
you?" he asked, feeling the discussion was now
fair game. "How many times have you been
married?"

She laughed. "Only had one steady. When I was
a freshman in college, he was a senior. I thought
it was love, but when he graduated, I never heard
from him again."

"Literally?"

"He went on some kind of an overseas trip,
sent me a cheap souvenir, and that was the end
of it. He's married now."

"His loss."

"Thank you."

Buck felt bolder. "What was he, blind?" She didn't respond. Buck mentally kicked himself and tried to recover. "I mean, some guys don't know what they have."

She was still silent, and he felt like an idiot. *How can I be so successful at some things and such a klutz at others?* he wondered.

She stopped in front of a gourmet bakery shop. "You feel like a cookie?" she asked.

"Why? Do I look like one?"

"How did I know that was coming?" she said. "Buy me a cookie and I'll let that groaner die a natural death."

"Of old age, you mean," he said.

"Now *that* was funny."

Rayford was as earnest, honest, and forthright with Hattie as he had ever been. They sat across from each other in overstuffed chairs in the corner of a large, noisy room where they could not be heard by anyone else.

"Hattie," he said, "I'm not here to argue with you or even to have a conversation. There are things I must tell you, and I want you just to listen."

"I don't get to say anything? Because there may be things I'll want you to know, too."

"Of course I'll let you tell me anything you want, but this first part, my part, I don't want to be a dialogue. I have to get some things off my chest, and I want you to get the whole picture before you respond, OK?"

She shrugged. "I don't see how I have a choice."

"You had a choice, Hattie. You didn't have to come."

"I didn't really want to come. I told you that and you left that guilt-trip message, begging me to meet you here."

Rayford was frustrated. "You see what I didn't want to get into?" he said. "How can I apologize when all you want to do is argue about why you're here?"

"You want to apologize, Rayford? I would never stand in the way of that."

She was being sarcastic, but he had gotten her attention. "Yes, I do. Now will you let me?" She nodded. "Because I want to get through this, to set the record straight, to take all the blame I should, and then I want to tell you what I hinted at on the phone the other night."

"About how you've discovered what the vanishings are all about."

He held up a hand. "Don't get ahead of me."

"Sorry," she said, putting her hand over her mouth. "But why don't you just let me hear it when you answer Buck's questions tonight?"

Rayford rolled his eyes. "I was just wondering," she said. "Just a suggestion so you don't have to repeat yourself."

"Thank you," he said, "but I'll tell you why. This is so important and so personal that I need to tell you privately. And I don't mind telling it over and over, and if my guess is right, you won't mind hearing it again and again."

Hattie raised her eyebrows as if to say she would be surprised, but she said, "You have the floor. I won't interrupt again."

Rayford leaned forward and rested his elbows on his knees, gesturing as he spoke. "Hattie, I owe you a huge apology, and I want your forgiveness. We were friends. We enjoyed each other's company. I loved being with you and spending time with you. I found you beautiful and exciting, and I think you know I was interested in a relationship with you."

She looked surprised, but Rayford assumed that, had it not been for her pledge of silence, she would have told him he had a pretty laid-back way of showing interest. He continued.

"Probably the only reason I never pursued anything further with you was because I didn't have any experience in such things. But it was only a matter of time. If I had found you willing, I'd have eventually done something wrong."

She furrowed her brow and looked offended.

"Yes," he said, "it would have been wrong. I was married, not happily and not success- fully, but that was my fault. Still, I had made a vow, a commitment, and no matter how I justified my interest in you, it would have been wrong."

He could tell from her look that she disagreed. "Anyway, I led you on. I wasn't totally honest. But now I have to tell you how grateful I am that I didn't do something—well, stupid. It would not have been right for you either. I know I'm not your judge and jury, and your morals are your own decision. But there would have been no future for us.

"It isn't just that we're so far apart in age, but the fact is that the only real interest I had in you was physical. You have a right to hate me for that, and I'm not proud of it. I did not love you. You have to agree, that would have been no kind of a life for you."

She nodded, appearing to cloud up. He smiled. "I'll let you break your silence temporarily," he said. "I need to know that you at least forgive me."

"Sometimes I wonder if honesty is always the best policy," she said. "I might have been able to accept this if you had just said your wife's disap- pearance made you feel guilty about what we had going. I know we didn't really have anything going yet, but that would have been a kinder way to put it."

"Kinder but dishonest. Hattie, I'm through being dishonest. Everything in me would rather be kind and gentle and keep you from resenting me, but I just can't be phony anymore. I was not genuine for years."

"And now you are?"

"To the point where it's unattractive to you," he said. She nodded again. "Why would I want to do that? Everybody likes to be liked. I could have blamed this on something else, on my wife, whatever. But I want to be able to live with myself. I want to be able to convince you, when I talk about even more important things, that I have no ulterior motives."

Hattie's lips quivered. She pressed them together and looked down, a tear rolling down her cheek. It was all Rayford could do to keep from embracing her. There would be nothing sensual about it, but he couldn't afford to give a wrong signal. "Hattie," he said. "I'm so sorry. Forgive me."

She nodded, unable to speak. She tried to say something but couldn't regain her composure.

"Now, after all that," Rayford said, "I some-how have to convince you that I do care for you as a friend and as a person."

Hattie held up both hands, fighting not to cry.

She shook her head, as if not ready for this. "Don't," she managed. "Not right now."

"Hattie, I've got to."

"Please, give me a minute."

"Take your time, but don't run from me now," he said. "I would be no friend if I didn't tell you what I've found, what I've learned, what I'm discovering more of each day."

Hattie buried her face in her hands and cried. "I wasn't going to do this," she said. "I wasn't going to give you the satisfaction."

Rayford spoke as tenderly as he could. "Now you're going to offend *me,*" he said. "If you take nothing else from this conversation, you must know that your tears give me no satisfaction. Every one of them is a dagger to me. I'm responsible. I was wrong."

"Give me a minute," she said, hurrying off.

Rayford dug out Irene's Bible and quickly scanned some passages. He had decided not to sit talking to Hattie with the Bible open. He didn't want to embarrass or intimidate her, despite his newfound courage and determination.

"You're gonna find my dad's theory of the disappearings very interesting," Chloe said.

"Am I?" Buck said. She nodded and he noticed a dab of chocolate at the corner of her mouth.

He said, "May I?" extending his hand. She raised her chin and he transferred the chocolate to his thumb. Now what should he do? Wipe it on a napkin? Impulsively he put his thumb to his lips.

"Gross!" she said. "How embarrassing! What if I have the creeping crud or something?"

"Then now we've both got it," he said, and they laughed. Buck realized he was blushing, something he hadn't done for years, and so he changed the subject. "You say your dad's theory, as if maybe it's not yours, too. Do you two disagree?"

"He thinks we do, because I argue with him and give him a hard time about it. I just don't want to be too easy to convince, but if I had to be honest, I'd have to say we're pretty close. See, he thinks that—"

Buck held up a hand. "Oh, I'm sorry, don't tell me. I want to get it fresh from him, on tape."

"Oh. Excuse me."

"No, it's OK. I didn't mean to embarrass you, but that's just how I like to work. I'd love to hear your theory, too. We're going to get some college kids' ideas, but it would be unlikely we would use two people from the same family. Of course, you just told me that you pretty much agree with your father, so I'd better wait and hear them both at the same time."

She had fallen silent and looked serious. "I'm sorry, Chloe, I didn't mean to imply I'm not interested in *your* theory."

"It's not that," she said. "But you just kind of categorized me there."

"Categorized you?"

"As a college kid."

"Ooh, I did, didn't I? My fault. I know better. Collegians aren't kids. I don't see you as a kid, although you are a lot younger than I am."

"Collegians? I haven't heard that term in a while."

"I *am* showing my age, aren't I?"

"How old *are* you, Buck?"

"Thirty and a half, going on thirty-one," he said with a twinkle.

"I say, how old are you?" she shouted, as if talking to a deaf old man. Buck roared.

"I'd buy you another cookie, little girl, but I don't want to spoil your appetite."

"You'd better not. My dad loves good food, and he's buying tonight. Save room."

"I will, Chloe."

"Can I tell you something, without you thinking I'm weird?" she said.

"Too late," he said.

She frowned and punched him. "I was just going to say that I like the way you say my name."

"I didn't know there was any other way to say it," he said.

"Oh, there is. Even my friends slip into making it one syllable, like Cloy."

"Chloe," he repeated.

"Yeah," she said. "Like that. Two syllables, long *O*, long *E*."

"I like your name." He slipped into an old man's husky voice. "It's a young person's name. How old are you, kid?"

"Twenty and a half, going on twenty-one."

"Oh, my goodness," he said, still in character, "I'm consortin' with a minor!"

As they headed back toward the Pan-Con Club, Chloe said, "If you promise not to make a big deal of my youth, I won't make a big deal of your age."

"Deal," he said, a smile playing at his lips. "You play a lot older."

"I'll take that as a compliment," she said, smiling self-consciously as if she wasn't sure he was serious.

"Oh, do," he said. "Few people your age are as well-read and articulate as you are."

"That was definitely a compliment," she said.

"You catch on quick."

"Did you really interview Nicolae Carpathia?" He nodded. "We're almost buddies."

"No kidding?"

"Well, not really. But we hit it off."

"Tell me about him."

And so Buck did.

Hattie returned slightly refreshed but still puffy eyed and sat again as if ready for more punishment. Rayford reiterated that he was sincere about his apology, and she said, "Let's just put that behind us, shall we?"

"I need to know you forgive me," he said.

"You seem really hung up on that, Rayford. Would that let you off the hook, ease your conscience?"

"I guess maybe it would," he said. "Mostly it would tell me you believe I'm sincere."

"I believe it," she said. "It doesn't make it any more pleasant or easier to take, but if it makes you feel better, I do believe you mean it. And I don't hold grudges, so I guess that's forgiveness."

"I'll take what I can get," he said. "Now I want to be very honest with you."

"Uh-oh, there's more? Or is this where you educate me about what happened last week?"

"Yeah, this is it, but I need to tell you that Chloe advised against getting into this right now."

"In the same conversation as the, uh, other, you mean."

"Right."

"Smart girl," she said. "We must understand each other."

"Well, you're not that far apart in age."

"Wrong thing to say, Rayford. If you were going to use that you're-young-enough-to-be-my-daughter approach, you should have brought it up earlier."

"Not unless I fathered you when I was fifteen," Rayford said. "Anyway, Chloe is convinced you're not going to be in the mood for this just now."

"Why? Does this require some reaction? Do I have to buy into your idea or something?"

"That's my hope, but no. If it's something you can't handle right now, I'll understand. But I think you'll see the urgency of it."

Rayford felt much like Bruce Barnes had sounded the day they met. He was full of passion and persuasion, and he felt his prayers for courage and coherence were answered as he spoke. He told Hattie of his history with God, having been raised in a churchgoing home and how he and Irene had attended various churches throughout their marriage. He even told her that Irene's preoccupation with end-time events had been one thing that made him consider looking elsewhere for companionship.

Rayford could tell by Hattie's look that she knew where he was going, that he had now come to agree with Irene and had bought the whole package. Hatti sat motionless as he told the story of knowing what he would find at home that morning after they had landed at O'Hare.

He told her of calling the church, meeting Bruce, Bruce's story, the videotape, their studies, the prophecies from the Bible, the preachers in Israel that clearly paralleled the two witnesses spoken of in Revelation.

Rayford told her how he had prayed the prayer with the pastor as the videotape rolled and how he now felt so responsible for Chloe and wanted her to find God, too. Hattie stared at him. Nothing in her body language or expression encouraged him, but he kept going. He didn't ask her to pray with him. He simply told her he would no longer apologize for what he believed.

"You can see, at least, how if a person truly accepts this, he must tell other people. He would be no friend if he didn't." Hattie wouldn't even give him the satisfaction of a nod to concede that point.

After nearly half an hour, he exhausted his new knowledge, and he concluded, "Hattie, I want you to think about it, consider it, watch the tape, talk to Bruce if you want to. I can't make you believe. All I can do is make you aware of what I have come to accept as the truth. I care about you and wouldn't want you to miss out simply because no one ever told you."

Finally, Hattie sat back and sighed. "Well, that's sweet, Rayford. It really is. I appreciate your telling me all that. It hits me real strange and different, because I never knew that stuff was in the Bible. My family went to church when I was a kid, mostly on holidays or if we got invited, but I never heard anything like that. I *will* think about it. I sort of have to. Once you hear something like this, it's hard to put it out of your mind for a while. Is this what you're going to tell Buck Williams at dinner?"

"Word for word."

She chuckled. "Wonder if any of it will find its way into his magazine."

"Probably along with space aliens, germ gas, and death rays," Rayford said.

TWENTY-ONE

WHEN Buck and Chloe reconnected with Hattie and Chloe's father, it was clear Hattie had been crying. Buck didn't feel close enough to ask what was wrong, and she never offered.

Buck was glad for the opportunity to interview Rayford Steele, but his emotions were mixed. The reactions of the captain who had piloted the plane on which he had been a passenger when the disappearances occurred would add drama to his story. But even more, he wanted to spend time with Chloe. Buck would run back to the office, then home to change, and meet them later at the Carlisle. At the office he took a call from Stanton Bailey, asking how soon he could go to Chicago to get Lucinda Washington replaced. "Soon, but I don't want to miss developments at the U.N."

"Everything happening there tomorrow

morning you already know about from Plank,"
Bailey said. "Word I get is it's already starting
to come down. Plank assumes his new position
in the morning, denies Carpathia's interest,
reiterates what it would take, and we all wait
and see if anybody bites. I don't think they will."

"I wish they would," Buck said, still hoping
he could trust Carpathia and eager to see what
the man would do about Stonagal and Todd-
Cothran.

"I do, too," Bailey said, "but what are the
odds? He's a man for this time, but his global
disarmament and his reorganization plans are
too ambitious. It'll never happen."

"I know, but if you were deciding, wouldn't
you go along with it?"

"Yeah," Bailey said, sighing. "I probably
would. I'm so tired of war and violence. I'd
probably even go for moving the place to this
New Babylon."

"Maybe the U.N. delegates will be smart enough
to know the world is ready for Carpathia," Buck
said.

"Wouldn't that be too good to be true?" Bailey
said. "Don't bet the farm or hold your breath
or whatever it is you're not supposed to do when
the odds are against you."

Buck told his new boss he would fly to Chicago
the next morning and get back to New York by

Sunday night. "I'll get the lay of the land, find out who's solid in Chicago and whether we need to look at outside applicants."

"I'd prefer staying inside," Bailey said. "But it's my style to let you make those decisions."

Buck phoned Pan-Con Airlines, knowing Rayford Steele's flight left at eight the next morning. He told the reservation clerk his traveling companion was Chloe Steele. "Yes," she said, "Ms. Steele is flying complimentary in first class. There is a seat open next to her. Will you be a guest of the crew as well?"

"No."

He booked a cheap seat and charged it to the magazine, then upgraded to the seat next to Chloe. He would say nothing that night about going to Chicago.

It had been ages since Buck had worn a tie, but this was, after all, the Carlisle Hotel dining room. He wouldn't have gotten in without one. Fortunately they were directed to a private table in a little alcove where he could stash his bag without appearing gauche. His tablemates assumed he needed the bag for his equipment, not aware he had packed a change of clothes, too.

Chloe was radiant, looking five years older in a classy evening dress. It was clear she and Hattie had spent the late afternoon in a beauty salon.

Rayford thought his daughter looked stunning that evening, and he wondered what the magazine writer thought of her. Clearly this Williams guy was too old for her.

Rayford had spent his free hours before dinner napping and then praying that he would have the same courage and clarity he'd had with Hattie. He had no idea what she thought except that he was "sweet" for telling her everything. He wasn't sure whether that was sarcasm or condescension. He could only hope he had gotten through. That she had spent time alone with Chloe might have been good. Rayford hoped Chloe wasn't so antagonistic and closed minded that she had become an ally against him with Hattie.

At the restaurant Williams seemed to gaze at Chloe and ignore Hattie. Rayford considered this insensitive, but it didn't seem to bother Hattie. Maybe Hattie was matchmaking behind his back. Rayford himself had said nothing about Hattie's new look for the evening, but that was by design. She was striking and always had been, but he was not going down that path again.

During dinner Rayford kept the conversation light. Buck said to let him know when he was ready to be interviewed. After dessert Rayford spoke to the waiter privately. "We'd like to spend another hour or so here, if it's all right."

"Sir, we do have an extensive reservation list—"

"I wouldn't want this table to be less than profitable for you," Rayford said, pressing a large bill into the waiter's palm, "so boot us out whenever it becomes necessary."

The waiter peeked at the bill and slipped it into his pocket. "I'm sure you will not be disturbed," he said. And the water glasses were always full.

Rayford enjoyed answering Williams's initial questions about his job, his training, his background and upbringing, but he was eager to get on with his new mission in life. And finally the question came.

Buck tried to concentrate on the captain's answers but felt himself trying to impress Chloe, too. Everyone in the business knew he was one of the best in the world at interviewing. That and his ability to quickly sift through the stuff and make a readable, engaging article of it had made him who he was.

Buck had breezed through the preliminaries, and he liked this guy. Steele seemed honest and sincere, smart and articulate. He realized he had seen a lot of Rayford in Chloe. "I'm ready," he said, "to ask your idea of what happened on that fateful flight to London. Do you have a theory?"

The captain hesitated and smiled as if gathering himself. "I have more than a theory," he said.

"You may think this sounds crazy coming from a technically minded person like me, but I believe I have found the truth and know exactly what happened."

Buck knew this would play well in the magazine. "Gotta appreciate a man who knows his mind," he said. "Here's your chance to tell the world."

Chloe chose that moment to gently touch Buck's arm and ask if he minded if she excused herself for a moment.

"I'll join you," Hattie said.

Buck smiled, watching them go. "What was that?" he said. "A conspiracy? Were they supposed to leave me alone with you, or have they heard this before and don't want to rehash it?"

Rayford was privately frustrated, almost to the point of anger. That was the second time in a few hours that Chloe had somehow been spirited away at a crucial time. "I assure you that is not the case," he said, forcing himself to smile. He couldn't slow down and wait for their return. The question had been asked, he felt ready, and so he stepped off the edge of a social cliff, saying things he knew could get him categorized as a kook. As he had done with Hattie, he outlined his own spotty spiritual history and brought Williams up to the present in a little over half an hour, covering every detail he felt was relevant. At some point the women returned.

Buck sat without interrupting as this most lucid and earnest professional calmly propounded a theory that only three weeks before Buck would have found absurd. It sounded like things he had heard in church and from friends, but this guy had chapter and verse from the Bible to back it up. And this business of the two preachers in Jerusalem representing two witnesses predicted in the book of Revelation? Buck was aghast. He finally broke in.

"That's interesting," he said. "Have you heard the latest?" Buck told him what he had seen on CNN during his few brief minutes at his apartment. "Apparently thousands are making some sort of a pilgrimage to the Wailing Wall. They're lined up for miles, trying to get in and hear the preaching. Many are converting and going out themselves to preach. The authorities seem powerless to keep them out, despite the opposition of the Orthodox Jews. Anyone who comes against the preachers is struck dumb or paralyzed, and many of the old orthodox guard are joining forces with the preachers."

"Amazing," the pilot responded. "But even more amazing, it was all predicted in the Bible."

Buck was desperate to maintain his composure. He wasn't sure what he was hearing, but Steele was impressive. Maybe the man was reaching to link Bible prophecy with what was happening in Israel, but no one else had an explanation. What Steele had read to Buck from Revelation appeared clear. Maybe it was wrong. Maybe it was mumbo jumbo. But it was the only theory that tied the incidents so closely to any sort of explanation. What else would give Buck this constant case of the chills?

Buck focused on Captain Steele, his pulse racing, looking neither right nor left. He could not move. He was certain the women could hear his crashing heart. Was all this possible? Could it be true? Had he been exposed to a clear work of God in the destruction of the Russian air corps just to set him up for a moment like this? Could he shake his head and make it all go away? Could he sleep on it and come to his senses in the morning? Would a conversation with Bailey or Plank set him straight, snap him out of this silliness?

He sensed not. Something about this demanded attention. He wanted to believe something that tied everything together and made it make sense. But Buck also wanted to believe in Nicolae Carpathia. Maybe Buck was going through a scary time where he was vulnerable to impressive people. That wasn't like him, but then, who *was* himself these days? Who could be expected to be himself during times like these?

Buck didn't want to rationalize this away, to talk himself out of it. He wanted to ask Rayford Steele about his own sister-in-law and niece and nephew. But that would be personal, that would not relate to the story he was working on. This had not begun as a personal quest, a search for truth. This was merely a fact-finding mission, an element in a bigger story.

In no way did Buck even begin to think he was going to pick a favorite theory and espouse it as *Global Weekly*'s position. He was supposed to round up all the theories, from the plausible to the bizarre. Readers would add their own in the Letters column, or they would make a decision based on the credibility of the sources. This airline pilot, unless Buck made him look like a lunatic, would come off profound and convincing.

For the first time in his memory Buck Williams was speechless.

Rayford was certain he was not getting through. He only hoped this writer was astute enough to understand, to quote him correctly, and to represent his views in such a way that readers might look into Christianity. It was clear that Williams wasn't buying it personally. If Rayford had to guess, he'd say Williams was trying to hide a smirk—or else he was so amused, or amazed, that he couldn't frame a response.

Rayford had to remind himself that his purpose was to get through to Chloe first and then maybe to influence the reading public, if the thing found its way into print. If Cameron Williams thought Rayford was totally out to lunch, he might just leave him out, along with all his cockamamie views.

Buck did not trust himself to respond with coherence. He still had chills, yet he felt sticky with sweat. What was happening to him? He managed a whisper. "I want to thank you for your time, and for dinner," he said. "I will get back to you before using any of your quotes." That was nonsense, of course. He had said it only to give himself a reason to reconnect with the pilot. He might have a lot of personal questions about this, but he never allowed people he interviewed to see their quotes in advance. He trusted his tape recorder and his memory, and he had never been accused of misquoting.

Buck looked back up at the captain and saw

a strange look cross his face. He looked—what? Disappointed? Yes, then resigned.

Suddenly Buck remembered whom he was dealing with. This was an intelligent, educated man. Surely he knew that reporters never checked back with their sources. He probably thought he was getting a journalistic brush-off.

A rookie mistake, Buck, he reprimanded himself. *You just underestimated your own source.*

Buck was putting his equipment away when he noticed Chloe was crying, tears streaming down her face. What was it with these women? Hattie Durham had been weeping when she and the captain had finished talking that afternoon. Now Chloe.

Buck could identify, at least with Chloe. If she was crying because she had been moved by her father's sincerity and earnestness, it was no surprise. Buck had a lump in his throat, and for the first time since he had lain facedown in fear in Israel during the Russian attack, he wished he had a private place to cry.

"Could I ask you one more thing, off the record?" he said. "May I ask what you and Hattie were talking about this afternoon in the club?"

"Buck!" Hattie scolded. "That's none of your—"

"If you don't want to say, I'll understand," Buck said. "I was just curious."

"Well, much of it was personal," the captain said.

"Fair enough."

"But, Hattie, I don't see any harm in telling him that the rest of it was what we just went over. Do you?"

She shrugged.

"Still off the record, Hattie," Buck said, "do you mind if I ask your reaction to all this?"

"Why off the record?" Hattie snapped. "The opinions of a pilot are important but the opinions of a flight attendant aren't?"

"I'll put you on the machine if you want," he said. "I didn't know you wanted to be on the record."

"I don't," she said. "I just wanted to be asked. It's too late now."

"And you don't care to say what you think—"

"No, I'll tell you. I think Rayford is sincere and thoughtful. Whether he's right, I have no idea. That's all beyond me and very foreign. But I am convinced he believes it. Whether he should or not, with his background and all that, I don't know. Maybe he's susceptible to it because of losing his family."

Buck nodded, realizing he was closer to buying Rayford's theory than Hattie was. He glanced at Chloe, hoping she had composed herself and that he could draw her out. She still had a tissue pressed under her eyes.

"Please don't ask me right now," she said.

Rayford was not surprised at Hattie's response, but he was profoundly disappointed with Chloe's. He was convinced she didn't want to embarrass him by saying how off the wall he sounded. He should have been grateful, he guessed. At least she was still sensitive to his feelings. Maybe he should have been more sensitive to hers, but he had decided he couldn't let those gentilities remain priorities anymore. He was going to contend for the faith with her until she made a decision. For tonight, however, it was clear she had heard enough. He wouldn't be pushing her anymore. He only hoped he could sleep despite his remorse over her condition. He loved her so much.

"Mr. Williams," he said, standing and thrusting out his hand, "it's been a pleasure. The pastor I told you about in Illinois really has a handle on this stuff and knows much more than I do about the Antichrist and all. It might be worth a call if you want to know any more. Bruce Barnes, New Hope Village Church, Mount Prospect."

"I'll keep that in mind," Buck said.

Rayford was convinced Williams was merely being polite.

Talking to this Barnes was a great idea, Buck thought. Maybe he'd find the time the next day in Chicago. That way he could pursue this for himself and not confuse the professional angle with his own interest.

The foursome moseyed to the lobby. "I'm going to say my good-nights," Hattie said. "I've got the earlier flight tomorrow." She thanked Rayford for dinner, whispered something to Chloe—which seemed to get no response—and thanked Buck for his hospitality that morning. "I may just call Mr. Carpathia one of these days," she said. Buck resisted the urge to tell her what he knew about Carpathia's immediate future. He doubted the man would have time for her.

Chloe looked as if she wanted to follow Hattie to the elevators and yet wanted to say something to Buck as well. He was shocked when she said, "Give us a minute, will you, Daddy? I'll be right up."

Buck found himself flattered that Chloe had hung back to say good-bye personally, but she was still emotional. Her voice was quavery as she formally told him what a good time she had had that day. He tried to prolong the conversation.

"Your dad is a pretty impressive guy," he said.

"I know," she said. "Especially lately."

"I can see why you might agree with him on a lot of that stuff."

"You can?"

"Sure! I have a lot of thinking to do myself. You give him a hard time about it though, huh?"

"I used to. Not anymore."

"Why not?"

"You can see how much it means to him."

Buck nodded. She seemed on the edge emotionally again. He reached to take her hand. "It's been wonderful spending time with you," he said.

She chuckled, as if embarrassed about what she was thinking.

"What?" he pressed.

"Oh, nothing. It's silly."

"C'mon, what? We've both been silly today."

"Well, I feel stupid," she said. "I just met you and I'm really gonna miss you. If you get through Chicago, you have to call."

"It's a promise," Buck said. "I can't say when, but let's just say sooner than you think."

TWENTY-TWO

BUCK did not sleep well. Partly he was excited about his morning surprise. He could only hope Chloe would be happy about it. The larger part of his mind reeled with wonder. If this was true, all that Rayford Steele had postulated—and Buck knew instinctively that if any of it was true, all of it was true—why had it taken Buck a lifetime to come to it? Could he have been searching for this all the time, hardly knowing he was looking?

Yet even Captain Steele—an organized, analytical airline pilot—had missed it, and Steele claimed to have had a proponent, a devotee, almost a fanatic living under his own roof. Buck was so restless he had to leave his bed and pace. Strangely, somehow, he was not upset, not miserable. He was simply overwhelmed. None of this would have made a bit of sense to him just days

before, and now, for the first time since Israel,
he was unable to separate himself from his story.

The Holy Land attack had been a watershed
event in his life. He had stared his own mortality
in the face and had to acknowledge that something otherworldly—yes, supernatural, something
directly from God almighty—had been thrust
upon those dusty hills in the form of a fire in
the sky. And he had known beyond a doubt
for the first time in his life that unexplainable
things out there could not be dissected and evaluated scientifically from a detached Ivy League
perspective.

Buck had always prided himself on standing
apart from the pack, for including the human,
the everyday, the everyman element in his stories
when others resisted such vulnerability. This skill
allowed readers to identify with him, to taste and
feel and smell those things most important to
them. But he had still been able, even after his
closest brush with death, to let the reader live it
without revealing Buck's own deep angst about
the very existence of God. Now, that separation
seemed impossible. How could he cover this most
important story of his life, one that had already
probed closest to his soul, without subconsciously
revealing his private turmoil?

He was, he knew by the wee hours, leaning over
the line. He wasn't ready to pray yet, to try to

talk to a God he had ignored for so long. He
hadn't even prayed when he became convinced
of God's existence that night in Israel. What had
been the matter with him? Everyone in the world,
at least those intellectually honest with themselves, had to admit there was a God after that
night. Amazing coincidences had occurred before,
but that had defied all logic.

To win against the mighty Russians was an
upset, of course. But Israel's history was replete
with such legends. Yet to not defend yourself
and suffer no casualties? That was beyond all
comprehension—apart from the direct intervention of God.

Why, Buck wondered, hadn't that made more
of an impact on his own introspective inventory?
In the lonely darkness he came to the painful realization that he had long ago compartmentalized
this most basic of human needs and had rendered
it a nonissue. What did it say about him, what
despicable kind of a subhuman creature had he
become, that even the stark evidence of the Israel
miracle—for it could be called nothing less—had
not thawed his spirit's receptiveness to God?

Not that many months later came the great
disappearance of millions around the world.
Dozens had vanished from the plane in which
he was a passenger. What more did he need? It
already seemed as if he were living in a science

fiction thriller. Without question he had lived through the most cataclysmic event in history. Buck realized he'd not had a second to think in the last two weeks. Had it not been for the personal tragedies he had witnessed, he might have been more private in his approach to what appeared to be a universe out of control.

He wanted to meet this Bruce Barnes, not even pretending to be interviewing him for an article. Buck was on a personal quest now, looking to satisfy deep needs. For so many years he had rejected the idea of a personal God or that he had need of God—if there was one. The idea would take some getting used to. Captain Steele had talked about everyone being a sinner. Buck was not unrealistic about that. He knew his life would never stand up to the standards of a Sunday school teacher. But he had always hoped that if he faced God someday, his good would outweigh his bad and that relatively speaking, he was as good or better than the next guy. That would have to do.

Now, if Rayford Steele and all his Bible verses could be believed, it didn't make any difference how good Buck was or where he stood in relation to anybody else. One archaic phrase had struck him and rolled around in his head. *There is none righteous, no, not one.* Well, he had never considered himself righteous. Could he go the next level and admit his need for God, for forgiveness, for Christ?

Was it possible? Could he be on the cusp of becoming a born-again Christian? He had been almost relieved when Rayford Steele had used that term. Buck had read and even written about "those kinds" of people, but even at his level of worldly wisdom he had never quite understood the phrase. He had always considered the "born-again" label akin to "ultraright-winger" or "fundamentalist." Now, if he chose to take a step he had never dreamed of taking, if he could not somehow talk himself out of this truth he could no longer intellectually ignore, he would also take upon himself a task: educating the world on what that confusing little term really meant.

Buck finally dozed on the couch in his living room, despite a lamp shining close to his face. He slept soundly for a couple of hours but awoke in time to get to the airport. The prospect of surprising Chloe and traveling with her gave him a rush that helped overcome his fatigue. But even more exciting was the possibility that another answer man awaited him in Chicago, a man he trusted simply on the recommendation of a pilot who had seemed to speak the truth with authority. It would be fun someday to tell Rayford Steele how much that otherwise innocuous interview had meant to him. But Buck assumed Steele had already figured that out. That was probably why Steele had seemed so passionate.

If this signaled the soon beginning of the tribulation period predicted in the Bible, and Rayford had no doubt that it did, he wondered if there would be any joy in it. Bruce didn't seem to think there would be, aside from the few converts they might be privileged to win. So far Rayford felt he was a failure. While he was certain God had given him the words and the courage to say them, he felt he had done something wrong in communicating to Hattie. Maybe she was right. Maybe he had been self-serving. It had to appear to her that he was merely getting out from under his own load of guilt. But he knew better. Before God he believed his motives pure. Yet clearly he had not persuaded Hattie of more than that he was sincere and that he believed. What good was that? If he believed and she didn't, she had to assume he believed something bogus, or she would have to admit she was ignoring the truth. What he had told her carried no other option.

And his performance during the interview with Cameron Williams! At the time, Rayford had felt good about it, articulate, calm, rational. He knew he was discussing revolutionary, jarring stuff, but he felt God had enabled him to be lucid. Yet if he couldn't get any more reaction out of the reporter than polite deference, what kind of a witness could he be? From the depths of his soul Rayford wanted to be more productive. He believed he had wasted his life before this, and he had only a short period to make up for lost time. He was eternally grateful for his own salvation, but now he wanted to share it, to bring more people to Christ. The magazine interview had been an incredible opportunity, but in his gut he felt it had not come off well. Was it even worth the effort to pray for another chance? Rayford believed he had seen the last of Cameron Williams. He wouldn't be calling Bruce Barnes, and Rayford's quotes would never see the pages of *Global Weekly*.

As Rayford shaved and showered and dressed, he heard Chloe packing. She had obviously been embarrassed by him last night, probably even apologized to Mr. Williams for her father's absurd ramblings. At least she had tapped on his door and said good night when she came in. That was *something*, wasn't it?

Every time Rayford thought of Chloe, he felt a tightness in his chest, a great emptiness and grief. He could live with his other failures if he must, but his knees nearly buckled as he prayed silently for Chloe. *I cannot lose her*, he thought, and he believed he would trade his own salvation for hers if that was what it took.

With that commitment, he sensed God speaking to him, impressing upon him that that was precisely the burden required for winning people, for leading them to Christ. That was the attitude of Jesus himself, being willing to take on himself the punishment of men and women so they could live.

Rayford was emboldened anew as he prayed for Chloe, still fighting the nagging fear of failure. "God, I need encouragement," he breathed. "I need to know I haven't turned her off forever." She had said good night, but he had also heard her crying in bed.

He emerged in uniform and smiled at her as she stood by the door, dressed casually for travel. "Ready, sweetie?" he said tentatively.

She nodded and seemed to work up a smile, then embraced him tight and long, pressing her cheek against his chest. *Thank you,* he prayed silently, wondering if he should say anything. Was this the time? Dare he press now?

Again he felt deeply impressed of God, as if the Lord were speaking directly to his spirit, *Patience. Let her be. Let her be.* Keeping silent seemed as hard as anything he had ever done. Chloe said nothing either. They grabbed a light breakfast and headed to JFK.

Chloe was the first passenger on the plane. "I'll try to get back and see you," Rayford told her before heading to the cockpit.

"Don't worry if you can't," she said. "I'll understand."

Buck waited until everyone else had boarded. As he approached his seat next to Chloe, her body was turned toward the window, arms crossed, chin in her hand. Whether she even had her eyes open, Buck couldn't tell. He assumed she would turn to glance as he sat next to her, and he couldn't suppress a smile, anticipating her reaction and only slightly worried that she would be less positive than he hoped.

He sat and waited, but she did not turn. Was she sleeping? Staring? Meditating? Praying? Was it possible she was crying? Buck hoped not. He already cared for her enough to be bothered when she seemed in pain.

And now he had a problem. As he warily watched for the change in position that would allow Chloe to see him in her peripheral vision, he was suddenly awash in fatigue. His muscles and joints ached, his eyes burned. His head felt like lead. No way was he going to fall asleep and have her discover him dozing next to her.

Buck gestured to get the attendant's attention.

"Coke, please," he whispered. The temporary caffeine rush would allow him to stay awake a little longer.

When Chloe didn't move even to watch the safety instructions, Buck grew impatient. Still, he didn't want to reveal himself. He wanted to be discovered. And so he waited.

She must have grown weary of her position, because she stretched and used her feet to push her carry-on bag under the seat in front of her. She took a last sip of her juice and set it on the small tray between them. She stared at Buck's glove-leather boots, the ones he had worn the day before. Chloe's eyes traveled up to his smiling, expectant face.

Her reaction was more than worth the wait. She folded her hands and drew them to her mouth, her eyes filling. Then she took his hand in both of hers. "Oh, Buck," she whispered. "Oh, Buck."

"It's nice to see you, too," he said.

Chloe quickly let go of his hand as if catching herself. "I don't mean to act like a schoolgirl," she said, "but have you ever received a direct answer to prayer?"

Buck shot her a double take. "I thought your dad was the praying member of your family."

"He is," she said. "But I just tried out my first one in years, and God answered it."

"You prayed I would sit next to you?"

"Oh, no, I never would have dreamed of anything that impossible. How did you do it, Buck?"

He told her. "It wasn't hard once I knew your flight time, and I said I was traveling with you to get next to you."

"But why? Where are you going?"

"You don't know where this plane's going? San José, I hope."

She laughed.

"But come on now, Chloe. Finish your story. I've never been an answer to prayer before."

"It's kind of a long story."

"I think we've got time."

She took his hand again. "Buck, this is too special. This is the nicest thing anyone's done for me in a long time."

"You said you were going to miss me, but I didn't do it only for you. I've got business in Chicago."

She giggled and let go again. "I wasn't talking about you, Buck, though this is sweet. I was talking about God doing the nice thing for me."

Buck couldn't hide his embarrassment. "I knew that," he said.

And she told him her story. "You might have noticed I was pretty upset last night. I was so moved by my dad's story. I mean, I had heard it before. But all of a sudden he seemed so loving, so interested in people. Could you tell how important it was to him and how serious he was about it?"

"Who couldn't?"

"If I didn't know better, Buck, I would have thought he was trying to convince you personally rather than just answering your questions."

"I'm not so sure he wasn't."

"Did it offend you?"

"Not at all, Chloe. To tell you the truth, he was getting to me."

Chloe fell silent and shook her head. When she finally spoke she was nearly whispering, and Buck had to lean toward her to hear. He loved the sound of her voice. "Buck," she said, "he was getting to me, too, and I don't mean my dad."

"Too bizarre," he said. "I was up half the night thinking about this."

"It won't be long for either of us, will it?" she said. Buck didn't respond, but he knew what she meant.

"When do I get to be the answer to prayer?" he prodded.

"Oh, right. I was sitting there at dinner with my dad pouring his guts out to you, and I suddenly realized why he wanted me to be there when he said the same things to Hattie. I gave him such a hard time at first that he backed off on me, and now that he had the knowledge and the real need to convince me, he was afraid to come right at me.

He wanted me to get it indirectly. And I did. I
didn't hear how he started because Hattie and I
were in the ladies' room, but I had probably heard
that before. When I got back, I was transfixed.

"It wasn't that I was hearing anything new.
It was new to me when I heard it from Bruce
Barnes and saw that videotape, but my dad
showed such urgency and confidence. Buck,
there's no other explanation for those two guys
in Jerusalem, is there, except that they have to
be the two witnesses talked about in the Bible?"

Buck nodded.

"So, Dad and God were getting to me, but I
wasn't ready yet. I was crying because I love him
so much and because it's true. It's all true, Buck,
do you know that?"

"I think I do, Chloe."

"But still I couldn't talk to my dad about it. I
didn't know what was in my way. I've always been
so blasted independent. I knew he was frustrated
with me, maybe disappointed, and all I could do
was cry. I had to think, to try to pray, to sort it
out. Hattie was no help. She doesn't get it and
maybe never will. All she cared about was trivial
stuff, like trying to matchmake you and me."

Buck smiled and tried to look insulted. "That's
trivial?"

"Well, compared to what we're talking about
right now, I'd have to say so."

"Gotta give you that one," Buck said.

She laughed. "So I knew something was wrong with Dad because I talked to you for only, what, three minutes or so before I went up?"

"Less than that, probably."

"By the time I got to our suite, he was already in bed. So I told him good night, just to make sure he was still talking to me. He was. And then I tossed and turned, not ready to take the last step, crying about my dad's worrying so much about me and loving me so much."

"That's while I was up, probably," Buck said.

"But," Chloe said, "this is so out of character for me. Even though I'm there, I mean, I'm right there. You follow me?"

Buck nodded. "I've been going through the same thing."

"I've been convinced," she said, "but I'm still fighting. I'm supposed to be an intellectual. I have critical friends to answer to. Who's going to believe this? Who's going to think I haven't lost my mind?"

"Believe me, I understand," Buck said, amazed at the similarities between their journeys.

"So, I was stuck," she said. "I wasn't getting anywhere. I tried to encourage my dad by not being so distant, but I could tell he saw me suffering, but I don't think he had any idea how close I was. I got on this plane, desperate for some closure, pardon the psychobabble, and I started wondering if God answers your prayers before you're . . . um, you know, before you're actually a . . ."

"Born-again Christian," Buck offered.

"Exactly. I don't know why that's so hard for me to say. Maybe somebody who knows better can tell me for sure, but I prayed and I think God answered. Tell me this, Buck, just with your cognitive-reasoning skills. If there is a God and if this is all true, wouldn't he want us to know? I mean, God wouldn't make it hard to learn and he wouldn't, or I should say he *couldn't*, ignore a desperate prayer, could he?"

"I don't see how he could, no."

"Well, that's what I think. So I think it was a good test, a reasonable one, and that I wasn't out of line. I'm convinced God answered."

"And I was the answer."

"And you were the answer."

"Chloe, what exactly did you pray for?"

"Oh, well, the prayer itself wasn't that big of a deal, until it was answered. I just told God I needed a little more. I felt bad that all the stuff I'd heard and all that I knew from my dad wasn't enough. I just prayed really sincerely and said I would appreciate it if God could show me personally that he cared, that he knew what I was going through, and that he wanted me to know he was there."

Buck felt a strange emotion—that if he tried to

speak, his voice would be husky and he might be unable to finish a sentence. He pressed his hand over his mouth to compose himself. Chloe stared at him. "And you feel I was the answer to that prayer?" he said at last.

"No doubt in my mind. See, like I said, I wouldn't even have conceived of praying that you would wind up next to me on the biggest day of my life. I wasn't even sure I'd ever see you again. But it's as if God knew better than I did that there was no one I would rather see today than you."

Buck was touched, moved beyond expression. He had wanted to see her, too. Otherwise, he could have flown on Hattie's flight or any one of a dozen that would have gotten him to Chicago that morning. Buck just looked at her. "So, what are you going to do now, Chloe? It seems to me that God has called your bluff. It wasn't a bluff, exactly, but you asked and he delivered. Sounds like you're obligated."

"I have no choice," she agreed. "Not that I want one. From what I've gathered from Bruce Barnes and the tape and Dad, you don't have to have somebody lead you through this, and you don't have to be in a church or anything. Just like I prayed for a clearer sign, I can pray about this."

"Your dad made that clear last night."

"You want to join me?" she asked.

Buck hesitated. "Don't take this personally, Chloe, but I'm not ready."

"What more do you need? . . . Oh, I'm sorry, Buck. I'm doing just what my dad did the day he became a Christian. He could hardly help himself, and I was so awful to him. But if you're not ready, you're not ready."

"I won't need to be forced," Buck said. "Like you, I feel like I'm right on the doorstep. But I'm pretty careful, and I want to talk to this Barnes guy today. I have to tell you, though, my remaining doubts can hardly stand up to what's happening to you."

"You know, Buck," Chloe said, "I promise this will be the last thing I say about it, but I'm thinking the same way my dad did. I have this urge to tell you not to wait too long because you never know what might happen."

"I hear you," he said. "I'm going to have to take my chances this plane won't go down because I still feel I need to talk to Barnes, but you have a point."

Chloe turned and looked over her shoulder. "There are two vacant seats right there," she said. She stopped a passing attendant. "Can I give you a message for my dad?"

"Sure. Is he captain or first officer?"

"Captain. Please just tell him his daughter has extremely good news for him."

"Extremely good news," the attendant repeated.

Rayford was manually flying the plane as a diversion when his senior flight attendant gave him the message. He had no idea what it meant, but it was so unlike Chloe to initiate communication lately, he was intrigued.

He asked his first officer to take over. Rayford unstrapped himself and made his way out, surprised to see Cameron Williams. He hoped Williams wasn't the extent of Chloe's good news. Pleasant as it was to think the man might already be making good on his promise to look up Bruce Barnes, Rayford also hoped that Chloe wasn't about to announce some ill-advised whirlwind romance in the bud.

He shook hands with the writer and expressed his pleasant, but wary, surprise. Chloe reached for his neck with both hands and gently pulled him down to where she could whisper to him. "Daddy, could you and I sit back there for a couple of minutes so I can talk to you?"

Buck sensed disappointment in Captain Steele's eyes at first. He looked forward to telling the pilot why he was glad to be flying to Chicago.

Sitting next to Chloe had been only a bonus.
He peeked back at Steele with his daughter,
engaged in intense conversation and then praying
together. Buck wondered if there was any
airline regulation against that. He knew Rayford
couldn't fraternize for long.

In a few minutes Chloe stepped into the aisle,
and Rayford stood and embraced her. They
both appeared overcome with emotion. A
middle-aged couple across the aisle leaned out
and stared, brows raised. The captain noticed,
straightened, and headed toward the cockpit.
"My daughter," he said awkwardly, pointing
at Chloe, who smiled through her tears. "She's
my daughter."

The couple looked at each other and the
woman spoke. "Right. And I'm the queen of
England," she said, and Buck laughed out loud.

TWENTY-THREE

BUCK called New Hope Village Church to set up an early evening meeting with Bruce Barnes, then spent most of the afternoon at the Chicago bureau of *Global Weekly*. News of his becoming their boss had swept the place, and he was greeted with coolness by Lucinda Washington's former assistant, a young woman in sensible shoes. She told him in no uncertain terms, "Plank did nothing about replacing Lucinda, so I assumed I would move into her slot."

Her attitude and presumption alone made Buck say, "That's unlikely, but you'll be the first to know. I wouldn't be moving offices just yet."

The rest of the staff still grieved over Lucinda's disappearance and seemed grateful for Buck's visit. Steve Plank had hardly ever come to Chicago and had not been there since Lucinda had vanished.

Buck camped out in Lucinda's old office, interviewing key people at twenty-minute intervals.
He also told each about his writing assignment
and asked their personal theories of what had
happened. His final question to each was,
"Where do you think Lucinda Washington is
right now?" More than half said they didn't
want to be quoted but expressed variations of,
"If there's a heaven, that's where she is."

Near the end of the day, Buck was told that
CNN was live at the U.N. with big news. He
invited the staff into the office and they watched
together. "In the most dramatic and far-reaching
overhaul of an international organization anyone
can remember," came the report, "Romanian
president Nicolae Carpathia was catapulted into
reluctant leadership of the United Nations by a
nearly unanimous vote. Carpathia, who insisted
on sweeping changes in direction and jurisdiction
of the United Nations, in what appeared an
effort to gracefully decline the position, became
secretary-general here just moments ago.

"As late as this morning his press secretary
and spokesman, Steven Plank, former executive
editor of the *Global Weekly,* had denied Carpathia's interest in the job and outlined myriad
demands the Romanian would insist upon
before even considering the position. Plank said
the request for Carpathia's elevation came from

outgoing Secretary-General Mwangati Ngumo of Botswana. We asked Ngumo why he was stepping down."

Ngumo's face filled the screen, eyes downcast, his expression carefully masked. "I have long been aware that divided loyalties between my country and the United Nations have made me less effective in each role. I had to choose, and I am first and foremost a Botswanian. We have the opportunity now to become prosperous, due to the generosity of our friends in Israel. The time is right, and the new man is more than right. I will cooperate with him to the fullest."

"Would you, sir, have stepped down had Mr. Carpathia declined the position?"

Ngumo hesitated. "Yes," he said, "I would have. Perhaps not today, and not with as much confidence in the future of the United Nations, but yes, eventually."

The CNN reporter continued, "In only a matter of hours, every request Carpathia had outlined in an early morning press conference was moved as official business, voted upon, and ratified by the body. Within a year the United Nations head-quarters will move to New Babylon. The makeup of the Security Council will change to ten perma-nent members within the month, and a press conference is expected Monday morning in which

Carpathia will introduce several of his personal choices for delegates to that body.

"There is no guarantee, of course, that even member nations will unanimously go along with the move to destroy ninety percent of their military strength and turn over the remaining ten percent to the U.N. But several ambassadors expressed their confidence 'in equipping and arming an international peacekeeping body with a thorough-going pacifist and committed disarmament activist as its head.' Carpathia himself was quoted as saying, 'The U.N. will not need its military might if no one else has any, and I look forward to the day when even the U.N. disarms.'

"Also coming out of today's meetings was the announcement of a seven-year pact between U.N. members and Israel, guaranteeing its borders and promising peace. In exchange, Israel will allow the U.N. to selectively franchise the use of the fertilizer formula, developed by Nobel prizewinner Dr. Chaim Rosenzweig, which makes desert sands tillable and has made Israel a top exporter."

Buck stared as CNN broadcast Rosenzweig's excitement and unequivocal endorsement of Carpathia. The news also carried a report that Carpathia had asked several international groups already in New York for upcoming meetings to get together this weekend to hammer out proposals, resolutions, and accords. "I urge them to move quickly toward anything that contributes to world peace and a sense of global unity."

A reporter asked Carpathia if that included plans for one world religion and eventually one world government. His response: "I can think of little more encouraging than the religions of the world finally cooperating. Some of the worst examples of discord and infighting have been between groups whose overall mission is love among people. Every devotee of pure religion should welcome this potential. The day of hatred is past. Lovers of humankind are uniting."

The CNN anchor continued, "Among other developments today, there are rumors of the organization of groups espousing one world government. Carpathia was asked if he aspired to a position of leadership in such an organization."

Carpathia looked directly into the network pool camera and with moist eyes and thick voice said, "I am overwhelmed to have been asked to serve as secretary-general of the United Nations. I aspire to nothing else. While the idea of one world government resonates deep within me, I can say only that there are many more qualified candidates to lead such a venture. It would be my privilege to serve in any way I am asked, and while I do not see myself in the leadership role, I will commit the resources of the United Nations to such an effort, if asked."

Smooth, Buck thought, his mind reeling. As commentators and world leaders endorsed one world currency, one language, and even the largesse of Carpathia expressing his support for the rebuilding of the temple in Israel, the staff of *Global Weekly*'s Chicago bureau seemed in a mood to party. "This is the first time in years I've felt optimistic about society," one reporter said.

Another added, "This has to be the first time I've smiled since the disappearances. We're supposed to be objective and cynical, but how can you not like this? It'll take years to effect all this stuff, but someday, somewhere down the line, we're going to see world peace. No more weapons, no more wars, no more border disputes or bigotry based on language or religion. Whew! Who'd have believed it would come to this?"

Buck took a call from Steve Plank. "You been watching what's going on?" Plank said.

"Who hasn't?"

"Pretty exciting, isn't it?"

"Mind-boggling."

"Listen, Carpathia wants you here Monday morning."

"What for?"

"He likes you, man. Don't knock it. Before the press conference he's going to have a meeting with his top people and the ten delegates to the permanent Security Council."

"And he wants me there?"

"Yup. And you can guess who some of his top people are."

"Tell me."

"Well, one's obvious."

"Stonagal."

"Of course."

"And Todd-Cothran. I assume he'll move in as new ambassador from the U.K."

"Maybe not," Steve said. "Another Brit is there. I don't know his name, but he's also with this international finance group Stonagal runs."

"You think Carpathia told Stonagal to have someone else in the wings, in case Carpathia wants to squeeze Todd-Cothran out?"

"Could be, but nobody tells Stonagal anything."

"Not even Carpathia?"

"Especially not Carpathia. He knows who made him. But he's honest and sincere, Buck. Nicolae will not do anything illegal or underhanded or even too political. He's pure, man. Pure as the driven snow. So, can you make it?"

"Guess I'd better. How many press will be there?"

"You ready for this? Only you."

"You're kidding."

"I'm serious. He likes you, Buck."

"What's the catch?"

"No catch. He didn't ask for a thing, not even favorable coverage. He knows you have to be objective and fair. The media will get the whole scoop at the press conference afterward."

"Obviously I can't pass this up," Buck said, aware his voice sounded flat.

"What's the matter, Buck? This is history! This is the world the way we've always wanted it and hoped it would be."

"I hope you're right."

"I'm right. There's something else Carpathia wants."

"So there *is* a catch."

"No, nothing hinges on this. If you can't do it, you can't do it. You're still welcome Monday morning. But he wants to see that stewardess friend of yours again."

"Steve, no one calls them stews anymore. They're flight attendants."

"Whatever. Bring her with you if you can."

"Why doesn't he ask her himself? What am I now, a pimp?"

"C'mon, Buck. It's not like that. Lonely guy in a position like this? He can't be out hustling up dates. You introduced them, remember? He trusts you."

He must, Buck thought, *if he's inviting me to his big pre-press-conference meeting.* "I'll ask her," he said. "No promises."

"Don't let me down, buddy."

Rayford Steele was as happy as he had been since his own decision to receive Christ. To see Chloe smiling, to see her hungry to read Irene's Bible, to be able to pray with her and talk about everything together was more than he had dreamed of. "One thing we need to do," he said, "is to get you your own Bible. You're going to wear that one out."

"I want to join that core group of yours," she said. "I want to get all the stuff from Bruce firsthand. The only part that bothers me is that it sounds like things are going to get worse."

Late in the afternoon they dropped in on Bruce, who confirmed Chloe's view. "I'm thrilled to welcome you into the family," he said, "but you're right. God's people are in for dark days. Everybody is. I've been thinking and praying about what we're supposed to do as a church between now and the Glorious Appearing."

Chloe wanted to know all about that, so Bruce showed her from the Bible why he believed Christ would appear in seven years, at the end of the Tribulation. "Most Christians will be martyred or die from war, famine, plagues, or earth-quakes," he said.

Chloe smiled. "This isn't funny," she said, "but maybe I should have thought of that before I signed on. You're going to have trouble convincing people to join the cause with that in your sign-up brochure."

Bruce grimaced. "Yes, but the alternative is worse. We all missed out the first time around. We could be in heaven right now if we'd listened to our loved ones. Dying a horrible death during this period is not my preference, but I'd sure rather do it this way than while I was still lost. Everyone else is in danger of death, too. The only difference is, we have one more way to die than they do."

"As martyrs."

"Right."

Rayford sat listening, aware how his world had changed in such a short time. It had not been that long ago that he had been a respected pilot at the top of his profession, living a phony life, a shell of a man. Now here he was, talking secretly in the office of a local church with his daughter and a young pastor, trying to determine how they would survive seven years of tribulation follow-ing the Rapture of the church.

"We have our core group," Bruce said, "and Chloe, you're welcome to join us if you're serious about total commitment."

"What's the option?" she said. "If what you're saying is true, there's no room for dabbling."

"You're right. But I've also been thinking about a smaller group within the core. I'm looking for people of unusual intelligence and courage. I don't mean to disparage the sincerity of others in the church, especially those on the leadership team. But some of them are timid, some old, many infirm. I've been praying about sort of an inner circle of people who want to do more than just survive."

"What are you getting at?" Rayford asked. "Going on the offensive?"

"Something like that. It's one thing to hide in here, studying, figuring out what's going on so we can keep from being deceived. It's great to pray for the witnesses springing up out of Israel, and it's nice to know there are other pockets of believers all over the world. But doesn't part of you want to jump into the battle?"

Rayford was intrigued but not sure. Chloe was more eager. "A cause," she said. "Something not just to die for but to live for."

"Yes!"

"A group, a team, a force," Chloe said.

"You've got it. A force."

Chloe's eyes were bright with interest. Rayford loved her youth and her eagerness to commit to a cause that to her was only hours old. "And what is it you call this period?" she asked.

"The Tribulation," Bruce said.

"So your little group inside the group, a sort of Green Berets, would be your Tribulation force."

"Tribulation Force," Bruce said, looking at Rayford and rising to scribble it on his flip chart. "I like it. Make no mistake, it won't be fun. It would be the most dangerous cause a person could ever join. We would study, prepare, and speak out. When it becomes obvi-ous who the Antichrist is, the false prophet, the evil, counterfeit religion, we'll have to oppose them, speak out against them. We would be targeted. Christians content to hide in basements with their Bibles might escape everything but earthquakes and wars, but we will be vulnerable to everything.

"There will come a time, Chloe, that followers of Antichrist will be required to bear the sign of the beast. There are all kinds of theories on what form that might take, from a tattoo to a stamp on the forehead that might be detected only under infrared light. But obviously we would refuse to bear that mark. That very act of defiance will be a mark in itself. We will be the naked ones, the ones devoid of the protection of belonging to the majority. You still want to be part of the Tribulation Force?"

Rayford nodded and smiled at his daughter's firm reply. "I wouldn't miss it."

Two hours after the Steeles had left, Buck Williams parked his rental car in front of New Hope Village Church in Mount Prospect, Illinois. He had a sense of destiny tinged with fear. Who would this Bruce Barnes be? What would he look like? And would he be able to detect a non-Christian at a glance?

Buck sat in the car, his head in his hands. He was too analytical, he knew, to make a rash decision. Even his leaving home years before to pursue an education and become a journalist had been plotted for years. To his family it came like a thunderbolt, but to young Cameron Williams it was a logical next step, a part of his long-range plan.

Where Buck sat now was not part of any plan. Nothing that had happened since that ill-fated flight to Heathrow had fit into any predefined pattern for him. He had always liked the serendipity of life, but he processed it through a grid of logic, attacked it from a perspective of order. The firestorm of Israel had jarred him, but even then he had been acting from a standpoint of order. He had a career, a position, a role. He had been in Israel on assignment, and though he hadn't expected to become a war correspondent overnight, he had been prepared by the way he had ordered his life.

But nothing had prepared him for the disappearances or for the violent deaths of his friends. While he should have been prepared for this promotion, that hadn't been part of his plan, either. Now his theory article was bringing him close to flames he had never known were burning in his soul. He felt alone, exposed, vulnerable, and yet this meeting with Bruce Barnes had been his idea. Sure, the airline pilot had suggested it, but Buck could have ignored him without remorse. This trip had not been about getting in a few extra hours with the beautiful Chloe, and the Chicago bureau could have waited. He was here, he knew, for this meeting. Buck felt a bone weariness as he headed for the church.

It was a pleasant surprise to find that Bruce Barnes was someone near Buck's own age. He seemed bright and earnest, having that same authority and passion Rayford Steele exhibited. It had been a long time since Buck had been in a church. This one seemed innocuous enough, fairly new and modern, neat and efficient. He and the young pastor met in a modest office.

"Your friends, the Steeles, told me you might call," Barnes said.

Buck was struck by his honesty. In the world in which Buck moved, he might have kept that information to himself, that edge. But he realized that the pastor had no interest in an edge. There was nothing to hide here. In essence, Buck was looking for information and Bruce was interested in providing it.

"I want to tell you right off," Bruce said, "that I am aware of your work and respect your talent. But to be frank, I no longer have time for the pleasantries and small talk that used to characterize my work. We live in perilous times. I have a message and an answer for people genuinely seeking. I tell everyone in advance that I have quit apologizing for what I'm going to say. If that's a ground rule you can live with, I have all the time you need."

"Well, sir," Buck said, nearly staggered by the emotion and humility he heard in his own voice, "I appreciate that. I don't know how long I'll need, because I'm not here on business. It might have made sense to get a pastor's view for my story, but people can guess what pastors think, especially based on the other people I'm quoting."

"Like Captain Steele."

Buck nodded. "I'm here for myself, and I have to tell you frankly, I don't know where I am on this.

Not that long ago I would never have set foot in a place like this or dreamed anything intellectually worthwhile could come out of here. I know that wasn't exactly journalistically fair of me, but as long as you're being honest, I will be, too.

"I was impressed with Captain Steele. That's one smart guy, a good thinker, and he's into this. You seem like a bright person, and—I don't know. I'm listening, that's all I'll say."

Bruce began by telling Buck his life story, being raised in a Christian home, going to Bible college, marrying a Christian, becoming a pastor, the whole thing. He clarified that he knew the story of Christ and the way of forgiveness and a relationship with God. "I thought I had the best of both worlds. But the Scripture is clear that you can't serve two masters. You can't have it both ways. I discovered that truth in the severest way." And he told of losing his family and friends, everyone dear to him. He wept as he spoke. "The pain is every bit as great today as it was when it happened," he said.

Then Bruce outlined, as Rayford had done, the plan of salvation from beginning to end. Buck grew nervous, anxious. He wanted a break. He interrupted and asked if Bruce wanted to know a little more about him. "Sure," Bruce said.

Buck told of his own history, concentrating most on the Russia/Israel conflict and the roughly fourteen months since. "I can see," Bruce said at last, "that God is trying to get your attention."

"Well, he's got it," Buck said. "I just have to warn you, I'm not an easy sell. All this is interesting and sounds more plausible than ever, but it's just not me to jump into something."

"Nobody can force you or badger you into this, Mr. Williams, but I must also say again that we live in perilous times. We don't know how much pondering time we have."

"You sound like Chloe Steele."

"And she sounds like her father," Bruce said, smiling.

"And he, I guess, sounds like you. I can see why you all consider this so urgent, but like I say—"

"I understand," Bruce said. "If you have the time right now, let me take a different tack. I know you're a bright guy, so you might as well have all the information you need before you leave here."

Buck breathed easier. He had feared Bruce was about to pop the question, pushing him to pray the prayer both Rayford Steele and Chloe had talked about. He accepted that that would be part of it, that it would signal the transaction and start his relationship with God—someone he had never before really spoken to. But he wasn't ready. At least he didn't think he was. And he would not be pushed.

"I don't have to be back in New York until Monday morning," he said, "so I'll take as much time tonight as you'll give me."

"I don't mean to be morbid, Mr. Williams, but I have no family responsibilities anymore. I have a core group meeting tomorrow and church Sunday. You're welcome to attend. But I have enough energy to go to midnight if you do."

"I'm all yours."

Bruce spent the next several hours giving Buck a crash course in prophecy and the end times. Buck had heard much of the information about the Rapture and the two witnesses, and he had picked up snippets about the Antichrist. But when Bruce got to the parts about the great one-world religion that would spring up, the lying, so-called peacemaker who would bring blood-shed through war, the Antichrist who would divide the world into ten kingdoms, Buck's blood ran cold. He fell silent, no longer pepper-ing Bruce with questions or comments. He scrib-bled notes as fast as he could.

Did he dare tell this unpretentious man that he believed Nicolae Carpathia could be the very man the Scriptures talked about? Could all this be coincidental? His fingers began to shake when Bruce told of the prediction of a seven-year pact between Antichrist and Israel, of the rebuilding of

the temple, and even of Babylon becoming headquarters for a new world order.

Finally, as midnight came, Buck was overcome.
He felt a terrible fear deep in his gut. Bruce
Barnes could have had no knowledge whatever
of the plans of Nicolae Carpathia before they
had been announced on the news that afternoon.
At one point he thought of accusing Bruce of
having based everything he was saying on the
CNN report he had heard and seen, but even
if he had, here it was in black and white in the
Bible.

"Did you see the news today?" Buck asked.

"Not today," Bruce said. "I've been in meetings
since noon and grabbed a bite just before you got
here."

Buck told him what had happened at the U.N.
Bruce paled. "That's why we've been hearing all
those clicking sounds on my answering machine,"
Bruce said. "I turned the ringer off on the phone,
so the only way you can tell when a call comes in
is by the clicking on the answering machine.
People are calling to let me know. They do that
a lot. We talk about what the Bible says may
happen, and when it does, people check in."

"You think Carpathia is this Antichrist?"

"I don't see how I could come to any other
conclusion."

"But I really believed in the guy."

"Why not? Most of us did. Self-effacing, interested in the welfare of the people, humble, not looking for power or leadership. But the Antichrist is a deceiver. And he has the power to control men's minds. He can make people see lies as truth."

Buck told Bruce of his invitation to the pre-press-conference meeting.

"You must not go," Bruce said.

"I can't *not* go," Buck said. "This is the opportunity of a lifetime."

"I'm sorry," Bruce said. "I have no authority over you, but let me plead with you, warn you, about what happens next. The Antichrist will solidify his power with a show of strength."

"He already has."

"Yes, but it appears that all these long-range agreements he has been conceded will take months or years to effect. Now he has to show some potency. What might he do to entrench himself so solidly that no one can oppose him?"

"I don't know."

"He undoubtedly has ulterior motives for wanting you there."

"I'm no good to him."

"You would be if he controlled you."

"But he doesn't."

"If he is the evil one the Bible speaks of, there is

little he does not have the power to do. I warn you not to go there without protection."

"A bodyguard?"

"At least. But if Carpathia is the Antichrist, do you want to face him without God?"

Buck was taken aback. This conversation was bizarre enough without wondering if Bruce was using any means necessary to get him to convert. No doubt it had been a sincere and logical question, yet Buck felt pressured. "I see what you mean," he said slowly, "but I don't think I'm going to get hypnotized or anything."

"Mr. Williams, you have to do what you have to do, but I'm pleading with you. If you go into that meeting without God in your life, you will be in mortal and spiritual danger."

He told Buck about his conversation with the Steeles and how they had collectively come up with the idea of a Tribulation Force. "It's a band of serious-minded people who will boldly oppose the Antichrist. I just didn't expect that his identity would become so obvious so soon."

The Tribulation Force stirred something deep within Buck. It took him back to his earliest days as a writer, when he believed he had the power to change the world. He would stay up all hours of the night, plotting with his colleagues how they would have the courage and the audacity to stand up to oppression, to big government, to bigotry.

He had lost that fire and verve over the years as
he won accolades for his writing. He still wanted
to do the right things, but he had lost the passion
of the all-for-one and one-for-all philosophy as
his talent and celebrity began to outstrip those
same colleagues.

The idealist, the maverick in him, gravitated
toward such ideas, but he caught himself before
he talked himself into becoming a believer in
Christ just because of an exciting little club he
could join.

"Do you think I could sit in on your core group
meeting tomorrow?" he asked.

"I'm afraid not," Bruce said. "I think you'd find
it interesting and I personally believe it would
help convince you, but it is limited to our leadership team. Truth is, I'll be going over with them
tomorrow what you and I are talking about
tonight, so it would be a rerun for you anyway."

"And church Sunday?"

"You're very welcome, but I must say, it's going
to be the same theme I use every Sunday. You've
heard it from Ray Steele and you've heard it
from me. If hearing it one more time would help,
then come on out and see how many seekers
and finders there are. If it's anything like the last
two Sundays, it will be standing room only."

Buck stood and stretched. He had kept Bruce
long past midnight, and he apologized.

"No need," Bruce said. "This is what I do."

"Do you know where I can get a Bible?"

"I've got one you can have," Bruce said.

The next day the core group enthusiastically and emotionally welcomed its newest member, Chloe Steele. They spent much of the day studying the news and trying to determine the likelihood of Nicolae Carpathia's being the Antichrist. No one could argue otherwise.

Bruce told the story of Buck Williams, without using his name or mentioning his connection with Rayford and Chloe. Chloe cried silently as the group prayed for his safety and for his soul.

TWENTY-FOUR

BUCK spent Saturday holed up in the otherwise empty Chicago bureau office, getting a head start on his article on the theory behind the disappearances. His mind continually swirled, forcing him to think about Carpathia and what he would say in that piece about how the man seemed to be a perfect parallel to biblical prophecy. Fortunately, he could wait on writing that until after the big day Monday.

Around lunchtime, Buck reached Steve Plank at the Plaza Hotel in New York. "I'll be there Monday morning," he said, "but I'm not inviting Hattie Durham."

"Why not? It's a small request, friend to friend."

"You to me?"

"Nick to you."

"So now it's Nick, is it? Well, he and I are not close enough for that familiarity, and I don't provide female companionship even to my friends."

"Not even for me?"

"If I knew you would treat her with respect, Steve, I'd set you up with Hattie."

"You're really not going to do this for Carpathia?"

"No. Am I uninvited?"

"I'm not going to tell him."

"How are you going to explain it when she doesn't show?"

"I'll ask her myself, Buck, you prude."

Buck didn't say he would warn Hattie not to go. He asked Steve if he could get one more exclusive with Carpathia before starting his cover story on him.

"I'll see what I can do, but you can't even do a small favor and you want another break?"

"He likes me, you said. You know I'm going to do the complete piece on the guy. He needs this."

"If you watched TV yesterday, you know he doesn't need anything. We need him."

"Do we? Have you run into any schools of thought that link him to end-times events in the Bible?"

Steve Plank did not respond.

"Steve?"

"I'm here."

"Well, have you? Anybody that thinks he might

fill the bill for one of the villains of the book of Revelation?"

Steve said nothing.

"Hello, Steve."

"I'm still here."

"C'mon, old buddy. You're the press secretary. You know all. How's he going to respond if I hit him with that?"

Steve was still silent.

"Don't do this to me, Steve. I'm not saying that's where I am or that anybody who knows anything or who matters thinks that way. I'm doing the piece on what was behind the disappearances, and you know that takes me into all kinds of religious realms. Nobody anywhere has drawn any parallels here?"

This time when Steve said nothing, Buck merely looked at his watch, determined to wait him out. About twenty seconds after a loud silence, Steve spoke softly. "Buck, I have a two-word answer for you. Are you ready?"

"I'm ready."

"Staten Island."

"Are you tellin' me that—?"

"Don't say the name, Buck! You never know who's listening."

"So you're threatening me with—"

"I'm not threatening. I'm warning. Let me say I'm cautioning you."

"And let me remind you, Steve, that I don't warn well. You remember that, don't you, from ages ago when we worked together and you thought I was the toughest bird dog you'd ever sent on a story?"

"Just don't go sniffing the wrong brier patch, Buck."

"Let me ask you this then, Steve."

"Careful, please."

"You want to talk to me on another line?"

"No, Buck, I just want you to be careful what you say so I can be, too."

Buck began scribbling furiously on a yellow pad. "Fair enough," he said, writing, *Carpathia or Stonagal resp. for Eric Miller?* "What I want to know is this: If you think I should stay off the ferry, is it because of the guy behind the wheel, or because of the guy who supplies his fuel?"

"The latter," Steve said without hesitation.

Buck circled *Stonagal*. "Then you don't think the guy behind the wheel is even aware of what the fuel distributor does in his behalf."

"Correct."

"So if someone got too close to the pilot, the pilot might be protected and not even know it."

"Correct."

"But if he found out about it?"

"He'd deal with it."

"That's what I expect to see soon."

"I can't comment on that."

"Can you tell me who you really work for?"

"I work for who it appears to you I work for."

What in the world did that mean? Carpathia or Stonagal? How could he get Steve to say on a phone from within the Plaza that might be bugged?

"You work for the Romanian businessman?"

"Of course."

Buck nearly kicked himself. That could be either Carpathia or Stonagal. "You do?" he said, hoping for more.

"My boss moves mountains, doesn't he?" Steve said.

"He sure does," Buck said, circling *Carpathia* this time. "You must be pleased with everything going on these days."

"I am."

Buck scribbled, *Carpathia. End times. Antichrist?* "And you're telling me straight up that the other issue I raised is dangerous but also hogwash."

"Total roll in the muck."

"And I shouldn't even broach the subject with him, in spite of the fact that I'm a writer who covers all the bases and asks the tough questions?"

"If I thought you would consider mentioning it, I could not encourage the interview or the story."

"Boy, it didn't take long for you to become a company man."

After the core-group meeting, Rayford Steele talked privately with Bruce Barnes and was updated on the meeting with Buck. "I can't discuss the private matters," Bruce said, "but only one thing stands in the way of my being convinced that this Carpathia guy is the Antichrist. I can't make it compute geographically. Almost every end-times writer I respect believes the Antichrist will come out of Western Europe, maybe Greece or Italy or Turkey."

Rayford didn't know what to make of that. "You notice Carpathia doesn't look Romanian. Aren't they mostly dark?"

"Yeah. Let me call Mr. Williams. He gave me a number. I wonder how much more he knows about Carpathia." Bruce dialed and put Buck on the speakerphone. "Ray Steele is with me."

"Hey, Captain," Buck said.

"We're just doing some studying here," Bruce said, "and we've hit a snag." He told Buck what they had found and asked for more information.

"Well, he comes from a town, one of the larger university towns, called Cluj, and—"

"Oh, he does? I guess I thought he was from a

mountainous region, you know, because of his name."

"His name?" Buck repeated, doodling it on his legal pad.

"You know, being named after the Carpathian Mountains and all. Or does that name mean something else over there?"

Buck sat up straight and it hit him! Steve had been trying to tell him he worked for Stonagal and *not* Carpathia. And of course all the new U.N. delegates would feel beholden to Stonagal because he had introduced them to Carpathia. Maybe *Stonagal* was the Antichrist! Where had *his* lineage begun?

"Well," Buck said, trying to concentrate, "maybe he was named after the mountains, but he was born in Cluj and his ancestry, way back, is Roman. That accounts for the blond hair and blue eyes."

Bruce thanked him and asked if he would see Buck in church the next day. Rayford thought Buck sounded distracted and noncommittal. "I haven't ruled it out," Buck said.

Yes, Buck thought, hanging up. *I'll be there all right.* He wanted every last bit of input before he went to New York to write a story that could cost him his career and maybe his life. He didn't know

the truth, but he had never backed off from looking for it, and he wouldn't begin now. He phoned
Hattie Durham.

"Hattie," he said, "you're going to get a call
inviting you to New York."

"I already did."

"They wanted me to ask you, but I told them
to do it themselves."

"They did."

"They want you to see Carpathia again, provide
him some companionship next week if you're
free."

"I know and I am and I will."

"I'm advising you not to do it."

She laughed. "Right, I'm going to turn down
a date with the most powerful man in the world?
I don't think so."

"That would be my advice."

"Whatever for?"

"Because you don't strike me as that kind of
girl."

"First, I'm not a girl. I'm almost as old as you
are, and I don't need a parent or legal guardian."

"I'm talking as a friend."

"You're not my friend, Buck. It was obvious
you didn't even like me. I tried to shove you off
onto Rayford Steele's little girl, and I'm not sure
you even had the brains to pick up on that."

"Hattie, maybe I don't know you. But you

don't seem the type who would allow herself to be taken advantage of by a stranger."

"You're pretty much a stranger, and you're trying to tell me what to do."

"Well, *are* you that kind of a person? By not passing along the invitation, was I protecting you from something you might enjoy?"

"You'd better believe it."

"I can't talk you out of it?"

"You can't even try," she said, and she hung up.

Buck shook his head and leaned back in his chair, holding the yellow pad in front of him. *My boss moves mountains, Steve had said. Carpathia is a mountain. Stonagal is the mover and shaker behind him. Steve thinks he's really wired in deep. He's not only press secretary to the man Hattie Durham correctly called the most powerful man on earth, but Steve is also actually in league with the man behind the man.*

Buck wondered what Rayford or Chloe would do if they knew Hattie had been invited to New York to be Carpathia's companion for a few days. In the end, he decided it was none of his, or their, business.

Rayford and Chloe watched for Buck until the last minute the next morning, but they could no longer save a seat for him when the sanctuary and the balcony filled. When Bruce began his message, Chloe nudged her father and pointed out the window, down onto the walk before the front door. There, in a small crowd listening to an external speaker, was Buck. Rayford raised a celebratory fist and whispered to Chloe, "Wonder what you're going to pray for this morning?"

Bruce played the former pastor's videotape, told his own story again, talked briefly about prophecy, invited people to receive Christ, and then opened the microphone for personal accounts. As had happened the previous two weeks, people streamed forward and stood in line until well after one in the afternoon, eager to tell how they had now, finally, trusted Christ.

Chloe told her father she had wanted to be first, as he had been, but by the time she made her way down from the last row of the balcony, she was one of the last. She told her story, including the sign she believed God had given her in the form of a friend who sat beside her on the flight home. Rayford knew she could not see Buck over the crowd, and Rayford couldn't either.

When the meeting was over, Rayford and Chloe went outside to find Buck, but he was gone. They went for lunch with Bruce, and when they got home, Chloe found a note from Buck on the front door.

It isn't that I didn't want to say good-bye.
But I don't. I'll be back for bureau business
and maybe just to see you, if you'll allow it.
I've got a lot to think about right now, as
you know, and frankly, I don't want my
attraction to you to get in the way of that
thinking. And it would. You are a lovely
person, Chloe, and I was moved to tears by
your story. You had told me before, but to
hear it in that place and in that circumstance
this morning was beautiful. Would you do
something I have never asked anyone to do
for me ever before? Would you pray for me?
I will call you or see you soon. I promise.
Buck.

Buck felt more alone than ever on the flight
home. He was in coach on a full plane, but he
knew no one. He read several sections from the
Bible Bruce had given him and had marked for
him, prompting the woman next to him to ask
questions. He answered in such a way that she
could tell he was not in the mood for conversation. He didn't want to be rude, but neither did
he want to mislead anyone with his limited
knowledge.

Sleep was no easier for him that night, though
he refused to allow himself to pace. He was going

into a meeting in the morning that he had been warned to stay away from. Bruce Barnes had sounded convinced that if Nicolae Carpathia were the Antichrist, Buck ran the danger of being mentally overcome, brainwashed, hypnotized, or worse.

As he wearily showered and dressed in the morning, Buck concluded he had come a long way from thinking that the religious angle was on the fringe. He had gone from bemused puzzlement at people thinking their loved ones had flown to heaven to believing that much of what was happening had been foretold in the Bible. He was no longer wondering or doubting, he told himself. There was no other explanation for the two witnesses in Jerusalem. Nor for the disappearances.

And the furthest stretch of all, this business of an Antichrist who deceives so many . . . well, in Buck's mind it was no longer an issue of whether it was literal or true. He was long past that. He had already progressed to trying to decide who the Antichrist was: Carpathia or Stonagal. Buck still leaned toward Stonagal.

He slung his bag over his shoulder, tempted to take the gun from his bedside table but knowing he would never get it through the metal detectors. Anyway, he sensed, that was not the kind of protection he needed. What he needed was safekeeping for his mind and for his spirit.

All the way to the United Nations he agonized. *Do I pray?* he asked himself. *Do I "pray the prayer" as so many of those people said yesterday morning? Would I be doing it just to protect myself from the voodoo or the heebie-jeebies?* He decided that becoming a believer could not be for the purpose of having a good luck charm. That would cheapen it. Surely God didn't work that way. And if Bruce Barnes could be believed, there was no more protection for believers now, during this period, than there was for anyone else. Huge numbers of people were going to die in the next seven years, Christian or not. The question was, *then* where would they be?

There was only one reason to make the transaction, he decided—if he truly believed he could be forgiven and become one of God's people. God had become more than a force of nature or even a miracle worker to Buck, as God had been in the skies of Israel that night. It only made sense that if God made people, he would want to communicate with them, to connect with them.

Buck entered the U.N. through hordes of reporters already setting up for the press conference. Limousines disgorged VIPs, and crowds waited behind police barriers. Buck saw Stanton Bailey in a crowd near the door. "What are you doing here?" Buck said, realizing that in five years at *Global* he had never seen Bailey outside the building.

"Just taking advantage of my position so I can be at this press conference. Proud you're going to be in the preliminary meeting. Be sure to remember everything. Thanks for transmitting your first draft of the theory piece. I know you've got a lot to do yet, but it's a terrific start. Gonna be a winner."

"Thanks," Buck said, and Bailey gave him a thumbs-up. Buck realized that if that had happened a month before, he would have had to stifle a laugh at the corny old guy and would have told his colleagues what an idiot he worked for. Now he was strangely grateful for the encouragement. Bailey could have no hint what Buck was going through.

Chloe Steele told her father of her plans to finally look into local college classes that Monday. "And I was thinking," she said, "about trying to get together with Hattie for lunch."

"I thought you didn't care for her," Rayford said.

"I don't, but that's no excuse. She doesn't even know what's happened to me. She's not answering her phone. Any idea what her schedule is?"

"No, but I have to check my own. I'll see if she's flying today."

Rayford was told that not only was Hattie not scheduled that day but also that she had requested a thirty-day leave of absence. "That's odd," he told Chloe. "Maybe she's got family troubles out West."

"Maybe she's just taking some time off," Chloe said. "I'll call her later when I'm out. What are you doing today?"

"I promised Bruce I'd come over and watch that Carpathia press conference later this morning."

"What time's that?"

"Ten our time, I think."

"Well, if Hattie's not around for lunch, maybe I'll come by there."

"Call us either way, hon, and we'll wait for you."

Buck's credentials were waiting for him at an information desk in the U.N. lobby. He was directed up to a private conference room off the suite of offices into which Nicolae Carpathia had already moved. Buck was at least twenty minutes early, but as he emerged from the elevator he felt alone in a crowd. He saw no one he recognized as he began the long walk down a corridor of glass and steel leading to the room where he was to

join Steve, the ten designated ambassadors representing the permanent members of the new Security Council, several aides and advisers to the
new secretary-general (including Rosenzweig,
Stonagal, and various other members of his international brotherhood of financial wizards), and
of course, Carpathia himself.

Buck had always been energetic and confident.
Others had noticed his purposeful stride on assignment. Now his gait was slow and unsure, and with
every step his dread increased. The lights seemed
to grow dimmer, the walls close in. His pulse
increased and he had a sense of foreboding.

The gripping fear reminded him of Israel, when
he believed he was going to die. Was he about to
die? He couldn't imagine physical danger, yet
clearly people who got in Carpathia's way, or in
the way of Stonagal's plans for Carpathia, were
now dead. Would he be just another in a line
that stretched from Carpathia's business rival
in Romania years before, through Dirk Burton
and Alan Tompkins, to Eric Miller?

No, what he feared, he knew, was not mortal
danger. At least not now, not here. The closer
he got to the conference room, the more he was
repelled by a sense of evil, as if personified in
that place. Almost without thinking, Buck found
himself silently praying, *God, be with me.
Protect me.*

He felt no sense of relief. If anything, his thoughts of God made his recognition of evil more intense. He stopped ten feet from the open door, and though he heard laughter and banter, he was nearly paralyzed by the atmosphere of blackness. He wanted to be anywhere but there, and yet he knew he could not retreat. This was the room in which the new leaders of the world congregated, and any sane person would have given anything to be there.

Buck realized that what he really wanted was to have been there. He wished it were over, that he had seen this welcoming of new people, this brief speech of commitment or whatever it was to be, and was already writing about it.

He tried to force himself toward the door, his thoughts deafening. Again he cried out to God, and he felt a coward—just like everyone else, praying in the foxhole. He had ignored God for most of his life, and now when he felt the darkest anguish of his soul, he was figuratively on his knees.

Yet he did not belong to God. Not yet. He knew that. God had answered Chloe's prayer for a sign before she had actually made the spiritual transaction. Why couldn't he have answered Buck's plea for calm and peace?

Buck could not move until Steve Plank noticed

him. "Buck! We're almost ready to begin. Come on in."

But Buck felt terrible, panicky. "Steve, I need to run to the washroom. Do I have a minute?"

Steve glanced at his watch. "You've got five," he said. "And when you get back, you'll be right over there."

Steve pointed to a chair at one corner of a square block of tables. The journalist in Buck liked it. The perfect vantage point. His eyes darted to the nameplates in front of each spot. He would face the main table, where Carpathia had placed himself directly next to Stonagal . . . or had Stonagal been in charge of the seating? Next to Carpathia on the other side was a hastily hand-lettered nameplate with "Personal Assistant" written on it. "Is that you?" Buck said.

"Nope." Steve pointed at the corner opposite Buck's chair.

"Is Todd-Cothran here?" Buck said.

"Of course. Right there in the light gray."

The Brit looked insignificant enough. But just beyond him were both Stonagal—in charcoal—and Carpathia, looking perfect in a black suit, white shirt, electric-blue tie, and a gold stickpin. Buck shuddered at the sight of him, but Carpathia flashed a smile and waved him over. Buck signaled that he would be a minute.

"Now you've got only four minutes," Steve said. "Get going."

Buck put his bag in a corner next to a heavy-set, white-haired security guard, waved at his old friend Chaim Rosenzweig, and jogged to the washroom. He placed a janitor's bucket outside and locked the door. Buck backed up against the door, thrust his hands deep into his pockets, and dropped his chin to his chest, remembering Bruce's advice that he could talk to God the same way he talked to a friend. "God," he said, "I need you, and not just for this meeting."

And as he prayed he believed. This was no experiment, no halfhearted attempt. He wasn't just hoping or trying something out. Buck knew he was talking to God himself. He admitted he needed God, that he knew he was as lost and as sinful as anyone. He didn't specifically pray the prayer he had heard others talk about, but when he finished he had covered the same territory and the deal was done. Buck was not the type to go into anything lightly. As well as he knew anything, he knew there would be no turning back.

Buck headed to the conference room, more quickly this time but strangely with no more confidence. He hadn't prayed for courage or peace this time. This prayer had been for his own soul. He hadn't known what he would feel, but he didn't expect this continued sense of dread.

He didn't hesitate, however. When he walked in, everyone was in place—Carpathia, Stonagal, Todd-Cothran, Rosenzweig, Steve, and the financial powers and ambassadors. And one person Buck never expected—Hattie Durham. He stared, dumbfounded, as she took her place as Nicolae Carpathia's personal assistant. She winked at him, but he did not acknowledge her. He hurried to his bag, nodded his thanks to the armed guard, and took only a notebook to his seat.

While no special feeling had come with Buck's decision, he had a heightened sensitivity that something was happening here. There wasn't a doubt in his mind that the Antichrist of the Bible was in this room. And despite all he knew about Stonagal and what the man had engineered in England and despite the ill feeling that came over him as he observed his smugness, Buck sensed the truest, deepest, darkest spirit of evil as he watched Carpathia take his place. Nicolae waited till everyone was seated, then rose with pseudodignity.

"Gentlemen . . . and lady," he began, "this is an important moment. In a few minutes we will greet the press and introduce those of you who

shall be entrusted to lead the new world order
into a golden era. The global village has become
united, and we face the greatest task and the
greatest opportunity ever bestowed upon humankind."

TWENTY-FIVE

NICOLAE Carpathia stepped out from his place at the table and went to each person individually. He greeted each by name, asking him to stand, shaking his hand, and kissing him on both cheeks. He skipped Hattie and started with the new British ambassador.

"Mr. Todd-Cothran," he said, "you shall be introduced as the ambassador of the Great States of Britain, which now include much of Western and Eastern Europe. I welcome you to the team and confer upon you all the rights and privileges that go with your new station. May you display to me and to those in your charge the consistency and wisdom that have brought you to this position."

"Thank you, sir," Todd-Cothran said, and sat down as Carpathia moved on. Todd-Cothran appeared shocked, as did several others, when

Nicolae repeated the same sentiment, including precisely the same title—ambassador of the Great States of Britain—to the British financier next to him. Todd-Cothran smiled tolerantly. Obviously, Carpathia had merely misspoken and should have referred to the man as one of his financial advisers. Yet Buck had never seen Carpathia make such a slip.

All around the four-sided table configuration Carpathia went, one by one, saying exactly the same words to every ambassador, but customizing the litany to include the appropriate name and title. The recitation changed only slightly for his personal aides and advisers.

When Carpathia got to Buck he seemed to hesitate. Buck was slow on the draw, as if he wasn't sure he was to be included in this. Carpathia's warm smile welcomed him to stand. Buck was slightly off balance, trying to hold pen and notebook while shaking hands with the dramatic Carpathia. Nicolae's grip was firm and strong, and he maintained it throughout his recitation. He looked directly into Buck's eyes and spoke with quiet authority.

"Mr. Williams," he said, "I welcome you to the team and confer upon you all the rights and privileges that go with your station. . . ."

What was this? It was not what Buck expected, but it was so affirming, so flattering. He was not part of any team, and no rights or privileges should be conferred upon him! He shook his head slightly to signal that Carpathia was again confused, that he had apparently mistaken Buck for someone else. But Nicolae nodded slightly and smiled all the more, looking more deeply into Buck's eyes. He knew what he was doing.

"May you display to me and to those in your charge the consistency and wisdom that have brought you to this position."

Buck wanted to stand taller, to thank his mentor, his leader, the bestower of this honor. But no! It wasn't right! He didn't work for Carpathia. He was an independent journalist, not a supporter, not a follower, and certainly not an employee. His spirit resisted the temptation to say, "Thank you, sir," as everyone else had. He sensed and read the evil of the man and it was all he could do to keep from pointing at him and calling him the Antichrist. He could almost hear himself screaming it at Carpathia.

Nicolae still stared, still smiled, still gripped his hand. After an awkward silence, Buck heard chuckles, and Carpathia said, "You are most welcome, my slightly overcome and tongue-tied friend." The others laughed and applauded as Carpathia kissed him, but Buck did not smile. Neither did he thank the secretary-general. Bile rose in his throat.

As Carpathia moved on, Buck realized what he had endured. Had he not belonged to God he would have been swept into the web of this man of deceit. He could see it in the others' faces. They were honored beyond measure to be elevated to this tier of power and confidence, even Chaim Rosenzweig. Hattie seemed to melt in Carpathia's presence.

Bruce Barnes had pleaded with Buck not to attend this meeting, and now Buck knew why. Had he come in unprepared, had he not been prayed for by Bruce and Chloe and probably Captain Steele, who knows whether he would have made his decision and his commitment to Christ in time to have the power to resist the lure of acceptance and power?

Carpathia went through the ceremony with Steve, who gushed with pride. Nicolae eventually covered everyone in the room except the security guard, Hattie, and Jonathan Stonagal. He returned to his place and turned first to Hattie.

"Ms. Durham," he said, taking both her hands in his, "you shall be introduced as my personal assistant, having turned your back on a stellar career in the aviation industry. I welcome you to the team and confer upon you all the rights and privileges that go with your new station. May you display to me and to those in your charge the consistency and wisdom that have brought you to this position."

Buck tried to catch Hattie's eye and shake his head, but she was zeroed in on her new boss. Was this Buck's fault? He had introduced her to Carpathia in the first place. Was she still reachable? Would he have access? He glanced around the room. Everyone stared with beatific smiles as Hattie breathed her heartfelt thanks and sat down again.

Carpathia dramatically turned to Jonathan Stonagal. The latter smiled a knowing smile and stood regally. "Where do I begin, Jonathan, my friend?" Carpathia said. Stonagal dropped his head gratefully and others murmured their agreement that this indeed was the man among men in the room. Carpathia took Stonagal's hand and began formally, "Mr. Stonagal, you have meant more to me than anyone on earth." Stonagal looked up and smiled, locking eyes with Carpathia.

"I welcome you to the team," Carpathia said, "and confer upon you all the rights and privileges that go with your new station."

Stonagal flinched, clearly not interested in being considered a part of the team, to be welcomed by the very man he had maneuvered into the presidency of Romania and now the secretary-generalship of the United Nations. His smile froze, then disappeared as Carpathia continued, "May you display to me and to those in your charge the consistency and wisdom that have brought you to this position."

Rather than thanking Carpathia, Stonagal wrenched his hand away and glared at the younger man. Carpathia continued to gaze directly at him and spoke in quieter, warmer tones, "Mr. Stonagal, you may be seated."

"I will not!" Stonagal said.

"Sir, I have been having a bit of sport at your expense because I knew you would understand."

Stonagal reddened, clearly chagrined that he had overreacted. "I beg your pardon, Nicolae," Stonagal said, forcing a smile but obviously insulted at having been pushed into this shocking display.

"Please, my friend," Carpathia said. "Please be seated. Gentlemen, and lady, we have only a few minutes before we meet the media."

Buck's eyes were still on Stonagal, who was seething.

"I would like to present to you all just a bit of an object lesson in leadership, followership, and may I say, chain of command. Mr. Scott M. Otterness, would you approach me, please?" The guard in the corner jerked in surprise and hurried to Carpathia. "One of my leadership techniques is my power of observation, combined with a prodigious memory," Carpathia said.

Buck couldn't take his eyes off Stonagal, who appeared to be considering revenge for having been embarrassed. He seemed ready to stand at any second and put Carpathia in his place.

"Mr. Otterness here was surprised because we had not been introduced, had we, sir?"

"No, sir, Mr. Carpathia, sir, we had not."

"And yet I knew your name."

The aging guard smiled and nodded.

"I can also tell you the make and model and caliber of the weapon you carry on your hip. I will not look as you remove it and display it to this group."

Buck watched in horror as Mr. Otterness unsnapped the leather strap holding the huge gun in his holster. He fumbled for it and held it with two hands so everyone but Carpathia, who had averted his eyes, could see it. Stonagal, still red-faced, appeared to be hyperventilating.

"I observed, sir, that you were issued a thirty-eight caliber police special with a four-inch barrel, loaded with high-velocity hollow-point shells."

"You are correct," Otterness said gleefully.

"May I hold it, please?"

"Certainly, sir."

"Thank you. You may return to your post, guarding Mr. Williams's bag, which contains a tape recorder, a cellular phone, and a computer. Am I correct, Cameron?"

Buck stared at him, refusing to answer. He heard Stonagal grumble about "some sort of a parlor trick." Carpathia continued to look at Buck. Neither spoke. "What is this?" Stonagal whispered. "You're acting like a child."

"I would like to tell you all what you are about to see," Carpathia said, and Buck felt anew the wash of evil in the room. He wanted more than anything to rub the gooseflesh from his arms and run for his life. But he was frozen where he sat. The others seemed transfixed but not troubled, as he and Stonagal were.

"I am going to ask Mr. Stonagal to rise once more," Carpathia said, the large ugly weapon safely at his side. "Jonathan, if you please."

Stonagal sat staring at him. Carpathia smiled. "Jonathan, you know you can trust me. I love you for all you have meant to me, and I humbly ask you to assist me in this demonstration. I see part of my role as a teacher. You have said that yourself, and you have been my teacher for years."

Stonagal stood, wary and rigid.

"And now I am going to ask that we switch places."

Stonagal swore. "What is this?" he demanded.

"It will become clear quickly, and I will not need your help anymore."

To the others, Buck knew, it sounded as if Carpathia meant he would no longer need Stonagal's help for whatever this demonstration was. Just as he had sent the guard back to the corner unarmed, they had to assume he would thank Stonagal and let him return to his seat.

Stonagal, with a disgusted frown, stepped out and traded places with Carpathia. That put Carpathia to Stonagal's right. On Stonagal's left sat Hattie, and beyond her, Mr. Todd-Cothran.

"And now I am going to ask you to kneel, Jonathan," Carpathia said, his smile and his light tone having disappeared. To Buck it seemed as if everyone in the room sucked in a breath and held it.

"That I will not do," Stonagal said.

"Yes, you will," Carpathia said quietly. "Do it now."

"No, sir, I will not," Stonagal said. "Have you lost your mind? I will not be humiliated. If you think you have risen to a position over me, you are mistaken."

Carpathia raised the .38, cocked it, and stuck the barrel into Stonagal's right ear. The older man at first jerked away, but Carpathia said, "Move again and you are dead."

Several others stood, including Rosenzweig, who cried plaintively, "Nicolae!"

"Everyone be seated, please," Carpathia said, calm again. "Jonathan, on your knees."

Painfully, the old man crouched, using Hattie's chair for support. He did not face Carpathia or look at him. The gun was still in his ear. Hattie sat pale and frozen.

"My dear," Carpathia said, leaning toward her over Stonagal's head, "you will want to slide your chair back about three feet so as not to soil your outfit."

She did not move.

Stonagal began to whimper. "Nicolae, why are you doing this? I am your friend! I am no threat!"

"Begging does not become you, Jonathan. Please be quiet. Hattie," he continued, looking directly into her eyes now, "stand and move your chair back and be seated. Hair, skin, skull tissue, and brain matter will mostly be absorbed by Mr. Todd-Cothran and the others next to him. I do not want anything to get on you."

Hattie moved her chair back, her fingers trembling.

Stonagal whined, "No, Nicolae, no!"

Carpathia was in no hurry. "I am going to kill Mr. Stonagal with a painless hollow-point round to the brain which he will neither hear nor feel.

The rest of us will experience some ringing in our ears. This will be instructive for you all. You will understand cognitively that I am in charge, that I fear no man, and that no one can oppose me."

Mr. Otterness reached for his forehead, as if dizzy, and slumped to one knee. Buck considered a suicidal dive across the table for the gun, but he knew that others might die for his effort. He looked to Steve, who sat motionless as the others. Mr. Todd-Cothran shut his eyes and grimaced, as if expecting the report any second.

"When Mr. Stonagal is dead, I will tell you what you will remember. And lest anyone feel I have not been fair, let me not neglect to add that more than gore will wind up on Mr. Todd-Cothran's suit. A high-velocity bullet at this range will also kill him, which, as you know, Mr. Williams, is something I promised you I would deal with in due time."

Todd-Cothran opened his eyes at that news, and Buck heard himself shouting, "No!" as Carpathia pulled the trigger. The blast rattled the windows and even the door. Stonagal's head crashed into the toppling Todd-Cothran, and both were plainly dead before their entwined bodies reached the floor.

Several chairs rolled back from the table as their occupants covered their heads in fear. Buck stared, mouth open, as Carpathia calmly placed the gun in Stonagal's limp right hand and twisted his finger around the trigger.

Hattie shivered in her seat and appeared to try to emit a scream that would not come. Carpathia took the floor again.

"What we have just witnessed here," he said kindly, as if speaking to children, "was a horrible, tragic end to two otherwise extravagantly productive lives. These men were two I respected and admired more than any others in the world. What compelled Mr. Stonagal to rush the guard, disarm him, take his own life and that of his British colleague, I do not know and may never fully understand."

Buck fought within himself to keep his sanity, to maintain a clear mind, to—as his boss had told him on the way in—"remember everything."

Carpathia continued, his eyes moist. "All I can tell you is that Jonathan Stonagal told me as recently as at breakfast this morning that he felt personally responsible for two recent violent deaths in England and that he could no longer live with the guilt. Honestly, I thought he was going to turn himself in to international authorities later today. And if he had not, I would have had to. How he conspired with Mr. Todd-Cothran, which led to the deaths in England, I do not know. But if he was responsible, then in a sad way, perhaps justice was meted out here today.

"We are all horrified and traumatized by having witnessed this. Who would not be? My first act as secretary-general will be to close the U.N. for the remainder of the day and to pronounce my regrettable benedictory obituary on the lives of two old friends. I trust you will all be able to deal with this unfortunate occurrence and that it will not forever hamper your ability to serve in your strategic roles.

"Thank you, gentlemen. While Ms. Durham phones security, I will be polling you for your version of what happened here."

Hattie ran to the phone and could barely make herself understood in her hysteria. "Come quick! There's been a suicide and two men are dead! It was awful! Hurry!"

"Mr. Plank?" Carpathia said.

"That was unbelievable," Steve said, and Buck knew he was dead serious. "When Mr. Stonagal grabbed the gun, I thought he was going to kill us all!"

Carpathia called on the United States ambassador.

"Why, I've known Jonathan for years," he said. "Who would have thought he could do something like this?"

"I'm just glad you're all right, Mr. Secretary-General," Chaim Rosenzweig said.

"Well, I am not all right," Carpathia said. "And

I will not be all right for a long time. These were my friends."

And that's how it went, all around the room. Buck's body felt like lead, knowing Carpathia would eventually get to him and that he was the only one in the room not under Nicolae's hypnotic power. But what if Buck said so? Would he be killed next? Of course he would! He had to be. Could he lie? Should he?

He prayed desperately as Carpathia moved from man to man, making certain they had all seen what he wanted them to see and that they were sincerely convinced of it.

Silence, God seemed to impress upon Buck's heart. *Not a word!*

Buck was so grateful to feel the presence of God in the midst of this evil and mayhem that he was moved to tears. When Carpathia got to him Buck's cheeks were wet and he could not speak. He shook his head and held up a hand. "Awful, was it not, Cameron? The suicide that took Mr. Todd-Cothran with it?"

Buck could not speak and wouldn't have if he could. "You cared for and respected them both, Cameron, because you were unaware that they tried to have you killed in London." And Carpathia moved on to the guard.

"Why could you not keep him from taking your gun, Scott?"

The old man had risen. "It happened so fast! I knew who he was, an important rich man, and when he hurried over to me I didn't know what he wanted. He ripped that gun right out of my holster, and before I could react he had shot himself."

"Yes, yes," Carpathia said as security rushed into the room. Everyone talked at once as Carpathia retreated to a corner, sobbing over the loss of his friends.

A plainclothesman asked questions. Buck headed him off. "You have enough eyewitnesses here. Let me leave you my card and you can call if you need me, hm?" The cop traded cards with him and Buck was permitted to leave.

Buck grabbed his bag and sprinted for a cab, rushing back to the office. He shut and locked his office door and began furiously banging out every detail of the story. He had produced several pages when he received a call from Stanton Bailey. The old man could hardly catch his breath between his demanding questions, not allowing Buck to answer.

"Where have you been? Why weren't you at the press conference? Were you in there when Stonagal offed himself and took the Brit with him? You should have been here. There's prestige for us having you in there. How are you going to convince anybody you were in there when you didn't show up for the press conference? Cameron, what's the deal?"

"I hurried back here to get the story into the system."

"Don't you have an exclusive with Carpathia now?"

Buck had forgotten that, and Plank hadn't reconfirmed it. What was he supposed to do about that? He prayed but sensed no leading. How he needed to talk to Bruce or Chloe or even Captain Steele! "I'll call Steve and see," he said.

Buck knew he couldn't wait long to make the call, but he was desperate to know what to do. Should he allow himself to be in a room alone with Carpathia? And if he did, should he pretend to be under his mind control as everyone else seemed to be? If he hadn't seen this for himself, he wouldn't have believed it. Would he always be able to resist the influence with God's help? He didn't know.

He dialed Steve's pager and the call was returned a couple of minutes later. "Really busy here, Buck. What's up?"

"I was wondering if I've still got that exclusive with Carpathia."

"You're kidding, right? You heard what happened here and you want an exclusive?"

"Heard? I was there, Steve."

"Well, if you were here, then you probably know what happened before the press conference."

"Steve! I saw it with my own eyes."

"You're not following me, Buck. I'm saying if you were here for the press conference, you heard about the Stonagal suicide in the preliminary meeting, the one you were supposed to come to."

Buck didn't know what to say. "You saw me there, Steve."

"I didn't even see you at the press conference."

"I wasn't *at* the press conference, Steve, but I was in the room when Stonagal and Todd-Cothran died."

"I don't have time for this, Buck. It's not funny. You were supposed to be there, you weren't there. I resent it, Carpathia is offended, and no, no exclusive."

"I have credentials! I got them downstairs!"

"Then why didn't you use them?"

"I did!"

Steve hung up on him. Marge buzzed and said the boss was on the line again. "What's the deal with you not even going to that meeting?" Bailey said.

"I was there! You saw me go in!"

"Yeah, I saw you. You were that close. What did you do, find something more important to do? You got some fast talking to do, Cameron!"

"I'm telling you I was there! I'll show you my credentials."

"I just checked the credential list, and you're not on it."

"Of course I'm on it. I'll show 'em to you."

"Your name's there, I'm saying, but it's not checked off."

"Mr. Bailey, I'm looking at my credentials right now. They're in my hand."

"Your credentials don't mean dirt if you didn't use 'em, Cameron. Now where were you?"

"Read my story," Buck said. "You'll know exactly where I was."

"I just talked to three, four people who *were* there, including a U.N. guard and Carpathia's personal assistant, not to mention Plank. None of them saw you; you weren't there."

"A cop saw me! We traded cards!"

"I'm coming back to the office, Williams. If you're not there when I get there, you're fired."

"I'll be here."

Buck dug out the cop's card and called the number. "Precinct station," a voice said.

Buck read off the card, "Detective Sergeant Billy Cenni, please."

"What's the name again?"

"Cenni, or maybe it's a hard *C*? Kenny?"

"Don't recognize it. You got the right precinct?"

Buck repeated the number from the card.

"That's our number, but that ain't our guy."

"How would I locate him?"

"I'm busy here, pal. Call midtown."

"It's important. Do you have a department directory?"

"Listen, we got thousands of cops."

"Just look up C-E-N-N-I for me, will ya?"

"Just a minute." Soon he was back on. "Nothing, OK?"

"Could he be new?"

"He could be your sister for all I know."

"Where do I call?"

He gave Buck the number for police headquarters. Buck ran through the whole conversation again, but this time he had reached a pleasant young woman. "Let me check one more thing for you," she said. "I'll get personnel on the line because they won't tell you anything unless you're a uniformed officer anyway."

He listened as she spelled the name for personnel. "Uh-huh, uh-huh," she said. "Thank you. I'll tell him." And she came back to Buck. "Sir? Personnel says there is nobody in the New York Police Department named Cenni, and there never has been. If somebody's got a phony police business card dolled up, they'd like to see it."

All Buck could do now was try to convince Stanton Bailey.

Rayford Steele, Chloe, and Bruce Barnes watched the U.N. press conference, straining to see Buck. "Where is he?" Chloe said. "He has to be there somewhere. Everybody else from that meeting is there. Who's the girl?"

Rayford stood when he saw her and silently pointed at the screen. "Dad!" Chloe said. "You're not thinking what I'm thinking?"

"It sure looks like her," Rayford said.

"Shh," Bruce said, "he's introducing everybody."

"And my new personal assistant, having given up a career in the aviation industry . . ."

Rayford flopped into a chair. "I hope Buck wasn't behind that."

"Me, too," Bruce said. "That would mean he could have been sucked in, too."

The news of the Stonagal suicide and Todd-Cothran's accidental death stunned them. "Maybe Buck took my advice and didn't go," Bruce said. "I sure hope so."

"That doesn't sound like him," Chloe said.

"No, it doesn't," Rayford said.

"I know," Bruce said. "But I can hope. I don't want to find out that he's met with foul play.

Who knows what happened in there, and him going in with only our prayers?"

"I'd like to think that would be enough," Chloe said.

"No," Bruce said. "He needed the covering of God himself."

By the time Stanton Bailey stormed into Buck's office an hour later, Buck realized he was up against a force with which he could not compete. The record of his having been at that meeting had been erased, including from the minds of everyone in the room. He knew Steve wasn't faking it. He honestly believed Buck had not been there. The power Carpathia held over those people knew no limits. If Buck had needed any proof that his own faith was real and that God was now in his life, he had it. Had he not received Christ before entering that room, he was convinced he would be just another of Carpathia's puppets.

Bailey was not in a discussing mood, so Buck let the old man talk, not trying to defend himself. "I don't want any more of this nonsense about your having been there. I know you were in the building and I see your credentials, but you know and I know and everybody who *was* in there knows that you weren't. I don't know what you thought was more important, but you were wrong. This is unacceptable and unforgivable, Cameron. I can't have you as my executive editor."

"I'll gladly go back to senior writer," Buck said.

"Can't go along with that either, pal. I want you out of New York. I'm going to put you in the Chicago bureau."

"I'll be happy to run that for you."

Bailey shook his head. "You don't get it, do you, Cameron? I don't trust you. I should fire you. But I know you'd just wind up with somebody else."

"I don't want to be with anybody else."

"Good, because if you tried to jump to the competition, I'd have to tell them about this stunt. You're going to be a staff writer out of Chicago, working for the woman who was Lucinda's assistant there. I'm calling her today to give her the news. It'll mean a whopping cut in pay, especially considering what you would've gotten with the promotion. You take a few days off, get your things in order here, get that apartment sublet, and find yourself a place in Chicago. Someday I want you to come clean with me, son. That was the sorriest excuse for news gathering I've ever seen, and by one of the best in the business."

Mr. Bailey slammed the door.

Buck couldn't wait to talk to his friends in Illi-

nois, but he didn't want to call from his office
or his apartment, and he didn't know for sure
whether his cellular phone was safe. He packed
his stuff and took a cab to the airport, asking the
cabbie to stop at a pay phone a mile outside the
terminal.

Not getting an answer at the Steeles', he dialed
the church. Bruce answered and told him Chloe
and Rayford were there. "Put them on the
speakerphone," he said. "I'm taking the three
o'clock American flight to O'Hare. But let me
tell you this: Carpathia is your man, no question.
He fills the bill to the last detail. I felt your
prayers in the meeting. God protected me. I'm
moving to Chicago, and I want to be a member
of, what did you call it, Bruce?"

"The Tribulation Force?"

"That's it!"

"Does this mean—?" Chloe began.

"You know exactly what it means," Buck said.
"Count me in."

"What happened, Buck?" Chloe asked.

"I'd rather tell you about it in person," he said.
"But have I got a story for you! And you're the
only people I know who are going to believe it."

When his plane finally touched down, Buck
hurried up the jet way and through the gate
where he was joyously greeted by Chloe, Bruce,

and Rayford Steele. They all embraced him, even the staid captain. As they huddled in a corner, Bruce prayed, thanking God for their new brother and for protecting him.

They moved through the terminal toward the parking garage, striding four abreast, arms around each other's shoulders, knit with a common purpose. Rayford Steele, Chloe Steele, Buck Williams, and Bruce Barnes faced the gravest dangers anyone could face, and they knew their mission.

The task of the Tribulation Force was clear and their goal nothing less than to stand and fight the enemies of God during the seven most chaotic years the planet would ever see.

ABOUT THE AUTHORS

Jerry B. Jenkins (www.jerryjenkins.com) is the writer of the Left Behind series. He is author of more than one hundred books, of which eleven have reached the *New York Times* best-seller list. Former vice president for publishing for the Moody Bible Institute of Chicago, he also served many years as editor of *Moody* magazine and is now Moody's writer-at-large.

His writing has appeared in publications as varied as *Reader's Digest, Parade,* in-flight magazines, and many Christian periodicals. He has written books in four genres: biography, marriage and family, fiction for children, and fiction for adults.

Jenkins's biographies include books with Hank Aaron, Bill Gaither, Luis Palau, Walter Payton, Orel Hershiser, Nolan Ryan, Brett Butler, and Billy Graham, among many others.

Eight of his apocalyptic novels—*Left Behind, Tribulation Force, Nicolae, Soul Harvest, Apollyon, Assassins, The Indwelling,* and *The Mark*—have appeared on the Christian Booksellers Association's best-selling fiction list and the *Publishers Weekly* religion best-seller list. *Left Behind* was nominated for Book of the Year by the Evangelical Christian Publishers Association in 1997, 1998, 1999, and 2000. *The Indwelling* was number one on the *New York Times* best-seller list for four consecutive weeks.

As a marriage and family author and speaker, Jenkins has been a frequent guest on Dr. James Dobson's *Focus on the Family* radio program.

Jerry is also the writer of the nationally syndicated sports story comic strip *Gil Thorp,* distributed to newspapers across the United States by Tribune Media Services.

Jerry and his wife, Dianna, live in Colorado.

Dr. Tim LaHaye (www.timlahaye.com), who conceived the idea of fictionalizing an account of the Rapture and the Tribulation, is a noted author, minister, and nationally recognized speaker on Bible prophecy. He is the founder of both Tim LaHaye Ministries and The Pre-Trib Research Center. Presently Dr. LaHaye speaks at many of the major Bible prophecy conferences in the U.S. and Canada, where his nine current prophecy books are very popular.

Dr. LaHaye holds a doctor of ministry degree from Western Theological Seminary and a doctor of literature degree from Liberty University. For twenty-five years he pastored one of the nation's outstanding churches in San Diego, which grew to three locations. It was during that time that he founded two accredited Christian high schools, a Christian school system of ten schools, and Christian Heritage College.

Dr. LaHaye has written over forty books, with over 30 million copies in print in thirty-three languages. He has written books on a wide variety of subjects, such as family life, temperaments, and Bible prophecy. His current fiction works, written with Jerry B. Jenkins—*Left Behind, Tribulation Force, Nicolae, Soul Harvest, Apollyon, Assassins, The Indwelling,* and *The Mark*—have all reached number one on the Christian best-seller charts. Other works by Dr. LaHaye are *Spirit-Controlled Temperament; How to Be Happy Though Married; Revelation Unveiled; Understanding the Last Days; Rapture under Attack; Are We Living in the End Times?;* and the youth fiction series Left Behind: The Kids.

He is the father of four grown children and grandfather of nine. Snow skiing, waterskiing, motorcycling, golfing, vacationing with family, and jogging are among his leisure activities.

THE FUTURE IS CLEAR

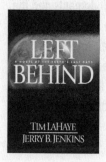

Left Behind®
A novel of the earth's last days . . .
In one cataclysmic moment, millions around the world
disappear. In the midst of global chaos, airline captain
Rayford Steele must search for his family, for answers,
for truth. As devastating as the disappearances have been,
the darkest days lie ahead.

0-8423-2911-0 Hardcover   0-8423-1675-2 Audio book—Cassette
0-8423-2912-9 Softcover   0-8423-4323-7 Audio book—CD

Tribulation Force
The continuing drama of those left behind . . .
Rayford Steele, Buck Williams, Bruce Barnes, and Chloe
Steele band together to form the Tribulation Force. Their
task is clear, and their goal nothing less than to stand and
fight the enemies of God during the seven most chaotic
years the planet will ever see.

0-8423-2913-7 Hardcover   0-8423-1787-2 Audio book—Cassette
0-8423-2921-8 Softcover   0-8423-4324-5 Audio book—CD

Nicolae
The rise of Antichrist . . .
The seven-year tribulation period is nearing the end of its
first quarter, when prophecy says "the wrath of the Lamb"
will be poured out upon the earth. Rayford Steele has
become the ears of the tribulation saints in the Carpathia
regime. A dramatic all-night rescue run from Israel through
the Sinai will hold you breathless to the end.

0-8423-2914-5 Hardcover   0-8423-1788-0 Audio book—Cassette
0-8423-2924-2 Softcover   0-8423-4355-5 Audio book—CD

Soul Harvest
The world takes sides . . .

As the world hurtles toward the Trumpet Judgments and the great soul harvest prophesied in Scripture, Rayford Steele and Buck Williams begin searching for their loved ones from different corners of the world. *Soul Harvest* takes you from Iraq to America, from six miles in the air to underground shelters, from desert sand to the bottom of the Tigris River, from hope to devastation and back again—all in a quest for truth and life.

0-8423-2915-3 Hardcover   0-8423-5175-2 Audio book—Cassette
0-8423-2925-0 Softcover   0-8423-4333-4 Audio book—CD

Apollyon
The Destroyer is unleashed . . .

In this acclaimed *New York Times* best-seller, Apollyon, the Destroyer, leads the plague of demon locusts as they torture the unsaved. Meanwhile, despite growing threats from Antichrist, the Tribulation Force gathers in Israel for the Conference of Witnesses.

0-8423-2916-1 Hardcover   0-8423-1933-6 Audio book—Cassette
0-8423-2926-9 Softcover   0-8423-4334-2 Audio book—CD

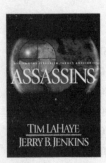

Assassins
Assignment: Jerusalem, Target: Antichrist

As a horde of 200 million demonic horsemen slays a third of the world's population, the Tribulation Force prepares for a future as fugitives. History and prophecy collide in Jerusalem for the most explosive episode yet of the continuing drama of those left behind.

0-8423-2920-X Hardcover   0-8423-1934-4 Audio book—Cassette
0-8423-2927-7 Softcover   0-8423-3682-6 Audio book—CD

The Indwelling
The Beast takes possession . . .
It's the midpoint of the seven-year Tribulation. As the world mourns the death of a renowned man, the Tribulation Force faces its most dangerous challenges yet. Time and eternity seem suspended, and the destiny of mankind hangs in the balance.

0-8423-2928-5 Hardcover   0-8423-1935-2 Audio book—Cassette
0-8423-2929-3 Softcover   0-8423-3966-3 Audio Book—CD

The Mark
The Beast rules the world . . .
His Excellency Global Community Potentate Nicolae Carpathia, resurrected and indwelt by the devil himself, tightens his grip as ruler of the world. The battle is launched for the very souls of men and women around the globe as sites are set up to begin administering the mark.

0-8423-3225-1 Hardcover   0-8423-3231-6 Audio book—Cassette
0-8423-3228-6 Softcover   0-8423-3968-X Audio book—CD

Watch for *Desecration* to arrive fall 2001

Left Behind®: The Kids
Four teens are left behind after the Rapture and band together to fight Satan's forces in this series for ten- to fourteen-year-olds.

Watch for the next Left Behind®: The Kids books, available fall 2001

Have You Been Left Behind®?
Based on the video that New Hope Village Church's pastor Vernon Billings created for those left behind after the Rapture. This video explains what happened and what the viewer can do now.

0-8423-5196-5 Video

An Experience in Sound and Drama

Dramatic broadcast performances of the first four books in the best-selling Left Behind series. Original music, sound effects, and professional actors make the action come alive. Experience the heart-stopping action and suspense of the end times for yourself. . . . Twelve half-hour episodes, on four CDs or three cassettes, for each title.

0-8423-5146-9 *Left Behind®: An Experience in Sound and Drama* CD

0-8423-5181-7 *Left Behind®: An Experience in Sound and Drama* cassette

0-8423-3584-6 *Tribulation Force: An Experience in Sound and Drama* CD

0-8423-3583-8 *Tribulation Force: An Experience in Sound and Drama* cassette

0-8423-3663-X *Nicolae: An Experience in Sound and Drama* CD

0-8423-3662-1 *Nicolae: An Experience in Sound and Drama* cassette

0-8423-3986-8 *Soul Harvest: An Experience in Sound and Drama* CD

0-8423-3985-X *Soul Harvest: An Experience in Sound and Drama* cassette

0-8423-4336-9 *Apollyon: An Experience in Sound and Drama* CD

0-8423-4335-0 *Apollyon: An Experience in Sound and Drama* cassette

0-8423-4338-5 *Assassins: An Experience in Sound and Drama* CD

0-8423-4337-7 *Assassins: An Experience in Sound and Drama* cassette

0-8423-4340-7 *The Indwelling: An Experience in Sound and Drama* CD (available fall 2001)

0-8423-4339-3 *The Indwelling: An Experience in Sound and Drama* cassette (available fall 2001)

Discover the latest about the Left Behind series
and interact with other readers at **www.leftbehind.com**